GW01179286

GANDHI'S TRAVELS IN TAMIL NADU

A. RAMASAMY (late), from Pudhuthamaraipatti village in Madurai district, Tamil Nadu, was a journalist who served as news editor of the dailies *ThamilNadu*, *Gramarajyam-Weekly* and *Dinamani*. A staunch Gandhian, he was secretary of the Gandhi Manram and the Harijan Seva Sangam, Madurai, and also translated works of Gandhian literature. He authored several books in Tamil, including *Ellayil Thollai*, *Porkalathil Bharatham*, *Lykkia Naadugal Sabai*, *Kulandhai Gandhi*, and *Thamizhnaattil Gandhi*, which took him three years to complete.

P. C. RAMAKRISHNA is a theatre actor and member of The Madras Players, India's oldest English theatre group. He has translated, dramatised and staged the Tamil novel *Karunai Kolai* by Sivasankari as *Mercy* in English. A leading voice professional who has lent his voice to documentaries, films and audio books, he is the author of *Find Your Voice*. He is also a co-translator of *Katha Vilasam*, a multi-author anthology of fifty Tamil short stories, edited by S. Ramakrishnan.

Mission Statement

This is an initiative of the Tamil Nadu Textbook and Educational Services Corporation (TNTB & ESC) under the aegis of one of the announcements for the year 2021–22, by Honourable Minister for School Education Thiru. Anbil Mahesh Poyyamozhi to identify and translate into English, Tamil literary works, that they might enhance the reach of Tamil antiquity, tradition and contemporaneity and enrich World literature and to also translate significant literary voices from other Dravidian languages into Tamil. Both ventures are to be undertaken as either independent or joint publications with collaborating publishers.

Members, Academic Advising Committee (Translation)

Dr. R. Balakrishnan, IAS, Researcher and Writer

Thiru. S. Ramakrishnan, Writer

Thiru. S. Madasamy, Educationist

Project Execution Team

Thiru. Dindigul I. Leoni, Chairperson, TNTB & ESC

Tmt. R. Gajalakshmi, IAS, Managing Director, TNTB & ESC

Dr. S. Kannappan, Member Secretary, TNTB & ESC

Thiru. R. Dhayalan, Financial Advisor, TNTB & ESC

Dr. T. S. Saravanan, Joint Director (Translations), TNTB & ESC

Thiru. P. A. Arumugam, Deputy Director (Publications), TNTB & ESC

Dr. P. Saravanan, Assistant Director (Publications), TNTB & ESC

Thiru. M. Appanasamy, Consultant, TNTB & ESC

Tmt. Mini Krishnan, Co-ordinating Editor, TNTB & ESC

GANDHI'S TRAVELS IN TAMIL NADU

A. RAMASAMY

Translated from the original Tamil by
P. C. RAMAKRISHNA

Orient BlackSwan

GANDHI'S TRAVELS IN TAMIL NADU

ORIENT BLACKSWAN PRIVATE LIMITED

Registered Office
3-6-752 Himayatnagar, Hyderabad 500 029, Telangana, India
e-mail: centraloffice@orientblackswan.com

Other Offices
Bengaluru, Chennai, Guwahati, Hyderabad, Kolkata,
Mumbai, New Delhi, Noida, Patna, Visakhapatnam

Originally published in Tamil as *Thamizhnaattil Gandhi* (Chennai: Vikatan Publications, 2013)

This English translation is published by arrangement with the Gandhian Literature Society, Madurai, copyright owner of the original Tamil work.

© Orient Blackswan Private Limited 2023
First published by Orient Blackswan Private Limited 2023

ISBN 978-93-5442-370-3

036435

Typeset in
Minion Pro 10.5/13
by Le Studio Graphique, Gurgaon 122 007

Printed in India at
Yash Printographics, Noida 201 301

Published by
Orient Blackswan Private Limited
3-6-752 Himayatnagar, Hyderabad 500 029, Telangana, India
e-mail: info@orientblackswan.com

CONTENTS

AUTHOR'S PREFACE

Mother, father, teacher, God—the man who was all of these to me, my father, Ma. Azhagarsamy—I bow to him, and humbly place this book at the golden feet of Tamil Nadu.

The object of this book is to highlight the connection and friendship the 'God among men', Mahatma Gandhi, had with the holy Tamil land. It is not a simple job to write about a great man and a celebrated land at the same time. I fully understand my limitations as I embark on this effort with respect and humility.

In my lifetime, there has been no holier time than the three years that I spent in preparing this book. I have toured from Delhi to the southernmost part of India. I have met many people who had been associated with Gandhiji. I have corresponded with many others, read books, pored over rare government documents and archives, examined daily newspapers faded with time, and extracted important and interesting details from essays written.

In his characteristically evocative language, Nehru said about Gandhi, "Everywhere he sat has become a temple". Hence I did not ignore even the remotest villages that this great soul visited. I have mentioned as many names as I could of people associated with him. After his first visit to Madras in 1896, because the number of welcome functions and the people he met increased greatly, I have in places included them within parentheses so as not to break the flow of the narrative. Such persons have been referred to only when the region to which they belong has been written about. Although the holy footprints of the Mahatma in Tamil Nadu can never fade with the passage of time, for the interested reader's ease, I have listed the details of the places he visited date-wise and provided a chronology at the end of the book.

Just as Narendranath Datta, better known as Swami Vivekananda, propagated the grace and greatness of his Guru, Bhagavan Ramakrishna Paramhamsa, so too the Tiruttani-born philosopher S. Radhakrishnan spoke of the glory of the Mahatma to the world. When Gandhiji visited Madras (now Chennai) in 1915, he was first met here by this great scholar, who then went on to spread his fame all over the world. In the twentieth century, it is Radhakrishnan's enunciation of Gandhiji's philosophical doctrine that made it easier for people to understand it, thus elevating the Mahatma in the eyes of the world. At that time, there were also others who served as Gandhiji's spokesmen to give his principles a more comprehensive form. In this effort, should not Tamil Nadu be proud of those illustrious Tamilians who became heirs to the Mahatma's legacy? Yes, if Nehru was the inheritor of Gandhiji's political legacy, then Dr Kumarappa was the heir to his economic thought, and Ariyanayakam to his tenets of basic education. As a touchstone on which to evaluate Gandhiji's philosophy and creed, and to act as his conscience was the political expert Rajaji; and if there was one man who followed Gandhiji's directives on prohibition, it was again Rajaji. Oh, Tamil land, be proud that you have given us the opportunity to serve such an *avatarapurushar*!

In the exemplary life of Gandhiji, Tamil Nadu has recorded several 'firsts'. In the front rank of Tamil martyrs figure Valliamma, Nagappan, Narayanasami and Selvan, among many others. Can Tamil land ever forget Tiruppur Kumaran who fell to police brutality while raising our national flag and leading a procession in 1932? It was Balasundaram, friend of the common man, who introduced the Indian coolies to Gandhiji while he was in South Africa. When thoughts of how to spread the *ahimsa* movement throughout India were exercising the mind of the great propounder of non-violence, it was in Tamil Nadu that Gandhiji found the way in a dream. The unbreakable connection he had all his life with students was born in Tamil Nadu. It was the Tamil student fraternity that first gave Gandhiji the title 'Father of the Nation' (though it was formalised when Subhas Chandra Bose addressed him so in 1944). It was also here that he first discarded his upper body clothing to make common cause with the poor and half-clothed mendicants. In the heroic struggle for freedom, it was in Tamil Nadu that the British parliamentary delegation held its discussions, recognising that India's freedom was inevitable. On Gandhiji's permanent return to India, it was in Tamil Nadu that he outlined in detail his plans for the future. Often when there was an impasse in the dialogue between the British government and Gandhiji, it was Srinivasa Sastri who became instrumental in removing the roadblocks. It was under the chairmanship of Salem Vijayaraghavachariar, at the Nagpur Congress session (1920), that Gandhiji's doctrine of ahimsa was fully and unanimously adopted by the Congress.

Gandhiji visited Tamil Nadu on the occasions listed below:

1. October 1896 (on his arrival from South Africa)
2. April 1915 (on his permanent return to India)
3. February 1916
4. September 1917
5. March 1919
6. August 1920
7. April 1921 (twice)
8. September 1921 (twice)
9. March 1925
10. August 1927 (for Khadi Yatra; thrice)
11. November 1927 (on his return from Sri Lanka; thrice)
12. 1927 (for Chennai Congress; thrice)
13. May 1929 (Tiruttani)
14. December 1933 (for Harijan Yatra)
15. January 1934 (for Harijan Yatra)
16. May 1936 (on his way to Bangalore)
17. June 1936 (on his return from Bangalore)
18. January 1937 (twice)
19. March 1937 (twice)
20. January 1946 (twice)

When I was writing and researching this book, I needed to arrive at decisions and affirm facts that sometimes ran contrary to the views held hitherto. For instance, there are many myths that have spread in Tamil Nadu around Thillaiyadi, near Tharangambadi, and Valliamma. One such myth is that she was born into a Harijan family in Thillaiyadi, and that Gandhiji had come there to take her away. People do not know that Valliamma attained a heroic death on 22 February 1914—several months before Gandhiji first visited

Thillaiyadi in 1915. Thillaiyadi Valliamma, as she is also known, was born in Johannesburg, and was a progressive-minded girl who studied in an English-medium school there.

Like Valliamma, Nagappan and Narayanasami, too, were born in South Africa. From my inquiries, there is no evidence that their ancestors lived in Thillaiyadi. It is possible that the people of Thillaiyadi had spoken about them to Gandhiji when he visited their village, and that Gandhiji may have later mentioned them in his historic address in Mayavaram. However, no one questions the pertinence of erecting memorials for Valliammal or other South African-born Tamil martyrs in Thillaiyadi. In that same village lived the widow and the family of Selvan—also martyred in South Africa during the Indian freedom struggle. Thillaiyadi was also the native place of T. A. Subramania Achari, who sacrificed so much in South Africa.

I have also stated in my book that the information regarding the exact day on which Gandhiji had his momentous dream, while he was staying in Rajaji's house in 1919, is incorrect. Professor Swaminathan, the chief editor of the English compilation on Gandhiji, has agreed with me.

In writing this book, many friends and well-wishers, from Delhi to Kanyakumari, have helped me. It is not possible for me to acknowledge each one of them here, but a few very important individuals need to be mentioned.

The managers of the Gandhi Publication Trust, particularly their head T. S. Avinashalingam, committee member Na. Ma. Ra. Subburaman, and the treasurer of the Gandhi Memorial Fund K. Arunachalam, have all actively supported me in this endeavour. K. Venkatasami, who waited eagerly for this publication to be completed and has been a source of constant encouragement, is now sadly no more. Professor Swaminathan, the aforementioned chief editor of the English compilation on Gandhiji, looked upon me as a younger brother, and offered many helpful suggestions. The chief editor of our group, Jayamani Subramaniam, lent his assistance with much affection. To the Khadi Department Secretary, Ve. Padmanabhan, I am indebted for introducing me to newspaper and magazine publishers in Chennai, and to teachers. Member of the Gandhi Memorial Trust, M. M. Viswanathan, was of great help to me whenever I needed it.

Associate editor of *Kalai Kalanjiyam*, S. Ramachandran, helped me with the first proofs of the book. N. Sivaramakrishnan of Jawahar Press took care of the printing efficiently. Bhargavi Radhakrishnan of the Government Information Department was of much assistance in making available numerous publications for my research.

Editors of *The Hindu, Mail, Swadesamithran, Ananda Vikatan* and many other dailies and journals allowed me to access old articles from their archives. The Tamil Nadu government authorities were also kind enough to give me permission to access their archives for official documents. I have drawn information from hundreds of publications. It is impossible for me to acknowledge all the sources. To each and every one of them I express my heartfelt gratitude.

If, upon reading this book, friends wish to add, modify or change any important details, they may please send it with supporting documents or references to the Secretary, Gandhi Memorial Trust, Madurai-13.

Vanakkam

Chennai, 19 November 1969

Your friend,

A. Ramasamy

PART I

IN SOUTH AFRICA

Overleaf image: Gandhi photographed in South Africa, 1909

1

BALASUNDARAM MEETS GANDHI

The new Indian lawyer

M. K. Gandhi, Bar-at-Law, was in his office chambers when Balasundaram came and stood before him. Balasundaram was a Tamil contract labourer. He had come to a white man, accepted a contract and become, in a way, a slave. The lawyer, however, was new. He had begun his practice only three or four months ago, but Balasundaram had heard of his empathy towards Indians. In any case, could poverty-stricken people like Balasundaram afford big lawyers? Hence he stood before this lawyer in torn clothes and in tears, having lost not only his dignity but his front teeth.

A few days ago, for some reason, his employer had thrashed him in rage, causing two of his front upper teeth to fall out. So much blood had poured from his mouth that the long turban he had used to stem its flow had got soaked with it.

Balasundaram went to the Magistrate to lodge a complaint. Observing his pathetic state the Magistrate was moved to pity. Directing that he leave his turban in custody of the court, he sent him to the hospital. After a few days he was better, and the hospital discharged him.

Dignity restored

Balasundaram came straight to Gandhiji. His condition even then did not permit him to speak clearly. He removed his turban and held it in his hand as he stood trembling before him. Removing the headgear and holding it in hand as a mark of respect was the accepted custom in South Africa at the time. It was not enough if a coloured man stood before a European with hands folded in greeting—the removal of headgear was mandatory. Observing that the Bar-at-Law was clad in an English suit made Balasundaram remove his turban.

The lawyer noticed this even before being concerned about what the man had come to say. "First tie your turban," he said to him. Balasundaram was elated and smiled, exposing all his teeth, including the two missing ones. That was his first victory. He realised from this one action that, with this lawyer, his dignity could be maintained.

Indian contract labourers

To be of service to Indians settled in South Africa, Gandhiji had recently established an association called the Natal Indian Congress. It catered to the interests of Indians born and brought up in South Africa, and Indian settlers working as clerks, but it did not cover Indian contract labourers who had come to work in that country. Gandhiji had been in fact yearning for the day when he could render service to this class of people.

Without knowing it, Balasundaram had thus brought together the contract labourers and their future leader. As directed, he wrote out his complaint on a piece of paper in Tamil. Fortunately, Gandhiji's clerk was a Tamilian, and Gandhiji asked him to translate the complaint. Then he sent Balasundaram to get treatment from a European doctor, who, in turn, wrote out the facts of his condition.

He was different

Even at that young age (he was not yet thirty), Gandhiji was different from other lawyers. Balasundaram pleaded strongly that the European who assaulted him be punished, but that was not Gandhiji's objective. "Is it not enough if you get your contract changed to another employer?" he asked. Balasundaram agreed. Gandhiji then wrote to the old employer, saying, "It is not my intention to punish you. If you accept your fault and agree to transfer this contract to another employer, it would be enough." The white man agreed.

However, the case of this Tamilian did not conclude so easily for Gandhiji. At every stage he encountered problems. He sent Balasundaram to the authority constituted for the welfare of contract labourers, and which alone had the power to allow the change or transfer of contract. But the head of the authority concerned ruled that Balasundaram must remain in his old job.

In the meantime there was a new development. The employer who had attacked Balasundaram rushed to the welfare authority, declaring that his wife insisted she needed that Indian labourer as he was a good worker whom she did not want to lose. The welfare authority sided with the white man. He then made Balasundaram unwittingly sign a paper to the effect that he had no complaint against his employer, and pronounced that the coolie and his employer had arrived at a compromise. Further, the authority wrote to Gandhiji that the employer was unwilling to allow Balasundaram's contract to be transferred to another.

Waves of anger washed over Gandhiji when he read that letter. What right did this authority have to obtain this kind of signature, he thought, as Balasundaram returned to him in tears and reported, "I cannot be transferred to another employer is what that authority has said."

The case begins

Gandhiji went to the welfare authority and pleaded his case fervently, but to no avail. Back in office, he wrote to Balasundaram's employer again to allow the transfer of his employment. He, too, did not relent. So the case went to the Magistrate's court. Having earlier seen the blood pouring from Balasundaram's mouth, the Magistrate was inclined to favour him. Gandhiji did not let go of his petition, insisting that he would withdraw it only if Balasundaram's employer consented to give the letter for transfer of employment. The Magistrate told the employer firmly, "You must accept this plea, else the consequences will be severe."

It was only after this that the employer relented. The welfare authority, however, did not. "If only another employer confirms his acceptance of taking Balasundaram into his employment will I permit the change" was the stand he took. Fortunately, a good employer (a preacher named Askew) conveyed his acceptance. Balasundaram's first employer was then handed the ultimatum by the Magistrate, and he conveyed his acceptance of the change in Balasundaram's employment. The welfare authority also relented subsequently.

Victory

Thus Balasundaram's case ended in victory. This served as a precedent, not only for contract labourers in South Africa, but for all such who were under the domination of the British in other countries. That there was a man willing to fight for them and their welfare in this world was something that brought them great joy. They gained a new confidence and courage. The fame of Balasundaram's lawyer spread all over Tamizhagam, his native place.

And thus it was that Gandhiji and the Tamils came closer. A new history was being written in India and the world.

2

VALLUVAR AND GANDHI

A special bond

When Swami Vivekananda met Bhagvan Ramakrishna Paramhamsa, there was an instant and singular affection generated between the teacher and the follower. Similarly, when Tamilians and Gandhiji met each other, there instinctively arose a special bond and respect between them. Those desirous of understanding the reason for this must refer to the principles of our great ancestor Valluvar, as enunciated in his treatise *Kural*.[1]

Rama and Krishna are both Vishnu's incarnations. That being so, rather than Rama declaring that he is Krishna, it would seem more appropriate for Valluvar to say that he is Gandhi—such was the similarity in their lives. Not that there are no differences between Valluvar and Gandhi, but they are few, very few.

"It is because of our previous births that I have such a close bond with Tamilians and Maharashtrians," Gandhiji has said many times.

It was only when Gandhiji was fighting for the rights of the people of South Africa and working to unite them that his political resolve and tenets began to evolve and to get strengthened. However, unlike most other political leaders, his way was direct, firm, full of love and truth. This perplexed many. "Truth and honesty in politics?" was the question that must have been raised in many minds at that time. The Tamil mind, however, clearly understood this.

The Tamil tradition

There were people of different faiths and languages who had settled in South Africa. Among them were Tamilians, Bengalis, Gujaratis and Punjabis. However, no one understood the doctrine and the methods of revolt laid down by Gandhiji more clearly and comprehensively than the Tamilian. Nurtured in the land of Valluvar, the Tamilian held Gandhiji high and showed him to the world. Gandhiji was amazed by the untiring cooperation of the Tamil people. It is only after he acquainted himself with and understood the vision of the Tamil poets and the holy tradition of the Tamil philosopher-saints that his amazement subsided.

Valluvar had discipline. He had substance. Pleasure, too. His belief in God was unshakeable. At the same time, for Valluvar, Siva and Vishnu were one. In his disciplined mind there was place for the domestic as well as for the ascetic. The spiritual Valluvar neither had contempt for politics, nor did he disregard it. In the 1330 short couplets of the *Kural*, 75 have been allocated to politics. Valluvar says: "It is neither food (paddy) nor is it the water that is the life of the nation. Indeed, it is the king." In his *Inbatthu-p-paal*, there is reasoning given for illicit love as also for chastity.

Valluvar's *Kural* and Gandhi's doctrine

It is with a prayer to God that Valluvar begins his great treatise. He asks: "What is gained by one who possesses knowledge, but who doesn't worship God?"

"One should preserve discipline and decorum, which gives excellence throughout life, like preserving your soul."

"Some trees offer all their parts as medicine. Likewise, philanthropists help others in every way."

"The earth bears it even if men dig for buildings and wells. Likewise, men should have the patience to bear everything."

"Repay those who do you injustice with kindness."

"He who has truth in his heart lives in the heart of all people."

"It is not the weapon that gives victory. It is the king's sceptre of justice."

"People of culture will even drink poison if given by their friends."

"Wealth should be gained from love and grace."

"If one wants to be in the hearts of noble persons, let him not take liquor."

"Those who are engaged in agriculture are great. All others depend on them."

"What else does a girl need but stability of mind?"

"Do not overeat, even if it does not affect your health."

"Always speak the truth. It is the best thing in the world."

"Do not think of doing evil to others, even if it is very small."

These are some sage and realistic pearls of wisdom that Valluvar has left the world a long time ago. Gandhiji's heart was filled with these principles. They were explicit in every action of his. Without them, there would be no Gandhi.

Whether the Tamilian has learnt the *Kural* or not, its tenets are unconsciously reflected in his thoughts, behaviour and speech. Without perhaps knowing that it is from the *Kural*, he has imbibed these principles. Thus, when he is in the presence of a great man who encapsulates these values, is there any wonder that he is drawn to him? Does not a mother's breast automatically produce milk when her child is on her lap? This is the only way we can explain the relationship between the Tamil people and the Mahatma. Should we say that it is like close friends meeting after years of separation? The main reason for this coming together was that the way of Gandhiji was also that of Valluvar.

Note

1. *Tirukkural*, a classic Tamil text of c. 500 CE or earlier.

3

THE PLIGHT OF TAMILIANS
ON GANDHI'S ARRIVAL

For a livelihood

The Tamilians who went to South Africa arrived there seeking a livelihood, not a life of luxury. Even though by chance some of them did become wealthy and lived comfortably, the majority of them eked out a hand-to-mouth existence. But the white people there grudged the few even that. Their objective was to see when they could be bundled and sent back to India, together with all the other Indians. At the same time, ironically, the same white people continued to lure Indians thousands of miles away to come to South Africa and work.

History

It is only by accidentally realising the mineral wealth and fertility of South Africa on their way to India that the white men decided to settle down in that land.[1] In order to exploit these riches to the hilt for a life of opulence and comfort, they needed people to toil for them in their plantations and mines. Such labourers had to be available at the lowest possible wages. Farm labourers in South Africa who owned some land were unwilling to offer themselves for this work. Hence, to further these commercial interests, labourers from other countries had to be brought in. The English in South Africa, who were part of the British Empire, made pacts with India and invited Indians to come. As per those agreements the first Indians landed in South Africa in 1860. Indians who reached there under such agreements were termed 'contract labourers'. To meet the needs of these contract labourers, Indian merchants also travelled to South Africa at a later date.

However, contrary to the expectations of the white people, a few of these Indians took to farming the plots of land they acquired, raised new varieties of vegetables and grains, and prospered as agriculturists. Indian merchants, with the help of workers from their own country, established shops in which they sold merchandise at low prices to overcome the competition from those run by white people, and gained economically.

The fact that the black people in South Africa chose to patronise the products of these Indian shops was something that the white locals resented deeply. Overcome by envy, and ignoring that they themselves had been instrumental in bringing Indians to work there under due agreement, the whites began trying to expel them from South Africa.

The agreement

The terms of the agreement, though, were different. Once the period of the agreement was over, Indians could return to their native land if they so wished. Alternatively, they could have the agreement extended by five years and remain in South Africa. In the event of neither of the above being invoked, the government would make a payment equivalent to the cost of sea passage, and the Indians could then stay on as independent citizens and undertake farming.

The agreement stipulated that: "Once the agreement period of the Indians who went as contract labourers was over, they should be permitted to stay on as free citizens." However, this condition laid down by the Indian government, along with other stipulations, was thrown to the winds by the Natal government.

There were four provinces in South Africa then—Natal, Cape, the Transvaal, and the Orange Free State. When Gandhiji first reached South Africa in 1893, the first two were under British control, and the latter two under the Dutch. The plight of Indians was unfavourable in all.

Consigned to slums

The Dutch turned out to be more vehement than the British in driving Indians out of the country. In 1885, restrictions were imposed on the activities of Indians in the Transvaal by the Dutch. At that time, as per the law they had promulgated in the Transvaal, Indians were prohibited from acquiring Dutch citizenship. They were permitted to live only in areas allocated to Indians, and to buy property there. Indian merchants had to get special licences. The Natal and other provincial governments followed suit. Indians were forced to live in and buy property in areas far removed from towns, where hygiene, electricity and basic civic facilities were unavailable. They were consigned to live in conditions akin to slums in India. Yet they were denied even the rights that people in Indian slums had.

The faces of racism

Racism showed its ugly face. South African law books referred to Indians as "some kinds of animals from Asia, or people without culture". In big cities like Pretoria and Johannesburg,[2] Indians were not allowed to walk on paths reserved for whites. A graduate from India was found walking on these paths once, and was held and pushed away. He wrote about this to the press, to no avail. He then brought it to the attention of the British government there, which replied: "We sympathise with you, but cannot interfere." Indians were denied permission to sit inside trams. An Indian Tamil, though dressed in European clothes, was once forced to travel on the footboard of a tram, despite seats being available.

To illustrate just how shamefully Indians were treated by the whites, the following letter, titled 'Coolie Traveller', written by a white man in *The Transvaal Leader* newspaper is a good example. The man recounted: "Some time back, from Potchefstroom to Park I was travelling by train. Two coolies were travelling on this train, and were in a different compartment. Still the disgust I felt did not diminish. After all, when they detrain, a white passenger is going to occupy those seats. He is going to be forced to use the same towel that these coolies have used to wipe their hands. He is going to be compelled to use the same cup that the coolies have used. I can say with certainty that he would not desire this. The Railways should therefore act with more concern for the general public."

One can only imagine what 'respect' that white man would have had for Tamils!

One day, a certain Police Superintendent Vernon went to the area where the Tamils had settled, in order to verify their entry documents. The officers accompanying Vernon spoke most degradingly of the Tamils. One of the terms used by the superintendent was particularly offensive. Gandhiji, speaking at a meeting in Johannesburg, referred to this and said: "That word used was shameful. It is not fit for me to repeat it here. I will not do it."

On trains and buses, in schools, eating places and on roads, racist feelings against Indians spread. Indians were not allowed to move within the four designated residential areas without permits. From Orange Free State, Indians were wholly evicted. In 1890–91, the total population of Indians in South Africa was approximately one and a half lakhs, and was largely concentrated in Natal. Contract labourers were mostly from Madras and Uttar Pradesh, while merchants and clerical workers were mainly from Gujarat.

False dignity

However, there was no unity among these one and a half lakh Indians in South Africa. The Parsees considered it below their dignity to refer to themselves as Indians and 'proudly' called themselves Parsees. The Muslim merchants declared they were Arabs. The white-collared Hindus considered themselves 'high-class' among the Indians in South Africa and did not mix with the others. Even so, there was still some social interaction between these three groups. But there was no such contact between the Indians who were labourers and these others beyond payment of wages.

Indians settled in South Africa could be classified into two categories. The first were the independent merchants and the people who worked for them; the second were the contract labourers. Indians who were independent did fight against the restrictions imposed on them. The Muslim merchants among them, however, were unable to get the support of their contract labourers. As in India, before the era of Gandhiji, Lokmanya Tilak and others, when Indians merely submitted their written grievances to the British authority and nothing more, these settlers in South Africa, too, had to be content submitting written petitions to the government.

'Coolies all'

Though the contract labourers in South Africa were largely Tamils, all Indians living and working there were tarred with the same brush of 'coolies' or '*saamys*'. Indian lawyers—including Gandhiji—and Indian merchants were referred to as 'coolie lawyers' and 'coolie merchants'. The South African leader Lieutenant Jan Smuts once referred to Indian society as a "society of coolies". Even law books started using the term 'coolie' for Indians. So did white people who had no animosity towards Indians. Strangely, Indians themselves also started referring to each other as coolies. Whether at the time of Gandhiji's entry into South Africa, or after he fought to remove the stains of racism, South African Indians, particularly the Tamilians, continued to live under the humiliation and injustice of racism.

Notes

1. The first white people settled in South Africa around 1652.
2. Johannesberg is the capital and largest city of Gauteng, which was then part of the Transvaal, South Africa's wealthiest province and the country's chief financial and industrial metropolis.

4

THE MORAL WAR OF
SOUTH AFRICAN INDIANS

Only if the history of Gandhiji's revolt in South Africa is known can
the central part played by Tamils in it be understood. So let us take
a brief look at that heroic revolt. A mere 250 Indians in Natal had
been granted voting rights, as though they were being given alms. In
that settlement European voters numbered 10,000. These Europeans
could not tolerate even those few Indians being given voting rights.
They decided to prevent them from reaching the ballot boxes (in
other words, not allow them to exercise their franchise). To this end
they prepared a motion to be submitted in the Natal Assembly. It was
on the day the Indians were according a farewell to Gandhiji that this
news was heard.

Journey deferred

Having arrived in South Africa in May 1893, Gandhiji had planned
to leave in end 1894, after completing all the work under his contract.
In these one and a half years, more than his work as a lawyer, it
was his service to the people which was the reason for the farewell
function. On that occasion, by chance Gandhiji came across this
news in a paper lying there. Explaining to the gathering the dangers
of being denied voting rights, he exhorted the Indians to oppose this
measure. "We know how to run a business. We have no idea how to
deal with political tangles and fight against them. Hence, please defer
your return by a month" is what the Indian community requested
of Gandhiji. He accepted their plea and drafted a memorandum to
be submitted to the Natal Assembly. However, before it could be
submitted, a second reading of the motion had been completed and

debate on it had begun in the Assembly. Some argued in ridicule, "We have brought forth a motion to deny Indians voting rights, and there has been no opposition to it. Is this not enough to prove that Indians are undeserving of being given such a right?" When Gandhiji submitted his memorandum, together with copies, to the Natal Assembly, newspapers carried large headlines supporting the Indian stand. Even so, the third reading of the motion was somehow conducted.

A memorandum to the Empress

Gandhiji then decided to obtain signatures to a memorandum from all adult Indians and submit it to the Home Minister. About 10,000 signatures were obtained and the Home Minister was requested to appeal to the Empress of Britain to use her veto power to quash the motion brought before the Natal Assembly.

A month elapsed before any reply was received. Gandhiji made preparations once again to return to India. Once more the Indians clamoured for him to stay, and he acquiesced. He enrolled himself as a lawyer in the Natal High Court.

Natal Indian Congress

Having decided to stay back, Gandhiji established the Natal Indian Congress on 22 August 1894 with the approval of the Indian National Congress. Under the Presidentship of Abdulla Haji Adam, a leading Indian and with Gandhiji as secretary, the Natal Indian Congress was constituted with persons of high standing. Of the 23 people selected as vice presidents of this organisation, Duraisamy Pillai, Ramasamy Naidu, Murugesa Pillai, and Rangasamy Padayachi were Tamils. (A name Nayana also features, but it is not known whether he was a Tamil. If he was, then there were five Tamils in all). Outside of this committee, Muthukrishnan, Subbu Naidu, R. Kandasamy Naidu, Perumal Naidu, Rayappan, and V. Narayana Batthar were the other Tamils who were member-functionaries.

In addition to Gandhiji as secretary, five Indians were selected as co-signatories on cheques. One of them, Duraisamy Pillai, was greatly instrumental in raising funds for the organisation. P. Perumal

Naidu helped in the membership drive. Somasundaram was engaged in translating into Tamil the court proceedings and in the distribution of circulars. In the beginning, the attendance of Tamils in the meetings of the Natal Indian Congress was low, and even when they did attend they were unpunctual. Still, after the meetings took place, and particularly after Gandhiji visited Madras Presidency[1] in 1896, Balasundaram kept fuelling their enthusiasm and ensured their active participation.

People in India were enraged at the denial of voting rights to Indians by the South African government. In December 1894, at the All India Congress meeting in Madras, the first motion that was tabled read: "The Indian people request that the decision of the South African Government to withdraw voting rights to Indians there be immediately revoked by the British Empress, invoking her veto power."

A first victory

The Natal Indian Congress toiled tirelessly towards instituting the political and economic rights of Indians, alongside working for improvements within the Indian community. Its first efforts were crowned with success. The British Empress did not accord her approval to the motion denying franchise to Indians in South Africa. As a result there was anger in the Natal Assembly. An amendment motion was brought forward to implement their decision through the back door.

Arrival in India

Thereafter, in 1896, Gandhiji arrived in India to take his family to South Africa. He also travelled to Bombay, Madras, and Calcutta and spoke about the travails of Indians in South Africa. (His Madras visit is dealt with separately later in this book). Around this time, due to the incorrect reportage of Gandhiji's speeches by the Reuters press agency, the Europeans in Natal rose up in anger against him. Later, once the truth was explained, they were pacified to some extent.

Return to South Africa

In 1899, when a conflict broke out between the British and the Dutch in South Africa (the Second Boer War, 1899–1902), Gandhiji stood in favour of the British, and established a 1100-strong Indian ambulance brigade, which rendered yeoman service. In 1901, on his return to India, Gandhiji began working as a lawyer in Bombay. However, whenever Britain's minister Neville Chamberlain came to South Africa, he would invite Gandhi to take up the cause of Indians there. In a meeting with him in December 1902, when Gandhi put forward the petitions of the Indians, Chamberlain responded: "The provinces of South Africa are under self rule; you have to reach agreements with them individually. We cannot interfere in this," and spread his hands in helplessness. Thereafter Gandhiji made up his mind to stay on in South Africa and fight the unjust and discriminatory laws. In 1914, when the Indian demands were successfully met, he returned to India. Gandhiji lived in South Africa for more than 20 years—a period of great struggles, interspersed with many difficult challenges and changes.

The Transvaal law

The humiliation that Indians had to endure was at its height in the Transvaal. The Transvaal government sought to obtain the identification of every Indian resident there, treating them like criminals. As per a bill enacted and published in the 22 August 1906 *Transvaal Gazette*, every Indian above the age of eight, male or female, was mandated to get his or her fingerprints recorded. Those who did not were either subject to fines or imprisonment, and at times, through a judicial decree, even exiled.

At any given time government authorities had the right to descend on Indians to verify whether they had complied with these regulations. Even after the Boer War, when Britain assumed power, Gandhiji was distraught that there was no end to the suffering of Indians. He realised that if the bill was not opposed, it would become law, which would sound the death knell to Indians in South Africa. Hence, a conference of important people was held, every clause of this emergency bill discussed, and it was decided to publicly demonstrate against it. On behalf of the British Indian Association, under Gandhiji's leadership, a mediation committee met the ministers of the government and explained the problems that the bill would cause Indians. They were told that the representation would be considered carefully. Despite this, the bill became law on 4 September 1906.

The next week, on 11 September, a large meeting of Indians took place at the Youth Empire theatre in Johannesburg. About 3000 representatives from the various sectors of the Transvaal attended this meeting and adopted the resolution: "We will not bow to the emergency law. If forced, we will accept the punishments meted out." The entire gathering rose and raised their hands, taking this pledge in the name of God. This was the historic start of the satyagraha by Indians under Gandhiji's leadership. The proceedings of this meeting were translated into four languages, one of them being Tamil.

Britain's deception

The Indian protest was, however, completely ignored by the Transvaal government. The only way out was for the British Empire to deny giving approval to this bill. To this end, a mediation committee consisting of Gandhiji, H. O. Ali, and others proceeded to England in 1906, and stayed there for six weeks, meeting the ministers. As Gandhiji and Ali were returning by ship, news was received that Britain had not given assent to this bill. The government, however, played a trick in the process. Hitherto the Transvaal province had not been given full administrative authority. Britain secretly declared that once the Transvaal had a government with full authority, they could give their assent to the bill. As per this, from 1 July 1907, the bill received Britain's assent.

The compromise

Later, Gandhiji formed the Satyagraha Sangam to oppose this law. They demonstrated in front of registration offices. Despite registrations being postponed, the efforts of the government resulted in the registration of 511 Indians. Many, including Gandhiji, who had refused to register, were imprisoned. Thereafter, at the initiative of Albert Carder, Gandhi and Jan Smuts agreed to come to a compromise.

The terms were that if the Indians came on their own to register, without any government pressure, the law would be rescinded for Asians, and the Indians arrested would be released.

In effect, Smuts deceived Gandhi, for he did not rescind the law, but on the contrary, passed a new law governing Indians who had voluntarily come to register. Gandhiji rose in anger. He exhorted the Indians to burn all the registration papers in a massive meeting. He made the protest against the law—that no Indians could enter the Transvaal afresh—an essential part of his satyagraha. A few well-placed Indians defied this ban and crossed over from Natal to the Transvaal, and were promptly arrested. Indian merchants on the streets who refused to show their licences when demanded by the authorities were sent to prison. The restrictions imposed by the government increased. Indians in jail were subjected to torture, including Gandhiji who was kept under rigorous imprisonment. Previously, citing the shortage of space in jails and the cost of keeping them imprisoned in the Transvaal, the government had, under the guise of transfer, sent several Indians to the provinces of Natal and Orange Free State. Now, however, they started repatriating them to India. Opposing this, Gandhiji filed a case in the South African Supreme Court, arguing that it was against the law to exile Indians from the country. The Supreme Court upheld this plea. Subsequently, some white people began to target Indians who had been prominently involved in the satyagraha, by destroying their livelihood. This resulted in many Indians becoming paupers. Indians who were active in the satyagraha began to tire. Again, in 1909, Gandhiji set sail for England. But he did not succeed in his mission there.

Tolstoy Farm

At the same time, there was also a lack of funds to continue the struggle because of a financial squeeze. A few Indian industrialists, government organisations and kings of princely states sent funds. A German named Hermann Kallenbach (1871–1945) bought an 1100-acre farm, 21 miles from Johannesburg, and gifted it to Gandhiji. Gandhiji named it the Tolstoy Farm. Because of this, those who had sacrificed their livelihoods in the satyagraha could find some comfort in working and making a living on this farm. The families of satyagrahis who had gone to jail could now live in one place that was organised like in a cooperative combine. Gujaratis, Tamils, Telugu-speaking people and many other Indians found their homes here.

In the beginning, when the Tolstoy Farm was being established, Kallenbach, Gandhiji and his two sons chose their living quarters. They were in the process of allotting the houses for the satyagrahis. Around that time, some Tamil women, together with Thambi Naidu, Gopal Naidu and others came there, and they began to inspect the houses, as if to rent the premises. Gandhiji and others cooked and served food for the guests. Kallenbach showed them around the farm. All of them expressed happiness in coming to settle on the Tolstoy Farm. Gopal Naidu stayed back. The road roller used to lay the roads in the farm was pulled by Chinnan, Kuppusamy, Manilal Gandhi, Gandhiji and others. Gopal Naidu was given the job of cooking. The responsibility for maintaining hygiene on the farm and the work of purchasing supplies from Johannesbuurg were entrusted to Thambi Naidu ('Thambi' in Tamil means younger brother).

In the school established on Tolstoy Farm, there were children of different age groups, and they spoke different languages. Kallenbach, Gandhiji and others functioned as teachers for these children, but except for Gandhiji, no one knew Tamil. Hence, to the limited extent that he could, Gandhiji himself taught students some Tamil. The first students who studied under Gandhiji were Gopal, Chinnan, Kuppusamy, and Kuppusamy's two sons.

The peace agreement

The satyagraha revolt continued vigorously for four years. In February 1911, the South African government announced the removal of the racist regulations, and allowed educated people, irrespective of community, to enter the Transvaal. Pursuant to the agreement arrived at between Gandhi and Smuts, Indians were permitted to carry on their businesses in South Africa. From June 1911, the jailed satyagrahis were also released.

In 1912, on Gandhiji's invitation, Gopal Krishna Gokhale[2] toured South Africa. Wherever he went everybody, including the white people, accorded Gokhale a special welcome. Until the end of 1912, the peace agreement was not broken. However, the moment Gokhale left for India, Smuts declared that he would not rescind the 'three-gold tax'. It was when Gandhiji was considering staging a satyagraha against this strangling measure that the High Court announced a horrible judgement.

Notes

1. In Gandhi's time, and till 1969, Madras was the name of both the state and the city. After Independence in 1947, Madras Presidency became Madras Province, and Madras State in 1950, which was renamed Tamil Nadu in 1969.

2. Gopal Krishna Gokhale (1866–1915), Indian nationalist leader and social reformer, whom Gandhiji considered his mentor.

5

TAMIL WOMEN IN THE STRUGGLE

The legacy of Kannagi

Imbued with the spirit of uncompromising loyalty and integrity exemplified by Kannagi, the fiery protagonist of the *Cilappatikaram*, the seething anger of Tamil women was witnessed by the South African government during one of the demonstrations held by Gandhiji. Legend has it that, with an anklet in hand, a woman stormed into the palace of the Pandyan king and shook the foundations of royal authority, leaving the king, queen and ministers trembling in fear at the terrible curse that she hurled upon the city in her rage at the injustice done to her and her husband. Unaware of the mettle of Tamil women, the South African government looked on them as pathetic persons whose pride could be easily dented. But the women showed themselves to be latter-day Kannagis.

Law exceeding limits

In a case on 14 March 1913, a judge of the High Court of South Africa, a man named Sears, pronounced the judgement that only marriages registered as per South African law, and under Christian traditions, were deemed valid, and that marriages of Hindus and Zoroastrians, whether solemnised in India or South Africa, were invalid. Therefore, under this law, women who were married under Indian traditions, and were living with their husbands in South Africa, were not recognised as wives but, shamefully, as concubines. Their children, too, were denied legal right to their property. It was decided, therefore, to exhort the women to join the satyagraha in protest against this law.

When the women living on Tolstoy Farm were first approached, they gladly came forward. Gandhiji, as was his wont, explained to them in detail the perils of participating in such a protest. He warned them that they could face restrictions on food and clothing; there could be restrictions on their movement; they could be given arduous work in prison; warders could speak very rudely, and so on. Despite this, 11 brave-hearted women from the Tolstoy Farm volunteered to enter this battlefield. Of these 11 women, 10 were Tamil. Could there be a better example of the heroism and courage of Tamil women? The intrepid women from the Tolstoy Farm who enlisted their names for this satyagraha were: 1) Tirumathi[1] Thambi Naidu, 2) Tirumathi N. Pillai, 3) Tirumathi K. Muruge Pillai, 4) Tirumathi A. Perumal Naidu, 5) Tirumathi P. K. Naidu, 6) Tirumathi K. Chinnasamy Naidu, 7) Tirumathi N. S. Pillai, 8) Tirumathi R. Amuthalingam, 9) Tirumathi Bhavani Dayal, 10) Tirumathi Meenakshi Pillai, and 11) Tirumathi Bhagyam Murugesa Pillai. Other than Tirumathi Bhavani Dayal, all were Tamil.

When these 11 women gave their names for the satyagraha, one of them was pregnant while five others had babes in arms. It is true that these shining stars of womanhood were prepared to court imprisonment, but the Transvaal government was reluctant to arrest them. When these women entered an area called Vereeniging inside Transvaal without entry permits, they were not arrested. Even when they sold merchandise on the streets, the police did not act. As a result their protest reached a point of stagnation.

Women in prison

Gandhiji was unsure what to do. As a strategic measure, he sent his co-workers from Phoenix Farm (established in 1904 near Durban as a residence for satyagrahis, and to publish the *Indian Opinion* magazine), without entry permits, to the Transvaal, and made arrangements for the women who were in the Transvaal to enter Natal. Should the women not be arrested even there, he directed them to go straight to the Newcastle coal mines and to urge the workers there to go on strike. As most of the workers in the Newcastle mines were Tamils, Gandhiji was confident that they would yield to the persuasion of their Tamil sisters and strike work. As per this plan, among the 11 people from Phoenix Farm who were sent were

Solomon Rayappan, Rajas Govind, V. Govindarajulu, and Kuppusamy Moonlight Mudaliar. In this group it is important to note that, for the first time, Kasturba Gandhi, too, went. Gandhiji's scheme succeeded. As soon as this Phoenix group crossed the border into the Transvaal, they were arrested (23 September 1913). What was surprising was that the women who entered Natal from the Transvaal without entry permits were still not arrested. Hearing that the Phoenix Farm group had been arrested while they were not roused the women from Tolstoy Farm even further. More and more people came forward to join the demonstrations. The entire family of Thambi Naidu, including his sister-in-law and mother-in-law, joined the protest. It was at this time that the young Valliamma also joined.

As Gandhiji had instructed them, the women went straight to Newcastle and spoke to the coal miners there about the harshness of the three-gold tax. Moved by the appeal of their Indian sisters, the miners struck work. Could the government remain silent after this? Treating as illegal entrants those who had instigated the Newcastle workers to strike, the government gave each of them a rigorous three-month imprisonment, and sent the women to the same prison where the Phoenix Farm group had been incarcerated (21 October 1913).

Maritzburg[2]—where Gandhiji was evicted from the first-class compartment of a train, and where he pledged to begin the struggle for the rights of black people—it was here that these women were imprisoned. That the women were jailed together with thieves and murderers in the same cells enraged Indians, both in South Africa and in India. They were subjected to nameless tortures. Food given to them was virtually inedible. They were allotted strenuous laundry work. They were not allowed any food from the outside almost to the end of their sentence. But these women did not lose heart. In fact, their numbers increased by the day.

The heroism of Tamil women

Tamil literature is replete with instances of courageous women in ancient times, who, on hearing the war drums, have proudly sent their husbands or brothers or sisters to battle. The poet Okkoor Maasaathiyaar has sung of a woman who loses her husband in war on one day, her father on another day, and yet fetches her son playing on the street, clothes him in white, combs his hair, gives him a spear, and sends him off to battle. That this is not just a fable or imagination, but the reality of the heroism rushing through the blood of Tamil women was experienced by Gandhiji in South Africa. In December 1909, there was a conference of Tamil women. Speaking on this occasion, Gandhiji said in praise: "All the women participating in this conference are satyagrahis who have willingly sent their husbands or siblings and family members to jail. They have displayed their fearlessness to their motherland."

In February 1910, Gandhiji witnessed a moving incident. Two women, Tirumathi Ammakkannu and Tirumathi Pakkirisamy, came to his lawyer's chambers and removed all their jewellery—earrings, nose rings, chains, bangles, and even the chains that held their mangalsutra. They also took an oath that till the struggle ended, they would wear no jewellery. "My eldest son is being taken to prison. In a few days my husband will also be arrested. In such circumstances I shall not be able to wear any jewellery," said Tirumathi Pakkirisamy.

The "women who courted imprisonment were not highly educated. In fact, the majority of them were illiterate, nor were they aware of the noble principles of nationalism," Gandhiji said. But when they realised that the pride of Indians was at stake, they did not baulk at any sacrifice. This selflessness and faith can neither be expressed in words nor measured. Many of these women, after serving their terms of imprisonment, had been reduced to skin and bones. One of them, in fact, lost her life days after being released. She was the fearless Valliammal.

Notes

1. 'Tirumathi' is the honorific prefix used to address adult Tamil women.
2. Shortened popular version of Pietermaritzburg.

6

THREE MARTYRS
Valliammal, Nagappan and Narayanasami

Valliammal, a martyr like no other

The protests and satyagrahas led by Gandhiji were not just one or two, but many. The bravehearts who sacrificed their lives in such protests too were not a few, but many. But no one touched the Mahatma's heart as deeply as Valliammal. One reason for this could be the fact that she was martyred at the very dawn of his public and political life. Another could be that she was a girl, and so very young, when she willingly sacrificed her life for a cause she believed in.

Valliammal was the daughter of R. Munusamy Mudaliar, a grocery and department store owner of Johannesburg, who originally hailed from Puducheri, and her mother Janaki was from Thillaiyadi, a nearby village in Thanjavur district. Her father was one of the first Indian settlers in the Transvaal. Valliammal was born in Johannesburg. Even in her childhood her family was considered a modern and progressive family, and she was brought up in a modern way. She studied in a government school there.

The reason for victory

In his book *Satyagraha in South Africa*, Gandhiji talks about the sacrifices that brought the movement victory. He strongly believed that the fruits of the movement were obtained by the purity of the sacrifices made and that the martyrdom of one or more persons, with no concern for reward, was the reason behind the victory of the Indian revolt in South Africa. But who was that person or persons? Gandhiji answers: "Nobody can say whose sacrifice it was that was dear to God and gave spiritual succour, but we do know one thing—Valliammai's sacrifice was instrumental in our victory. Likewise the martyrdom of other sisters."

And so I write about Valliammai.

A martyr at sixteen

When Valliammal died she was just sixteen. Born in 1898 as the eldest child of her parents, she passed away on 22 February 1914. Her family itself was one of martyrs. Before she went to prison, her father had undergone imprisonment. Her mother, Janaki, went to jail along with her.

The issue that made the teenager boil with indignation and rage was the ruling that marriages under Indian traditions would not be considered valid. When she thought, "If one were to accept this rule, my mother would not be the legal wife of my father, and I would not be their legitimate daughter," she felt as if her heart would explode.

Valluvar said: "Just as the Himalayan deer cannot survive without its hair, human beings cannot exist without their dignity." Is not this an irrefutable truth?

Her father was unwell at the time. Admitting him in the hospital, Valliammal and her mother Janaki girded up their loins to oppose this rule.

Revolt and imprisonment

On 29 October 1913, young Valliammal joined the courageous band of women who were marching from Johannesburg to Newcastle (a distance of about 310 kilometres). She did not consider her duty done just by joining the ranks of these women. When the satyagrahis halted at Charlestown, Dundee, Ladysmith, Maritzburg and Durban, she performed her duties diligently. As her group was not arrested, they re-entered the Transvaal. On 22 December 1913, in a place called Volksrust,[1] Valliammal and her mother were arrested along with the other women and sentenced to three months' rigorous imprisonment at the Maritzburg jail.

Health worsens

Soon after she was incarcerated, Valliammal's health rapidly deteriorated. She was bedridden in prison. As per the terms of the interim agreement between Gandhiji and Jan Smuts, she was released before completing her full sentence, on 11 February 1914. However, she was already gravely ill by then. Valliammal died on 22 February 2014, within two days of her being brought home to Johannesbuurg, Gandhiji has written. Hence, one must assume that she was kept at the place where she was released for a few days. Had she not been released ahead of time, Valliammal would have died in prison. It was just before she was brought back to Johannesburg that her father had recovered from surgery, and returned home.

Moved to pity

On the day Valliammal was released from prison, Gandhiji and Henry Polak[2] had visited the jail. Valliammal staggered out in a condition so weak that she would have fainted if not supported. The satyagrahis, following utmost discipline in jail, had not requested for any mattresses or stretchers. Placing Valliammal upon a rug, her mother Janaki, Gandhiji and Polak gently carried her out.

Valliammal was a young, healthy, attractive girl. When Gandhiji saw her body so wasted and ravaged by illness, he was moved to pity and agonised that he should have been the cause. Visiting her at home, he asked her in great sorrow,

"Valliamma, do you not regret having had to go to jail?"

"Regret? Even now I am ready to go back to jail," was the brave girl's response.

"But, if this results in your death?"

"I am not worried about it. Who would not be prepared to lay down their lives for their motherland?"

Within days of this conversation, Valliammal left her mortal coil. The body hitherto clothed in flesh and bone became the object of veneration.

Gandhiji's heartfelt tribute

In *Indian Opinion*, Gandhiji wrote: "We mourn the loss of a precious daughter of India. With never a question of 'why' or 'what for', she realised and discharged her duty. She was a shining example of the mental strength of women in enduring suffering, of their self-esteem and dignity, which, I am sure, will not be forgotten by Indian society."

On another occasion, he said, "As I speak, the image of this young girl comes before my eyes. She has sacrificed herself for truth. Faith was her weapon. She did not have the education I had. She did not know what satyagraha was, nor was she aware what benefit would accrue to Indians through this satyagraha. Yet, driven by a limitless urge to serve her motherland, she went to jail, lost her health completely, and died in a few days thereafter."

Whenever he made a reference to Valliammal, Gandhiji would be overcome with emotion. "Perhaps the death of Valliammal was a greater shock to me than that of my own sibling (Lakshmidas Gandhi)," he said once. In another tribute he said: "When one considers the sacrifice of Valliammal, Nagappan and Narayanasami, the service of all other Indians combined (including mine) appears small in comparison."

Her name will endure

As a heartfelt tribute to Valliammal's sacrifice, the Indian community in South Africa decided to instal a memorial in her name, 'Valliammal Mandapam', which Gandhiji mentions in *Satyagraha in South Africa*. Gandhiji's words were inscribed on her memorial in golden letters: "Through her service, she has established an institution. Her pristine image is embedded in people's hearts even to this day. As long as India lives, Valliammal's name in the history of South African satyagraha will endure."

It has indeed endured.

As if to prove that men were not inferior to women in this respect, a few young Tamil men too sacrificed their lives in the satyagraha led by Gandhiji; prominent among them were Nagappan and Narayanasami.

Nagappan, the fearless

Gandhiji was in London for discussions with the British ministers to try and resolve the problems being faced by South African Indians, when he received news that his eldest son, Harilal, had been arrested in South Africa. He consoled himself with the thought of Nagappan, the Tamil youth whose noble example he cited in the *Indian Opinion*:

"Nagappa, when you laid down your life for your motherland, were you also not a young man? I consider your sacrifice a blessing that was given to your family. Though you are no more, you will live on. Hence, why should I be distressed to hear that my son is in prison?"

The stories of Valliammal, Nagappan and Narayanasami tell us that these fearless Tamil heroes would rather give up their lives than compromise their pride and dignity. The three were not yet twenty when they fought like lions for the cause of their motherland and gladly sacrificed their lives. Should it not make Tamilians proud that Gandhiji recalled their martyrdom wherever he went, before addressing any gathering?

Prison or hell?

Seeing that the extreme and harsh conditions in prisons did not deter the Indian satyagrahis from courting imprisonment, the Transvaal government began to consider other ways of subduing them. Like moving heavy stones inch by inch, when measures to exile Indian prisoners from South Africa were enforced, although a few backed out, those with hearts as impermeable as diamond continued to put up a determined stand against the atrocities. The inhuman treatment they were subjected to in prison would be enough to demoralise and break any ordinary soul.

Desisting from the earlier practice of housing all prisoners in one place or a common enclosure, the Johannesburg jail authorities now separated the Indian prisoners, so that they could be tortured with impunity. The tasks allotted to the male *ahimsa* followers included digging, breaking stones and laying roads. In the freezing cold, Indian prisoners were led out for road work without adequate warm clothing or blankets. They were denied proper nourishing food. Once when they were taken to an open field for work, Nagappan contracted double pneumonia, and later died of it. The lack of double blankets and adequate food were what had caused the pneumonia.

No medical treatment

Nagappan was kept in solitary confinement under heavy guard for ten days. During those ten days, the jail authorities tortured him. Confined on 21 June and released on 30 June 1909, almost near death,

Nagappan breathed his last on 6 July 1909. When fever racked his body, the South African warders denied him medical facilities. On his release, the doctor who attended on Nagappan in jail, W. Godfrey, declared: "The cause of his death was double pneumonia, brought about by inhuman treatment by his warders in jail. In fact, if all those reports are true, his death has been hastened by such actions."

Learning of the circumstances leading to Nagappan's death, Gandhiji—at the time on board a ship sailing to England, to find a solution to the South African impasse—was deeply affected. This youth had carried out all his duties in jail without demur. Despite being subjected to hellish torture, not for a day did he regret going to prison. "The satyagraha must succeed" was his life's motto. Like meeting an old friend after a long time, Nagappan embraced death.

False judicial inquiry

Referring to Nagappan's death, the people of Madras State wrote to the British Parliament, protesting the heinous treatment of Indian prisoners by the South African government. The evidence of two witnesses to Nagappan's torture, Veeramuthu and A. A. Mudali, was recorded in their letter. A demand from the South African Indian community reinforcing the need for judicial inquiry into Nagappan's death was also sent. A South Africa-British India Association had been formed in London to look after the interests of Indians under British rule in South Africa. The secretary of this association, S. W. Rich, argued on their behalf. The first inquiry into Nagappan's death was held by the Johannesburg Fort governor, Bateman. The findings of that inquiry being adverse enraged the people. Publications like the *Transvaal Leader*, issued in Johannesburg, opposed the findings of the inquiry. A large number of people sent letters to these journals. The authorities ordered a formal judicial inquiry. The Resident Magistrate of Pretoria, Major A. J. Nixon, conducted the inquiry. The findings of this inquiry too were not favourable to the Indians. The fact that a government official went on record to say that "The inquiry conducted by the government into Nagappan's death was no more than an eyewash" is ample testimony to how contrary to justice it was. Appeals by the Indian and European groups to reopen the inquiry also fell on deaf ears.

Gandhiji's praise

In the effort to raise a memorial for Nagappan, Tirumathi Vagil (who was involved with the women's movement in Europe) was of great assistance. In Bloemfontein jail, a memorial stone was laid in memory of Valliammal and Nagappan in July 1915, and unveiled by Tirumathi Philip. Speaking on the occasion, Gandhiji said:

> Nagappan's face is not as clear before my eyes as Valliammal's, but I can well imagine the tortures that brave young man would have endured in the freezing cold imposed on him by his captors.
>
> I now realise how unnecessary it was to send him there. However, at that time, we were all preoccupied with what good we could do by the satyagraha, and turned their attention to that. Today we all accept how firm Nagappan had been in his resolve. He came out of incarceration with his body ravaged by sickness. He then said, 'What does it matter? We can die only once. If necessary I am ready to go to jail again.' What he said came true. The soul that had not known failure left his body. Born in South Africa, Nagappan was uneducated. By experience he learnt to speak English and Zulu. He had the capacity and patience to endure any kind of suffering, and fearlessness to lay down his life for the sake of his motherland. What more can one ask of a man?

Another young man like this was Narayanasami.

Narayanasami, the African Tamil

Narayanasami was a Tamilian born and brought up in South Africa. Till his exile, he had never been to India. Exiled to India and while returning to South Africa, A. Narayanasami fell victim to untold suffering and became a martyr to the cause. The extreme hardships pursuant to the exile took his life (on 16 October 1910), Gandhiji wrote in the *Satyagraha in South Africa*.

Travails in travel

After being exiled to India, the South African Indians, in protest against the measure, were returning by ship to South Africa in September 1910 on board the S.S. *Sultan*. They had been invited by

Polak, Gandhiji's friend and associate. Narayanasami was one of the passengers. The authorities refused to let them disembark in Durban. Hence Narayanasami and 31 other Indians set sail for Port Elizabeth. There too they were denied permission. They decided then to return to India, and so came back to Durban. Narayanasami and other satyagrahis on the ship had been denied boots and caps, and made to travel as deck passengers. As their clothes had been stolen at Port Elizabeth, they were forced to make the journey in the cold weather without adequate protection. Had not the Indians in Cape Town been generous in their help, the travellers would have had to go hungry till Durban. Some were helped with clothes. Enduring all these hardships, the satyagrahis had already spent more than two months on board ship. When they finally reached Durban, the High Court of South Africa ruled that they should not be taken out of the limits of Natal. Giving a twisted interpretation to the ruling, the local minister ordered that they be whisked away to Delagoa Bay (now Maputo Bay). This was the cause of Narayanasami's death—he was forced to go hungry, and already weakened by prolonged near-starvation conditions, passed away at Lourenço Marques (now Maputo, capital of Mozambique). Describing Nagappan's death as murder, Gandhiji wrote that Narayanasami's was a murder too.

Narayanasami was a gentle, law-abiding person. When he was exiled to India from South Africa, he was in good health. However, six weeks of sea voyage, the extreme and varying weather conditions, and the different ships he had to change to, told on his health, which worsened considerably. When his ship halted at Table Bay, no one, including lawyers, was allowed to visit Narayanasami or his fellow satyagrahis. Only after the High Court ruled on their petition was this permitted.

The complete satyagrahi

Gandhiji categorically declared: "We say that if one goes against the law, and is thereby punished, we should have no objection. This position has been accepted by most satyagrahis. Even when their protest against laws that offend their conscience is met with simple punishments, they do not bother to escape from them. However, I can affirm with certainty that, in this matter (Narayanasami's), when the torture is so severe as to result in a virtual death sentence, it cannot be accepted." He later praised Narayanasami in *Indian Opinion*, writing that, "Narayanasami deserves the garland of praise that is due to no other major satyagrahi. He was a complete satyagrahi. Hail to the parents who begot Nagappan and Narayanasami!"

When the Duke of Connaught visited South Africa (on 31 October 1910), one reason Indians did not participate in his welcome could have been the death of Narayanasami.

Other martyrs

Not just Valliammal, Nagappan and Narayanasami, there were numerous other unsung Tamil heroes who sacrificed their lives in this struggle. Selvan, Soosai and Pachaiyappan were shot dead by European plantation owners. To offer condolences to their families, Gandhiji came in 1915 to Tharangambadi (formerly Tranquebar in the then Madras State). There were countless other Tamilians who answered the Mahatma's call for satyagraha and joined him in his holy crusade against British imperialism. A leader among them could be said to be Thambi Naidu.

Notes

1. Near the Natal, now KwaZulu-Natal, provincial border, about 240 kilometres from Johannesburg.

2. Henry Polak (1882–1959), a British-born Jewish lawyer, journalist and activist who worked in close collaboration with Gandhi.

7

THAMBI NAIDU AND OTHER MARTYRS

Without parallel

At a public meeting in 1911, towards the last stages of the South African struggle, Gandhiji declared: "The personal sacrifice that Thambi Naidu has made has no parallel." There were two people who were always mentioned by Gandhiji with reference to the South African struggle—one was Sohrabji, a Parsee, and the other was Thambi Naidu, a Tamil.

Refusal to comply

In 1907, owing to their refusal to have their fingerprints recorded as per the 'Black Law', separate cases were filed against Gandhiji, the Tamil leader Thambi Naidu, and the Chinese leader, Leung Quinn. The magistrate who heard these cases ruled that all three should be sent out of the Transvaal. They did not, however, comply. The date fixed for their banishment, 10 January 1908, went by. These cases came up again in the High Court. All three accepted that they had defied the government orders. They were consequently given two months' simple imprisonment and incarcerated in the same cell.

A true patriot

Thambi Naidu was among the first lot of Indians participating in the South African struggle to be arrested. Born to parents who migrated to Mauritius from India, he made his living as a hire-vehicle contractor and merchant. He had no higher education, but his rich experiences served him well, and he taught himself to speak and write in English. He could also speak Hindi, Telugu, and Odiya. Many admired his sagacity in finding solutions to tangled problems. Although Thambi

Naidu had never been to his motherland, India, his patriotism was unquestioned—his love for the motherland was present in every drop of his blood. When the Black Law in the Transvaal came into force, Thambi Naidu was among those who stoutly opposed it. "I would rather die than submit to this law" is what he would thunder in Tamil at public meetings of Indians, where he was a regular and key speaker.

A natural leader

Thambi Naidu was the leader in all demonstration groups. Being indefatigable, his conviction in the movement was apparent on his face. He never considered any work difficult or unworthy, nor did he fail in its implementation. Whether chairing a public meeting, leading a protest march, lifting weights, or cooking, Thambi Naidu was always at the forefront. The hygiene work on Gandhi's Tolstoy Farm and the job of making purchases from Johannesburg for the farm were entrusted to him.

The number of Indian prisoners in South African jails at first was few. They had not considered cooking for themselves. But the numbers increased, and food in prison was unpalatable. They obtained permission to cook for themselves. Thambi Naidu turned out to be an excellent cook. Gandhiji was an expert in serving. Not content to be idle in jail, Thambi Naidu learnt Gujarati and tailoring.

Against the Black Law

In the revolt against the Black Law, when Gandhiji and others were in jail, the efforts of Albert Cartwright, editor of *The Transvaal Leader*, resulted in a compromise, whereby Indians would register on their own, and after a majority of them registered, the government would rescind this law. When the copies of this agreement were handed over by Cartwright, Gandhiji, Leung Quinn and Thambi Naidu were joint signatories, establishing the kind of influence Thambi Naidu wielded among Indians.

Mir Alam's attack

Thereafter, convening a meeting of Indians, Gandhiji explained the terms of this agreement, emphasising the difference between Indians being forced to record their fingerprints and doing so voluntarily. Thambi Naidu tirelessly assisted Gandhiji in this, as also in helping the registering authority to get this done. When Gandhiji went to their office to register the document, in anger at this misperceived betrayal, a Pathan named Mir Alam and some others blocked his path and hit him with a heavy stick. Exclaiming 'Hey Ram!' Gandhiji fell to the ground. Yusuf Mian and Thambi Naidu, who had accompanied Gandhiji, prevented Mir Alam and the others from doing further damage, thus saving Gandhiji from a worse fate. The ire of Mir Alam and his confederates then turned to these two, and they were severely thrashed.

Extend punishment

In July 1908, Thambi Naidu, Ko Krisnasamy Pillai, Veerasamy Naicker, and Gandhiji's eldest son, Harilal, together with some other Indians, were arrested for selling merchandise without a licence. Of these, Thambi Naidu, Krishnasamy Pillai and Harilal Gandhi, through their lawyer, Gandhiji, requested the court to award them as stringent a punishment as possible. In his argument, Gandhiji told the court that, were they to be released soon, they would commit the same offence again; hence by awarding extended punishment, the court would not only save time, but the offenders' health too would not be much affected. However, only Thambi Naidu was given a sentence of two weeks' rigorous imprisonment, the other two for just one week. After this, C. Rangasamy Pillai, Suba Veerasamy Naicker, Ramasamy and M. Sivalingam Pillai were arrested and given one week's rigorous imprisonment.

The hero rises

This time when the intrepid Thambi Naidu was jailed, Gandhiji wrote praising him. "There are only few Indians who can equal the courage of Thambi Naidu. He was leading a hand-to-mouth existence. His wife was expecting, and was full-term. Without caring about any of this he went back to jail after being released. Even in prison he behaves in exemplary fashion. The jail authorities speak highly of his behaviour. Still, he has not resorted to flattery, behaving appropriately like the leader of a demonstration. I am confident that Indian society will bring forth such heroes."

Loss of child

Thambi Naidu's wife delivered a still-born male child. In jail, Thambi Naidu did not know of this. Gandhiji felt deep sorrow at this loss. "The Transvaal government is responsible for the death of this child," he said. "It is because Shri Naidu was imprisoned that the child met with such a fate. I had occasion to visit Shrimathi Naidu on the day he was taken to prison, and she was in a very pathetic state. Another woman would not have been able to bear with such courage her husband being sent to jail a second time. Particularly in the condition she was in, one could not have expected to see this fortitude in any woman," he wrote in the *Indian Opinion*. On 10 August 1908, in a public meeting of Indians, Gandhiji reiterated in his speech, "The sin of killing Naidu's child rests squarely on Lieutenant Smuts. "When Naidu went to jail, his wife was in labour. Her child was still-born. Who, other than Lieutenant Smuts, could be responsible for this? Lieutenant Smuts is a Christian. He believes that there is a world beyond this one. He will have to answer for this there."

Even after enduring such hardship and great personal loss, Thambi Naidu's resolve did not diminish after being released from prison. To praise his efforts, a meeting was organised.

Failed agreement

On 26 September 1908, unable to reach any sort of understanding with the Indians, Smuts brought in a new law. The way it was introduced did not find favour with Gandhiji. Exhorting that no precipitous action be resorted to by the Indians, he said that first there should be an effort to reach an agreement with the government. A person called Hosken spelt out the terms of a possible agreement, and invited six Indians to speak on their behalf. Thambi Naidu was one of them. However, as Gandhiji's response to some of the terms laid down by Hosken was not accepted by Smuts, this attempt at an agreement failed.

Kicking the habit

Thambi Naidu used to drink a lot of coffee and tea, and he was a smoker. He would need coffee or tea every hour. In prison, however, he gave up these habits. "During the period of revolt I shall not grow my moustache," was another resolution he took. "As long as such heroes are there among Indians, our struggle will surely achieve victory," said Gandhiji, lauding him. There were some weak-minded prisoners who would secretly manage to get food brought to them. Because of such arrangements, even prisoners who did not smoke or chew tobacco began to indulge in these vices in jail. Gandhiji admonished them saying that not only should they be ashamed of their behaviour, but they should follow Naidu's example.

A braveheart

In later days, when Gandhiji spoke of the valour of Sardar Patel, he would refer to the heroism of Thambi Naidu in South Africa and say, "He was like a lion … a braveheart". On 6 December 1909, detailing the rebellious situation in South Africa, Gandhiji wrote to Gokhale, saying:

> Among the prisoners in jail, Naidu is the most courageous. In this struggle I do not know if there is anyone like him who understands the motives behind our actions. Although he was born in Mauritius, he is a more dedicated Indian than most others. He has sacrificed himself completely for the cause. Even if *I* compromise, he has written to me saying he will remain in jail alone and die in a Transvaal prison.

No welcome

In January 1910, Thambi Naidu, N. S. Padayachi, N. Gopal and N. S. Pillai, together with other Indians, were released from jail. At that time they received no congratulatory letters or telegrams of appreciation from the general public. Distressed by this, Gandhiji wrote in the *Indian Opinion* that he regretted that the welcome an eminent patriot like Naidu should have received on being released was not accorded to him and the others.

Lodging a protest

When Thambi Naidu was in Deep Klup jail, adequate food was denied to the inmates, leading to their near-starvation. When Thambi Naidu complained about this to the prison doctor, he was abused with the word 'Boer'.[1] This pained Gandhiji considerably, and he wrote to the prison authority complaining against this official. "The British Indian Association considers Thambi Naidu to be a person with a fearless disposition. He is not a person to lie. When he complained to the jail doctor about the semi-starved condition of the prisoners, he has been called 'Boer'."

Rearrested

One could say that the South African government was reluctant to keep Thambi Naidu out of jail. It had become routine for the police to rearrest him as soon as he was released. On 6 June 1910, he was arrested for the sixth time. It was just on the morning of his release after three months that Thambi Naidu had seen his son. The government did not seem to be able to bear the father and son spending even a day together. He was rearrested the same afternoon. In the major race revolt of 1913, 300 persons were led from Newcastle by Thambi Naidu. On 21 November of that year, when a strike was announced in Maritzburg, he was arrested.

Anger restrained

Thambi Naidu, who had courageously spearheaded protests against tortures and restrictions of the government, went on to become the President of the Tamil Welfare Sangam. In his last days in Johannesburg, amidst all these achievements, there was just one shortcoming according to Gandhiji. In *The South African Chronicle*, Gandhiji wrote: "If only he was not quick to anger and indignation, he would have become the leader of the Indians in South Africa. During the Transvaal demonstration, he did not give way to anger. His sterling qualities shone like sparkling jewels and diamonds. In later years, though, his anger became his worst enemy. I hear it came in the way of his good intentions and deeds."

P. K. Naidu

The movement gathers momentum

When the Indians were demonstrating against the government's insistence on entry permits into the Transvaal (February 1909), Gandhiji and seven others refused to show their permits at a place called Volksrust, and were sentenced to three months' rigorous imprisonment. While in prison, Gandhiji made strenuous efforts to learn Tamil as a measure of his gratitude to the Tamilians. Roused by these arrests, the struggle gained momentum.

Always ready

Seeing that the Indians were unwilling to yield, the South African government ordered the prisoners to be exiled to India. The Indians so exiled felt the need for a guide. When hours were left for the first ship carrying the exiled prisoners to depart, they requested Gandhiji to send someone with them as a guide. Gandhiji summoned his associate P. K. Naidu (PKN), and asked him, "Can you take these poor brethren to India?"

PKN: Why not?
Gandhiji: But the ship is about to sail.
PKN: Let it.
Gandhiji: But your clothes and food?
PKN: As far as clothes are concerned, the suit I am wearing now is enough. Adequate food I will get on the ship.

Gandhiji was delighted to find someone so full of conviction and ready. "I will prove that I am a disciplined soldier," declared P. K. Naidu as he boarded the ship.

Gandhiji's praise

P. K. Naidu had the rare ability to tackle any task however complicated and whatever the circumstances. "To illustrate the devotion to truth, when Sudhan was asked to jump into a a vessel of boiling oil, he did so without demur, and with a smile. Every satyagrahi's mental make-up should be so. Naidu was a prime example of this," Gandhiji wrote in praise. Born in South Africa, Naidu demonstrated that he was a pre-eminent satyagrahi by participating in all the protests, and repeatedly submitting to imprisonment. He served as a member of the Tamil Welfare Sangam.

Gandhiji's disapproval

At times, anger would get the better of P. K. Naidu, leading to his behaving violently. On one occasion a verbal exchange between him and another person from Madras city on the subject of registration turned ugly and ended in fisticuffs. The Madras resident had, against the resolve of the satyagrahis, gone and registered himself with the authorities, which led to his being assaulted by P. K. Naidu. When, after an inquiry by a magistrate, Naidu was fined ten rupees, his friends paid the amount for him. The magistrate went on record to say that he should have awarded a jail sentence in this case rather than imposing a fine.

Gandhiji also strongly felt that Naidu should not have got off with a fine, and wrote in the *Indian Opinion*: "I do not feel any pity for ... Naidu. Such actions only bring us disgrace. There is no place for violence in protest. Paying a fine to get freedom is worse than the offence. The friends who paid this fine too should be ashamed. To prevent others registering themselves by use of violence is to have not understood the very nature of this satyagraha."

This incident shows how strict Gandhiji was. The *Kural* says: "To prevent someone when on the wrong path by showing him the right one, and to share with him his sorrow—is this not true friendship?"

Expert barber

From the time the Indian protest started in South Africa, P. K. Naidu had been part of it. In January 1908, when Gandhiji refused to register under the law, he and five others were given two months' simple imprisonment. P. K. Naidu was one of them. Thambi Naidu joined Gandhiji in prison after four days. P. K. Naidu was expert in hair-cutting, more adept than Gandhiji, as he himself admitted. In prison, they spent two hours daily in this service for the inmates, some of whom may have in turn learnt the skill from them.

The trouble maker

Among the Indian leaders considered offenders in the eyes of the Transvaal authorities, one was P. K. Naidu. When he was released from prison in 1908, the authorities hardly waited for him to meet his family before rearresting him after a further inquiry, with a sentence of three months' rigorous imprisonment. For this, and for serving in the Indian ambulance service during the Boer War, he was awarded the war medal. P. K. Naidu's letter from prison, to Gandhiji and Rayappan's mother, reflect his courage. Gandhiji read out this letter at a public meeting, and exhorted others to follow Naidu's example. This time, when released from jail, a co-worker called Rari Naidu and Gandhiji's son, Manilal Gandhi, were with him.

Gandhi's letter to Polak

Gandhiji held P. K. Naidu's honesty and forthrightness in esteem. As Naidu was not proficient in English, he would seek the help of one P. S. Iyer to write to others for him. P. S. Iyer, owner and editor of *The Durban Chronicle*, had strongly protested the imposition of the three-gold law, and had formed the '3-Gold Protest League' for this purpose. He was able to influence the European-run *The Natal Mercury* and *Pretoria News* and obtain their support for the movement. But Gandhiji doubted Iyer's integrity and believed that, with his knowledge of English, Iyer was misleading Naidu. Gandhiji wrote a letter to Naidu asking him to be careful of Iyer, and also referred to this in another letter to Polak.

> Naidu had sent to me an article written in connection with the 3-Gold tax for correction. This could have been written by either Naidu or Iyer. Though you have written extensively in a letter of yours, I am still not convinced of Iyer's good intentions. He is a time server.
>
> He will write something today, and something quite opposite on another occasion. He is a completely untrustworthy man. I am reluctant to see him participating in any common endeavour. I tremble when he praises me. In fact I secretly admire him when he abuses me in front of four people, and covertly opposes me, because only then do I feel confident that he would not ask

me any favours in the work he does. That he is a Brahmin, and has a better command over English than P. K. Naidu, is used by him to lead him astray.

I pity P. K. Naidu, because, in character, he is way above Iyer.

Intrepid service

On 6 November 1913, the army of footsoldiers led by Gandhiji was formidable—it comprised 2,037 men, 127 women and 57 children. In the journey of such a large army, the service rendered by P. K. Naidu was commendable and a matter of pride for Tamils. On the first four nights, exhausted by the walk, the marchers rested in Palmsford, about eight miles from Volksrust, within the limits of the Transvaal.

After completing his work, Gandhiji, too, prepared to rest for the night. Just then a European police officer came up to him with a torch in hand and said, "I am arresting you". Gandhiji immediately woke P. K. Naidu, who was asleep near him, and instructed him what to do in his absence. Without hesitation, Naidu took charge of the group after Gandhiji's arrest. Gandhiji came out of jail on his own recognisance, and resumed charge. Again on 8 November 1913, Gandhiji, P. K. Naidu and four others were arrested. Realising that his presence was now essential for the struggle, Gandhiji again arranged for bail personally and obtained his release. P. K. Naidu went to prison.

Joseph Rayappan

Having set fire to their certificates, the Indians resolved to oppose not only the Black Law, but the ruling on exile. At first, educated Indians wanted to test whether they would be permitted to enter the Transvaal. Sohrabji Shapoorji Adjania, a young Parsee man described by Gandhiji as "pure gold," and who played a major role in the South African revolt as a strong proponent of ethics, intimated the government in advance and entered the Transvaal. He was not stopped till he reached Johannesburg, when he was ordered to leave the Transvaal within seven days. When he did not comply, a case was filed against him. It was heard, and Adjania was given one month's rigorous imprisonment.

Unpermitted commerce

The Indians were not fazed by the dilatory tactics of the government. Under the leadership of Seth Dawood Mohammed, a large group came to the Natal border and entered the Transvaal. They were arrested by the Transvaal police and produced before the magistrate, who ruled that they should leave the Transvaal within seven days. As they did not comply with that order, they were arrested again and taken out of the Transvaal. However, they still did not yield and re-entered the Transvaal. They were arrested and brought to court once more. The magistrate did not show any leniency. Seeing this, the Transvaal Indians were roused. To purify themselves for sacrifice, many desired to court arrest. Selling merchandise on the streets by declaring the prices required government permission. Hence they did so without permission, and were promptly arrested. One of the people who courted arrest was Joseph Rayappan.

A comprehensive work ethic

Less talk and more work was what defined Joseph Rayappan, B.A., L.L.B. (Cantab). Born to Tamil contract labourers in Natal, he completed his graduation from Cambridge University, in England, and his education as a barrister in Lincoln's Inn. Other than Gandhi, there were perhaps only three or four Indians who had a barrister's degree; one of them was Rayappan. But, rather than make money as a lawyer, he opted to join the protest movement, and despite being subjected to exile and enormous hardship, cheerfully endured it. Born and brought up in South Africa, Rayappan was raised with European habits, such as wearing shoes outside the house, speaking English at home and so on. So, rather than calling him an Indian, it would have been more appropriate to call him a South African. Yet, in his patriotism towards India and love for his Indian brethren, he was second to none.

Service while studying

In 1906, when he was still a student in England, he participated in activities that were supportive of the South African rebellion. He and another Tamil student, Rathinam Batthar, together with three other

South African Indian students, opposed the Asian (Amendment) Emergency Bill, by submitting a memorandum to the British minister, Elgin Prabhu. Under Gandhiji's leadership, the Transvaal Indian Mediation Group reached England, and Rayappan, along with Rathinam Batthar, rendered whatever assistance they could to them.

As a struggling, indigent student, Rayappan suffered a lot in England. Realising his predicament (and possibly on Gandhiji's behest), in 1908 Henry Polak sent him the fifty pounds he had received as reward from the British India Society. Even so, without adequate funds, Rayappan was unable to return to the Transvaal after completing his studies. Hence, a donation was collected and sent to him from the Transvaal, after which he was able to return in 1909.

Imprisonment

Within days of Rayappan's return, he had barely settled in his native Durban with his mother and family, when the call of the nation reached him. In December 1909, under Gandhiji's leadership, Joseph Rayappan, an Indian school teacher Samuel Joseph, translator and clerk David Andrew, Manilal Gandhi and others crossed the Transvaal border. They reached Johannesburg without being stopped or arrested. There, Rayappan, Joseph, Andrew and Manilal were invited to a gathering where 40 eminent European men and women were present, some of whom spoke about them in glowing terms. After this, the four carried fruit baskets and went about the streets quoting prices and selling goods without licence. Rayappan, Andrew and Joseph were arrested and evicted from the Transvaal. When they re-entered, the police arrested them and filed a case. The magistrate awarded each of them three months' imprisonment. When barrister Rayappan was jailed, some Europeans also commiserated.

The upholder of sarvodaya

Even at a young age, Joseph Rayappan had grasped the tenets of *sarvodaya* (service to all). Determination to live a life of physical labour and service to the poor became his way of existence. He did not consider any work below his dignity, and did not differentiate it from intellectual pursuits. In crowded markets, it was a familiar sight to see him carrying loads on his head. He would chop wood, wash clothes, and work as a labourer at railway stations, loading and unloading goods. In July 1910, on the day that he was released from jail, he went to Phoenix Farm and started working there. In the one-week interval between his release and exile, his work routine included cutting trees, sawing wood, loading and unloading of railway wagon goods and carrying them to trucks, drawing water, and washing clothes, together with a group of youngsters he had commandeered to help, demonstrating his commitment to the movement. At first, Rayappan travelled in the first-class compartment of the train. Once he asked Gandhiji, "Should I travel in the third class compartment?" to which Gandhiji replied, "Who am I to tell you that you should travel in first, second or third class? Who is going to respect your barrister's degree in prison?" Thereafter, Rayappan travelled only third class.

Travails in prison

Indian prisoners were treated like common thieves and murderers. Rayappan was forced to endure all kinds of hardships in prison. He and the three other Indian prisoners with him were transported in a garbage truck from the jail where they were initially incarcerated to Deep Klup prison. They were made to walk two miles barefoot, without headgear, kept starving, made to stand barefoot on the freezing floor and forced to walk barebodied in the biting wind. Some warders treated them like animals or worse. All this served only to strengthen their resolve not to admit defeat.

After this, Rayappan went to Durban to meet his mother and other relatives, before returning to join the protests. For a second time he was given six weeks' rigorous imprisonment. His associates followed him into jail. On his release, he was exiled again. However, he re-entered the Transvaal, and received three months' rigorous imprisonment.

Welcome to Gokhale

When Gokhale visited South Africa, the responsibility of welcoming him and arranging his tours was taken up by Gandhiji, assisted by Rayappan. In Durban's Town Hall, in the welcome accorded to Gokhale, the inscription on the gold plate presented to him was read out by Rayappan.

An exemplary, educated man

In the 29 January 1910 issue of *Indian Opinion*, Gandhiji writes about Rayappan in the article, 'Educated Indians', citing his life and work as exemplary and worthy of emulation.

> Rayappan sold products on the streets shouting out their prices. He is a barrister. Could anyone have believed that such a barrister would move from street to street as a vendor? But satyagraha means making the impossible possible. Rayappan's actions were useful not only to him, but a blessing to his family. Had he started work as a barrister, he would have earned some money from Indians, but it would be arguable whether such money could have been earned honestly. It is also uncertain whether his earnings would have been commensurate with his qualifications. He would have fallen into debt, leaving him and his relatives heartbroken. In the end everybody would have suffered. Today, however, Rayappan is poor. Through his example of hard work, his family, too, would have learnt to become self-reliant and happy. Will Indians follow the example of Rayappan? The answer to this is difficult. Those who can will lead happy lives. Uneducated Indians tend to look upon educated Indians as themselves. Hence such Indians become quite useless. In this context, what is the duty of an educated Indian? It is to do the kind of work an uneducated Indian does and so earn his livelihood. It is only by doing so that they would truly be of help to the uneducated.

Joseph Rayappan's relative, Solomon Rayappan (who was permitted to remain in the Transvaal in 1912) also participated in the revolt and went to jail.

Rathinam Batthar, Gandhi's favourite

In 1906, Gandhiji and H. O. Ali went to London as mediators. Despite his many preoccupations at the time and some physical afflictions, Gandhiji devoted attention to the education of an 18-year-old boy and took care of his food and clothing. The boy was Y. Rathinam Batthar, who was born in Durban to an impoverished Tamil family. He did his graduation and went to London for Bar-at-Law studies. Feeling that his education as a barrister and his ability to serve the nation was not enough, Gandhiji took pains to make him study French and other languages at home. He even wrote letters to educationists like Professor Paramanand, J. C. Mukerjee, J. H. Polak, E. J. Beck and others in this regard and met some of them personally, showing his keen interest in the boy.

Gandhiji praised him, saying, "Mr. Rathinam Batthar is a person with qualities meriting appreciation. At this young age, if he is given good training, he has the potential to turn into a man of high abilities." He completed his Bar-at-Law studies, returned to South Africa and, like Rayappan, plunged into social work, rather than making money out of law practice.

T. Lazarus, the man who gave shelter

To exhort the Newcastle coalminers to strike work, the women who travelled to Newcastle from Tolstoy Farm in the Transvaal needed a place to stay. Under the stringent regulations imposed, people were hesitant to offer them shelter. The government was clamping down on anyone who came forward to help. Well-to-do Indians and other merchants were ready to help, but they were neither prepared to sacrifice their commercial interests nor go to jail. Then, one Tamilian enthusiastically came forward to offer his residence for the women to stay. He was T. Lazarus. A middle-class Christian, he had been a contract labourer himself and hence knew about the three-gold tax. He too had voiced his protest against it, and sympathised with the plight of the Transvaal women.

A refuge for Gandhiji too

As soon as news of the imprisonment of these women spread, the entire Newcastle coal factory labour force struck work and came out of the mines. Hearing this, Gandhiji rushed from Phoenix Farm. How could merchants who had refused accommodation to these women agree to host Gandhiji? He was in a quandary as to where to stay in Newcastle. Thus Lazarus's home became Gandhiji's refuge as well.

The house becomes a hostel

After Gandhiji arrived, the number of workers who came to see him grew. That house became a hostel. The mine owners had subjected the workers to enormous hardships, forcing them to leave their homes in Newcastle. As a result, hundreds of labourers landed up at Lazarus's house to meet Gandhiji. The kitchen fires burned day and night. Both Lazarus and his wife showed themselves equal to the occasion. They welcomed and served all cheerfully. Lazarus was ready to go to prison—even if it meant that his family would be ruined.

Vincent Lawrence

Balasundaram was certainly the one who was responsible for bringing the Tamils closer to Gandhiji. But the first Tamilian to interact with Gandhiji and function as his ghost writer was most likely Vincent Lawrence. He was the one who translated what Balasundaram said to Gandhiji. He also taught Tamil to those who did not know the language. Later, Lawrence almost became a member of Gandhiji's family and stayed with them for four and a half years. He and his wife were devout Roman Catholics. For his commendable work for the Christian faith, the Pope presented Lawrence with a gold medallion.

The fight with Mehtab

One day, when there was a bitter fight between Gandhiji and his old friend, Sheikh Mehtab, it was Lawrence who intervened to keep Mehtab from assaulting Gandhiji. Mehtab was Gandhiji's schoolmate. His vices, even during his schooldays, were known to Gandhiji, but he befriended him, believing he could reform him.

On reaching South Africa, Gandhiji invited his old friend to look after his house, as his work had become pressing. But, discovering him at home one day with a prostitute, Gandhiji got enraged and ordered him to leave the house. The heated argument that resulted between the two led to Mehtab threatening to assault Gandhiji, when Lawrence stepped in and caught Mehtab from behind. It was Gandhiji who separated them as they were rolling on the floor.

Lawrence was prepared to go to any lengths for Gandhiji, such was his loyalty. While working with Gandhiji, Lawrence would often assist him during public meetings. On occasions when Lawrence could not return home till 9 p.m. due to the work pressure, he would expose himself to police action as per the curfew regulations imposed then.

V. A. Chettiar

A family of jailbirds

A person who took a significant part in the protest, and was the head of the Tamil Welfare Sangam, V. A. Chettiar, was chosen as a representative of the Indian mediation group that went to London in 1909. On the threshold of his departure for London, the government arrested him (for the second time), preventing him from making the trip. About 55 years of age, Chettiar had been a resident of Johannesburg for over 10 years. At the time Chettiar went to jail for the second time, his son, then only 19, had been jailed five times already. Hence we can well realise the burning patriotism of the young man.

When jailed for the second time, Chettiar was quite sick. Even so, the Transvaal government decided to exile him. By 1910, when he was imprisoned a third time, his son had been arrested seven times. Concerned about Chettiar's health, Gandhiji requested the government by a letter to treat him well.

With Chettiar and his son going in and out of jail so many times, there was no one to look after his family, which descended deeper and deeper into poverty. A well-to-do man at one time, Chettiar became a pauper by 1910. He met the expenses of his house by selling their jewellery items one after the other. Aware of all this, Gandhiji declared,

> If anyone feels that a society with such brave people cannot attain its goal, he should only be an atheist. The example of Chettiar will give even pessimistic Indians goose pimples. He is an elderly man, the leader of the Tamil society. His son has been imprisoned several times. Now the government has ordered the exile of his daughter to India. Without fearing arrest, Chettiar had been working on the outside. He, too, has now been arrested. He is indifferent even to his ill health.
>
> He has lost all his wealth. Still, rather than surrendering, his feelings of dignity, national welfare, and even death in protection of his oath, run through every drop of his blood.

The *Indian Opinion* of 14 May 1910, carried a photograph of Chettiar with a written tribute to him, his son, and the Tamil society.

In August 1912, Chettiar returned from South Africa to his homeland. Before his departure, on 1 August, a farewell function was organised. About 300 people, including Europeans favourable to the movement, attended. Paying tributes to Chettiar, Gandhiji, Rev. Dr Ross, Rev. Toke, Hosken and others spoke at this function.

Munusamy

It had become usual for the South African government to levy fines on protestors, their refusing to pay, and courting imprisonment. Thousands of such people went to jail. Because of the high cost of maintaining these prisoners, the government was determined to consider how best to force the people to pay up their fines. Towards this, they began to auction the properties of Indians, in some cases confiscating them. As an example, the magistrate who heard the case of Munusamy fined him two pounds. He refused to pay this, and he was promptly jailed. The government then confiscated his house valued at 250 pounds.

All for the good

There is a humorous incident concerning a person who thrived while in prison. Raju Naidu, a Tamil, who had been given a prison sentence, suffered severe stomach cramps there. His reason for this gave everybody cause for amusement. "I drink 30 cups of tea through the day. However, I do not get it here. That is the reason for my stomach disorder," he said. His request for tea was not granted. Instead he was given some medicine, bread and milk. His stomach ailment vanished and he became well. Raju Naidu was a calm-tempered associate.

Jack Mudali

The agreement between Gandhiji and Smuts, that Indians may voluntarily record their fingerprints and register themselves, and that the government would thereafter withdraw the cases against them, was opposed by Mir Ali and his Pathani confederates. To dispel the mistaken understanding of some Indians in the Transvaal, as also some in Natal, Gandhiji came to Johannesburg from Durban and explained this agreement at a large public meeting. At the end of this meeting, armed with a huge stick, a belligerent Pathan came up on stage. Immediately all the lights were switched off. His efforts were not successful. Some who were alert to ensure that no harm should come to Gandhiji protected him. After the meeting, as Gandhiji was leaving for Phoenix Ashram, an entire platoon of people under a Tamilian called Jack Mudali accompanied him as escort. Jack Mudali was born and brought up in Natal. In his time there was no one who could match him in boxing skills. Whether against whites or blacks, he stood guard, always watchful when Gandhiji rested at Phoenix Farm—such was his devotion to Gandhiji.

James Duraisamy

When the British Indian Society was formed to safeguard the welfare of Indians, Tamils joined in large numbers. A Tamilian called James Duraisamy made it a habit to come to the office of this society and work without any remuneration. Referring to this, Gandhiji wrote in the *Indian Opinion* of 19 September 1908: "As Duraisamy was engaged in no other employment, he has been taken for work in the society without remuneration. No doubt it is necessary for Indians to take up honest employment to make a living. Everybody cannot leave his job and become servers of society. Duraisamy has other means to earn a livelihood, hence he is in a position to help the society with his work." Gandhiji conveyed to his readers that it was indeed necessary for them to work at an honest job to look after their families.

Manikkam Pillai

The tacit approval of the British government towards the misdeeds and tortures perpetrated by the Transvaal government was apparent in the exile of the student Manikkam Pillai from the Transvaal to India. Because he was a student, he was permitted to enter the Transvaal. The authorities connected with Asian affairs knew his father well. Manikkam Pillai was fluent in English. He was exiled despite his protestations that he was born in South Africa, was a student, and was thus legitimately permitted to enter Natal. Returning to Natal from exile in India, Manikkam Pillai re-entered the Transvaal, got arrested, and was sent to prison.

The exiled

Like Manikkam Pillai, other educated persons, too, were exiled, among them, R. S. C. Pillai, and T. A. Subramania Achari. Two Tamil brothers, who were born in South Africa, were also exiled. R. S. N. Mudali had lived in South Africa for twenty years, yet the magistrate who heard his case and knew of this, passed his order of exile.

Munian

When the Indian nationalist leader Gokhale visited South Africa, despite the assurances given by ministers and the government that the three-gold tax would be rescinded, a person called Munian suffered distress. Even after his paying this tax, he was found guilty of contempt of court, and given 14 days' jail sentence.

Sam

In the printing press at Phoenix Farm, there was a Tamilian foreman. Known as Sam, he was a good hunter. Suganlal Gandhi pleaded with Gandhiji to request Sam to give up hunting. Gandhiji, however, said that he could not force Sam to do this, but would try and persuade him in stages to do so. T. Pillai was one of the leaders of the group of 200 that marched from Newcastle to Volksrust.

Duraisamy Pillai

Kumbakonam V. Duraisamy Pillai was one who, at a young age, took part in Gandhiji's satyagraha and went to jail. When the author of this book met him, he recounted an anecdote.

> As Indians in South Africa followed different faiths, with idols and pictures of deities at home, the South Africans would chant:
>
> *Sami, Sami, ring the bell*
> *Coolie, Coolie, go to hell*
>
> Subjected to such demeaning conditions, it was Gandhiji who instilled in [the Indians] self-esteem and made them lift their heads high. I shared the same prison cell with him. Vernon was the name of the judge who heard my case. He told me that he would release me if I apologised. Since I refused, he handed

me six months' rigorous imprisonment. For two days they kept me in Johannesburg, but I still did not apologise. Thereafter, they moved me about three miles away to Deep Klup prison. Manilal Gandhi, Joseph Rayappan, C. K. Naidu and others were lodged there. After the term of my imprisonment, I stayed in Johannesburg for a while, before coming to India in 1913. I was well acquainted with the South African martyr, Valliammal, her father, Munisamy Mudaliar, her mother, Janakiammal, her brother and sisters. There was only a distance of 500 feet between my house and their shop.

Several others

Thousands of Tamils who took part in the South African movement went to jail. A partial list of Tamils who served jail terms is given below:

Kandasamy Pillai

C. Kanda Mudali

Ganga Padayachi

Gabriel Anthony

Ganapathy N. Pillai

Karumutthu Pillai

Kuppu

Govindasami N. Pillai

Govind

Govindasamy

Gopal N.

P. Krishnasami Naidu

Krishnasami Pillai

Saveri Pillai

Sana

Saminathan

Naidu V.

Naidu S. P.

Naicker

Pakkiri Mudali

Pavadai Naidu S.

Padayachi M. P.

Padayachi V.

Bana Padayachi

Chinnasamy

Chinnapa Rengasami

Subbarayulu Naidu

Subbayya Naidu K.

Chetty N.

Chetty S.

Chetty P.

R. Chokkalingam Pillai

Muthaiah Naidu

Munusamy Moonlight

David Anthony

Thambi Naidu

Natesan M.

Narasimhulu

Nayana Naidu

Nagappan Naidu

Maduramuthu Padayachi V.

Munusamy Naidu

Oorthan V.

Rengasamy Naidu S.

Munusamy

Munusamy Ellari

Mohan Anthony

Raju Naidu

Padayachi R. K.
Pakkiri Naidu
Perumal Naidu
Pillai S. R.
Pillai
Pillai A. N.
Pillai A. S.
Pillai C. M.
Pillai A. A.
Peter N. K.
Pillai Peter V. N.
Peter Anthony
Maduramuthu Batthar
Maduramuthu
Maduramuthu Pillai S.
Hala Padayachi
Edward Warmley
Ellari Munusamy
John Lazarus

Ranga Padayachi
Rama
Raja Francis
Ramasamy
Rome John
Rengasamy Naidu N.
Lakshmanan Varadachalam
Vallu Padayachi
Veerthu
Veerasamy Naicker Suba
Appasamy V.
Amirthalinga Chetty
Appasamy Naicker
Appu Chetty
Haridan Abraham Jameson R.

Exiled Tamils

Munusamy Chellan
Munusamy Paul
Muthu Manian
Murugan L.
Munusamy R.
Munusamy S.
Chellaiah
Chella Batthar
Pillai N. G.
Pillai N. K.
Chinnasamy Pillai K.
Chinnasamy Paul (16 years old)
Govind Chetty
Govindasamy L.
Veera Pillai
Veerasamy Naidu
Subbaiah Naidu

Subramania Achary P. A.
Tommy Govindasamy
Joe Chinnan
Daniel Arumugam
Toby Sabi
Arumugam T.
Peter Moonlight
Narayanasami C.
John Edward
Appan

Gandhiji's headache

That a few Tamils were ready to adopt base tactics was exemplified by C. M. Pillai. In 1906, when Gandhiji and H. O. Ali had gone to London on behalf of the Indians, Dr W. Godfrey and C. M. Pillai sent a petition to the British government complaining against Gandhiji. An alumnus of Edinburgh University, Dr Godfrey was a practising lawyer in South Africa, and had argued on behalf of Indians several times in court. Pillai was a translator by profession, but also an alcoholic and could be termed a loafer and a rowdy. Signed by 437 British Indians, the petition said that Gandhiji had no right to represent the South African Indians in Britain.

Dr Godfrey, who had been involved with Gandhiji's movement in South Africa, had expected that he too would be part of the delegation to London led by Gandhiji. He was, however, not included. Aggrieved by this omission, he, together with Pillai, misused the authority of the British India Association, obtained 437 signatures on blank paper, and sent the petition off to London. This petition said that Gandhiji had taken on the opposition of government as his sole occupation. According to the petition:

> Gandhi is a paid government protestor, from which profession he has amassed enormous wealth. In 1896, he was beaten and chased away by the whites. His activities have resulted in much wrongdoing. He has caused a rift between the whites and the blacks. The head of the British India Association, Abdul Ghani, knows nothing of all this. Ali (he had accompanied Gandhiji to London) is a revolutionary. In government matters he would want the authority of the Caliph to prevail. Because he bows to the British India Association, more Indians are reluctant to sign the petition.

Gandhiji was forced to explain in London the intention behind this petition, and a question was raised in British Parliament—testimony to the waves this petition created. On 14 November 1906, Churchill announced that he himself was going to examine the veracity of this petition. C. M. Pillai's actions thus caused considerable trouble to Gandhiji. Nevertheless, Pillai did participate later in the Indian struggle, and even went to jail, where he was found to be a bibliophile.

Another example of dubious behaviour was Ponnusamy, a washerman, who was in the habit of accusing Indians of wrongdoing and giving false evidence against them. On one occasion when Indians filed a case against him in court, the jury held him guilty, and the judge sentenced him to 18 months' rigorous imprisonment.

Note

1. The term 'Boer', derived from the Afrikaans word for farmer, was used to describe the people in southern Africa who traced their ancestry to Dutch, German and French Huguenot settlers who arrived in the Cape of Good Hope from 1652.

8

THE OVERALL CONTRIBUTION OF TAMILS

There are examples galore of how committed the Tamils were to Gandhiji's movement, how much they were a part of his reformist principles, and how effectively they were associated with him. In 1896, the Tamils presented Gandhiji with a gold ornament. In 1897, when India was gripped by famine, Gandhiji had initiated a cotton development fund in South Africa. Receipts for contribution to the fund were printed in Tamil and English. In 1898, to help on the British side in the Boer War, the Tamils, P. K. Naidu, J. Rayappan, M. Rayappan, R. Mudali, V. Lawrence and R. Govind were associated under Gandhiji.

When Professor Paramanand came to Johannesburg from London, among the fifteen signatories to the welcome accorded to him by the South African Indians, seven were Tamils. The leader of this welcome committee was a Tamil, V. M. Mudaliar. During the Boer War, on the side of the British an Indian ambulance brigade was formed. Of the 20 Indians in it, 12 were from Madras State (Andhra was a part of it at that time). In every public meeting, whatever be the language in which the speech was delivered, it was customary to translate it into Tamil, establishing that a large portion of the audience were Tamils.

At times, to explain the problems of Indians, a separate meeting of South Indians was held. In this, the majority would be Tamils. In August 1908, at such a meeting, among those who attended were P. K. Naidu, W. J. R. Naidu, S. Matthews, S. Lingam, T. N. Naidu, S. Kumarasami, S. Veerasamy, Thambi Naidu, S. P. Padayachi, R. K. Naidu, R. Dhandapani and K. K. Samy.

Deep Klup prison

The Tamils owned or managed several shops. Some were trolley contractors, others street vendors. Those employed earned between 6 to 15 pounds a month while those who were self-employed or merchants earned between 20 to 30 pounds. Because of joining the satyagraha, all these people lost their jobs and earnings and became paupers. It became necessary to financially assist these families out of the satyagraha funds. Still, these people never despaired. As the intensity of the protests increased, the repressive measures of the government got worse. The government had earmarked certain prisons where dangerous criminals, and those that the government wanted to subdue, were lodged. There were such prisons in the Transvaal too, one of them being Deep Klup jail, with a particularly sadistic jailer. He tortured prisoners to get work out of them. Many Indians showed that they could efficiently finish the work allotted to them. Yet, unable to bear the persecution meted out to them by that jailer, in 1910 they went on a hunger strike, demanding that, "...transfer this jailer, or send us to a different prison". This was in all respects a justifiable hunger strike. Normally all measures adopted in Transvaal prisons were harsh, but the suffering in this prison was particularly so. As the Indians' hunger strike continued, they were transferred to another prison.

To find snakes and scorpions in jail cells was not an uncommon occurrence. Once a snake entered the cell in which Daniel Arumugam and others were lodged. Arumugam was half asleep when the snake coiled itself around his neck. He woke up in alarm and threw it away from his body. Fortunately, the light was still on in the cell (in many of the cells in Deep Klup there were no lights). Arumugam woke up the person next to him as the snake was moving towards him. All the prisoners had by then got up. Someone brought a slipper from a neighbouring cell and killed the snake. This was not an isolated incident. It was in Deep Klup prison that a majority of Tamils were incarcerated. Every wall in that prison will tell a thousand stories of the agonies of Tamils who were confined within them.

Another horrible prison

Some Tamils were sent to the Pretoria prisoners' reserve camp, where the treatment was equally harsh. There were no bathing facilities. There was only one water trough for washing the clothes of 200 prisoners. When melted butter was requested with food, fat was mixed and given. The gruel they received was mostly liquid with little or no grain. They were given only half the standard ration. Digging, cutting trees, breaking stones, laying roads and pulling road rollers were the jobs assigned to them. Even though many of the prisoners in this jail were above 60, they would be sent long distances in the freezing cold without adequate clothing to cut grass in the fields.

On 23 August 1908, Gandhiji, addressing a massive public meeting in Johannesburg, said, "I have seen [the Indians'] suffering with back-breaking work in prison. They had no experience of carrying sandbags, but they were coerced into lifting these in prison. This was the prison protocol, which gave them all body sores." On hearing this, the people gathered at the meeting openly shed tears and cries of "Shame! Shame!" rent the air.

Sons proffered

I share another shining example of the patriotism of the Tamils in South Africa. Just before Gandhiji was to finally leave South Africa for India (on 14 January 1914), the Johannesburg citizens held a farewell function for him, Kasturba and Kallenbach. At that function, a prominent Tamil, C. K. T. Naidu, on behalf of himself and his wife, formally offered his four sons to Gandhiji for service in India. This intensely moved not just Gandhiji and Kasturba, but the entire gathering. In his reply to the farewell, Gandhiji said:

> Naidu and his life-partner have been jail birds for a long time. By giving their four sons in adoption, observing the necessary rituals, they have conferred their rights on the children to us. I do not know whether we have the competence to accept this responsibility, but I can give the assurance that we shall make all efforts to do so. Both at Tolstoy Farm, and later at Phoenix Farm, these four boys have been my students in the school I ran for Satyagrahi's children. When Shrimathi Naidu was in prison,

these four boys had been taken to Johannesburg. I wondered then whether we had lost these gems. But they have now come back to me.

It is in part the praiseworthy contribution of Tamils in the struggles of Indians in South Africa and their zeal and commitment to the cause that made Viceroy Hardinge take the unprecedented step of criticising the South African government in a speech in Madras (24 November 1913).

Exceeding expectations

Tamilians conducted themselves all along in a manner to merit the praise heaped on them by Gandhiji, unconcerned whether such praise was given to people speaking other languages. The moment they understood that Gandhiji's movement was based on truth, they jumped into the fire of his protests with fearless hearts. Not only did they accept imprisonment, but they were instrumental in raising substantial amounts of money for the cause. There was no Tamil leader out of prison all through 1909. Gandhiji said several times, "The Tamils have even exceeded my expectations of them." In fact, in Pretoria division, there was not a single Tamil out of prison.

Others should be ashamed

Many of them had made no arrangements for their families to survive while they were jailed. Gandhiji stipulated that the merchants of those places should look after them. In June 1909, there was a directive which demanded that all those named Ashwath in charge of shops will be arrested. As a consequence, every day, many owned up to that name and courted arrest. Majority of them were Tamils. "Other Indian communities should be ashamed of themselves," observed Gandhiji.

Madras takes pride of place

When Polak visited Madras in 1909, he sent telegrams to Gandhiji, who was then in London, about the public meetings held at various places, and the support of the people here. Because Gandhiji had visited Madras in October 1896, he had some idea about the people there. Hence, in his reply to Polak, he wrote, "Madras, to the extent of surprising all, takes pride of place in our conflict. The people there are heroes in their accomplishments, completing any work to 100% satisfaction. If they cannot, they would rather not take up the work."

Support to exiles

G. A. Natesan ensured that the Tamils who had been exiled to India from South Africa were not treated like orphans by the people of Tamil Nadu. The assistance he extended to the exiles and the funds he raised for the South African movement were praised by Gandhiji several times. On 23 August 1910, there was a large public meeting at Victoria Mandapam in Madras to decide on the sending back of South African Indians exiled to India from the Transvaal. The meeting was chaired by Sir S. Subramania Iyer, and Mrs Annie Besant attended. There was frequent correspondence between Natesan and Gandhiji.

Letter to Gokhale

In a letter dated 23 April 1909, Gandhiji wrote to Gokhale about the Tamil brethren.

> These days the South African authorities have shown keenness in arresting Indians, particularly Tamils. There have been none better than the Tamils who have participated in our struggle. Courageous as they are, they accept to go to jail time and again. With a view to dent the fearlessness of the Tamils, the Asia division not only wishes to obliterate them, but wishes to see that our financial resources are denuded by overspending. But I can only assure you that, whatever happens, neither the Tamil men, [nor] their wives or family will ever behave in such a way as to bring dishonour to our country while they are there.

Yes, indeed they did not.

What was the benefit?

Some may ask what was the benefit, if any, that accrued to the Tamils by such non-submission to wrongs inflicted. Was going to prison and sacrificing their lives the only 'benefits'? No, they did receive an unexpected gain. Before Gandhiji returned to his motherland (as he had said), whatever demands the Tamils had fought for were attained. The Tamils in South Africa who participated in the satyagraha gained many advantages. For example, the Tamil community there, which had been fragmented by minor differences, was now united and inspired by one aim—to work together for the nation. People outside the community and in the world at large also came to know how many heroes and heroines there were in Tamil Nadu. In sum, it can be said that the Tamils emerged with renewed spiritual vigour and determination after going through the fire of sacrifice.

9

GANDHIJI'S PRAISE FOR TAMILS

It was the moment of Gandhiji's departure from South Africa to India. The Tamils arranged a big farewell for him. He opened his heart out at that event in an emotional speech, and the words he spoke should remain encased in pearls in the history of the Tamils. He said:

> When I met the Tamils it felt like I was meeting my own brothers and sisters. It seemed an emotion that had been nurtured in me for so many years. The reason for that is very simple. I am of the opinion that, among the Indians, the people who bore the brunt of the revolution were Tamils. A majority of those who laid down their lives in this satyagraha are from Tamil families. I had been this morning to the church cemetery at a gathering to honour the memories of a dear sister and brother by raising memorials for them. Both of them were Tamils. In addition to this, Narayanasami's bones are drowned in the Delagoa Bay. He, too, was a Tamil. The exiles were Tamils, and the people to come out of prison last were Tamils. Those who hawked their merchandise on the streets and lost everything were all Tamils. A majority of satyagrahis at the Tolstoy Farm were also Tamils.
>
> Whichever aspect you look at, the Tamils have proved that they are the greatest examples of the greatest tradition. I do not exaggerate one bit. The unquestioned belief that the Tamils have had in God and truth has, for long years, been the life giving strength for all of us. Among the women who went to jail, the majority were Tamils. Who were the people defying the authority, unafraid of being arrested, who went from house to house, mine to mine in Newcastle, exhorting the workers to lay down their tools and strike work? Who were they? Again, Tamil sisters. Who were those who prepared these women for protests? Definitely Tamils. Who were they who subsisted on

one dried piece of bread and an ounce of sugar? Largely Tamils. In this matter, even if the sacrifice of people from Calcutta has to be highly commended, the majority were Tamils.

Notwithstanding their strong response to the final clarion call, [the people from Calcutta] were not comparable to the Tamils. Though, by the end of the protests, they had more or less reached the levels established by the Tamils, there is no doubt that over these last eight years, the Tamils have been the supporting pillars of this movement. From the very outset they exhibited their abilities. Their presence in Johannesburg was minimal … yet if one looks at the number of times they went in and out of prison, it seemed much more. When [communities] were required as a whole to seek arrest and go to prison, the Tamils did it. Hence, when I attend a gathering of Tamils, it feels as if I am coming to a place where I am bound by ties of blood. Such courage, … such belief … such duty consciousness. The Tamils have shown they have it all.

However, they have not boasted about this one little bit. What I spoke is not in their language, though I have been keen to do so. Yet it was not possible for me. Still they fought with conviction. This has been a great and historic experience. I will guard it all my life like a treasure. How can I describe this association with them? I know they do not expect me to, either. Still, if I have to explain this, I should say … Whatever they and their friends have done for this movement has achieved fruition. They did not expect a result beyond the satisfaction of their conscience. They fought for their right to enter the Cape Province under a British regime, and they achieved it. They fought against the harsh laws of the Orange Free State, and won. The three-gold tax became a thing of the past. The women who went to prison, putting their marriages in jeopardy, can today claim to be proud wives of their husbands.

Gandhiji's praise

It was thus that Gandhiji extolled the Tamil people, who owed their heritage to Valluvar. In India or elsewhere, one has not read of so much praise being heaped by him on any other people. What better example does the Tamilian need? Who could have been better qualified than the Mahatma to exemplify a people who have been sung about in *Tholkkappiyam*[1] by Valluvar, by the Sangam poets Kamban and Ilango, and who belong to a land that has nurtured a Kannagi and a Valliamma?

A few drawbacks

Amidst all this praise, the ahimsa warrior has, however, not failed to point out a few drawbacks among the Tamils. In that historic speech he went on to add:

> The Tamils have the same sense of jealousy seen in other communities, too. Though at the time of the protests, this meanness was not in evidence, it was apparent in their actions afterwards. If only they could overcome these petty jealousies, and differences of opinion, be receptive to new ideas they receive in future, they would reach greater heights. Not only this pettiness ... like other communities the Tamils, too, are prone to verbal arguments on trifling issues, and fist fights. I desire that, to prove themselves worthy of service to their motherland, the Tamils need to give up these faults. However much I emphasise this is not enough. Also, if you have elected a leader, you must follow him. Instead, if you lend an ear to everything you hear on the street as you come and go, the efficacy with which you wish to function will be eroded. You must not worry if someone else succeeds. If you do not meet with success in this world, a greater success awaits you in the world beyond. We did not fight for wordly success ... a true satyagrahi does not do that. You should not worry about money or wealth. At all times your thoughts should be on higher issues. As a constituent of the society, you must strive to improve the lot of the society as a whole. One more thing ... I know something about Madras. I am aware how strong caste feelings there are in it. If you bring the same caste conflicts into South Africa, your mission here would be a waste. There are some advantages of caste, but to use them in a malafide manner, by terming some castes higher and some lower, will only result in your ruin. You do not belong to a high or low caste. You are Indians ... you are Tamils. Do not ever forget this. I have said this about Tamils, but it applies to the entire society, but because I expect so much from you, it is largely addressed to you.

It was thus that Gandhiji spoke at the farewell function organised by Tamils. While praising their sterling qualities, Gandhiji did not hesitate to point out their drawbacks. It was with the desire that Tamils should improve themselves that he outlined these faults. We are aware that these faults are still mingled in our blood. But that Gandhiji should have discovered them so minutely shows how closely he interacted with them. This relationship was not an ordinary one, but with a divine and spiritual element in it,.

Learn from them

On another occasion on 24 May 1909, in a gathering largely of Gujaratis, Gandhiji said: "We have a magazine for ourselves: we are able to air our views in it. The Tamils have no magazine in their language, but their strength is in how diligently they discharge their duties. They are God-fearing. We should learn from them, and follow [in] their footsteps. If we do so, we should very soon get victory."

Repaying the debt

When Nagappan and Narayanasami laid down their lives, Gandhiji said, "The debt that other Indians owe the Tamils is increasing by the day. Their fame is increasing day by day. After all this is over, how are we going to repay the Tamils? The ideal way to do this is for others to learn from their examples and silently work for our motherland. If we do not do so, it would amount to us Indians disrespecting ourselves!"

For Gandhiji, being in the gathering of Tamils, and speaking in praise of them, was as sweet as tasting a delicious fruit. One day (14 December 1908), when Gandhiji had been to Johannesburg on the invitation of Tamils, he was offered a garland. Gandhiji removed it from his neck, and put it on the neck of an elder Tamil chairing the meeting, saying: "Truly it is the Tamil who deserves to be so garlanded, as the Tamil society has so effectively demonstrated its ability in this protest. Hence, I honour your own leader with the garland you have put on me."

Everybody witnessed the high esteem Gandhiji that held the Tamil community in by this gesture.

Glory is theirs

When Gandhiji spoke about somebody's courage, it was usual for him to compare it with that of Tamils. Once, extolling the bravery of Parsees in an article of 20 February 1909, he wrote:

> Like the Tamils, I can say that the Parsees, too, fought till the last man. Before the Parsees and the Tamils, other Indians, Muslims, Hindus and others, should bow their heads in shame. When these two communities are there in our midst, why should we take the examples of anybody else challenging the courage of Indians? The Tamils and Parsees have raised their own victory flags. Although, at the end of the revolution, everyone will reap the benefits, the glory belongs to them alone. They will become the 'government'. It is only they who have a right to this. All of us will be citizens under them.

In the South African protest, when courting arrest for the third time, Indians of other communities hesitated and backed out. But the Parsees and Tamils exhibited the determination to accept incarceration yet again.

My people

In a letter to G. A. Natesan on 21 July 1910, Gandhiji wrote, "You have said that the courageous satyagrahis who were exiled belong to your state. I wish to assume the right to celebrate them as belonging to mine also."

Note

1. The most ancient text of Tamil grammar and the oldest long work of Tamil literature, variously dated between the first millennium BCE and the second century CE.

10

INDIAN OPINION

Tamil edition stopped

For Europeans in South Africa to be informed of Indian views from time to time, and to instil a consciousness of their rights among Indians, Gandhiji started a weekly newsletter, *Indian Opinion*. It was printed at Phoenix Farm, some 13 miles from Durban, in English, Gujarati, Tamil and Hindi, and demonstrated Gandhiji's realisation that the views of Tamils should be reflected in it. However, after some time, few people could be found capable enough to write articles in Tamil and Hindi, besides, suitable compositors were not available (as such people had to necessarily settle in Phoenix Farm). In addition, there was the cost of engaging such persons that could not be met. Hence, editions in these two languages were discontinued. Gandhiji tried his best to surmount these problems and continue the Hindi and Tamil editions by trying to persuade his close relative, Gokuldas, to learn Tamil to be able to compose in it, in addition to Gujarati and English.

The Tamil edition of the newsletter used to contain the horoscope for the week, prices of commodities, and details of ships leaving South Africa for India. It carried the banner of *Indian Opinion* in bold letters in Tamil and the words *Kadavul Thunai* (grace of God) under the sign of Vinayaka.

Great effort

Gandhiji's intense desire was to read the Tamil articles in the newsletter himself and to understand them first-hand. On 17 April 1905, in a letter to Suganlal Gandhi from Johannesburg, he wrote, "I am learning Tamil very actively. If everything goes well, I should be able to read and understand the Tamil articles by myself." For this, he ordered G. U. Pope's Tamil essays and other books, and read them. Not only did he make efforts to understand the essays, he wished to become the editor of the Tamil newsletter and get ready to bring it out. He also tried to prepare Madanlal for it.

However, at one stage, both the Hindi and Tamil editions failed to be published in the manner Gandhiji wanted. Translators could not be found even for the articles written by him in English and Gujarati, with the result that, with much sorrow and reluctance on his part, the Hindi and Tamil editions had to be discontinued.

Eminent Tamils

Gandhiji had often written moving articles in praise of prominent Tamils. For instance, in the *Indian Opinion* of 21 October 1905, writing about the royal Dewan of Thiruvangur, Sir T. Madhavarao, born in Kumbakonam, he says that, but for the presence of Madhavarao, the Thiruvangur Maharaja would have lost the Thiruvangur princedom.

Born into an impoverished family, Sir T. Muthuswami Iyer, through his unflagging efforts and intellectual ability, rose to the position of a high court judge. Writing about him in the issue of 11 November 1905, Gandhiji said, "his judgements appear completely fair, moral, and in no way inferior to the judgements of the English judges."

When Dr Sathyanathan, MA, LLB, of Madras passed away, in a tribute to the eminent professor, Gandhiji wrote: "He commanded respect from all quarters for his knowledge and humility. [By] nominating him as Assistant Director in the Education Department, the government [demonstrated its] respect and belief in his ability."

PART II

IN INDIA

Overleaf image: Gandhi during the Salt March, March 1930

11

IN BALASUNDARAM'S LAND

Departure to India

In 1896, on the day before Gandhiji was to leave for India from South Africa (4 June), to commemorate his services to India as the secretary of the Natal Indian Congress, the Gujaratis and Tamils of Durban organised a meeting at the Indian Pavilion. In that enthusiastic gathering, Gandhiji, in his reply to the farewell speeches, pointed out that the Tamils had so far not shown much interest in the Congress, and that they should now join it in large numbers. From that one assumes that, in 1896, till he came to Madras, there was not much presence of Tamils in the Natal Indian Congress. But thereafter, their numbers and involvement steadily increased. Gandhiji's visit to Madras must have acted as a spur to this.

To bring his family, and to acquaint the Indian authorities and general public with the travails of Indians in South Africa, Gandhiji left for India on 5 June 1896. Prominent Indian citizens in South Africa sent a letter to the effect that Mohandas Karamchand Gandhi was coming on their behalf to make known the plight of South African Indians. Forty-one persons, including the Tamils, A. C. Pillai, K. S. Pillai (and company), and Narayana Batthar had signed this letter.

Footprint in Tamil Nadu

14 October 1896 was the date on which Gandhiji first set foot in Tamil Nadu. Born on 2 October 1869, he was then 27 years and 12 days old. It was fated that he would return several times to Madras—to tumultuous welcome as a great leader in the future.

Even at that young age, M. K. Gandhi came to Madras as a leader. The newspapers here gave a lot of importance to his speeches and words of advice. His visit captured headlines. The Reuters[1] news agency sent reports on the visit to London. However, the misrepresentation by London in their news despatches to South Africa became a matter of much misunderstanding, causing him considerable misery.

The *Green Pamphlet*

During his one-month-long ship voyage to India, Gandhi learnt Tamil and Urdu. Alighting in Calcutta, he boarded the train to Rajkot. On board the ship, he had written an article on the travails of British Indians in South Africa, which he now got printed as a pamphlet, and distributed. As it was bound with a green cover, this came to be known as the *Green Pamphlet*. It served as a plea to Indians concerning the problems faced by one lakh Indians in South Africa. Till that time, no similar publication had been issued in subjugated India. In it, Gandhiji had disclosed in detail the many torments endured by Indians in Natal, Cape Colony, the Transvaal, and Orange Free State, as well as Balasundaram's story. Even at that time, he was 'Ahimsa Gandhi' and wrote, "We did not care about the attacks on Indians there, and that is the attitude I want from you." But in those days, how many could have understood the nuances of ahimsa?

From Rajkot, Gandhi went to Bombay and Poona, met prominent men like Ranade, Badruddin Tayabji, Ferozeshah Mehta, Lokmanya Bal Gangadhar Tilak and Dr Bhandarkar, explained to them the South African situation, obtained their support, and then reached Madras. From here Gandhi went to Calcutta, and met Surendranath Banerjee, Maharaja Jyotindra Mohan Tagore, and Sanders Mudaliar, editor of the newspaper *The Englishman*, and returned to Bombay to take the ship back to South Africa with his family.

The *Hindu* welcome

Within three days of Gandhi's arrival in India (on 17 October 1896), there was a notable write-up in *The Hindu* which read: "From South Africa as the representative of the trust of our brethren there, Thiru. M. K. Gandhi is in our city, and our citizens are here to listen to him, hear what he has to say, and what position he takes." Clearly, Gandhi was expected to address a public meeting here. *The Hindu* (which began as a weekly in 1878, and became a daily in 1889) expressed the confidence that Gandhiji would discover the wholehearted fellowship and kinship that the people of Madras had for Tamilians beyond the seas.

A memorandum

The renowned judge, Justice Subramania Iyer, the noteworthy lawyers Norton, Sir Bhashyam Iyengar, the editor of *Madras Standard* Parameswaran Pillai and Panapakkam Ananthacharlu were all taken with this young man, and gave him their support. (Sir B. Iyengar, P. Pillai and P. Ananthacharlu later praised Gandhi at a public meeting). Forty prominent people from various walks of life affixed their signatures on a memorandum to conduct a meeting under the auspices of the Madras Mahajana Sabha to speak about the travails of South African Indians. The first signatory was the Raja Sir Ramasami Mudaliar.

The seed of a leader

The seed that would sprout to accord him a singular position in world leadership was indeed already manifest in the 27-year-old Gandhi. His voice was unique. If one listens to his speeches or reads his letters even today, it is difficult to change a word. "Every word that I say in my pronouncements today I can convert into reality" is what he had the confidence to say with complete conviction. What he said dispassionately then has become a pathfinder for young people wanting to enter politics today. The reverberations of his visits to cities like Madras and other states were felt in the people's responses through telegrams of support received from places like Salem.

Newspaper publicity

Before public meetings were held, several newspapers of Madras advertised his arrival and wrote articles. *Madras Mail* wrote:

> M. K. Gandhi, Barrister-at-Law, who has already issued a pamphlet on the hardship of South African Indians, is now in Madras. He has the confidence that, by negotiation, he can improve the lot of British Indians. Some English dailies have

written that his manifesto is not true, and that, in some quarters it has only served to whip up the emotions of people. Gandhi has refuted this in a letter to *Times of India*. If one reads his manifesto carefully, one will realise that it contains the correct and honest resolution to the problem ... Gandhi has all our sympathies. Nevertheless, how the plight of British Indians in South Africa, namely the workers, can be removed is what is difficult to understand at this point. Please attend Monday's meeting in large numbers.

Public meeting

On 26 October 1896, at the meeting held in the evening at Pachaiyappan Hall, chaired by P. Ananthacharlu, Justice Subramania Iyer, Sankaraier Se. Adam, N. Subramaniam, and a large assembly of dignitaries were present. (Later, writing in *Sathya Sodhanai*, Gandhiji said, "I recall the public meeting was presided over by Dr Subramaniam." But it was in fact chaired by P. Ananthacharlu). Although Gandhiji's speech was long, the audience heard it attentively. Telegrams and letters of support for this meeting received from Salem, Tiruchirapalli, Srirangam and Kannur were read out by Renga Chettiar. Similar expressions of support and good wishes for Gandhiji's mission were received from Raja Sethupathi. (In 1893, Sethupathi had put in strenuous efforts to send Vivekananda to America. His support for public causes was conspicuous). Parameswaram Pillai also spoke at this meeting.

Powerful speech

Gandhiji had spoken at several meetings in Bombay, Poona, Madras, Calcutta, and elsewhere, but the hard-hitting speech he made in Madras was perhaps unmatched in impact. In some ways it can be compared with Vivekananda's historic oration in Chicago, after which thousands had run up just to touch Vivekananda. When Gandhiji finished his speech at Pachaiyappan Hall, there was such a rush to buy the *Green Pamphlet*, which he had brought along, that it was sold out, and he had to order another 10,000 copies for printing. Could Madras—Balasundaram's hometown—ever forget the grace conferred upon its son by Gandhiji?

Referring to the Madras visit, Gandhiji wrote in *Sathya Sodhanai*: "…The people [of Madras] were bursting with enthusiasm. The Balasundaram incident melted everyone's hearts. Even though I had to speak in English…, I got the feeling of being at home. Everybody I met showered me with affection, and exhibited much excitement at my objectives. Is there any barrier that cannot be overcome by love?"

Just before his arrival in Madras, the Natal Agent General from London had issued a notification pointing out drawbacks in the *Green Pamphlet*. Hence, Gandhiji took the opportunity to counter it at this meeting, categorically highlighting with numerous examples that everything he had said in the pamphlet was true. Speaking rhetorically to the authorities in London, he said:

> Respected people … we are all youngsters, lacking experience. You are older to us … brothers who are more free than us. At first, I felt that Indians could help the South African Indians in a significant way. Thereafter, realising that subservient India could not assist the South African Indians in any manner, I returned to serve the cause of India's freedom. This is something the Natal Agent General has the right to tell you. We can only complain against our tormentors. You have heard our cries of anguish. If it continues, the repercussions are on you.

His speeches in India angered the Europeans in Natal, particularly his reference to the attack on Balasundaram, which was reported by Reuters. This must have been the main cause of his being assaulted as he landed in Durban.

Learning Tamil and labour laws

Gandhiji stayed in Madras for two weeks. After arriving on 14 October 1896, he delivered an oration on 26 October. He spent those two weeks preparing his speech which he gave for printing at the Pricecurent Press and had it distributed to the gathering at the meeting. "The Indians in South Africa belong largely to Madras and Bengal. Hence you have, even in the normal course, a particular empathy towards the problems of South African Indians," he wrote in his preface to the speech. Having started learning Tamil during his voyage to India, he collected Tamil books while in Madras to further his knowledge.

In addition, he studied the labour laws prevalent in India. Gandhiji encouraged artistes by giving them money and enjoyed acts of street performers during his stay. The guards, gardeners and workmen at the hotel where he stayed here gave him much respect. (His expenditure statement shows that he lived and dined well. His 14-day stay at the Buckingham Hotel cost Rs 7440. In those days decent vegetarian food was available for three and four annas; Gandhiji's breakfast cost Rs 160 and lunch Rs 1130.)

Letter to Gokhale

Gandhiji conducted regular and proper correspondence by mail. On his way to Madras, in a letter dated 18 October to Gokhale, whom he had met in Poona, Gandhiji wrote that attempts were being made in an Australian province to prevent Indians from settling there, and if this was not countered, Indians would lose the status of refugees in that country. On the day of his speech (26 October 1896), he visited the Hindu Brahmagnana High School in Madras, escorted by Ramaswami Iyer, BA, LLB, and was shown round the classrooms. He remarked, "I have had the good fortune to visit this institution. As a Gujarati Hindu, I was filled with pride when I heard that some Gujarati patrons had also been responsible for establishing this institution. May this institution flourish. It is fully equipped to do so. I wish that such institutions are established all over India to promote Aryan culture."

Peaceful attendance

The Hindu reported the next day on the crowd that had gathered at Gandhiji's meeting. "Gandhiji was reading out his long speech in a low and soft voice. It is natural to expect some restlessness in the crowd. However, they were disciplined and quiet…This shows how completely they identified themselves with the sufferings of the Natal Indians." All newspapers gave due importance to his speech in their reportage. The editor of *Madras Standard* gave his word that whatever Gandhiji wrote would find a place in his paper.

The decision

After Gandhiji concluded his speech, the gathering voiced its complete support for the cause of the South African Indians. At the subsequent meeting it was decided that the British governments of South Africa and India should be immediately informed and asked to rectify the drawbacks in the system. P. Ananthacharlu was authorised to get a resolution signed and sent; Sankara Nair, G. Subramania Iyer, N. Subramaniam, J. Adam and Haji Batcha Sahib were also authorised in the matter. Another resolution—to the effect that no more contract labourers should be sent to Natal from India—proposed by Parameswaran Pillai and seconded by M. Veeraraghavachari, had already been adopted in Bombay when Gandhi had spoken there. Contract labourers in Natal were mostly Tamils; hence this new resolution was added.

Press support for Gandhiji

The day after Gandhiji's speech, the *Mail* editorial of 27 October 1896 read:

> Gandhi said that the anger against Indians in South Africa was because the whites there had not properly understood them. This does not somehow appear to be correct. In his speech Gandhi said, 'We realise that it would not be possible to mitigate the hardships and ill treatment of South African Indians at the hands of the whites merely by representation to the British government for intervention. Nor have we requested for this. There are honest people in all communities. The newspapers must bring this situation to the notice of such people. It is only when they openly condemn this brutality will we see the decrease of this intensity. At the same time, we do appeal to the British government to ensure that this anger does not get transformed into law. We trust our appeal will not be in vain.' Gandhi has the sympathy of all in India. The British government must see to it that any law governing the British citizen does not permit discrimination and divisive feelings. Should it allow it, it would not be doing its duty.

Also on 27 October 1896, *The Hindu* editorial observed:

> We believe that the efforts of Gandhiji to shape public opinion
> in India will prove to be helpful to the repressed people in
> South Africa. Gandhiji is a Hindu Barrister-at-Law, practising
> as a lawyer in Natal. He has embarked on a patriotic movement
> to mitigate the suffering of Indians there by highlighting
> them before the Indian and British governments to gain their
> understanding and sympathy. We need hardly say that in this
> noble mission of his, the heartfelt support and active help of
> Indian society and its people is there in full measure, as he
> makes efforts here in India.

Departure

On Tuesday, 27 October evening, Gandhiji left Madras for Calcutta.
Before leaving, he wrote a letter of thanks to all newspapers here.
We gather from this letter how successful Gandhiji considered the
meeting was, and what thoughts it had inspired in him.

> The general public of Madras understood yesterday that the
> demands of South African Indians had your full support. Their
> gathering in large numbers was praiseworthy. If I do not express
> my gratitude to them I would be failing in my duty. In truth, that
> meeting was a big success. It appeared that each person wished
> to outdo the other in making the meeting such a success. For this
> to happen, your heartfelt support was instrumental, and I thank
> you for it. It showed your belief in the truth of our movement,
> and threw up some drawbacks, too, which were important.
>
> To the respected secretary of the Madras Mahajana Sabha is
> due my special thanks. By toiling tirelessly and with enthusiasm
> for this meeting, he has made our agenda his own. With your
> continued sympathy and support for our cause, which I believe
> will be given, I feel sure we will get justice.

Income and expenditure statement

Gandhiji was careful about his income and expenditure. As much as
he was a Brahmin in his personal life, a Kshatriya in fighting against
an oppressor and a Shudra in his duty consciousness, he was a Vysya
in matters of income and expenditure control. He would not ignore

even a half or quarter anna in his accounts. He rendered accounts for Rs 49 and 11 annas as railway fare from Bombay to Madras. The meticulous accounts Gandhiji maintained during his stay in Madras can be seen in the table below.

Table of expenditure, 1 October to 28 October 1896, Madras

Item	Rs	Anna	Pice
1 OCTOBER			
Madras railway station	0	4	0
Guide	0	4	0
Porter	0	2	0
Vehicle hire (full day)	4	2	3
Artiste	0	0	6
Newspapers, envelopes	2	10	0
Vehicle hire from station	1	8	0
15 OCTOBER			
Vehicle hire	4	6	0
Postman	0	10	0
Newspapers	0	4	0
Tram	0	1	0
16 OCTOBER			
Stamps	1	0	0
Vehicle hire	2	3	0
Newspaper	0	8	0
Laundry	1	0	0
17 OCTOBER			
Newspaper	0	14	0
Vehicle hire (Full day)	4	3	0
18 OCTOBER			
Vehicle hire (half day)	2	3	0
Donation to Andrews[i]	7	0	0
Sulphur ointment (for eczema[ii])	0	2	0

(Contd)

Table (Contd)

Item	Rs	Anna	Pice
19 OCTOBER			
Tram fare	0	9	0
To Dinshaw Vacha (telegram) (an Indian leader)	1	6	0
Newspapers	1	0	0
20 OCTOBER			
Laundry	0	4	0
Newspapers	0	12	0
Fan puller	0	2	0
21 OCTOBER			
Note paper	0	14	0
Ink, pins	0	3	0
Tape	0	1	0
Native physician	0	8	0
Newspapers	0	10	0
Lace	0	1	0
22 OCTOBER			
Vehicle hire	2	4	0
Sweet	0	5	3
Photo	0	6	0
Newspapers	0	10	0
Tram	0	13	0
23 OCTOBER			
Vehicle hire	5	0	0
Tram	0	10	0
Stamps	0	8	0
24 OCTOBER			
For school children	0	13	0
Vehicle hire	2	10	0
Andrews	0	8	0

(Contd)

Table (Contd)

Item	Rs	Anna	Pice
Tram	0	1	0
Post boy	0	4	0
Newspapers	0	10	0
Laundry boy	0	12	0
East India Assam coolies[iii]	1	0	0
Assemblies[iv]	0	6	0
Main admin notices[v]	5	0	0
Assembly laws[vi]	0	6	0
Foreign notices[vii]	2	0	0
South African government notices (concerning drawbacks)[viii]	0	8	0
Spiritual progress notices[ix] (Madras District Town laws)	1	0	0
Main Madras institutions[x]	0	10	0
Tamil books[xi]	4	12	6
Andrews for books	1	9	0
26 OCTOBER			
Tamil books compendium[xii]	7	0	7
Vehicle hire	0	8	0
Tram fare	0	4	0
Newspapers	0	8	0
Vehicle hire			
27 OCTOBER	2	4	0
Vehicle hire	3	4	0
Internal telegrams	18	12	0
Madras Standard			
Telegrams on account	30	0	0
Tips to butlers	0	9	0
Waiter	1	0	0
Cleaner	0	8	0

(Contd)

Table (Contd)

Item	Rs	Anna	Pice
Cooks	1	0	0
Gardeners	0	2	0
Security guards	0	2	0
Baggage to Calcutta	3	0	0
Andrews	5	0	0
Hotel account	74	4	0
Newspapers	0	10	0
Laundry man	0	12	0
Pankha puller (for 14 days)	3	4	0
Fare to Calcutta	122	7	0
Guide	0	2	0
Stamps	0	4	0
Lunch at Arakkonam	1	0	0
28 OCTOBER			
Breakfast	1	6	9
Lunch	1	13	9
Newspapers	0	10	0
Water	0	0	6
Guard	0	8	0
Afternoon meal	2	8	6
Porter	0	2	0

Notes to Table: [i] Charles Freer Andrews (1871–1940), an English priest, a close associate and lifelong friend of Gandhi.

[ii] The eczema Gandhiji had developed on his skin during his voyage had not improved till this time.

[iii, iv, vi, and x] Books for studying various laws prevalent in India.

[v, vii to ix] Kinds of notices required to be sent to Parliament in those days.

[xi and xii] These show the seriousness of Gandhiji's intent in learning Tamil.

A cherished memory

Gandhiji cherished the memory of this visit to Madras and the welcome accorded to him then all his life. In 1915, when he visited

Madras again, he said in the welcome meeting arranged for him on the grounds north of Victoria general hall:

> In 1896, I experienced the time awareness of people in Madras, that I had not felt in any other State. I came in 1896 as a man unknown to you, arguing on behalf of people with no future before them. I found that Madras had the nuanced ability to discriminate between what was good and what was bad. I wanted to create awareness all over India about the plight of Indians in South Africa. However, you are the people (of Madras) who understood the problems fully.

There were shouts of "Hear! Hear!" from the crowd at this.

About 37 years after his first visit, when Gandhiji revisited Madras in December 1933, he referred to the reception given to him by students in emotional terms: "I am not new to you. Neither are you to me. Even in 1896, when many of you were not yet born, I was introduced to the student community. The labourers and true Tamil people alone knew me somewhat then. I still remember the welcome students gave me at that time."

Note

1. Established in London in 1851 by the German-born Paul Reuter.

12

EXPLORATORY TOUR, 1915

Seeds of nationalism

Almost a hundred years before Independence, the seeds of nationalism had already sprouted in Tamil Nadu. The embryo of the Indian National Congress was conceived in the city of Madras, the reason being that nationalistic fervour had gripped the Tamil people before the Congress had been thought of. The Congress had not considered fighting for our country's freedom at the beginning. Only an educated few participated in the birth of national feeling in Tamil Nadu. Independence was not the main objective at that time. The Madras People's Society and the Hindu Debate Forum had been established here by educated people, and, through these, they spread the feeling of nationalism. Sending representations to the British government was their main business. The members of these societies took pride in considering India as one country, and its traditions as the noblest. They did not like the East India Company conducting its affairs on purely business and trading terms, without any consideration for aspects of law and governance. Hence, their first demands, as stated in their memorandum to the British government in 1855, were that:

1. The British government should immediately take over the governance of India from the East India Company.

2. Thereafter, they should provide responsible governance under the rule of law. Education and tradition have empowered the people of India to appropriately participate in such a government.

The old and the new

Chanting the war cry of '*Vel Vel Vetri Vel*' when going into battle, and returning in triumph after vanquishing the enemy has been the tradition of the brave Tamils. The duty of the Tamil son of the soil has been expressed in song by a Sangam[1] poet, who said: "It is the duty of the son to wield his shining sword in battle, and kill the elephant, returning victorious."

The great Tamil army under Kattabomman (1760–99) raised the battle cry, "Get out, English white man," meeting the British in battle, and the army led by the Sivagangai brothers sacrificed themselves to enemy bullets (towards the end of the eighteenth century). Later in history, we cannot forget the Tamil youth who participated in the Resistance Movement. Analysing the political awareness of the Tamils, scholars have concluded that, following the footsteps of Valluvar, Tamils were aware of the tenets of the laws of governance, and were determined not to allow any violence. As an example, in his research publication, *Madras Administration*, Dr B. S. Baliga (1908–58) wrote: "In 1857 there arose the Sepoy Mutiny. However it did not find any echoes in the Madras State. The truth is that the people of this region did not believe that violence is the way to achieve their objectives."

A change of hands

There was a clamour all over India that the British government should take over the administration of India. At the end, it did succeed. Queen Victoria took over the governance in 1877. Although this brought cheer to the Tamil nationalists, it did not fully satisfy them. Their demand was not only for the abolition of (East India) Company rule, but for a responsible representative government. Hence they started working towards it.

Indian National Congress

The British government did not give in, determined to uphold the glory of their empire. They did give some representation to Indians in town councils and taluka boards, but the representative government that the Tamil nationalists demanded did not come about. In its place, the Indian National Congress was established in March 1885. This was one reason for the awakening of national feeling and fervour among the educated. In Madras, its districts and district capitals, many pamphlets and newspapers were started, and wrote criticising the taxes imposed by the government, especially the tax on salt.

The Congress in Madras

In 1897, the third annual session of the Indian National Congress was held in Madras with great success. It served to whip up nationalist feelings several notches higher in the state. Under the presidentship of Badruddin Tayabji, the representatives from Madras at this Congress meeting were T. Madhava Rao, S. Subramania Iyer, Rangayya Naidu, G. Subramania Iyer, Sabhapathy Mudaliar, S. A. Swaminatha Iyer, P. Somasundaram Chetty, C. Vijayaraghavachariar, prominent lawyer, Norton, and A. O. Hume. The Madras Mahajana Sabha, born a year before the Congress, helped to spread the nationalist agenda of the Congress in Madras State, and particularly in Madras city. Conducting meetings in almost all districts through the year, they debated on various problems and sought solutions. Many issues, including self-governance, discarding foreign cloth, the ban on foreign articles, establishment of Indian industries, giving new life to panchayats, and prohibition, were discussed in these meetings. The decisions of the district-level meetings were sent to the government. But the government was implacable.

Gandhiji arrived, and the government seemed to wake up.

Gandhiji arrives

A poet rightly said: "The man, who, without thought of his own happiness, makes all efforts to remove the sorrow of another by taking it on himself, is like a pillar." The time seemed right for such a man to step forward with a single-minded goal: working towards removing the misery of his Indian brethren without a thought to his own comfort.

Before coming to Madras

On 9 January 1915, Gandhiji arrived in Bombay with his wife Kasturba, with the decision to stay in India permanently, and to serve his motherland lifelong. Having lived abroad for years, he announced that it would be inappropriate for him to take decisions just yet on the problems in India as he was still to get fully abreast of them, and so he would, for now, accept the counsel of Gokhale. In India, Gandhi took to wearing the Indian Kathiawari kurta, turban, and dhoti tied in the *panchakacham* style. He found the '*naveena nagarik*' (new citizen) environment of Bombay a bit alien. He went to Poona, met Gokhale, and went on to Rajkot and Porbandar. From there he went to Bolpur in Bengal to meet with his fellow ashramites who had returned with him from South Africa, and to Shantiniketan to meet poet Rabindranath Tagore (who had recently won the Nobel Prize, Asia's first, in Literature, in 1913). Tagore, however, was not there.

India tour

As Gokhale passed away (on 19 February 1915) while Gandhiji was in Shantiniketan, Gandhiji returned to Poona with Kasturba. Thereafter, to acquaint himself with the situation in the country, he toured almost every region of India. He went to Rangoon,[2] via Calcutta, and again returned to Shantiniketan, to be welcomed by Tagore himself this time. When he went to Hardwar to participate in the Kumbh mela, together with his ashramites, elaborate banquets were arranged for him. This, however, did not please Gandhiji, and he took a vow that on any one day henceforth he would not partake of more than five varieties of food. Even in Madras he confined his meals to fruits, cashew nuts and such sources of nutrition. He stuck to his vow in Hardwar, not eating anything after sundown. He went to the Gurukulam, met with Munshiramji (who later became known as Swami Chirathananda), and returned to Madras.

Why he came to Madras

One of the reasons Gandhi came to Madras was, as per Gokhale's advice, to assess the situation in the country. But there was also another purpose. He went to Tharangambadi, to which many of the South African Indians who had sacrificed their lives in the struggle in South Africa, belonged. Gandhiji wanted to meet their widows to console them.

Though people had begun to refer to Gandhi as 'Mahatma' even while he was in South Africa, that title was not so prevalent when he toured Tamil Nadu, and the newspapers and people here still referred to him as Mister or Sri Gandhi. The honorific of 'Mahatma' became associated with him in 1919. Many in India were not aware that his movement was called satyagraha. Enlightened individuals like Subramania Iyer, who understood its principles, called it a 'spiritual opposition'. People also did not know much about Gandhi then. A journalist who met Kasturba wrote that she and her husband were Brahmins (when in fact they were Vysyas). In a function to honour Gandhiji, Krishnaswami Iyer, in his welcome address, called him a Maharashtrian. Be that as it may, Gandhiji's fame had started to spread in Madras State. His association with G. A. Natesan, what was said about him by people who had returned from South Africa, the resolutions being adopted by the Congress on the problems encountered in South Africa, the newspaper articles highlighting the issues in South Africa—all these helped to shape Gandhiji's ultimate victory in South Africa.

Above all, there was an important factor, as enunciated by Valluvar ages ago: "One who makes his own life an example is worshipped by all living beings."

A hero's welcome

It was because the people of Madras were well acquainted with the history of his South African struggles that Gandhiji and Kasturba were accorded the kind of welcome fit for a monarch on their triumphant return from battle. Individuals, civic organisations, government establishments and social welfare societies vied with each other to stand in the forefront of the reception accorded to him on 27 April 1915. In the welcome given by students, V. S. Srinivasa Sastri, who presided, said the Gandhis were hard-pressed to cope with their adulation.

There were welcome functions, meetings and felicitations every day for the service Gandhiji had rendered in South Africa. The welcome citation in Tharangambadi read: "To Sriman Gandhi, the leader of Indians in South Africa, this respectful welcome citation by the people in and around Tharangambadi". Every such meeting was attended by high court judges, senior officials, and prominent citizens, cutting across differences of belief or party. When Gandhiji later entered politics, however, they could not come close to him.

Plans for the future

D. G. Tendulkar, in his eight-volume biography, *Mahatma* (1951) writes: "In Madras, Gandhiji had felt he was in fact staying with his South African colleagues. Hence his views seemed natural when expressed. About his future plans, it looked as though he outlined the blueprint here." In other words, Gandhiji unveiled his plans for the future of India in Tamil Nadu.

During this visit, Gandhi's speeches—on ahimsa, caste abolition, *swadeshi*, the right to protest, and more—gave shape to India's political and economic problems. In an interview to *Associated Press* on 23 April 1915, he said, "I want to run an ashram here on the lines of the ashram in South Africa. The aim of the ashram is to prepare youngsters for national service. … the youngsters … who have come with me from South Africa are involved in this effort of mine."

Mammoth crowd

There were no banners proclaiming his arrival. Still, when the Delhi Express from Hardwar steamed into Central Station in Madras on the evening of 17 April 1915, the mammoth crowd that waited to welcome Gandhiji and Kasturba was like nothing ever seen here. A human sea thronged the station to get a glimpse of Gandhiji. The list of prominent persons gathered to receive him included S. Srinivasa Iyengar, P. N. Sarma, Dewan Bahadur L. A. Govindaraghava Iyer, Dewan Bahadur Karunakara Menon, C. R. Thiruvenkatachari, Khan Bahadur Walji Lalji Seth, Yakub Hassan, G. A. Natesan, T. Rangachari, Annie Besant, C. P. Ramaswami Iyer, Vidyasagar Pandya, S. Gurusamy Chetty, G. Narayanasamy Chetty, C. S. Govindaraja Mudaliar, B. B. Wadia, C. Handu, Krishnaswami Iyer, V. V. Srinivasa Iyengar and V. Ramadas. Many in the multitude were students.

Gandhiji not found!

When the train arrived, at first Gandhiji could not be found. Some searched for him in the first-class compartment, some in the

second-class compartment, doubting whether he would have travelled
second class. Nobody thought of checking the third-class bogie.
Would such a big leader, a noted lawyer belonging to a prominent
family, travel third class? They looked at each other, perplexed. The
crowd grew restless. Then the train guard arrived and said, "Gandhiji
and his wife have indeed arrived—there they are, in that last bogie".
Rushing to the end of the train, the people found an unexpectedly
lean and tired-looking Gandhiji standing at the entrance of the
compartment. After four days' journey, his clothes had become dirty.
The couple alighted with their bundles of baggage, looking like some
villagers travelling from the north of India.

As soon as the crowd espied Gandhiji, an army of people gathered
near his compartment. After all, don't the Tamils have a reputation for
greeting visitors enthusiastically! As per the state protocol for security
of VIP arrivals at the time, 12 policemen had been deployed for crowd
management. But nobody knew where they were, leaving Gandhiji
and the crowd to fend for themselves!

Hail Gandhiji! Hail Kasturba!

Formality required L. A. Govindaraghava Iyer to receive Gandhiji
with a garland, but the crowd stood in his way. Ultimately, somehow
finding a passage, he managed to garland Gandhiji, as cries of "Hail,
Gandhiji! Hail, Kasturba! Our hero, hail! Vande Mataram!" rent the
air. It looked as if the crowd would bodily lift and carry both the
train and Gandhiji from there! Thereafter, it was a veritable flood
of garlands. The women offered turmeric, kumkum and flowers to
Kasturba. Gandhiji thanked the crowd and was escorted to the chariot
that waited.

A human chariot

Students rushed forward in large numbers. The horses were unyoked,
and the students themselves began to pull the chariot. They pulled it
up to Natesan and Company building on Sunguram Chetty Street, as
Gandhiji and Kasturba stood in the chariot greeting all with folded
hands. On either side of the narrow streets thronged crowds, chanting
"Jai to Gandhiji!"

They reached Natesan and Company building. There were no microphones then, and everybody had to speak loudly. Expressing his gratitude to those who welcomed him, Gandhiji said: "I thank you for your affection. As we have journeyed for four days, I am extremely tired. As long as I am here, I will listen to the grievances of people between 3 p.m. and 5 p.m. every day." In anticipation of his visit, Ganesh and Company had printed more than 10,000 copies of his biographical sketch in three languages, Tamil, Telugu and English, to be distributed free. People did not know the kind of simple life Gandhiji had led. Hence, for the stay of the Gandhi couple, two rooms had been furnished with cots, tables and chairs. Gandhiji looked at these for a while and smiled. "Oho, has your son-in-law from South Africa come to his wife's home?" he asked in jest. He requested that the bedcovers be removed from the cots. In the room allotted to Kasturba, he made them take away all the chairs and tables placed there. Until all these were removed he did not speak freely to anyone.

Work or food?

Gandhiji woke up early, finished his ablutions, and washed and dried his own clothes before attending to his duties. He completed these chores before dawn. After that he would go for a stroll on the beach along with P. Natesan, assistant editor of G. A. Natesan's *Indian Review*. The first time he did so, he was offered coffee before proceeding.

Gandhiji's response was: "I do not touch that beverage. What comes first, work or food?" P. Natesan said: "Coffee, of course." Gandhiji firmly replied: "No, it is work." And saying so, he walked on. Natesan hurriedly gulped his coffee down and ran to catch up with him.

The press welcome

The Hindu welcomed the Gandhi couple with an editorial which read:

> The Gandhi couple returned, armed with a simple, yet difficult to use, weapon of truthful opposition, to fight for their motherland. The enthusiastic welcome accorded by the public on their arrival here illustrates the great respect and adulation

they have for them. Gandhiji had never held back his admiration for the endurance and humility of Tamil satyagrahis.

Now, one of the objects of his visit to Madras is to establish good connections with those who have returned from South Africa. Another is to spread the swadeshi movement to improve the economic conditions of Indians. He also feels that for self-esteem to develop among Indians, the study of their mother tongue is highly essential.

The *Swadesamithran* wrote in its editorial: "Although he was a citizen of India, having stayed for long years in South Africa, wherever he went in India, his exhortation to the people that it is possible to exercise their rights in fighting against repression, while preserving their dignity, will be etched in stone for generations to come."

Man of destiny

The extent to which Gandhiji's visit instilled happiness in the minds of the people can be gauged from the article in *Swadesamithran* by Pandit K. T. Srinivasachariar (6 May 1915 issue) in which he referred to Gandhiji as an '*avatara purushan*' (man of destiny).

> Mr Gandhi's foremost quality is that he loves the common man, and then only others. From the time he alighted at Central Station till he reached G. A. Natesan's place, the common folk who saw him, from fruit sellers to coolies, with palms joined in respect, praised him, saying, 'O, great soul who have come down for the uplift of the poor ...'. A beggar laid down the begging bowl in his hands and praised him … with tears in his eyes. An aged Mohammedan cartman did likewise.

About Gandhiji's meeting with Subramania Iyer, Srinivasachariar writes:

> On Monday 19 April, 1915, at 5 p.m., in Subramania Iyer's house, I was speaking about the sterling qualities of Mr Gandhi, when G. A. Natesan, together with Gandhiji came to see Iyer. The moment he saw him, … Iyer's inner tiredness seemed to vanish, and the brightness on his face was as though he had seen God's true likeness, much like that of a sadhu who witnesses divinity. Sir Iyer welcomed Mr. Gandhi, and introduced me to him. As they were conversing largely in English on worldly matters, I

heard Gandhiji using two Indian language words 'shanthi' and 'abhayam'. After they took leave of each other, I asked Iyer in what context these two words had been uttered. Sir Iyer told me that, according to Gandhiji, if our minds were always in peace (shanthi), we would ... not be in a state of fear (i.e. in abhayam), and resultantly, we will not feel any physical tiredness. This could be well understood by the people in Madras who were familiar with the teachings of the Puranas.

Srinivasachariar went on to say it was everyone's duty to worship a man like Gandhi.

> The advantage of Mr Gandhi having been so warmly welcomed by the intelligentsia and spiritual leaders alike was the hope that at least one aspect of Gandhiji's character should resonate with and inspire such a trait in the psyche of those welcoming him, as well as the common man. It is our country's duty to wholeheartedly and affectionately worship such a man.

Meeting G. Subramania Iyer

Gandhiji spent two days meeting and talking to people from all walks of life. To meet the distinguished nationalist and newspaper editor, G. Subramania Iyer, Gandhiji went to his house along with V. S. Srinivasa Sastri and G. A. Natesan. Iyer was then suffering from leprosy, despite which he strived to serve the nation as best he could, and was despondent that he could not do more. Iyer told Gandhiji that India was proud of the work Gandhiji was doing. "...look at me. I have become powerless to do anything because of my illness. Of what use am I to the nation?" he added, in tears.

Deeply moved, Gandhiji consoled Iyer saying, "Do not worry, you have done yeoman service for our country. There is no reason for you to be dispirited," and he wiped his tears with his own towel. He also wiped the puss oozing from Subramania Iyer's boils with his cloth. Recalling this incident later, V. S. Sastri lauded Gandhiji's compassion, saying that it could not be described in words.

Gokhale Club

Touring the country as per the wishes of his mentor Gokhale, it was members of the Gokhale Club in the Indian Labour Society building that Gandhiji first met and addressed in Madras, on 20 April 1915. It was an association of young people committed to look into people's problems, following the path shown by elders. Gandhiji dwelt on the objectives with which the Phoenix Farm had been established, and the conditions governing the induction of its members. "It is essential for the service of the country that one must adopt *brahmacharyam* (celibacy). Hence, only such people were admitted into Phoenix Farm," he said.

Someone asked him, "Are you saying that the whole of India should adopt brahmacharyam and accept poverty?"

"Certainly," replied Gandhiji. "I would say so without any hesitation. But, at the same time, because this rigour cannot be practised all over the country, I suggest that the following two concepts should be adhered to. One is truth, and the other is ahimsa. Ahimsa does not merely refer to [not] harming the body; it also has to deal with not hurting the mind."

Gandhi emphasised peaceful opposition to the government. "It (satyagraha) is a difficult weapon, and should be used only as a last resort, as when there is a threat to the dignity of a nation and similar such issues." Later, when he spoke about producing all goods by hand, he declared that he was against all kinds of machines.

Foresight

A Tamilian, who chaired a meeting that Gandhiji addressed on 21 April 1915, said:

> I am 73 years old. In all these years I have not had such a privilege, as today, to chair a welcome meeting for Gandhiji. We have gathered here to honour a very great man of India. … the man to have raised India's status in the world. Every house in India knows his name. This land has been blessed to have received the footprints of Gandhiji and his wife. This city itself has thus attained purity. … The events in his life, from the day he set foot in South Africa to this day, must be written about in all the languages of India in a befitting manner, and must be made available to every man, woman and child to read. However, although the work he has done so far is great, if we see the work that he has been destined by divine decree to do here, what he

has achieved so far should be considered only a past experience. Had he continued as a lawyer, he would have become a judge. If he had been in Bombay or any other part of India, he might not have had the opportunity to realise the strength of the soul (he has defined satyagraha as the strength of the soul). He would not have been able to use the power of peaceful opposition. His work from now on would not be confined to that of Gokhale, expertly pointing out the rights of Indians under the law in the Assembly. It will consist of people working together for the betterment of people. In South Africa, from dust, he created a precious stone. When he starts his work in India, true sanyasis will join him, and will strive, not for their redemption, but for that of crores of people. When the stamp of Gandhiji falls on thousands of workers, the Indian people as a whole will be uplifted. The strength of soul that Gandhiji is trying to generate is the power that India needs ... not army power.

A tribute

Gandhi's speech was made at a time when he had not yet assessed what work he should do in India, and the principles of his satyagraha were not yet known. How well this Tamilian had foreseen Gandhiji's future work and stature! The tribute above was delivered by Sir S. Subramania Iyer, in the open ground outside Victoria General Hall, on behalf of the India South Africa League, where Gandhiji and Kasturba were being welcomed. The Bishop of Madras, who was the president of the League, but could not be present on the occasion as he was travelling out of Madras on work, however, sent a message to the meeting: "There have been many who have striven for the nation, but there has been no one who can better you. You stand as a symbol of the divinity in an intellectual, and his intelligence. Mrs Gandhi represents in our eyes the essence of the virtues of womanhood. She walks with you in the short and long term, through gain and sorrow, at home and in prison."

This tribute was read out by G. A. Natesan, although he did not put it in a casket and hand it over, as was done in those days. He told the gathering that he was giving it as it is, because Gandhiji did not want such a casket.

Gandhiji's response, and praise for Tamils

Gandhiji rose and expressed thanks on his and his wife's behalf for the special welcome accorded to them. He said: "If at all we are even somewhat worthy of this welcome, it is due to be placed at my guru Gokhale's feet. It is because of his inspiration that, an exile, I was serving in another country. I am sure that, though we have not rushed to Madras, you will not misunderstand us, and have place in your hearts for us always."

He went on to speak about his visit to Madras in 1896, and the welcome he had received then. The first function Gandhiji attended and addressed concerning Indian politics was in Madras. There were no dramatic gestures, no fiery calls or high emotional moments. He stood and spoke in a calm voice that was not overlaid with modulated sympathy, yet his words were imbued with dignity and beauty. There was a singular inner strength to his speech, otherwise devoid of drama, which filled the hearts of the listeners. Gandhiji fashioned one garland of praise after another for the Tamils, and said:

> You have praised highly in your welcome speech the little work that I have done. Let us assume that I am worthy of even one-tenth of the praise you have heaped on me. How then will you praise those who have sacrificed their lives for the cause of the South African Indians' struggle? How can I extol enough the service and sacrifice for their motherland in the face of enormous tortures and indignities by 16- and 17-year-old youngsters, like Nagappan and Narayanasami? What praise can you offer for that beautiful 17-year-old girl, Valliamma, released from Maritzburg prison as skin and bones, contracting fever, and laying down her life within a month? Indeed, God has specially selected, from among Indians, people from Madras to shoulder this onerous responsibility. In periods of difficulty, do you know that the Madrasi in Johannesburg would not respect another Madrasi, if he refused to go to jail? I cannot accept the fact that those noble men and jewels among women undertook these privations upon my inspiration, as you seem to think. It is they, who, with their conviction, and work, without seeking any recompense, who have been my inspiration. It is their unshakeable belief in God that made them carry on the work. It is a sin for us to accept praise for the sacrifices they have made.

The Tamils understood that, although Gandhiji said that it was the Tamils who inspired him in his work, it was a measure of his humility. There was no doubt whatsoever that Gandhiji showed the way to the Tamils in South Africa, as Annie Besant and others said in their speeches afterwards.

Dharmic strength

The Hindu English language newspaper brought out an editorial on this meeting.

> The nationalism of those involved in political work, or those associated with organisations that encourage revolt, and their service mindedness therefrom, is very different to the intense nationalism advocated by Gandhiji, based on spiritual values. The latter is much nobler. This humble heroic figure is clad in only simple clothes. Yet his words inspire the emotions in people. They demonstrate his inner dharmic strength, Godfearing nature, and spiritual belief. In the face of innumerable problems, and in the present-day world, it is these qualities that help him in restoring the tolerance and dignity of this nation. Our country can well discern in him a worthy and qualified leader.

What *The Hindu* wrote went on to become true in later years.

The *Swadesamithran* wrote: "If Madras has had the good fortune of welcoming Mr Gandhi and his wife, true children of our Bharata Mata, and presenting the welcome address, we should indeed say that yesterday was an auspicious day. The honour of formally receiving Mr Gandhi in person, was honour indeed. India's pathetic situation, and its hard-hearted civilians were well understood by Gandhiji, who can be counted as a proud son of our nation, as per the likes of the late Gokhale and Dadabhai Nowroji."

In her newspaper *New India*, Annie Besant (1847–1933), the British social reformer, theosophist and political activist who settled in India, wrote, "We expect that he would undertake much greater work here than he did in South Africa, because, through his words and deeds, he is one who has the ability to urge people forward."

At Cosmopolitan Club

At the reception given to Gandhiji by the Cosmopolitan Club on 22 April 1915, the secretary, T. Rangachariar, introduced the prominent people to Gandhiji. The president of the club, Sir C. Sankaran had also come. The vice president, Thyagaraja Chetty, garlanded Gandhiji. There was a concert, after which Gandhiji, in his reply to the welcome address, said that he had a 'fight' with the leaders of the society. In those days, the so-called leaders of society, wearing fashionable clothes, met in clubs over tea parties, made speeches and dispersed, considering their responsibilities done. Gandhiji did not like this. He believed that simple attire, meeting the oppressed, empathising with them and giving them a helping hand to be the duties of society and its leaders.

"One who believes in justice and discipline, and uses it for the betterment of others, will be lauded by the world" is a valuable saying. It is thus no surprise that Gandhiji opposed the '*durbar* leadership' culture prevalent at that time, and wished to change it. In the Gandhian era, it was a welcome change that leaders emerged whose aim was to serve the people. At first, Gandhiji was unwilling to speak at a club. It is only after the persuasion of a few club members that he agreed. Referring to this, *The Hindu* wrote:

> Gandhiji said in his speech that there was a fight between the society leaders and him. Although he did not specify the nature of the fight, it was not difficult to guess what it must have been.
>
> There would have been no better place than the Cosmopolitan Club to say this, because, although it was called 'Cosmoplolitan Club' (the meaning of cosmopolitan being 'broad-minded'), it was in fact a place where only the affluent met. Gandhiji's aim, on the other hand, is to see how best such people identify themselves with the ethos of the common man.

Gandhiji's speech at the Cosmopolitan Club created quite a stir in the press. Welcoming Gandhiji's stand, *Swadesamithran* wrote in its editorial:

> Those who call themselves leaders of people have no love for the common man, said Gandhiji openly [while disclosing] what he had in his mind. They do not appear to be concerned about

the joys and sorrows, gains and losses of the common man, and thus have no real affection for them, is what we guess Gandhiji observed wherever he went.

The methods they have for the progress of India are not in conformance with those of Gandhiji. What is the combined experience of the leaders who went to receive Mr Gandhi, when he arrived? Where did they go searching for him? Was it not in the first-class compartment? What was the result? They concluded that Mr Gandhi had not come. But, where, in fact, was he? ... in the third-class compartment, giving no room for doubt that this was indeed him. This alone is enough to show the different mindset of these leaders and that of Mr Gandhi ... and how indeed different it was. The return of Mr Gandhi to India, and his plans for the progress, along with efforts and discipline that he is going to put in for it, are going to be at variance to what is being done now, is our impression.

This surmise of *Swadesamithran* turned out to be true.

The Congress welcome

We cannot think of the Congress Party without Gandhiji, but in 1915, there was not such a close bond between him and the Congress. He was looked upon as a nationalist who had fought for the cause of South African Indians. The welcome accorded to him by the Madras District Congress assumes singular importance. The Madras Mahajana Sabha and the Madras District Congress joined to arrange this welcome. In those days, there were no organisations in Madras other than these involved intensely in the national effort. The welcome and tea party for the Gandhi couple was arranged by both these organisations in Humayun Manzil, the residence of the president of the Madras Mahajana Sabha, Nawab Syed Mohammed. After the meeting there was a flute recital by R. Jagannatha Pillai, and a rendition of Kumbakonam Kandasamy Mudaliar on the harmonium. The Gandhi couple arrived with the Kuruppam Raja. Nawab Syed Mohammed Bahadur read out the welcome address.

Gandhiji's response

Gandhiji spoke briefly in his response to the welcome address. "They say that the green colour one sees in the distance is always pleasing to the eye. This is the reason why the work done by us so many miles away appears great to you. Now we have come to serve among you, and you are going to be observing us closely. Hence I request that whatever faults that may be seen in our work here may be forgiven with a broad mind" he said in all humility.

Apart from the hardship and rigorous imprisonment, which were a part of the South African struggle, even the fruits of his dignity and self-esteem were used by Gandhiji for the general good. The humility with which he spoke about his work in South Africa was an object lesson to the people gathered at this welcome.

"Humility is a virtue for all, but humility in a leader is special," said Valluvar.

One of the persons mainly responsible for arranging this welcome was C. Gopal Menon. On 23 April 1915, Gandhiji rested for the night at Tayabji's home.

24 April 1915, Special welcome for Ba

On 24 April 1915, at the special welcome arranged for Kasturba Gandhi (1869–1944, born Kasturbai Gokuldas Kapadia), more than 150 women attended, a large gathering in those days, in Anna Pillai Street, Georgetown, organised on behalf of Brahma Samaj under the presidentship of Tirumathi Adinarayanayya. The women were given fruits, sweets, betel leaves and nuts. Tirumathi Alamelu Mangammal in her welcome speech said that Kasturba would surely secure a permanent place in India's history. Kasturbai responded with her thanks in English.

Party by lawyers

When F. S. M. Corbett, then advocate general of Madras, told Gandhiji that he should thank the British government at the party organised by lawyers in Madras, Gandhiji was taken by surprise. However, he accepted their invitation. The reception by the lawyers was the third function organised for Gandhiji in Madras. Lawyers from other cities too came to attend this meeting. Together with the advocates and judges, there were about 150 persons. The advocate general presided over this meeting, which was held at People's Park, near Moore Market. Chief Justice John Wallis was the chief guest. High Court judges C. Sankaran Nair, T. V. Seshagiri Iyer, C. V. Kumaraswami Sastri, Tayabji, and Cootes Trotter, Small Causes judges Rao Bahadur V. Krishnaswami Rao Mudaliar, V. V. Srinivasa Iyengar, K. Srinivasa Iyengar, W. T. Barton, T. Chamier, V. Tirumalai Pillai, T. Prakasam, J. Krishna Rao and J. S. Rozario were some of the notable persons at this meeting. As desired by the advocate general, Gandhiji thanked the British government in his speech. He still had faith in and respect for the British government. Many people had asked Gandhiji before the meeting how, as a patriotic Indian, he could speak in consonance with the British government. Gandhiji offered his rationale for that at this meeting.

British democracy

Other than in the British Empire, whether Gandhiji's satyagraha would have been possible under German Nazism or Italian fascism is a question that must have been asked for a long time. While a definite 'yes' or 'no' answer to this question may not be forthcoming, in his speech at the lawyers' meeting Gandhiji accepted that there was more freedom under British rule for such a movement to be possible.

> This belief of mine is based on selfishness. As a satyagrahi I have found that I had some level of freedom under the British rule that I could not have received elsewhere. The satyagrahi needs to carry on his protest under any circumstances, and it is under British governance that he is able to do the kind of work he likes. He is given the liberty to act as per the dictates of his conscience. It cannot be said that in all governments such a situation exists, but [it] is true that it does in the British. I do not favour even such a government. I have said often that 'a government that rules least is the best government'. I realised that in the British empire there is a possibility of less government. Further, it is here that I have the right to protest. That is why I record my faith in the British rule.

Strong opposition

There were echoes of opposition in Madras from some quarters to this speech. As in other parts of India, there were people in Madras too who felt that Gandhiji, who considered himself a student of Gokhale, would faithfully follow in his footsteps. They did not like that Gandhiji gave the example of South Africa in saying that there, he had been given the scope to protest against the government. Observing that Gokhale would not have wanted him to speak thus, one K. R. Guruswami Iyer of Tirunelveli (then Tinnevelly) wrote a letter of objection to the press, while conceding that Gandhiji had probably done so under pressure, and that he might have said the same thing in a different way had he been given time.

Welcome by Muslim League

To know how the Muslim League of those days functioned, we may note the reception Gandhiji and Kasturba were given at Lawley Hall on Mount Road. Yakub Hassan welcomed Gandhiji to the meeting and said, "Give some place for South India in your heart," and further added: "Muslims and Hindus are proud to be equal beneficiaries of your work. I assure you from my heart that in any national endeavour of yours the Muslims will cooperate fully." Clearly, rather than asking for the special welfare of Muslims, the League sought the welfare of South India as a whole.

A promise must be kept

Gandhiji was a Vysya by birth and a Kshatriya in life. He took up Hassan on his assurance, and said: "You have made a promise that you will give your cooperation to whatever measures I plan to take up. Making a promise is one thing, to fulfil it is another. I will demand this promise of yours to be fulfilled at a later time, and I warn you that I will be very strict in it being implemented. When I ask this of you later, you will be in a quandary."

Gandhi cited the examples of several Muslims in South Africa who were true to their word in spite of enduring much hardship. The words of those who speak only the truth will indeed find fruition later.

If one looks at future events, one can see how prophetic his words turned out to be.

25 April 1915, Welcome by women

The date 25 April 1915 being a Sunday, there were more welcome functions for the Gandhis than on other days. In the Abheda United Anand Samaj building on Ramasamy Street in Mannady, the women of the Samaj welcomed the Gandhi couple in the manner of honouring great *maharishi*s and their wives, by washing their feet, adorning their foreheads with kumkum, and escorting them to their seats. Thereafter, one by one, they went and prostrated before the couple, and sang traditional songs for their welfare in Sanskrit, Tamil and Telugu. Gandhiji conversed with the people. The secretary of the Samaj, Sister Thayarammal, the editor of *Women's Education*, who welcomed them said, "Gandhi is Rama. Kasturba can be compared in all ways to Sita Devi. As long as the story of India is told, Indians will not forget Gandhi and Kasturba." Gandhiji was then 45 years old and Kasturba, older to him by a few months, was 46. He in turn praised them for offering the translations of their welcome and songs in Tamil, and as Sanskrit slokas.

Welcome by Seva Sangam

That evening, at the Seva Sangam meeting in Ranade Hall, attended by several luminaries, Gandhiji's views, as expressed in his speech, were testimony to how he had matured in his service consciousness to society. Emphasising that social service should be neither for personal aggrandisement nor for seeking status, he said:

> Social service should be undertaken with full humility and self-effacement. Gokhale has said that true service is its own reward. This is what I would like to reiterate here. Merely because he does not get praise from others should not deter a social worker from carrying out his duties in an enthusiastic manner. Rather than a half-hearted effort in social work, it is better not to undertake it at all.

Questions and answers

Gandhiji also responded to the questions of the Seva Sangam members.

Q: Seva Sangam members are able to devote only a few hours every week for service. What is your advice to them?
Gandhiji: Even if it is for a few hours, it should be with full involvement. If the right persons take up social service, success is assured.
Q: In night schools, what are your views on Dalit and Hindu children being allowed to mingle?
G: At least in night schools we must do this. There is nothing wrong in it. Since the time spent for teaching in these schools is limited, neither the Dalit nor caste students will be affected adversely.

When asked about physical labour, Gandhiji said it is not wrong for a boy of the cobbler caste, who had studied up to M.A., to remain a cobbler all his life.

Q: Is it necessary to define the limits of teaching in primary schools? What are your views?
G: It is desirable. However, at the same time, it is not mandatory that primary classes must educate everyone on hygiene. Even those who cannot read or write can follow the hygiene practices on their own.
Q: How can we remove alcoholism?
G: This is very difficult. It can only be overcome by the intervention of important community members.

Money is not important

At the end of this dialogue, Gandhiji said:

> Money is not essential for social service—only people. People full of affection, duty consciousness, and faith in their work alone are required. If such people take up social work, money will automatically find its way. Much social service can be done without money. Unless he descends many steps, a man cannot appreciate the travails of the common man. However rich a man is, if he takes up this work only to serve his own means to prosperity, he cannot render true service. A camel can pass through the eye of a needle, but such a man cannot achieve any success.

Welcoming this speech, *Swadesamithran* wrote in an editorial:

> People should not think that they are to be denied carrying on the professions their families have been engaged in for generations. There can be no embargo in continuing to use one's body and hand tools to make products. Nobody should think that they need give up such professions for social service. A young man, whose family for generations have been shoemakers, and has completed his M.A., should not be required to give up his profession, Mr Gandhi said. His profession does not become beneath him. In fact the quality of his work will improve. Now, holy souls like Mr Gandhi have made service to the nation their profession … if our youngsters are prepared to follow his path, the future of India will not just be dark, but emerge with some brightness.

Welcome by Vysyas

At Vasanta Mandapam on Govindappa Naicken Street, on behalf of the Arya Vysya Sabha, Salli Gurusamy Chetty said in his welcome address that, as Gandhiji was born in the Vysya community, this special welcome had been organised for him. The women belonging to this community had also come. The Sabha secretary, C. Venkatachalam expressed the confidence that Gandhiji would lead Indian politics.

In response, Gandhiji categorically said that problems for Indians in South Africa could resurface at any time, notwithstanding the current compromise reached. "In South Africa, Indians are competing with Europeans in agriculture and commerce. Whatever be the other troubles for Indians, this is the main problem. Though, for the time being, there is a compromise in place there, the bitterness continues, and will do so until there is this competitiveness."

Welcome by Bohras

The Bohra Muslims organised a welcome for Gandhiji in the Muhammad Ali Fazal Ali building. Interestingly, G. A. Natesan, a Hindu, welcomed Gandhiji on their behalf. The Bohra president said that Madras State was a foremost example of good relations between Hindus and Muslims. Gandhiji responded that in India since the aims of both Hindus and Muslims were the same, there can be no room for problems. A money garland was offered to him.

26 April 1915, Dinner at 'Luz'

The next day, on the evening of 26 April 1915, at S. Srinivasa Iyengar's residence at 'Luz' (which means 'light' in Portuguese), Mylapore, a traditional Indian dinner was organised, accompanied by a vocal concert of C. R. Srinivasa Iyengar, accompanied by the late Tirukkodikaval Krishna Iyer's son, Rama Iyer on the violin. A Vedam recitation was also arranged. At the dinner, S. Srinivasa Iyengar's daughter, S. Ambujammal, had a photograph taken of Gandhiji and Kasturba. The menu contained boiled manila nuts, tender coconut shavings, apples, oranges, almonds, other fruits and nuts, buttermilk, and tender coconut water. Would such a menu be considered appropriate for a garden party today?

About Kasturba, Ambujammal said:

> Wearing a simple, pure white *pavadai* and *davani*, a small, slender figure, a face suffused with life experience, reflecting motherly love, a look of internal yearning, bright eyes, a full-sleeved white blouse, a pair of iron bangles—there was no other ornamentation. She looked the modern wife of a poor householder. That was Kasturba Gandhi.
>
> I was very young, just fifteen. Mrs Gandhi looked at me and smiled. I felt that she was smiling in sympathy at the diamond jewellery that my entire body was decked in. Immediately I felt like flinging them all away in anger. The moment passed, as I realised it would be bad behaviour to do so, and sat back as before. She, though, continued to converse affectionately with my mother.
>
> The next evening, Mrs Gandhi alone came to our house. My mother took her to the Ladies Recreation Club in Mylapore, and introduced her to the many ladies there. I, too, went with them, dressed up like a doll.

Welcome by Christians

At the welcome given by Christians at the house of Rev. T. Subramaniam belonging to the Wesleyan Mission, on Peters Road,

Royapettah, European and Indian padres attended in large numbers. Rev. Subramaniam had lived in South Africa, and known Gandhiji at that time. M. T. Devadas, Bar-at-Law and V. Sakkarai Chettiar, on behalf of the Christians, welcomed Gandhiji and spoke. In his reply, Gandhiji described his association with Christians while in South Africa.

27 April 1915, Inspection of institutions

On the morning of 27 April 1915, Gandhiji, along with G. A. Natesan, visited the Ramakrishna Students' Home, Venkataramani Ayurveda Hospital and Sanskrit College (established by the late Krishnaswami Iyer), and observed their working. He wrote his comments in the visitors' books of each of these institutions. For the Ramakrishna Students' Home, Gandhi's comments in Gujarati were: "I am delighted beyond words to visit this institution. The enthusiasm of those running it is immeasurable. Experience will show that this would yield all manner of benefits."

'Father of the Nation'

The first person to formally honour Gandhiji with the title 'Father of the Nation' was Subhas Chandra Bose, on 6 July 1944. But much before that, it was the students of Madras who first publicly addressed him as such. On 27 April 1915, when Gandhiji visited the Young Men's Christian Association (YMCA) building, in their welcome address, read out by Chinnasamy, the students said: "Your untarnished humility, your severe simplicity, your enthusiasm born out of tireless strength of mind, your patriotism, unaffected even an iota by any selfishness, your affection that has spread throughout the world, fuelled by your inner spiritual strength, have all elevated you to the status of 'Father of the Nation'. As children, we wait to be guided by your passion and direction."

At this meeting, attended by a multitude of students and the general public, V. S. Srinivasa Sastri, who was presiding, said: "Gandhiji reminds us of our ancient spiritual heritage. If he is a *rishi* of old, his wife is a *rishi patni*." (Kasturba was not present at this meeting.)

Message to students

In his response, Gandhiji said: "Gokhale's advice to us is enshrined in the Articles of the Indian Labour Association. I accept that as my signpost. Those Articles specify that the political life of our nation must follow the spiritual path. Politics cannot be separated from spiritualism. If that happens, politics will descend to a level that is banal." Addressing the students, he said:

> Students, not just the students of Madras, but to the students all over India, I am going to ask one question. Does your education help you to realise your national aims? Or is it just a factory to prepare you for government jobs? I am one who strongly opposes modernity. We should conduct our lives on the examples set by our rishis. We should propagate not just physical well-being, but tidings of affection. It is only then that, using your spiritual strength, you can win over those who rule you, without shedding of blood. Look into yourselves—wherever you see iniquities, fight against them. If someone threatens your rights, oppose them, but without your enemy shedding a drop of blood.

This raised a debate among the intelligentsia: Gandhiji acknowledged Gokhale to be his guru. But Gokhale favoured the Western system of education. Education and culture cannot be separated. If Gokhale advocated the Western system of education, doesn't it also mean that he was in favour of Western culture? But Gandhiji is completely against modern education and modern culture. So, how could Gandhiji's principles be in consonance with those of Gokhale? One of them must be wrong!

After the students' meeting, the YMCA Graduates Club accorded a welcome to Gandhi, where C. G. Spencer presided, and lawyer Sir P. Chinnaiah spoke.

Visit to the slums

The next day, 28 April 1915, to the questions on education and discipline raised by the Pachaiyappa High School teachers at the welcome arranged for him, Gandhiji offered detailed responses. He said even low-caste persons must be given the opportunity to prove themselves. He visited the slums of Madras and observed first-hand the conditions of people living there. He also visited a dyeing unit in Washermanpet, a weaving factory run by Rao Bahadur Thyagaraja Chettiar, and several handloom units, and enquired about the running costs and wages, and whether the workers were financially self-sufficient.

Annie Besant's welcome

If Lokmanya Tilak was then the shining sun of Indian politics in the west, Annie Besant was the luminous moon in the south. In her *New India* publication, she publicised Gandhiji's visit in detail. She had been at the railway station to welcome him. From Gandhiji's diary we learn that he had met her on the day of his arrival. She participated in some of the welcome meetings for him. She also arranged for a welcome, with a veena recital, for the Gandhi couple at Blavatsky Park inside the Adyar Brahmagnana Circle, where judges, lawyers, merchants and other notables were invited. Prior to this meeting, Gandhiji visited the various units run by the Brahmagnana Sangam, including a printing press, a school for Dalits in an interior village, and the administrative office. In a symbolic move to show respect for Gandhiji's philosophy, the meeting was held under a banyan tree. In her welcome address, departing from convention, Annie Besant recited a poem by James Russell Lowell, 'The Present Crisis' (1845), which Gandhiji listened to intently, as it was so apt for the occasion.

A disappointment

Gandhiji had great respect for Annie Besant and her service to the country and had a marked appreciation for her organisations. After dinner that evening, Dr Besant wrote in her diary: "He visited one of our Dalit schools. As one well versed in the printing profession, he came to our printing unit. Our welcome was held under the large banyan tree. More than 200 guests had come. We were all extremely happy."

It was arranged that Gandhiji and Kasturba would stay at the Adyar Brahmagnana Sabha premises. However, an incident that took place in the interim did not allow him to stay there. During his visit to the various units run by Dr Besant, he was first shown the massive office, and the ornate chairs and tables in the rooms. Nearby, he was shown a simple shed where the 'untouchables' were taught—at that time there were no schools for them. Gandhiji felt it loathsome that there should be impressive buildings for one class of people, and just a shed for others. He therefore did not wish to stay the night there, but decided to go to G. A. Natesan's office in Georgetown. When he communicated this to Natesan, Natesan tried his best to talk him out of it, saying, "Dr Besant would misunderstand, not only you but me." But Gandhiji was determined, and he left Adyar despite it being late.

Arya Patasala

In Thambu Chetty Street, when Gandhiji and Kasturba visited the Arya Patasala, run in memory of Lakshmi, the school correspondent, C. Ramanujam Chettiar, Georgetown Schools' sub-assistant inspector, N. Swaminatha Iyer, Dr M. Krishnaswami Iyer, and A. Kumaraswami Iyer took him around the classes. This was followed by a concert of Bhavani Ammal on the veena and vocals by Rajathi Lakshmi. Gandhiji said the school was fortunate to have a person of the stature of C. Ramanujam Chettiar at its helm.

29 April 1915, Welcome by Gujaratis

Just as the Vysya community in Madras had welcomed Gandhiji as one of their own, the Gujaratis in Madras got together and gave him a rousing welcome on 29 April 1915. In the 'Govind Vilas' Bungalow on Peters Road, Royapettah, its owner, Lod Govind Das and Gokuldas Goverdhandas welcomed the Gandhi couple. "The Gujarati community is proud that a great man like Gandhiji belongs to our community," said Lod Govind Das. Dewan Bahadur Govind Das Chathurbhuj Das read out the welcome in Gujarati. Songs in praise of Gandhiji were sung in Gujarati and English. Gandhiji replied in Gujarati and said, "The welfare of other communities in Madras is your welfare. Hence you must cooperate with them and join in service." He also thanked the people of Madras city and State for giving so much space to the Gujaratis. On behalf of the Gujarati community in Madras, Lod Govind Das presented a purse to Gandhiji, accepting which Gandhiji said, "I do not accept such purses from anyone in my individual capacity, but only for use in social work."

Initiation of disciples

Many youngsters wondered how a great political leader like Gandhiji could lead a life of such austerity. They approached him and expressed their wish to be part of the ashram that he was planning to develop. (When Gandhiji visited Madras in 1915, he could not start the ashram.) Gandhiji made up his mind at that time that some of those keen should join him later. In a letter from Madras he wrote that he would be bringing some of these youngsters from here. In the manner of a formal initiation, one of them took an oath before him in Madras. Earlier, Anna Harihara Sharma had accompanied Gandhiji to Rangoon, and expressed the desire to join his ashram. After Gandhiji's return to India from South Africa, Anna Harihara was the first Tamilian to join him at Shantiniketan. Another person desirous of joining the ashram, Krishnaswami Sharma, met Gandhiji on 22 April 1915, shared the details of his background, and said that he wished to devote his life to the service of the nation; he joined the ashram in November. Likewise, Gandhiji accepted the request of Alluri Ramaraj, a graduate, who joined the ashram in July. Krishnaswami Varadachariar was another who met him and discussed with him the religious observances he had to undertake.

An intrusion

One day, in a room in G. A. Natesan's office on Sunkuram Chetty Street, Gandhiji was preoccupied in discussions with some people, including Swaminathan, chief editor of the translated works of Gandhiji. Just then, a well-placed person in Madras arrived, and he said, "Mr Gandhi, I do not think I am intruding in your work..." Normally, if it were anyone else, Gandhiji would have typically responded, "No problem." But on this occasion, combining both truth and tact, he said, "Yes, you have interrupted my work. Yet, you are here, and I will give you a minute. Please tell me what you have in mind within this time." Impressed by this, the editor later recounted,

"As a student, I can never forget this firm, clear response; it was an example to me."

The martyrs of Tharangambadi

Although Tamils from several parts of the state had gone to South Africa, a large number of them belonged to a few locations. Tharangambadi had sent many to South Africa, and several who returned from Natal settled down there. Many of them were known to Gandhiji. He learnt that the widows of two martyrs who were shot dead in South Africa were in Tharangambadi. Gandhiji could never forget that these people shared his joys and sorrows there. Hence, he wished to go and visit them. T. A. Subramania Achary, who had participated in the South African revolt, belonged to Thillaiyadi. During the non-cooperation movement in 1930, he wrote a letter in which he says that, on his invitation, Gandhiji came to Tharangambadi (about 250 km/155 miles from Madras city). To meet those heroes, Gandhiji left by the Thoothukudi Express on 29 April 1915, along with Kasturba. V. S. Srinivasa Sastri accompanied him from Egmore railway station.

Sembanarkoil

On the morning of 30 April 1915, the Gandhi couple got down at Mayavaram and proceeded to Tharangambadi via Sembanarkoil. The people of Mayavaram seated them in a two-horse chariot and took them in procession to the school hall. From there, en route to Tharangambadi, the East Sembanarkoil public accorded them a reception under the presidentship of Rao Sahib Vaidyanatha Iyer.

Welcome at Tharangambadi

Much like the reception accorded to warriors of old returning triumphant from battle was the welcome given to the Gandhi couple at the Fort grounds in Tharangambadi. The committee formed under the leadership of K. C. Subramaniam, Bar-at-Law, had taken pains to arrange this reception. The Thanjai Band played as the couple entered. Fireworks lit up the sky. The committee members and the 200 satyagrahis who had returned from South Africa gathered at the grounds and greeted the couple with garlands and glad handshakes, and took them to the Daniskar Palace, where their stay had been arranged.

Meeting the heroes

Gandhiji expressed the wish that he and his wife wanted to meet all his Tamil brethren who had fought shoulder to shoulder with him in South Africa. Knowing that Gandhiji was coming to Tharangambadi, those heroes had come there from neighbouring villages. As they stood in line, Gandhiji and Kasturba individually enquired after their welfare. At the dinner that followed, the Gandhi couple were served palm fruit (*nungu*), tender coconut water, peanuts, fruits, etc.

There was a public reception that evening at the Fort grounds. Attractive banners had been put up. The dais was decorated with plantain tree pillars, much like a marriage *muhurtha mandapam*. About 3000 people from Tharangambadi and its outskirts, including officials, lawyers, teachers and others thronged the grounds. Both sides of the road from Daniskar Palace to the meeting pandal were lined with members of the welcoming group. As the Gandhi couple made their way, the band struck up a tune and fireworks were let off.

K. C. Subramaniam, as president of the meeting, spoke about the greatness of Gandhiji. "With never a selfish thought and with determination, Gandhiji is toiling for the people of our country. In knowledge, he is comparable to the ancient rishis. This noble soul has forsaken his bodily needs and desires. Hence there can be no impediment in the future to his fame and victory."

Amidst old friends

In the midst of tigers, even a tiger cub sports a confident walk goes a saying. In the company of his old friends, the satyagrahis, Gandhiji's enthusiasm was considerable. The speeches he made at Mayavaram and Tharangambadi show how much of a rebel he was. Of the two widows of the martyrs he had come to meet, he could meet one (Selvan's widow).

Speaking of why he had come to Tharangambadi, Gandhiji said: "… I have come to see how I could help the widows of the two martyrs who were shot [dead] in South Africa. I have met one of them. The other lady belongs to Madurai, I will meet her too before leaving this State." (It is not known whether Gandhiji met that lady, but on this trip he did not visit Madurai).

He then asked the old heroes of non-violence who had gathered, "I hope you all have returned from Transvaal with the same ... determination as of old?"

On behalf of the satyagrahis, T. A. Subramania Achary replied, "Yes, we have all come with the same determination."

Gandhiji added in English, "You used the weapon of spirituality in the South African satyagraha. I trust you would not have left it behind there. Here too when the occasion demands, you should not hesitate to use that weapon."

Gandhiji's speech (in English) was translated by P. A. Muthu Thandavaraya Pillai. Thereafter, V. S. Srinivasa Sastri explained what the concept of Gandhiji's spiritual strength was. The meeting concluded with votes of thanks from Rev. Samuel and M. P. Guruswami Iyer.

Plaints of the depressed

The event that shook Gandhiji significantly followed. A memorandum outlining the problems of the Indian depressed classes was read out to him on their behalf. They had submitted that they had no access to drinking water, could not own, buy or sell land, nor could they approach courts for redress. They could not have known then how deeply and emotionally Gandhiji would be affected by this. Gandhiji seethed with rage on hearing this, but did not express it, and merely said, "We should pay special attention to these depressed classes. We must work towards this till they are able to get equal status among caste Hindus without any discrimination, and obtain the same rights." However, in Mayavaram, he gave full vent to his emotions.

Invitations

Gandhiji received telegrams in Tharangambadi inviting him to visit Thanjavur and Kumbakonam. However, he did not accept the invitations, regretting that his programme had already been drawn up by his office. That night, the Gandhi couple, together with Sastri, were taken in a two-horse-drawn chariot around the streets of Tharangambadi.

Welcome at Thillaiyadi

On the morning of 1 May 1915, Gandhiji went to Ramapuram and Thillaiyadi and met the families of the satyagrahis who had fought with him in South Africa. According to Subramania Achary, the first village Gandhiji set foot on in Tamil Nadu was Thillaiyadi. Hence Gandhiji must have visited Thillaiyadi before going to Ramapuram. There was a small welcome organised by Subramania Achary in Thillaiyadi. (There is no mention or record anywhere that Gandhiji referred to Thillaiyadi as Valliammal's village. Had he been so informed, he would have spoken in praise of it there.)

Selvan's son

When Gandhiji met the widow of Selvan in Tharangambadi, he requested her to send her son to be with him. At first, she refused, saying angrily that Gandhiji was the cause of her husband's death. However, eventually he succeeded in his efforts to obtain her approval to send her son with him. He said that he would send her five rupees every month. Selvan's family had stayed with him on Phoenix Farm, and Gandhiji vividly remembered this boy, named Naicker, recalling him as a mischievous child. He took him along, and reached Mayavaram. (Later, Naicker's brother and his mother went to the Sabarmati Ashram.)

Welcome at Mayavaram

In Mayavaram, Gandhiji and Kasturba were accorded a welcome at the Victoria Town Hall. In what was virtually the Town Council's welcome to him, under the presidentship of V. K. Ramanujachariar, the entire elite of the town was present, and an address was read out by M. S. Natesa Iyer, the president of the town council. In his response to the welcome, Gandhiji spoke about the unacceptable plight of the depressed classes in Tharangambadi as follows.

Who is a Brahmin?

> I received by chance the welcome by my brothers of the depressed classes in Tharangambadi. They have no water facilities. They have no freedom to buy or sell land. They

also tell me they are unable to approach the courts. Who is responsible for this state of affairs? Can we allow such a situation to continue? Is this Hindu religion?—I really do not know. In my readings abroad I learnt that it is not [in] Hindu religion to ride roughshod over the backs of the depressed people. But if this is in fact the advocacy of Hindu religion, I am violently against it. Who is responsible for delineating one class of people as untouchables? I see that, wherever they are, Brahmins are looked upon with respect. If they alone are considered worthy of respect, this sin squarely devolves upon them. Remember what the *Bhagavad Gita* tells us: 'The true Brahmin is one who does not discriminate between a pundit and an uninformed person'. Do the Brahmins in Mayavaram look upon themselves and the Dalits as equal? This is my response to your welcome address. Even though you are not expecting this, I am going to say these words at the cost of giving you pain. If Brahmins have to attain their past glory, this is the way. If the Brahmins decide to treat the depressed classes in Mayavaram as equal in all respects, will the other communities say they will not follow? But, if the Brahmins continue to claim that their present status is as a result of penance of previous birth, I condemn them as sinners who will destroy our nation.

Difference of opinion

It was thus vehemently that Gandhiji spoke on that day. In his presidential address at this meeting, V. K. Ramanujachariar had at first requested Gandhiji to explain the differences of opinion and arguments on certain matters with other leaders. As a reply to this Gandhiji said:

> ... I have had no fights with our nation's leaders, but I only made it seem so, because some things that I have heard go against my self-respect and the pride of this nation. I am trying to understand the logic behind the measures undertaken by these leaders in fulfilling the holy task in hand, but have been unable to. Perhaps I am not competent enough to do so. Their words and actions do not appeal to me. For example, there is a decision on 'swadeshi' in the Congress programme, which has been printed in English, which tells me that, in truth, you have

not embraced 'swadeshi'. I have no hatred for English. But when you kill the mother tongue, and, in its place, develop the English language, it means that you have not used the 'swadeshi' concept correctly. If you think I do not know Tamil, one, you should teach me, or alternatively deliver your welcome address in Tamil and translate it to me.

In 1927, when he went to Thoothukudi (then called Tuticorin), he said, "At one place in Madras I was given a welcome speech in English. You might have known that I had immediately objected to it." Perhaps it is this meeting that he referred to, because, if we see the news appearing in the press, they write that the need for welcome addresses in Tamil was perceived only at this meeting. In the 4 May 1915 issue of *Swadesamithran*, it was written that:

> As the upper-class people in Madras do not give enough importance to the national languages, their development is hampered. But for some years now, because the public have begun to show interest in general matters, proceedings at major conferences and meetings are being conducted in the national languages. It is hoped that this important change will now not be given up. This exhortation of Mr Gandhi in respect of the presiding speech in the presence of the general public will not, we believe, be in vain.

Looms of Mayavaram

Speaking of the weaving looms of Mayavaram, Gandhiji said,

> When I went via Mayavaram, I enquired whether handloom was being made there, and there were weavers. I was told that there were 50 weaving units in Mayavaram, producing saris. Does this mean that our 'swadeshi' is for women alone? When I look at the men, it does not appear that they wear fabrics made here. (A voice from the crowd is heard to say: '...There are 1000 weaving units here.') Then, it is even worse. If these thousand units produced fabrics for both women and men, there would be no poverty in India, is it not? I wish to know how much you and your leaders favour foreign-made cloth. I know that, without much expense, the nation's clothing needs can be met by swadeshi cloth. Hence, keeping this in mind, what can I teach

to the leaders who have brought the Congress decision on this matter? At the feet of my leaders, and at the feet of you all in Mayavaram, I ask: Let them tell me the inner meaning of this. Is nationalism the chasing away of those who have no roof above their heads, and who scream for food and water?' By saying things you do not like, will the students' respect for me increase, or will I get the blessings of elders?… I doubt this seriously. Give me a little space in your vast hearts. I will learn from you in all humility. If you cannot teach me, it will appear that I renew my fight against the leaders.

When he finished his speech, veena music and snacks followed. S. Kuppuswami Iyer, K. Kesava Iyer, and S. Sundaram, who spoke after Gandhiji, said that the advices of Gandhiji would be taken up. This speech in 1915, in a town like Mayavaram, must have severely impacted the large number of priests residing there. G. A. Natesan said that Gandhiji's speech, expounding such realities at the spiritual centre of Mayavaram, raised fierce arguments. The following is an example of how there were some salutary repercussions of this speech. On 8 May 1915, in the issue of *Swadesamithran*, one Vindu Nemi wrote a letter to the editor:

In the last couple of weeks, we had kept the Gandhi couple in a vehicle … we led them in procession in horse-drawn chariots and motor cars. We took them to meetings here and there, and to some prominent people's houses, and welcomed them. We read welcome speeches. Garden gatherings, music concerts and tea parties were arranged. We praised, sang and danced. It was Gandhi here, Gandhi there, and a festival of Gandhi. These virtuous people left yesterday. It need not be said how difficult the parting was. So much for that. What was the result of this visit? What is it that we learn from his good nature, good deeds and good conduct? How many among us have started to follow his path for the welfare of common folk? Or, has it been just empty words and promises? Without doing anything, without working with enthusiasm, merely to organise such meetings once in a blue moon, and put on an outward show, will only lead to ridicule … what a sham!

At G. A. Natesan's house

Gandhiji returned to Madras on 2 May 1915. He discussed with Natesan the uplift of the depressed classes, and the eradication of untouchability. Student leaders also met him. The fact that Gandhiji arrived at Natesan's house, bringing with him Selvan's son, Naicker, caused a minor earthquake. With the exception of Natesan, all others in his house were followers of vedic rituals, particularly his aged mother. But Gandhiji had not considered any of this. He was in the habit of assuming that others were like him. Two years before Gandhiji came, Natesan had presided over a conference of the depressed classes, and criticised their treatment by the higher classes. Gandhiji knew this, and had read Natesan's speech. This was enough for Gandhiji. He concluded that as Natesan opposed untouchability everybody in his house must be of the same view. Hence, he had no second thoughts about taking this boy with him to Natesan's house. But Natesan was in a fix. On the one hand was his respect for Gandhiji, and on the other his concern for his mother's feelings. Gandhiji quickly realised the dilemma Natesan was in, and in his own way tried to find a way out of this problem—which he soon did. Either because of a change in environment or for some other reason, Naicker fell sick. In his free time Gandhiji attended to him. Natesan's mother observed this. Whatever her feelings were about untouchability or equality, this touched her deeply. She had a change of heart. She also understood the boy's predicament. In later years, Gandhiji referred to this in a letter to Natesan: "How magnanimously your mother behaved towards Naicker! You had doubted whether you could change her views. As social reformers we face these problems, but do not realise that reforms should start at home. To reform ourselves becomes the biggest problem."

At V. S. S. Sastri's house

Thinking about the confusion caused in Natesan's house when he went with Naicker, Gandhiji wanted to cancel his visit to V. S. Srinivasa Sastri's house the next day. Like Natesan's mother, Sastri's mother, too, was of a conservative bent. "Natesan, please inform Sastri that I am not coming to Sastri's house tomorrow," he said. "I have given your mother enough mental agitation; should I give Sastri's mother the same?" Natesan conveyed this to Sastri, but Sastri insisted that Gandhiji should still come to his house with Naicker. "Natesan, if Gandhiji could change your mother, who is so stubbornly adherent to vedic views, it should be easier with my mother. Further, when I joined the Indian Workers' Union, we had taken an oath that caste and religion will not play a part [in our lives], and that we would all partake of food together. Hence, as planned, Gandhiji must come home." Thus, on 3 May 1915, Gandhiji and Naicker went to Sastri's house for dinner.

Naturopathy

How Gandhiji cured this boy has been written about by G. A. Natesan's brother's son, G. V. Kalyanam, who was then staying in Natesan's house, in the *Mail* (2 November 1968), as under:

> The Harijan boy developed high fever that night. Early morning the next day, Gandhiji brought the shivering boy downstairs, removed all his clothes, made him sit under the tap, and opened it. My uncle was greatly concerned, and said that he would summon his doctor, but Gandhiji strongly objected. My uncle's confusion increased. 'Gandhi, do not commit a murder in my house,' he shouted, to which Gandhiji calmly replied, 'No, be quiet, Natesan, you do not know.' Thereafter, he carried the boy upstairs and set him down on the bed. He cut up a melon, pulped it, and gave it to the boy, who was running a temperature of 104 degrees. He then told his attendant that, if he did not return by 11 a.m., he should give the remaining amount of fruit to the boy, and left. However, by 10 a.m., the boy's fever subsided and he went out to play.

Second class

Gandhiji was a man of strict principles, but on small matters, he could be flexible on occasion. He had arrived in Madras in a third-class compartment to experience the hardships of passengers travelling by that class, and to be one with the poor people. However, on the persuasion of some prominent local persons, he travelled from Madras to Nellore by second class. In those days, State conferences were held. The Madras State conference would include Madras, Andhra and part of Mysore and Kerala. When Gandhiji came to Madras, this conference was held in Nellore, and he was invited to it. Hence, along with Naicker, the Gandhi couple went there.

3 to 6 May 1915, Nellore conference

On the evening of 3 May 1915, Gandhiji reached Nellore to participate in the conference and was put up at the residence of the District Collector, Dewan Bahadur Ramachandra Rao. Leaders such as Mrs Besant, V. K. Ramanujachari, Srinivasa Iyengar, G. A. Natesan, C. P. Ramaswami Iyer, Lod Govind Das, V. S. Srinivasa Sastri, K. Chidambaranatha Mudaliar and George Joseph participated as representatives of (what is present-day) Tamil Nadu. Such conferences used to be attended even by important government officials. The Nellore Collector attended. Issues pertaining to education and social problems were discussed and debated. After paying tribute to the memory of late Gokhale, a decision was taken to request the British government to extend the tenure of the then Viceroy, Lord Hardinge. After that, a motion of thanks to the Gandhi couple for having made great sacrifices in South Africa was adopted. Natesan, who had tabled this motion, praised Gandhiji's heroic efforts in South Africa which were testimony to the fact that man can realise his full humanity; similarly, Kasturba had realised the pinnacle of women's achievement.

Annie Besant's tribute

Annie Besant spoke in favour of adopting this motion. From her speech about the satyagraha movement in 1915, it was evident what stand she would take in the future, abjuring violence and taking the oath of peaceful non-cooperation. She said:

> The weapon of peaceful opposition had been adopted in South Africa and yielded positive results. Earlier, on a couple of occasions, this weapon had been employed in England, too, but it is the first time in an Indian struggle it has been used in South Africa. When people under an oppressive government suffer immeasurable affronts to their dignity, there is no better weapon than peaceful non-cooperation. I pay my tribute to

Gandhiji, not only for the work he has done in South Africa, but for having most intelligently used this weapon there. He restored the dignity of Indians in South Africa, and proved to the world that India was indeed a land of culture. Kasturba, on her part, stands as a shining example to women in future of how she served with her husband, as a companion, giving support and encouragement.

As much as all these tributes paid to Gandhiji were significant, his response to them was likewise. "Do not spoil us by over-praising us for the work that we have done in South Africa. This could lead to our becoming arrogant, and, as a result, we may not be able to do as much as you expect of us, leading to your disappointment and dislike," he said, in a warning laced with humility.

In Madras again

After staying for three days in Nellore, he returned to Madras on 7 May by Calcutta Mail. Before leaving that night by Bangalore Mail, he participated in a meeting of the South Africa India League, and went to Sowcarpet to inaugurate a book store. In the evening he saw *Harishchandra*, a play staged by Suguna Vilas Sabha.

The South Africa India League had been established to carry forward the protest of South African Indians. In the meeting of the League held at G. A. Natesan's house, Gandhiji made an announcement with reference to the South African Indian revolt.

"There are 30 satyagrahis and their families in India, including the wives and children of two satyagrahis who were shot and killed there. Hence it is my suggestion that the remaining funds of the League be used to give them assistance. At a time of great pressure these people have aided the revolt in South Africa, for which, on behalf of South African Indians, I express my gratitude. Further, for the help that G. A. Natesan rendered for the welfare of exiled Transvaal Indians, I give my heartfelt thanks on their behalf."

As the work of the League was over, it was decided to disband it and hand over the funds contained therein to Gandhiji for deployment. Seeing off Gandhiji to Bangalore that night at the station were V. S. Srinivasa Sastri, S. Srinivasa Iyengar, Pandya and

T. K. Venkatarama Sastri. G. A. Natesan accompanied Gandhiji to Bangalore.

Gandhi and Kasturba

The occasional differences of opinion between husband and wife did happen with Gandhiji and Kasturba too. The frequent reason for this was Gandhiji's stubbornness in holding fast to his principles and practices. Gandhiji was stricter with workers than with common folk, he was stricter with his associates, more so with his relatives, even more with his children, and most of all with his wife. This time when they had come to Madras, their small fights on some matters were in evidence. On this, G. A. Natesan has written:

> When they stayed in Madras, I have observed Kasturba looking sad on some occasions. When I brought this to the notice of Gandhiji, he would say, 'She has brought this upon herself. It seems her grandchildren want to buy fancy clothes, and are asking for money. So she wants money.' I then jocularly told Gandhiji that he was indeed a troublesome husband, to which he replied, 'Look here, you are blaming me unnecessarily. If I bow to her demands, it would be contrary to my own principles. She knows what they are. She has been with me for long. I told her that she could go back to her home, set up a separate family with all conveniences for her people, so that the children could be happy. But it is she who has not accepted it. As a faithful Indian wife she wishes to follow me wherever I go.

This shows that, with her gentle nature, Kasturba was like a backbone of steel in upholding the tenets of her husband.

Support for satyagraha

Along with praise for Gandhiji and Kasturba was heard praise for the peaceful non-cooperation movement. In every welcome accorded to the Gandhis, there were references to peaceful non-cooperation too. This repeated expression of support for the peaceful non-cooperation method of satyagraha was not liked by some. A representative of this group of people wrote a letter to the editor of the *Mail* that the concept of peaceful non-cooperation may not be a panacea.

It is said that the same method, as adopted in South Africa, would be employed here. This is a dangerous concept, and should be immediately and firmly opposed. Politicians cannot adopt the way of peaceful non-cooperation. As peaceful non-cooperation requires enormous patience, strong mind [and] firm determination, no political party, from the time of Adam, has been able to adopt it. Further, there is only a slender line separating peaceful non-cooperation and direct opposition, with the danger that movement from one to the other is easy. It is not suitable for any nation, more so in nations that do not have political stability. In South Africa, Gandhiji had full control over people who followed him. It cannot be expected that the same support will be forthcoming here. Even in South Africa, did it not lead to chaos and firing? I therefore feel that, soon, Gandhi will become the centre of such confusion here.

Even today, there is lack of unanimity in support of a moral war using the ahimsa principle.

Ahimsa as a political tool

Just as the Tamils in South Africa had understood Gandhiji's principles and accepted his leadership, the Tamils of the motherland India soon took to him, too. After his Mayavaram speech, *The Hindu* carried an article titled 'Indian Publicity' which talked about his ahimsa principle as a political tool.

[Gandhiji] puts forward [ahimsa] as a superior measure in political work. It is a measure that defines the merit in righteousness, and the correlation between word and deed. It is not just a measure to inspire honest good work by the common man for his prosperity, but will be of use to several in India to obtain degrees and positions with fulsome praise, or to enthusiastically live one's life. A few months ago, a man who was praised all over India, who practises what he preaches, and expects others to do so, has suddenly found awareness among people. When Gandhiji asks some questions, they run into a quandary. Why should the indignities heaped on Indians in South Africa be suffered by the depressed classes in India? The Congress has moved a resolution that Swadeshi should be encouraged ... then why are prominent leaders still not following it? All our conferences and meetings seem to be intrinsically without truth and non-actionable … why? When Gandhiji asks all these questions, why does he appear to be just a hero of South Africa, who has been successful in self-rule there, and be looked on here as a 'theoretical politician' or 'a mere idealist'?

Gandhiji's diary

The following entries in Gandhiji's diary, from 17 April 1915 to 7 May 1915, have been excerpted from his account of his visit to Madras.

April 17th, Saturday: Reached Madras in the evening. There was a big crowd at the railway station. They pulled the vehicle themselves. Met Mrs Besant. Stayed with Natesan.

April 18th, Sunday: Started to meet people.

April 19th, Monday: Started to meet people.

April 20th, Tuesday: Met several persons.

April 21st, Wednesday: Welcome by South Africa League.

April 22nd, Thursday: Krishnaswami Sarma has studied up to Matriculation. He passed out in 1907. Knows Tamil and Telugu. Has studied the *Bhagavad Gita*. Has spent 3 years in jail. Assistant editor in *Indu Nesan*. Has embraced brahmacharyam throughout his life. In addition, he has taken oath of truth and honesty. Wishes to fully devote himself to the service of the nation. He has land and property in Kancheepuram, from which he gets an annual income of Rs. 200. He is in Cosmopolitan Club.

April 23rd, Friday: Welcome of Mahajana Sabha. Slept at Tayabji's house at night.

April 24th, Saturday: Muslim League meeting. Dinner with lawyers.

April 25th, Sunday: Dinner with Bohra friends. Social Service League (women's) meeting.

April 26th, Monday: At Mr Subramaniam's house.[3] Rev. Padiriyar, programme in the absence of S. Srinivasa Iyengar.

April 27th, Tuesday: Programme in Mr Simon's house. Y.M.C.A. programme. Welcome by students.

April 28th, Wednesday: Discussion with teachers of Pachaiyappa's college. Programme at Mrs Besant's house. Alluri Ram Raj's decision to join me. Age 29. Has lost both parents. Language Telugu. Does not know Tamil. B.A. Knows Sanskrit. Has two elder brothers. Has always been a brahmachari. A vegetarian for 15 years. Is willing to take six pledges. Has not asked for rail fare. Will come in July.

April 29th, Thursday: Spoke to Ram Ratan in the morning. Has taken the required pledge on Wednesday. Krishnamachari Varadachari. Age 25. Married 6 years. Has no parents. Has no responsibility to provide for anyone. Has passed matriculation. Has been working for 3 years. Venkatappa Sethuram Iyer. Age 33. Married in 1889. Has 3 children, boy 7, and 2 girls, 9 and 2. Parents are alive. Does not have to help anybody. Both have some property. Has passed matriculation. Knows a little Sanskrit. Dinner at Govind Das's house.

April 30th, Friday: Reached Mayavaram in the morning. Left for Tharangambadi by tonga. Got down on the way at Sembanarkoil. Evening meeting at Tharangambadi. Welcome by depressed class people.

May 1st, Saturday: Went in the morning to Ramapuram and Thillaiyadi. Started in the evening for Mayavaram. Welcome there. 1000 looms. Women producing textiles. Left at night by train for Madras. Selvan's son, Naicker, accompanied me.

May 2nd, Sunday: Reached Madras. Discussion with Natesan about depressed classes. Met students.

May 3rd, Monday: Went to Sastri's house for lunch. Left for Nellore in the evening. Stayed there with Dewan Bahadur Ramachandra Rao. Naicker and Ada came with me. C. Srinivasa Iyengar gave Rs 500. I handed the money over to Natesan.

May 4th, Tuesday: Ada fell sick. Did not like the fruit diet. Ate cooked food. Gave that food to Naicker also. Participated in the conference. Saw a Telugu play called *Prahlada Akkayyan*.

May 5th, Wednesday: Went to the conference. Community conference and Sanatana Conference also were held.

May 6th, Thursday: Went to both conferences. Saw swadeshi cloth. There was a decision about us. In the evening welcome by students. Reply to that.

May 7th, Friday: Started in the morning. Reached Madras. Meeting of the League. *Harischandra* play in Suguna Vilas Sabha. Left for Bombay with Sundaram.

Gandhiji's letter

After this tour, when he reached Bombay, Gandhiji wrote the following letter:

Dear G. A. Natesan,

How can I ever thank you enough for the extraordinary affection you have displayed towards me? I have accepted all this as your service to the nation. I will try to be worthy of it. Yes, Madras is still very much in my mind for the respect I have for it.

We reached here without any major inconvenience. Sundaram is developing very well. Naicker is another gem. Mrs Gandhi remembers you often.

Please send me some Tamil books. I need books both for the beginner, as well as those suitable for people like Sundaram, who are older. I need all the books of Dr Pope. ... would you please look into this at the earliest? Please also send those blankets.

To your mother and wife, and to all friends, please tell them that we enquired after them.

Yours
Affectionately
M. K. Gandhi

Notes

1. 'Sangam', meaning a noble union or gathering, is the earliest known Tamil literature, said to date between 100 BCE to 250 CE.

2. Now Yangon, in Burma (now Myanmar), which was part of British India till 1937.

3. The house of Subramaniam referred to here is where the Indian Christians welcomed Gandhiji.

13

THE BESANT-GANDHI WAR, 1916

Starting the ashram at Kosrab

After his return from Madras, the first task Gandhiji undertook was to establish an ashram at a village called Kosrab, on the outskirts of Ahmedabad. Among the 25 people who found place in the ashram at that time, 13 were Tamils. The other 12 were from different parts of India. This shows how significant the contribution of Tamils was, even at the outset, in India and in Gandhiji's own life. According to the conditions laid down by Gandhiji, those who joined the ashram had to take the oath of practising the 11 virtues: truth, ahimsa, *brahmacharyam* (celibacy), control of the tongue, non-thieving, non-amassing of wealth, swadeshi, hard work, courage, equality of all religions, and abolishment of untouchability.

Not an enemy

For the services rendered by Gandhiji to the people, the British government conferred the Kaiser-i-Hind gold medal on him in June 1915. This meant that, till then, the government did not consider him an enemy. As per normal practice, when political leaders who were considered enemies of the government travelled from one state to another, the State Home Secretary would warn the people of the various districts by a Home Ministry communication of the possible repercussions such people may have to face from them. It is not known whether any such notification was issued in 1915–16 with reference to Gandhiji's visit to Madras.

The meeting at Benares

There is nothing of note to mention about Gandhiji's participation in the Congress and Muslim League conferences held at Bombay. The ending of his self-imposed political 'silence' of one year in 1916 coincided with the invitation of Madan Mohan Malaviya (1861–1946) to Gandhi to address a Benares Hindu University meeting. Viceroy Hardinge, who had come to lay the foundation stone at this meeting, was under heavy police escort. In fact, it seemed as if the entire city of Benares had been taken over by the police. Gandhiji took this, and the pomp of the arrangements for the meeting, as the main subject of his address. He explained in detail the loss to India in education though studies in the English medium. Our progress can only be achieved through farmers and workers, not through lawyers, doctors, and rich people, he said emphatically.

Referring to those who wished to oppose the government through violence, he said that while their daredevilry may be admired, the fight against authority from the outside was undesirable. "Some advocates of violence," Gandhiji said, "have told me that, but for their actions and use of bullets, they could not have created a separatist movement." At this, Annie Besant intervened and said, "Please stop this." Gandhiji turned to the Raja of Darbhanga, who was presiding over the meeting, and said, "If you desire I should end my speech, I shall defer to it. I look to your orders. If you feel that my speaking thus is of no service to the nation or the British government, I am ready to stop." The audience, however, erupted with cries of "Speak, please continue…" The Raja, too, said, "Please say whatever you wish to say." As Gandhiji continued, there were further interruptions. Thinking that the people gathered would lose patience, Gandhiji placated them, saying: "Friends, do not feel aggrieved by these interruptions. Mrs Besant's intervention is also because she loves India." Even so, before he could finish, he was again interrupted. Some of those sitting on the dais walked out, and much confusion and chaos reigned. Even the president left the stage.

Argument

As a sequel to this incident, there was a sustained argument between Annie Besant and Gandhiji. She spoke fiercely criticising his speech. After visiting Poona, Hardwar and Karachi, when Gandhij visited Madras again, the Madras government sent a communication to the Indian government on the repercussions of this disagreement between her and Gandhiji, which said:

> The Madras newspapers have taken great interest in the interventions Mrs Besant made during Gandhiji's address in Benares. Mrs Besant, too, has issued several communications. These are mostly contradictory of each other. It does not appear that what she says is 100% true, according to them. Mr Gandhi has refuted her views. The newspapers here are largely against Mrs Besant. It seems that her popularity is greatly on the wane.

New India reports

The *New India* issue published by Annie Besant covered the Benares event, under the by-line of their special correspondent, as follows:

> Organised on the pretext of discussing a sinful deed, the salutary ending of the meeting was ultimately destroyed. Gandhiji, who had garnered respect and affection all over India on account of the extreme heroism shown by him in South Africa, is turning out to be a veritable child in matters of politics. That he does not speak now with the same intensity in his ideas is giving scope for total misunderstanding in the minds of people. He spoke the other day, giving completely wrong interpretations to misgovernment and violence. If a politician had spoken in this manner, he would have been soundly criticised. But those who continue to believe that Gandhiji would not have said all this with any wrong intentions are those who would regard his speech as coming from a person having no touch with reality... that of an idealist.
>
> As Gandhiji spoke on in this manner, Mrs Annie Besant requested the president, Raja of Darbhanga, to stop him.
>
> However, not knowing whether he was going to speak on, or whether he was going to offer any explanations, the Darbhanga Raja allowed Gandhiji to continue.

At the end, all the Rajas seated on the stage got up and walked away. Pandit Madan Mohan Malaviya apologised to the crowd for this wrongful address. Gandhiji had indicated, he said, that he was going to address the students condemning misgovernance, but, to the surprise of everyone, his speech seemed to be sympathetic to, and in favour of it.

Rajaji condemns Besant

This news was despatched telegraphically to the press. The Tamil people were enraged by it, and felt that likening Gandhiji to an infant in politics was reprehensible. Perhaps Annie Besant herself had written this under the guise of the 'special correspondent', they conjectured.

It was at this point that the tributary of Chakravarthi Rajagopalachari's political career joined the river of Gandhiji's. Rajaji had heard about the successful revolt Gandhiji had spearheaded in South Africa, but there had been no correspondence or interaction between them so far. Rajaji had special praise for Gandhiji's methods. Hence Annie Besant's slight of Gandhiji, the hero of South Africa, at the Benares meeting, pained him. He wrote a letter to *The Hindu* (12 June 1916) condemning Annie Besant's action.

'A child in politics'

Many others too wrote to the papers in a similar vein. Some took up cudgels against Besant on an individual basis. Kasturi Ranga Iyengar wrote:

I cannot think for a moment that the honourable nationalist, Gandhiji, who enjoyed the trust of the Raja, and who knew the nuances of service, would have said anything objectionable in that large gathering. Besant knows Gandhiji very well, and has already spoken in praise of this worthy son of the soil. Hence, she should have exercised her intelligence and forethought. If she could not immediately realise what conclusion Gandhiji was leading to, she should have waited till he completed his speech. However, without doing so, she took strong action … and it should have been her duty to explain such an action to the public. She has called Gandhiji a "child" in politics. It would be interesting to compare her view with that of eminent leaders [of] Britain and India .... Nowhere has Gandhiji said that violence should be used as an instrument for obtaining India's freedom ... and never will. If there were other 'children' like Gandhi, more than Mrs Besant and a thousand other politicians, they would be successful in freeing India. People have been angered by the action of Mrs Besant.

If one section of the Indian people and press condemned Besant's action, on the other side were the Anglo-Indian papers, writing in her favour. This was not surprising in the days of British rule.

Malaviya counters

Madan Mohan Malaviya sent a telegram to the *New India* publication, which read: "The news, that I had said Gandhiji had spoken sympathetically about violence, and that it should be adopted, is erroneous. Gandhiji's speech did grieve some of the dignitaries assembled on the stage. It is for that I apologised. His aim was only to exhort students to stay away from those who resort to violence."

Rajaji responds

In response to Rajaji's objection to how *New India* had reported the meeting at Benares, the publication in an editorial outlined the difficulties faced by newspapers, and further stated that, while Besant was in Benares, she should not be blamed for the telegrams received and headlines appearing in Madras. To this, Rajaji thundered in response:

> Let these headings be on one side. Are Annie Besant or her special correspondent competent to call Gandhiji a 'mere child'? Are they qualified to send a telegram 'Gandhiji is a politician who advocates wrong actions, and such politicians should be condemned,' and print the telegram in their paper? As Indians, we have every right to condemn the stand taken by *New India* that Gandhiji is a mere idealist, unaware of and inexperienced in the ways of the world. Such presentation of news has forced us to find out who is the cause of it all.
>
> Now a new thing is being said that Annie Besant had in fact sent a telegram not to publish such news about Gandhiji, and,

because *New India* was a paper that did not enjoy the patronage of the government, the telegram did not reach on time, leading to such news being published, seemingly not approved by her. So…what punishment was handed out by Annie Besant to that special correspondent who was put in this position by her? Did she write this news herself, or give her approval earlier, and later wish to stop it?

Gandhiji arrives in Madras

It was in the midst of this heated debate raging about the Benares meeting that Gandhiji arrived in Madras. This time he stayed for about five days, visiting no other city in the state in that period. Arriving on 13 February 1916, he left on 17 February, as he was required to speak at a public meeting on Gokhale's memorial day at Poona on 19 February. While Gandhiji did not receive as tumultuous a welcome as he had in 1915, when he came as a hero of South Africa, there was no significant decrease in his audiences wherever he spoke, particularly among students. The Benares issue featured along with other matters. After all, was not Madras the state capital, and the base of Annie Besant?

13 February 1916, Madras Central Station

Gandhiji arrived in Madras by Delhi Express on 13 February 1916, along with Sohrabji Rustomji (son of one of the leaders of the Peace Protestors Organisation). Srinivasa Sastri, Indian Workers Sangam's H. Hanumantha Rao, and crowds of people went to the railway station to welcome him. No one knew for certain that Gandhiji was arriving by this train; hence many people, exhausted by waiting for each train and not finding him, left disheartened. Students, who had been waiting since morning, had also left, with the result that when Gandhiji arrived, there was only a small crowd at the station. After conversing with a few people, he got into a car to go to Mrs Whitehat's house. He was their guest at their Teynampet Bishop's house. Not aware that he had arrived early that morning, some people went that evening to Central Station to meet the 6 p.m. train.

An announcement

S. Srinivasa Iyengar and G. A. Natesan met Gandhiji at Mrs Whitehat's house in the evening for a discussion. Information of his visit was published in the *Swadesamithran* on 14 February 1916, on page 3, in the second column, as the ninth news item under a small heading, 'M. K. Gandhi'. In those days a major national daily like the *Swadesamithran* made only such a small announcement of his visit. It shows also the degree of importance it accorded to his visit.

Missionary conference

The Christian priests of Madras were by and large sympathetic to the objectives of Indians. However, the swadeshi concept was still a puzzle to them; they wished to hear about it from Gandhiji. Therefore, at Rev. W. S. Ferguson's house in Vepery (a suburb in the north of Madras city), a 'Missionary Conference' was held at night on 14 February 1916. The speech that Gandhiji delivered there on swadeshi was one of his best. The press were not allowed inside, hence this speech did not get the prominence it merited. G. A. Natesan, in his book *Gandhiji's Speeches and Writings*, has shared the details of this meeting.

The substance of Gandhiji's speech

The important points that Gandhiji emphasised in his speech were as follows.

> Service to people near us and in our neighbourhood, rather than service to people in distant places; and, in turn, to utilise the service of such people ... this feeling in us is what is called swadeshi.
>
> Hence, what is swadeshi in religion? I must utilise the circumstances present around me. That should be my inner religion. If there is any fault in it, I must work towards its removal. What is political swadeshi? I must make use of the local institutions that have been established.
>
> *Swadeshi economy*
> What is swadeshi in [the] economy? I must use the articles manufactured by the people near me. If such units producing

these articles are in disrepair of any kind, we must aid in their rectifying those defects and working smoothly. If we are able to bring this concept of swadeshi into practice, it will be the yardstick of progress. Do we believe that we can bring back the age in which Jesus lived? But we do not give up our efforts to do so, do we not? Likewise, while we may not for several generations manage to achieve 100% swadeshi, we should never give up our efforts.

Christian duty

Therefore, if there is any substance in what I am saying, the Christian padres should note one important thing. This country is indebted to the sterling service rendered by Christians in the past, and are continuing to render in the present. But, if only they would give up the idea of conversion into their faith, and continue to do their religious work, they would be rendering greater service to the present. I say this with all humility. My heart is dominated by the teachings of the *Bhagavad Gita* on equality.

Caste

This is religion-based, and I do not stand by it. I look to your assistance in political matters, too. I am not one who believes that there is no connection between discipline and politics. Politics that is not in conformity with discipline is a corpse to be buried. It is with the swadeshi concept that I am establishing our internal institutions. Village Panchayats attract my mind. India is truly a republic, which is why it has survived the shocks that it has suffered. The Rajas merely imposed taxes ... they had no interaction with the people. The travails of people in society brought by time have been addressed by caste. In fact, political needs, too, are being served by caste. Through caste, villagers have been tackling, not only their internal matters, but the torments of their rulers.

Language

For literate people like us, our education is being imparted through a foreign language. This cannot inspire any change in the common people. We want to be representatives of the common people, but fail. If, over the last 50 years, we had been educated in our mother tongues, our elders, workers, and people around us would have shared our knowledge. Like the

Ramayana and *Mahabharata*, every house would have known of the discoveries of [Acharya P. C.] Ray or [Acharya J. C.] Bose. Had our mother tongue been the medium of instruction in educational institutions, our progress today would have been spectacular. The village hygiene problems would have long ago been solved. Village Panchayats would, in their own way, have functioned with life-giving force, and India would have today been enjoying a self-governance suited to its needs.

Cause of poverty

Let us now come to the last part of swadeshi. We are staying away from swadeshi to the extent of destroying our progress in the economy and industry sectors. This is the main cause of poverty that our common people are being roasted in today. If we had chosen not to buy a single foreign-made product, India would today have been a land of milk and honey. If swadeshi had been the concept adopted, we could have discarded Lancashire without any difficulty. I do not advocate swadeshi as a weapon to take revenge on the British, but as a timely measure for all to follow.

Self-sufficiency

If we were to adopt the swadeshi principle, we should find out whether there are people around us capable of manufacturing products. Let us assume that there are are people available in our neighbourhood, who are in search of good jobs. If such people do not possess the skill to make these products, we should give them proper training. Every village, then, will become self-sufficient. Only such products as a village is unable to manufacture should be sourced from other villages.

A life doctrine

There is yet another objection to swadeshi, to which also I will respond. The opposers of this claim that it is based on self-interest, and will not be relevant in the modern world. They believe that swadeshi is a return to the primitive age, but I emphasise that this is in fact the principle that will engender humility and affection. If I am not able to provide for my own family, it is arrogance to believe that I can begin working for the world. Instead, devoting my full attention to the needs of my family, and, through that, the nation ... why, mankind itself ... is an eminently better approach. It might appear that, in the swadeshi life doctrine, I work only for the service of my country, ignoring other nations. However, I do not contemplate harming any other country. On the one hand, if my patriotism is only for my land, I am not competing with any other country, or displaying enmity towards them. My service is in fact for the whole world. Hence, this is the proper method to embrace ahimsa and love for all.

The last word

D. G. Tendulkar, who has written Gandhiji's biography, has said that this speech of Gandhiji was the last word on swadeshi, so eloquently, firmly and precisely had he spoken. It was Gandhiji's habit to write and read out his speeches. The Christian padres of Madras had said they were keen to understand the tenets of swadeshi, and they were educated and knowledgeable; hence Gandhiji had prepared this well-researched speech for them.

'When shall I come?'

Gandhiji had earmarked a time for students to meet him in G. A. Natesan's company building. On 15 February 1916, some students of Victoria Hostel met him, and requested that he visit their hostel. Among them was P. N. Ramasubramaniam, who later became a doctor in Madurai. Gandhiji enquired when he should visit the hostel. The students replied that he could do so whenever he wished. Gandhiji said, "I will come early tomorrow morning at 4 a.m." The students were taken aback and thought perhaps he meant 4 p.m. When he clarified, they said, "But no one would be awake at that time." Gandhiji replied, "Then why did you say I could come when I wished? You could have told me the time firmly."

Victoria Hostel

Finally it was decided that Gandhiji would visit the students at 5.30 a.m., which he did, on 16 February 1916. In the food section he noticed several categories, such as Smartha (followers of Adi Guru Shankaracharya), Iyengar, Andhra, and Karnataka, and was not only surprised, but gently chided the students too. Later, after going round the dining room facilities, the warden took him to the room (number 180) of P. N. Ramasubramaniam, who had been in that hostel the longest. Gandhiji complimented Ramasubramaniam on the cleanliness of his room. When V. S. Srinivasa Sastri informed Gandhiji that Ramasubramaniam's father was a noted doctor, Gandhiji commented with pleasure, "Oh, you are from a traditional doctor's family."[1]

At 6 a.m. the welcome to Gandhiji in Victoria Hostel began. After lauding his sacrifices in South Africa, the students asked Gandhiji whether he had any advice for them. He told them that if they adopted the path of righteousness, it would lead to God.

The ashram pledge

The Tamils regarded Gandhiji not merely as a politician, but as one who served the cause of politics with the attitude of a sage. Hence, many, particularly students, were keen to know details about his ashram, its establishment and working. Even after Gandhiji left Madras, several queries on this were directed to G. A. Natesan, then editor of the *Indian Review*. In reply, it was the practice of both Gandhiji and Natesan to refer to the speech that Gandhiji gave at the YMCA (education wing), under the presidentship of Rev. George Briton Trik (of the Madras Christian College). In this speech, titled 'Ashram Pledges' (excerpted below), Gandhiji talks at length of what he expects from those who wished to join his ashram, and from all Indians in general.

> Today, it has become imperative for all nations to foster discipline. More than in other countries, it is vitally necessary in ours. I say this from my own experience. This is the view of the great patriot, Gokhale, too. Our Sastras tell us that we should adopt certain life practices and truths. If we do not, we would become powerless to understand properly the demands of time. We have given these precepts our full belief over the years, and have tried to adopt them in our lives. It is for those who are of similar conviction as I am that I established this ashram. For each one who wishes to be a member of this ashram, I would like to place before you today the practices to be followed.

Prahlada's oath

There are 5 'isms'. The first one is truth. This is not truth as we normally understand it. ... it is the performance of a given principle, whatever profit or gain comes in the way of its accomplishment. It is the truth for which Prahlada was willing to sacrifice himself. He did not even try to escape the punishment handed out to him. Instead, he bore it all with a smile on his face. Ultimately truth triumphed. He did not hold the view that, sometime in his life, he could prove that truth will win. Although, on one side, it might have been true, if, on the other hand, he had to give up his life in the face of the tortures heaped upon him, he would still have been happy. I desire that all of us should be followers of that kind of truth.

Having spoken in general terms about truth, to illustrate, Gandhiji then recounted an incident from 1915 when Swaminathan was with him.

It was only a small incident but, as strands of hay indicate which way the wind is blowing, such incidents do, too. I was speaking with a friend yesterday. He said he wished to speak with me alone ... At that time a third person entered, asking politely whether he was interrupting us. My friend replied, 'No, there is no secret here.' Hearing this, I was a bit surprised, as the very reason he had drawn me aside to speak was because he had something to say in private. Still, I would consider his politeness beyond requirement. He seemed to suggest that our conversation was not private enough for the third person not to join in.

This is against the concept of truth that I am talking about. Do you know what my friend should have said with extreme politeness, yet firmly? 'Yes, as you have rightly said, you are interrupting.' If we, too, like that friend of mine, continue, for the sake of politeness, to say what we do not feel, we will become a nation of hypocrites.

Then he proceeded to elaborate on what he meant by ahimsa.

The meaning of ahimsa is 'not to kill', but to me that word has a mountain of meaning. It signifies to me a nobility in everything. You should not deal in violence towards anyone. Even to those who consider you their enemy, you should have no thoughts of violence. This is the true meaning of ahimsa. The person who adopts ahimsa does not believe anyone is his enemy. An eye for an eye takes us away from the path of ahimsa. ... if, because of the actions of a friend, or that of one who considers himself your enemy, we give place to anger, I say that we are moving far away from this concept of ahimsa. When I say you should not get angry, it is not just that you should not be affected by the words. I mean that you should have no thoughts that you, or others, or God should punish him. Even if you entertain such thoughts you are acting against the tenets of ahimsa. Those who join the ashram must embrace this concept of ahimsa. You should not think because you do this you are following the practice of ahimsa ... it only means that you are trying to. To come near this objective, you will need to spend several sleepless nights. If we have lived a religious life, you and I have to adopt this way. ... The man who believes in the fruits of Hindutva will find that, when he does succeed, the world will be at his feet, although he does not actually want that to happen.

After ahimsa, Gandhiji speaks of the necessity of celibacy for serving the nation.

Brahmacharyam

Those who wish to serve the country, and those who are desirous of living a disciplined existence, must embrace the concept of brahmacharyam. Even if they are married, they must take this pledge. Marriage brings a man and woman together, that is all. By being married they become friends for this life and the next. But in my concept of a disciplined marriage, I do not feel that sex is a necessity.

Control the tongue

He that wants to control his animal instincts can do so easily by controlling his tongue. However, in the ashram pledge, I consider this to be one of the most difficult. One should not go to coffee and tea shops. One should attain bodily good and mental satisfaction through the eating of wholesome food. We should be willing to forgo flavours like cardamom and clove in our diet.... otherwise these will tend to evoke limitless and unnecessary desires that will enslave our taste.

Non-acquisition of wealth

In a way we are all thieves. If I acquire something that is of no immediate use to me, it would amount to my having stolen it

from someone else who is in need of it. I can firmly state that
to resort to nature, which produces everything that we need, is
the correct approach. If only each one takes just what he needs,
there would be no poverty in the world, and nobody will die
of starvation. As long as this imbalance exists, we will continue
to be thieves. I am not a socialist. I do not propose to snatch
the wealth of the rich. If I do so, I will be moving away from
the path of ahimsa. If someone has more wealth than me, so
be it. But I shall not hold on to anything beyond what I need in
life. In India there are 30 lakh people who barely get one meal a
day. Till these 30 lakh people get food and clothing, we have no
right to desire anything. We might even have to fast to achieve
this. From this concept of thievery arises the principle of non-
acquisition of wealth.

Swadeshi

Till we have contempt for those near us, and satisfy our wants
by the acquisition of products from far-off places, we exceed one
of the holy tenets of our life. As long as there is a barber in your
own village, you should not look for some expert hairdresser
who comes from Madras. If the local barber of your village has
to learn the skills of his counterpart from Madras, you must
provide him training. This is swadeshi. If certain products are
yet not available in India, we must decide to do without them.

Fearlessness

Gandhiji believed that, "Educated people in India are subject to
trepidation.... By upholding truth, you will be free of fear. Hence, the
Bhagavad Gita says that the main quality a Brahmin must possess is
fearlessness. Fearing the repercussions in speaking the truth, we avoid
it altogether. Those who fear God will never fear such consequences."

The curse of untouchability

Speaking emphatically against untouchability, he said: "When India
was in an extremely depressed state, untouchability continued to be
rampant. This is a curse. Till this is removed, it must be considered that
the Almighty rightly subjects us to punishment. I cannot understand
how a person can be considered untouchable, based on his trade."

Education in mother tongue

> Except a few of us, the majority of people cannot become experts
> in the English language, not being able to express in English as
> well as we can in our mother tongue. Can what we have absorbed
> as children suddenly be uprooted from our minds? But when we
> are educated in a foreign language and begin to elevate our lives,
> we do try to erase this early learning, which is why there are big
> gaps in our lives. Although we feel untouchability is wrong, we
> are hesitant to apply it within our own homes.

Physical toil

Gandhi strongly felt that, "We need to still realise the importance of
physical toil. Even though a barber's or cobbler's son is studying in
college, it does not mean that he has to forsake the trade of his father.
I say that the profession of a barber is equal to that of a doctor."

Politics

Gandhiji said students who wished to join his ashram must first
implement some or all of these pledges in their own lives and try to
live as they would in an ashram. Only after fulfilling these 11 pledges,
and thus preparing oneself internally, should one enter politics, he
said. "There is no politics without discipline," he warned. His advice
to students needs close attention.

> For students to throng the political platforms in our country is
> not a good sign. This does not mean that, as students, you should
> not learn about politics. In fact, you can learn it from childhood
> itself. We teach the children at our ashram about the political
> structures of our country. But first, we desire that children
> should acquire discipline. Your lives will not be complete if
> you just pass out from colleges with discipline and awareness
> of politics … you must first equip yourselves to deal with the
> vicissitudes of life. However, the situation today is diametrically
> opposite. The chapter on political awareness gets over with
> student life. The student begins to search for a job immediately
> as he leaves college.

Newness of his views

In 1916, Gandhi's views were new not only for students but even for older people. After his speech, the president at this meeting said: "Gandhiji has enunciated several high moral principles. I feel that the practice of all these is going to be difficult."

The *Swadesamithran* used to carry a review column titled, '*Tharasu*' (meaning, weighing scale). One Kalidasan, in his review of Gandhiji's speech to the students, wrote:

> The four pledges of truth, ahimsa, [possessing only what one needs] and fearlessness that he advocates are exemplary virtues. All should follow these to whatever extent they can. But it is an error to say that, if someone hits me, I should not retaliate.
>
> Swadeshi, caste equality, patriotism and God-fearing nature should be adopted in life immediately. If not, our country will fall into ruin. If control of one's tongue and brahmacharyam are practised now and then, it will be beneficial. This advice is unnecessary for poor people. Their tongues are anyway tied. Sri Gandhi has not said that brahmacharyam is the practice to be adopted across all castes. If that happens, the country will soon be denuded of people. Gandhi spoke of 11 pledges. I give you here a 12th, that is: 'Search for meaning in life with whatever efforts you can, and reach great heights.' The whole country should adopt this 12th pledge.

Gandhi-Jinnah-Besant

At that time, Annie Besant and Muhammad Ali Jinnah (1876–1948) were emphasising that students should not involve themselves in politics. The same week, when Jinnah spoke to Muslim students in Bombay, and Annie Besant to students at the Hindu Sangam meeting in Pachaiyappa's College in Madras, they both reiterated that while students should *prepare* themselves for politics, they should desist from *entering* it. This shows that Gandhiji, Annie Besant and Jinnah were all of the same mind vis-à-vis this issue, and exhorted students in like manner.

Besant praises Gandhi

Before Gandhiji's speech at the YMCA, a person had submitted a note that the Benares imbroglio may be explained. Gandhiji, by way of response, began his speech by saying, "You do not have to give so much importance to that event—it is like water under the bridge, which comes and goes."

This pleased Annie Besant immensely, and she wrote an editorial in *New India*, titled, 'Visionary and Politician,' in which she praised Gandhiji effusively.

India's Mazzini

Comparing Gandhi to the visionary Italian leader G. Mazzini (1805–72), Besant referred to "the excellent speech" made by Gandhi at YMCA, and said that "he has taken on this great responsibility. He is indeed born to carry out such work. Suffering all the tortures heaped upon him fearlessly, he has led India on the path of peaceful opposition."

Besant could have stopped short after offering such encomiums in her article. But no, she raised the old issue again.

> To call him an infant in politics cannot offend his dignity, because his life has not led him to the path of politics. He led and obtained victory for people who had lost hope. It was a conflict that needed to be resolved by peaceful protest. However, in the fight to obtain freedom in the political arena, which is fraught with more dangers, he is still required ... not as a visionary, but as a politician. Gandhiji says that to talk of time, place, and circumstance is a betrayal of truth. But, as one who has modestly been involved as a politician, I believe that these are vital necessities in the great drama of politics.

Different paths, one goal

Besant also referred to Gandhi's comment of "water under the bridge" and said:

> In the morning, Gandhiji referred to the Benares incident as 'water under the bridge, that comes and goes, and we should not make too much of it.' I agree wholeheartedly. One or two newspapers made a big issue of it. Just as I was indifferent to the

muck they threw at me, Gandhiji made little of the bouquets they offered him. In each our own way we seek to serve God and the people. Our paths may be different…our goal is the same.

Gandhiji's reply to Besant

However, despite Annie Besant's praise, Gandhiji was not going to let her have the last word—because she had reiterated her view that he was an infant in politics, and then gone on to offer a further explanation for it. Hence, Besant's editorial served only to add fuel to the fire already smouldering among Gandhiji's supporters. Ultimately, he found it necessary to issue a clarification. Besant's piece had come out on 16 February 1916 evening. Gandhiji must have read it the same evening and drafted his response, sending a copy to *New India*, which is why its headlines referred to it the next morning itself, that is, 17 February 1916.

Contradictions

In his response Gandhiji wrote, "Mrs Besant has written as though I had whispered something to the kings. If I were to believe my eyes and ears, it seems I need to reiterate my old statements." He then referred to where she sat that day on the dais, and added:

> When I was speaking, Mrs. Besant was seated more or less near me. When the president, Darbhanga Maharaja, got up, she got up, too. I ended my speech before the rajas exited the dais. Mrs. Besant, at that time, was discussing about this with some others. Even if she had not heeded my request not to interrupt while I was speaking, and was not in agreement with my views, I calmly told her that she could have spoken after I finished my speech. However, she retorted somewhat impatiently, 'How could we remain silent when your speech served to directly silence us all? You should not have expressed such views.' So, how can I take it that it was for my benefit only that she interrupted my speech?

Gandhi went on to say that, "It is still a puzzle to me as to what, in the views expressed by me in my speech, prompted her to interrupt as she did," adding further, that, "It did not seem to me that the students who had gathered at the meeting would have been adversely affected by this speech. In fact, some students met me the next day to say that they had understood me correctly."

The mystery sentence

> Hence, to give full justice to Mrs. Besant and myself, I offer the following thoughts. The sentence that 'drove' the rajas out of the dais, which sentence seemed to be supportive of the British government, is what has been referred to as the offending sentence. But in an earlier communication she has said that my speech was in the hands of a secret service authority. Her not releasing that sentence, therefore, is of not an iota of use to me. She could have at least released the sentences that were offensive, causing her to interrupt, and the rajas to walk out.
>
> If Besant had not intervened, I would have completed my speech within minutes thereafter. What I had spoken about anarchy, too, would not have been misunderstood.

Besant's response

The result of Gandhiji's reference to the Benares meeting in *New India*, 17 February 1916, was strange. Besant wrote:

> It is only yesterday that Gandhiji wisely referred to the Benares incident as a small issue, but he has changed his stance and given a long rejoinder to the Press. He is staying with Christian padres. Hence he has been influenced by them to change his views. He is now functioning as a songbird of the Christians. The ruling classes will be happy with this. Large efforts are being undertaken to turn the student community away from Mrs. Besant, but this victory will be short-lived.

Gandhiji shot off a reply to Besant: "You have written in your editorial that, at the behest of Christian evangelism, I have recounted the Benares event. I state here that my announcements have no connection with the spread of Christianity, nor indeed with any religion."

'In defence of Gandhi'

The nineteenth issue of *New India* carried Besant's response, under a rather curious headline that read 'In Defence of M. K. Gandhi', in which she wrote:

When the meeting was in progress, the students became angry at the way the C.I.D. officials conducted themselves. Many students had been held in custody at their colleges themselves. For some days, some prominent persons were being arrested and treated harshly. It was in that tinder box situation that the meeting was held. Many in the meeting did not know about Gandhiji's principle of peaceful opposition. Hence, even though Gandhiji warned against the adverse effects of throwing of grenades, I feared that they would construe that he was in favour of such action.

I felt it was injudicious on the part of Gandhiji to say that it is only by force that England would leave India. But, at the same time (as I myself have been earnestly working towards self rule), had I said what he did, I would not have been understood in similar fashion. My statement would have sounded like a threat, but Gandhiji cannot be made to understand this, because what he unequivocally told the crowd was, 'You are not competent yet for self rule.' The words that came from Gandhiji's mouth could not be considered as intentioned towards protest. Hence I cannot count him as a straightforward politician. He will place at stake his life and those of his followers only, but not those of his enemies.

When, in a country, anarchy is understood to refer to the use of firearms and explosives, it is not sagacious on his part to bravely declare, 'I am an anarchist'. Like Tolstoy, Gandhiji is a believer in the 'non-government' principle. There are lots of similarities between them ... when divine principle shows a man the path from within, he can afford to have contempt for outside laws.

For a man like Gandhiji, who leads a life of selflessness and purity, a life that day in and day out eschews personal desires, what is the need for laws from the outside? Such people are treasure houses of heroism and virtue to inspire people. That is why some of Gandhiji's views, if not relevant to the present day world, but are of significance for the future generations, and if his politics leads him in that direction, which we may consider not practical, why, even serving to completely block the change in future government establishment—when such a man is subjected to attack by the Anglo-Indian government, or

the authoritarian classes, we will stand around him in thousands
and lakhs to protect him.

Clash of titans

The stinging arguments and counter-arguments that flew back and
forth between the leaders on two sides of the Indian political spectrum
seemed like a clash of titans. Since these took place in the 'battlefield'
of Madras, the city elders were able to witness them first-hand.

On 18 February 1916 evening, the headlines of the *Madras Mail*
roused strong sentiments, and stoked the anger of the Tamil people
yet again. The *Mail* opined that it was wrong to compare Gandhiji
with Tolstoy, but Annie Besant objected to it, and wrote:

> *Madras Mail* has openly expressed its displeasure in Gandhiji
> being compared to Tolstoy. Except in literature, Gandhiji is in all
> ways superior to Tolstoy. Tolstoy lived as a farmer, made shoes
> for a living. Gandhiji, too, lives in similar fashion, and works for
> the service of society. The Russian government hated Tolstoy …
> so also the South African government which hated Gandhiji.
> But, on behalf of his people, Gandhiji has suffered much
> hardship. Tolstoy, though, had not gone through that. Both are
> visionaries, and have been lauded by people from far off places.

The Hindu criticises

The Hindu took up the cudgels even more vehemently against the
Madras Mail in its editorial.

> The *Mail* has written that, if whatever Besant says has been
> actually spoken by Gandhiji, … he should withdraw from
> public life, or he must be prepared to face the enmity of all
> right-minded people in India. A man who is reported as having
> aired such degrading views has no right to speak about general
> problems. When Gandhiji speaks next, instead of waxing
> eloquent about the simple life, and singing about pristine fields,
> he should respond to this criticism. …
>
> Last night's issue of the *Madras Mail* contained some insane
> statements. It has refuted that Annie Besant found fault with
> Gandhiji's speech in a public meeting. It castigates Gandhiji for

making degrading statements, that Gandhiji should make his entire speech available, and that the leaders who left the dais and the rajas should approve it (but this speech is not available with Gandhiji). In this way, Gandhiji must prove that he is opposed to the discrimination and arrogance of the Anglo-Indian authorities ... This is a condemnable and impolite way to dishonour a great man.

'A hero of service'

Under the auspices of the Madras Social Service League, students organised a welcome to Gandhiji in the Madras Christian College grounds with unbounded enthusiasm. It was initially decided to hold this in Anderson Hall, but they had to change the venue owing to the huge crowds that came. In fact, even the open grounds were not enough. Students were sitting in the courtyard, on walls and terraces. It became quite difficult for Mrs Whitehat and her husband, the Head Bishop of Madras, Mr Whitehat, to escort Gandhiji to the dais through this milling crowd. There were shouts of 'Hail, Gandhiji!' all around. It was a problem for Mr Whitehat to restore order and start the meeting as president and head of the Social Service League. He introduced Gandhiji as "a hero of service not given to idle talk." Rao Bahadur T. Vijayaraghavachariar proposed the vote of thanks at this meeting.

Gandhiji began his speech saying that there were a number of officials present on that day (16 February 1916), and that he had not had much time to think about his speech.

> There is a condition, not only for social service, but for any kind of service in the world, which is that the person so engaged in service must be qualified for it. At times, is it not a fact that the work of some, instead of being of assistance, turns out to be a burden? I enumerated 11 pledges to be taken at the Y.M.C.A. meeting this morning. We should move forward with truth in one hand and fearlessness in the other. Truth without discipline will lead only to danger. A life without discipline is a life without principles, and a life without principles is like a rudderless boat.

Change is important

Before arriving at this meeting, Mrs Whitehat had taken Gandhiji to the slums behind the house where he was staying. The students of the Social Service League had done commendable work to improve the conditions there. Lauding their work, Gandhiji said, "This slum is in fact cleaner than some other slums that are in the centre of Madras city. I can confidently say that it is an example for cleanliness and hygiene." He went on to say,

> We should not leave the responsibility of cleanliness only to the Municipality in cities. Social service organisations must work towards this patiently. Unless the people themselves clamour for progress, the town council can do very little. The reprimand of authorities will not work either. 'It is better to leave a drunkard as he is, rather than threaten him to stop drinking at the point of a knife,' said a wise man. I am in agreement with him. In spite of our best efforts, if a drunkard insists on drinking, it is better we let him be. There is no cleanliness even in our temples. Because of that we should not just leave them under the control of the government or town council. Once they go to school, students forget our temples. If we are to be worthy of such schools, we should bring in improvements in the education system. We are caught in a faulty education system. We should not be pointed a finger at by the next generation for doing nothing about this.

Speaking about the travails of people travelling by third class, Gandhi said, "Looking at your white shirts, they will start thinking themselves inferior. Do not begin to dominate them. If you do so, you cannot be considered suitable for social service."

Education in mother tongue

On 17 February 1916, before Gandhiji's departure, a debate was arranged in the evening at Anderson Hall under the auspices of the several associations in the Madras Christian College, on the topic, 'Should mother tongue be the medium of instruction in our schools and colleges?' Evidently this issue had exercised the minds of people in Madras from before 1916. Gandhiji said,

There has been one improvement. In High Schools it has been accepted by all sections that the mother tongue should be the medium of instruction, and it has also been implemented. In Colleges, however, although we have decided that the mother tongue medium could be brought in, it has been implemented only here and there. Till time solves this problem, it will remain as an itch in our inner palm.

In the debate, A. S. Rajan, Ramanathan, Muthugopalan, and Mohammed Hanif participated from among the students. Offering his views at the end, Gandhiji said:

In colleges and schools, if [the] mother tongue is adopted as the medium of instruction, there will be no problems of race. Our country's people will consider themselves to be part of one nation. Even before the advent of the British we have functioned as citizens of one nation and one religion. For our country to progress, people in authority must solve this problem soon. Arguments against the use of mother tongue in education are baseless and without foundation. Hence the best way to solve this issue is by the people themselves. When persons are educated in their mother tongue, the authorities will automatically start adopting it as benefiting the administration. If our mother tongue has not achieved the prominence of English, is it not our duty to ensure its development? Unless our mother tongue grows into prominence, the self-rule that we desire will never be realised.

Leaving for Poona

Thus, after waging a protracted war of words with Annie Besant, and emerging victorious, obtaining the people's good wishes, and outlining the path of service to the nation through his definitive speeches, Gandhiji left for Poona on the night of 17 February 1916. For Madras, and indeed for India itself, this visit proved to be historic.

Note

1. Based on the author's interview with P. N. Ramasubramaniam.

14

EN ROUTE TO RANCHI, 1917

First success

The period around 1916 in Indian politics can be termed as the age of Tilak, Besant and Jinnah. Their voices reverberated at innumerable conferences. There was no conflict then between the Muslim League and the Congress. It was after setting foot in India, touring the country exhaustively for two years, acquainting himself with the situation prevailing at different places, and addressing various gatherings, that Gandhiji got down to work. As in South Africa, here too he took up the problems of contract labourers first.

He gave an ultimatum to the British government to stop sending Indian contract labourers to other places in the British Empire. Bowing to this pressure, the Viceroy agreed to suspend sending out such persons temporarily (from January 1920, this was stopped permanently). In this manner, the dream of Gandhiji in South Africa was realised on his return to India.

Home Rule

The Home Rule Movement, which spread all over India, shook Britain. The regions in which it gained momentum were Maharashtra in the west and Madras in the south, which is why the Madras government sought the help of the Justice Party (set up in Madras in November 1916). It was because of the Home Rule Movement that Annie Besant and her followers were arrested, and later released after a short incarceration, on the intervention of Montague Crook, a minister in the British government.

Unannounced Madras visit

After successfully launching the Champaran Satyagraha, Gandhiji began to shine as a star in the Indian political firmament. It was the first moral war that he undertook in India, at the end of which an inquiry commission was established, with Gandhiji as a member. The commission was to meet at Ranchi. To participate in it, he came to Madras on the morning of 14 September 1917, from Ahmedabad en route to Ranchi. After 1915, when he permanently returned to India from South Africa, to a tumultuous welcome in Madras, this visit in 1917 was the only time that Gandhiji arrived in Madras without notice, unannounced.

New India news

It is doubtful if the press knew about his visit to Madras, because there was no news of it in the papers, except in Annie Besant's *New India*, where it appeared under the heading 'M. K. Gandhi', which read: "Our respected son of India arrived this morning from Ahmedabad. He will be here till tomorrow evening. He will meet several people tomorrow for discussions."

Besant, B. P. Wadia (1888–1958) and George Arundale (1878–1945) were in prison at this time. They were released three days after Gandhiji's departure, that is, on 17 September 1917.

Travails of journey

It is not known whom Gandhiji met and had discussions with during this visit, or in whose house he stayed (it can only be guessed that he stayed at G. A. Natesan's house). His itinerary was from Ahmedabad to Bombay, Bombay to Madras, Madras to Poona, and from Poona to Ranchi. In a letter from Ranchi to Maganlal Gandhi (1883–1928, a cousin), the weariness caused by all this travel comes through: "It is 12 days since I left you. Out of 11 days, I have spent 9 days on the train. It is only two nights that I spent at a friend's house. Yet my health has not been affected. After 11 days I have been able to get proper food only today."

The only firm details of this visit are that Gandhi was to start on 11 September from Ahmedabad for Madras, to arrive here on 14 September and reach Poona on 17 September. Hence, it can be construed that he left Madras on 15 September night.

Third-class travel

Writing about the hardship he encountered in third-class travel from Bombay to Madras, and generally about the problems faced by third-class passengers, Gandhi wrote a letter to the editor of *The Leader*. He copied this letter suggesting various improvements that were required in train travel, and sent it to the Delhi Commerce and Labour Department Secretary.

When he started for Poona from here, the train compartment he entered was small, with seating for nine persons. However, 12 persons boarded the compartment. When Gandhiji entrained, there was no seat for him. A passenger 'friend' requested others to shift and make room for Gandhiji. It is not known who this 'friend' was (G. A. Natesan, perhaps?). Gandhiji jokingly said that he found his place in the toilet. "There was a tap in it, but no water. If I said it was unhygienic enough to cause an infectious disease, no one would have contradicted me. The compartment itself was filthy. The planks were all full of dust. It is doubtful whether in its lifetime, the compartment would have ever seen soap or water."

There were two modern and distinguished Tamil men in the compartment. One informed Gandhiji that he had paid a bribe at Madras Central Station to get a ticket to travel. The other passenger said that he himself had paid five rupees for it.

15

THE MORAL WAR BEGINS, 1919

Enrolling people for the War

After handling a strike by Ahmedabad factory workers, and the revolt of farmers in Kheda (a district of Gujarat) in 1918, ensuring justice for them, Gandhiji found himself faced with the need to plunge into another challenging situation. In connection with World War I (July 1914–November 1918), Gandhiji was invited by the authorities to a conference in Delhi in April 1919. He participated in it, and conveyed his concurrence with the resolution to gather men for the War. As always, not content with mere talk, he sprang into action, and travelled to numerous villages in Gujarat, enrolling people for the War. He did not flag in his efforts even though his health had deteriorated.

Montagu's communication

As the Emperor's representative in India, Edwin Montagu released in July 1918 a communication containing a blueprint drawn up by Viceroy Chelmsford, detailing the composition of the government and the improvements to be effected after the War. This was a communication eagerly awaited by the leaders and the people of India. One section of politicians opposed it, while another was strongly in favour. Gandhiji, however, said, "This communication should not be deferred in its entirety. We should look at it dispassionately. We should fight without any conditions for the victory of Britain. At the same time we should fight to the last for the improvements that need to be made for us." To discuss this, at the special Congress meeting in Bombay, under the presidentship of Syed Hassan Imam, a resolution was adopted, praising the Chelmsford-Montagu plan to initiate responsible governance in India, stating, at the same time, that the improvements contemplated were disappointing. To explain this stand of the Congress to British leaders, Tilak went to England. Gandhiji was not in a condition to travel owing to ill health.

The Rowlatt Act

Once World War I ended, Britain seemed to forget about the prior assurances it had given. Further, anticipating there would be a widespread revolt in India for self-governance, and to equip themselves to counter it, it set up a commission under Justice Sidney Rowlatt to look into all possible anti-government activities likely to happen. In the communication it sent to the Indian government, the commission, after travelling all over the country, said that there were rebel groups plotting to overthrow the government through the use of violence, and that unless a separate law was brought in to curb them, the government was in danger of being toppled. With a view ostensibly to reform the outdated defence laws and give them new shape, and to amend the criminal law with respect to offenders, a Bill (in the name of Rowlatt) was introduced in the Indian Legislature. The nation rose up in anger against this. As per the government's assessment, anti-government offenders numbered only 300. For these 300 people, a law that sought to drag 30,000 into the same net—how could the people countenance such a law? At that time the Muslims had their own particular grievance: they were angered at the treatment meted out to the vanquished Turkish caliph by Britain.

Gandhiji rises

Even as he lay sick in Sabarmati Ashram, Gandhiji could not keep silent at this grave injustice. Taking a pledge to launch a satyagraha there, he came to Bombay and set up a satyagraha organisation. The work of obtaining signatures for the satyagraha went on apace. Thereafter he also went to Delhi. But despite all this, the government introduced the Indian Criminal Law Bill No. 1, and the Criminal Law Emergency Authority Bill. Of these, the second bill became law, the Rowlatt Act, in 1919, while Gandhiji was in Madras. It was later repealed in 1922.

18 March 1919, Madras Central

There was as in the past a large crowd when Gandhiji arrived at Central Station. Despite being told not to throng the railway station in large numbers and disturb Gandhij, who was recovering from a heart ailment, multitudes had gathered. At a time of great political turmoil, the news that Gandhiji planned a satyagraha made the press accord importance to his visit. The newspapers, that had hitherto devoted a single column to his arrival, wrote three full columns on this occasion. The huge crowd at the railway station conducted themselves with discipline. Gandhiji was welcomed with garlands by members of the Rowlatt Act opposition group, viz. Kasturi Ranga Iyengar, A. Rangaswami Iyengar and S. Sathyamurthi.

Gandhiji compared with Jesus

Swadesamithran, that had published this story, had compared Gandhiji with Jesus. "History tells us that Christ had exhorted such of his disciples who wished to follow him to carry the Cross and come with him. Gandhi is a symbol of truth—hence, more than the words of others, it is his words that must make us follow him. He carries the Cross and asks us to follow. Will the people of India forsake their self-interest and follow him?"

Satyagraha Pledge

Gandhiji declared that the Rowlatt Act should be opposed by peaceful satyagraha. Those who wished to join should take the 'Satyagraha Pledge', he said, circulating this pledge to all. It was at this time that the words 'satyagraha' and 'satyagrahi' became widely known throughout the country. In all the main cities of India, meetings of the supporters of the satyagraha movement were held, including Madras, where they were held even before Gandhiji's arrival. The first meeting against the Rowlatt Act was in fact held at Madras.

V. O. Chidambaram Pillai

A few days before Gandhiji arrived, a meeting was held in Madras to oppose the Rowlatt Act and take the satyagraha pledge. Among those who attended this meeting was V. O. Chidambaram Pillai (V. O. C.), also known by his adopted pseudonym 'Kappalottiya Tamizhan', which means 'the Tamil helmsman'. How well he understood the value of spiritual strength may be gleaned from the speech he made at the time (as reported in *The Hindu*, 10 March 1919).

> Western people are clever in spreading animal instincts. In the fight between this animal strength and spiritual power, the victory to spiritual power is guaranteed. This would serve as the best example to show who the true believers of our country's spiritual power are. Under the leadership of Mahatma Gandhi, this is the time for India to show its peaceful opposition. If we are firm in this, it will certainly help in our realising 'self rule', said 'Kappalottiya Tamizhan'.

S. Sathyamurthi

Speaking at the same meeting, the nationalist S. Sathyamurthi praised Gandhiji's spiritual strength, adding that this was an opportunity that comes once in a lifetime, which no one should let slip. Those gentlemen engaged hitherto in 'guerilla[1] warfare' should at least now give it up and fight openly alongside Gandhiji, with the flag held high. Gandhiji, possessing the patriotism given to visionaries from birth, a clear objective and foresight, had come up with the plan to counter this law after several sleepless nights, and hence everyone should follow him, said Sathyamurthi.

S. Somasundara Bharathi

At this time in Madras city, among those spreading the word of satyagraha like a hurricane was the Tamil scholar, S. Somasundara Bharathi. He said that it was wrong to translate 'satyagraha' as peaceful opposition, because 'satyagraha' did not mean opposition at all (*The Hindu*, 24 March 1919), revealing that he had understood Gandhiji's principles well.

The opposition of moderates

Not everyone thought that satyagraha was the only way or the best way. This group, known as the 'moderates', took the stand that an unjust law must be challenged (even if peacefully) not through direct action, but by discussions within and outside the legislature. They accepted that the Rowlatt (Emergency) Bill was against the tenets of justice, and they strongly opposed its becoming law, but they did not think that satyagraha was the right way to oppose it. This could be done, they believed, by making an appeal to the British Empire. Hence, as soon as Gandhiji reached Madras, they got together and issued a statement containing their views. G. A. Natesan was also one of the moderates. Even earlier, leaders such as Srinivasa Sastri and Surendranath Banerji had also issued a notice to the effect that satyagraha was not the proper way to oppose this bill. However, they were strongly criticised by nationalists like V. O. Chidambaram Pillai, S. Sathyamurthi, and Kasturi Ranga Iyengar. The public too did not support them.

Subramania Iyer's stand

When Dr S. Subramania Iyer welcomed Gandhiji in 1915, he was Sir S. Subramania Iyer. He had retired as a judge of the Madras High Court, was the honorary president of the All India Home Rule League, and also a member of the Congress. In 1917, the arrest of Annie Besant and her associates had pained him. He gave up his knighthood, and decided to continue peaceful protest, for which he prepared a pledge. Gandhiji, deciding that he would be a staunch support for the satyagraha movement, invited him to be the vice-president of the Satyagraha Sabha. But Subramania Iyer declined; he was an admirer of Besant, and involved with her politics. Gandhiji, however, asked him to explain to Besant that there was no politics in satyagraha, and that by joining the movement, there was no danger of Iyer's political affiliations being affected.

Gandhiji sends a message

The political methodology advocated by the moderates did not appeal, not only to the common people, but the intellectuals as well. *The Hindu* criticised their approach, and said that the people needed to find ways of preserving their dignity after their rights had been so flagrantly violated by the government. Gandhiji's visit had also served to awaken their sense of duty-consciousness. Those who opposed Gandhiji's activities may have discussed within the legislature and outside, and raised storms of protest, but when it came to action, they had shown hesitation. So, before making any announcement, they should first try to understand what 'satyagraha' means, wrote *The Hindu*.

It was in such circumstances that Gandhiji arrived in Madras. At a public meeting at the Marina Beach the evening before his arrival, attended by Andhra Kesari T. Prakasam, and S. Sathyamurthi, Sarojini Naidu (1879–1949) read out a message sent by Gandhiji to the people. It said: "Those who merely sign the satyagraha pledge will not contribute to its success; it is those who *act* according to it who will."

Public meeting

When Gandhiji arrived in the evening, he addressed, for the first time, a meeting on the Marina Beach. The emotional crowd gathered there, a veritable sea of humanity, seemed to tacitly declare that they were ready for non-violent protest. The newspapers estimated that there were around 15,000 people at that meeting, a large number of them women—in 1919 that was a mammoth crowd. The meeting had been organised to welcome the Mahatma, and to explain to the people that there was no alternative to taking the pledge of satyagraha to oppose the imposition of the Rowlatt Act. Kasturi Ranga Iyengar, who had invited Gandhiji to Madras, presided over this meeting. Those who participated included A. Rangaswami Iyengar, Sarojini Naidu, George Joseph, S. Sathyamurthi, and C. Rajagopalachari. An Englishman named Gilbert Slater[2] also attended.

The term 'Mahatma' was used for the first time in a sentence of the resolutions passed at this meeting. It was between 1917 and 1919 in Madras that this honorific began to be used for Gandhiji, and it gained prevalence during the 1919 Civil Disobedience Movement.

Gandhiji's preface

Gandhiji could not stand and talk loudly at the time. Doctors had advised him not to speak at length. Hence, he had written out his speech and given it to his secretary, Mahadev Desai, to read out. However, aware that the large and enthusiastic crowd was eager to hear his voice, Gandhiji spoke for a few minutes in the beginning, but even this he could not do loudly enough. As a result S. Sathyamurthi, in a ringing baritone, had to repeat what he said for the audience.

Apologising to the people for speaking while seated, Gandhiji said in his preface: "Be warned before you sign the satyagraha pledge. But once you have signed it, do not turn your backs to it. God will give you strength to carry out this pledge."

Action imperative

In the speech read out by Mahadev Desai, Gandhiji emphasised the difference between this meeting and any other.

> At other meetings, people can listen to the speakers and leave, but in this meeting it is not enough if you merely listen. You must translate it into action. The magnanimity of people will be called in question. A few noted leaders in our country have questioned the suitability of satyagraha for the nation's welfare. Sastri is a politician who has sacrificed everything for the good of our country. He has no equal to his honesty and probity. He is second to none in service to the nation. I have a bond with those who have opposed the signing of the satyagraha pledge, but with deep sadness I have to differ from them. Is not our conscience a voice that compels us to act, even against the wishes of friends and relatives? I have no disrespect whatsoever for those who have found it not possible to sign this pledge. ...[You], too, must not harbour any grievance towards them. Such grievance would be against the spirit of satyagraha. In fact, I am happy that there is difference of opinion among leaders. Differences between friends is even more laudable, because it helps to serve as a warning to us to stay on the right path.

After Gandhiji's speech, three persons spoke in three languages. George Joseph of Madurai spoke in English, Chidambaram Pillai in Tamil, and Hari Sarvottama Rao in Telugu. The vote of thanks was given by T. V. Gopalasamy Mudaliar. The satyagraha pledge document was placed in the house where Gandhiji was staying. A few went there to sign it.

Workers' meeting

On 19 March 1919, Gandhiji participated in the Madras workers' meeting. As the strike of the tramway workers was ongoing, it was a time of intense activity for workers' unions. The meeting, under the presidentship of trade union leader B. B. Wadia, brought South Africa to Gandhiji's mind. He recalled the contract labourers from Madras, and emotionally recounted how he had lived, worked and eaten with these workers over the years that he had spent there. He regretted that he could not speak in Tamil at this meeting.

Education is essential

Addressing the workers, Gandhi said:

> Money cannot achieve anything without workers, nor can workers do anything without money. Part of the profit your employers earn from your labour is distributed amongst you as wages. Hence, it is your situation that gives you the advantage. However, there are at the same time several responsibilities that you have to undertake. Firstly, you must be honest people. For this to be reflected, you must be educated. You can learn at any age. It is only then that you will be aware of your duties and rights. Do you wish to waste your money in drink and gambling?

20 March 1919, Triplicane beach

At a meeting on 20 March 1919, in frail health, and with difficulty, Gandhiji attended a meeting organised to thank him for coming to Madras and strengthening the satyagraha movement. An objective of the meeting was to felicitate P. N. Sarma of Andhra, who had been a member of the Central Legislature, and had resigned from it. Another aim was to request the Viceroy not to give his assent to the Rowlatt Bill. The meeting was held at Triplicane Beach, under overcast conditions, with rain forecast. Still, the crowd of over 10,000 people that had gathered reiterated their commitment to the satyagraha movement. There were also some at this meeting who opposed the movement. C. Vijayaraghavachariar of Salem, who presided, said that Gandhiji ought to have presided, but could not owing to ill health. Sarojini Naidu, T. P. Gopalasami Mudaliar, S. Somasundara Bharathi,

Dr Avadhanulu, and Mir Sulthan Moideen Sahib spoke. The vote of thanks to Gandhiji proposed by S. Sathyamurthi was seconded by T. A. Adhinarayana Chetty from Madras.

Gandhiji's clarification

In response to those who were opposed to his plan for satyagraha, Gandhiji clarified that as the satyagrahi's weapons were truth and ahimsa, there need be no fear of violence being resorted to. He reiterated and emphasised the qualities of a true satyagrahi as one who: should not forsake truth, whatever the hardship; should always try and treat his enemies with affection; and, whatever be the maltreatment meted out by authorities, or opposition to his views from others, he must be ready to tolerate them. "If he does so, not only will the Rowlatt bill be given up, the satyagraha movement will be accepted as a powerful weapon by the people," Gandhiji said. This is what happened.

21 March 1919, Tram workers' strike

The tram workers' strike was continuing. About 1,000 tram workers came to where Gandhiji was staying on 21 March 1919 to seek his advice. They were aware that Gandhiji was concerned with the problems of workers, and also that he would not arrive at any solution in haste or anger. He invited one of the workers to sit beside him, and asked him some questions.

Gandhi: For how much longer can you hold out under this strike?
Worker: We are not tired. We can manage for another 10 or 15 days.
Gandhi: What will you do if the strike extends beyond that period?
Worker: I believe we can hold out for another 10 days beyond that.

Gandhiji told the workers that though he had not had the opportunity of examining their demands in detail, he believed that they must be true, and the strike they had undertaken justified. He praised the discipline and solidarity of the tramway workers. Then he outlined some of his important principles governing strikes:

1. If employers refuse to concede the just demands of workers, going on strike was the only rightful weapon available to them.

2. If a strike has to succeed, the first condition is that the demands must be just.

3. Those going on strike must not indulge in any violence at any time against either the employer or workers who decide not to join the strike.

4. Whatever the hardship during the period of strike, they must all be borne patiently.

5. Demands must always be submitted in writing. At the time an agreement or compromise is about to be reached, these demands must not be multiplied.

6. If mediators are appointed to resolve the issue, such mediation must be accepted by the workers.

7. If the strike extends interminably, the workers should seek some temporary employment. There is no work beneath one's dignity.

Gandhiji's words were translated for the workers by C. Rajagopalachari.

23 March 1919, Opposing the Rowlatt Bill

Prominent leaders met to consider the actions to be taken with respect to the Rowlatt bill. At that meeting, the actions taken till then in Bombay were examined. Thereafter Gandhiji shared his own 'dream vision' of how he proposed to oppose the Rowlatt bill. He requested that the second Sunday of April, that is, 6 April 1919 be observed as a "day of shame and prayer," if, and after, the news was received that the second Rowlatt bill was accepted by the Viceroy. Gandhiji suggested the following ways to do this:

1. Adults should fast from the meal of one night for 24 hours. To prepare for the opposition to this bill, not only satyagrahis, but all those who oppose this bill must also join in this fast.

2. All establishments, including markets and commercial establishments, other than those considered essential for the public, must be closed on that day. Government employees, too, must observe this.

3. All through the day on 6 April, across India, including in villages and towns, meetings must be held in which resolutions must be passed demanding the withdrawal of both the Rowlatt bills.

Gandhiji released a circular detailing these measures. The circular, signed by him on 23 March, was published in the newspapers of 24 March 1919.

Satyagraha sabhas

The circular issued from Madras reached nationwide. To implement these measures, satyagraha sabhas were organised. The satyagraha sabha in Madras had Gandhiji as president, and Dr Subramania Iyer, C. Vijayaraghavachariar, M. C. Nanjunda Rao, S. Kasturi Ranga Iyengar and T. Prakasam were elected vice-presidents. A. Rangaswami Iyengar, C. Rajagopalachari, T. Adhinarayana Chettiar and G. Hari Sarvottama Rao were elected secretaries, and T. V. Venkatarama Iyer the treasurer. (Dr Subramania Iyer had declined the vice-presidentship.)

The idea that shook India

Although it was four years since Gandhiji had returned from South Africa, and toured India from north to south and from west to east, and conducted the Kheda and Champaran campaigns, he had not yet undertaken any action on an all-India scale. He was contemplating such an action against the Rowlatt bill, but he was still unaware of just what shape this mass protest would take. While he was staying at Kasturi Ranga Iyengar's house, where Rajaji was also staying at the time and practising as a lawyer, the idea appeared to Gandhiji in a dream. (It may be interesting to note here that it was after a dream that Swami Vivekananda had in Madras that he decided to go to America in 1893). People may think that the idea of a nationwide fast and strike occurred to Gandhiji because he was constantly thinking about it, but Gandhiji himself has called it a 'dream' in his essays and autobiography, a holy dream that he saw in the early hours of the morning. Many believe that what one dreams in the early morning finds fruition. This dream of Gandhiji did not just fructify—it shook India to its very roots, and prised open the eyes of the British government.

In comparison to the volcanic eruption of ahimsa, the South African revolt appeared small. This was a movement that heralded powerful new changes and awakening in the Indian polity. It made the whole world sit up and believe that Gandhiji's new principles would be the precursor of a new world order. In every nook and corner of India, in every household, the word 'Mahatma' resonated.

Rajaji—The force behind

When he first announced his plan of a mass *hartal* or strike against the Rowlatt bill, Gandhiji had strong doubts whether all of India would accept it. Recalling the events of 1919 later, he has acknowledged this with humility in his autobiography, which was published in Tamil as *Sathya Sodhanai.*

> I have ever felt at home in the south. Thanks to my South African work I felt I had some sort of special right over the Tamils and Telugus, and the good people of the south have never belied my belief. The invitation had come over the signature of the late Sjt. Kasturi Ranga Iyengar. But the man behind the invitation, as I subsequently learnt on my way to Madras, was Rajagopalachari. This might be said to be my first acquaintance with him....
>
> Rajagopalachari had then only recently left Salem to settle down for legal practice in Madras[3] at the pressing invitation of friends like the late Sjt. Kasturi Ranga Iyengar...with a view to taking a more active part in public life. It was with him that we had put up in Madras. This discovery I made only after we had stayed with him for a couple of days. For, since the bungalow that we were staying in belonged to Sjt. Kasturi Ranga Iyengar, I was under the impression that we were his guests. Mahadev Desai, however, corrected me. He very soon formed a close acquaintance with Rajagopalachari, who, from his innate shyness, kept himself constantly in the background. But Mahadev put me on my guard. "You should cultivate this man," he said to me one day.
>
> And so I did. We daily discussed together plans of the fight, but beyond the holding of public meetings I could not then think of any other programme. I felt myself at a loss to discover how to offer civil disobedience against the Rowlatt Bill if it was finally passed into law. One could disobey it only if the Government gave one the opportunity for it. Failing that, could we civilly disobey other laws? And if so, where was the line to be drawn? These and a host of similar questions formed the theme of these discussions of ours.[4]

The dream

Gandhiji further tells us,

> While these cogitations were still going on, news was received
> that the Rowlatt Bill had been published as an Act. That night
> I fell asleep while thinking over the question. Towards the
> small hours of the morning I woke up somewhat earlier than
> usual. I was still in that twilight condition between sleep and
> consciousness when suddenly the idea broke upon me—it was
> as if in a dream. Early in the morning I related the whole story
> to Rajagopalachari.
>
> "The idea came to me last night in a dream that we should
> call upon the country to observe a general *hartal.* Satyagraha
> is a process of self-purification, and ours is a sacred fight, and
> it seems to me to be in the fitness of things that it should be
> commenced with an act of self-purification. Let all the people of
> India, therefore, suspend their business on that day and observe
> the day as one of fasting and prayer. The Musalmans may not
> fast for more than one day; so the duration of the fast should
> be 24 hours. It is very difficult to say whether all the provinces
> would respond to this appeal of ours or not, but I feel fairly sure
> of Bombay, Madras, Bihar and Sindh. I think we should have
> every reason to feel satisfied even if all these places observe the
> *hartal* fittingly."
>
> Rajagopalachari was at once taken up with my suggestion.
> Other friends too welcomed it.... The date of the *hartal* was first
> fixed on the 30th March 1919, but was subsequently changed
> to 6th April. The people thus had only a short notice of the
> *hartal....*
>
> But who knows how it all came about? The whole of India
> from one end to the other, towns as well as villages, observed a
> complete *hartal* on that day. It was a most wonderful spectacle.[5]

Gandhiji does not mention the date of his dream, but he does tell us
that it was a few days after he reached Madras, on 18 March, and after
learning that the second Rowlatt bill received the Viceroy's assent to
become law, on 22 March evening. It thus transpires that Gandhiji
possibly had his dream on 23 March early morning, wrote his brief
proposing the nationwide fast and strike on 23 March, which the
newspapers published on 24 March 1919.

Farewell

In 1919, when Gandhiji came to Madras, he did not stay, as he had previously, in the house of G. A. Natesan, the reason being that Natesan's brother's son, G. V. Kalyanam (then a small boy) was suffering from an attack of typhoid. He went one day to Natesan's house to enquire about the boy. As the boy was upstairs, Gandhiji went up to where he lay, lifted him up on his shoulders and then sat the boy on his lap, all the while talking to the others. It was a sight to behold. Need one say that after having known them for so long, he had become one of the family?

Subramania Bharathi

V. Ramasamy (Va. Ra.) says that during this visit of Gandhiji, he met Subramania Bharathi—a fact that Rajaji confirms. It was about 2 p.m. Gandhiji was reclining on a mattress, speaking with his secretary, Mahadev Desai, as Salem barrister, Adhinarayana Chettiar, was peeling sweet lime and squeezing it as juice for Gandhiji to drink. In one part of the room, the *Swadesamithran* editor, A. Rangaswami Iyengar, and S. Sathyamurthi were in conversation, leaning against the wall. Rajaji and the others were standing about. At the entrance to the room, Va. Ra. stood guard. There were strict orders not to allow anyone in.

Bharathi arrived. Having been introduced to Va. Ra. in Pondicherry, Bharathi greeted him with "*Enna voy!*" (What, my friend!), and walked into the room. He went straight up to Gandhiji, greeted him and, sitting down next to him on the mattress, said, "Mr Gandhi, I am going to speak at a beach meeting in Triplicane this evening. Could you please preside over it?"

"What is my programme for the evening?" enquired Gandhiji of Mahadev Desai. It turned out that he had another engagement. He said, "I cannot come today. Can you postpone your meeting till tomorrow?"

"I cannot. I will take your leave, Mr Gandhi. I bless the movement that you are about to start." With these words, Bharathi left.

When he had gone, Gandhiji asked, "Who was that?" No one answered. It was Rajagopalachari who said, "He is the national poet of our state." On hearing this, Gandhiji supposedly said, "He must be guarded carefully. Is there no one in Madras to do this?"

Protect this prodigy

This interesting incident exemplifies the natures of both Subramania Bharathi and Gandhiji very well. When all others stood before Gandhiji in awe and respect, Bharathi treated himself as an equal and sat next to him, surprising everyone. Further, the blessing Bharathi gave to Gandhiji's future movement may have filled those present with amazement, but not Gandhiji. 'Is it not your duty to protect this prodigy?' was the one sentence through which he roused the Tamil consciousness. When he met Gandhiji, Rajaji said that Bharathi had the appearance of an ascetic immersed in Vedanta. Perhaps the physical and mental turmoil he had undergone had made him so.

Bharathi's foresight

In his book, *Chitra Bharathi*, Ra. Aa. Padmanabhan has described this meeting of Subramania Bharathi and Gandhiji aptly, and said: "Among Indian leaders, of the very few who had first recognised the greatness of Mahatma Gandhi was Bharathi." When young Gandhi as a barrister was working for the welfare of Indians in South Africa in 1908, the poet had seen his worth, and praised him in the daily *India*, of which he was then editor. "Gandhi's satyagraha is based on truth, and reflects Indian tradition. He is the leader of the future," Bharathi had written with unusual foresight at a time when Indian leaders neither knew Gandhi nor saw his future potential. Bharathi had also collected funds for the Indian protest in South Africa, contributing Rs 5 himself, and sent the money to South Africa.

When Gandhi was arrested by the South African government in 1908 upon his return from London, where he had gone on behalf of South African Indians, Bharathi had expressed his views through a cartoon, whose caption read: "The cow called Gandhi, that went to England to speak for the welfare of its calves, the Indians, has returned to be imprisoned again in Transvaal. The authoritarian tigers of South Africa, not realising his softness, have put him behind bars." In later years, Bharathi praised Gandhi in song: '*Vaazhga nee yemman...*

Puvikkulle mudhanmai pettraai (Long live, you…you have attained primacy upon this earth).'

Propagating satyagraha and ahimsa

To spread the word of satyagraha in Thanjavur, Trichy, Madurai, Thoothukudi and Nagapattinam, Gandhiji left for Thanjavur by train on 23 March 1919 night. When he came to Madras in 1915, although he visited Tharangambadi and Mayavaram, his objective then was to visit his South Africa colleagues and enquire about their welfare. In his visits of 1916–17, he did not proceed beyond Madras. It was in 1919 that he went on his first political tour in the then Madras State south of the state capital, accompanied by Dr Kalelkar, Mahadev Desai and Dr T. S. S. Rajan. At every city meeting that Gandhiji participated in, the resolution to oppose the Rowlatt Act was adopted. Many took the satyagraha pledge in front of Gandhiji by appending their signatures.

Ardently preaching the concept of ahimsa, Gandhiji reiterated that the Rowlatt Act could not eschew violence; the satyagraha movement alone could do so. India would show the world that satyagraha was not just a weapon of protest, but an instrument of productive power. "Do you want the violent means adopted by foreign countries, or the method of ahimsa practised for generations in India?" was the question he repeatedly asked his audience. He cited the mythological example of Prahlada, and the courage and sacrifice of the three young Tamil martyrs, Nagappan, Narayanasami and Valliammal, who laid down their lives in the moral war in South Africa. These three names served as a '*Tharaka Mantra*' to rouse the Tamil conscience.

In Thanjavur

On 24 March 1919, Gandhiji reached Thanjavur. A public meeting was held at Besant Lodge in the afternoon, with V. P. Madhava Rao presiding. At this meeting, about 50 people signed and took the satyagraha pledge, a majority of them Muslims and merchants from Rajagiri. One question being widely raised was: was it right on the part of Gandhiji to have said that government employees could participate to some extent in the satyagraha? Another was, could government employees take part in politics?

Responding to these, Gandhiji clarified: "I have said that government employees could participate in the fast I have called for everyone on 6 April. I accept that government employees should not take part in politics. But we need not prevent them to act as per their conscience, or to express themselves about the travails of their country."

He further said: "When meetings are held opposing the Rowlatt Act, if the occasion arises to speak about the government, or its laws, only dignified language must be used. Those who take the pledge must ensure that no danger should accrue to the rights or lives of others."

25 March 1919, Trichy

Gandhiji left for Trichy from Thanjavur on the morning of 25 March 1919, and stayed at the house of Mirasdar Subbarama Iyer in Chintamani. The people of Trichy welcomed the Mahatma with enormous enthusiasm, for which he offered profuse thanks at the end of the meeting. A mammoth procession had been originally planned. Had it taken place, the welcome would have been even more spectacular, but it was dropped on Gandhiji's request. Pleading exhaustion, he said he would not be able to take the rigours of a procession. On behalf of the people of Trichy, Professor T. K. Balasubramania Iyer presented the welcome address in a casket, etched with the motif of Lord Ranganatha in repose, to Gandhiji. Pandit T. Sourirayan sang songs he had composed on Gandhiji.

Gandhiji regretted that the people gathered were unfamiliar with the national language, Hindi, and that he himself could not speak Tamil, hence he was constrained to speak in English. He said:

> In the Transvaal protest, you have observed in your welcome address, that the spirit has come out successful. The time is now fast approaching to test your belief in this. If you approach this problem with the steadfast belief of Valliammal, you will see these bills being given up. There is only one reason I have for organising public meetings and passing resolutions ... to implement such resolutions and to establish [that] this nation has the strength to stage a satyagraha on these matters.

26 March 1919, Madurai

He reached Madurai by Boat Mail[6] on the afternoon of 26 March 1919. On his way from Trichy, at Dindigul railway station, the secretary of the Tax Collectors' Association of that town, S. Ramaswami Iyer, and its members, welcomed him. In the evening, at the public meeting in the (old) Madurai College grounds, with K. Rama Iyengar presiding, Gandhiji in passing made a comparison between Hindi and Tamil, and said: "I know a little bit about the Tamil language. It is a beautiful, musical language, but its literature is very difficult to learn. Hindi literature, on the other hand, is simple even for a child."

Temple visit

At the Madurai meeting, more than 20 persons signed and took the satyagraha pledge. The newspapers said that Gandhiji visited 'the temple' and other places, and left for Thoothukudi the same night. When one refers to 'the temple' in Madurai, it is normally understood to be the Meenakshi temple. However, since Gandhiji said, in 1927, that he had *not* visited the Meenakshi temple, it must then be presumed that the temple he did visit in 1919 was some other one.

'Think before you sign'

In Madurai, Gandhiji put up at the house of well-known lawyer George Joseph, one of the foremost supporters of the satyagraha movement. Those who wished to meet Gandhiji and sign the satyagraha pledge went to Joseph's bungalow, situated north of the Vaigai bridge. Far from compelling or luring anyone to sign, Gandhiji was clear and firm with them. Sangilia Pillai, a long-time Congressman and a merchant, was one of those who met him at George Joseph's house to sign the pledge. Gandhiji said: "Think carefully before signing this pledge. Those who sign this pledge must be prepared to lay down their lives. Not only that, you should not expect any monetary gain. If you are ready to undertake these two conditions, sign the pledge."

Sangilia Pillai replied: "Mahatmaji, what can I do if I get run over by a car when I am on my way, or become afflicted with cholera? Instead, is not being part of this holy movement better?" Pleased with this response, Gandhiji permitted him to sign the pledge. Krishna Kundh, Pathra Ayyasamy, Sundaram Pillai and Sozhavandan Munagal Pattabhiramayya were among those who signed the pledge in Madurai.

At Virudhunagar station

Gandhiji did not get down at Virudhunagar railway station. R. T. P. Subramania Nadar of this town, who later went on to participate in the freedom struggle, and become an important spokesman for Gandhi's principle of sarvodaya (progress of all), was just a boy at the time studying in the fourth grade. Despite his tender years, he had a great admiration for Gandhiji, and a passion for the freedom movement. He had gone to the railway station along with a few friends to see Gandhiji.

Gandhiji told his young audience: "You are students, and should not get involved in politics. However, the opposition to the Rowlatt Act is a one-time movement. So go to the villages and spread the satyagraha news." Then he asked them: "Are you ready to go to jail?"

The children looked at him in some confusion. Then a mathematics teacher who had accompanied them replied, "Yes."

Gandhi: How many?

Teacher: One for sure.

Gandhi: What is the population of this town?

Teacher: 25,000.

Gandhi: (Laughing aloud) If I can get one satyagrahi out of 25,000, it is enough.

(Based on the interview of R. T. P. Subramania Nadar.)

In Thoothukudi

Gandhiji reached Thoothukudi on 23 March 1919. He was taken in a procession from the station along decorated streets to his place of temporary residence. There was a larger procession in the evening. The salutary results of his having passed through Madurai, Thanjavur and Srirangam were also seen at the Thoothukudi public meeting, where he extolled the hoary traditions of South Indian temples.

This is more or less the southernmost part of India. The religious fervour that I have seen all the way from Madras to here has taken me by surprise. The South of India is replete with temples. Nowhere else can one see such profusion. Immeasurable amounts of money have been poured in to endow these temples with artistic splendour. There is nothing else that exemplifies our religious awareness more truly than these.

Praise for audience

Gandhiji was pleased with the meeting at Thoothukudi because he said no one applauded or cried 'Hear! Hear!' or 'Shame, shame!' while he was speaking.

> It is with concern for my health that you have not raised these cries. I request that you give the same respect to all speeches of satyagrahis. By shouting 'hear! hear!' or 'shame, shame!', applauding loudly, you distract attention. If you refrain from doing so, you can concentrate on what is being spoken. By this, the concentration of the speaker, too, will not get disturbed. I would say this should be the practice, not only at satyagraha meetings, but any other meeting…. Whether you observe this at other meetings or not, I am confident that you will do so at satyagraha meetings.

28 March 1919, Thanjavur

He started from Thoothukudi in the morning on 28 March 1919, and arrived in Thanjavur at about 9 p.m., after changing trains at Madurai. At Madurai junction, hundreds had gathered to welcome Gandhiji with garlands, and to send him on his way. At Thanjavur station, prominent citizens of the town and a large number of the common people welcomed him. That night, Gandhiji stayed at the residence of Rao Bahadur K. S. Srinivasa Pillai. On 29 March morning, he left Thanjavur for Nagapatnam on a special invitation of the workers' association there. As majority of those who attended that meeting were workers, he spoke at length on workers' problems.

> I hope those who head the workers' associations make them aware of the pride in work. If we consider farmers and workers together, they would constitute the majority of India's population.

In India, as in the world, the future does not belong to the higher classes alone—it is [as much] for the common people. Hence, it is important that workers understand their position in society. It is not necessary that there should be struggle, as in Western countries, between workers and industry leaders.

Referring to his call for a nationwide strike on Sunday, 6 April 1919, Gandhiji clarified that those asked to work that day by their employers must not join the strike. "Only such workers who have the approval from their employers not to work on Sunday may refrain from working. Acting against the just orders of employers will not constitute lawful opposition," he added.

Praise for Tamil ethos

In Nagapatnam, Gandhiji again praised the Tamil ethos.

> More than in any other part of the country, you have carefully guarded the outer aspects of our Indian tradition. You have unshakeable faith in God. Looking at you, I am reminded of our great sages. ... even our forbears could not have lived as simple a life as you are leading. Along with the wonderful way in which you have preserved the external facets of our tradition, you must now acquire the inner consciousness of our great rishis. If only you could do that, you will become a strong force in India. I pray to the almighty that He give you the strength to protect the honour of our country, and be instrumental in realising its blissful state.

'Satyagraha will forestall Bolshevism'

On 30 March 1919, as he had to leave urgently for Vijayawada that evening, after arriving in Madras, Gandhiji could not attend the meeting to oppose the Rowlatt Act, arranged by K. V. Rangaswami Iyengar in Triplicane under the auspices of the Satyagraha Sabha. S. Sathyamurti read out Gandhiji's speech contained in his letter mentioning his inability to attend. In this letter, Gandhiji responded to possible objections to his satyagraha movement. Notable was his comparison between Bolshevism and 'Gandhism'.

> Some friends of mine have shared their fears about Bolshevism already making rapid strides, and that my concept of satyagraha

only increases those fears. I say that if there is anything that will prevent the entry of Bolshevism into our country, it is satyagraha. Bolshevism is a natural product of modern culture. This modernity is devoid of any good feeling, and is a worshipper of worldly objects. Without any consideration to the nuances of life, it is directed solely towards material advancement. Unlimited consumption is the basis of this doctrine, whereas the control of such consumption is the object of satyagraha. If our country can adopt satyagraha as a main tenet in our political and social life, there is no need to fear the spread of Bolshevism. If, instead, ... we choose to act in a manner that makes rabid violence more desirable than truth and love, we will discover in a few years that in this most holy land, Bolshevism will begin to reign supreme.

Some political experts have since said that to arrest the spread of communism, Gandhism is the answer. Gandhiji was indeed farsighted. "Wise persons anticipate events. The ignorant do not," says the *Tirukkural*.

In his letter, Gandhiji also mentions the benefits gained on this tour.

I had gone to Thanjavur, Tiruchirappalli, Madurai, Thoothukudi and Nagapattinam. The crowds that had come to the meetings numbered not less than 30,000. They were people who had a right to warn us, who had reservations, and who had acquired these rights like us by serving their motherland. These people expressed the fear: 'Our objective may be laudable. We may be keen on seeing that violence does not spread. However, those who join the movement could well lose their self-control under severe emotion and resort to violence, why, the national objective itself may suffer.' But, in this State, as I visited various towns, it was a fact that, out of concern for my health, the people refrained from clamour and noise at meetings. More than this, they did so out of an awareness that they should be disciplined. The leaders of this movement also emphasised the need for self-control. These experiences fill me with great confidence about the future.

Whatever fears our friends may have of the dangers ahead, I do not share [them]. The several meetings that I have attended reinforce my confidence in the future.

Looking back in 1946

The deep impression this visit made on the Mahatma was evident in the speech he gave on his last visit to Madras, on 22 January 1946 at a prayer meeting. It was at Madras that he had begun the fight against the Rowlatt Act, and Gandhiji paid his tribute to that moment in these words: "Rajaji, as I had seen him then for the first time, remains the same even today. It was also on that occasion that I had met (the late) Salem C. Vijayaraghavachariar. The holy satyagraha movement was started at Rajaji's home on 6 April [1919]. The satyagraha that was born that day has most amazingly awoken our nation."

Notes

1. The word *guerilla* was coined about 1809.

2. Gilbert Slater (1864–1938), economist and social reformer, was Professor of Economics at the University of Madras, 1915–21.

3. *Author's note*: When Gandhiji had come to Madras in 1919, though C. Rajagopalachari was practising law there, he was not yet considered a Madras resident; the newspapers referred to him as Salem C. Rajagopalachari.

4. M. K. Gandhi, *An Autobiography or My Experiments with Truth*, translated from the original Gujarati by Mahadev Desai (Ahmedabad: Navajivan, 1948), 507–508. Available at https://www.mkgandhi.org/ebks/An-Autobiography.pdf (accessed 18 November 2022).

5. Ibid., 508–509.

6. Also known as the Indo-Ceylon Express, an express train connecting Rameswaram with Madras city, inaugurated in 1914, then a combined train and steamer ferry service between India and Ceylon (now Sri Lanka).

16

IN THE THICK OF
NON-COOPERATION, 1920

Arrest on the train

Misunderstanding Gandhiji's call for general strike on the second Sunday of April, Delhi organised the strike and protest procession on Sunday 6 April 1919. Many in the procession lost their lives in the police firing. Hence, Gandhiji, who had gone to Bombay from Madras, began the satyagraha there on 6 April with a general strike, and entrained the next day for Delhi en route to Amritsar.

On the way, the police forced him to detrain at a place called Palwal, and took him, changing several trains on the way, including goods trains, first- and third-class compartments, finally to Bombay, declaring, "Now you have been set free." Angered at Gandhiji's arrest, people turned violent at some places in Ahmedabad and Amritsar. This was severely criticised by Gandhiji, who went on a three-day fast as penance.

Jallianwallah Bagh

An unerasable stain on the British rule was the Jallianwallah Bagh massacre that took place on 20 April 1919. A peaceful meeting of unarmed men, women, the elderly and children was surrounded and fired at under the orders of Brigadier General R. E. H. Dyer, and 379 persons were shot dead in cold blood. Arrests were rampant in other parts of India. All this grieved Gandhiji. More than the police action, the violence resorted to by people in a few places was what pained him. Leaders in Indian public life like Rabindranath Tagore called for a re-consideration of the protest against the Rowlatt Act. Gandhiji also felt that the protest had begun before the people were adequately prepared for it. He, therefore, halted the protest on 18 April. He got immersed in elucidating the concept of ahimsa in the weekly journals *Navajivan* in Gujarati, and *Young India* in English.

With the Viceroy's permission, Gandhiji went to the Punjab to assuage the emotions of the people. After discussing details of the Jallianwalla Bagh massacre with the Congress officials, he returned to Delhi, and, on 24 April, participated in the Khilafat conference organised enthusiastically by Hindus and Muslims. The term 'Non-Cooperation' was first used by him at this conference.

Amritsar Congress

In December 1919, the Amritsar Congress conference took place. This was the last Congress session in which Bal Gangadhar Tilak (1856–1920) participated. At this session the Congress adopted the resolutions that General Dyer of the Military Commission be removed from his post, and that Chelmsford be reinstated as Viceroy. Inclined to punish anyone indulging in violence, Gandhiji brought in a resolution condemning such violence, which was adopted. It was also resolved to revive traditional practices such as hand-spinning and weaving.

The Khilafat Movement

Gandhiji outlined his nationwide plan of non-violent protests in the beginning of 1920. The date 19 March 1920 was adopted as the date of protest against the British stand on the Khilafat.[1] Resulting from the events at Amritsar, 6 to 13 April 1920 was declared the 'National Week'. As a precursor to correcting the wrongs of the government, Gandhiji declared that if the Rowlatt Act was not repealed, cooperation with the government would not be possible. Tilak did not concur with this fully. Gandhiji had at that time accepted the post of president of the All India Home Rule organisation. While Tilak desired that the country's attention be directed towards the legislature, Gandhiji said that it was not possible to remain silent till the Punjab and Khilafat issues were resolved. At the same time Indian Muslims were unwilling to accept the compromise formula suggested by Turkey, and arrived at between the Allied nations of Britain and France. On 28 May 1920, the All India Khilafat Group met and accepted Gandhiji's non-cooperation scheme. Simultaneously, Gandhiji increased the thrust of the swadeshi movement. On 7 July 1920, four aspects of Gandhiji's non-cooperation plan were announced:

1. Titles and honorary posts should be given up;
2. People should be relieved from salaried government posts;
3. People should remove themselves from police and army services; and
4. No taxes should be paid.

Tilak's death

The non-cooperation movement started on 1 August 1920. On that day Tilak passed away. Gandhi's political guru, Gopal Krishna Gokhale, passed away in 1915, just a week after Gandhiji returned from South Africa to work in India. It was almost as if, in dying, Gokhale had said, "My political heir has arrived. I have served my purpose." Likewise, Tilak's death, too, happened at a crucial phase in India's history. "The freedom struggle that I desired has begun. … My work is done," is what Tilak seemed to have felt before he passed away. When Gandhiji visited Madras in August 1920, he assumed leadership of the national struggle. Tilak was not yet 64 when he died, while Gokhale was only 48.

Nationalist fervour in Tamilnadu

Before World War I, youngsters teeming with nationalistic fervour in Madras had engaged in acts of violence against the government. It was around that time that the Tirunelveli Collector Robert William d' Escourt Ashe was murdered (on 17 June 1911), V. O. Chidambaram Pillai embarked on his shipping trade, and the national poet Subramania Bharathi's poems were being sung by nationalists all over the state. Accused of having spoken against the government, persons like V. O. Chidambaram Pillai and Subramania Siva were arrested.

Yet, this sense of nationalism had not spread among the common people. As far as Madras was concerned, it was Annie Besant's Home Rule movement that had to an extent spread among them, that too among a few. When Gandhiji started the non-cooperation movement, it roused public emotion, both among those who were politically active and those who were not.

A special affection for Tamils

The non-cooperation movement set in motion a chain of events nationwide: general strikes, processions and protest meetings began to take place at regular intervals, even as the nature and expression of Indian nationalism began to change. Owing to the popular protests against liquor shops, government revenues from liquor sales dropped significantly. Charkhas began to spin across the country and households started making khadi. Young men's associations and Congress youth wings were being formed. The most crucial of all these changes was the new-born confidence that an ordinary Indian could challenge the might of the British government. Madras played a vital role throughout. Tamil political leaders who were in the vanguard of the movement at the time were Kasturi Ranga Iyengar, Srinivasa Iyengar, C. Vijayaraghavachariar, Rajagopalachari, S. Sathyamurthi, V. O. Chidambaram Pillai, Kalyanasundara Mudaliar, Singaravelu Chettiar, E. V. Ramasami Naicker, Dr P. Varadarajulu Naidu, Sarojini Naidu and Yakub Hassan, among others. Newspapers such as *The Hindu, Desa Bhakthan* and *Swadesamithran* rendered invaluable service. Gandhiji's special affection for the people of Madras and Tamils in general stemmed from the fact that they had so closely assisted him in his struggle in South Africa. In the struggles that he initiated in India too, the Tamils stood with him and gladly sacrificed themselves to the cause. Madras participated energetically in matters of administration, whether it was in the interests of khadi, or prohibition or caste abolition. And till his dying day, Tamil Nadu always held a special place in Gandhiji's heart.

The Justice Party

The Justice Party was formed in the Madras Presidency in 1916 to protect the welfare and interests of non-Brahmins, and to achieve governance through the rule of law. Step by step, in the period of Home Rule, non-cooperation and Khilafat, this party grew with the approval of the government. P. Thyagaraja Chetty, and Dr. T. M. Nair were the leaders of the Justice Party. In 1919, it accepted the improvements announced by the government, and was installed in power.

Support for the movement

Around August 1919, based on a rumour that Gandhiji was coming to Madras, the State government, using provisions of the Indian Defence Law, pronounced a ban on his entering the state. The local satyagrahis gathered in Madras to deliberate on whether to continue the protest or not. Some, like Krishnaswami Sarma spoke openly at meetings that it was not proper on the part of Gandhiji to halt the satyagraha struggle. As a celebration of Gandhiji's 50th birthday, it was decided at a meeting presided over by Dr Subramania Iyer to raise money for the Punjab Improvement Fund under the name of 'Gandhi Fund'. In June 1920, at a state-level meeting in Tirunelveli, with S. Srinivasa Iyengar presiding, the Punjab situation, Khilafat problems, non-cooperation struggles, among others were discussed. Moderates like Annie Besant and C. P. Ramaswami Iyer also took part in this meeting and offered their views, which, however, did not find acceptance. Rajaji and Muslim students endeavoured to further the non-cooperation tenets, by attempting to bring in a resolution. It was in this situation that Gandhiji and Shaukat Ali reached Madras. In early August, many started discarding their titles (including honorary ones). When Gandhiji came to tour Madras State, unannounced, several more followed suit. Yakub Hassan personally arranged for Gandhiji's visit. The State government may have intended to ban this tour, but were dissuaded from doing so by a communication from the Central government.

Gandhi criticises Empire

Gandhiji had taken to touring all over India to make people aware of the non-cooperation movement. If his Madras visit was a part of that initiative, we must examine why he came here first. There was no other occasion when he had criticised the British empire and the British government in India as much as then. He spoke about ending this 'Ravana Rajya' and establishing 'Rama Rajya'. Even Gandhiji's associates were surprised at his vehemence. Some others even commented that such aggressive speech ran counter to his own tenets of ahimsa. Gandhiji, however, was unfazed.

A hurricane tour

It was almost a hurricane tour. For two days, he went to Kallikkottai and Mangalore. From there, via Salem, Bangalore and Madras on the next day, he went to Bezawada (now, Vijayawada). It was not just a tour of present-day Tamil Nadu, but encompassed Mysore (now, Karnataka), Andhra and Kerala as well. He wrote in *Navajivan*: "Except in Madras, we could not spend a continuous 24 hours anywhere else. Even in Madras, when I first went there, I was able to stay for more than 24 hours. After that (as it was a midway place), we were able to stay for a few hours there, as we travelled to and fro. From Salem to Bangalore, a distance of 123 miles, we travelled by car. To have undertaken such a hurricane tour was extreme."

This time, as Gandhiji had come for the Khilafat-sponsored protest, the places he visited were predominantly Muslim. This tour helped to establish for Gandhiji and Maulana[2] Shaukat Ali that, in the non-cooperation movement, Hindus and Muslims could work together. There was a massive welcome wherever they went. Thousands of rupee-bundles were given to them. When they reached Madras, as Shaukat Ali fell ill, he did not go with Gandhiji to Ambur (about 118 miles from Madras) and Vellore, but he accompanied him to all the other towns. Gandhiji received a hero's welcome everywhere.

The Mahatma and the Maulana in Madras

Thanks to the station master, Barlow, the compartment in which Gandhiji and Maulana Shaukat Ali were travelling to Madras was detached at Madras Central Railway Station, and placed at the end of the platform so that people could receive them. There was such a chaotic crowd to meet and garland them on 12 August 1920 that there were fears of a stampede, and it took Gandhiji and Shaukat Ali half an hour to negotiate a way through the crowd and reach the car in which they were to be taken in procession. The *Swadesamithran* reported: "As the Mahatma and the Maulana got down from the car, it ... seemed as if some divine beings had descended from the '*Pushpaka Vimana*' [a celestial aeroplane] and set foot on earth to give darshan."

Notable among those who had come to receive them were the Madras Central Khilafat group president Khan Bahadur Khuddoos Basha Sahib, State Congress president S. Kasturi Ranga Iyengar, Yakub Hassan, Vidyasagar Pandya, Duraiswami Iyengar, Abdul Hakim, C. Rajagopalachari, V. Kalyanasundara Mudaliar, V. V. K. Iyer, Challa Gurusamy Chetty, Adhinarayana Chetty and S. Sathyamurthi. Crescent flags were prominently visible (the crescent moon-and-star was the Turkish symbol, here signifying the Khilafat movement). The workers of Simpson and Company and the government press took an important part in the movement.

Gandhiji and Shaukat Ali stayed as guests of Haji Abdul Rahim Sahib at 63, Purasawalkkam Road, 'Sait Gardens'. Before reaching Madras, they were also welcomed at Arakkonam with *nadaswaram* music by a crowd led by Krishnaswami Sarma, and the Vellore Khilafat group secretary, Shahbuddeen. Many leaders, prominent persons and workers visited Gandhiji at his place of stay to learn the details of the non-cooperation movement.

A reporter of the *Mail* also met him and asked him several rather pointed questions. "Even after the experience of the satyagraha last year, do you still feel it is wise to conduct the non-cooperation movement now?"

"Certainly," Gandhiji replied confidently, adding that, "I feel people are better disciplined now. Moreover, the risks of opposition to law are not there … The non-cooperation movement is not a people's movement against law. I do not desire that the people cut off their ties with government. It is only for the government to become aware of the feelings of the people."

At Triplicane beach

Gandhiji and the Maulana arrived twenty minutes late for the public meeting at Triplicane beach that evening (12 August 1920). The English version of the 'Gandhi' book refers to the speech made by Gandhiji at this meeting as "the emotions of a visionary". He said:

> The day on which India begins to depend on the power of the sword will be the day my life will end. There is a definite goal

for India. Our ancestors have discovered through centuries of experience that any law based on violence is never permanent for mankind. Rather, a doctrine that is founded on selflessness and penance is the true one. As I firmly believe in this, I have adopted it, and will always do so. I am not an opponent of [the] English. Neither am I against the British, or any government. I am an opponent of untruth and injustice. As long as the government indulges in injustice, it can consider me its enemy. … albeit a heartless one. Even if I have to lay down my life in this effort, I shall consider it my good fortune.

Faith in Tamil people

At this meeting, under the presidentship of Khan Bahadur Khuddoos Basha, Gandhiji spoke in the same vein for an hour. National newspapers reported that the likes of the crowd of 25,000 plus that had gathered at this meeting near the aquarium on Triplicane beach had not been seen elsewhere in the state. Compared to his previous visit, Gandhiji seemed to be in good health, although he still could not stand and speak loudly. He went into more detail than before about tenets of the non-cooperation movement, and did not fail either to reiterate his faith in the Tamil people.

> I have immeasurable faith in you and the people of Tamilnadu. It is a faith that has grown from the time I had first been associated with Tamil coolies in South Africa. Madras is in no way inferior to any other State. It will stand in the forefront of sacrifice. It will translate into action every promise it makes.

It is worthy of note that at a time when Andhra and Madras were one state, Gandhiji chose to refer only to 'Tamil coolies' in South Africa.

On student participation in politics

Leading lawyer S. Srinivasa Iyengar raised the question whether the non-cooperation movement was against the political establishment. There were also those who felt that some aspects of 'non-cooperation' as articulated by Gandhiji were impractical, while other aspects were unclear and could thus be misunderstood. *Swadesamithran* had highlighted this in its editorial:

> The troublesome aspects of the non-cooperation movement should be discarded by schools and colleges, he [Gandhi] has said. Students above the age of 16, should, if necessary go against their parents, their schools and colleges, and act according to their conscience. He has also said that such students must act with dignity and self control. This gives room for more misinterpretation.

Some leaders felt that the movement was too extreme, whilst others thought it was not strong or effective enough as a political tool. V. S. Srinivasa Sastri did not accept the non-cooperation idea. He also strongly objected to Gandhiji's statement that students should avoid going to schools and colleges if they were 'conscience-bound'. Gandhiji's question to Sastri was: "Would he send his children to a school that runs based on what it has robbed from Sastri?" Gandhiji was forced to respond at length to these and other questions at the meeting on Triplicane beach.

"Students must learn about matters of politics, but should not involve themselves directly" was Gandhiji's general view. "But would not students staying away from schools and colleges in the non-cooperation movement amount to their participation in politics?" was what he was asked. Gandhiji had earlier said that students could participate in politics by staying away from school and college. It was not his idea that, by so doing, students would be directly involving themselves in politics. His view was that parents could pull their children out of certain schools and send them to those with a national fervour.

The Khilafat pledge

The Congress had planned to decide at the Amritsar conference what their response to the Khilafat movement should be. However, before that, Gandhiji announced what his view was. "In the Khilafat problem, the Muslims have decided in conscience to oppose the government. Their pride is in my hands. Hence, even if Congress on its own decides to meet and pass a resolution opposing their decision, I will not accept it, but will stand on my own and encourage them to go ahead with their protest." Supporting those who believed in him steadfastly through any difficult circumstances was one of Gandhiji's virtues. He did say later, "If the Kashmir people believe the Indian government, I will, if necessary, send the army to protect them."

A poet once said: "The hallmark of good friendship is to be steadfast at all times, having the strength to uphold moral values."

Swadesamithran disagrees

The *Swadesamithran* editorial, while welcoming other aspects of Gandhiji's speech, voiced its disagreement on one issue.

> Although our respect for Gandhiji is boundless, his advice in the matter of boycotting the legislature is not acceptable. At the end of December, if matters continue to remain as they are now, the representatives could stay away from the legislature. If, however, there is a change, the places could be divided in the legislature. If, on the other hand, they do not attend the legislature from now itself, it would amount to giving way to those who plan to do ill to our country. Hence we request that the Mahatma reconsider this matter.

Gandhiji respectfully responded: "Among the most influential Tamil papers that are published from Madras is *Swadesamithran*, which is read by many. Whatever matters it writes about are important. Its editor has said that, in the pursuit of the non-cooperation movement, there will be some difficulties. Therefore, I will, to the extent possible, offer my response to it." In his essay in *Young India*, Gandhiji wrote: "It is more important for those who have faith in non-cooperation to attend the legislature, than the moderates or others. Moreover, you cannot adopt the tenets of non-cooperation after accepting to cooperate. Being a member of the legislature you cannot dismiss a clerk who wipes the tables there."

Swadesamithran responds

The *Swadesamithran* did not let it go at that, and published three editorials reiterating its views, and seeking clarification. "We have no doubt that there is no more powerful weapon than non-cooperation that the Mahatma is advocating," it duly conceded, but went on to argue that it was essential to note and address the fundamental confusion in it.

Although the Mahatma has read all our editorials on this matter and offered his consoling response in *Young India*, which we have respectfully gone through, we must be excused for not accepting his arguments. When those in the Police and armed services ask for discharge from their jobs, it seems that the Mahatma feels the country would continue to require their services. However, if, after resigning from government service, as per Gandhiji's design, they work without pay for the social cause, which government would they be forcing through their non-cooperation? … and indeed, would they not in fact be helping the government in spending less, and so being more comfortable? … Moreover, how will they eke out their livelihood? How will they support their families? Gandhiji has written that the Khilafat committee is seized of these difficulties, and is considering solutions to them seriously. Will not the public want to know what those solutions are?

Further, when Mahatma Gandhi wrote his response in *Young India*, he asks how it is just for clerks to ask for being relieved from work in the legislature, without stopping to cooperate in their jobs. Members of the legislature and clerks should not believe they are serving in their individual capacities. Clerks are paid by the government for the work they do for the government. Legislators form the ministry of the people, and come forward to work for them, sacrificing their salary. They are in a position to remain in the legislature, stop working for the government, and fulfill the aspirations of the people. Hence, they could discipline themselves, refuse to sit in the legislature, and thereby cause major difficulties in the functioning of the government. This could be a national movement, not an individual protest. Therefore, we urge that the Congress should get together and take a comprehensive decision on this.

Other battles in press

On 13 August 1920, after Gandhiji's arrival in Madras, on his advice, a secret meeting was held to discuss the Khilafat and Punjab movements, at which V. S. Srinivasa Sastri, G. A. Natesan, C. P. Ramaswami Iyer, Rao Bahadur T. Rangachari, T. S. S. Rajan, George Joseph, Khuddoos Basha Sahib, and Yakub Hassan participated. The Anglo-Indian papers, including the *Mail* of Madras, roundly criticised the non-cooperation movement as expected. The *Mail* carried an editorial, based on Gandhiji's interview by its reporter, which observed: "If one were to say in base terms, Gandhiji believes more in ignorance than intelligence. The weaknesses and hazards in his schemes are due to this."

An entirely different argument, on whether or not to adopt non-cooperation, was raging between *The Hindu* editor S. Kasturi Ranga Iyengar and Annie Besant. "*The Hindu* editor has accepted the principle of non-cooperation. Hence, was it not but natural that he should also accept the scheme laid out by Gandhiji?" asked Besant. To which Iyengar's response was: "The non-cooperation scheme is not some divine pronouncement. It is just another scheme like many others. The nation is bigger than the individual."

Meeting at Jumma Mosque

Speaking at the meeting of Muslims at Jumma Mosque that day, Gandhiji focussed on exhorting the people to surrender their titles, resign from government jobs, and withdraw from the armed forces, for Indians to become the masters of their destiny in their own country. "Until those with titles give them up, honorary magistrates resign from their posts, lawyers desist from practising law, school children [stop] attending government-run schools, or those assisted by government, and be encouraged to adopt swadeshi, leaders give up travelling in their motor cars, wear khadi, and walk barefoot, we cannot ask government employees and sepoys to resign their jobs," he said.

This time Gandhiji's speeches in Madras inspired changes in the lives of many, especially the youth. The head of the Law College refused permission for a meeting organised by the college students. So the students held their meeting at the newly opened Ambi's Café. It was there that N. S. Varadachari met Gandhiji for the first time, and possibly K. Santhanam also met him there. Varadachari joined the Sabarmati Ashram and stayed there for two or three years; he joined the Madras Khadi Service later. Santhanam joined the khadi movement, and the Congress, and went on to become the governor of a state.

14 August 1920, Ambur and Vellore

On 14 August 1920, Gandhiji went to Ambur and Vellore. In Ambur, a few Honorary Magistrates, Bangi Hayat Basha Sahib, Malik Abdul Rahman Sahib, Mohammed Kasim, and H. N. Chengalappa submitted resignation letters to the government. Gandhiji took part in the North Arcot Khilafat Conference there. On his way to Vellore after the conference, Muslim schoolchildren welcomed him. Reaching Vellore by car (accompanied by Rajaji and Yakub Hassan), a 4000-strong crowd, led by a few prominent persons at the Hazrat Bagh railway crossing, welcomed Gandhiji and led him to the Fort grounds, where a public meeting was to be held. The speech that Gandhiji gave at this meeting, attended by over 20,000 people, was translated into Hindustani by Yakub Hassan, and into Tamil by Rajaji. As the people requested Gandhiji to speak a little in Hindustani, he obliged. He stayed overnight at the Subedar Bungalow, and started by the early morning 4 a.m. mail for Madras.

15 August 1920, Madras Congress Committee meeting

On the evening of 15 August 1920, the Madras Congress Committee met under the presidentship of Kasturi Ranga Iyengar, and discussed for four hours the non-cooperation movement, concluding that its principles be accepted, and that the Committee should meet one more time to reconsider the details. At the Tirunelveli conference it had been decided that, although the Khilafat issues had not been satisfactorily resolved, the people of this country should consider it their duty to follow the non-cooperation movement step by step. Rajaji suggested at the Madras conference of the Congress Committee that this resolution be sent to the All India Congress Committee. Kasturi Ranga Iyengar said that only if the Congress, as a whole, met to ratify the non-cooperation movement could it be fully adopted, and Gandhiji's scheme considered a national movement. It was possible for non-cooperation to continue even after elections; but to ask lawyers to abstain from courts, and stop children from attending school, was not possible, he said. The boycott of foreign goods could also be made part of the non-cooperation movement, he said.

Three views

The Madras Congress Committee meeting—in which neither Gandhiji nor Maulana Shaukat Ali participated—was a good opportunity to assess the different kinds of views circulating at the time in Madras political circles about the non-cooperation protest. Broadly, three kinds of views were expressed at this meeting. The Moderates held that the non-cooperation protest would upset the government as its methods were anti-government. Others felt it would be beneficial only if it did not ban legislators from attending the legislature, and that this ban should hence be lifted. Lawyers belonging to the Congress Party, however, were in favour of adopting the non-cooperation movement in its entirety.

A new problem

A few Muslims in the Madras Congress were against Gandhiji, a Hindu, being president of the Khilafat movement. Saadullah Basha Sahib raised this issue at the committee meeting and said that as the Khilafat problem was religion-based, it could only be resolved by a Muslim leader ordained by the Ulema (a body of Muslim scholars with specialist knowledge of Islamic sacred law and theology), and that therefore, until such time, he could not accept Gandhiji's doctrine. Yakub Hassan's response was that Basha Sahib was clearly unaware that the Central Khilafat conveners had already obtained the Ulema's approval.

Annie Besant's views

Annie Besant's views on non-cooperation was different from that of others. The movement was not wrong, but other than in this way, could a responsible government not be formed, is what she asked. She emphatically approved attending the legislature. The resolutions of the legislators against the government on the Khilafat and Punjab issues would be far more effective than conducting hundreds of public meetings, she said. At the same time, she also agreed with Gandhiji's declaration that, whatever the Congress decided, he would continue his work on the non-cooperation movement. She accepted that this was based on each one's conscience. "Mr Venkatarama Iyer's statement, that no one is bigger than the Congress, is no doubt correct, but what he said does not apply to Gandhiji alone, because he stands by his conscience," she said at the Madras Congress Committee meeting (as reported by *Swadesamithran* on 17 August 1920).

G. A. Natesan and V. O. C. Pillai's views

G. A. Natesan, Gandhiji's friend and longtime associate during the South African struggle, did not approve of the non-cooperation protest. "Embracing such a movement so expansively would amount to murdering our national life," he said. V. O. Chidambaram Pillai, who had supported the satyagraha movement in 1919, did not concur with the non-cooperation movement in 1920. Mutual cooperation was the principle he advanced (*Swadesamithran*, 17 August 1920). "My aim is to inculcate truth and strength in people. Adopting non-cooperation will induce cowardice in them. Nevertheless, finally, I am willing to abide by the decisions of this committee," he added.

Rajaji

Of the Madras leaders who understood Gandhiji's non-cooperation doctrine, and abided by it, Rajaji could be considered the foremost. He made special efforts to ensure that other leaders and the general public should also comprehend and follow it. He knew the protest would succeed only if all the leaders joined in, and realised that Gandhiji sought to awaken both the individual conscience and the collective acceptance of the country's leaders. Between the achievement of these two objectives, Rajaji requested Congress leaders to be prepared for whatever sacrifices were necessary. And if such agreement was not possible, he wished that at least, as a first step, they should refrain from exercising their vote on the matter.

Debates within Congress

Thus, while there was much debate within the Congress about whether to go ahead with the non-cooperation movement, there were many, particularly the educated, not belonging to the higher classes, who welcomed Gandhiji's movement. One of them, belonging to the Justice Party, wrote in a letter to *The Hindu* (on 27 August 1920) that non-violent non-cooperation would not be against the law, and that it was the ultimate and only way in which our objectives could be achieved. Generally, since Gandhiji had specified that there would be no violence attached to this movement, some were of the view that it could be practised as a test case on a national scale. The biggest gain of Gandhiji's Madras visit was the impetus it provided for people to think deeply about this subject.

Workers' meeting

To give workers an opportunity to hear Gandhiji's speech, a meeting was arranged by the Central Labour Board, under the presidentship of B. B. Wadia, at the beach near the Madras High Court. Gandhi's views on strikes, labour rights, and the importance of 'mediators' are evident from his speech.

> It is possible for a nation to survive without crorepatis or industrialists, but it cannot function without workers. There is no shame in being a worker. You have every right to demand wages for your work. It is also your duty to work, commensurate to the wages you receive. It is my experience in several places that industrialists do not fulfil their responsibilities to the extent that workers perform their duties as per their conscience. What, and how much, the workers can do to get the industrialists to fulfil their obligations is the next question. Wadia and other leaders must, before arranging for you to acquire literacy, educate you on human matters and relationships. What are the rights of workers, and to what extent you could exercise them, should also be taught. All over the world today we are witnessing strikes. Even on trivial matters workers are striking work. Strikes will cease once there is more cooperation and discipline among workers. Commensurate with mental growth, workers will begin to repose faith in the decisions of mediators. Thereby, in the place of strikes, the decisions of mediators will prevail.

16 August 1920, Madras tour

On Sunday (15 August 1920) night, Gandhiji left by the Boat Mail along with Shaukat Ali, and reached Kumbakonam on Monday morning (16 August). On the way, large crowds welcomed him at Chinglepet, Villupuram, Cuddalore, Chidambaram and Mayavaram stations. On his earlier trips to Madras State, Gandhiji had on several occasions got down at Kudandhai (another name for Kumbakonam) and visited places nearby. When Gandhiji arrived, the town was well decorated. From within Kumbakonam and outside (particularly from Rajagiri, Nachiarkoil and Thanjavur), thousands had gathered to see Gandhiji. With fireworks going off from the railway station onwards, and the band playing (musicians of the neighbouring *mutt*s and the Kudandhai temple had also come to welcome him, it seems), he was taken in procession to Porter Mandapam, where Gandhiji and Shaukat Ali addressed a gathering of more than 15,000 people. At this meeting, chaired by Rao Bahadur N. Krishnaswami Iyengar, the Social Service Sangam, Khilafat Committee, Congress Committee, and Jain Association presented welcome addresses. Notably the welcome of the Khilafat Committee was read out by Rao Bahadur N. Krishnaswami Iyengar, and the one on behalf of the Muslim Association by N. Dhandapani Pillai. At the Jain Association welcome, Gandhiji was referred to as a Jain, which he corrected to say that he was a Vysya. The Muslims of Rajagiri handed over a cloth bundle containing cash for the Khilafat movement through Abdul Majid.

At Needamangalam

It had been planned that Gandhiji would go by car from Thanjavur to Nagapattinam, but because of his frail health, the idea of such a long trip was given up. The leaders took the train to Nagapattinam. At Pandaravadai railway station en route, Muslims of the neighbouring hamlets handed over a cloth purse of money. At Needamangalam, people within a 10-mile radius of the place gathered to see Gandhiji. Of these, the majority were from Mannargudi, and students.

With Mannargudi students

At this time, there was a feud between the Mannargudi Wesleyan Mission college students and the college president. When B. G. Tilak died, the students had requested that the college be closed for a day in his memory. Arguments arose between the students and the college president, who had reportedly used certain 'wrong' words, which the students insisted he retract. It was at that time that Gandhiji reached Needamangalam. On that date the college board members were scheduled to visit, but the students, without attending college, got on to a train en masse and came to Needamangalam. Those who could not find place on the train walked. Many of them, not halting at Needamangalam, went along with Gandhiji to Nagapattinam. From Needamangalam to Nagapattinam, there were large crowds all along the way. When they reached Tiruvarur it was midday.

At Nagapattinam

There was a problematic situation at Nagapattinam. Gandhiji's train, bound for Nagore, was surrounded by a mass of people, not allowing even a fly to get through. There was clamour all around that they wanted to see Gandhiji. Many were perched on top of the train, which could not proceed for about two hours. At Nagapattinam, the Nagore Muslim League and the Nagapattinam League presented separate cloth bundles of cash.

Welcome at Nagore

At Nagore railway station, more than 10,000 people had gathered. Festoons were strung up, and streets were decorated with lights, as Gandhiji and Shaukat Ali were taken in procession. At a dargah, with a lawyer named Malim Sahib presiding, the meeting took place, in which a large number of Muslim women participated. "This shows the extent to which the Khilafat problem has hurt the Muslim sentiment, and the non-cooperation movement touched their hearts," said Gandhiji in his speech.

On his return journey, he made a speech at Needamangalam, before they returned to Thanjavur. At a meeting in Krishna Vilas Theatre, under the presidentship of V. P. Madhava Rao, Gandhiji said, "If only a man acts according to his conscience, he need not wait for someone else to take the lead in any matter. It is his duty to follow his conscience at all times." His speech was translated by E. Suryanarayana Iyer. They went from Thanjavur to Trichy.

Welcome at Trichy

The grand welcome Gandhiji and Shaukat Ali received in Trichy would scarce be given even to kings. Arriving at around 1.30 p.m., they were met at the station by numerous prominent people with garlands, and taken to the bungalow of Dr Rajan by car. For their smooth reception at the station, no platform tickets were sold that day. Workers interested in the non-cooperation movement and others sought clarifications and details, which Gandhiji readily gave. A historic and grand procession started from Palakkaranai (now Palakkarai, the main residential and densely populated area in Trichy), amidst fireworks. It went for about a mile through the big shopping street, and reached Shauk Grounds, the venue of the meeting. There were festoons all the way and pandals. The flower pandal erected in front of the Fort market by merchants was exquisite. Every shop was decorated with plantain trees as if celebrating a festival. No event had been jointly celebrated so spiritedly by both Hindus and Muslims, was the word going around in excitement. Mohammed Basith Sahib led the Muslim crowd, that maintained peace and decorum throughout the procession and the meeting. Many were on horses in front of the car in which Gandhiji and Shaukat Ali travelled. Much ahead, groups of Boy Scouts marched. From balconies along the way, women showered the leaders with flowers, rose water and camphor. All the *nadaswaram* and *thavil* vidwans from Trichy and surrounding areas walked in front with their troupes, making divine music. It took an hour and a half to cover a mile, before the procession reached the meeting venue.

In Trichy, a never-before-seen crowd had gathered for the public meeting. A beautifully decorated canopied vehicle had been arranged for the leaders to sit in. They were placed on a raised dais in a newly erected pandal. People had come from Madurai, Dindigul, Pudukkotai. Newspapers reported that more than 20,000 people had gathered. The secretary of the Trichy Khilafat committee, V. S. Muhammad Ibrahim, Dr Abdul Subhan Sahib and Dr Sastri gave welcome addresses in Tamil, Hindustani and English respectively. The representatives of the Dindigul Khilafat committee, and the Tirupparaithurai (a village in Trichy district) Gandhi Sangam also read out their addresses.

The students of Tiruchirappalli offered a beautiful garland, which Gandhiji accepted with pleasure. Dr T. S. S. Rajan proposed a vote of thanks. Retailers presented a cloth bundle of cash. When Gandhiji spoke, he said that he expected great work from places like Trichy and Madurai. His mention of Madurai indicated the faith he had in the people of that city. He responded to the objections raised by Kasturi Ranga Iyengar, one by one.

A humorous lesson

As Gandhiji was speaking, there arose some commotion and disturbance in one section of the gathering. Without getting angry or perturbed, he dealt with it in a humorous way. When some quiet returned, he said, "We have learnt a good lesson in cooperation and non-cooperation." The crowd resounded with laughter. He continued:

> Some youngsters here (pointing to where the disturbance had occurred) started to fight. This is a lesson that non-cooperation teaches us. However, it is a dangerous weapon. Even if one person decides to pledge non-cooperation, it can serve to cause confusion to the entire assembly. This is what we have seen here. Likewise, you have also seen what cooperative strength can achieve (Laughter). You lifted that heavy chair together and took it away. Each of you lent a finger to it, and it was enough. This government exists, not because of its arms strength, but because of people's cooperation ('Hear! Hear!'). The direct opposite is also true, that is, if cooperation is denied, the government will fall (Laughter). Our friend (Kasturi Ranga Iyengar) said that we must avoid foreign goods. Of all the ways that I have recommended, this is the most difficult, because it will lead to losses of lakhs of rupees to merchants. Further, it is a measure to punish the British. All the measures that I have recommended are those of self-denial, not of punishment. O, people of Tiruchirappalli! You need not wait for all of India ... if you have not already begun the non-cooperation activities, start tomorrow itself.

There was a thunderous ovation. Gandhiji's response to Kasturi Ranga Iyengar's objections reflected his respect for him. It became unnecessary for these two leaders to continue their arguments thereafter. Iyengar acted as per his word. After the non-cooperation movement was adopted at the Calcutta Congress, he accepted it as a loyal Congressman. He also wrote to Gandhiji saying that he would no longer oppose the movement, which delighted Gandhiji.

18 August 1920, Erode

Along with Syed Mutthuja Sahib, and the Madurai lawyer, George Joseph, the leaders left Tiruchirappalli at night on 18 August 1920 for Kallikkottai, reaching Erode at 3.30 a.m., where more than 10,000 people had gathered, chanting, 'Allahu Akbar' and 'Vande Mataram'. The leaders were led to an adorned dais at a corner of the station. Three welcome addresses were read out. Gandhiji, speaking briefly, said, "This is an hour to pray to God, not to conduct a public meeting. Hence, to give you all strength, Mohammedans should pray to Allah. Hindus should pray to their God to be given strength to provide succour to Muslims brothers who have been subject to hardship."

Salem

After leaving Kallikkottai, Gandhiji and Maulana Shaukat Ali reached Salem on 20 August night. On the way, in Tiruppur, Desa Bhaktha Samajam members had organised a reception. Near the railway station a public meeting was held, where both leaders were welcomed. For the Khilafat Fund, a purse was handed over by T. S. Duraiswami Iyer on behalf of the people. M. V. Karuppannan Chettiar presented hand-spun 100 hanks. Gandhiji and Shaukat Ali left together by train after the meeting. The crowd was so thick that even a prominent person like Dr Varadarajulu Naidu could not get near the two leaders at the station; their stay had been arranged at his residence. In Sevapettai, in connection with the Mahatma's arrival, food was served to 4000 poor people and hundreds of others. At the welcome organised, Angamuthu Chettiar, a merchant, presided.

Tap opening ceremony

A staunch nationalist, T. P. Chinnakrishnan Chettiar had installed as charity two water taps, which were ceremonially opened by Gandhiji and Shaukat Ali. Louis Fisher[3] has written with wonder that, along with macro national problems, Gandhiji could also devote his attention to micro issues. On 21 August 1920, in Salem he accomplished two such tasks. One was the inauguration of a public tap to provide free water to people, and the other was to participate in a non-cooperation conference to expound his principles. Gandhiji spoke at the Salem Khilafat conference about his non-cooperation tenets. In the evening, the two leaders attended a meeting at Bengar, where they stayed for about four hours, before starting that night itself for Bombay via Madras.

In Madras again

Reaching Madras on 22 August 1920, the leaders stayed in the city for a while, and left for Bezawada. During their brief stay, they were met for discussions by the Khilafat Committee members. Gandhiji spoke at a meeting of Law College students. He had received a letter written by a Christian girl in support of the Khilafat that morning. Reading it out at the students' meeting, he praised the girl for realising that not only Hindus but Christians too needed to participate in the religious struggle of Muslims. "Likewise, if the Christians faced any problems, he guaranteed his support. "Hindus are the brothers of Muslims. God will proclaim a new edict, I am sure, that there should be no dispute between them," he added with emphasis.

Brahmins and non-Brahmins

A problem that had plagued Madras for long was brought to Gandhiji's attention as he was addressing the students. Asked for his views on the Brahmin–non-Brahmin tangle, he replied:

> In the Brahmin–non-Brahmin issue, at every stage, Brahmins should yield ground. This is their duty. The number of posts demanded by non-Brahmins must be given to them. If it were in my power, I would give even more. It is because of the suspicion non-Brahmins have against the Brahmins that they are demanding thus. Brahmins have been for long years occupying important posts. But owing to their arrogance in declaring themselves superior, the difference there exists between them and others is quite horrible. It is as terrible as the difference the Europeans celebrate as existing between themselves and black people. (*The Hindu*, 23 August 1920).

Fierce arguments

Unsurprisingly, Gandhiji's comments gave rise to severe arguments. Some said that his observations were based on faulty information. "It is wrong to state that availability of more or less posts is under the authority of Brahmins. Like others, Brahmins, too, will not desire to ruin themselves, nor will they wish to be denied the power to serve society. As Gandhiji himself accepts, history amply demonstrates that Brahmins have served the nation excellently. It cannot just be stopped now," responded some, on behalf of Brahmins.

As this issue snowballed, S. Narayanan of Madras explained what happened at a meeting in Madras in which Gandhiji took part. He was the one who had raised this problem at this meeting with Gandhiji. Saying that the full text of what Gandhiji said at that meeting was not released, he clarified what he stated, as follows:

> If a non-Brahmin asks me for my house, I, as a Brahmin will give it to him. Till now Brahmins have been leading dignified and upright lives. Hence their affluence has been growing. This is why, among non-Brahmins, the feeling of inferiority has crept in, because of which their faith in Brahmins has been eroded. It is something they have developed themselves. If this lack of faith has to be erased and integrity established, the Brahmin must yield whatever he has to the non-Brahmin. You (Brahmins) in truth, should consider them as brothers, and prove to them that, as they have given you their trust, you, too, will give them yours.

The disagreements abated for the time following this.

Not a minority

The problem of Brahmins and non-Brahmins was brought to Gandhiji's attention many times. As far as Madras was concerned, one does not know when the problem began. Even Swami Vivekananda has spoken of this. Each time this issue was brought before Gandhiji, he tried to respond to it in broad, general terms. There were specific problems as well as general ones. There were problems, as in Cheramadevi, which were complex and to which there were no easy solutions. However, in offering solutions to these problems, Gandhiji advocated certain basic principles, from which he did not waver in his lifetime. A few months before his death, Gandhiji received a letter from some Brahmins, in a minority in Madras, that they were suffering from the inability to obtain positions in government service or in colleges, and that the anti-Brahmin lobby alone was the cause of such misfortune.

Gandhiji referred to this at his prayer meeting in Delhi, followed by advice on what he thought the Brahmins should do in this situation. This advice, given just a few months before Gandhiji's death, could be taken as his considered view.

> I sympathise with the situation Brahmins find themselves in, although, unlike them, I have no sense of betrayal or regret. Firstly, I cannot accept their claim to be a minority. If we belong to the same nation, where is the question of majority or minority? I could also declare myself to be in the minority and complain that benefits are not reaching me. Hence, my appeal to Brahmin friends is to forget considering themselves a separate community. Should they desist from referring to themselves as in the minority, they will, as small drops go to make the mighty ocean, add to the glory of the Indian (or Hindu) nation. If we count the crores of village folk in the 7 lakh villages of India, to what extent are these in government and college jobs? It is my view that Brahmin friends should be pleased, in fact, that government and college posts are unavailable to them. There will only be a very few of them. Those who do not hanker after government and college posts only are the true servants of India. Is education confined within the four walls of a classroom? ... I wish to bring to their attention the concept and benefits of basic education. If only they would realise ... that our rights emerge from the performance of our duties, they would readily know that nobody has been given a right that they alone should join a government college. If any boy or girl has that right, it is they whose rights have been dealt with violent contempt. A Brahmin's duty is to reach God and help others to do so. If he does that, in whatever society, he should be given food and clothing by that society to lead a dignified life.

An indelible impression

In 1920, Gandhiji recorded in *Navajivan* (29 August 1920) the impact of his Madras tour.

The Tamil people have made an indelible impression in my heart in a unique way. In Madras, my friend and I made speeches in English. In the gathering where the Muslims predominated, Shaukat Ali spoke in Hindustani, and the crowd heard him in full patience. This gave rise to a good thought within me. The trust of the Madras public is boundless, as is their belief. However, I cannot say that there was any immediate benefit from this tour. At every place some lawyers had given up their practice, some others had left their office posts. A few had given up their ideas of becoming legislators. But when I see the affection the people have for me, I must say that as much success as I expected was not realised. It is not difficult to find the reasons for this. Some leaders did not have belief in non-cooperation. Those who did were not ready to make sacrifices. A third category were persons without integrity … those who would say one thing and do something else. If the condition of leaders itself was so, it is no surprise that the public could not be moved to immediate action. This experience shows that it is only through the purity of the non-cooperation movement that the situation can attain purity. Hypocrisy and cobwebs of dust will get exposed. Without such purification, people cannot progress. Some other States spoke against the non-cooperation movement making rapid strides. Crowds raised their voices and caused confusion at these meetings. But Tamilnadu alone was different.

It is on this happy note that Gandhiji ended his article in *Navajivan* that reflected his special delight with Madras.

Notes

1. The Khilafat movement of 1919 in India was a pan-Islamic call to reclaim the Ottoman caliph as a symbol of unity among Indian Muslims during British rule, and a protest against the sanctions imposed by the Treaty of Sèvres on the caliph and Ottoman Empire after World War I. The idea of a separate nation for Indian Muslims had its origins in the Khilafat, which was initially bolstered by Gandhi's non-cooperation movement, but fell apart after the abolition of the caliphate in 1924.

2. The word *maulana* is used to address a Muslim man revered for his religious knowledge and scholarship.

3. Louis Fisher (1896–1970), American journalist who wrote a biography of Gandhi, 1950.

17

THE GOLDEN AGE OF
NATIONAL SERVICE, 1921

Intense activity

Gandhi presented a picture of intense activity. The derision of
Viceroy Reading (1860–1935, Viceroy, 1921–26), that all the actions
of Gandhiji amounted to mere stupidity, served only to increase his
creativity and enthusiasm, not diminish it. Like a hurricane he kept
touring all over the country without pause. On the one hand, he
criticised and contained the violent instincts of people, and, on the other,
he urged people who were hesitant to make sacrifices for the country
by infusing new spirit in them, to do something for the service of the
nation. His non-cooperation protest bound closely not only Hindus
and Muslims, but people across religion, caste and language.

Three boycotts

At the Calcutta Congress session (in 1917), elements of Gandhiji's non-
cooperation protest had been adopted by an overwhelming majority.
The initial objectives of this protest were Khilafat, and rectification
of the injustices in Punjab. However, Salem Vijayaraghavachariar
and Pandit Motilal Nehru suggested that there was a more important
objective—that of obtaining *swaraj* (self-rule) or *swarajya*—which
Gandhiji accepted, and showed the way to rightful action. He
asserted that if the people followed the measures he was advocating,
India would attain freedom in a year. The courts should be ignored,
legislatures should not be attended, and foreign cloth should be
boycotted: these were his three 'mantras'. Those who mocked this
non-cooperation movement witnessed its increasing intensity day by
day, till they could mock no more.

Gandhiji explained further the basic truths about the protest that people had accepted as the centre of their actions. He strongly condemned the 'copying' of European culture. He explained the greatness of India's rich composite culture. Together with protest against the government was conducted the work of self-determination. He vowed that he would not eat unless he spun yarn for half an hour daily. In November, he introduced in Gujarat National University, Ahmedabad, the scheme for protecting and infusing new life into Indian languages. It gave Hindus the opportunity to study the Koran, and Muslims, to study the Hindu scriptures.

The Nagpur Congress

When the Congress met at Nagpur in December 1920, C. Vijayaraghavachariar, who presided, and several other leaders raised objections to specific measures in Gandhiji's non-cooperation movement. C. R. Das, together with other representatives who had come from Bengal, urged Gandhiji to reconsider his directive to boycott courts, and for lawyers to abstain from practice, but Gandhiji remained firm on this; ultimately, his resolution was unanimously adopted. He also obtained the support of those who had opposed it. It was at this session that the resolution "Lawful and peaceful means to achieve swarajya—the Congress objective" was adopted. "Through truth and ahimsa …" was the phrase Gandhiji had desired.

It was on the basis of the consensus that the phraseology was finalised. After the Congress adopted this, Gandhiji declared happily, "I have now truly joined the Congress." This Congress also adopted important resolutions relating to Hindu-Muslim unity, abolition of untouchability, and khadi. The Congress states were bifurcated on the basis of language. Steps were taken towards establishing Congress branches in villages. In the elections to the Legislative Assembly held in November 1920, since two-thirds of the voters abstained from voting, it may be said that Gandhiji had already achieved a great victory. At the Nagpur Congress in December, this victory elevated him further. As the Nagpur session turned out to be a truly people's Congress, Gandhiji became its sole and permanent leader.

At this time in several other countries under the British Empire, protests against Britain and struggles for freedom were brewing. India being one of the largest countries, the authorities felt that something should be done against the movement led by Gandhiji. Some moderates broke off their association with the Congress. V. S. Srinivasa Sastri, who had hitherto been attending its conferences, declared that he no longer had any interest in it.

A golden period

A close relative of the Emperor George V, Prince Arthur, the Duke of Connaught and Strathearn (a son of Queen Victoria), came to India and opened the new Central Legislative Assembly, Council of State, and Chamber of Princes. On Gandhiji's behest, the people treated his visit with contempt. In Bengal, thousands of college students came out of their colleges. National Education Centres appeared in Patna, Aligarh, Ahmedabad, Bombay, Benares and Delhi. The joint effort of Gandhiji and Mohammed Ali Jauhar (1878–1931) resulted in the establishment of the Jamia Millia Islamia, a central university in Aligarh in 1920. Students left schools and colleges. Leading lawyers like Motilal Nehru (1861–1931), C. R. Das (1870–1925), Vallabhbhai Patel (1875–1950), Rajendra Prasad (1884–1963) and Rajagopalachari left their practice and took up national service, followed by many lawyers all over the country. Subhas Chandra Bose (1897–1945) gave up his I.C.S. post. Jamnalal Bajaj contributed one lakh rupees to the Tilak Swarajya Fund. Muslim women who voluntarily blindfolded themselves and attended meetings were permitted by Muslim leaders to do so, accepting that, "Gandhiji is a pure human being, and can go anywhere." This was in many ways a golden period of national service.

Meeting in Madras

At the end of March 1921, the All India Congress Committee which met at Bezawada resolved that one crore rupees be collected for the Tilak Swarajya Fund; this money got collected well before the expected date. Seeing the widespread public enthusiasm in the struggle, government restrictions became more and more stringent. The Mahatma counselled the people to be patient. As soon as the Congress meeting in Bezawada was over, he toured Andhra, and arrived in Madras on 8 April 1921. He took part in a massive public meeting here, and started the same night for Bombay. A few days before he arrived here, the Ali brothers, Shaukat Ali and Md. Ali Jauhar, arrived in Madras from Bezawada and went on to Bangalore via Erode.

Anti-British emotions run high

At that time, when the nationalist fervour was rising to a crescendo, the massive crowds that came to see Gandhiji in Madras, their limitless enthusiasm and their eagerness to hear him speak came as no surprise. The women in particular showered their wholehearted support. Thousands of rupees worth of gold jewels were offered at his meetings. The emotion against the British and the government was at fever pitch. A similar kind of emotion was seen during the Salt Satyagraha and the 1942 Quit India Movement. However, it cannot be conclusively said whether, in 1942, the same 'ahimsa' feeling experienced in 1912 was evident. The Madras government had begun to accept that there was some success in Gandhiji's pronouncements.

Non-cooperation versus pro-cooperation

At this time, there was a sustained and vehement argument between the proponents of non-cooperation and those who advocated cooperation in Madras. Annie Besant was the leader of the pro-cooperation group. In *New India*, she wrote criticising Gandhiji's non-cooperation movement. No living saint has ever headed politics, she wrote. The national press responded that, it is only because a living saint was involving himself in national matters that politics was being spiritually enriched, and at a time when sparks of violence were sought to be ignited, he was counselling that India dealt with the issues with sobriety.

The Anglo-Indian papers, however, criticised not only the non-cooperation movement but also the Madras government. They advocated that the proponents of the movement be severely proceeded against and crushed. And even if no such action were taken, "should not a counter argument to non-cooperation at least be incited," wrote the *Mail* in Madras. It went on to say that, it is every loyalist's wish that the government should create an effective opposition to the non-cooperation movement, and play an important part in it. This was what responsible newspapers have been pointing out over the last few weeks. Yet, the result is failure. The effective steps that other States have been taking to control these sponsors of rebellion are not being matched by our State, which we feel is shameful. As termites eat into strong wood, making them weak and old, the non-cooperation proponents will go on to ruin India's faith.

Public meeting

From Nellore, Gandhiji, Kasturba and their fourth (and youngest) son, Devdas, came to Madras by Calcutta Mail. As desired by Gandhiji, a satyagraha week had been observed on the beach between 6 and 13 April 1921. Rajaji had informed a few others that this visit of Gandhiji's was special, and that in order to avoid the crowds, they had decided to discreetly detrain at Basin Bridge junction, a fact known only to the leaders. However, the public somehow got scent of it and gathered there in large numbers. There is no limit to public awareness in these matters.

Gandhiji stayed at Ramji Kalyanji's bungalow in Santhome, where he had discussions with leaders of the non-cooperation movement. In the evening, a meeting with Marwaris was held at Kushaldas Hall, after which a public meeting on the beach took place.

Propriety

The propriety displayed by Gandhiji was evident when, on this occasion, he decided not to stay at the residence of G. A. Natesan. He had communicated this to Natesan through Mahadev Desai. "It is at your house that he will get peace, Gandhiji says, but he does not want to put you to any embarrassment," wrote Mahadev Desai. Would the votaries of the non-cooperation movement desire that Gandhiji stay in the house of one who was not in support of it? After a few days, Gandhiji wrote a letter to Natesan on this:

> I should not cause you problems by the meeting of true non-cooperation supporters or otherwise in your house. Likewise,

I should not embarrass them either by not being able to freely discuss matters that you are not in favour of at your residence. I may not be able to meet you, but wherever those in Madras hold me captive, I look forward to your dropping in there at least to show your face.

Massive turnout at beach meeting

Although the meeting was scheduled for the evening at 6 p.m., people started arriving at the beach in droves from 3 p.m. onwards. Hindus, Muslims, Christians … nearly 50,000 people had gathered. Madras could legitimately feel proud at the turnout, with several noted personages in attendance. Shop owners voluntarily shut down their establishments to show their respect for Gandhiji and his movement. By 6 p.m., the crowd on the beach was a sight for the gods. A sea of people stretched between the beach-front aquarium and the old engineering college. Senior government officials could see this from a distance. Some Europeans were also spotted in the crowd. Gandhiji's speech in English of approximately one hour was translated by A. Rangaswami Iyengar into Tamil.

Lawyers barred

A large number of lawyers had come to hear Gandhiji. Before the meeting began, Swami Gitananda Yogi suddenly got up and said that as the lawyers had not given up their practice in line with Gandhiji's advice, they should not be allowed to sit along with the VIPs, nor allowed to speak. This shows that the general public did not respect those who went against Gandhiji's tenets.

Paper flowers

With Kasturi Ranga Iyengar presiding, Brahmin priests from the nearby Ganesha temple in Tiruvallikkeni came and offered 'purna kumbham' to Gandhiji, to the chanting of the vedas, wishing him a long life. They sprinkled holy water and 'akshatha' on Gandhiji and Kasturba, and circumambulated them. Gandhiji took up the paper flower garland that was on the pot. In his address of thanks for this welcome, he did not miss making a reference to this. "The flowers around the pot were paper flowers. The cloth covering it was also foreign cloth, a symbol of slavery. Our nation has natural flowers in plenty. I greatly regret the use of paper flowers in vedic rites." Saying this, he flung the paper garland into the air, to resounding applause from the crowd.

The Brahmin–non-Brahmin issue

Gandhiji began his speech right at the point at which he had finished in 1920, and said: "Ahimsa is the main element of our non-cooperation movement, but this ahimsa has to cross several problem areas. However much one is provoked to anger, one must not submit to it. It is most important that our speech and action should not contain even the slightest danger of violence."

He then took up the issue of Brahmins and non-Brahmins, and his speech largely centred around this. The difference was that, when he had spoken to the Law College students, his advice was directed to Brahmins. On this occasion, his words were meant for the non-Brahmins. His mention of the Brahmin–non-Brahmin issue itself was singular. The fact that the State government was seized of this issue, and that some non-Brahmins were victimised by the government were the main reasons for his advice during this speech. "This government does not have the issue of Hindu-Muslim fighting to occupy itself; hence it is using the opportunity to widen the split between Brahmins and non-Brahmins," he said, evoking applause. He went on to say, "Just as we solved the differences between Hindus and Muslims, we should resolve the issues between Brahmins and non-Brahmins." He reminded people of what he had said to the Law College students.

> I have no doubt in my mind that it is the legacy of Brahmins that is the pride of Hindu religion. If the non-Brahmins seek to demean this 'brahmaneeyam' in order to elevate themselves, it would be fundamentally wrong. Even in this Kaliyuga, Brahmins stand in the forefront of selflessness and sacrifice. All over India, the Brahmins have been responsible for making the people of all classes aware of their rights, and offering advice to them on such matters…

Gandhiji admitted that there were faults on both sides. At the same time, he advised non-Brahmins: "You must realise that you cannot improve your lot by fighting with Brahmins or denigrating them in any way. This will only spell the decline of Hindu religion. Let not the non-Brahmins attempt to rise out of the ashes of 'brahmaneeyam'. If the non-Brahmins find themselves unable to wholeheartedly participate in this movement, let them at least not get caught in the deceit of the government and stand as barriers to this progress."

Abolish untouchability

Turning next to the abolishment of untouchability, Gandhiji said that the Brahmin–non-Brahmin problem was nothing compared to the grievances directed against the Hindu religion by the Adi Dravidars and 'untouchables', whom Hindu society treats like lepers. As a result, the British Empire has begun to look at us as lepers, too. Both Brahmins and non-Brahmins are responsible for the plight of these castes, Gandhiji iterated.

> We treat our brothers as untouchables … it is the same feeling that makes us be looked on as slaves is my definite conclusion as a Hindu of sanatana dharma. I take the liberty of saying so because I have studied our 'sastras' to the extent possible. I have understood the tenets of our religion. I have lived as a sanatani, having absorbed over the past 30 years the teachings of our Vedas and Upanishads. Hence, in spite of any Hindu feeling that what I say is wrong, I would entreat you to accept what I say from the strength of my own experiences. Nothing in our sastras permits us to label anyone as untouchable. I feel fulfilled to be a Hindu, and to die as one for it at any time. But from the moment I consider a person as untouchable, I will cease to call myself a Hindu. Untouchability is a curse, and I invite Brahmins and non-Brahmins alike to fight against it. At the same time, one should not think that eradication of untouchability is one thing, and inter-caste marriages, sharing meals together, are another. As the *Bhagavad Gita* says, if we can give the same place in our hearts to the Brahmin and the chandala, the problem between Brahmins and non-Brahmins will cease to exist at that very moment.

The meeting concluded, and, when Gandhiji returned to where he was staying, he had a long discussion with Sathyamurthi, and left by the night mail with Kasturba for Bombay.

Swadesamithran's endorsement

The *Swadesamithran* endorsed Gandhiji's speech fully in its editorial. "Had the leaders of the non-Brahmin community witnessed the massive crowds on the beach, they would no longer [have] had cause to complain, because the majority of this crowd were non-Brahmins. The silence at the meeting, and their rapt attention to the speech of Gandhiji outlining the principles of non-cooperation, would have shown them how involved they were. Realising that there were more non-Brahmins at the meeting must have prompted Gandhiji to advise them on good thinking yesterday."

A few regrets

This speech, though, did not please some non-Brahmins. They wrote letters to Gandhiji. Of these, the letter from Kandasamy of Madras was published by Gandhiji in *Young India* (27 April 1921), together with his response.

> The reference to non-Brahmins in Gandhiji's speech has hurt their sentiments. It would have [been] better if he had not spoken about it at all. From his speech it seems clear that he is unaware of Dravidian culture, and the objectives of the non-Brahmin movement. The singular features of the Dravidian traditions of South India, as different from other parts of the country, do not seem to have been understood by him.
>
> When he extolled the contribution made to religion and culture in India by Brahmins, it appeared that he had Northern India in mind. He is causing friction among non-Brahmins. If you consider the literature, religion, principles, etc., of the South of India, the non-Brahmins have contributed as much, if not more, than Brahmins. If Gandhiji truly desires to heal the rift between the Brahmins and non-Brahmins in South India, let him examine it with an open mind, unclouded by prejudice on either side. It is only then that he will find a solution.

In his response, Gandhiji wrote:

> I have received several letters like this. It is clear that those who have sent these letters have understood me wrongly. I did not read my speech, as reported in the papers. Hence I cannot say

whether there is any error in the reporting. Nobody has forgotten the excellence of the Dravidian tradition. But, at the same time, one should not belittle the service Brahmins have done to the facets of this Dravidian culture, Hindu religion, or humanity. I warn those who have written such letters not to maintain that Dravidian is South and Aryan is North. India, today, is a conglomeration of not just these two, but other cultures.

Gandhiji cautioned us against the dangers of speaking divisively of the North and South back in 1921 itself, showing his far-sightedness. We know only too well how, in the future, these divisive tendencies whipped up the emotions of people.

18

REVOLUTION IN APPAREL

National Flag

Gandhiji realised in 1921 that India needed to have a national flag. Based on the suggestion of P. Venkatayya of Masulipatnam National College, he created the national flag. At this time, Rabindranath Tagore, who was in Europe, had criticised the non-cooperation movement from a spiritual angle, with which view Gandhiji did not agree. He said the votaries of cooperation could at least accept the construct of his movement. As this was a new movement, he found the need to explain its aspects at every meeting. He did not hold the English in contempt, but wrote that India was only asking for justice.

Talks with the Viceroy

Viceroy Reading was aware of the problems being faced by the government, and invited Gandhiji for discussions. They met six times for talks. The Viceroy brought to the attention of Gandhiji that the speeches of the Ali brothers were inciting violence. Gandhiji accepted that there was scope for misinterpretation in their messages, and handed over a letter from them regretting that their speeches lent themselves to such actions.

The Khilafat resolution

At the end of July 1921, the All India Congress Comitttee that met at Bombay resolved that, from August, Congressmen would not only *not* wear foreign clothes, but would publicly burn them, as also express contempt for the impending visit of the Prince of Wales. A resolution to boycott liquor shops was also adopted. Ahead of this, the

Khilafat conference in Karachi had passed a revolutionary resolution that Muslims would not be part of the British army, and that, if, by Christmas, no decision regarding the Khilafat was forthcoming, a resolve to announce an 'Independent Indian Republic' would be taken at the Ahmedabad Congress meeting. In July, August and September, Gandhiji appealed for a unanimous action by people to avoid foreign clothing. On 31 July 1921, Gandhiji himself burnt foreign cloth. All over India, foreign cloth was set fire to. Gandhiji travelled around the country, exhorting people to take up his weapons of silent revolution. Karachi in the west to Dibrugarh in the east, Rawalpindi in the north to Thoothukudi in the south formed the vast ambit of his influence.

The Moplas

The Moplas of Malabar, members of the largest Muslim community in Kerala, thinking that the British rule was over, and that they had obtained freedom, announced in August 1921 that they had established the Khilafat rule there. Gandhiji and Maulana Mohammed Ali set out to assuage the feelings of the Moplas. En route, at Waltair railway station in Andhra, Mohammed Ali was arrested, consequent to the resolution passed at the Karachi Khilafat Conference. Shaukat Ali and some other leaders were also arrested later.

By April 1921, as a result of the visit of Gandhiji and the Ali brothers, the non-cooperation movement in Madras had gained momentum. The activists worked hard to spread its tenets. The most difficult decision of Gandhiji to implement was to stop students from attending government-aided schools, and to send them to national schools. But Madras did not hesitate to swallow even that bitter pill. In a few places like Salem and Kallidaikurichi, efforts were afoot to establish national schools.

Boycott of liquor shops

Perusal of a letter from the Madras government to the Central government at the end of August shows how successful the boycott of liquor shops was.

> All over the State, sales in liquor shops have decreased. In several districts such shops have even been put up for auction, but the

income even from that is very low. In other districts there have been no takers for this auction, and the shops are unable to be sold. The non-cooperation proponents are claiming this to be a success of their movement. The broadcasting of the movement in some places gives no room for doubt that the boycott of liquor shops has been a major contributory to this. There are other reasons, too, but, compared to boycott of liquor shops, the burning of foreign cloth is nothing.

Madras tour

Before Gandhiji came, Rajaji and S. Srinivasa Iyengar had sent him a telegram in July, requesting that he undertake a two-week tour of Madras. Gandhiji replied telegraphically that, being occupied with work relating to the convening of the All India Congress Committee, he could not visit Madras till August. In September, on being reminded by Dr T. S. S. Rajan, Gandhiji agreed to a brief tour, subject to the condition that he be allowed three hours of silence daily. Accordingly his tour schedule was drawn up. Gandhiji said that he could not stay for long. Dr Rajan announced that Gandhiji would visit Cuddalore, Parangippettai, Kumbakonam, Tiruchirapalli, Devakottai, Madurai, Tirunelveli, Dindigul, Erode, Coimbatore, Kallikkottai, and Salem, and no other place in Madras. He reminded the Tamil people that they should show themselves as heroes of service before the Mahatma. "When the Mahatma comes, there should be no commotion or processions. It is only the work of swadeshi that must be importantly undertaken. Persons of every district must compete with one another in showing the improvements made in the matters of prohibition of liquor and swadeshi."

Subramania Bharathi's death

The 13 September 1921 issue of *Swadesamithran* and other papers carried the news of Subramania Bharathi's death: "The celebrated poet of the south, Sri Subramania Bharathi is no more." This meant that Gandhiji came to Madras just a few days after the death of Bharathi, but it does not appear that Gandhiji made any mention of him during his tour. Bharathi's greatness was, it would seem, neither recognised nor appreciated yet by the Madras of that time.

Conflicting views

People contributed generously to the Tilak Swarajya Fund and the Khilafat Fund. On his tour, the Mahatma and Maulana Subhani were accompanied by Yakub Hassan, Rajaji, Dr T. S. S. Rajan, and the secretary of the Madras Congress Committee, K. Rajagopalan. Officials of municipalities did not participate in Gandhiji's welcome; one reason could be that he had raised his flag against the British Empire. Dr Rajan, who accompanied Gandhiji, translated his speeches into Tamil at most of the meetings. Ministers of the Madras government were, for one reason or another, travelling in the vicinity at the same time as Gandhiji's tour. At the non-Brahmin convention, many ministers condemned Gandhiji's non-cooperation movement against the government. However, amidst Gandhiji's own speeches, theirs were rendered ineffective, much as stars fade when the sun rises. Maulana Subhani's presence alongside Gandhiji during the tour helped assuage the anger felt by Madras Hindus pursuant to the confusion caused by the Mopla revolt. At every meeting, Maulana Subhani exhorted the people to follow Gandhiji's principles, adhere to swadeshi, cast off foreign cloth, and be prepared to make any sacrifice for the country. He also condemned as anti-religious that some Moplas were forcibly converting Hindus. Gandhiji realised that Madras was a place beset with a myriad complex problems.

Problematic situation

Before Gandhiji's arrival in Madras, *The Hindu* carried headlines that he was coming at a difficult time, and that it was necessary for him to spread the word about his non-cooperation movement. National newspapers had also written that certain tenets of non-cooperation required amendment as otherwise their implementation may not be possible. Completely discarding foreign cloth, it was felt, did not make economic sense. Further, the problems of workers in Madras were rife. The Brahmin–non-Brahmin issue and the problem of untouchables (or 'panchamars', as they were called) could not be denied. If at all one measure had found full support, it was prohibition. Governmental oppression was severe and mounting throughout.

Untouchability

This time, Gandhiji gave greater weight to the issue of eradication of untouchability. "On one side the Brahmins, and on the other, the non-Brahmins… both are responsible for crushing to pieces the 'outcasts'. Tamilnadu abounds in temples, and there is a great deal of faith among the people. Persons with Vaishnavite caste marks on their foreheads, long hair, and bare bodies are seen wandering around like the 'Maharishis' of old, but their religion stops short of mere appearance" Gandhiji wrote. In the land of Ramanuja,[1] it surprised him to witness such a dangerously widespread mindset. Nevertheless, he did not lose heart, fervently believing that he could change the mentality of Tamils on untouchability. "The whole world treats us like lepers…is not at least 20% of that due to our treating some of our own people as untouchables?" he asked repeatedly.

The government view

A communiqué of the Madras government stated the usual success that a visit of Gandhiji to the state achieved: "In general, Mr Gandhi lays emphasis on ahimsa, but when he leaves this State, people often forget his advices. At the same time, his visit awakens and gives life to his non-cooperation movement even in places which are slow to rise." The government also acknowledged that while big crowds gathered at Gandhiji's meetings, there were more who came for the fun of it rather than those who wished to take him up on his advice. The crowds seen in places where the affluent Nattukkottai Chettiars lived were motivated to attend because of a newspaper article extolling the special powers that Gandhiji supposedly had. It was the Rai Chokkalingam-edited *Oozhiyan* publication that the government was referring to.

15 September 1921, At Basin Bridge station

At the Basin Bridge railway junction, where Kasturi Ranga Iyengar, A. Rangaswami Iyengar, Sathyamurthi, Rajaji and T. Prakasam spoke, the Calcutta Mail compartment in which Gandhiji was travelling (with his group from Calcutta) was disconnected, attached to a special train and brought to Madras. As usual a huge crowd had gathered at Central Station on 15 September 1921 to welcome him. From there, Gandhiji was taken in procession to Ramji Kalyanji's residence on Sullivan Street, Santhome. Along with Gandhiji, the wife of Maulana Mohammed Ali, Maulana Subhani of Kanpur, and Konda Venkatasubbaiah arrived in Madras. At the railway station, the first person to garland the Mahatma was T. V. Venkatarama Iyer.

A word portrait

An artist working for the *Mail* who had met Gandhiji drew a portrait of him, using words alone. Recalling his interaction with the Mahatma, he wrote:

> When we reached, Gandhiji asked, 'How much will they contribute to the Malabar rehabilitation fund?' We said that we would contribute some small amount. Thereafter, Rajaji took us into Gandhiji's chamber. He was having his meal at that time. He silently shook our hand and motioned us to sit, but, as we declined, he went on to finish his meal. A special feature in the centre of the room was a spinning wheel. Gandhiji spoke to my friend, the *Mail* reporter in soft tones. There was none of the fiery speech that one had come to expect from national leaders. He gave me the permission to draw as many pictures as I wished, as he sat erect and continued to converse, every now and then stopping to write something down. His face resembled that of the Ireland leader Éamon de Valera [1882–1975], and the attraction of his face reflected in his talk.

The Maulana's arrest

In the evening, with Yakub Hassan presiding at a large Madras Congress Committee meeting, Gandhiji condemned the government oppression, reiterating that there was no alternative to the non-cooperation movement for India. Normally, the Madras beachfront would be heavily crowded for Gandhiji's speeches, but when the news reached of Maulana Mohammed Ali's arrest, there was no controlling the crowds and their agitation. Gandhiji spoke in a resounding voice for over an hour. The Muslims had requested for a ten-minute break in the speech to observe namaz. The foregoing part of the speech was translated by A. Rangaswami Iyengar, and the latter by Sathyamurthi.

Gandhiji referred to Mohammed Ali's arrest, and the chaos caused by the Mopla revolt in Malabar. On the subject of swadeshi he pointed out to the women in the crowd that Begum Mohammed Ali was wearing khadi, while, regrettably, most of them were not, which made his heart break. He stressed on the merits of the spinning wheel. "We are not asking for swarajya for the upper classes alone. It is for the people considered untouchable, the common people all over India, and the poor," he emphasised.

Swadesamithran, in its editorial on this meeting, wrote, "There is no way except the spiritual path to attain swarajya. People should accept the Mahatma's words as a guru's teaching that, whatever the provocation to anger, we should not waver from our path."

Malabar travel ban on Gandhiji

When Gandhiji reached Madras, there was a letter for him from the chief secretary to the government, which said that, as there was martial law in force in Malabar, it was inadvisable for Gandhiji to visit or stay there. The nationalist newspapers condemned this letter. "It is sheer nonsense," wrote *The Hindu*. Somewhat more angrily, *Swadesamithran* wrote: "It is understood that the Mahatma has been prohibited from going to Kallikkottai. Peace will reign wherever Gandhiji's feet touch. Hence, if there is any chaos there, it will be cleared as soon as the Mahatma reaches. In fact, the government should escort the Mahatma with all honours to Malabar. If they do not, it would amount to disrespecting the Goddess who has come to your doorstep. When will wisdom dawn on these authoritarian classes?"

There were unpleasant echoes of the Malabar conflict in Madras. When Gandhiji had arrived in Madurai earlier, the Madurai Town Council had been enthusiastic to give the welcome address. After the onset of the Malabar problem, as some of the Town Council members kept away, there was a line of thinking that the welcome should not be given this time. In Trichy, too, there was difference of opinion between Muslims and Hindus on this issue.

A Gujarati audience

In Govindappa Naicken Street, George Town in Madras city, at the meeting arranged by Gujarati women in Soundarya Mahal, Gandhiji spoke in Gujarati as most of the women who attended were Gujaratis. Only a few were Tamil or Urdu-speaking. None of the women who came wore khadi. Expectedly, Gandhiji was dismayed at this, and emphasised the need to wear khadi in his speech.

Cloth merchants' meeting

Gandhiji had been saying that, not only should people desist from wearing foreign cloth, but merchants must stop selling them. There were, however, several problems faced by merchants in this matter. It was to discuss this that Ramji Kalyanji, vice-president of the Madras Cloth Merchants' Association, invited Gandhiji for the meeting. On the previous day, the cloth merchants had got together and resolved that it was impossible not to trade in foreign cloth. Still, they attended this meeting only to hear what Gandhiji had to say. The meeting took place at the Association Building in George Town.

Moosa Sait, G. Venkatasubbaiah Chetty, and P. Jayannan Chettiar, the prominent participants in the discussions, pointed out the difficulties that would be encountered in the overnight suspension on sale of foreign cloth. They said:

> Some merchants had already entered into agreements with mills in England. The arrival of those stocks cannot be stopped. Some other merchants procure stocks on credit. Hence, if a sudden embargo is put on such stocks, the creditors would demand their money back. If the merchants were to sell cloth and pay off their creditors, they would be left with no money to purchase swadeshi cloth. Should the new business begin in a small way, it would be impossible to settle the old rent for the shops, licence fees, salaries, etc. Moreover, there are European merchants operating in Madras. If we stop selling foreign cloth, they would take advantage of this opportunity and increase their profits. Therefore, as lawyers were given time to suspend their legal practice, cloth merchants, too, should be given time.

Gandhiji's views

While agreeing that the boycott of foreign cloth depended on its acceptance by the general public, Gandhiji said: "I do not say that existing agreements should be annulled. If the merchants make up their minds, it is possible that people's views in the matter of cloth can be influenced. Merchants should give up buying stocks on credit. It is always bad for business." He added that, while problems will arise out of the ban of foreign cloth for merchants, such sacrifices had to be made for the freedom of our country.

Though they heard him out, the merchants remained dissatisfied. The meeting ended without any decision being arrived at. Gandhiji left for the workers' meeting on the beach. In a communication later to the Central government, the State government wrote that the cloth merchants had interrupted and cross-questioned Gandhiji.

Split among workers

About 10,000 workers belonging to different industrial establishments were on strike at the time in Madras. But there was a split among them—Harijan workers had returned to work, leading to anger amongst the rest. They created a situation demanding that such workers stop work compulsorily. There were constant fights and arguments. Hence, a meeting had been arranged on the beachfront opposite Madras High Court, as an opportunity for Gandhiji to pacify the workers, and obtain their support for the non-cooperation movement. The meeting was attended by workers, industrialists and leaders in government. The majority of striking workers were from Buckingham Carnatic Mills. Gandhiji's speech was translated by M. S. Subramania Iyer. As the cloth merchants' meeting had ended in an exchange of strong words, Gandhiji could not arrive on time for this meeting. He emphasised that there should be no split among the workers and that they should work together. Throughout this tour, at all the meetings, his focus remained on swadeshi, and he himself burned foreign cloth at several places. Gandhiji's speech to the workers was welcomed even by the *Mail*, which conceded that there was reason in his demand, though the workers might not have understood it.

An incident

In his book *The Way Shown by Gandhi*, Akkoor Ananthachari has referred to a little-known incident, and recounts:

> In 1921, at the start of the non-cooperation movement, when Gandhiji had visited Madras, a prostitute had come wanting to meet him. However, no one desired that she should be allowed. The Mahatma agreed to see her after hearing that she hated her profession. He found out the reasons why she had descended to this profession, and his sympathy for her grew. He urged her to marry a man of her choice, which she did. She plunged into national service for many years thereafter, made sacrifices, removed the stigma of her past, and died in the country's cause.

This incident occurred either during Gandhiji's first visit to Madras in 1921, or the second.

17 September 1921, To Cuddalore

On 17 September 1921, the Mahatma started for Cuddalore via Villupuram and Parangippettai. The plan was to return from Cuddalore the same evening, spend the night at Parangippettai, and start the next morning for Kumbakonam. Gandhiji's relative, Prabhudas, and a disciple of Maulana Subhani, Anwaruddin, were accompanying him. At Villupuram railway junction, Gandhiji was escorted to a dais erected on the platform, and welcomed by V. T. Ramaswami Iyer on behalf of the South Arcot District Congress Committee. Because of this, and delays at other places, they reached Tiruppapuliyur half an hour behind schedule.

At Parangippettai

Via Panruti, Gandhiji reached Parangippettai, and laid the foundation stone for the Christian National School of Culture Building. This school was affiliated to the Seva Sadan established nearby by a Dutch woman, Anne Marie Peterson (d. 1961). There was mutual respect between her and Gandhiji. The fact that she kept and treasured all her life a pair of sandals belonging to him speaks volumes of her devotion. It was at her request to lay the foundation stone for the school that Gandhiji included it in his tour schedule.

A Christian debate

Thereafter, he was in a hurry to reach Cuddalore, but the Christian crowd assembled there were insistent that they speak to him of the Christian religion, and that he should consider being part of it. "Can such a good man not join the Christian religion?" was the wish expressed by them. Gandhiji enthusiastically joined the discussion, and he told them, "In South Africa, a majority of my friends were Christians. I had also felt in my life, on occasion, whether I should embrace the Christian faith. However, the Lord showed me a different path."

A Christian lady said, "We have faith that even now you will embrace the Christian religion. It is our belief that there is no redemption for those who do not embrace this faith. Jesus alone is the Prince of Peace." Shaking his head and smiling, Gandhiji said,

> That is your belief. In the same way I believe Hinduism is the faith that leads to redemption. Muslims have the same faith in their religion. The fact is that, if we understand the underlying tenets of every religion, anger and the feeling of discrimination will be erased. The basic principles of every religion should serve to purify man. Of all religions, the most scientific is Hindu religion, which is why I love it the most.

Cuddalore meeting

Gandhiji was to leave Parangippettai around 6 p.m., and go to Cuddalore by car. However he was two hours late. In the meantime, people from ten to fifteen miles around had collected in Cuddalore. Horse carts, bullock carts and hired vehicles choked the town. Large crowds had thronged from Tiruvannamalai, Panruti, Chidambaram, and Pondicherry. Shutting shop early, shop owners and their staff arrived at the meeting venue to 'purchase the product' of Gandhiji. Tens of thousands waited eagerly near the river for the Mahatma. Khadi-clad volunteers from Panruti and Cuddalore, holding welcome signs woven on khadi cloth, maintained order and peace in the crowd. The moon shed its light on the occasion as it drifted across the sky, its beams reflecting off the waves in the river. Prior to Gandhiji's arrival, the volunteers collected foreign cloth from the crowd to consign them to the Fire God. The leaders kept announcing news of Gandhiji's impending arrival at any moment. The crowd's enthusiasm knew no bounds. A high decorated dais had been erected, the path to it lined with flowers. A portion in front of the dais, from where the Mahatma was to enter, was to be kept free of crowds, but in their unbridled excitement, people filled that area too. Confusion reigned for a time. Meanwhile, the flames from the pile of burning foreign cloth were seen touching the skies. It was a sign that the Mahatma had arrived. He ascended the dais and waved at the crowd, requesting all to settle down. Everyone sat down quietly in their places and peace reigned. Cuddalore shone in the serene beauty of the moonlight and breathed in the cool river breeze. Gandhiji spoke for an hour, of ahimsa, discipline, hand-spinning, swadeshi, Hindu-Muslim unity and good treatment of Harijans. M. K. Acharya translated his speech into Tamil.

A new era begins

Clad in khadi, S. Srinivasa Iyengar enhanced the solemn dignity of the meeting. He had come there as a lawyer, but the organisers decided to utilise his presence there to preside over the meeting. Hitherto in Cuddalore, at public meetings, leading lawyers and public figures were always accorded special honours and allotted reserved seats. But at this meeting, everyone, including ordinary citizens, was seated randomly. Knowledgeable people realised that a new era had begun—the Gandhian era, where workers, farmers, and the common people enjoyed equal status with those in privileged positions.

Women's welcome

A welcome on behalf of South Arcot, and another one on behalf of women, were given. The women's welcome address was read out by Asalambikai, who later sang the 'Gandhi Puranam'. The Panruti welcome was separate. The welcome of the South Arcot District Congress Committee was read out by its secretary, Krishnasami Chetty. Saranga Chetty handed over a purse to Gandhiji.

Gandhiji said that love born out of confusion is blind love. "What India needs most today is love tempered by wisdom. Whatever else the word 'swarajya' might mean, it most certainly means discipline."

Train to Trichy

Coming via Erode to Parangippettai, Gandhiji stayed near Kumarakoil in a newly-restored old mansion. After breakfast here, he was to leave for Kumbakonam, but the person who had promised to bring transport had not arrived. Gandhiji looked at his watch, and decided to start immediately without breakfast so as to be on time. This saddened Anne Marie Peterson. Reaching Parangippettai railway station, and after addressing a small gathering, he boarded the train to Trichy.

Duraisamy Pillai

Duraisamy Pillai, who had undergone imprisonment with Gandhiji in South Africa, met Gandhiji and informed him that he was now at Swamimalai. Gandhiji told him, "I want you to come to Sabarmati Ashram with me." Pillai replied, "I am now married, and have started a rice mill. Hence it would not permit me to come." Gandhiji replied, "Then join the Indian National Congress, and work in it till freedom is obtained. Even if you have to lay down your life, it should not matter." Pillai accepted this, and from that moment on, he served the Congress, until India won independence. In 1930, as per Gandhiji's command, he participated in the Vedaranyam Salt Satyagraha, barely five days after his wife delivered a child. Of the many associations that served the nation in the freedom struggle, he became the leader of one. In the anti-law movement, when Duraisamy Pillai was imprisoned for four years in Madurai jail, his life partner, Tulavambal Achiyar, passed away.

When Gandhiji reached Thanjavur, as he was observing his day of silence, people could only see him, not speak to him.

Untouchability in Madurai

In an article for *Navajivan*, Gandhiji dwelt on the evils of untouchability prevalent in Madurai at that time.

> I am writing this letter from Kumbakonam in Madras State. This town is famous for its temples. Many educated Dravidars live here. But Brahmins believe that even if the shadow of a scavenger

falls on them, they would be rendered unclean. Such scavengers are also roundly abused, if not given a sound thrashing. There is no place like Madras State comparable in the harsh treatment meted out to the untouchables. An untouchable cannot even consider walking along the streets on which Brahmins reside. They are purposely kept in ignorance. There are persons to attend to an animal, if wounded; but only God should protect the untouchables.

Rumours

There came the news that Maulana Shaukat Ali had been arrested. Rumours were afloat that Gandhiji might also be arrested. In Madras, based on the rumour that the Mahatma had been arrested, people started marching towards newspaper offices. The Congress Working Committee was to meet at Ahmedabad on 6 October. Gandhiji had sent a circular to a select 23 persons from all over India, among them Yakub Hassan, C. Rajagopalachari and Kasturi Ranga Iyengar, that it would be good to meet at Bombay on 4 October to discuss matters.

18 September 1921, Trichy

Before Gandhiji reached the Trichy railway station on 18 September 1921, a large crowd assembled there. The stationmaster said he would not issue more than 50 platform tickets; as a result some prominent people of the town were forced to stand outside. Fortunately, the District Transport Superintendent happened to pass that way. Seeing the massive crowd outside the station, he permitted them to enter free of charge. When Gandhiji arrived, people stood in line to receive him on the platform. Those who could not enter stood in lines outside the station even at a late hour. Gandhiji and Maulana Subhani stayed at the residences of Dr Rajan and Khwaja Mian respectively.

The day after Gandhiji reached Trichy, one of the noble sons of Tamilnadu, Va. Ve. Su. Iyer was sentenced to nine months' simple imprisonment for an article that he had written. Around this time, the government also demanded land tax from 'Kappalottiya Tamizhan', V. O. Chidambaram Pillai.

Arguments at Trichy Town Council

On 20 September 1921, at a public meeting, Gandhiji was accorded a welcome on behalf of the Trichy Town Council, but how the decision to give such a welcome was reached is another story. At the meeting convened to discuss the welcome, the question of where it should be given came up. Council Member K. V. Jambunatha Iyer opined that, as a large crowd was expected, all programmes should be conducted at the Chowk Grounds. Council president, Khan Bahadur Khalifullah Sahib, disagreed and said he was not prepared to read the welcome address in the presence of 30,000 people. Jambunatha Iyer said the Khan Bahadur should either go by the Council's decision, or step down as president. The matter was put to vote and a decision taken. Nevertheless, as the Council president did not attend the meeting ('owing to unforeseen circumstances'), Council member Moulvi Syed Murtuza Sahib read the welcome in English, and T. V. Narasapillai the Tamil translation.

Long speech

The day of the public meeting at Trichy happened to be Gandhiji's day of silence. Hence, the meeting began at 8 p.m. to accommodate his breaking his silence. From the Kallathur village of Udayarpalayam, cotton garlands were sent for garlanding the Mahatma and other leaders. Dr T. V. Swaminatha Sastri, District Congress Committee secretary, handing over a collection of Rs 15,000 to the Tilak Swarajya Fund, announced that Trichy was in the forefront of these collections. It was 11 p.m. when the meeting ended. The volunteers maintaining peace and order at the meeting came in for praise. The speech that Gandhiji made at this Trichy public meeting was the longest after the one he delivered in Madras. The arrest of Shaukat Ali and others must have grieved him considerably. Hence his speech was in the nature of a huge challenge thrown.

> Not all of you would have known that Maulana Shaukat Ali was arrested in Bombay on 17th. The same 'honour' was given to Dr. Kitchlew in Punjab. The arrest of the Ali brothers was based on the accusation that they were thwarting the trust in the army. This is not a new crime.

> In September last year, I myself have committed it …
> at the Congress meeting in Calcutta … I say even now…
> this government has sucked our nation like a sponge. It has
> denigrated the Islam faith in front of the whole world. This is
> the government that is responsible for the Jallianwalla Bagh
> massacre.
>
> Hence, I issue a call to all those who call themselves Indians
> in the armed forces… and those who work in the government…
> to understand the principles of swadeshi, and come out of their
> jobs.

Gandhiji warned people against anger and violence, and praised them
for remaining calm in the face of government provocations.

> The students of Kumbakonam, Madras … asked me what their
> duty was in these difficult times. My advice was to come out of
> government-run and government-aided schools. I praised the
> students in Trichy for having done so. At the same time, I do
> sympathise with those who find themselves unable to do so. If
> they were so minded, they could as well serve the country, while
> continuing in such schools. They could devote one or two hours
> daily for the work of India's welfare. However, those who do
> leave their schools and colleges, and [those who] suspend their
> law practice should not demean those students and lawyers who
> are not able to act likewise.

Pudukkottai

The Pudukkottai[2] 'Durbar' must once have been powerful, perhaps
even more than the British. The British government that arrested
the Ali brothers allowed Gandhiji to tour in Madras, but the
Pudukkottai Durbar put a ban on Gandhiji's movement from Trichy
via Pudukkottai to Chettinad. As per the order promulgated by the
administrator of the Pudukkottai princedom, Sir Sidney Burn, I.C.S.,
and sent to Gandhiji through a messenger, he could not pass through
Pudukkottai, and that, should he do so, he would be stopped at the
border by the Pudukkottai police.

Gandhiji's reply was succinct. He did not wish to create trouble for
the Pudukkottai administrator, in the light of his having suspended the
non-cooperation movement temporarily. "Sir, Your letter of 18th has

been received. I had thought of going to Chettinad via Pudukkottai, but in view of your letter I am changing my route."

Do not ill-treat a messenger

The treatment that the Pudukkottai police official, who had come to deliver the letter to Gandhiji, received at the hands of Dr Rajan and its aftermath are worth recalling. In *Dinamani Kadir* (17 December 1967), R. Krishnaswami has referred to this as follows:

> It would have been about 10 in the morning, when a senior police official came to see Gandhiji, and handed over the communication from the Durbar that Gandhiji was prevented from entering the Pudukkottai princedom. Gandhiji accepted the letter and sent the official away. In a little while, the Congress workers and others who had gathered there were invited to lunch. They were being served on plantain leaves by Dr. Rajan and some volunteers, when Dr. Rajan noticed that police official also sitting in line to be served. That was all…. he put the serving vessel he had in his hand down, went to the official and yelled, 'Hey…who was it that invited you to sit here? Get up! … So, you have sat down to eat, have you?' The official's face fell, and he got up in a hurry and ran out. This incident reached the ears of Gandhiji. Deeply hurt, he sent for Dr. Rajan. 'What have you done, Rajan? It is against the tenets of ahimsa. That official merely did his duty… is this how he should be treated? Till you apologise to him and make him sit down to eat, I shall not partake of any food.' Guessing that the police official should have just reached the bus terminus, Dr. Rajan went there directly. He was indeed there as expected. Dr. Rajan said, '… I apologise for what I did. The Mahatma is very angry with me, and asked me to apologise to you. He wants you to come and eat, otherwise he says he will fast. Come, let's go.' The official was greatly moved, and, together, they returned to the house.

20 September 1921, Srirangam

On the morning of 20 September 1921, Gandhiji went to the Srirangam Town Council office and received their welcome, etched on a palm leaf. President of the Town Council, P. Srinivasaraghava

Iyengar, read the welcome address, and presented it in a silver casket. The three types of duties of a town council that the Mahatma outlined in his speech are edifying even to this day: 1) each town council should ensure that people living within its jurisdiction avoid wearing foreign cloth, and wear only khadi; 2) they should completely abstain from alcohol; and 3) there should be not even a hint of untouchability being practised.

He then proceeded to the Coronation Hall nearby, where he was accorded a welcome, with T. V. Seshadri Iyer reading the address on behalf of the people. This had been artistically printed in gold letters on palm leaf by Sri Vani Vilas Press. Among the gifts offered to Gandhiji were rice bags. He praised the handiwork of the welcome address on palm leaf but remarked: "The only drawback is that, instead of printing it in your language or any other Indian language, you have chosen to do so in English."

Every time Gandhiji spoke in English he felt a sense of humiliation, which is why, out of the funds collected from friends, he was working towards the spread of Hindi in Madras State. Many belonging to the Brahmin community were seen seated together in traditional garb. Addressing them, Gandhiji said, "When our women come out wearing foreign clothes in various colours, I feel sad to see them. On the other hand, you, who are seated without any upper cloth, and with tilaks on your forehead, look so resplendent. But when you, too, go yearning for foreign clothes, I despair at the fate of our nation."

Karur incident

There was an incident at Karur. As a shed owner had refused to contribute to the Tilak Swarajya Fund, some people had got together and demolished his shed. The police arrested 40 members of the Karur Congress Committee. Bringing this to the notice of Gandhiji, the people of Karur requested him to come there. However, he could not go. From Trichy he sent a letter to the Karur Congress Committee members, which said: "I regret that I am unable to come to Karur. I am aware how efficiently you have handled the liquor prohibition issue, but I am grieved at the way you have harmed the shed owner in the matter of the Tilak Swarajya Fund."

In Pudukkottai

Gandhiji rerouted his trip, and reached Chettinad via Dindigul and Madurai. Expecting Gandhiji to travel via Pudukkottai, the Congress Committee had prepared to welcome him at their office, as also the public there, with much ardour, and had made ready the purse to be handed over to him. The Town Council had adopted a resolution to welcome him. The Pudukkottai administration, however, used its veto power to annul this Resolution. The anger and disappointment this caused among the people was considerable. The people of Alangudi and Kulathur, who had been anxiously waiting for Gandhiji's arrival, took the purse they had collected and rushed to Karaikudi, to somehow get to meet Gandhiji and hand over the purse to him. Many others also went in the hope that the Mahatma would come there.

The expectant crowds that came from Alangudi, Kulathur and Annavasal and nearby places were large. Carrying garlanded pictures of Tilak, Gandhiji and the Ali brothers, they went around the four main streets with the resolution: "The Pudukkottai administration's order has betrayed the people's expectations, and the welcome address of the Pudukkottai Congress Committee would be read out in Karaikudi."

In Dindigul

Gandhiji was then travelling via Dindigul to Madurai. This was an unexpected bonus for Dindigul. There were elaborate decorations, with large crowds thronging the railway station. From the 20 members of the Dindigul Town administration, however, only 10 persons had come. The Town Council meeting was held at noon. Its president, R. Ramasamy Naidu read out the welcome in Tamil. The public meeting was held at 3 p.m. at the Hill Fort grounds. Having rested briefly at Kalastri Devasthanam building, Gandhiji arrived at the meeting.

Originally it was planned that Gandhiji would travel via Pudukkottai to Karaikudi, and thereafter to Madurai. But once it was known that his plans had changed and he was proceeding directly to Madurai, the Dindigul representatives rushed to Trichy and requested that he come via their town. Gandhiji said that it was on the basis of that invitation that he had come to Dindigul. It was usual for Gandhiji to refer to himself in good humour as a 'Baniya,' in other words, as belonging to the Vysya community. Here, too, in typical Baniya fashion, he said:

> Your representatives came to Trichy and requested me and Maulana Sahib to come to your town. I expected from that invitation that I would find extraordinary support for the non-cooperation movement here. I had expected, too, that all of you would be wearing khadi, and there would be a spinning wheel in each of your houses. But, in direct contrast, what do I find? Only more noise. There is no doubt much enthusiasm, but, if we were to get swarajya, and if the Ali brothers were to be released from jail, should not our enthusiasm be better directed?

It is said in the *Tirukkural*: To accomplish one task through another is like employing an elephant to catch another elephant.

Gandhiji had gathered the relevant information and said: "There are only 300 spinning wheels in Dindigul. If we assume that each family, on an average, consists of 5 persons, should there not be 6000 spinning wheels here?" He did not stop with that, and further warned: "I have heard that you enter into trifling dissensions with each other. As you are all serving your self-interest, we shall definitely not attain swarajya."

In Madurai

There had been much excitement in Madurai for quite some days. The people were eagerly awaiting Gandhiji's arrival and preparing to receive him wearing khadi. The tailors were busy stitching khadi shirts and caps. The sale of khadi dhoties was in full swing. The ladies, too, were not far behind; many had blouses stitched in khadi. But the Dravida Sangam sent a circular to Dravidians not to participate in the welcome to Gandhiji. A few questions were printed so that Gandhiji could respond. The enthusiasm of the people increased.

When Gandhiji's train reached Madurai, the 10,000 people who had gathered at the railway station were orderly. Gandhiji was led out of the station, seated in a car, and driven to the nearby Madurai College grounds. As all along the route there were big crowds, the short distance could be covered only after many stops. At the meeting grounds there were more than 50,000 people. In the ensuing noise, Gandhiji's speech could barely be heard.

District Congress Committee members, Madurai merchant offices' clerical staff, and the Madurai Ramanathapuram District Mahajana Sabha members gave welcome addresses to Gandhiji. S. D. Krishnan Iyer had a welcome typed which was handed over in a khadi bag. He translated Gandhiji's speech. Nationalist and stage actor, Vishwanath Das, had been keeping the crowd occupied and quiet with his songs. It was on this occasion that the future leader K. Kamaraj (1903–75) saw Gandhiji for the first time. He was then an ordinary worker.

Students

P. K. Ramachari, who became secretary of the Madras District Harijan Seva Sangam, was then a small boy. Along with P. V. Subbaiah, Rajaram M. Konda and L. R. Muthukrishnan, he had discontinued his studies at the S.S.L.C. or secondary school leaving certificate stage, at the call of the non-cooperation movement. They had gone with great fervour to Chozhavandan to welcome Gandhiji, and travelled on the same train to Madurai. In the Madurai public meeting, Gandhiji introduced with pride these four youngsters, who had come out of their schools in response to the non-cooperation movement.

So much noise!

The noise made by the crowd must have vexed Gandhiji, because he completed his speech quickly. Some of it was not audible to the crowd. He said, "Although thousands of welcome addresses have been offered by you, they would not be enough for us to attain swarajya. This noise pains me greatly. I regret that I have come to Madurai just to hear this useless noise. If you desire a rule of justice, you must work the spinning wheel. That is the symbol of peace, the sign of Hindu-Muslim unity." In Madurai, he stayed as a guest of Ramji Kalyanji at his house on Mel Masi street. That night, members of the Madurai Girls' Association, Gujarati merchants, and Muslim youth association members met him and offered welcome addresses and purses.

The Chozhavandan issue

When Gandhiji was in Madurai, an issue concerning the leaders in Chozhavandan (a town panchayat, i.e. in transition from rural to urban, in Madurai district) was brought to his attention. Two leaders of the non-cooperation movement in Madurai district were lawyer George Joseph, and Munkala Pattabhiramayya of Chozhavandan. When liquor shops were put up for auction in Nilakkottai, a demonstration was staged by Munkala Pattabhiramayya, Mattaparai Venkatarama Iyer, Madurai Maulana Sahib, Irumbadi Nallathambi Pillai, Chozhavandan Thirumeni, and Mattaparai Dasan, among others. They were arrested and charged with looting. Except Pattabhiramayya, the others decided to go to court and argue wrongful arrest. Pattabhiramayya did not do so; it was the practice for those charged with demonstrating against liquor shops to accept their guilt and go to jail. Hence, when Gandhiji was in Madurai, the others met him to seek his advice. Should they fight the case or not was their query. He replied, "Tell the court what actually happened. You need not concern yourself with what did not take place. If you had committed a wrong, accept it. If the charge is for an offence not committed, object only to that. Do not argue against it."

Change of attire

On 22 September 1921, Gandhiji undertook the radical measure of appearing bare-torsoed in public, clothed only below the waist. If a common man was seen in this garb, it would be taken as a normal occurrence, but the Mahatma's appearance became an international incident. It is with just a cloth around his waist as a half dhoti that he met viceroys, the British Emperor, and other world leaders, which invited Churchill's disparaging comment, calling Gandhiji a "half-naked fakir". It was as a temporary measure that he adopted this dress, but it became his habit subsequently, something that did not change till his dying day. Nobody had expected that such a historic decision would be taken by Gandhiji in this matter at Madurai, nor would he himself have planned to do so there, and from that date. His heart must have nurtured this wish over a period, which gained fruition in the temple towns of Meenakshi and Chokkanathar. Gandhiji's saintly mentor-poet, the ninth-century Tamil saint and poet Manickavasagar, had described Nataraja, Lord Siva in his form as the cosmic dancer, as 'Picchai Deva' or the Beggar Lord. Hence, appearing as a beggar among the beggars in Madurai, a low caste among the low castes, this holy mendicant-like garb of Gandhiji seemed appropriate to the place. Surprisingly, this was not reported by the newspapers at the time. Perhaps they realised only later that Gandhiji was capable of taking such extraordinary steps. *The Hindu* and *Swadesamithran* published the clarification given by Gandhiji on this.

In a news item sent from Tirunelveli, newspapers wrote that the Mahatma appeared without an upper cloth. In *Navajivan* of 21 January 1921, under the heading, 'My full cloth,' Gandhiji wrote about how his appearance with just a dhoti tied at his waist came about. The changes he adopted in Madurai were effected after deep thought, and he never worried about having to change them later. He added, "I did this under unavoidable circumstances. Such a revolutionary change in attire was made … at Madurai."

Why the change

That he should discard the upper cloth was a thought that occurred to him at Barisal and in Khulna (both towns in present-day Bangladesh). He saw people there, desperately poor and famine-stricken, moving around almost naked. He was asked, when he decided to send them caps and clothes, whether burning of foreign cloth was justified. After Mohammed Ali was arrested in Walveedar, Gandhiji went to speak to the people there. He thought of removing his shirt and cap, but did not. In the first instance he felt it would be seen as self-aggrandisement, and in the second that it would cause confusion. How he finally did so the third time in Madurai, Gandhiji has himself described.

> In my Madras tour, I had the third opportunity. 'If one wanted to wear khadi, there was not enough khadi available. Even were it available, there was not enough money,' the people told me. 'If we were to discard all our foreign cloth, what would we … wear?' complained the workers. This stayed in my mind, and I realised that there was a point in this argument. This plight of the poor took hold of me, and I shared my concern with Maulana Asad Subhani, Rajagopalachariar, and Dr. Rajan. I told

them that henceforward I would wear only waist cloth. Maulana
understood my distress and accepted my decision. The others
were shaken. They felt that some people would be confused and
not understand the reason for this change, while others might
think I was mad. They added that people might not follow me
as they had done earlier. I examined these arguments. I realised
that whenever I had talked to people about wearing only waist
cloth, if they could not get khadi, but throw out foreign cloth, I
did have reservations in my mind. As long as I wore a shirt and
dhoti, there would not be enough strength in my words. The
shortage of swadeshi cloth in Madras State also added to my
dilemma. I saw the overflowing affection of the people, but it felt
like insubstantial bubbles. I discussed my decision again with
my friends, but they did not offer any new arguments. It was
almost the end of September. What should I do to enforce the
discard of foreign cloth before the end of the month?…This was
the question agitating me. It was in this state of mind that we
reached Madurai on 22nd night [It was the 21st night: Gandhiji
had made a mistake]. I decided that at least till October 31st
I should wear only a dhoti around my waist. The next day
morning I attended and spoke at the Madurai weavers meeting
wearing just the dhoti.

As soon as Gandhiji reduced his clothing, the Maulana too reduced
his own apparel to the extent acceptable to his religion. Rajaji,
Dr Rajan, and other leaders keenly observed how the people reacted
to this change. Gandhiji had done so with the objective that people
should discard foreign cloth. In a letter to Mahadev Desai, Gandhiji
wrote that he took this step as he could not control the distress he felt.
The day on which he started wearing just the dhoti in Madurai, he
made an announcement to the people giving his reasons.

> It has been almost been one year since the All India Congress
> appealed to the people to shun foreign cloth, and there are only
> a few days left for the year to be completed. Still, many declare
> that they cannot discard foreign cloth. If the reason for that
> is non-availability of adequate cloth, they should be content
> wearing only waist cloth (and, on required occasions, upper
> cloth). It is to set an example that I have discarded shirt and cap
> and decided to wear just a dhoti around my waist at least till
> October 31st.

He added that if freedom was not obtained before the year was out, this dress of his would serve as the apparel appropriate for mourning. He attached much importance to khadi. He said he was ready to suspend all other activities in the promotion of swadeshi for the rest of the year, including strikes.

Saurashtra community

Early one morning, as was his habit, Gandhiji awoke and requested Virudhunagar Palani Kumaru Pillai, a national co-worker, to hold his dhoti as he tied it. He then went to a place called Gandhi Pottal, where a meeting of people from Saurashtra was being held. A dais was placed in the west corner, facing east. Those who had seen Gandhiji the previous day with turban and upper body cloth were surprised to see him now merely dhoti-clad. On this visit to Madurai, the two persons responsible for arranging his meetings were T. R. Padmanabha Iyer and Krishna Kundhu. At this meeting, representatives of various Saurashtra organisations gave welcome addresses and purses. To them Gandhiji advised, "I hear that some among the Saurashtra community are addicted to alcohol. They should make all possible efforts to rid themselves of it."

Melur

From this meeting Gandhiji and his group went to Chettinad, a region in Madras State which then enjoyed much prosperity. In expectation of the visit, an air of festivity prevailed in that area. At places, Gandhiji's car was stopped for a few seconds and flower petals were showered on him in a show of affection by the people. People said that Chettinad acquired enhanced status because of this visit. At Melur en route, union leader Kasi Chettiar garlanded Gandhiji.

Tirupatthur

The crowd that had gathered in Tirupatthur was more than 10,000, conducting themselves patiently and with discipline. Gandhiji mentioned the statistics of how much khadi could be produced in the country to adequately clothe everyone. Until the poor and the affluent alike were able to obtain it, he would continue to be clad as he

was then, he declared. He was greatly pleased when, in the welcome
address presented in Tirupatthur, it was stated that the alcohol
habit had been largely given up. Maulana Subhani said, "If Muslims
act as per the dictates of Islam, they could emulate the Mahatma's
way of dressing, because the Mahatma is in fact dressed in the way
recommended by the Prophet" (as reported in *Swadesamithran*, 27
September 1921).

Kanadukathan

Having been welcomed at Karaikudi and Palavangudi, Gandhiji
reached Kanadukathan at noon. He was welcomed in a beautiful
pandal, with a crowd of 5,000 people sitting patiently, which must
have pleased Gandhiji. Several welcome addresses on behalf of many
associations were read out, and purses presented. After telling them
that all foreign articles must be discarded, he went to Kottaiyur via
Pallathur and Velangudi. There, too, there was a massive pandal, and,
noticeably, the presence of a large number of women.

Karaikudi–Pudukkottai

At Karaikudi, Gandhiji saw not only the local people but also leaders
of the Pudukkottai princedom, lawyers, merchants, Town Council
members, landlords and the common people waiting to welcome him.
It seemed that Karaikudi had been overrun by Pudukkottai (the two
places are about 27 miles apart). On behalf of various organisations
of Pudukkottai, welcome addresses and purses were presented to the
Mahatma. "The day I hear that in Pudukkottai, a lakh and twenty
thousand spinning wheels are in operation, I will be there," he said.

When it became known that members of the Pudukkottai Town
Council had gone to Karaikudi and read out a welcome address to
Gandhiji, the Pudukkottai Durbar did not remain silent. Individual
'notices' were served on the Council members, G. Sundaresa Sastrigal,
G. Sundaresa Iyer, S. Viswanatha Iyer, and K. Balusamy Chetty.

> It has come to the knowledge of the Durbar that, on behalf of
> the people of Pudukkottai town, you read out a welcome to
> Gandhiji at Karaikudi, signing it as members of the Pudukkottai
> Town Council. Mr. Gandhiji is a sworn enemy of the British

government. It was as a consequence of this he was prevented from travelling through Pudukkottai. In spite of the Resolution of 18th being annulled by the Administration of this princedom, your having signed the welcome address to him is considered an offence. Hence, please reply within one week of receipt of this notice why you should not be removed from the Council and legislature positions, and be prevented from contesting future elections.

Anticipating this, S. Viswanatha Iyer resigned from his post. How was the post more important than Gandhiji, is what he felt.

Many women of Karaikudi met Gandhiji and gave welcome addresses and purses. In the public meeting held at night, he found it difficult to pass through the crowd and reach the dais. Hence he spoke from his car. Since his speech from one corner of the 25,000-strong crowd could not be heard by most, there was much noise. On behalf of eight associations in Karaikudi, eight welcome addresses and eight purses were presented.

Gandhi Meiyappa Chettiar

When Gandhiji came to Karaikudi in 1921, Subramaniya Siva[3] welcomed him. Most of the arrangements for the welcome were made by Gandhi Meiyappa Chettiar, so named for his great admiration for Gandhiji. The Hindu Religious Association read out an invocatory welcome to him. Rai Chokkalingam narrates an interesting incident.

> From the day on which Gandhiji came to Karaikudi in 1921, I started wearing khadi along with some others. In Karaikudi, after Gandhiji had settled down at the residence of Thiru Sa. Na. Sa. Th. Sathappa Chettiar, I went with some others and prostrated before him. Amaravathi Pudur Lakshmanan Chettiar was among those who prostrated likewise. But he was not wearing khadi at that time. Gandhiji in good humour told him, 'You have touched my feet without donning khadi.' Lakshmanan Chettiar went on the same day to buy and wear khadi. He never wore anything but khadi thereafter. When Gandhiji came home in Karaikudi, he asked in Tamil, 'Please bring water.' In 1921, Thiru Subramania Siva was in Karaikudi, and was one of the main persons in welcoming Gandhiji (At that time Siva had been

in Karaikudi for about a year, along with 'Kalki' Sadasivam[4]).
The subject of *Tirukkural* came up during Gandhiji's visit. Then
Gandhiji said, 'I know about *Tirukkural*....Tiruvalluvar was a
great teacher.'

Devakottai

Stopping the car for a few minutes at Amaravathi Pudur, and receiving
welcome addresses, Gandhiji and party proceeded to Devakottai,
going straight to the venue of the public meeting. Welcome addresses
were delivered and purses handed over on behalf of the Dharma Vysya
Sangam and Swami Vivekananda Sangam. One welcome was etched
on a gold plate. But what gave Gandhiji the greatest pleasure was a
young girl presenting him with yarn spun out of 100s count cotton on
behalf of the Viswakarma community. He praised her. In responding
to the vote of thanks by the president, he mentioned that Chettinad
was famous for hand spinning and weaving for generations, and that
spinning wheels were presented as part of the dowry at weddings. "In
Devakottai, every house should have a spinning wheel, very much like
having a horse [elsewhere]," said Gandhiji. "If you also wear rough
cloth like I do, I can assure you that not only in India, but in Rangoon
and other places, too, your money lending profession would prosper.
Like the people in Andhra, I notice that men here, too, prefer to wear
rings and earstuds embedded with precious stones. If only you could
donate these to the Tilak Swarajya Fund, and take to wearing simple
ornamentation, as before, how much better it would be," he added.

Debate on caste

Gandhiji noticed the popularity of khadi in Chettinad. When he
undertook a khadi tour in 1927, he would return to Karaikudi every
day. On that tour, Sa. Ganesan, as the leader of a small group of
workers, served Gandhiji in his daily routines. At that time, he and
some others, along with noted writer Va. Ramasamy, engaged in
debate with Gandhiji as to whether caste divisions were necessary. This
debate went on over three days, half an hour each day. "You say there
should be no discrimination of castes, but at the same time maintain
that caste divisions are necessary—is this not self-contradictory?"
they asked. To this, Gandhiji responded as follows:

Varnasramam, or caste divisions, are based on trades. If trades are hereditary, the effects of time and money will be countered. Each trade will grow to the maximum. High caste or low caste on the basis of trades should not be predicated. Hence caste divisions on the basis of trades is beneficial to society. But to prevent any caste person to mix and converse, or to cause them hardship and exclusion in any manner is what is wrong. Therefore, caste differences are separate, treatment as high and low caste is separate. In my view, therefore, as you can see, there is no contradiction. (Interview with Sa. Ganesan)

23 September 1921, Meeting Bhaskardas

Gandhiji came to Madurai from Karaikudi on 23 September 1921 and entrained for Tirunelveli. In the next compartment to Gandhiji's were Kamaraj and some other workers. Noted playwright, Bhaskardas, garlanded Gandhiji at the station, and presented him with a book of his poems. One of the poems began '*Gandhiji is an extremely poor sanyasi,*', a popular song that was sung in many plays in those days. Dr Rajan explained the meaning of this poem to Gandhiji, who laughed aloud on hearing it. It was the word 'sanyasi' applied to him that tickled him.

Tirunelveli

It was evening when he reached Tirunelveli. The programme was delayed because of the Pudukkottai tangle but this news had not reached the interior sections of Tirunelveli, with the result that people had begun to gather the previous day. Tirunelveli town was chock-full of people, and it appeared that a new era had dawned in the district, where the only lawyer who had quit his profession in response to the non-cooperation call was Tirukoodasundaram Pillai. Because of his and his associates' determined efforts, a large number of people were seen wearing khadi in the crowds that came for the meeting. There was much demand for the khadi bales brought by G. Subramaniam from the swadeshi stores in Thoothukudi. There was not enough khadi cloth to meet the demand.

Gangaikondan

Tirukoodasundaram Pillai went to Maniyachi and joined the Mahatma and his group. As the crowd anticipated at Tirunelveli railway station was large, which would make it difficult for him to detrain, Gandhiji was asked to get down at Gangaikondan station, and was taken by car to the residence of Abodharana Iyer in Tirunelveli. The crowd that waited at Tirunelveli raiway station for Gandhiji was enraged. They were tactfully dealt with by the stationmaster Gopala Iyer, and made to disperse.

A public meeting was held in the Kailaspuram (a township about 11 miles from Trichy) beachfront, with the merchant, S. K. Sheikh Moideen Sahib, presiding, attended by an estimated 20,000 people, who remained orderly even after it became dark. Many had come from the neighbouring villages and also from Thoothukudi. Sundaram Pillai read and handed over a welcome address printed on khadi cloth. *Swadesamithran* reported that, like the Tamils, the Mahatma presented a smiling picture of being seated bare-bodied on the dais, with just an upper cloth. The first half of Gandhiji's speech was translated by T. R. Mahadeva Iyer, and the second by Dr Rajan. On behalf of the people of Tirunelveli, Mahadeva Iyer presented a purse.

The issue of Nadars

Gandhiji said, "You are facing the Brahmin–non-Brahmin problem, as also the Nadar-lower castes issue." As reported in the *Swadesamithran* of 27 September 1921, Gandhiji had said,

> The complaint of Nadars needs to be specially looked into. The Nadars [now, 'an Other Backward Class'], who are in the forefront of business in Madras, and living under very prosperous conditions, observing high religious discipline, are not being accorded equal status in temples, and if such a situation were to continue, we will not get freedom even in a hundred years. Hence, Nadars should be given equal status. This problem is connected to untouchability.

When the meeting ended at night, Gandhiji went to his place of stay, met some prominent persons, and discussed politics. The next morning he met the Quilon nationalist professor and leader of the

Ezhavas (one of the lower castes in Kerala), T. K. Madhavan, who explained the problem of his caste. Gandhiji started for Trichy by the morning train from Tirunelveli on 24 September 1921. En route at Madurai, he prepared a notice for Indian Muslims on the importance of ahimsa. Ko Venkatachalapathy, who went on later to become a prominent 'Gandhi-vaadi', was then a small boy, who saw Gandhiji at Tirumangalam.

25 September 1921, Coimbatore

Gandhiji went to Coimbatore on 25 September 1921 via Trichy, Erode and Tiruppur. A high dais was put up near Tiruppur railway station, festooned with khadi cloth, and occupied by a few women working on the spinning wheel. This special arrangement, appreciated by Gandhiji, had been made by Karuppannan Chettiar, a Tiruppur cloth merchant dealing in khadi, who later became the head of the khadi movement in Madras. Thousands of people sat patiently when Gandhiji arrived. Karuppannan Chettiar welcomed him with a khadi garland. Blessing the crowd, Gandhiji proceeded to Coimbatore.

The shuttle train that brought Gandhiji from Erode reached Singanallur, where the Coimbatore Town administration's vice president, K. Subramania Mudaliar, Sulthan Sahib, and N. S. Ramasami Iyengar welcomed him, and took him by car to Coimbatore.

Town Council welcome

The welcome accorded by the Coimbatore Town Council had its sidelights. Although they had brought Gandhiji from the railway station to Coronation Park, they found it difficult to escort him to the high dais erected there, as massive crowds surrounded them. Ultimately, Gandhiji was bodily lifted by a *pehlwan*, a wrestler or bodybuilder, and seated on the dais. With C. S. Rathinasabapathy Mudaliar presiding, the Town Council did not support Gandhiji's non-cooperation movement. Still, they did not wish that a great man who had come to their town should not be properly honoured (whether to welcome Gandhiji or not had been debated briefly by the Town Council, and decided in favour by a small majority). Thus in their welcome address, they dwelt only on those principles of Gandhiji that were acceptable to them. While concurring with the issues of prohibition, untouchability, and swadeshi, they said they could not understand why swarajya cannot be obtained through cooperation with the government, or by reform in the legislative system. Being a seeker of truth, Gandhiji appreciated this admission of the Town Council, and in his response said:

> For the last 30 years, I have been cooperating with the government, but I came to the sad conclusion that such cooperation was in fact causing great loss to the nation. As soon as I realised this, I patiently sat down to find another way, and decided that non-cooperation with this government was the only way to solve this problem. ... The Town Council says it is against my views, but they could still carry out three of my advices: 1) abolish untouchability within the control area of the Council, 2) introduce spinning wheels in all the boys' and girls' schools in their jurisdiction, and 3) take care of the welfare of untouchables. I desire that the Town Council must fight strenuously with the government for the introduction of prohibition.

Workers of Pothanur

In Coimbatore, Gandhiji was accorded welcome at various venues. To the workers of Pothanur gathered at Besant House he advised that they should remain united. It was at this gathering that Ayya Muthu, who went on to render yeoman service for the growth of khadi, met Gandhiji for the first time. Normally accustomed to wearing Western dress, he went clad in khadi to this meeting. Later, under the leadership of Gandhiji, he and his wife went to jail several times. They were also fully involved in administration. After this, Gandhiji visited the house of future Central government minister and financial expert, R. K. Shanmugam Chettiar, where he was seated on a decorated dais and offered '*Purna Kumbham*,' accompanied by the chanting of mantras as a welcome. The crowds that had gathered at Coronation Park and Besant House turned up here to see Gandhiji. The large crowd conducted itself well, helped by the presence of some 200 volunteers. On behalf of the people of Coimbatore town, the Congress and Khilafat committees, the Coimbatore Viswakarma Society, grain merchants and commercial associations, greetings were offered. Parameswaran Chettiar presented a purse on behalf of the grain merchants.

But it pained Gandhiji that one group of people was conspicuous by its absence. "I am disappointed that there is no welcome from my Panchama [members of the lowest caste group in India, Harijan/'untouchable'] friends. They seem embarrassed even to approach me," he said.

The auction at Devakottai

It was thought that the attractive articles presented at Devakottai would fetch a good price, and hence they were put up for auction with Rajaji as the auctioneer; the articles fetched approximately Rs1500. Ponni Naicker of Peelamedu bought the articles. It was nearly midnight when Gandhiji returned to his temporary residence.

Many were disappointed that the non-cooperation idea had not spread adequately. This was expressed in a letter from M. Bhakthavatsalam (future chief minister of Madras) to the editor of *The Hindu* at the end of the tour. He desired that every village should have a 'grama sabha' and all adults should join the Congress and receive political education. Instead of impressing on the leaders the necessity to discard foreign cloth, it would be more advantageous to spread the word among the people, he declared. Gandhiji's tour certainly gave a new impetus to the non-cooperation movement.

26–27 September 1921, Salem

On 26 September 1921, he observed a day of silence. When Gandhiji started from Coimbatore at night and reached Salem, he, along with the Salem Town Council president, Venkatappa Chettiar, Dr Varadarajulu Naidu, and Adinarayana Chettiar saw spinning wheels in operation at Kallakurichi. The merchants of Sevvappettai donated a generous amount to start a school for spinning. Bangaru Chettiar read out the welcome. Praising the national spirit of the Salem merchants, Gandhiji exhorted them to employ their acumen in business in all ways beneficial to the country. Then he went to the Town Hall and responded to the welcome oration read by the president, Venkatappa Chettiar, by especially praising the beauty of the container in which it was presented, and the efforts of the Town Council that had enabled the non-cooperation movement to make strides there. He asked them to devote the same attention to ahimsa, Hindu-Muslim unity, swadeshi and other issues.

Rajaji's service

Where the Coimbatore Town Council had expressed reservations in adopting some of Gandhiji's principles, the Salem Town Council fully accepted them and promised due compliance—on khadi, untouchability abolition, prohibition and the use of Hindi. They asserted that they would implement these measures to the maximum extent allowed by their Council. In the welcome of the Salem Town Council, it was noted that when Rajaji was its president, he had seen to it that all liquor shops were shut down, but after his tenure, the government had permitted their revival.

Gandhiji said: "I greatly appreciate your progress. I can expect nothing less from a town that has produced an All India Congress Committee leader like C. Vijayaraghavachariar, and a chief secretary like Rajaji. The swadeshi concept has spread in Salem more than anywhere else in this State."

The 'panchama' members of the Salem Town Council were later introduced to Gandhiji. It was afternoon before Gandhiji returned to Asthampatti, where he was staying. In honour of his visit, 4,000 poor people were fed.

Women donate generously

There were several programmes lined up for Gandhiji in the evening. At the meeting of women, he exhorted them to discard foreign silk clothes and don khadi. Many women took off their jewels and offered them to him. Dr Varadarajulu Naidu's wife offered him all her jewellery. Thereafter, prominent weavers and merchants met and held discussions with Gandhiji. The Education Society refused government grant for eight schools, which became national schools on this occasion. Students who had come out of government-aided primary and high schools were accommodated in schools run by the Congress Committee. Gandhiji expressed his happiness at seeing these students spinning cloth. He proceeded to the Salem Literary Association gathering, where he unveiled a portrait of Lokmanya Tilak, painted by local artist, V. V. Lingam. At a public meeting in the Council Food Court grounds, welcome addresses were offered on behalf of the District Congress Committee, and the Kshatriya Merchants' Association. With Salem C. Vijayaraghavachariar presiding, Gandhiji's speech dealt with discarding foreign cloth, use of khadi, abolition of untouchability, among others. After this meeting he went to the station to leave for Tirupati.

Weakness for jewellery

Before coming to Madras this time, Tamil women's fondness for Kanchipuram silk saris and heavy jewellery was brought to Gandhiji's notice by a friend. In a pained letter to Gandhiji, this Vaishnavite, who was part of the non-cooperation movement, wrote:

> Women in Tamilnadu are proving to be a barrier to this movement. Some of them are clinging to the past. The bad habits of the West have taken hold of several of these women belonging to the Brahmin community. They drink coffee at least thrice a day, and are of the view that drinking even more cups signifies modernity. It is the same with dress. Instead of wearing modest clothes like good domestic women, they hanker after foreign clothes. In the matter of jewellery, Brahmin women surpass all others. Among these, the worst offenders are Vaishnavite women. When men go seeking the simple life, the women are turning out to be spendthrifts. Even when they go to worship in a temple they do not think of wearing simple cotton clothes. They seem to desire at all times saris with heavy zari and great amounts of jewellery.

Gandhiji shared the following views in his response (11 August 1921):

> My heart grieves at the desire of Tamil sisters, more than in other parts of the country, desiring to hold on to past glory. Nevertheless, this letter should be a warning to my Tamil sisters. They should return to the simplicity of the past instead. I can assure them that God would be happier if they discard rich clothing and adopt khadi saris. Our temples have not been established for the display of ostentation, but as symbols of

devotion and simplicity. There needs to be continued education in Madras on the points raised by my friend in his letter.

The lure of silk saris

Once again the same person had written to Gandhiji about the lure of silk saris among women here, and the fact that, as women in the south did not wear white saris, unlike their counterparts in the north, khadi could not make as much headway here. He had also pointed out that families were being ruined because of this craze of women for silk. This letter was written to Gandhiji a few weeks before he came here. It appears that the letter caused Gandhiji anguish. In *Young India* (25 August 1921), he wrote:

> I hesitate to come to Madras. My friend writes that Tamil women have an over-fondness for silk saris. My view is the same. In a place like Madras, which is so hot and humid, a fabric like silk is inappropriate. In a poor country like India, to spend Rs.100 on a sari is a sinful expense. Madras is a State that sends out the maximum number of people abroad as slaves. Giving the spinning wheel new life is the surest way to solve the problem of people being forced to go abroad for work. Even if tax is fully abolished, the Indian farmer cannot just live off his land.

Disappointment

Unlike Gandhiji's other tours, this one caused him considerable dissatisfaction, and he expressed it in writing:

> My tour was a disappointment. I have always had praise for the people of Madras. I have several times seen the ability in them to overcome any kind of hardship. But in the matter of swadeshi, it has taken a back seat. If only it would wake up, so much could be achieved. Compared to the intelligence of Tamil women, the women of Gujarat pale into insignificance.
>
> The women here are extremely sharp. No other women in India have as much skill in their hands. The women elsewhere have the ability to sell products that are even considered useless.

Gandhiji was dismayed that Tamil women were not wearing khadi. He had praised the Muslim women of Madras for wearing pristine white apparel.

There is no shortage of Congress workers in other parts of India, but very few who possess the intelligence, integrity and ability of Rajagopalachari, who has understood our struggle through and through. In difficult situations he is able to remain steadfast and calm.

Then, why am I disappointed with Madras? There are two reasons. One, because the love for English is embedded here deeply, Those who know English in Madras do not care about Tamil. The Bengalis, too, love English, but they do not forsake their own Bengali language. I must say that Madras has abandoned Tamil. As a result, not only has the growth of Tamil been stifled, there has resulted a huge divide between the English- and Tamil-speaking people. Rajagopalachari and his associates are undertaking all measures to redress this problem, but it will take time. (Gandhi Publication, English translation, chapter 21, page 233)

We can gauge from this how strongly Gandhiji felt about Tamil, and the need for it to grow.

The other main cause of my disappointment is that, although the Tamil people have true faith in religion, they are ruled by a blind belief in ritual. Hence, only the outward trappings of religion are visible. … the inner core has been forgotten. More than in any other part of India, lower-caste people are facing hardship here. Again, the Brahmin–non-Brahmin divide is more apparent here than anywhere else. No other people, on the other hand, spend as much money on vibhuti, sandal paste, or kumkum, nor do other parts expend as much on upkeep of temples as in Tamilnadu. As a result, on one side, educated people find fault with whatever is done outside their religion. On the other, there is darkness and ignorance among the priests.

In such a situation, if darkness is dispelled, light would automatically shine. Once common people begin to realise the darkness within themselves, it would fade away by itself. That is why, in the midst of darkness, I see light. Congress workers tell me that, without any special efforts on their part, people have started taking to the spinning wheel. Khadi is being produced even where Congress workers are not putting in any effort. Thousands have taken to wearing khadi caps. The majority of Congress workers [here the reference to 'majority' is noteworthy, as in 1921, it was not yet compulsory for Congress workers to wear khadi] are fully wearing khadi. If you ask me of my experience, I would say that, in spite of this, I have not lost the faith that swarajya would be attained before the year is out.

That Bengal has disappointed me there is no doubt. [But] Tamilnadu has disappointed me much more. Congress workers must reinforce faith in the spinning wheel. … true labour is what I believe [in]. I expected this in Bengal and was disappointed. The situation is the same here. This is what makes me apprehensive.

Gandhiji sent the above letter to Mahadev Desai on his way to Coimbatore.

Purses presented

The details of purses presented to Gandhiji during this tour were as below:

Samarna Fund: Rs. 7122-2-6
Khilafat Fund: Rs. 153-1-9
Tilak Swarajya Fund: Rs. 23,209-6-0

When Rajaji announced these figures, there were articles as yet unauctioned.

What he said in Madras

When he returned from Madras, Gandhiji released in *Young India* (in two issues of 20 and 27 October 1921) a letter written by R. Krishnaswami Iyer, a lawyer well-versed in the shastras, claiming that there is justification in the sastras for untouchability, also quoting from *Manusmriti* and other authorities. Gandhiji's response to this was also published.

> I spoke in Madras mainly about the ill-treatment and irrational behaviour towards untouchables. Do we treat untouchables in the same way as we treat our mothers and sisters sometimes? Even if I admit my ignorance of the sastras, I can claim to have understood the essence of Hindu religion.
>
> If we continue to practise the kind of untouchability that has been in vogue till now, it would cast a major stain on our religion. To interpret the 'Smritis' wrongly would amount to

offending the basic concept of love intrinsic in our religion. I would, therefore, not hesitate to say that untouchability is the work of the devil. God has endowed Sri Iyer with a few attributes. I entreat him to use those attributes for the service of untouchables. He would then realise the practical, life-giving aspects of our Hindu sastras, as I have.

The Brahmin farmers

Gandhiji was a revolutionary, although some called him a retrograde thinker because of his staunch belief in the caste system. This was, however, the view of people who were unsure of what he meant by the caste system, and his definition of it. They did not know that Gandhiji was a strong opponent of the common misconceptions about caste divisions as held in the past. In 1921, in Thanjavur district, two Brahmin brothers had taken up agriculture, because of which the Brahmin community ostracised them. When the Sankaracharya from Kumbakonam came there, he declared that he would not accept any tribute from Brahmins who committed the sin of physical toil. But these two brothers did not flag in their efforts, and continued to labour on their fields. When one of them wrote a letter to Gandhiji explaining their circumstances, he praised their courage. "Expulsion from an oppressive society is indeed special. You must welcome it. To say that a Brahmin must not wield the plough is a disgrace to the caste system, and against the teachings of *Bhagavad Gita*."

Notes

1. Ramanuja (1017–1137), iconic Tamil Hindu philosopher, theologian, exponent of Vaishnavism and social reformer.

2. Pudukkottai was a kingdom, and later a princely state in British India, from 1680 to 1948.

3. Subramaniya Siva (1884–1925), freedom fighter, writer and 'pure Tamil movement' activist.

4. 'Kalki' Sadasivam (1902–97), freedom fighter, journalist and film producer, husband of legendary Carnatic vocalist and Bharat Ratna, M. S. Subbulakshmi.

19

KANYAKUMARI DARSHAN, 1925

A personal choice

The leaders in Bombay sent out a circular that in Gandhiji's view, the decision of individuals to join as employees of the British government, or join the Navy, responsible for the fall or failure of Indian enterprise, thus bringing down the honour of our country, was their personal choice. The Congress Working Committee later approved and adopted this circular.

Gandhiji meets Tagore

At this time, in September 1921, Gandhiji and Tagore met and discussed the state of politics, but there was no confluence of views; rather, there was an open war of words between them. Tagore felt that, however eminent a person might be, a large country like India cannot be run on one individual's likes and predispositions or otherwise. He also opposed Gandhiji's single-minded exhortation for hand-spinning, to the exclusion of other human industry and activity. Gandhiji had enormous respect for Tagore, and so responded with humility, yet firmness. He said that the Indian people had taken to the spinning wheel, not just because he had said so, but only after thoughtful consideration. He persuaded the poet to consider it holy work and ply the spinning wheel himself.

People's rage

The two-year rigorous imprisonment handed out to the Ali brothers at this time enraged the people. Gandhiji, nevertheless, requested the leaders and the people to show patience. He informed them that he was about to start a protest against the iniquitous laws at Bardoli, a town in Gujarat, and that the effects of that should be studied before proceeding likewise in other places.

The Prince of Wales

The Prince of Wales (traditionally, heir to the British throne) arrived in India at this time. Wherever he went, he was met with strikes and shop closures. A few persons had gone to receive him in Bombay. When Gandhiji heard that the public, angered by this, attacked them and the police force that had been deployed for their protection, he went there and made the crowds disperse, and arranged for first-aid for the injured policemen. He then learnt that such incidents were happening all over the country. Deciding that it was not an appropriate time to begin a protest movement, he temporarily deferred the Bardoli protest, and went on fast to restore peace.

The Madras incident

On the day the Prince of Wales came to Madras, the call for strike was successful. However, incidents of violence were aplenty. There were some policemen in the crowd. Stones were thrown by the public in front of Wellington Talkies. A shot fired by someone from the top of the theatre building resulted in one person's death on the spot. Some others were wounded. As a result, the crowds stormed into the theatre in anger and broke windows and furniture. They also entered the house of the then Minister, Sir Thyagaraja Chettiar, and prevented him from going out to welcome the Prince of Wales.

Gandhiji's worry

When Gandhiji heard about this from Dr Rajan, he was grieved. The success of the strike gave him no pleasure. He was concerned about the violence that accompanied the strike, and, in the *Young India* issue of 19 January 1922, he strongly condemned it.

> The destruction of property cannot be passed off as the work of antisocial elements. It only shows that the people of Madras are not yet ready for the non-cooperation movement and self-rule. Those who claim competence to this right should have been able

to control the compulsions of violence. This [was] not a peaceful strike, because, had shop owners decided to keep their shops open, they would have suffered the same fate as that hapless theatre owner. I believe that the firing by the theatre owner was justified, as otherwise his theatre would have been entered into and reduced to rubble. Further, the intrusion into Sir Thyagaraja Chettiar's house is an act of cowardice, and people taking law into their own hands. This could be because of violent crowds, but it certainly is not the path to be taken by votaries of non-cooperation. Like Bombay, Madras, too, has taught us a lesson. To create the environment for swarajya, we need to work so much more. We should have the belief the peaceful protest will lead us to victory. Or, is it that we believe ahimsa is what we practise for indulging in violence? If so, we should change our attitude. However, I am still of the firm conviction that India has acquired the required level of awareness on ahimsa.

Deeply anguished every time he heard of such incidents from any corner of India, Gandhiji reiterated his criticism of violence in the *Navajivan* issue of 22 January 1922, and said, "What do these incidents teach us? When this rule ends, we will be governed by hooligans … we will not be in governance."

The onus on Congress

On the day of the general strike, many wrote to Gandhiji about the destructive events that took place in Madras. V. R. Rajagopalan of Madras Rajdhani College wrote about how people travelling by trams, including girl students, were attacked. Gandhiji released this letter, saying that the future of India must be wary of such actions, and he hoped that the Madras Congress Committee would accept responsibility for these wrongs.

Subramania Siva

At this time, the government blamed those practising non-cooperation in Madras, saying that they were not acting as per the rules of the establishment, and were betraying the government. The first person to be so accused was the nationalist Subramania Siva. The government said that he had initially claimed ill health and promised to stay away from politics for a specified period, but later said that he had given no such assurance.

Citing this, Gandhiji wrote: "Subramania Siva is a noted worker. I am sure that, like Yakub Hassan, he will explain the complete circumstances of his actions, and state that, had he apologised at all, it would have been in a moment of weakness. If he had given an assurance to stay away from politics for a year, he must honour his words."

Siva's clarification

In a few days, Subramania Siva made public his clarifications to the people and Gandhiji.

> Referring to my release from prison, the government communication about me and my condition at that time could have been misinterpreted by the people of my country. This communication seems to suggest that it was on the basis of my assurances that the government released me from prison. But the order received by the Superintendent of Central Jail, Tiruchirapalli, said: "Under IPC .... the Governor unconditionally repeals the sentence of prisoner Subramania Siva"—that is all. The word 'unconditionally' has been used there, and there is nothing contained of any assurance that I have given, or any other conditions accepted by me. The main reason for my release could have been the recommendation made by the Surgeon General and the District Medical Officer. Hence, I wish to inform the people that I have the right to act as I want.

Siva further said,

> A word about my determination. After my incarceration, I was seriously ill, to the extent that I thought my life was threatened. It was at that stage that I gave an assurance to the government that, should I be released, I would not be involved in politics. Some may interpret this as a weakness on my part, but if they understand the context in which such assurance was given, I believe I have the right to be forgiven.

The given word

Gandhiji's response to Subramania Siva, published in the *Young India* issue of 9 March 1922, indicates just how strict a leader he was. He wrote:

> Whilst it must be expected that one should not ask for forgiveness even when subjected to extreme torture, people should not find fault with the way a person acts under such torment. Siva is right in expecting that he should not be castigated by people for asking forgiveness under duress, but the important aspect to be realised here is that, once you have asked for forgiveness and given an assurance, it should have been adhered to faithfully. Siva should not have used the word 'unconditionally' in his release order to his advantage.

Government oppression

To counter violent incidents, the oppression of the government increased. Ban orders were promulgated all over the country. These were flouted by leaders and workers. Prominent leaders like C. R. Das (1870–1925), Lala Lajpat Rai (1865–1928), Motilal Nehru (1861–1931), Maulana Abul Kalam Azad (1888–1958) and Jawaharlal Nehru (1889–1964), and thousands of workers were arrested. Gandhiji was not. In the Congress Conference at Ahmedabad in December 1921, speaking on the compromise resolution with the government brought forward for debate, Gandhiji said, "I am no doubt a man for compromise, but do not desire the peace of the cemetery."

He brought in the resolution that that there should be opposition to the laws imposed by government, and that this protest should be non-violent in nature. Public meetings should be held all over the country despite the government's ban orders. Workers should join together and peacefully offer themselves for arrest. The resolution introduced by Gandhiji was adopted by the Congress. Though India did not obtain her freedom within one year—as promised by Gandhiji—Indians attained this freedom in their minds. About 30,000 people were arrested in these protests. Many thousands more were ready to be arrested. Gandhiji became the leading light of the Congress. "Prison has become our paradise—a place of pilgrimage," was the clarion call given by Nehru.

Gandhi praises E. V. R.

At the time when E. V. Ramasamy Naicker[1] was dealing with the issue of prohibition in Erode, Gandhiji praised his efforts. "Madras and Andhra are slowly moving forward. I will not be surprised if, like in Bengal, 1500 persons ... get arrested there. In the matter of prohibition, Erode alone is working courageously, with the result that E. V. Ramasamy Naicker has been gifted with one month's simple imprisonment. In this small town, already 37 people have been arrested. Now, Naicker's wife and sister are going to stage a protest," wrote Gandhiji in the *Young India* issue of 22 December 1921.

In the same issue, he also wrote about Rajaji demanding that, in the case brought against him, he be given as long a sentence of imprisonment as possible: "I trust the magistrate will accept Rajaji's demand. His ill health is causing concern to his fellow workers. Hence I believe that the magistrate would transfer the care that is now being given by his friends to the prison authorities."

All-party conference

Thanks to the efforts of Madan Mohan Malaviya and Muhammad Ali Jinnah, a conference of all parties was held in Bombay. On one side this conference deplored the oppressive measures of the government, and, on the other, the Congress was requested that, in the pendency of compromise talks with the government, the protests be deferred. In the all-party committee appointed to examine this issue were Rao Bahadur T. Rangachariar, Srinivasa Sastri, Sir P. S. Sivaswami Iyer, S. Srinivasa Iyengar and C. Rajagopalachari. On the recommendation of this committee, the Congress postponed its protests. The compromise efforts, however, were not successful.

Chauri Chaura

On 31 January 1922, the period for which Gandhiji had agreed to suspend the protest was over, and he sent an ultimatum to Viceroy Reading. The Viceroy, however, did not accept any of his demands. At this time, in Chauri Chaura, a village in Gorakhpur district of the United Provinces (now Uttar Pradesh), there was an incident of violence. Following a peaceful procession, some members of the police force standing by jeered at the dispersing crowd. Heated arguments ensued, and the police resorted to firing. It was only after their supply of bullets was exhausted that the police returned to the police station. The enraged crowd stormed the police station and set it on fire. When 22 policemen rushed out to escape the flames, they were hacked to pieces and thrown into the flames.

'God's warning'

When news spread of the policemen having been burnt alive, Gandhiji was shocked. Pleading with the Congress Working Committee to stop the nationwide non-cooperation protest, he went into determinate action. He fasted for five days as atonement for the violence. God has given us a warning for the third time that India is not yet ready to start a protest against laws, he declared. "Madras gave me a warning, but I ignored it. Now, through Chauri Chaura, God has issued another clear warning to me as to his intention." This move of Gandhiji was resisted by Motilal Nehru, Lajpat Rai and other associates. Nevertheless, at the All India Congress Committee meeting in Delhi, Gandhiji's diktat prevailed.

Six years' rigorous imprisonment

For condemning the British government's unjust rule in a series of articles in *Young India*, Gandhiji was arrested from Sabarmati Ashram on 10 March 1922. C. N. Broomfield, the Sessions Judge who tried his case, sentenced him to six years' rigorous imprisonment. Held initially in Sabarmati jail, he was shifted to Yerawada jail in Poona (now Pune, Maharashtra) where he faced much hardship. During Gandhiji's incarceration in Yerawada jail, Rajaji and George Joseph took over the editorship responsibilities of *Young India*.

Protests against government laws

A committee consisting of Hakim Ajmal Khan, Pandit Motilal Nehru, Rajagopalachariar, Dr Ansari, Vitthalbhai Patel (brother of Vallabhbhai Patel) and Kasturi Ranga Iyengar was constituted to consider whether the protest against the government could be restarted. It concluded that for the time being such protest was not possible. It approved the attending of the legislature by Motilal Nehru, Hakim Ajmal Khan and Vitthalbhai Patel. In December, when the Congress met at Gaya under the presidentship of C. R. Das, he said that attending the legislatures was acceptable. Rajaji brought in a resolution not to attend the legislature. By a large majority it was adopted, and the Congress decided that the non-cooperation movement should continue.

The Swaraj Party

On 1 January 1923, C. R. Das and Motilal Nehru (within the Congress) started the Swaraj Party. There were constant power struggles within the Congress between the Swaraj Party members and others, with the Swaraj Party on the ascendant at times. Ultimately, the Swaraj Party was given permission to contest the 1923 elections.

'A very strange leader'

As president of the Congress in 1923, Maulana Mohamed Ali opined that it would be good if Gandhiji could lead the country from the outside. At this time, in Turkey, as Mustafa Kemal Pasha was elected President, the Khilafat advocates found an unexpected resolution to their problem there. As a result, all those involved in the Khilafat movement in India lost their enthusiasm. The Hindu-Muslim imbroglio eased. In August 1923, under Pandit Malaviya's leadership, at the Hindu Mahasabha meeting, Hindus showed renewed fervour. On another front, extremists started raising their heads in Bengal. The Alipore treason trials happened at this time. Annie Besant, commenting sarcastically on the fate of the present-day politics, said, "Nowadays, a strange kind of revolution is taking place in India. After Tilak, we seem to have found a very strange leader, and the protest, too, is being undertaken in very peculiar ways."

Srinivasa Sastri

The relationship between Srinivasa Sastri (1869–1946) and Gandhiji was as close as that of brothers. When Gandhiji was in Yerawada jail, he was so severely afflicted by an ailment that he had to be rushed to the Sassoon General Hospital in Poona, where he underwent an emergency appendectomy on 12 January 1924, as it was diagnosed that unless surgery was performed immediately, there was danger to his life. "Do you wish to see any of your friends?" he was asked by the hospital authorities, to which Gandhiji mentioned the names of three friends, among whom was Srinivasa Sastri, and it was in the latter's presence that he signed the surgery authorisation form. It was no ordinary task to stand with Gandhiji in those days and get the surgery done. Sastri's plight, in the event of the surgery running into any risk, and his subsequently having to face the wrath of the people, was unenviable. This is why a story by Kothamangalam Subbu (1910–74), titled 'Gandhi Mahan', included a song which went as follows:

> With the responsibility of the nation on Srinivasa Sastri
> He performed his duty to save the Mahatma.
> Had Gandhi died, the country would have thrashed Sastri,
> Thrown soot at him without mercy, for sure, if surgery failed.
> No one else would have given permission for surgery.
> In this situation, Sastri took on the responsibility,
> With no thought of himself, no hesitation.
> Gandhiji came back from the dead, and all was fine.

Indian Review in jail

In 1922, when Gandhiji was in Yerawada jail, he heard from his visitors that the government had permitted newspapers to be supplied in prison. He, therefore, wrote to the jail superintendent to provide him with issues of the *Indian Review*; this showed the respect Gandhiji had for G. A. Natesan and the magazine of which he was the editor.

Sangu Ganesan

As the doctors attending on Gandhiji declared that he needed sea breeze for improvement in his health, he was released from prison unconditionally. He went to a Juhu beach resort to recuperate. S. Ganesan collated and published as books the articles Gandhiji had written in *Young India* from 1919 to 1924. The dedicated interest that Ganesan took in the writings and speeches of Gandhiji was known to all. Hence, if anybody desired to read Gandhiji's writings, he would direct them to S. Ganesan's publishing house. Gandhiji once wrote a letter to Albert C. Mayer (on 15 March 1924) in the USA, saying,

"There are book sellers in Madras by the name of S. Ganesan, who have published most of my articles that have appeared in *Young India*, of which I am the editor. You can find what you need from his publications."

The case against Periyar

Cases were filed in June 1924 against the nationalists from Madras including Periyar E. V. Ramasamy Naicker (EVR). Rajaji, who had gone to Bombay, hastened back to Madras, hearing that the case against EVR was coming up for hearing on 18 October 1924, ignoring even the invitation of Devdas Gandhi to stay for an extra day. "I have to be in Madras on 18th as the final hearing of Ramasamy Naicker's case is coming up on that date. You know that he has been charged with treason. He could be given an extended sentence. He has been the head and master of our Congress activities," Rajaji wrote in a letter, dated 16 October 1924, to Gandhiji from the train.

Periyar and Gandhi

Periyar has personally shared with the author of this book his views at length and several details, referring to the close association he had with Gandhiji. A few excerpts from this correspondence are shared here.

> I had faith in Gandhiji when I was in the Congress. It was 1921, I think, when Gandhiji had come to Erode. He came to our house, where I met him for the first time.
> Gandhiji wrote letters to me twice. At one time he praised the work I was doing. The second time was when I was suffering from severe pain in my hand. "I think this could be because you have been at the spinning wheel for too long. Hence, till the pain subsides, please refrain from hand spinning," he wrote. It was a time when protests against the government were at fever pitch. Thousands of men and women had joined these protests, and been arrested. At that time, Sir Sankaran Nair organised a conference to discuss about taking up peace talks with the government to achieve a political compromise. He laid down a condition that the protests should be suspended before the talks began. Gandhiji did not accept it. "It is not in my hands to stop

this protest. It is in the hands of Erode E. V. Ramasamy's sister, wife and others," he said at that conference.

There was a reason for Gandhiji to speak thus. On that occasion, my wife, who had taken part in the protest, had gone to jail, and many had followed her. Our family had a good influence in Erode. Further, I had served as the Town Council president, with the result that more than the expected number of our friends and associates courted imprisonment. The authorities had to consider promulgation of Section 144 in that area. They, however, desisted, fearing that it might lead to more unmanageable protests. Let individual cases against the protestors begin … we shall consider this ban at that time, was perhaps their reasoning. This became a test case all over India, that Section 144 had been fought and victory obtained. When I was active in the Congress at that time, I was also involved deeply in the spread of Hindi. I started a school in Erode to teach Hindi. That school was inaugurated by Pandit Motilal Nehru. I was also involved with the issue of prohibition in those days. To succeed in this I had the coconut trees in my garden cut down, which was followed by many of my friends in their orchards. There was a question as to whether or not the Congress should contest elections in 1924. My view was that it should not. But Gandhiji gave permission to contest the elections. After this I offered an alternative suggestion. If the elections were to be contested, half the seats should be allotted to Brahmins and the other half to other communities. I took this as a resolution to be moved at the Kanchipuram District Congress Conference. However, this was turned down at this conference. I came out of the Congress. Thereafter, when I had gone to Bangalore to recuperate from an illness, Gandhiji invited me for a compromise. I went along with Thiru Ramanathan, but could not accept his compromise. Finally, Gandhiji listed three things that I should do: 1) The Congress should be disbanded; 2) government should be constituted without the basis of religion; and 3) the Brahmins should involve themselves in religion and allow the non-Brahmins to educate themselves and take up jobs.

I was the President of the Khadi Board first established in Tamilnadu for five years. I set up khadi outlets in important towns, and acquired buildings in these places for the spread of khadi sales. K. Santhanam was the the secretary of the Board.

There was difference of opinion between us in the matter of appointment of persons. Gandhiji intervened and resolved this to some extent. Thereafter, all the khadi boards were integrated into an All India 'Charkha' Sangam. The State khadi boards thereby lost their authority, which grieved me.

Rajaji and Gandhi

It is doubtful whether Gandhiji would have corresponded with any other Tamil leader, or in fact with any other Indian, to the extent he did with Rajaji. The topics of their correspondence ranged from hand spinning to elevated spiritual principles and philosophical questions. Gandhiji opened up even on his innermost emotions and doubts in his letters to Rajaji. In a letter dated 16 July 1925 to Rajaji, for instance, he wrote: "I am in some world where I do not wish to be affected by my mind and body, but at the same time am being constantly tested. My soul is in a world separate from my body. But I am troubled in that world. … want to be troubled."

Such deeply private thoughts he shared with very few.

The split in Congress widens

In June 1924, at the Congress Committee meeting in Ahmedabad, Gandhiji did not consent to changing the resolution he had brought up concerning the extremist Gopinath Saha, as a result of which there was a major 'battle' in the party between him and C. R. Das; Gandhiji won by a slender majority. Noting that some of his closest associates had voted against his resolution, Gandhiji openly wept.

There was nothing comparable to this split in the history of those times. Those who were against any alteration to the resolution on non-cooperation passed in Calcutta were dubbed 'resistors of change'. Stating that the actions taken under that resolution were not as effective as expected, the Swaraj Party members advocated a return to the Legislatures to continue working for the nation. The split between the Swaraj Party members and those who did not want change was further compounded by that between Hindus and Muslims, not just in the south, but throughout India, and the rift between the Brahmins and non-Brahmins. To help restore Hindu-Muslim unity, promote khadi and eradicate untouchability, Gandhiji announced in August-end that he would be willing to temporarily suspend the non-cooperation movement. Even Annie Besant, considered to be Gandhiji's political adversary, accepted his three measures completely, and wrote that if those in charge of the Congress accept this, she would even consider returning to the Congress.

Disturbances

From March 1922 till February 1924, when Gandhiji was in prison, the non-cooperation movement had gone somewhat off the rails. Members of the Swaraj Party re-entering the legislatures was seen by Gandhiji as going against the foundational credo of the non-cooperation movement. Without labouring much on this issue, however, he went about trying to bridge the divide within the Congress towards unity. When he was in prison, the trust between Hindus and Muslims dwindled, leading to feelings of hate intensifying in 1924. There were many disturbances. The heartfelt desire to quench this fire, and finding no other option, led Gandhiji to embark on a 21-day fast that he began from the house of Mohammed Ali in Delhi.

The Madras leaders

As he started his fast, Rajaji and Srinivasa Iyengar, fearing that Gandhiji's frail health would not allow him to withstand its rigours, attempted to stop him. Rajaji sent this telegram to Gandhiji: "Your present health will only lead to your death. Hence please immediately give up your fast.' But in such matters, what Gandhiji decided was unshakeable. Telegrams flew thick and fast between him and Rajaji. Gandhiji was clear in his telegram. "I can successfully complete the fast of 21 days. Initially, I had thought to go on fast for 40 days, but, then, I felt I could undertake a 21-day fast without much trouble, and so reduced the duration." He gave a similar reply to the telegram sent by Srinivasa Iyengar.

An agreement in Calcutta

When this problem had ceased, a fresh one arose. In an emergency enactment by the Bengal Governor, the residences of prominent leaders like C. R. Das and Subhas Chandra Bose were raided and, since no revolvers or arms were found, circulars of the Swaraj Party were confiscated. Though considerably weakened by his fast, Gandhiji left for Calcutta, where there was an agreement between him, Das and Motilal Nehru. With a view to strengthening the hands of Nehru and Das, Gandhiji yielded ground to them on several issues. A communiqué was issued jointly by the three of them to the effect that, barring the issue of swaraj or self-rule, the Congress would defer all its other measures relating to non-cooperation. Gandhiji accepted that, as agreed between him and the Swaraj Party members, that the Swaraj Party, on behalf of the Congress, could attend the legislatures. In return, the Swaraj Party agreed that, as members of the Congress, they would encourage daily hand spinning of yarn.

Differences of opinion

Referring to the agreement with the Swaraj Party, Gandhiji was aware that there would be differences of opinion in the Madras Congress. Therefore, in November 1924, when the Madras political conference was held at Tiruvannamalai (about 120 miles from Madras city), he wrote a letter to the effect that he hoped the agreement arrived at between him and the Swaraj Party would be understood in the proper context by the conference. He believed that, whilst there may be differences within the people here on political issues, they had the attitude to go along with each other.

Opponents of change

All over India, those who were opponents of change condemned Gandhiji, without understanding his mind or motives, for apparently yielding to the Swaraj Party. The All India Congress Committee approved this agreement. Rajaji clarified how much Gandhiji had to concede in order to reach this agreement. Gandhiji knew that among those who did not want this change was his most trusted ally, Rajaji. Hence, to placate him, he kept explaining and justifying his reasons for giving ground. If the measures contained in a resolution were incapable of being translated into action, we should all quit the Congress, Rajaji declared in a letter, which Gandhiji agreed with.

However, he added that it was difficult to predict whether a resolution was actionable or not. Despite Gandhiji's continuing efforts to placate him, Rajaji remained unconvinced.

Rajaji's call to spin

At the end of this argument, Rajaji's belief in the value of the charkha grew. He wrote in the *Young India* issue dated 15 April 1925:

> The spinning wheel constitutes our faith [and] happiness and is our guardian angel. In our waking hours we must work at it, and dream about it at night. Initially I had not realised its value, hence I thought that the Mahatma was treading a path without truth and light. But now I see it very clearly, and trust that all those with the same doubts as me would also see the truth. Spin the charkha, spin, and spin it continuously. Inspire others to do likewise. This is our only mantra, our 'Gayathri.'

Thus, prominent leaders who were major opponents of change started entertaining similar thoughts, and khadi ashrams sprung up across the country. For example, Babu Rajendra Prasad started the Sadaqat Ashram in Patna. Sardar Vallabhbhai Patel established the Swarajya Ashram in Bardoli. On 6 February 1925, Rajaji, too, started the Gandhi Ashram in Puduppalayam, near Tiruchengode (not far from Erode in northwestern Madras State), with khadi spinning as a major activity. One of those who came for the inauguration of this ashram was E. V. Ramasamy. Gandhi Ashram was the first of several such ashrams established, some others being Tiruvennaippatti Gandhi Mission Sangam, Kiruba Ashram, Kalluppatti Gandhi Niketanam, Tirupatthur Kiritthu Gurukulam, Gandhi Gramam and Keezh Mungiledi Ashram. The services rendered by these establishments were significant. Their primary aim was to awaken the national consciousness and prepare the masses for freedom. They also inspired people, especially rural people, into social service and education-related work, making them ideal citizens of a free country.

Gandhiji is Congress president

Gandhiji became president of the Congress at the Belgaum conference in December 1924. That year, Dr Subramaniam and P. K. Naidu had passed away, and Gandhiji paid obituary tributes to them during his presidential address. There was dissension among Gandhiji's associates on his becoming Congress president, with some strongly in favour, and some against. Among close friends who supported his presidentship was Rajaji (Gandhi book, English, chapter 24, page 536). The Gandhi-Motilal Nehru-C. R. Das accord was approved. Since opponents of change would not normally support measures introduced, Gandhiji did not include them in the Congress Working Committee. Dr Varadarajulu Naidu from Madras was taken on as a member of the Working Committee.

L. K. Tulasiram's promise

When a meeting of the representatives from Madras was held separately at the Belgaum session, L. K. Tulasiram of Madurai sent a note to Gandhiji that, by April 1926, he would ensure that 10,000 spinning wheels were working in Madurai city alone. Gandhiji was delighted, and wrote in *Young India*: "If it is possible for Madurai city alone to get 10,000 spinning wheels, does it not mean the introduction of 10,000 Congress members? And if Madurai gets 10,000 members, how many will the whole of Tamilnadu get?"

Disagreements

There were constant disagreements between Gandhiji and Salem Vijayaraghavachariar. Letters had been exchanged between them on whether, after India got freedom, there should be continued relationship with the British. Vijayaraghavachariar wrote, "The connection with the British will be required for a long time—most probably for a century." Gandhiji did not agree.

After the Congress conference, Gandhiji, as a first step, undertook the tour of Kathiawar, Central India, Bengal, Malabar, and Tiruvangur, a village in Kerala. It was on the way to Vaikkom, a town in Kerala, that he came to Madras. In the last week of January, he went to Delhi to preside over the All Party Conference. That differences of opinion between him and the Ali brothers had surfaced was first known through him only then.

Satyagraha

Gandhiji was impressed with the decision taken to stage a satyagraha in Vaikkom town of the Tiruvangur princely domain, to permit Harijans to use the street leading to the temple. His view was not to seek freedom from the governance of princely domains by means of satyagraha. However, the satyagraha undertaken for the specific issue of allowing Harijans access to the temple street had his approval. Against invitations received from various states, he considered it more worthwile to visit this place. Therefore, in 1925, if he came to Madras State and some of its towns at all, it was to and from Vaikkom.

7 March 1925, Madras Central

A massive welcome awaited Gandhiji's arrival at Madras Central station on 7 March 1925. Every feasible vantage point, including on trees, the nearby hospital, and terraces of buildings near the station was taken. Leaders were walking to and fro on the platform, anxiously awaiting the arrival of the train, which, however, had been halted at Basin Bridge, because of the welcome of Perambur workers there. The welcome of the Perambur Congress Committee was read out by its representative, Bhakthavatsulu. It was as if a new life had been imparted by the arrival of Gandhiji, which was mentioned in their welcome. But Gandhiji had little time to linger. So he accepted the welcome, responded to it in a few affectionate sentences of thanks, and was on his way.

At Madras Central station, C. R. Reddy, S. Satyamurthi, V. Kalyanasundara Mudaliar, Dr Varadarajulu Naidu, Alladi Krishnaswami Iyer and K. V. Rangaswami Iyengar were among the many leaders who received him. S. Srinivasa Iyengar travelled with Gandhiji from Basin Bridge.

Government welcome

Almost unknowingly, the state gave an official welcome to Gandhiji. As though the presence of Surendranath Aliya, Ramachandra Udayar and Adikesavulu Naicker was not enough, policemen lined the railway station with their rifles. There were mounted police outside the station. So many had turned up that it took half an hour for

Gandhiji to come out of the station and get into the car which could not move because it was surrounded on all sides by crowds. Gandhiji rose and pleaded, "Please allow the car to move." The people no doubt wished to catch a glimpse of Gandhiji. As he got up, he was visible to all. There were cries of 'Victory to Gandhiji' and 'Allahu Akbar' as the people moved aside to let his car pass. It took the route through Periamet, Chinthadripet, Swami Nayakan Road, Napier Park, Mount Road and Royapettah, to the residence of Srinivasa Iyengar on Luz Church road, where Gandhiji would stay.

Sharanalayam

Once when Gandhiji had visited Kakinada (in Andhra), he was met by some women of ill repute. He advised them to return to the pure life. His advice was not in vain. There was an institution established in Kilpauk (in Madras city), named Sharanalayam, run by Yamini Purnathilakamma. When Gandhiji came to Madras, the first function he took part in was at this institution, where he accepted the welcome address of one Tilakamma.

Municipal Society

The welcome organised by the Municipal Society was impressive, and remarkable in terms of passes being given to hundreds of bonafide entrants, with throngs of people gathered outside the venue. If there was one glitch, it was that the police had not given permission to fly the Congress flag at the meeting. Even the odd flags which were placed at the entrance were confiscated by the police. When it was disclosed that this was done at the behest of the Commissioner of the Society, a resolution condemning his decision was passed at the meeting. European officials did not attend. The Municipal Society had declared the day as a holiday for its staff.

'Your streets are filthy'

After Dr Usman delivered the welcome address, Gandhiji's response followed, and he began on an unexpectedly harsh note, which was necessary for what he had to say: "Madras city is not new to me. I have stayed in this city enough times to study its cleanliness. The streets of your city are extremely filthy. Even adults dirty your streets, hence, compared to other cities, your streets are most unclean. I have myself felt like taking a broom and sweeping your streets when I have had to go through them."

There was no mention of Gandhiji's contribution to khadi in the welcome address. He pointed this out. "Of the small service that I have done for humanity, khadi is among the foremost," he said, exhorting the Municipal Council to take note of it, and to accord khadi a place in every municipal school.

'Khadi, khadi, khadi!'

When some girl students of an arts college met Gandhiji in the afternoon, he advised them to learn spinning. He sat in a broad verandah of Srinivasa Iyengar's house, working on the spinning wheel, as he gave interviews to the press. Their questions were largely about the prevailing political environment at that time.

The *Swadesamithran* journalist asked him: "What are your thoughts about awakening people from their lethargy and infusing them with new energy?"

The *Free Press of India* representative asked: "Assuming that the government introduces fresh oppressive measures, what would be your message to the nation?"

The *Swarajya* correspondent asked: "What is your message for South India?"

Gandhiji's response to all three was: "Khadi, khadi, khadi!"

Beach meeting

The public meeting held on the Tiruvallikeni beach front was huge. Women were present in large numbers. In contrast to the lack of Congress flags at the Municipal Council meeting, there were flags galore here. Gandhiji made his way to the dais through the crowd with difficulty. The meeting was held in Tilak Building. With Srinivasa Iyengar presiding, Satyamurthi translated Gandhiji's speech. The welcome addresses, numbering 11, threatened to be as long as Hanuman's tail! Adi Kesavulu Naicker on behalf of the Madras Congress, Janab S. A. Shafi Mohammed for the State Khilafat

Committee, Madras Mahajan Sabha's C. Gopala Menon, Central Workers' Association's V. Sakkarai Chettiar, Adi Dravidar's (Tiruvallur education society) Jayavelan, and Hindi Prachar Sabha's K. Bhashyam read out addresses of welcome. On behalf of the Andhra Congress and Royapuram Congress Committees too welcomes were read.

No taste for politics

In response to all these welcome addresses, the truth enunciated by Gandhiji should have pleased *New India*. In 1916, that publication had termed Gandhiji an infant in politics, which had then given rise to a public exchange of views. But when Gandhiji spoke about his connection with politics, seemingly in line with what *New India* had written earlier, it was to be expected that they would give it importance—and they did. What Gandhiji said (in March 1925) was this:

> You might have all come here expecting me to speak about the present situation of politics in India, but I am not going to speak on any matters today that are political. I have no taste for it. Although it might be an important constituent in the working of the Congress organisation, I have decided not to worry about it. I am not fond of it, though it does not mean others should not have faith in it. In my time, I have in a way made up my mind about the kind of work I should engage in. If we do what we need to do, there will automatically be daylight after the night. It is most important to improve ourselves…. such awareness that comes from within is the best.

Learn Hindi

On the Hindi language issue, Gandhiji said:

> It is only for you to learn Hindi that Rs. 75,000 has been brought from North India to be spent here, but you are still in a situation of not being able to understand me if I speak in Hindi. At least I should have learnt enough Tamil to have been able to speak to you. Had my incarceration in Yerawada jail been for the full term of sentence, I would have attained this felicity. However, on account of ill health, I was denied this good fortune.

After the meeting, he went straight to Madras Central station and left by Mettuppalayam Mail for Vaikkom.

Erode

The next morning at Erode, prominent Congressmen and surging crowds met him. Because of the chaos caused by the crowds, whoever was appointed to read the welcome address could not reach Gandhiji, nor could he come out and receive it. The railway workers' association's conference was to be held that day. On behalf of the South Indian Railway workers conference a welcome address had been prepared. Among those who had come to Erode railway station to welcome the Mahatma was E. V. Ramasamy Naicker. At Tiruppur, since the crowds were lined up in orderly fashion, it was possible to see him.

Pothanur

At Pothanur (now a panchayat town in Namakkal district), there was some time available for Gandhiji to stand on a chair and speak to the public. He asked them, "How many of you are wearing khadi?" Many hands were raised. "How many of you are spinning?" he asked. Only a few raised their hands. This saddened him. He exhorted everybody to take to spinning, and work for eradication of untouchability.

Oranges for Gandhiji

At Pothanur railway station, a photographer wished to take a photograph of Gandhiji. "You are not wearing khadi. I will not allow you to photograph me," he said firmly. As the train was leaving, a youngster came running clutching two oranges in both hands. Vikramanarayanan (the boy's name) was keen that somehow he should reach the fruits to Gandhiji. The train started, but he ran alongside and managed to hand over the fruits to the Mahatma, who smilingly patted the boy on his back and accepted the fruits. That made the boy's day. One of the people who had come to the station was C. P. Subbaiah Mudaliar (1895–1967), who later served as vice-president of the Indian National Congress.

14 March 1925, Kanyakumari

Kanyakumari, at the southernmost tip of India and Madras, surrounded on three sides by seas and an ocean, is where the feet of Bharata Mata rest. That is where Eswari, as a virgin, undertakes penance, desiring to obtain Eswara of the Himalayas as her husband. For those engaged in the spiritual life, Kanyakumari is an incomparable place of pilgrimage. Even when it was under the rule of the Tiruvangur princedom, the Tamil people had always considered it as part of their province. "It is the holy land called Thenkumari by the Tamils," sang a poet about the glory of Tamilnadu in literature. When Bharathiar sang, "Meditate in Kumari, the edge of the ocean," Kanyakumari was not then part of Madras State, but part of Tiruvangur royalty.

The nation remembers with respect 'Rajarishi' Vivekananda, who came on foot from the Himalayas, and decided to travel to America while meditating on a rock in the ocean at Kanyakumari. It was also here that the father of 'Bhoodaan' Acharya Vinoba Bhave (1895–1982) declared: "Till my work is over, I will travel only on foot."

Welcome at Kanyakumari

Having started for Vakkom (in Trivandrum) from Madras on a Saturday, Gandhiji arrived in Kanyakumari from Trivandrum the next Saturday, 14 March 1925. Resting briefly at the British Resident's House (as a guest of the Tiruvangur prince), he came to stand at the steps of the confluence of three seas, caressing the feet of Bharata Mata and the Goddess. A large wave drenched the Mahatma from head to toe. He smiled and remarked, "It looks like the ocean-mother is welcoming me here."

'Kanyakumari Darshan'

The extent to which Kanyakumari stoked Gandhiji's faith is seen in his essay titled 'Kanyakumari Darshan', in the *Navajivan* issue of 29 March 1925, excerpts of which are produced below.

> I was persuaded by the government guest house authorities to witness the majestic sight of the setting sun before leaving. But our tight schedule did not permit us to stay that long to

enjoy that good fortune. I had to be satisfied with receiving the blessings of the ocean mother through the waves on my feet.

...As far as I am concerned, it was the nectar of spiritualism that was important. As I stood with my feet being washed by the waves at the bathing ghat, an associate of mine said, 'See that stone there?.... that was where Vivekananda meditated.' Whether Vivekananda actually did so or not, it was clear he could. A good swimmer could reach that rock. What else could be found on that island-like rock but peace? The sound of waves, like the seven notes of music would certainly have inspired anyone to meditate. Hence my spiritual desire was truly awakened. The steps on which I stood, and the area around it, could accommodate approximately a hundred persons. I felt like stitting there and reading the *Bhagavad Gita*, but I controlled that desire. I merely meditated on the Giver of the *Gita*, Lord Krishna, as I sat down quietly.

Purifying ourselves in this manner, we proceeded to the temple. Among the heroes of the war against untouchability, I am one. I call myself a scavenger. Hence, I was in doubt whether I could enter the temple or not. I told the temple official that I need not be taken where I was not supposed to go. He told me that the darshan of the Goddess was possible only after 5.30 p.m., and that we had come there at 4 p.m. Hence he offered to first show me around other places. The ban imposed on us was that we could not enter the sanctum of the Goddess, ... a general ban that was imposed on all who had returned from abroad. I said that I would gladly accept this ban, but the temple official, after this conversation, took me into the temple.

Going thus around the temple is itself a means of purification and prayer to the idol of the Goddess. There is no aspect of untouchability in such an activity. That God can be seen through either the Koran or Bible also is a faith that amounts to physically being in front of the idol. There is no discriminatory factor in this either. A Hindu goes beyond this and desires to pray to God in His Physical image. Should he wish to worship God through His stone, gold or silver image, he, too, is deserving of 'Moksha'. As I went around the temple, all these thoughts became clear to me.

But, here, too, my happiness was not untinged by sadness. I had been allowed to go around the full 'prakaram', but, as I had returned from England, I was not permitted to go inside. The ban imposed was on such persons who had been tainted in this fashion, or by birth. How can we countenance this? Can we allow the Kanyakumari Goddess to be tainted? Has this practice been in vogue since time immemorial? It could not be, said my inner soul, and were it so, it is a sin. Merely because a sinful deed has been practised over generations, it cannot become sinless or attain any special distinction. Hence every Hindu must make great efforts to remove this taint from our society. I began to believe that it was in fact his duty to do so.

Nagercoil

Gandhiji left Kanyakumari and went to Balaramapuram (an urbanised panchayat in Trivandrum), and inspected the school for Pulayars (untouchables) run under the auspices of Swarajya Vidya Sangam. Awaiting his arrival, the town of Nagercoil (in Kanyakumari district) wore a festive look, thanks to the efforts of Dr Emberumal Naidu. The Municipality, Nanjil Nadu Farmer's Association, and Scott Christian College students read welcome addresses. On behalf of Nagercoil and Suchindram (a panchayat town in Kanyakumari district), a purse was presented to Gandhiji. He left for Trivandrum the same night.

In Tiruppur

On Tuesday night, he started from Vaikkom, went on Wednesday to Alwaye, Trissur and Palakkad, reaching Tiruppur (now a city in Tamil Nadu) on 19 March 1925, Thursday. The shuttle train from Palakkad stopped as usual for an hour at Pothanur. The plan was for Gandhiji to detrain here and proceed to Tiruppur by car, but, considering the state of his health, and his lack of sleep the previous night, it was decided that he would travel by the same train. It thus gave him the opportunity to rest for an hour. Many women had come from Coimbatore to see him with garlands made of khadi. Gandhiji's halt for an hour here enabled the railway workers' union to welcome him. An address read out by the union leader, S. S. Ramaswami Iyengar, mentioned that among railway workers there was neither any Hindu-Muslim conflict, nor untouchability, which pleased the Mahatma.

The distinction of Tiruppur was that a majority of people who had come to welcome him were wearing khadi. As he was being led in procession to the house of Asher Sait, he saw the large crowds that had gathered, and got up on to a balcony so that all could see him. Before coming to this town, Jayaraman Naicker of Varakkudaippalayam had been doing penance for rain, observing fast for 48 days. Gandhiji gave him an interview and enquired about the conditions of his fast. "You and I have undertaken fast for different reasons. Hence I feel pleased to meet such an associate of mine," he told him affectionately.

Khadi producers

In the afternoon, Gandhiji met those who were keen on khadi. K. Santhanam, secretary of the Madras Khadi Board, was told that khadi outlets should be established in all important towns. In those days, khadi had not come into vogue in Kerala. When Gandhiji went there, many had complained to him that they were unable to get khadi. Hence, at a meeting with the Kerala State Congress Committee, Gandhiji said that khadi sales outlets should be opened in Kerala too (in good humour, he spun Santhanam's spinning wheel and said that it felt good. Santhanam was later instrumental in spreading Gandhiji's views through his writing. B. R. Ambedkar, 1891–1956, wrote a book in which he criticised Gandhiji's views on the Harijan issue; Santhanam wrote a book as a response to this). Sankarappa Chettiar, R. T. Muthusamy Chettiar, K. V. Muthuswami Iyer and Uthukkuzhi Pazhaniappa Thevar, who took interest in the production and sales of khadi, also met Gandhiji. As those involved in the production of khadi were poor, they requested that their stocks be sold on priority. Seeing khadi being produced for people in the south at Iduvampalayam (a locality in Tiruppur) filled Gandhiji with happiness. He also inspected the Congress Khadi Vastralayam and its sales outlet there.

The 'khadi king'

On behalf of Tiruppur Town Administration, and other organisations, welcome addresses were read out to Gandhiji. Muslims read out a separate welcome in Urdu. In the Town Administration's welcome,

Tiruppur was described as the khadi capital, and Gandhiji as its king. "If there is any place that can be called the khadi capital, it is Tiruppur, but to refer to me as khadi king is inappropriate," said Gandhiji with humility. He then proceeded to give examples of the exquisite varieties of khadi cloth being produced in Tiruppur. On behalf of the general public, the people of Velampalayam, and on behalf of Gujaratis, separate purses were presented. Cancelling his trip to Gandhi Ashram from Tiruppur by car, Gandhiji started by train after the meeting was over.

He wrote in *Young India* (16 April 1925), praising Tiruppur: "The production and quality of khadi has grown considerably. Many important measures are being undertaken to bring down the price of khadi, and to make it longer lasting. Tiruppur is the main centre where all these efforts are taking place."

At Gandhi Ashram

Within a few weeks of the inauguration of Gandhi Ashram, Gandhiji came and rested for two days there, much to the pleasure of the Ashram. A cottage had been especially erected for his stay in a grove in front of the Ashram. In the visitors' book at the Ashram, Gandhiji wrote: "I came here on 19 March 1925 evening to visit the Ashram and meet the Ashram people. I spent two happy days at the thatched cottage [put up] separately for me."

Rathinasabapathy Gounder

The next day, on 20 March 1925, after writing articles for *Young India* and *Navajivan*, Gandhiji went to the house of Mirasdar Rathinasabapathy Gounder[2] in the afternoon, and was glad to see several women working on spinning wheels. In the setting up of Gandhi Ashram, Gounder had offered much assistance to Rajaji. Other Gounder Mirasdars had come, too, who declared that they were deeply involved in khadi and hand spinning. At the Ashram prayer time, there was great enthusiasm. In that tiny village, interacting in the mango grove with Gandhiji and the ambience of the Ashram felt like communion with the divine. Rajaji, Agnes Balaji Rao, Ramanathan,

K. Subramaniam and Santhanam participated in this meeting, at which Gandhiji spoke about various kinds of prayer.

Why harmonium?

Gandhiji took rest the next day too, attended prayers in the evening, and spoke about the running of the Ashram. When he spoke at night at the public meeting in Puduppalayam, his references to the harmonium and 'bhakti' songs showed how well informed he was:

> When I saw your musical instruments, I desired to hear your songs sung in your own individual style. I believe that songs have a special place in the fabric of a nation. But there are many kinds of songs. There are songs of discrimination, songs that elevate, and songs that depress. If all songs truly promoted our feelings of 'bhakti', they would necessarily ennoble us. From ancient times in India, such have been the songs. … there have been instruments that we could call our own. Instead of these, the harmonium is being used these days. Can we not go back to the stringed instruments of old? As far as I am concerned, more than the harmonium, it is the sounds of those instruments that echo in my heart, filling me with peace and tranquility.

Kamadhenu

Gandhiji then spoke about the economy of khadi and expressed sadness over many in the gathering not wearing khadi.

> I request those without spinning wheels at home to introduce them. The spinning wheel is our Kamadhenu. Rathinasabapathy Gounder has in his house not one spinning wheel, but several, and when I went to his house, I was delighted to see yesterday the women of his house at work on these wheels. He himself was wearing cloth woven out of yarn spun on the spinning wheels at home. His entire family was wearing khadi. God has given him much wealth. Spinning the wheel or wearing khadi is not for the money....it is for our country and its spiritual upliftment that he does so.

He praised Rathinasabapathy Gounder and his wife at other meetings too.

No free food

Before coming to speak here, Gandhiji was given a donation for feeding the poor. Gandhiji's response was:

> I do not believe in the free feeding of those who have arms and legs, and are capable of finding work. Affluent people, who think that they are doing service by giving money to the poor, are mistaken in my opinion. Such service should be done only to the blind and deaf, who do not have the capacity to find work. Hence, after discussing with Rajagopalachariar, I have decided to use this money to make available cloth at low prices to people in this gathering or in this village. If the really poor register themselves here, and give an assurance that they will wear only khadi henceforward, cloth at lower prices than sold in shops will be made available to them.
>
> If the money now donated is not found enough for all the poor people in this gathering to purchase khadi, I will find more donations for this. But one thing ... they must take an oath only to wear khadi from now on.

The Devadasi way

Members of the Coimbatore District 'Sengunthar' (weaver community) Association had come from Puduppalayam to read out a welcome to Gandhiji. In Tamil, they dwelt on the hardships faced by their sisters who had come through the *devadasi* system. Gandhiji's response was practical, suggesting ways to come out of it: (1) enlist all families in which a girl was compulsorily forced into this system, meet them, and explain how wrong it was; and (2) women who were forced into this profession must be found other work. Spinning alone would not make ends meet for them. They could learn weaving, tailoring and embroidery on khadi too. Since the number of devadasis was not large, this was not expected to be difficult.

Muthulakshmi Reddy

Gandhiji wished that there was at least one person with the strength to dedicate his life to render this service. This person was Dr Muthulakshmi Reddy, whom Gandhiji met in 1925 or 1927. An interesting incident took place at this meeting. Lakshmana Mudaliar, who read out the welcome address on behalf of the Sengunthar Mahajana association, handed over his ear studs and ring as his donation to Gandhiji, who returned them to him, saying that he should use the money out of these jewels as principal, and work for the improvement of the lot of devadasis.

Tiruchengode

When Gandhiji went to Tiruchengode (now a town in Tamil Nadu), he thanked the Tiruchengode Union members, Congress Committee members, and the Youth Swarajya Association for their welcome. Dr Rajan translated his speech. The advice Gandhiji gave at this meeting on khadi was precise. "Today, khadi is the only answer to India's poverty. This is the simple solution to the problem that the intelligentsia has struggled to overcome for generations. The best service you can render to your motherland is wearing khadi."

Harijan boys

The way in which Harijan boys had been nurtured at the ashram gave Gandhiji much satisfaction. He told the local people, "Go to the ashram, and see how Harijan boys have been brought up. Can you distinguish them from boys belonging to other castes? The Harijan boys are as good, clean and God-fearing as the Brahmin boys are."

Foresight

On Sunday, 22 March 1925, the first function Gandhiji attended was at Narayankad Social Seva Sangam at Egmore, where he received the welcome given by T. V. Seshagiri Iyer on behalf of the oppressed classes residing in that area. Speaking at this meeting, he said: "Without the spinning wheel and khadi, no society will achieve fulfilment. You may perhaps laugh, hearing me say this. A time will come when a social worker who does not adopt khadi and learn to spin the spinning wheel will not be considered a social server at all." We now realise how far-sighted Gandhiji was.

He further added: "A harder task master than the Yerawada jail authority is here with me today…S. Srinivasa Iyengar. Hence he spoke about khadi and education alone at this meeting, and has left for the next meeting. I am not against the present system of education, But, as far as my life is concerned, it takes only second place. This education is of no use unless it prepares us for service to our country."

Gandhiji inspected the Whitehat memorial and the Narayankod slum during this visit.

The example of Sita

In Tulasingaperumal Street of Tiruvallikeni, when Gandhiji went to witness a spinning wheel competition among women, he noticed them wearing other kinds of clothes while so competing. On the one hand this saddened him, and on the other it pleased him. In his reply in English (translated into Tamil by S. Srinivasa Iyengar) to the welcome address of Tirumathi Chinnaswami Iyengar, Gandhiji said:

> The redemption of India is in the hands of women. Unless women participate on equal terms with men, my dream of a 'Ramarajyam', that is swarajya, cannot be realised. I have spoken at women's meetings that swarajya is 'Ramarajyam'. Unless there are thousands of Sitas, how can 'Ramarajyam' be established? When Sita walked across India, she was not clad in foreign clothes like you are. Only modern women tell me that khadi is a rough cloth to wear.

Gandhiji exhibited the depth of his feeling at the end of the meeting when he said that participation of people in the meeting, who continued to wear foreign cloth, gave him unbearable sadness. "I do not wish to any more keep hearing my own voice. I just trust that my words this afternoon find some resonance in your hearts."

Kasturi Ranga Iyengar

One of the persons who lent his shoulder to Gandhiji in the freedom struggle was Kasturi Ranga Iyengar, the editor of *The Hindu*, one of India's foremost dailies. He helped Gandhiji in several ways through this newspaper. Not only did he join forces with Gandhiji in fighting against the British Empire, but he had fought with Gandhiji himself. Was he not a part of the same Madras which celebrated the famous saying, 'Even if Siva's third eye opens, what is said is said'? If what

Gandhiji advocated went against his conscience, Kasturi Ranga fearlessly told him so. It was because of this that Gandhiji was fond of him. Hence, when he passed away on 12 December 1923, Gandhiji was grief-stricken. Unveiling his portrait in *The Hindu* office on this day (the office was at the south of the Roundtana), he considered it an honour. The elite of Madras city had assembled to witness the full-length portrait of a newspaper mogul being unveiled by a toothless 54-year-old man clad in just a dhoti up to his knees. The function was held, with Srinivasa Sastri presiding, on an upper floor of the building. On behalf of the paper, its editor, Rangaswami Iyengar, welcomed Gandhiji. Unveiling the portrait that was painted by artist Nagappan, Gandhiji, in his thanks, said that it was his privilege to do so, and that the participation of Srinivasa Sastri in the function was an added bonus.

India's '*Times*'

Gandhiji spoke generously in praise of both Kasturi Ranga Iyengar and *The Hindu*. About Iyengar he said:

> In the world of Indian newspapers, he represented some important aspects. His way was unique, his ironical comments and criticism special. You could not avoid praising him, whether he wrote in your favour or against. His love for the country was unwavering. On several occasions I have found myself not in consonance with his views, but have always respected his decision, because, through his arguments I could analyse the strengths and weaknesses of my views. I have many times been led to believe that he [had] reached a position of such eminence in this State that the editor of *The Times* enjoys in England.

Speaking in praise of his paper, Gandhi said:

> Once a person reads *The Hindu*, he need not go elsewhere to get news about the world. One cannot be without certain newspapers ... *The Hindu* is one among them. The passing away of Kasturi Ranga Iyengar will be condoled not just by people in South India, but by those in the north as well, who like to read what *The Hindu* writes about problems besetting India.

Gandhiji wished greater success for *The Hindu*.

Madras Mail

In the midst of this speech, he also praised the *Madras Mail*, though indirectly. He said that if a person in Madras read both *The Hindu* and the *Mail*, he would be acquainted with whatever is required to be known on both sides of the coin on issues, based on which he could make up his mind. Kasturi Ranga Iyengar's son, K. Srinivasa Iyengar, presented a silver spinning wheel to Gandhiji.

Cosmopolitan Club

When Gandhiji went to Cosmopolitan Club, the Club's vice-president, Justice C. V. Kumarasamy Chetty, received Gandhiji at the entrance, and escorted him in, while V. Azhwar Chetty read out the welcome. The Club's secretary, Dr Venkataswamy, honoured him with a khadi garland, signifying that those in the higher echelons of society were also aware of the compulsions of the time.

"Whether the Indian government or the British government is in power, the problem of poverty among people must be resolved. The spinning wheel is the one instrument that will rescue them from this," Gandhiji said, and went straight to the public meeting on the beach.

Public meeting

There was massive attendance at the beach meeting. Yakub Hassan, who was in the chair, said in his welcome address, "The crowd gathered here exposes the lie of the government that Gandhiji is a gun without bullets, and that he has lost the support of people." Welcome addresses were read out on behalf of the Gujarati Sevak Mandir, Amara Bala Vilasini Sabha, and Nowroji Gokhale Union. At this time, there was widespread criticism that Congress, from being a political organisation, was becoming a social service establishment. Gandhiji's emphasis on khadi and prohibition, not favoured by such critics, was cited as examples of this change in focus. Yakub Hassan pointed out to Gandhiji that this view was now gaining ground.

Gandhiji said in reply:

> I am one who is against Congress being either a social service organisation or a governmental association. If we ignore the

economic problems of society, we cannot achieve freedom. Till Swarajya Party is one limb of it, Congress will be a political organisation. Those who are desirous of climbing the political ladder could well do so through the Swarajya Party. But my politics does not extend beyond the spinning wheel.

The speech turns

Gandhiji's speech was then interrupted by a friend, and so took a different direction. When this person handed over a list of questions to Gandhiji, he proceeded to respond to those questions one by one. "If walking on the street leading to the temple at Vaikkom is permitted to the lower classes, would you thereafter also allow them into the temple? What is your definition of 'Sanatani Hindu'? Should Brahmins sit together and eat with meat-eating non-Brahmins? What are your views on caste divisions? What is the duty of voters in the coming elections? Would you say we should not vote?"—these were the kind of questions engaging the vedic society of those days. We can perhaps surmise how Gandhiji might have responded to them today, but his answer to the question, "Should we vote in the elections?" makes one ponder.

Conditions for casting vote

Elaborating his views on voting, Gandhiji said,

> If someone said they wished to vote, I would first see whether they are wearing khadi. If not, I would lock up the voting sheet in my box. If they are, I would ask them politely, 'Are you wearing khadi just for this occasion, or do you wear it at all other times?' If the answer is 'no', I would again lock up the voting sheet. If the answer is 'yes', I would ask further, 'Good, do you spend at least half an hour daily for spinning?' If I receive a satisfactory reply, and if he was a Hindu, I would ask, 'Among my views, would you accept the one on eradication of untouchability?' Thereafter, 'Would you accept prohibition? Even if all our schools were closed, would you support bringing in this measure?' If still the answer is 'yes', I would examine what their views were on the Brahmin–non-Brahmin problem, and, if completely satisfied with their replies, I would allow them to vote.

Students' forum

After his meeting on the beach, Gandhiji was invited to a group discussion in the evening by students at Gokhale Hall. Receiving their welcome, he spoke of the long association he had with students.

> Till today, I have been regularly meeting students, with the result that I am well aware of the aspirations of the student world. You have requested that I should not lose faith in the student community. How can I lose faith? I have myself been a student. It was in Madras, as I recall, that at a students' meeting, I addressed them as 'my fellow students'. A student should consider his duties before he looks upon his rights. Students must understand the needs of common men, and work for their welfare. Your true education begins only when you leave your schools and colleges. The basis for service and genuine effort lies in the spinning wheel.

'I am your co-worker'

At a workers' meeting, the Choolai (now a developed residential area in central Chennai) Congress, and Madras Literary Society read their welcome addresses. M. S. Subramania Iyer translated Gandhiji's speech. Having addressed students as "fellow students" earlier, Gandhiji now introduced himself to the assembled workers as "I am your co-worker." He explained why he considered himself a worker, and said: "I take pride in being addressed as a spinner, weaver, farmer, scavenger, etc. A person like me will share as much of life's ups and downs that you undergo, the reason being that the future of India lies in your hands." Thereafter he was given a list of workers' grievances. His response underlines how closely he had observed the lives of workers.

> Workers are given to the drinking habit. Many squander their money in gambling. Not working towards peace with one another, you are fighting amongst yourselves. You are envious of one another. On many occasions you do not honestly complete the work assigned to you. You do not consult proper advisors. Whenever something wrong happens, you lose patience, and start believing that violence would redress the wrong. You behave disgustingly towards the lower caste people. If night

schools are opened for you, you do not attend them, nor do you send your children to school. You do not understand at most times what the meaning of a country is, and live for yourselves rather than for your nation. You do not think of those who are poorer than you. You do not wear khadi.

Students in khadi

How delighted Gandhiji would have been if he could visit a students' hostel where all the students wore khadi! Early next morning, on 24 March 1925, his wish was fulfilled when he met the Ramakrishna Home students. The secretary of this home, Rao Bahadur Ramaswami Iyengar, welcomed Gandhiji and his associates and took them around. In his speech to the students, Gandhiji expressed his happiness on hearing that all of them wore khadi, and that all the students of this home were also being trained in hand weaving. He told the students, "Instead of working merely for your livelihood, if you spin and weave with the feeling of sacrificing for the nation, good things will come to you, and the nation, too, will benefit."

'Biggest cooperative in the world'

From there he went to Mylapore Sanskrit College, and accepted a welcome address read out by a student in a North Indian language. At the Tiruvallikeni Urban Cooperative Society in Big Street, Tiruvallikeni, the head of the warehouse, C. V. Ram Menon read out the welcome. Gandhiji, in his speech, said:

> I am running the biggest cooperative society in the world. You may not accept it now, but, in time, you will. I am in the business of enrolling 30 crore people into one cooperative society. Your slogan is 'All for one and one for all'. If you analyse this slogan deeply, you will find the message of the spinning wheel intrinsically embedded in it. Hence, I invite all you cooperators to join my larger cooperative.

Hindi school

When he visited the Hindi Prachar Sabha on the same street, he had to, against his will, speak in English. G. N. Ramaswami Iyer,

V. O. Chidambaram Pillai, Nageswara Rao Panthulu, K. Santhanam, K. Bhashyam, Prakasam, and Alladi Krishnaswami Iyer were among those present. In the end, K. Bhashyam placated the Mahatma somewhat by reading out the vote of thanks in Hindi.

Ayurveda

At the Madras Ayurveda Vaidyasala on Mount Road, its director, N. Ramacharlu, welcomed Gandhiji and presented 25 gold coins. On behalf of the general public, seeking Gandhiji's blessings, the granddaughter of Desachariar presented him a gold coin. Gandhiji told her with a smile that it should not have been wrapped in foreign cloth. The views he expressed at this Ayurveda meet are relevant even today.

> Ancient medicine men have given their lives for research. They have cured diseases without an iota of recompense. Today's doctors must follow these two examples. The Ayurveda practitioners of today are living in this pride of ancient wisdom. The diagnosis of disease is still in its infancy here, not having advanced to the level of the Western nations. Even if there are drawbacks in the Western systems, there is humility and research. The arrogance and desire to get rich quick is predominant among doctors here. Ayurveda cannot be served by such an attitude.

On hearing him speak, some may have begun to doubt why he was invited. Gandhiji then expressed a view that paraphrased what Valluvar had said: "Friendship does not mean that two people pass the time in laughter. It is the pointing out of the wrong deeds of each other."

Prohibition, a Himalayan task

Under the presidentship of Annie Besant, at the prohibition advocates' meeting in Gokhale Hall, Gandhiji spoke emotionally, saying that his mother had inculcated the right ideas in him from a young age, with the result that the concept of prohibition grew step by step in him. When he had spoken about it to the Indians in South Africa, they had asked him, "Westerners can drink, and we cannot, is it?" He had then laughed, and replied: "If I could influence the members of legislature to forfeit their income from liquor, I would do so immediately. If I am told that children cannot be educated without this income, I am ready to pull out these children from the schools." Gandhiji agreed with Dr Besant when she said in her presidential address that unless we know the reasons for why the drinking habit develops, we cannot put a stop to it. Pointing out that it was the poverty and pathetic situation of workers in Bombay that led them to drink, Gandhiji said,

> Hence, by mere speech alone we cannot stop the drinking habit of some. I do not know how serious a problem this is to men and women in the slums of Madras, but if you analyse the causes deeply, you will be highly disturbed. It is not something that can be achieved by one person. This Himalayan task is to be undertaken by each one of you, wherever you are.

Women's Christian College

In the afternoon, when Gandhiji visited the Women's Christian College, the principal, Ms McDougal welcomed him. Before starting his speech, he wanted to know how many Christian girls were present in the gathering. Almost everyone raised her hand. Wherever Gandhiji met educated girls, he told them that the question which always arose in his mind was:

> 'What will India do with these modern girls?' In other parts of the world, education is tailored to where students are going to live in the future. But in India, the world of students is divorced from the people. You must see whether there is a connection between academics and domestic life. If you ask me, I would say that the message you can carry to our villages is that of the spinning wheel.

Manual scavengers' meet

Near the Maniyakkara Hall, at a gathering of manual scavengers, as per Gandhiji's desire, a welcome was read out to him in Telugu, to which Gandhiji replied in Hindi, translated by G. Rangaiah Naidu in Telugu. Emphasising the importance of bathing, wearing clean clothes and observing cleanliness, he advised the manual scavengers to pray to God morning and evening, and he exhorted them not to give up their profession.

In Sowcarpet, Multanis, Marwaris and Gujaratis presented purses to Gandhiji.

The Iyengar feast

That evening, at the grand dinner hosted for Gandhiji by Srinivasa Iyengar, the elite of Madras as well as those of other cities had been invited. The Raja of Ramanathapuram and N. Gopalaswami Iyengar were present, for instance. Gandhiji was running a temperature. Normally, he was against taking medicines. He declared that he was going to fast. This pained Srinivasa Iyengar and his wife. The lady desired that somehow or the other Gandhiji should be made to eat well, and she summoned the family physician, Dr S. Rangachariar, to help convince Gandhiji. Putting on his dentures, Gandhiji reluctantly partook of some bread and fruit juice. Dr Rangachariar noticed this, and he advised the Mahatma, "Bapuji, I believe the amount you eat is more than you require for your life and work schedule. Instead of wearing your dentures for eating and drinking fruit juice, it is better that you enjoy what you eat. At unavoidable times alone, you can drink fruit juice."

The lady of the house wailed aloud in Tamil, "I sent for the family doctor to get Gandhiji to eat more, instead of which he has given this sort of advice! ... Had I known this would happen, I would have sent for some other doctor. I never thought that these two crazy men would end up agreeing with each other!" It was her great affection and respect for Gandhiji that made her speak thus. Dr Rangachariar's suggestions did not please Mrs Iyengar, but Gandhiji heartily approved. Everybody laughed at her remarks. Gandhiji did not comprehend at first, but when someone translated for him what she had said, he too broke into laughter.

Peddanayakanpettai

The final function Gandhiji participated in before leaving Madras was the Congress meeting at Peddanayakanpettai. At the gathering of more than 20,000 people, it was difficult for him even to reach the dais. The welcome address on behalf of the Congress Sabha was read out by S. Venkatasubramaniam Chettiar. It was not enough just to gather in thousands, Gandhiji said—the enthusiasm must be shown in action. If everyone followed the divine path, and did not harbour ill-will towards others, we would obtain our freedom sooner than expected, he added. When the meeting started, there was much clamour. Gandhiji said, "If you must shout slogans, do so musically, and not at random. At specific points, when the leader shouts a slogan, you must repeat after him. If we want to become warriors for our nation's freedom, you must behave like war heroes do. Even if thousands are gathered, you must conduct yourselves in a disciplined and noise-free manner."

Gandhiji's speech was translated by M. S. Sharma. From the meeting Gandhiji left for the railway station. Although he promised the crowd that he would return in three months, it was two years before he could.

Gandhiji hijacked

An interesting incident took place in Madras during this tour, which Gandhiji later wrote about in the *Young India* issue of 30 April 1925.

> In Madras, Srinivasa Iyengar and I took part in a function. The crowds were in a frenzy of emotion. We were travelling by car to reach the venue of another function. The 'bhakthas' wanted to take us through an unscheduled route. I pleaded with them that there was no time, as did the others with me. Iyengar explained the state of my health, but to no avail. I do not say we were kidnapped, but [were] certainly taken astray by the car. They could not understand our anxiety, and it became quite a nuisance. We pulled in the reins at one stage, and got down from the car. The crowd could well have carried me away, if they had wanted. This is an example of the danger involved with crowds. People with good intentions become thoughtless in situations like this.

On which street this happened or when, and why a different "unscheduled" route was chosen is not known.

In the train compartment

Gandhiji left for Bombay by train, along with Ramdas Gandhi (1897–1969), the Mahatma's third son, and others. There was a large crowd waiting at the station. Gandhiji went directly to his compartment and sat down. The people grew restive at not being able to see him. So they were allowed in one by one to see him in the compartment. When the large number of Muslims who had come went and garlanded him, Gandhiji noted with disappointment their foreign clothes, and said, "Why can't you wear khadi?" As the train pulled out of the station for Bombay, cries of 'Vande Mataram' and 'Jai to Mahatma Gandhi' drowned out the engine's piercing whistle.

All efforts for khadi

What Gandhiji had emphasised in this tour was briefly reported by *Swadesamithran.*

> At this time the issue which he emotionally and emphatically stressed on was … khadi. Other administrative measures like social unity, eradication of untouchability, were also dealt with. The greatest problem affecting our nation is poverty. He said that priority attention should be devoted to this problem. His focus on social unity and economic freedom as foundations for swarajya will be accepted by all. For economic freedom, khadi was essential.

In 1925, those responsible for political administration in Madras were well aware that the khadi movement had not yet taken root here. The views expressed by *Swadesamithran* after Gandhiji's tour found echoes in the views of leaders of the government.

> The Tamil people have great affection for the Mahatma, and share his fondness for khadi, but it must be seen and accepted, … how much the khadi movement has spread and how much it has not. At a time when we are happy that Gandhiji has indicated his returning to Madras in three months, we believe that all efforts will be made for the spread of khadi before he comes.

After this tour, Madras girded up its loins to work for promoting khadi. When Gandhiji had come in 1921, he lamented that the state had not done enough for khadi. In 1925, though he did not overtly express disappointment, he did not lavish praise either on this issue (except in Tiruppur). Hence, those involved in khadi promotion now put their heart and soul into it. In 1927, Gandhiji undertook a special khadi tour to Madras. But before that, we must look at two slices of history.

Notes

1. Erode Venkatappa Ramasamy (1879–1973), revered as Periyar, was a path-breaking Tamil social activist and politician who started the Self-Respect Movement and Dravidar Kazhagam, and is known as the 'Father of the Dravidian movement'. He famously dropped his caste title 'Naicker' from his name in 1929.

2. 'Mirasdar' is a hereditary landowner, and a title; 'Gounder' is a title used by several communities in Madras State.

20

THE CHERAMADEVI TANGLE

Beginnings

With the aim of running a *gurukulam*[1] on the pattern of the olden days, to inculcate nationalism among the young, V. Ve. Subramaniam Iyer[2] started the Bharadwaj Gurukulam in Cheramadevi, a panchayat town in Tirunelveli district of Madras State. In those days there was strong support from the general public for setting up such educational institutions by eminent citizens. So when a reputed lawyer and staunch nationalist like V. Ve. Su. Iyer came forward to establish such an institution, and bought land for the purpose, the support he received in response was immense. The Madras Congress Committee donated Rs 5,000 out of its national education fund. Affluent Tamilians and people in favour of such a system also donated liberally for the cause.

T. R. Mahadeva Iyer

In this endeavour of V. Ve. Su. Iyer, T. R. Mahadeva Iyer was his right-hand man. He had participated in the nationalist struggle, gone to jail several times, and had great faith in the *sanatana*[3] system. He travelled to Malaya to raise money for the Gurukulam, and successfully collected more than Rs 20,000 from businessmen there who belonged to Madras. However, instead of bringing back this money with him, Mahadeva Iyer advised them to send it later.

The problem

It was at a time when the Bharadwaj Gurukulam had achieved commendable growth and success that a problem arose—one that shook the whole of Madras State. That even the Mahatma could not untangle it showed its gravity and how twisted it had become. There were about 20 students who resided and studied in the Gurukulam; among them the number of Brahmin students was negligible. These few individuals would not sit and eat with the other students, and had to be served separately.

If this had happened in any other institution at that time, the Tamil people would not have tolerated it. But such a situation in a national gurukulam, that too run by a reputed public intellectual like V. Ve. Su. Iyer, caused them much distress. Dr Varadarajulu Naidu took up cudgels against this. V. Kalyanasundara Mudaliar, Periyar E. V. Ramasamy Naicker and other leaders supported him. In a jointly raised three-point objection, they said:

1. Iyer has every right to run a Gurukulam started as per his desire, but he should have made known his preference at the time of raising of funds for it. To now say that, as per parental wishes, Brahmin boys are being served food in a separate place is unjustified.
2. Did Iyer start the Gurukulam as per the desire of such parents, or was there a higher objective?
3. An ashram that induces caste discrimination in impressionable children is not justified when one raises funds for it from the public.

V. V. S. Iyer speaks to Gandhi

Even Brahmins like Dr T. S. S. Rajan pointed out to Va. Ve. Su. Iyer that to separate only a few students at meal times was not correct, but Iyer was not swayed, and declared that he could not force such children to sit and eat with others. Finally, this problem reached the Mahatma. In 1925, when Gandhiji visited Vaikkom, Iyer went there to meet and discuss with him.

Iyer had known Gandhiji when he went to London from South Africa in 1909. At a dinner organised in London by Dr. Rajan, Va. Ve. Su. Iyer, V. D. Savarkar (1883–1966) and others, Gandhiji was the guest of honour. Gandhiji arrived without announcing who he was, and helped in carrying water, cleaning vessels, and cutting vegetables. When it was later revealed that he was in fact Mahatma Gandhi, all were astonished. This incident is now part of folklore. Iyer and Savarkar visited Gandhiji where he was staying in London, on three days, and asked him several questions, to all of which Gandhiji responded appropriately. These exchanges feature prominently in *Hind Swaraj or Indian Home Rule*, a historically important book written by Gandhiji (1909).

The fact that Iyer chose to go to Vaikkom and raise this matter with Gandhiji was not liked by those who were on the side of the non-Brahmins. Thiru Vi. Ka. expressed his views in *Nava Sakthi*.

> I did not like Sriman V. Ve. Su. Iyer going to Vaikkom and raising the problem of eating together arising in the Tamil Gurukulam to Gandhiji, and seeking a decision. Who does not know of the Mahatma's views on eating together? The Tamil Gurukulam is running owing to contributions from people of different beliefs. Before asking for donations, Sriman Iyer had not said anything about eating together. Later he has found an excuse that parents had so requested. After that it was proposed that every one of the boys would be given the sacred thread to wear, and a common feast be arranged. Now it is being said that it is the wish of the Mahatma. So … can it be said that everything is as per the Mahatma's desire? Had not Iyer opposed the boycott of the Legislature proposed by Gandhiji?

Saiful Islam, Dravidan and other Tamil publications also wrote supporting the stand of non-Brahmins.

Gandhiji's views

At Vaikkom, Gandhiji did not speak in detail with Iyer. He shot off a three-line reply to his letter. He thought it would be better to hear both sides of the issue after Dr Varadarajulu Naidu arrived. But the daily papers reported their versions of what Gandhiji was supposed to have said to Iyer. When Dr Naidu went to Vaikkom and met him, Gandhiji conveyed his views to him on the problem on a sheet of paper, since it was his day of silence. His views were: 1) for now, since some of the *brahmacharis* or celibates at the Gurukulam had been told by their parents to eat separately, their sentiments must be respected; 2) as far as the future was concerned, brahmacharis whose parents objected to common eating should not be admitted; 3) it seems that you have accepted that the cooks at the Gurukulam must necessarily be Brahmins; and 4) you seem to object only to the separation of Brahmin boys from non-Brahmins; this is acceptable.

A secret meeting

After coming to Madras, Gandhiji convened a meeting of select prominent persons (11th date in the month of Panguni, Tamil name for the month from 14 March to 13 April) to find a solution to this problem. Though the meeting was held in secret, the newsapapers reported what Gandhiji and Iyer had agreed upon: the brahmacharis in the Gurukulam should sit together and eat; the cooks in the Gurukulam must be Brahmin; and that in special circumstances, students residing outside could be admitted to the school.

Iyer agreed to this, but Naidu and his supporters opposed the decision that cooks should only be Brahmin. Hence, on this occasion, the mediation on the Gurukulam issue did not meet with success.

V. V. S. Iyer's death

In the meantime, the non-Brahmins in the Congress Committee condemned the action of Va. Ve. Su. Iyer, and demanded that the money they had given to the Gurukulam be returned. In Ipoh city of Malaya, the Tamil residents of the town resolved that, if the rule of students eating together was not brought into force, they would not send the amounts collected for the Bharadwaj Gurukulam from Malaya. Iyer, on his part, was unshaken in his resolve. With neither side yielding ground, the problem remained unsolved. During this impasse, Iyer passed away. The Gurukulam having been established in 1922, its problems arose in 1924. Iyer lost his life in a waterfall in 1925. The running of the Gurukulam was taken up by Mahadeva Iyer, but he could not continue. The ashram stopped functioning, but he was unwilling to hand over the responsibility to anyone else.

In 1925, after Iyer passed away, Gandhiji wrote his obituary in *Young India*.

> Thiru Va. Ve. Su. Iyer's demise in the waterfall will be condoled, like myself, by all readers of *Young India*. Many years ago I had the opportunity to meet him in London. He was then a noted revolutionary. Step by step, his extreme views decreased, but the fire of nationalism continued to burn within him. He was a committed non-cooperation movement supporter. Finally I respected him as an eminent, honest, and hard-working

nationalist in the functioning of the Gurukulam in Cheramadevi. May his soul rest in peace.

Contested claims

After Iyer's death, the Nattukkottai Nagaratthars (a Tamil caste and mercantile community) raised funds for the Gurukulam. They declared that the running of the Gurukulam was now their right as they had raised the funds. But Va. Ve. Su. Iyer's close associate T. R. Mahadeva Iyer claimed that right as his. In July 1927, he went to Bangalore, and presented both sides of the contested claims to run the Gurukulam. However, Gandhiji wrote to him that the funds of the Gurukulam should be handed over to a committee. Thereafter, Dr Varadarajulu met Gandhiji in Bangalore, and Gandhiji declared that no further mediation was required in this matter, and the funds of the Gurukulam should be handed over to the committee immediately. However, Mahadeva Iyer did not comply. It was at that time that Gandhiji came to Madras on his khadi tour.

Notes

1. *Gurukulam* (or *gurukul*) is an ancient Indian traditional education system, where the *shishya* (disciple/novice) lives near or with the guru at an ashram; the guru-shishya tradition is a sacred one in Hinduism.

2. Varahaneri Venkatesa Subramaniam Iyer (1881–1925) was a revolutionary from Tamil Nadu who fought against British rule in India. He is also considered the father of the modern Tamil short story.

3. Sanatana dharma is in Hinduism a traditional, 'eternal' or absolute set of duties or religiously ordained practices incumbent upon Hindus.

21

KHADI

Khadi—Praised by the virtuous
Khadi—Blessed by the gods of paradise
Khadi—Respected by monarchs
Khadi—Sung in words sweet as honey
Khadi—That makes young maidens fall in love
Khadi—That makes people's sadness disappear
Khadi—That invokes all salutary thought
O, Indians! Wear this khadi with pleasure

—'Mugavai Kanna Murugan', Bharatwaji

Those days

There was a time when textiles from India were being exported and worn all over the world. It was a time when all fabrics were hand-spun and woven. The crushing of the handloom professions in Madras was the result, not so much of British rule, as the Industrial Revolution in Britain. In the sixteenth, seventeenth and eighteenth centuries, shiploads of textiles from Madras were being exported to England and the rest of Europe. The East India Company established weavers' colonies in several parts of Madras, produced hand-woven textiles and exported them to Britain. Cloth merchants in Madras, Cuddalore, Masulipatnam, Kanchipuram, Madurai and Salem were paid advances to get high quality textiles produced at these centres for export to Britain. In the eighteenth century, as the exports of such textiles from India were increasing, Britain, to protect its own domestic textile industry from being crushed, promulgated a law that British citizens should not patronise Indian textiles. The situation of great demand for Indian textiles in Britain turned upside down overnight. During the Industrial Revolution, many textile units sprang up in England. The spinning and weaving outfits in India were destroyed by the imposition of various crippling measures, in the wake of Britain looking for markets for its own textiles and raw materials. The spinning and weaving industries of Madras were no exception to this destruction.

Charkha Day

It was because of his undying love for khadi and the spinning wheel or *charkha* that Gandhiji declared his birthday to be celebrated by people as 'Charkha Day'. When asked by leaders to take over the position of president of the Indian National Congress, he at first declined, but on repeated persuasion, he said, "If you wish I will take on this post just once, but I should not be forced to continue in it the next year," and accepted it. But he was the Mahatma: it must be noted in golden letters that till his last days, he remained the head of the Charkha Sangam, and that this was the only position he held till his death.

Gandhiji's travails

However, to discover the wonders of the charkha, the troubles that Gandhiji had to undergo were not few. Nobel Prize-winning scientists could not have put in more tireless efforts in their work. His discovery of the spinning wheel is a big story. His putting it to profitable use is another. Even after making its use profitable, it took him a long time to create awareness about it among the people. It is only after the Congress adopted the spinning wheel as its symbol that this became possible.

The principle of khadi

Khadi played a central and vital part in our freedom struggle, with the common people, nationalists, leaders and everyone involved in the struggle being exhorted to wear khadi alongside boycotting foreign cloth. That Gandhiji sought to further elevate the status and spread of khadi was appreciated by only a few in those days. Those involved in intensive work relating to khadi were naturally also connected with the swadeshi movement and the opposition to foreign cloth. Unlike today, there were no 'fine' fabrics, colours and varieties of design in the khadi cloth of that time. The cloth produced was more or less like sack cloth, and unbleached, but that it still found eager buyers and enjoyed brisk sales is testimony to the untiring toil, day and night, by thousands of unnamed khadi workers across the country—a tremendous sacrifice, without consideration for compensation or recognition.

Avoid ostentation

Gandhiji considered khadi to be a symbol of the poor, hence he did not permit people involved in khadi work to travel by car even at personal cost. He considered travel by car to be ostentatious and believed it would destroy the faith of humble spinners and weavers, sending them the wrong signals. Further, he did not approve of spending thousands of rupees on constructing large buildings for Charkha Sangams. He favoured serving the cause of khadi in the simplest ways. When Ayya Muthu was the secretary, he requested Gandhiji to permit him to own a car at his personal expense, but Gandhiji did not approve. When Muthu was in charge of a khadi unit, and had made good profits, he asked Gandhiji for permission to construct a warehouse for the Charkha Sangam at a cost of Rs 13,000. Gandhiji refused. He declared that any profit made should be spent for the welfare of spinners, weavers and the common people, and to counteract the fluctuations in cotton prices.

The Tamil tradition

Madras was among a handful of states adopting and promoting khadi owing to the following reasons. In 1921, the share given to Madras out of the Tilak Swarajya Fund had been specifically earmarked for the growth of khadi. The funds initially made available by the Congress were utilised for khadi work under its overall supervision. As far as khadi production was concerned, until 1937, Kerala was considered part of Madras. K. Santhanam was appointed the first secretary of the Khadi Board in Madras. He had only one person to help him, a 17-year-old boy, who later became a professor in the Thanjavur Sarvodaya Institution, N. Ramaswami. In 1921, when the khadi movement started, in Tiruppur, Karuppannan Chettiar, P. A. Asher and others started production of khadi by putting in their own funds, helped by loans from the Madras Congress Committee. Under the administration of N. Ramaswami (a relative of Periyar), a khadi *vastralayam* or shop selling clothing and textiles functioned in Erode. This was the Congress Committee's vastralayam, under Periyar's supervision.

Other milestones

At the outset, Periyar had a great regard for khadi and he sold khadi by carrying bundles on his head. Kandasamy Gupta in Tirunelveli district, and Rangasamy Raja in Rajapalayam not only manufactured and provided villagers with spinning wheels at their own cost, encouraging them to spin, they even bought the yarn from them. Investing a lot of money, Kandasamy Gupta established a spinning factory with 4,000 spinners, which was later merged with the All India Charkha Sangam. Kongu Krishnasamy and several others were also active in promoting khadi.

K. Santhanam

In 1923, after K. Santhanam took over the responsibility of khadi work, he established the Tiruppur Khadi Board office, and went on to make improvements in the private khadi producing units in Tiruppur, Rajapalayam, Disayanvilai (now Thisayanvilai), Tirumangalam, etc. His name became the stamp of quality for the sale of khadi items to the eager buyers. The public was protected from the purchase of fake khadi products. The Madras Khadi Board helped the producers and sellers of khadi with investments. From September 1925, the Madras branch of the All India Charkha Sangam contributed to the khadi work reaching great heights here. Tiruppur, in those days, was known as the Lancashire of khadi. Till 1925, as secretary of the Madras Khadi Board, Santhanam, along with Varadachari, K. A. Subramaniam, Ramanathan, W. P. Ignatius and M. G. Vasudevayya, was deeply involved in the administration of khadi. It was the practice for the Mahatma to consult Rajaji before appointing the secretary in Madras. All through 1923 Gandhiji was in jail. He sent Shankarlal Bangar to decide in consultation with Rajaji the organisation of khadi. Rajaji,

Bangar and Santhanam went on a khadi tour of the state, which was why, in 1925, when Gandhiji visited Madras, the khadi organisation had to an extent earned a good name here.

Other Khadi Board administrators

After Santhanam, the Madras branch of the Khadi Board was administered by Thanga Perumal Pillai (the person who worked as his helper was the later-known celebrated writer, 'Kalki' Krishnamurthi), S. Ramanathan, N. S. Varadachari, N. Narayanan, Kovai A. Ayyamuthu, S. Ramanathan, K. M. Sankararajan, Na. Ramasamy and N. N. Subramanian. Thereafter, the headquarters itself took on this work in Madras. In the 1950s and 1960s, the Madras Sarvodaya Sangam was engaged in khadi work. The spread and success of khadi in Madras was due to the indefatigable efforts of all these people. Other individuals who contributed to the spread of khadi in this state included Muthuranga Mudaliar, 'Kalki' Krishnamurthi, owner of *Kalki* magazine, T. Sadasivam, and R. Parthasarathi. Songs of the Tamil national poet, Subramania Bharathi and the Namakkal poet Ramalingam Pillai, as also performers like Viswanath Das and K. B. Sundarambal, who sang on stage, helped in khadi developing strong roots in this state. The credit for the expansion of the Tiruppur Central Vastralayam goes to W. P. Ignatius.

Khadi, district by district

1. *Salem District*: The Gandhi Ashram in Puduppalayam, established by Rajaji, gave the khadi movement in Madras, and particularly in Salem district, a new fillip. The main activity of the Gandhi Ashram was the production of khadi. The surrounding villages and towns such as Tiruppur, Dharapuram (in Tiruppur district) and Tiruchengode were often in the grip of drought and shortages. Khadi production provided the poor of these places with some small income.

2. *Coimbatore District*: In Kaanoor of Coimbatore district, the credit for establishing a self-supporting khadi unit in 1921 goes to C. Balaji Rao, a lawyer in Coimbatore, who left his practice and settled down in the village to run this unit. Two politicians in Coimbatore district who worked for the growth of khadi were C. P. Subbaiah, and Subri.

V. A. Krishnamurthi, a lawyer, who became the first administrator of the Madras Khadi Vastralayam.

3. *South Arcot District*: In the forefront of khadi propagation in this district were Kandasamy Padayachi, Thittakudi Rangasamy Pillai, Balakrishnan Pillai, and Narayana Iyer (related by marriage to Vaidyanatha Iyer).

4. *Thanjavur District*: Alangudi Viswanatha Iyer, Adhiramapattinam Janab Meeran Sahib and Mannargudi Dr Muthkrishna Iyer were involved in khadi production in this district from 1902.

5. *Tiruchi District*: In 1920–22, Dr T. S. S. Rajan and Dr T. V. Swaminatha Sastri played important roles in the development of khadi.

6. *Madurai District*: Lawyer N. Narayana Iyer left his practice at the very beginning, and engaged seriously in khadi production in Tirumangalam and Kundathur. In those days, people involved in politics considered growth of khadi as their life-breath. Prominent among them was Madurai A. Vaidyanatha Iyer. Others who served the cause of khadi for several years significantly were Subbaier, A. Subbarayulu, N. M. R. Subbaraman, Ka. Arunachalam, A. N. Rajan, P. K. Ramachari, Madurakavi Reddiar, Vedarama Iyer, T. R. Padmanabha Iyer, advocate Sivaramakrishna Iyer, Srinivasavaradan and his wife, Padmasini ammal (Madurai), Ko. Venkatachalapathy, R. Gurusamy (Kalluppatti), G. Ramachandran, Tirumathi Soundaram Ramachandran (Gandhi Gram), T. R. Mahadeva Iyer, Kuppuswami Iyer, Amirthalinga Iyer (Dindigul) and several others.

7. *Ramanathapuram District*: G. P. Rangasamy Raja of Rajapalayam and G. A. Pettharaja worked for the growth of khadi from the beginning. S. P. Srinivasa Iyengar (Ramanathapuram), P. S. Krishnaswami Iyengar (Manamadurai, now in Sivaganga District), Rama Iyer (Paramakudi) and Rathina Pillai too played important roles. In Virudhunagar, Prakasa Nadar, Arunachala Nadar and Sankaralinga Nadar showed great interest in khadi.

8. *Tirunelveli District*: Dr Sankara Iyer, Yagneswara Sharma, A. N. Sivaraman (editor of *Dinamani*), Gomathi Sankara Dikshitar and his family, K. R. Krishna Iyer, Harihara Sarma, Soma Iyer, advocate V. Subramaniam, Ponnaiah Pillai, V. Sivaraman, Ramachandra Iyer, A. P. C. Veerabahu, Nammazhwar, S. N. Subramania Iyer, S. V. Sivasubramania Nadar, Tirukoodasundaram Pillai, Subramania Iyer, S. N. Somayajulu, V. S. Pathy, A. K. Muthaiah Asari, and many others featured in khadi work.

9. *Kanyakumari District*: In this district, the persons who were involved
from the outset in khadi work were Dr Emberumal Naidu and his
associates Kasi Padaram and Natarajan. Dr Naidu had 10 looms
in his house to produce khadi cloth. There was a close connection
betweem him and Gandhiji. Returning from Gandhi Niketan,
G. Ramachandran became the manager of the Nagercoil Khadi
Vastralayam, and worked for the production and sales of khadi.

Madras is first

In 1923, the value of khadi produced in Madras State was below
Rs 5 lakhs. By 1944–45, it had grown to Rs 32 lakhs. If one discounts
the inflation caused by World War II (1939–1945), this represented
a three-fold increase in production value. In 1944–45, Madras was
the state that produced the maximum khadi cloth in India at 30 lakh
square yards followed by Bihar, Maharashtra and Uttar Pradesh.

Investments

Under the industrial growth plan after the War, the Indian government
allotted 3,52,000 spindles for Madras. Of these, 2,00,000 spindles were
earmarked for coarse yarn, and 1,52,000 spindles for fine yarn. This
allocation was made by the Central government at the request of the
Madras government for the nine units already operating in the state
and the 25 new units to be started. The Indian government approved
the investments in these units and the licence for imports. The
construction of buildings for the new units was in progress, equity
raised, and arrangements made for machinery. Thus, work on the new
units was at different stages of completion.

T. Prakasam

In 1946, as per Gandhiji's recommendations, T. Prakasam (1872–
1957, then chief minister of Madras Presidency, and later, the first
chief minister of Andhra State) approved the concerted khadi work
to be undertaken in five places under the Madras government.
Prakasam desired that these schemes should be inaugurated on
2 October, the Mahatma's birthday, with his blessings. Gandhiji made
some stringent stipulations: 1) no new yarn or cloth units should be

started; 2) spindles should not be increased in existing units; and 3) permission given earlier for additional spindles should be revoked. Prakasam accepted these conditions, and returned the extra spindles allotted by the Indian government.

Betrayal of trust

The spinning wheels already earmarked for Madras were not accepted back by the Indian government. It was considered a betrayal of trust by the Madras government, and a lawsuit was threatened. This stand of the Indian government was not accepted by the T. Prakasam ministry, which wrote to them to change their position.

At this juncture, the ministry in the Madras State changed. When the new ministry under Omandur Ramasamy Reddiar took charge, it decided to get back the surrendered spindles. Without adopting any of the three conditions imposed by Gandhiji, the new ministry took on the responsibility of swiftly implementing the khadi programme. Ko. Venkatachalam was appointed head of the Charkha Development Authority. With the cooperation of the Charkha Sangam, he made the programme a success. The complete focus on khadi production was considered pivotal to it. S. Ramasamy, secretary of the Khadi Board, ran this scheme for about three and a half years.

Gandhian heirs

J. C. Kumarappa

Thus, new life was given to the khadi programme, that had more or less died. As the progenitor of the concept, Gandhiji could be called the 'Father of Khadi' all over India. In some ways, Rajaji could be called the 'Father of Khadi' in Madras, which enjoyed the unique right and pride in spreading khadi as a village enterprise. Just as Jawaharlal Nehru was Gandhiji's heir in politics, and Vinoba Bhave his spiritual heir, so J. C. Kumarappa (1892–1960) could be termed as Gandhi's heir in the field of economics. A Tamilian, he created a formal foundation and structure for Gandhiji's economic thought. From the time he joined hands with Gandhiji till the very end, he worked without break for Gandhian economics. The services he and his brother, Bharathan Kumarappa rendered towards spreading

Gandhian principles are noteworthy. Bharathan Kumarappa (1896–1957) was skilled in English. He compiled many of Gandhiji's essays on a variety of subjects as books, writing the introductions for the compilations himself, which are deemed to be worthy pieces of writing in their own right.

Ariyanayagam

The heir to Gandhiji's tenets on basic education was another Tamilian, Ariyanayagam, from Jaffna, Ceylon (now Sri Lanka). He and his wife, Asha Devi (1901–72), spent their lifetime giving working shape to his concepts on education. They lived in Wardha, in Maharashtra, spreading among children this education system overseen by 'Bapu' (a title conferred on Gandhiji by Netaji Subhas Bose, on 6 July 1944 in his condolence message on the death of Kasturba Gandhi), untangling problems they encountered from time to time through discussions with him, making course corrections, and improving content and delivery. Ariyanayagam had not only extensively toured abroad, but deeply studied diverse systems of children's education, earning recognition and several prestigious awards in the process.

Rajaji

Likewise, when it comes to the cause of prohibition, Rajaji must be termed the kingpin. No one else in India has done as much as him for this issue. Giving up a profession that would have enriched him, he was regularly seen, khadi bag in hand, containing dhotis, shirts and towels, *Vimochanam* magazine and a few posters, going from village to village to create awareness for prohibition, earning him praise from all quarters. It could be said that Rajaji surrendered his body, wealth, and soul for the cause of prohibition.

Let us now come to the khadi tour of 1927.

22

KHADI TOUR, 1927

Khadi tour

To explain his administrative principles, chiefly on khadi, Gandhiji toured Gujarat and Bengal in 1925. His tour of Bengal was similar to the Noakhali tour that he undertook in later years. Through thorny paths, bushes, marshes, river and streams he walked and went by boat, reaching tiny hamlets in remote interior areas. At one of these places, a youngster walked up to Gandhiji and said indignantly, "In Kanyakumari, you were not allowed inside the sanctum of the Goddess. Who are they to have prevented you from entering? Are you not the sun of this world?" Gandhiji smilingly replied, "Yes, one, there should have been some justice in their preventing me. Or, if I was indeed the sun of the world, I should have not found it necessary to get their permission to go inside."

The demise of C. R. Das

When Gandhiji reached Khulna in Assam, he received the news of C. R. Das passing away in Darjeeling. Leaving aside his tour engagements in Assam, Gandhiji rushed to Calcutta for Das's funeral. He was one of those who carried the bier. He stayed on for several days in Bengal to console and offer succour to the people who felt bereft having lost one of their most precious and beloved sons, Chittaranjan Das.

Swaraj Party merges with Congress

On 22 September, an All India Congress Committee meeting was convened in Patna. Because of the disagreements at Belgaum, the

Swaraj Party's responsibilities were removed. An amended rule was introduced that those who paid four annas per year, or those who gave 2000 hanks of yarn, could become members of the Congress. From being a branch of the Congress, the Swaraj Party was now merged with the Indian National Congress. Another important decision taken at Patna was the establishment of the All India Charkha Sangam.

Government post or service?

At this time, the government was providing much encouragement to parties that opposed the Congress. One party that benefited from this was the Madras Justice Party. When there was a fierce debate going on among Swaraj Party members on whether they should accept government posts as a measure of responsible cooperation, or continue with non-cooperation, Gandhiji, who was at the time touring Bihar, Uttar Pradesh and Kutch, did not offer his views. Completing his tour, he went to Sabarmati Ashram, on the banks of the Sabarmati river in Ahmedabad, to rest.

Tagore's opposition

Many intellectuals did not like Gandhiji speaking in praise of the charkha, including Rabindranath Tagore. The acrimonious debate between Tagore and Gandhiji on this matter is well known.

In the midst of all his preoccupations with work, promoting khadi, the freedom struggle and raging political debates, Gandhiji continued to write his life story once a week in his Gujarati journal *Navajivan*, and his English weekly, *Young India*, from 1925–1929. The serialised writings were later collected and published as *An Autobiography or The Story of My Experiments with Truth*, and translated into Tamil by Kalki Krishnamurthy as *Sathya Sodhanai*.

Elections

Gandhiji attended the Kanpur Congress session in April 1925, presided over by Sarojini Naidu. The Hindu Mahasabha meeting also took place in that pandal. At the same time, under the presidentship of Maulana Azad, the Khilafat Conference too met. In 1926, avoiding outside tours, Gandhiji concentrated on the development of the Sabarmati Ashram, and the work of the Charkha Sangam.

When the general elections were held in November, the Swaraj Party suffered great losses everywhere except in Madras State. Those who had left the Swaraj Party on account of policy differences won. The disharmony between the Hindu and Muslim communities was highlighted in the election propaganda.

Swami Sirathananda's death

A vow of silence undertaken by Gandhiji in 1926 came to an end in December when he travelled to Gauhati. At Sorbhog railway station, he received the news that Swami Sirathananda (also known as Swami Shraddhanand (1856–1926), a holy man of the Arya Samaj, and Indian independence activist), had been stabbed to death. At the Gauhati Congress session in late December 1926, presided over by Srinivasa Iyengar, Gandhiji condoled C. R. Das's death and moved an obituary resolution. It was at this Congress session that it was resolved that every Congressman who desired to vote should wear khadi. Annie Besant decided to join the Congress again, and this was welcomed by all.

Nandi Hills

In 1927, in Comilla, at Kasi Gandhi Ashram, at Benares Hindu University and wherever else he went, Gandhiji's speeches had the same refrain: khadi, khadi, khadi. On 9 January—Sirathananda Memorial Day—Gandhiji and Pandit Malaviya walked up to the Dashashwamedha Ghat in Benares, completed the obsequies, and went to the Kasi Vishwanath temple to pray. Thereafter Gandhiji's tour of Bihar, and the Central Provinces (parts of present-day Madhya Pradesh, Chhattisgarh and Maharashtra) began. He completed this in the middle of March, and proceeded to the Kangri Gurukulam (in Hardwar, now in Uttarakhand), where Swami Sirathananda had stayed. When Gandhiji left for Mysore via Bombay, his health was affected, and he was advised by doctors to take rest, which he did, staying at Nandi Hills, a town in Karnataka.

Gujarat floods, Bihar quake

Whilst Gandhiji was making strenuous efforts to complete the work
he planned to accomplish, he allowed nothing whatsoever to deter
him from reaching his self-determined goal. The Mysore tour was
coming to an end, and he was about to come to Madras. At that time,
Gujarat was reeling under heavy rain and floods. Thousands lost their
homes; many were left clinging to trees for days without food or water
to escape being swept away by the swirling floodwaters. But Gandhiji
did not visit Gujarat, although it was his home state. "I am not resting
here. Not only Gujarat, I am fighting against the hardships faced by all
of India," he said. Seven years later, on his Harijan tour, while he was
travelling to Madras via Kanyakumari, a massive earthquake struck
Bihar, leaving thousands dead. Despite frantic requests asking him to
come there immediately, Gandhiji resolutely completed his Madras
Harijan tour before visiting Bihar.

Krishnagiri

After staying in Mysore for four months, Gandhiji entered Madras
on 24 August, the day he left Bangalore via Hosur and Krishnagiri
(in Madras State). He returned to Bangalore after visiting these two
towns to get a day's rest. There was a tumultuous welcome for him on
the highway entrance into Hosur. P. Seetharamaiah on behalf of the
townspeople, and Nanja Reddy on behalf of the farmers, accorded
welcomes and offered purses. "The only way to eradicate poverty is
through the spread of charkha. The Moderates may have a different
approach, but alleviation of extreme hunger among the very poor,
and ensuring a somewhat comfortable life for them is the essence of
the principle of swarajya," Gandhiji said.

On way to Krishnagiri, the people led by S. N. Venkatarama
Chetty welcomed Gandhiji and handed over a purse at Soolagiri
(or Sholagiri, a large village in Krishnagiri district). He was taken in
procession to Puduppettai (a suburb in Madras city), near Coronation
Hall, Krishnagiri. At the reception in the evening, on behalf of Union
Board Krishnagiri Cooperative Society, and the general public,
welcome addresses were read out to Gandhiji by S. S. Sundaresa Iyer
and O. Venkata Rao, respectively.

'Donate only if you have faith'

Gandhiji unveiled a portrait of Chittaranjan Das, and spoke briefly to say, "Here, on behalf of the Cooperative Society, I was welcomed. Their work is good, no doubt, but unless they include the charkha and khadi in it, the Cooperative will not attain completion." When persons went into the crowd to collect money, he warned, "Those alone who have faith in the charkha need give money." At the end of this meeting, a youngster from Palakkottai, P. V. Pattalam Chetty, proudly handed over to Gandhiji the yarn he had spun. Seeing a gold chain bracelet on his right wrist, Gandhiji said, "Normally, only women wear gold bangles, but you have worn a chain. Why?" When the youngster replied that he would take it off, Gandhiji said, "Then, can you donate it wholeheartedly to the Khadi Fund?" The youth promptly removed it and gave it to Gandhiji.

The government's view

There were disturbing bits of information contained in the communication sent to Delhi by the Madras government on Gandhiji's Krishnagiri visit.

> Hosur is a smaller town than Krishnagiri, lower in economic status, too. That being so, it is surprising that khadi sales in Krishnagiri are less than in Hosur. He emphasised the importance of Hindu-Muslim unity. But the incidents that took place in the town were in direct contrast to this. Some Muslim leaders had printed and distributed a pamphlet containing references to the murder of Swami Sirathananda, the explanations given by Gandhiji to Islamic texts and dicourses, the judgement in the Rangeela Rasool trial, and the anger existing between the Hindus and Muslims. Muslims did not participate in the welcome given to Gandhiji. The next day, on the main road Gandhiji travelled on, rotting leather and wooden footwear had been placed between two trees, as a reflection of the anger of some. There was a board in the middle, on which a charkha was drawn and obscene words had been written against Gandhiji. (It was construed to have been the handiwork of some irresponsible elements). The Muslim leaders decided to send a letter of apology to Gandhiji on this matter. However, in the

meantime, the Hindus distributed a printed rejoinder to this pamphlet. Abuses like "sons of prostitutes" and "pigs" were used in this rejoinder. This was being distributed from a motor car with music being played.

In the meantime, a cabinet consisting of Dr P. Subramaniam, A. Ranganatha Mudaliar, and Dewan Bahadur R. N. Arogyasamy Mudaliar, took office in the Madras government. All three had contested the elections as Independents.

Vellore

Gandhiji, and Kasturba Gandhi, along with Gangadhar Rao Deshpande and Rajaji, arrived in Vellore by Bangalore Express, and were received by the prominent persons and taken to their town. The North Arcot district officials, led by Rao Bahadur K. Krishnasamy Naidu, came to where Gandhiji was staying, and read out the welcome address of the district. In the evening, although entry to the students' meeting at Cobb Memorial Hall was only by passes, there was no shortage of crowds, with college students streaming in and several government officials. While a college student, Natesan, sang the invocatory song, another student, Swaminathan, read out the welcome in English, and Tamil pandit, K. Venugopala Naicker sang a welcome song in Tamil. Displaying exemplary duty consciousness, the president of the meeting attended despite a death in his family. Acknowledging this, Gandhiji said, "I commend you highly for giving permission for the meeting to be held here, and your show of affection to me by attending this meeting in spite of your personal tragedy."

'Heed my words'

Addressing the students, Gandhiji said, "When you leave school and enter your [adult] lives, you will have to become helpful to the people of little means. In one's mother tongue, the word 'student' translates to the beautiful term 'brahmachari,' which means, 'seeker after truth' and 'Godfearing.' Do not discard the combined wisdom of our sages and great men without analysing them." He considered his speech to students in Vellore important because, when he later addressed students in Madras, Gandhiji said, "After much consideration I had given the students in Vellore advice, which has been reported verbatim in *The Hindu* newspaper. I ask those who have not read it to do so, and those who have, to read it again."

Advice to lady doctors

The next day, speaking at a Ladies' Medical College meeting, Gandhiji's advice to the women medical students was: "Many people enter the medical field thinking there is much income to be had in it. Women should not get caught in this desire for money." He admitted that women doctors and nurses were urgently required for India.

Meeting at Gandhi Grounds

In the evening, at the public meeting held in the Gandhi Grounds, one out of seven or eight people in the gathering was a woman. After a musical performance by Narasimhulu Naidu's troupe, on behalf of the Taluk Congress Committee, its secretary Dr Ranganna read the welcome address and presented a purse. The town khadi shop too presented a welcome address. Gandhiji recalled his previous visit to this town with Maulana Shaukat Ali, and its associated incidents. The Hindu-Muslim discord seen in the north was not evidenced here, he said, which had given him much happiness then. Before arriving at the public meeting, Gandhiji inaugurated the Deshbandhu Chittaranjan Das Park and planted a sapling there. The Vellore Town Administration and the Taluk Board presented their welcome speeches on silver plates. Prior to this, some Indian Christians of town colleges met and discussed matters with Gandhiji.

'Mouna' Swami

The 'Mouna' Swami (or silent sage) near Vellore met Gandhiji, as reported by Dr Varadachanar in the *Dinamani* 14 April 1927 special issue:

> When Gandhiji came to Vellore, he had been told by someone of the 'Mouna Swami', who had requested Gandhiji to be brought to him. Devadas Gandhi, who accompanied Gandhiji, approached the Mouna Swami and asked him some questions, to which the Swami replied in writing. He did not answer the

questions, 'Where do you hail from?' and 'How old are you?' When Gandhiji started from Vellore, he invited the Swami to ride with him in his car, which the Swami accepted. After touring with him for five days, he returned to Vellore. Even after the Swami returned to his ashram, he remained in Gandhiji's heart. Writing in *Young India*, he lauded the service of 'Mouna Swami', and exhorted other holy men to follow his example.

1 September 1927, Gudiyattam

On 1 September 1927, Gandhiji went by car in the morning to Gudiyattam (now a municipality in Vellore district in Tamil Nadu). In their welcome address, the people of that town revealed that just a few days before his arrival, there had been a Hindu-Muslim clash, and added that, "Your frail health is in a way a blessing in disguise. If you had come as originally scheduled, you would have been extremely saddened at our plight. It is only now that we have overcome it and come together." He participated in the public meeting that evening and returned the same night to Vellore.

In their ardent wish to meet Gandhiji, a large crowd surrounded the Moosa Bari bungalow where he was staying. From there to the meeting venue the roads were chock-a-block. It was difficult to maintain the peace. Several requests by Rajaji were of no avail. Gandhiji came forward on his own, got into the car, drove up to a shaded spot on the road, and sat down. When the crowd got wind of this, they felt greatly chastened, fearing that, because of their disorderly behaviour, he might not even come to the meeting. However, at exactly 5.30 p.m, the appointed hour, Gandhiji appeared on the stage. Welcome addresses were offered on behalf of the public, and the Taluk Congress Committee (the latter by Shannmuganatha Swamigal). On the way, Pallikonda (a town panchayat in Vellore district) residents gathered on the road presented Gandhiji with a purse in two silver bowls.

2 September 1927, Arni

The next day, he went to Arni (Arani, now a major commercial town in Tamil Nadu), and via several villages, returned at night to Vellore. En route, in Arcot (now an urban area in Ranipet district of Tamil Nadu), at the crowded meeting on the banks of the Palar river, the

Walajah (now Walajapet, another town in Ranipet district) Taluk Congress Committee, the Gandhi welcome group, and the Union Board members read out welcome speeches. A purse from Arcot and its surrounding villages, and a welcome from Ammur village were also presented. Union Board President, A. N. Annamalai Mudaliar presented two purses to Gandhiji. Although Gandhiji arrived that morning at V. G. Seshachalam Chettiar's house in Arni, where he was staying, the public assembled there to see him did not disperse till two o'clock in the afternoon. This was Gandhiji's first visit to Arni, hence there were massive crowds that came to see him from Tiruvannamalai, Polur, Calambur, Timiri, Sethupattu, Vandavasi, Desur, Veeranamur and Tiruvatthipuram. To facilitate the movement of these crowds arriving from all over, shops in Arni had downed their shutters. Although tickets for the meeting, held at Parasurama Naicker's Rice Mill, had been sold, permitting only those who had paid to attend, more than 2000 people attended. Gandhiji delivered his speech briefly, and invited all to come and hear his longer speech at the public meeting.

Before that, he attended the women's meeting, where a large number of children came. A small girl, dressed for the occasion, read the welcome address on behalf of the wife of Parasurama Naicker, and handed over the address on a silver plate. Gandhiji lifted the child, kissed her, and asked, "Child, why are you wearing jewels? Why have you not asked your father to buy a khadi *pavadai* [a traditional skirt] for you? Henceforth, do not wear jewels—wear only khadi." And with that, he put a khadi garland round the child's neck.

Two things

At the Arni Fort grounds, thousands had gathered for the public meeting. On behalf of the Union Board and several other organisations, welcome addresses were offered. Thereafter Gandhiji returned to Madras. On the day Gandhiji returned to Madras, *The Hindu* reminded the people of two things: "It is only recently that Gandhiji has recovered from severe illness. People should behave in such a manner as to not cause any discomfort to him. He has come here to raise money for the Khadi Fund, hence people may generously donate to it."

3 September 1927, S. S. Iyengar's house

With Kasturba and Rajaji, Gandhiji reached the home of S. Srinivasa Iyengar by car on 3 September 1927. Iyengar's grandson Krishnaswami garlanded Gandhiji, as Iyengar's wife and family members welcomed him. Dewan Bahadur R. Ramachandra Rao and C. F. Andrews met and spoke with Gandhiji. Having returned from East Africa, Andrews explained the conditions prevalent there. Workers came to meet Gandhiji at the house through the day. A workers' meeting was also held, in which Gandhiji took part. M. Bhakthavatsalam, future chief minister of Tamil Nadu, met Gandhiji here for the first time. He was then a student of the Law College in Broadway, Madras, (established in 1920). Gandhiji's words left such a deep impression on him that he forgot to take his usual tram that day and got on to another one by mistake. After entering public life, this was his first opportunity to meet Gandhiji. Later, Bhakthavatsalam went along with Gandhiji on his tour of Chinglepet district.

Peravallur

On the evening of Gandhiji's arrival in Madras, he laid the foundation stone for the M. S. M. Railway Employees Society on Perambur Highway, and spoke at a workers' meeting at the neighbouring village of Peravallur. These were his first programmes after reaching Madras. It was fitting that Gandhiji, who had come to spread the word about khadi to the poor, should have laid the foundation stone for the workers' building. "Khadi is for workers even poorer than you," he told them. The Society president, Panchatchara Asari, proposed the vote of thanks. Kasturba Gandhi unveiled a painting of Bharata Mata. In the meeting on Peravallur grounds, M. S. M Railway Employees Society, Perambur Congress Committee and Peravallur Gandhi Sangam presented purses for the Khadi Fund. The Gandhi Sangam had constituted a chit fund system, of which Gandhiji approved. On behalf of Gandhi Sangam, P. Bhakthavatsulu Naidu presented the welcome address.

For an autograph

Gandhiji then attended a students' meeting at Stanes Building on Mount Road, where V. C. Rangasamy presented a purse on behalf of the students. The maximum amount had been contributed by a student, Anandbai, who was duly praised by Gandhiji. When two Americans came up to request for his autograph, Gandhiji demurred at first. But, on repeated persuasion, he agreed, provided they promised to wear khadi. The two thought for a while, and then agreed. Gandhiji gave them his autograph.

4 September 1927, YMCA

The next day, 4 September 1927, by the time Gandhiji retired for the night, he was more than usually exhausted, such was his gruelling schedule. His speeches had been lengthy. From the function at YMCA that morning till the public meeting on the beach in the evening, there were back-to-back engagements. He had some breathing time in the forenoon, but even that was taken up by workers and leaders coming to meet him. His speech at YMCA, with Mukherji presiding, can only be termed a spiritual discourse.

Khadi and spiritualism

A Christian padre in Vellore had met Gandhiji and said, "When you speak about spiritualism, it is a delight to hear you, but suddenly you introduce khadi into it—what is the connection between khadi and spiritualism?" Gandhiji replied, "Virtue and religious life must be seen in action. Jesus has said that the man who does not show this in action cannot hope to find salvation."

The padre continued, "Can you go against the current trend and turn the people's attention to khadi?"

"You have not understood India," was Gandhiji's reply. This discussion was cited by Gandhiji at the public meeting, where he went on to say how khadi was the permanent answer for India.

He wept for the poor

On the way from Arcot to Arni, Gandhiji was greatly affected by the extreme poverty he saw in the villages.

> They are wearing less clothes than I am. What are you going to do for such poor people? Your beautiful sisters wear silk saris.

Is it difficult for you to persuade them to give up these and wear only khadi, that has been tirelessly woven by poor people? Why, does khadi weigh too much, and silk does not? Is the 18 'muzham' sari not heavy, but khadi is? Do our poor sisters in the villages not wear saris?

Even as he was saying all this to his companions, his voice choked and tears came streaming down. He then said firmly,

Those poor people are not going around naked. We, who are overclothed, are the ones who are naked. The message of the charkha is indeed spiritual, which is why it has the power to make an important economic change in our country. I will take this message to the poorest of the poor with full faith in God.

You may laugh at me, and think that this is all the politics I know. But I have not lost faith in you, because I have not lost faith in God. Therefore, the faith I have in the charkha can never be eroded.

Hindus and the *Gita*

When the Tiruvallikeni Hindu High School students presented a purse to him in Singarachariar Hall, Gandhiji asked them, "You call yourselves Hindus…have you read the *Bhagavad Gita*?" Of the more than thousand gathered there, only six people lifted their hands. His talk that day was on the need for Hindus to learn Sanskrit and read the *Gita*. At least one statement made by N. S. Varadachariar at this meeting must have given Gandhiji satisfaction. When he explained the tenets of the Sangam, he said that, out of the donations made by the old boys' association, the first beneficiary would be the boy who displays interest in spinning or any handicraft. The Sangam president, T. V. Muthukrishna Iyer read the welcome address. Another news that pleased Gandhiji was that this was a school where Srinivasa Sastri had been a professor.

State scouts

In anticipation of Gandhiji's visit, the State Scouts Association had decorated their headquarters, Vennala Park, beautifully. Boxing, wrestling and other sports of the Scouts were exhibited in his presence.

The vice-president of the Madras District Council, T. S. Ramaswami Iyer, read out the welcome. In the midst of all this fanfare, Gandhiji was focused on his service.

"My dear brothers, I am no doubt delighted to have witnessed all your sporting activities. However, I will not derive full satisfaction unless your service begins from where it ought to begin. You must wear khadi. It is from that your service must start."

Gandhiji's speech was translated by T. S. Ramaswami Iyer. From there Gandhiji went to the Khadi Vastralayam, and then to the public meeting on the beach.

Foreign loudspeakers

At the public meeting, the large crowd was able to hear Gandhiji's speech clearly, thanks to the loudspeakers provided by the Adyar Brahmagnana Sangam. But in their official communication sent to Delhi on this tour, the Madras government ridiculed this. "On September 4th, at the public meeting held on the beach, speakers discovered by a foreign country were used. No one opposed it. The funds raised by Gandhiji in Madras were not up to his expectations. Hence he made an impassioned appeal for more contributions. In Chinglepet, the members of the Wesleyan Mission had taken an important part in his welcome. A lady read out his welcome address."

Gandhiji's speech in English was simultaneously translated by Rajaji and Satyamurthi. As the Congress conference was to convene in a few months at Madras, Gandhiji made a mention of it. He requested the Brahmin–non-Brahmin differences not to come in the way of the arrangements, and for resolving all conflict between the two communities. He spoke emotionally about khadi. "You refuse to see this simple service right in front of your eyes. I ask on behalf of the nation and crores of poor people, please wake up from this slumber."

The crowd at the meeting stretched from the aquarium on the beach to the office of the Chief Engineer. Gujarati service volunteers in large numbers stood on the road and supervised the crowd's peace and orderliness. Muthuranga Mudaliar, who presided, presented a purse on behalf of the people of Madras city, Purasawakkam workers, Indian Industrial Company employees, the public of Jambazaar and students. On behalf of Purasawakkam workers, Adi Dravidars, and several other organisations, welcome addresses were presented.

Let us at this juncture look at some of the general aspects of this tour.

Purses

During this tour, in every town and almost at every meeting (particularly the public meetings), purses were presented to Gandhiji for the Khadi Fund. All the gifts that he received were generally auctioned, and the proceeds utilised for the fund. At some places, meetings were ticketed, and the collections were taken into the Khadi Fund. When Gandhiji was undertaking this tour, S. Ramanathan was the secretary of the Charkha Sangam. Accompanying Gandhiji were Kasturba Gandhi, Kumari Lakshmi, Rajaji, Mahadev Desai and Kaka Kalelkar (1885–1981, Indian independence activist). The to-be daughter-in-law, Lakshmi (although she did not know it at that time), had a good opportunity to get to know Kasturba during this tour.

Health

In 1927, when Gandhiji was about 58 years old, he was frail and could not speak loudly. At times, even persons sitting next to him found it difficult to hear what he was saying. He needed to be frequently examined by a doctor. A separate railway compartment earmarked for Gandhiji and his group was of some comfort for him. Because of his failing health, he could not visit some places originally scheduled in the tour. Hence, either Kasturba Gandhi or Mahadev Desai went to receive the welcome addresses and collect the money for the Khadi Fund. On this tour, many welcome addresses were handed over without being read.

Brahmins–non-Brahmins

In every town that Gandhiji visited, not only did he speak about the growth of khadi, but he was compelled to address the Brahmin–non-Brahmin problem, such was the major dimension this issue had taken in 1927, becoming a serious impediment to the national movement. Hence, many requested that he must help find some resolution to this vexing problem. Gandhiji had been encouraging all the Brahmins and non-Brahmins he met to find a solution by themselves. The complaint of non-Brahmins was that the Brahmins had Gandhiji in the palm of their hands. Prominent Justice Party leaders were roped in to meet Gandhiji. The issue was placed before him. Gandhiji heard it all carefully, and suggested a way out. To the non-Brahmin leaders who came to discuss it with him, he said, "Ensure that the Brahmin tradition is protected."

A long tour

Khadi being central to Gandhiji's thinking, it was no surprise that this 'khadi tour' of his was so long: two days in Mayavaram (now Mayiladuthurai, a town 281 km from Chennai), four days in Tiruchi, six days in Chettinad (a region mainly in the Sivaganga district of Tamil Nadu), and the tour continued. Owing to his frail health, Gandhiji could not participate in more than one or two functions in a day, requiring him to stay longer at each place to complete his engagements. Of all the tours undertaken by him in Madras, this was the longest.

A servant of the poor

Gandhiji often reminded the crowds that he had come not as the Mahatma, but as a servant of 'Daridra Narayanas' (the poor). It was not enough to donate to the Khadi Fund, he reiterated, but to give liberally for the uplift of the poverty-stricken from the problems besieging them. However, no amount of money or jewels donated would be of any use unless people wore khadi, he warned. He asked that khadi production units be started in many places. If adequate numbers of spinners and weavers were available in those towns, he would have no objection to such units being started, he constantly declared.

For and against khadi

Khadi was wholeheartedly welcomed by the national newspapers and magazines. Only a few, like the *Mail* did not support it, even while not being strongly opposed to it. The *Mail* suggested that Gandhiji had an ulterior motive in promoting khadi: he was using khadi, not as an economic answer to the country's myriad problems, but as an instrument to unite the people of the nation. "How many people can be employed in an activity that cannot provide adequate income?" was the question it asked. In its reply, the *Swadesamithran* said: "Our *Mail* editor seems to have looked at the effect khadi will have on our economy with some trepidation. The time has come for India to produce its own clothes, but we think he is more worried about what will happen to Lancashire."

Supporters of prohibition

In Tiruvallikeni Mani Iyer Hall, Gandhiji had come to speak about prohibition with those who were in favour, where he was welcomed by Sir T. Sadasiva Iyer. Objections raised against prohibition were also discussed, and Gandhiji replied to each of them. The Excise Department minister suggested that prohibition be introduced in two districts as a trial measure, which Gandhiji did not accept.

> This is the wrong way. If it fails in those places, it would cast a shadow on the entire programme to be implemented elsewhere. Unless some people give money to purposely create disturbances in this matter, the Indian people have no objection to prohibition being introduced. Further, successful introduction of prohibition in India will serve as a salutary example to other nations. …
>
> Ask a drunkard's wife to be patient. What will she think of you then? I consider myself the wife of thousands of drunkards, hence I cannot tolerate this. Rather than be in the midst of thousands of drunkards, it is better that our country remain a land of poor people. If the education system in our country is going to be affected by the introduction of prohibition, I am ready to let India be without education.

'My personal institution'

At that time the Hindi Prachar Sabha was in Tiruvallikeni, to which Gandhiji went from this meeting. On behalf of the Hindi Premi Mandal, and the Hindi Prachar Sabha employees and workers, separate welcome speeches were read. "I look upon this as my personal institution. Reading a welcome address to me here amounts to my welcoming myself," Gandhiji said. He presented certificates and awards to students successful in the examinations. Yogi Suddhananda Bharathi, who met Gandhiji here, recounted: "I told Gandhiji that I would give him all the money I had and go off to the Himalayas. Gandhiji replied, 'Keep your money, but you should not go away to the Himalayas. Conduct your penance here. Service of the nation is the highest penance.' I acted accordingly."

S. S. Satyamurthi

S. S. Satyamurthi (1887–1943, independence activist, and mentor of K. Kamaraj) privately met Gandhiji at Srinivasa Iyengar's house (on 3 September 1927), and discussed several issues, including the next Congress conference in Madras, the Madras Legislative Assembly, the Neill Statue Satyagraha (to remove the statue on Mount Road of Colonel James G. S. Neill, who played a major role in crushing the Rebellion of 1857), and other contentious matters. Satyamurthi wholeheartedly accepted the leadership of Gandhiji. But although he supported the decisions of the Congress under Gandhiji, and implemented them, Satyamurthi was not strictly speaking a 'Gandhivadi'. He believed it was wrong to mix spiritual matters with politics. He also openly discussed his differences of opinion with Gandhiji and other leaders. Despite this, when it came to implementing Gandhiji's decisions within the Congress, Satyamurthi was more a 'Gandhivadi' than many others. In his last days, having witnessed Gandhiji's extraordinary efforts, Satyamurthi poignantly acknowledged his greatness, saying that this was indeed a land where mahatmas and maharishis lived and imparted words of wisdom.

The James Neill statue

At the time of the 1857 Sepoy Mutiny, a statue of the inglorious Brigadier General James Neill (1810–57) of the Madras Fusiliers, reviled as the 'Butcher of Allahabad' and killed during the siege of Lucknow, was erected at a prominent place on Mount Road, opposite the police station in Madras. For some time before Gandhiji arrived on this tour, the clamour for removing this statue had been growing louder. Two youths from Madurai who attempted to break the statue were arrested and a case registered against them by the government, which incensed the people. Referring to this in *Young India*, Gandhiji lauded their heroism, and declared: "This statue must be immediately taken down by the Madras Municipality." But this was not done, and the demonstrations continued. When Gandhiji came, the Congress members debated whether to continue the demonstrations or call a temporary halt. T. Kuzhandai, M. S. Subramania Iyer, Krishnasamy Pavalar and Nithyanandam were in the forefront of these debates. Their leader Satyamurthi also showed keen interest in the issue. The Neill statue exemplifies how minutely Gandhiji analysed each issue before taking a decision. He read the legend written at the base of the statue, and declared that what was written was a falsification of history, and that for it to be permitted to remain there was an affront to the nation.

The legend on the statue reads: "A Lieutenant Colonel of the Madras Fusiliers Regiment of the British government, James George Smith Neill was a devoted and self-confident war hero. It is accepted that he stood against and was in the forefront of the Bengal uprising. He honourably laid down his life in the liberation of Lakshmanapuri on 25th September 1857." The Neill statue is now housed in the Madras Government Museum.

A relative of Sir Thomas Munro who served as Governor, Neill was sent to North India to quell what was known as the first war of freedom—the revolt led by the Rani of Jhansi in 1857, where the atrocities committed by him were considerable. Gandhiji knew that he was shot dead by a sniper from the terrace of a house. "A statue is a lifeless object. There is no harm in breaking it, neither is the act violent. However, there should be no harm to the police station personnel nearby. It would not be appropriate to [perform] satyagraha either. Throw mud on it—that would be enough for you to show your protest," he said.

Gandhiji was informed that those who had tried to break this statue were Somayajulu and Srinivasavaradan. "After the failure of the Madurai 'Pattakatthi' Satyagraha (Sabre)?" he asked. Revolting against the Madurai Arms Law, people who were prevented from walking with sabres in hand showed their defiance by doing so on the roads. The Neill statue issue came close on the heels of this, and this is what Gandhiji was referring to. A worker immediately interrupted, "This is not a failure at all. We walked on the roads freely with sabres in hand—no one did anything to us." Gandhiji replied,

> You are fooling yourselves thinking it to be a victory. Seeing that you were carrying just tin sticks in your hands, and that you did not have the support of the public, the government let you go. Merely because you were not arrested does not mean that you achieved victory. Only if the government scrapped the Arms Act, and allowed you to go out on to the streets with weapons of your choice, can your efforts be termed successful. Remember, however, that it is not possible. Even a free nation cannot survive without Military law.

Thereafter Gandhiji declared that the Congress could not formally participate in any satyagraha for the removal of the Neill statue, but that the youngsters should continue their protests. If the young people proved themselves qualified to undertake such a protest, the Congress would rally behind them, he added.

The next day, the workers wrote down their decision, and brought it to Gandhiji. They had decided not to stop the demonstration, for which their main reason was the unification of national feeing through this endeavour. But if Gandhiji openly called for suspension of this protest, they were prepared to do so. Then, addressing Satyamurthi, Gandhiji asked, "What do you say to this?" to which Satyamurthi replied, "There is no objection to Congress taking up this problem." The Congress Committee secretary, Kuzhandai, asked that the matter be deferred by three months.

7 September 1927, Pachaiyappa's College

An attractive welcome address printed on khadi was made by the students of Pachaiyappa's College, and read by a student, V. C. Gopalan. The principal, Chinnathambi, handed over a purse to Gandhiji, saying, "This is a Hindu institution, run on donations from Hindus." Gandhiji spoke expansively at this meeting, on 7 September 1927, for more than an hour. He shared his views on charkha, widows' remarriage, cigarette smoking, and several other issues. But above all else was the old memory of this hallowed hall that touched his heart. When Gandhiji had first come to Madras in 1896, it was in this hall that he had spoken. He mentioned it in his speech, saying, how proud he was to meet the students at that time.

> You must all take an oath that you will not wear anything other than khadi. If you have not so pledged till now, you must do so. Otherwise the funds you have given me will be of no use whatsoever, and only be a burden. A great man from Madras had said that when he died, there would be no need to look for firewood for his funeral pyre—the wood from all his spinning wheels would suffice. Do not belie the words of this visionary.

Important meeting

This meeting proved to be critical on many counts. Muslims and lower-caste students were not being admitted in Pachaiyappa's College at that time. People in the crowd brought this to the notice of Gandhiji, who was upset on hearing this. "Pachaiyappa's College considers itself a Hindu institution, but the fact that lower-caste students are not admitted here brings disrepute to it. Further, to hear that Muslims, too, are denied admission is like pouring hot oil into my ears. I wish to convey my recommendation to the Trustees and Principal of this college to relook at this policy." He reminded them that the High Court decision was to include students of all communities in an institution.

Widow remarriage

One issue that Gandhiji raised at this meeting was revolutionary and radical in concept, and it led to strong opposition. He exhorted every umarried man to take a pledge to only marry a widow.

> How can a girl of 10 or 15 be considered as having accepted to marry? Not having lived with her husband, how could she then be considered a widow? That is why I will term them just young girls. I do not say that they are not widows, but it is your duty to marry such girls is what I say. If such widowed girls are not available, do not get married. If Brahmin boys are unable to get widowed girls from among Brahmins, they should look to marry such girls from other communities. God will forgive them.

He also spoke here about the marriageable age for girls. "They should be at least 16 years old to be married. They could be married even after 20," he said, adding, "I have met girls of 20 who are as pure as Sita."

Royapuram

At the S. I. A. A. Grounds of People's Park, a public meeting was held in which, on behalf of the workers of the Madras Tramways Union, the union leader S. A. Shafi Mohammed handed over a purse to Gandhiji. After this, at the public meeting in the Royapuram Stone Monument Grounds, multiple purses were presented to him. This was the first time Gandhiji was being welcomed in the Royapuram area. When he spoke about the Neill protest here, his words had a timeless appeal.

> Satyagraha has great power, and it has the potential for good. Misused even slightly, it can result in danger, like one drop of poison polluting an entire pitcher of water. There should be no secret in satyagraha, no fear, no self-interest. A little selfishness would destroy the movement. Money is not essential for satyagraha. The importance of satyagraha is in the effort that you make. The more difficulties you overcome, the greater the success.

After Gandhiji spoke, several persons took off their jewels and offered them to him. When the son of Janakiram Naidu garlanded him and offered him some diamonds and gemstones, Gandhiji blessed him.

8 September 1927, Kanchipuram

The next morning, 8 September 1927, Gandhiji reached the temple town of Kanchipuram (or Kanchi) by car. Large numbers of people had arrived the previous night by carts and on foot from Arni and Vandavasi. Gandhiji stayed in the house of V. Rajagopala Iyengar, a government forest contractor. In the grounds near the market, a public meeting was held in the evening. On behalf of the township, the general public, students, and Chinglepet District Congress Committee, welcome addresses and purses were presented. These welcome addresses were often in the form of questions. Gandhiji answered in detail every question that was raised, and lauded the efforts of Kanchipuram for the spread of the charkha, while exhorting the town to do more. "Some Town administrations showed much interest in the charkha to start with, but flagged in their efforts thereafter, causing the movement to die. Here, one or two members of the Town administration should take special interest in the spread of awareness of the charkha."

Question: What more should we do for the extremely poor?
Gandhiji: You must make your children wear khadi. All employees of the Town administration must wear khadi. Complete prohibition should be introduced.
Question: You must do something to bring down the discord between Brahmins and non-Brahmins.
Gandhiji: I am always ready to do whatever is required for the resolution of this problem. I am not in a position to say anything more definite at this stage.

The pride of Kanchipuram

The pride of Kanchipuram was brought out in the welcome address. Referring to it, Gandhiji said: "Your town of Kanchi is revered as a famous holy place all over India. But in sinful deeds, it is very much like other places. A holy place presupposes that most of the people living there are pure of heart. Untouchability and purity of heart are contradictory to one another."

A chit was sent to him that he speak about child widows. He shared the same thoughts here that he had in a previous meeting, and reiterated: "If only I had the authority, I would force the parents of very child widow to get her remarried."

Health check-up

Before coming to Kanchipuram, Dr Rangachariar, who examined Gandhiji, said that his blood pressure was on the higher side. Having participated in innumerable functions in Madras, he was exhausted. Hence, everyone was closely monitoring his health. Consequently, en route to Kanchipuram, he chose not to reply to the welcome offered on behalf of the Poonamallee Union Board.

The gold sovereign

In the auction at Kanchi, there was an unusual incident. In the purse presented to Gandhiji by the Pachaiyappa Cultural Centre, there was a gold sovereign. When it was auctioned, it was bought by Kalyanasundaram Iyer for Rs 1690; however, not only did he return the sovereign, but he also added Rs 3 to it. It was auctioned yet again. Another person bought it for Rs 1490, but he too returned the gold sovereign.

Leather slippers

On Thursday morning, the Perambur Arundhatiyars offered a handsome, gratitude-filled welcome address, and presented both Gandhiji and Kasturba with leather slippers. Gandhiji praised the beauty of the slippers. "I have myself stitched slippers. Even today I can stitch slippers to some extent, but not as beautifully as these. Instead of killing animals to make slippers, it is better to use the skin of animals that have died naturally," he added. He also said that stitching footwear was an honourable profession, and no one need be ashamed of doing so. In the meetings he attended in Madras, the leather workers' meeting was an important one. Some people noticed that the slippers he was wearing were old and had worn out in several places. This was why slippers were presented to him by two persons. They pledged that henceforth they would use only the skins from animals that had died naturally to make leather footwear. However, on visiting their homes and seeing their living conditions, Gandhiji realised that it would indeed be difficult for them to follow his advice, and he, therefore, exhorted them to follow his advice to the extent possible.

North Indian welcome

After returning to Madras from Kanchi, there was a reception early morning the next day, 9 September 1927, at Ekambareswarar Agraharam, where, on behalf of people from North India, including Gujaratis, Marwaris, Sindhis and Kathiawaris, Jawari Govindbhai Purushottam Das read out the welcome address and presented a purse. On behalf of the National Workers' Union, S. S. Dase presented a small purse for the Khadi Fund. The welcome was given in Hindi, to which Gandhiji replied in his mother tongue, Gujarati, and said: "Much of the cloth trade is handled by you. You earn money out of this from simple folk. This is a sin, for which you have to make atonement. Hence I entreat you to start the marketing of khadi. This is your true work, not mine."

Women's meeting

A women's meeting was organised at Tiruvallikeni Singarachariar Hall by Dr Muthulakshmi Reddy, who read the welcome, Tirumathi Lakshmipathy, who presented a purse on behalf of the women, M. E. Cousins, and Lady Sadasiva Iyer. Dr Reddy brought to Gandhiji's attention some major problems faced by women. "We have tried to the best of our ability to get the age of consent for married girls raised to 16, and unmarried girls to 18," she said, and went on to explain in detail the repressive treatment that devadasis routinely faced in temples and in society at large. This was an issue more serious than the advocacy of prohibition, Dr Reddy said, and requested that, along with untouchability and prohibition, Gandhiji also incude the devadasi issue in his speeches, to help raise people's awareness on it and to hasten its end. This request bore fruit immediately, because in most places thereafter, Gandhiji spoke condemning the treatment of devadasis.

Gandhiji's response and advice

Responding at length to Dr Muthulakshmi Reddy's welcome address in his speech, Gandhiji said, "I am very happy to hear that Dr Muthulakshmi Reddy is the Deputy Leader of the Legislative Assembly. I am a proponent of non-cooperation; yet, on behalf of the women of India, I believe that she can do much good work. I ask her not to completely copy the ways of the Western world. She should develop an Indian ambience in the legislature. She should not forget the welfare of women at any stage."

What Dr Reddy had said in her welcome speech was:

> In Hindu society, there is no legal protection or assistance for women. Neither do they have rights. They are forced to be

subservient to their husbands. Their joys and sorrows are in the hands of their husbands. This helpless situation of subjugation [of women] by men is growing. Noted lawgiver, Manu, has said 'Where women are admired, God dwells.' Yet, in another place he has said, 'The wife and the slave have no right to property.' We are observing this directly in front of us today. The wife is not allowed to enjoy any right to her husband's property. She could perhaps ask her husband for living expenses, but has no right to the income that she brings in together with him. Further, the daughter has no right to her father's property. If you consider the right to marriage, it is the same. A Hindu man is allowed to marry any number of women, even when his wife or wives are alive, whereas a woman discarded and disowned by her husband is not allowed to remarry. From the above laws in force, does it not appear that there is one law for men and another for women? How could anyone with self-respect countenance this? Hence, we want justice, equality, and equal rights.

Gandhiji's response to Dr Reddy's speech was thoughtful and deliberate.

Your welcome address was very long. It is doubtful whether some of the women gathered here may have understood its implications fully. I have not time enough to respond in detail to all the questions that you have raised, but I shall certainly look into them later. I do accept that women have a share in rights. If one reads the Hindu shastras, they affirm this. In the Hindu shastras, the concept of 'Ardhanari' is very special. That alone is enough to confirm equal rights for men and women. In English it is termed 'better half'. Although in our country women have been celebrated over the years, there are several atrocities and hardships they are being subjected to today. You must work towards removal of superstitions and other irrational practices forced upon women. If you are prepared for this, first stop getting your daughters married before they turn 16. (*Laughter*). If you have daughters widowed in childhood, you must come forward to get them remarried.

Gandhiji's advice on jewellery to the women present at this meeting also deserves special mention: "I notice that many of the women who are sitting around me are wearing expensive jewellery. Just one of those jewels would provide food for a starving man. Men who toil by the sweat of their brow have no concept of gold, diamonds or silver. Only women's groups know this, and can do something about it."

Dr Muthulakshmi Reddy

The pioneering work done by Dr Muthulakshmi Reddy for the cause of women's welfare and emancipation is well known. There were also others besides her who brought the plight of devadasis, in particular, and women in general, to Gandhiji's attention. On his previous tour, a group of devadasis had met him. But it was Dr Reddy who put their issue into perspective, initiated debate on it, and brought a Bill in the Legislature. She also explained to Gandhiji the deleterious effects of this ancient devadasi custom, and expressly requested him to speak about it wherever he went. An extensive correspondence followed between Gandhiji and Dr Reddy on the subject of women's rights, which Gandhiji wrote about in *Young India* also.

Dr Reddy poignantly recalled her first meeting with Gandhiji in her welcome address to him at the All India Women's Meet.

> I had no opportunity to personally meet the Father of the Nation, Gandhiji [before this], although I had read about the satyagraha he had undertaken in South Africa through newspapers. I went to see him in Madras at Srinivasa Iyengar's residence in 1927. When he saw me he stood up and greeted me like a mother seeing her child, by saying, 'You are now a member of the Legislative Assembly, are you not? What service are you going to do for women there?' I then showed him the Bill I was seeking to introduce in the Assembly, seeking his blessings. Immediately, and without hesitation, he said, 'This bill has my wholehearted blessings. I will write in *Young India* that the general public should support it.' Not only was he true to his word, but it led to a lasting connection between us on women's issues. His childlike nature captivated me.

The extent and impact of Gandhiji's contribution to women's emancipation can be seen in what Dr Reddy wrote on the subject in 1961.

> In 1927, when the Mahatma toured South India, the Indian Women's Association ... had dealt with the issues of child

marriage, abolition of the devadasi system, dowry, the right [of women] to father's and husband's property, educational parity, equal rights, etc. Thanks to the writings and persuasion of the Mahatma, support of national-minded men, and the concerted and continued efforts of women, in free India, today, women occupy significant positions in Legislatures, Parliament and educational institutions. Women-unfriendly laws are being scrapped, specifically child marriage, which has been mostly abolished. The devadasi system prevalent in Tamilnadu temples has faded away. We might say that most of these happened during the Mahatma's lifetime itself. After our country attained freedom, women have started getting equal rights in property. The oppressive dowry stem has also been declared illegal. The education status of village women and their economy has been improving. It is imperative that men and women must collaborate to set right such inequalities through amendments in law.

Deshbandhu Chittaranjan Das

Of special significance was Gandhiji unveiling the portrait of his political 'guru', Deshbandhu Chittaranjan Das, at Satyamurthi Mahajana Sabha. The portrait, presented by Gandhiji, was received on behalf of the Mahajana Sabha by T. V. Venkatarama Iyer. Unveiling Das's portrait, Iyer praised Gandhiji's spiritualism over his politics, while at the same time also requesting him to take more active part in politics. Iyer said,

> Let our political objective be the working towards the freedom of India. Anyone who calls himself an Indian cannot be without a political objective. This country will not accept any political credo not founded on spiritualism. Even if others misunderstand me, I must make my position clear. I will not hesitate even to sacrifice India's freedom in the pursuit of truth, because a freedom based on untruth is no freedom at all.

On this occasion, Serfoji Rao of the Press Photo Bureau presented Gandhiji an album of photographs covering his tour of Madras and surrounding areas.

Adambakkam

The General Public Workers' Association at St Thomas Mount in Adambakkam had been rendering commendable services for the people. It was running five night schools, a free dispensary and a library, and had erected at its own cost 15 street lights. This association, together with the Jain public, arranged a reception for Gandhiji that evening at Adambakkam. This was Gandhiji's final engagement before he left Madras. Praising the association's work, he said, "When you undertake a cleanliness drive, do not leave it half done—it will only lead to more danger."

Satisfaction

The overall enthusiasm people showed for khadi in Madras gave Gandhiji cause for some satisfaction. Before leaving for Cuddalore, he duly conceded that, "Wherever I went, I spoke only of khadi. But the people never tired of it. Many who were not wearing khadi came up and apologised to me. Purses for khadi were also plenty, as were sales of khadi." He was pleased and proud that the concept of khadi was finally well-ingrained.

10 September 1927, Cuddalore

Gandhiji left by Trivandrum Express for Cuddalore on the night of 9 September 1927. As people anticipated that he would finish his Madras tour, go to Ceylon, and then straight to Orissa from there, there was a huge crowd, particularly of students and women, to see him off at the railway station. The Egmore District Railway Superintendent, Shield, had made special arrangements for women to meet Gandhiji at the station.

The train reached Cuddalore on 10 September 1927, at 3.30 a.m. The compartment in which Gandhiji travelled was delinked at Cuddalore, and the train went on to Trivandrum as usual. As it was a very early hour, the station officials had made arrangements for Gandhiji to sleep in the compartment on arrival. At 6 a.m., the Town Council president, Venugopala Naidu, his committee members and the public welcomed him and escorted him to the bungalow of the Nattukkottai Chettiars in Tiruppapuliyur, where Gandhiji would stay.

In the welcome address of the Town Council, it was requested that Gandhiji use all his influence to solve the Brahmin–non-Brahmin problem. Gandhiji, however, said that he would respond to this request only in his speech at the public meeting in the evening. He stayed as a guest of Tiruppapuliyur Rao Bahadur T. N. Muthaiah Chettiar, in Ramachandrapuram.

Students' meeting

From the Cuddalore Town Council office, Gandhiji went to the students' welcome at the YMCA building. At the meeting presided over by Venugopala Naidu, on behalf of the students, P. Swaminatha Iyer presented a purse. Reverend Lang, who welcomed Gandhiji, said that he should speak keeping in mind that it was not a gathering of holy men. Gandhiji responded humorously, while enunciating principles worthy of emulation by sages, and said:

> Had you all been holy men (sanyasis), I would have been put in a grave problem. I have not yet reached that stage. But I am making all efforts to see that I attain that state, and I would be very happy to speak to a gathering where everybody is making similar efforts. In my efforts towards this, I have discovered some truths. 1) The growth of society depends on the growth of an individual. 2) For the growth of an individual, what is required is humility. 3) The individual desiring to do service must elevate himself to be pure-hearted. 4) A pure heart can only be achieved through spiritualism and prayer. 5) Those who want to serve must always be alert. 6) Self-effort is very important, but without God's grace, such effort will come to nought. 7) If you have true belief in God, it will act as your shield.

Public meeting

At a well-organised public meeting held at the Collectors' Office Grounds, Krishnasamy Chettiar on behalf of the District Congress Committee, Srinivasa Iyengar on behalf of the Cuddalore Lawyers' Association and Swarajya Party, and Venkatarama Reddiar and A. P. Reddiar on behalf of the Tindivanam general public, read speeches of welcome and presented purses. Gandhiji's response covered all the welcome addresses presented to him since the morning. Eager surging crowds greeted Gandhiji and his associates on the way at the railway station, making him wonder if it was the people's great love for him or hooliganism that he had been put to so much trouble.

> The train stopped for some time at three stations. The crowds surrounded my compartment and demanded that I show myself at the window. I, however, said firmly that it was not possible, making them very angry. All that anger was turned to the associates who were travelling with me. I had stretched out due to extreme exhaustion, but could not sleep because of the commotion caused by the crowd. I could not decide whether this unruliness was due to affection or hooliganism. Had I shown my face at the window, it is true that my co-passengers would have been happy, but I could not oblige.

Gandhiji requested those who had genuine affection for him not to come at night and disturb him. He said, "On the way I saw a poster which said: 'Love the poor, you will automatically love Gandhiji,'" and added that if everyone followed this, it would be enough.

No solution in sight

After speaking about the charkha, Gandhiji addressed the issue of Brahmins and non-Brahmins raised by the Town Council, admitting that he had no solution in sight, and that he did not in fact know why there was a conflict of interest between them in the first place; he once again advised both sides to come to a mutual understanding.

> I do not have any firm solution to this difficult problem. Even now, I am unable to understand what is the difference of views between them. First the non-Brahmins met me, and said that they would clarify their stand during my tour. The Brahmins, though, never said anything to me. In my lifetime, although I am not a Brahmin, I have spent a considerable amount of time among Brahmins. Hence, some people feel that the shadow of Brahmin thinking has fallen over me, which is why I sometimes feel that non-Brahmins think they cannot get any justice from me in this matter. However, in spite of my ill health, I am prepared to hear both sides carefully. The advice I will give Brahmins is this: 'You are treasure houses of knowledge and symbols of truth. You have accepted a life of poverty also. Hence, give to the

non-Brahmins whatever they want. Take only what they leave for you.'

To the non-Brahmins I say: 'You are greater in numbers. You are also more wealthy. So, what is it that you want? Do not be guilty of generating another kind of untouchability. Do not kick aside the bonds that you have had for generations with Brahmins out of anger. Criticise them, if you must, but do not curse brahmaneeyam. I have come across Brahmins who support the Hindu faith without any fanfare. You perhaps do not even know them. Do not, therefore, believe that I am on the side of Brahmins because I say this, nor feel that I am in favour of Brahmins who are lawyers, ministers and judges. That is not my intention at all. All I wish to say is that both Brahmins and non-Brahmins must free themselves of all wrongs. The non-Brahmins must first understand what their drawbacks are, and then make efforts to overcome them.

11 September 1927, Chidambaram

As Gandhiji was too exhausted to travel, he could not go to Nellikuppam (now a municipality in Cuddalore district, Tamil Nadu). Hence, Kasturba went in his place. After Nellikuppam, the next meeting was at Kotthuvapalli. The plan was to take Gandhiji in a procession from Chidambaram railway station to Nandanarpalli, but as he did not wish to do so, he was taken there directly by car. At the Nandanar Mutt, after Gandhiji laid the foundation stone for the Nandanar temple, the South Arcot Adi Dravidar Mahajana Sabha members accorded him a welcome, read out by Swami Sugajananda. In the inscribed history of the mutt, named after the revered Tamil saint and devotee of Lord Shiva, Nandanar (of about sixth to eighth century), it was stated that: "Realising that the growth of our society cannot happen without education, handicraft, and belief in God, we, through our own efforts, established the temple, mutt, art and handicraft centre in the name of Nandanar in 1926."

Gandhiji was happy for the opportunity to lay the foundation stone for the first such Nandanar temple in Chidambaram, and believed that it would be a temple where one could directly commune with God, as Nandanar had done, and where everybody could enter. "Nandanar did not wish to enter a temple of just stone and sand; he desired the redemption of spirit. Like him, you, too, must aspire for inner purity," Gandhiji said.

A brave request

In the welcome address, there was a brave request made to Gandhiji. "We shall work towards the growth of khadi and abolition of untouchability. For the swarajya and khadi funds, as you have toured all over the country, we request that you make a separate tour for untouchability eradication, and raise funds for it." This request made in a holy place like Nandanar's Chidambaram found fulfilment. In 1934, Gandhiji specifically made a tour to eradicate 'untouchability'.

Nandanar's spirituality

Opposite the railway station, in Kotthangudi Gardens, Gandhiji spoke eloquently about Nandanar's spirituality. Professor Swaminathan, vice-president of Sri Meenakshi College, was present along with students of the college, members of the Chidambaram Town Administration, Arumuga Navalar School students, and the chief editor of Mahatma Gandhi's English compendium. Professor Swaminathan had made the arrangements for Gandhiji's welcome. On behalf of Sri Meenakshi College students, the Lawyers' Association, the Lawyers' Clerks' Association, Paranjothi Swamigal, and the Chidambaram general public, welcome addresses and purses were presented. Gandhiji was in a hurry as he had to leave by train from Chidambaram at 7 p.m., but still managed to find time to speak cogently about Nandanar's principles. Referring to an essay by Rajaji in *Young India* about Nandanar, which had moved him, he said:

> From the time I read this essay, I decided that Chidambaram must be one of the places in my tour. I do not claim that I am the first satyagrahi. I say that everyone can be a satyagrahi. My entire being feels elevated at having come to the place where Nandanar's holy feet have rested. When I have to leave this place in a few moments, my mind will be greatly saddened. Do you know how much I wish that the people of Chidambaram at least do not differentiate between Brahmins and 'Panchamars'? Nandanar withstood the arrogance of Brahmins. That showed

him to be not in a bad light, but a highly elevated status. Adi Dravidars and 'Panchamars' must live according to the doctrine of Nandanar. 1) With a pure heart and sacrifice, Nandanar came forward to break the barriers before him. 2) He did not even descend to ask for his rights. 3) He shamed them through his high prayers, purity and behaviour. If truth be told, God himself came down and opened the eyes of those who had punished him. Why cannot each one of us do today what Nandanar did then? If you could do that, you will transform our nation into one filled with virtuous people.

Moving on then to his favourite subject, Gandhiji said:

At the same time, mere wearing of khadi will not constitute our following Nandanar's footsteps. What is khadi awareness? 1) When we start to wear khadi in the morning, we must remember that we do so in the name of poor people. 2) We must live a life of simplicity at all times. 3) We must always be patient. The people working on spinning wheels and looms know exactly what this means. 4) You must have unshakeable faith in truth and ahimsa. 5) You must practise brotherhood with all living beings.

The Nandanar temple at Chidambaram, a sacred repository of lofty principles, was indeed the appropriate place for Gandhiji to enunciate his philosophy.

Mayavaram

At about 9 p.m., the train was to have reached Mayavaram. On account of the huge crowds assembled at the station at that hour, the time of the train's arrival was kept secret, bearing in mind the difficulty of receiving Gandhiji there and the problems he would face. But somehow the crowds got wind of this, and thronged the station. Hence, with no other recourse, Gandhiji was made to alight at Needur railway station, north of Mayavaram, and taken to the residence of Mayavaram Taluk Board vice-president, S. Thillainayagam Pillai (Ranga Vilas) in Tiruvazhundur on the banks of the Kaveri. The crowds returned disappointed from Mayavaram station.

12 September 1927, Day of Silence

Monday was Gandhiji's day of silence, and therefore no function had been organised for him on this day. People in thousands, nevertheless, flocked to his place of residence to see him. In honour of his visit, all the schools under the town administration had declared a holiday. The school children, along with others, had also been trained on how to conduct themselves in an orderly fashion at the public meeting the next day.

13 September 1927, Raja Park

The next day, at the public meeting in Raja Park, the conduct of the school children, Congress workers, and police personnel was exemplary, thanks to the training given. A traditional welcome was offered by the Mayavaram Town Council, Taluk Board, Town Council High School teachers, students, Mayavaram High School students, Tiruchampalli Sembanarkoil Congress Sabha, the Kuvalaikkal villagers of Nannilam taluk, and the Tharangambadi South India Depressed Classes Sangam. On behalf of the people of Mayavaram town, Karkudi R. Chinnaiah Pillai, on behalf of Kuvalaikkal villagers, Natesa Iyer, and on behalf of Kodai Vilagam people, S. Sambandham Pillai, and others presented purses. A few days before Gandhiji's arrival, a benefit drama, acted in by Velunayar Ananthanarayana Iyer, was staged under the auspices of the Sri Ranga Vinodha Sabha for raising funds for the khadi movement.

Inculcate cleanliness

The absence of cleanliness was a key reason for Gandhiji to leave early. There were beautiful ponds and orchards close to where he was staying. One had only to cross a bamboo bridge to reach the pond. But when he went there, he found people performing their ablutions, and the air had an unbearable stink. At the same spot, he saw a young girl filling her pot with drinking water. All this pained Gandhiji, and he mentioned it at the meeting. "There is a huge mistake in all this, that is certain. The first thing a Town Council should ensure is cleanliness and pure water to drink." To those who wished to become town council members, Gandhiji said:

You should not join the Council for the mere status that you get. You should keep your town clean, and approach it with the mentality of a scavenger. You have so many schools. Give those students a day's leave and ask them to clean the roads. Ask them to spread the word among the public about the importance of keeping your streets and water clean. What is the use if cleanliness is not properly inculcated in schools?

Gandhiji considered this speech in Mayavaram important, because in Tiruchi, on account of his inability to address the public, he said, "I will bring to your attention the speech I gave in Mayavaram."

Panchamars of Tharangambadi

The conflict between landowners and the Harijan Workers' Organisation had existed in one form or another even in those days. The welcome address of the Tharamgambadi South India Depressed Classes Association raised complaints that their predicament was caused by caste Hindus, that the government did not offer them any posts, their annual income was less than Rs 40, while their expenses were Rs 120, and that for most of the year they went without work. Gandhiji's response was clear and measured.

> I do not know how far these accusations are true. I will ascertain this from my discussions with others later. Still, the depressed classes have my full sympathies. I also accept when they say that they are the true owners of the land. However, they need not despair to the extent they have stated in their welcome address. They need to depend on hard work and faith in their own strength. No one can then assail them, and they need not be subservient to anyone. Without your hard work, the land will only remain as bushes.

Having advised the depressed classes thus, Gandhiji then turned to the landowners.

> Even if the complaints in this welcome are true to some extent, they give a very poor impression of the landowners. You should not bite the ears of those who lean on you. These are the workers who bring fertility to your land, making it flower and bear fruit. You must therefore treat them as members of your household,

and share the profits from your land with them. To say that your own workers are untouchable is a sin.

When Gandhiji had visited Tharangambadi in 1915, there were problems raised by the Panchamars; these were firmly dealt with by him only now at Mayavaram.

Isai Velallar

In the afternoon, members of the Isai Velallar community, a minstrel community traditionally engaged as performers of classical dance and music in Hindu temples and courts of patrons, met Gandhiji. He enquired in detail about their lifestyle, the system of devadasis attached to temples, and their sordid existence. "Can you not adopt other professions?" he asked them. "We cannot make ends meet unless we pursue our traditional professions," replied a woman who had come as a spokesperson for the community. Gandhiji said, "Write to me after deep consideration how many of you are willing to make efforts to work at other professions. I will arrange for you to get honest and honourable jobs that occupy you for eight hours per day happily."

This meeting took place about two hours before the public meeting, and Gandhiji mentioned it with much sadness there.

> By calling them devadasis, we are denigrating God. We drag His name to satisfy our lustful pursuits. To ensure the continuance of this class of people to justify the leading of characterless lives by some, leaves a very bad taste. When I met those women, I did not see any sin in their eyes. I can confidently state that, like all other women, they are capable of living modest lives. What difference can there be between them and our own sisters? In fact, all of them were willing to change their lives based on the conditions I laid down. If they cannot, I would still not find fault with them. It is the fault of the repressive society they are entangled in, I would say.

14 September 1927, Kumbakonam

The next day, Gandhiji left for Kumbakonam in the morning by the Madurai Passenger train. It was his practice to take a walk mornings and evenings. That morning, when he was being driven to the railway station, Gandhiji got down in the middle and walked to the station. In Kumbakonam, to avoid the crowds, Gandhiji and some of his entourage detrained at Tiruvidaimarudur (now a panchayat town in Thanjavur district of Tamil Nadu) station, while Kasturba and others went on to Kumbakonam to receive the honours. In Kumbakonam, Gandhiji stayed at Panthulu Iyer's house, where he was received with *purna kumbham*, an auspicious ceremonial greeting as part of Hindu custom. He did not miss out on the welcome benefits either. The Tiruvavaduthurai Adhinam High School students and teachers presented him with a purse before he left the station.

Public meeting

The Kumbakonam public meeting took place at Town High School Grounds. M. C. N. Muthukumara Chetty, the Town Council president, C. N. Lakshmivarada Iyengar, Taluka Board president, Ramachandra Sastri of the Indian Publishing house, Siva Gurunatha Chettiar of the Tamil Sangam, and Muthuraman for the college students, presented welcome addresses on behalf of their respective organisations. Purses were presented on behalf of the general public, and Jains, by V. Panthulu Iyer; on behalf of Saurashtra people, by Bhadraswami Iyer; on behalf of college students, Tiruvidaimarudur school students and teachers, by A. S. Kalyanasundaram Sastrigal; by Krishnamurthi Iyer, on behalf of townfolk, and Tirupperinthiru Tiruvavaduthurai Pandara Sannidhi. Girl students of Saraswathi School, and Gopalakrishna Pillai gave cotton hanks to Gandhiji. In the spinning competition, the winner T. Krishnaswami Iyengar received a gold medal, instituted by Periasamy Batthar, from Gandhiji. Gandhiji was met by student representatives, who invited him to speak at a separate meeting for students, but Gandhiji declined, citing ill health not permitting him to address two meetings. However, at this public meeting, he specifically directed his advice to students.

Arguments with Hindu priests

At the Madras Pachaiyappa College students' meeting, Gandhiji's advice exhorting students to marry young widows deeply troubled orthodox Brahmins and vedic scholars in Kumbakonam. When

Gandhiji arrived, they requested time from him to discuss this issue. He agreed to meet them at 8 o'clock that evening. Referring to this, he said at the public meeting: "The views that I had expressed at the students' meeting were after much consideration. I do not see the need to change one word in them. Not only untouchability, but child marriage, too, has no place in our society."

The sanatanis and other orthodox Hindu factions asked in anger: "Why should Gandhiji, who seems to find fault with Hindus, not apply the same yardstick for Muslims and Christians?" Gandhiji replied: "As I am a Hindu, I am well versed with the Hindu faith. I do not have as much knowledge about the Muslim and Christian religions. As a good physician diagnoses in detail the condition of his patient, and then proceeds to treat him, I wish to do the same."

There is a single sound on one side of the mortar, but two on either side of the *maddalam*, a South Indian percussion instrument. Likewise there were arguments on either side of Gandhiji's views. Orthodox Brahmins, opposing the views on child marriage, were enraged and, after Gandhiji left, convened a meeting in Kumbakonam to pass a resolution condemning it. On the other hand, the association of non-Brahmin youth in Madras passed a resolution that it was caste divisions that stood as a barrier to progress.

Respect for Gandhiji

That night, Government College Sanskrit pandit, R. V. Krishnamachariar, and seven other pandits on behalf of the orthodox Hindus, came to meet Gandhiji. Although they had differences of opinion with him in principle, many among them held Gandhiji in high esteem. This was illustrated by what their leader Krishnamachariar Swamigal said: "We can never speak lowly of the Mahatma's pure heart and adherence to truth. His pleasant countenance and patient outlook captivate all opponents who meet him." The anger of the pandits likewise evaporated on seeing Gandhiji. "His radiance makes him appear more than a mere human," they said.

However, in their publication, *Arya Dharmam*, they criticised him as a man in disguise who espoused only North Indian views for Indian society as a whole. There was no agreement between them at the end of this meeting. The pandits emphasised that the shastras must be interpreted on the bedrock of 'sruti' and 'smriti'. The Mahatma responded that, as far he was aware, there was no place in the shastras for untouchability, and any shastra that went against the conscience of people was not acceptable to him. When he later referred to this in Mannargudi, Gandhiji said:

> If I were to speak the truth about untouchables, the sanatanis are willing to change their minds. They have not thrown out all my views. If one were to look from the point of view of people's welfare, they agree that the argument appears to be in my favour. If all the pandits were of this view, I would not worry about what interpretation they give to the shastras.

15 September 1927, Mannargudi

The next morning, he reached Mannargudi (a town in the Thiruvarur district of Tamil Nadu) by car, and stayed at Sadagopa Mudaliar's house. An American lady, Miss Mayo, had written a book denigrating Indian customs and habits, and Gandhiji, in his response, had called it a drain inspector's book. This response, written in Madras, had just been published in *Young India* at the time Gandhiji reached Mannargudi. Miss Mayo had written that there was an obscene meaning to the Vaishnavite caste mark. Gandhiji asked the Vaishnavites who came to meet him in Madras about this, and they said there was no such thing; it was just how the American lady chose to interpret it.

Srinivasa Sastri's birthplace, Valangaiman

On the way to Mannargudi, Gandhiji inaugurated a free library named after Srinivasa Sastri in Valangaiman, his birthplace. Praising Sastri as one of India's greatest sons, Gandhiji expressed happiness at visiting Sastri's birthplace. Here, on behalf of the Swarajya Sabha, and the general public, welcome addresses and purses were offered. En route to Mannargudi, similar purses were presented to Gandhiji at Needamangalam (formerly, Yamunambalpuram), and Rasappan Chavadi. At Rasappan Chavadi, it was presented by Raghava Iyer. In Needamangalam, at the entrance to the Union Board Office, Gandhiji accepted the purse offered by the president K. Nataraja Pillai in the car itself, and blessed him.

The *Bhagavad Gita*

Schools and colleges were closed for the day in honour of Gandhiji's visit to Mannargudi. At the National High School, the principal, S. Vaidyanatha Iyer, read the welcome address, which mentioned that education in this school was based on the tenets of the Hindu religion. When Gandhiji asked, "How many of you know the *Bhagavad Gita*?" only one student raised his hand. Gandhiji appreciated the students for being honest, but expressed disappointment that, in a school which prided itself on education based on Hinduism's principles, only one student should be conversant with the *Gita*. Then he spoke about religious observances.

> South India is known for the maximum use of sandal paste and 'vibhuti' (sacred ash). All of you have vibhuti on your foreheads or tilaks of sandal paste. This is good practice, but if you do not understand the rationale behind this, it is of no use. Likewise, if you merely commit the *Bhagavad Gita* to memory and recite it, I will not be pleased. You must incorporate its message in your personal lives. If you study the *Bhagavad Gita* with an attitude of reverence, you will realise that there is no place for Hindu-Muslim discord, or Brahmin–non-Brahmin conflict suggested in it.

Gandhiji also asked the school principal a problematic question: "How many Muslim and Christian boys are there in your school? How many are there from depressed classes?"

Principal: There are 6 or 7 Muslim boys, 4 or 5 Christians. There are no applications received from those belonging to the depressed classes.
Gandhiji: If they were to apply, would you admit them?
Principal: I do not think there will be any problem.

Praise for Rev. Smyles

After this, at the rousing function organised at Finlay College by the staff and students, Gandhiji was happy to hear from the president of the institution, Rev. Smyles, that many students from the depressed classes were studying in it, and praised the president. "I am delighted at your efforts in admitting these students in your college," he said and, as it was a Christian institution, added, "The wrong behaviour of students is due to their having forgotten the tenets of their religion. At the same time I do not say that religion that encourages irrational behaviour should be blindly followed, and God-given traits forgotten."

P. Rajagopala Iyer of Palaiyur Sakthi Ashramam met Gandhiji and reported that there was enthusiastic welcome for the spinning wheel in the villages. Kasturba Gandhi unveiled a portrait of Bajaj at the Bajaj Spinning Unit.

Public meeting

A public meeting was held at the college grounds opposite the bungalow of Sadagopa Mudaliar, where Gandhiji was staying. He spoke here at length, also declaring with pleasure that, with the exception of Madras, in no place other than here in Mannargudi was there such a collection of funds for the movement. Perhaps his long speech was a result of this, in which he dealt with the recurring issues of the need for Hindi, importance of charkha, eradication of untouchability, child marriage, and prohibition. He had known that Mannargudi was traditionally a centre of weaving, and he requested its weavers to weave 100s count yarn.

Welcome addresses were presented on behalf of the Mannargudi Town Council, Mannargudi Taluk Board, Rajaji Library, Tagore Tilak Library and other institutions. Most of them were printed on khadi cloth, which pleased Gandhiji considerably. On behalf of the people of Mannargudi Taluk Board, K. S. Subramania Iyer handed over a purse. On behalf of the general public of Tiruthuraipoondi (a municipality in Tiruvarur) Taluk Board too a purse was presented.

The debate

Where Gandhiji was staying in Mannargudi, he was met by the Kottur Estate Sanskrit School president, U. Ve. Thilliambur Chakravarthiar Swami, who insisted that there was a foundation in the Hindu shastras for untouchability, and that Gandhiji's views were not supported by the shastras. There was a long and stirring debate between Chakravarthiar Swami and Gandhiji. At the outset the achariar praised Gandhiji lavishly, and ended up showing off his proficiency. This prompted Gandhiji to comment rather firmly to the person translating this exchange between them: "He is quoting shlokas that have no relevance to the subject. This does not show such a pandit in favourable light. In a court of law, if a lawyer argues thus, it will not be countenanced." Thereafter, the achariar came directly to the point.

Achariar: We can build houses for Harijans, donate food, buy them charkhas, but they should remain untouchable. When the Lord in the temple is brought out on the streets in procession on a chariot, they can worship, but they cannot enter the temple.

Gandhiji: It is not correct to select just one or two statements in our shastras and build your arguments around them.

Achariar: In the Kaliyuga, may we not accept in entirety the 'Parashara Smrithi?'

Gandhiji: No. We cannot accept any shastra 100% as our direction finder.

Achariar: Would you take only one part of a 'Smrithi' and leave another part out?

Gandhiji: I cannot accept that just because we accept one part, we should accept the whole.

Achariar: Then it means that you will take what is convenient to you and not that which is not?

Gandhiji: This is a good question. There is no hard and fast rule in our Hindu shastras. There are hundreds of treatises on our shastras. We have not even known some of them. Hence, when we examine what is right or wrong, we do not depend on any one text. We look at it in the context of our entire religion. There is a yardstick to evaluate every shastra and every action in our Hindu religion, and that is the truth. Whatever stems from truth must be accepted, whoever says it.

Achariar: Then, how is untouchability against truth?

Gandhiji: If I consider you an untouchable, will that conform to truth?

Achariar (in surprise): How could I be considered an untouchable? As there is difference between the fire at home and the fire in a funeral pyre, there is a difference between man and man.

Gandhiji: Oho! Then how could you say that you are 'touchable', and that Rajagopalachariar and me are 'untouchable'?

Achariar: There is a difference in body, thoughts, behaviour and virtue between me and a 'chandalan' (or chandala, member of a Hindu 'lower caste' engaged in disposing of corpses, and considered 'untouchable').

As this debate was going on, the time allotted by Gandhiji for the Sanskrit pandit came to an end, and he left by saying truthfully, "I did not come to argue with you, but merely have the good fortune of meeting you."

16 September 1927, Thanjavur

From Mannargudi, Gandhiji and his entourage arrived by Nagapattinam Passenger train at Thanjavur the next morning, 16 September 1927. Realising that to avoid crowds, Gandhiji had been alighting at earlier railway stations, the crowds in Thanjavur decided to wait for him at the dak or mail road crossing before the train entered Thanjavur. But on this occasion, Gandhiji got down at Thanjavur station itself. The public were again disappointed. Gandhiji and his group stayed at Ukkadai House in Thanjavur.

Meeting Justice Party leaders

Some Justice Party leaders met Gandhiji. He gave appointments to Panneerselvam and Umamaheswaran Pillai of the Justice Party, Ukkadai Thevar, Syed Tajuddin, Karkudi Chinnappa Pillai and Pattukkottai Dandapani Chettiar. He also met prominent persons like Pappanadu Zamindar and K. Natarajan. When the aged mother of K. Natarajan met Gandhiji, he welcomed her affectionately, and told her that there were soft khadi saris that could be worn by women. The meeting and discussion with Justice Party leaders turned out to be worthwhile on both sides as they had the opportunity to understand each other.

The discussion

Swadesamithran reported on details of the talks held between Gandhiji ('G') and the Justice Party leaders Panneerselvam ('P') and Umamaheswaran Pillai ('U'). It is an interesting and revealing exchange.

U: The Brahmin–non-Brahmin problem is becoming increasingly complex. Leaders need to meet and find a solution to this.

G: Non-Brahmins themselves talk about this in different voices. Although there are differences between Brahmins and non-Brahmins, Dr Varadarajulu feels that they will vanish in a short time, and does not want a person like me to interfere. But Erode Ramasamy Naicker is of the opinion that the torment by Brahmins in South India is intolerable, and I should arrive at some satisfactory solution. In recent times I have come across some progressive measures by Brahmins. When I had come to Madras a few years ago, I was sitting only in the portico of S. Srinivasa Iyengar's house. Today, I look upon his house as my own, and my wife even walks up to their kitchen.

P: The Brahmins hold on to their authority and their jobs, making it impossible for other classes to aspire for them.

G: I see from what you say that your main objective is to share both the authority and the jobs. I cannot be supportive of such a desire. No movement that does not benefit the people can have my sympathy.

U: Getting authority is only one of many demands. The abolition of social atrocities and improvement in religion-related matters are our other objectives.

G: It is good that there has been a change in the aims of your movement. You talk of improvements in matters of religion, but you have joined up with members of other religions, have you not?

U: As Hindu religious leaders were not responding to us, non-Hindus were inducted into our movement in the early days. Non-Brahmins are being insulted by Brahmins in several ways. The general public, too, has woken up to this.

G: We can examine and discard the present caste division, but can we erase the fundamental principle? A man does not become noble by mere birth.

P: Take the khadi movement. There is a complaint that Rajagopalachariar is not allowing non-Brahmins to join and work with you in this movement. It is true that S. Ramanathan is part of the khadi movement, but he, too, will be chased away by the Brahmins. (Rajaji and S. Ramanathan were both present during this exchange.)

G: Achariar has devoted his life to the khadi movement, and no money has been paid to him for this. I wrote and arranged to pay him some money. If people are willing to come forward and work with dedication in the khadi movement, I will ask Achariar to step aside. I, too, will withdraw. Achariar has his lawyer's profession in hand. Why should he forsake it and the remuneration it gives him to work here? Should we not consider this?

P: His objective is to benefit himself and his associates through khadi work. People are beguiled because they see him with you. It has become an electioneering point with him.

G: I do not see that kind of desire on the part of Achariar. One cannot say that there are no persons with disguises in the khadi movement. Even so, are they not wearing the disguise of khadi? Is that not a good thing at least?

Public meeting

This conversation highlights the views that were prevalent among the non-Brahmins in those days. Gandhiji referred to this conversation at the public meeting that evening.

> I had argued with certain friends here about the problems of Brahmins and non-Brahmins. This discussion pleased me. I have begun to understand the non-Brahmin movement a little better than before. I also noticed that they had formed a certain opinion of me that was disturbing to them. They feel that I am of the belief that persons are of high or low caste as per their birth. I explained to them that all men are born equal. If a Brahmin or anyone claims superiority due to birth, and non-Brahmins agitate against it, I support it completely. The man who claims such superiority is in fact not superior at all. However, in spite of all this, I do have belief in the system of caste division. Just as a person derives his physical appearance from his parents and forbears, he inherits their actions, too. By openly accepting this brings a full stop to our outworldly desires. It also helps in developing our spiritual strength. If only you could accept this premise, the Brahmin–non-Brahmin problem can be easily solved. If a Brahmin begins to earn money, he is no longer a Brahmin.

Gandhiji spoke for about an hour. He praised the intricate workmanship of the 'Viswakarmas' (a community or caste, named after the craftsman deity and divine architect Viswakarma) in the plate presented to him. "I am in admiration of the wonderful artistry of my Viswakarma friends, I am going to have it put as an exhibit in the Ahmedabad Gujarat Vidyapith museum."

Tiruchi

He went from this meeting to the railway station and boarded his special compartment. It was later attached to the Rameswaram Express at night, and he reached Tiruchi. There was no prior intimation of which train he was travelling by, and when it would arrive. Hence, except for some prominent people who received him at Tiruchi, there was no crowd.

Exhaustion

In the morning of 17 September 1927, Dr Rajan, a physician, examined Gandhiji. Other than extreme exhaustion, he did not find anything wrong, so he offered a piece of advice. There were several functions that had been organised for Gandhiji in Tiruchi. Dr Rajan suggested that, instead of speaking at every one of the functions, Gandhiji might indicate that he would say whatever he wanted at the public meeting. Gandhiji accepted this.

Foundation stone

There were many foundation stone-laying functions for Gandhiji. In the morning he laid the foundation stone for the Fort Market, and in the afternoon for the Golden Rock South Indian Railway Workers' Sangam building. In the grounds opposite the Fort Market, a welcome was arranged by the Town Council. The Town Council president, P. Rathinavelu Thevar, read out the welcome speech written on palm leaf. As per Dr. Rajan's advice, Gandhiji wrote out his response to the welcome, which Rajaji read out. When Gandhiji came to Golden Rock, there were thousands of railway workers, many of whom had come from Pothanur and Nagapattinam. The Workers' Union president, T. Krishnasamy Pillai, welcomed Gandhiji, who, in a written response, said, "Self-confidence and self-effort should be the motto of workers."

Lalgudi

At about 6 p.m., Gandhiji left for Lalgudi. Sethurathnam Iyer went with him and his group. Others in the party rode in the double-bullock drawn cart, arranged by Nochiyam Adimoola Vandavarayar, to cross the Kollidam river, a northern tributary of the Kaveri, north of Srirangam. But, as reported by *Swadesamithran*, Gandhiji preferred to walk across, not wanting to ride in the cart. In Adimoola Vandavarayar's house, he, along with the people of Manachanallur village presented purses to Gandhiji. Thereafter, Gandhiji reached Lalgudi by car.

A public meeting was held in Lalgudi YMCA Building. Based on a request made by the nationalist N. Halasyam to say a few words to satisfy the crowd, Gandhiji expressed his thanks briefly. On behalf of the Lalgudi Congress Committee, L. N. Paramasivan Pillai, on behalf of the Taluk Board, its president, L. D. Ramachandra Iyer, and on behalf of the Young Indians Association, S. S. Swaminatha Iyer, offered welcome addresses.

X-ray centre

In those days, when even speakers for sound amplification were rare at public meetings, one may imagine how much rarer X-ray equipment must have been. Through strenuous efforts, and at considerable expense, Dr Rajan had established an X-ray centre, and he requested Gandhiji to inaugurate it. This became a problem for Gandhiji, who was not used to inaugurating any enterprise that profited just one person. Further, Gandhiji did not encourage modern methods of medical treatment. Some of his friends therefore put it to him that he should not inaugurate this facility. Ultimately, however, Gandhiji did inaugurate it, on 18 September 1927, and he gave two main reasons for doing so. "The group under the leadership of Rajaji has included this function as part of my tour. Hence I must inaugurate it. Further, unless it is against 'dharma', it is my practice to yield to the requests of my friends" (*The Hindu*, 1927). The second reason was, even if it was going to profit one person, poor people can approach Dr Rajan and seek help in this matter.

Welcome in Sanskrit

The students of Tiruchi got together at Tiruchi National College, presented a hefty purse, and, quite unexpectedly, delivered their welcome address in Sanskrit. Gandhiji rose to speak, and asked those in the crowd who could understand Sanskrit to raise their hands. Very few people did, and Gandhiji went on to say that when an overwhelming majority of people could not understand it, the welcome should not have been composed in Sanskrit. At the same time, he requested students to learn Sanskrit. The people in the vanguard had thought that a welcome in Sanskrit would please Gandhiji. Acharya Kaka Kalelkar (1885–1981, independence activist, journalist, social reformer and a Gandhian), who had come to the function also thought that might be the case. But in fact it only saddened Gandhiji, who felt it would have been better if the welcome address had been written in Tamil, and thereafter translated into Hindi or Sanskrit. When he returned from this meeting, Kaka Kalelkar asked him, "It is only because of your love for Sanskrit that such a welcome was drafted; why did you not like it?"

Gandhiji's reply reveals his attentiveness to time and circumstance: "They offered this welcome on behalf of people from all walks of life. Hence it should have been prepared in a language that all understand. Further, in these parts, the Brahmin–non-Brahmin movements are very strong. I wonder whether this welcome in Sanskrit has been written as an echo of that conflict. This is why I expressed my regret" (Kaka Kalelkar interview).

The nationalism of Christians

In Puthur YMCA, Gandhiji attended a Christians' meeting, where he was welcomed by Rev. Sanford. Gandhiji said in his speech, "Christians, because they belong to this religion, need not forget their nation. The man who has willingly changed his religion must enlarge his vision of his country."

Devadasis

In the afternoon, in the Town Council General Hall, there was a women's gathering. Tirumathi Swaminatha Sastri and, on behalf of devadasis, Kumari Jeevarathinam, presented welcome speeches. When they mentioned that the jewels they were wearing were acquired bit by bit as a result of judicious savings made over years, Gandhiji could not accept this and firmly declared: "These have all been given to you by others, and not what you have earned through your own toil. They have been given to you as marriage gifts. Hence you must share it with your poor sisters." After the meeting, when Gandhiji was receiving jewels as donation from these women, it began to rain heavily, requiring a temporary halt to this donation.

Srirangam Town Council

The Srirangam Town Council had originally decided to collect not less than Rs 100 from each member of the Council for the Khadi Fund. But for some reason, this scheduled function at Srirangam on Gandhiji's visit fell through. Only the Council president, along with some of the members, visited Gandhiji where he was staying, and presented their welcome addresses and purse.

The next day, members of the Vivekananda Ashram too offered their welcome address. They gave him the visitors' book of the Ashram, and requested Gandhiji to write in it. He wrote: "Unless the people who are running this Ashram in the name of Vivekananda make all efforts to keep their surroundings clean, there is no value in naming the Ashram so."

21 September 1927, Public meeting

At this time a strong rumour was making the rounds that the Mahatma's health was a matter of concern, and that he was going to stop the Madras tour and return home. Some newspapers too carried this view. Gandhiji was forced to correct this. In Tiruchirappalli, his meeting was rescheduled. Because of rain, it did not take place the day before. Hence the revised arrangement was that he stay a day more, and leave on Wednesday morning for Pudukkottai.

At the public meeting held the next morning, Gandhiji spoke with some sadness: "The unity I felt when I visited Madras before I am not able to experience this time. [The Brahmin–non-Brahmin discord seems to have led him to make this statement.] Khadi, however, is a matter for the general public, and in this I do not see any differences of opinion."

In this meeting, Gandhiji spoke, not so much about khadi, but the pollution that was beginning to threaten the waters of the Kaveri. On behalf of the Tiruchirappalli general public, District Committee president, M. R. Sethurathinam Iyer presented the welcome address and a purse.

Priceless

An incident at the public meeting caused a slight diversion. The Town Council president, P. R. Thevar, presented to Gandhiji his three-stone studded ring for the Khadi Fund. When Gandhiji asked him for the value of the ring, Thevar said he did not know, prompting Gandhiji to remark humourously, "He does not know its price because he has so much money."

Pudukkottai

In the evening Gandhiji reached Pudukkottai. Kasturba and he took a couple of hours' rest in the bungalow of Annamalai Chettiar, known as S. A., before proceeding to the public meeting. The welcome given to him mentioned that there had been no rain in those parts for a long time, but, as Gandhiji started speaking, a slight drizzle started. He prepared to halt his speech, but perhaps because it did not want to interrupt him, the drizzle stopped! Gandhiji finished whatever he had to say. The president of the reception group, K. Swaminatha Iyer, presented the welcome address and purse at the meeting.

Township administration

A resolution had been placed for a welcome to Gandhiji to be given on behalf of the Pudukkottai Town administration. When the resolution came up, there were 11 members, including the president. As seven members voted against it, it did not go through; two members elected by the people had voted against the resolution, while two other members did not attend the public meeting. A meeting was organised by the public and a resolution was passed condemning these four.

This was the first time Gandhiji was coming to Pudukkottai. Until he arrived, the people had been apprehensive that some ban may be placed against his entry, because on the previous occasion, the Durbar had promulgated such a ban, and the people had been forced to welcome him in Karaikudi.

22 September 1927, Kanadukathan

Ramachandrapuram, in Pudukkottai, was under the princedom. The following day, on Gandhiji's arrival here, S. T. Nagappa Chettiar, Trustee of Sri Bhumiswara Free High School, and the Principal, V. Santhanam Iyengar, separately presented welcome addresses and purses to him. Thereafter, he visited T. S. R. M. Free Medical Dispensary, where its founder, Ramasamy Chettiar, presented a purse. After this there was the welcome by Nagarathars (a Tamil mercantile community and caste). From here, via Kothamangalam (a municipality in the Ernakulam district of Kerala), Gandhiji went to Kanadukathan (now a town panchayat in Karaikudi taluk of Tamil Nadu), and stayed at the bungalow of Shanmugam Chettiar. When he spoke here, he asked for many more khadi shops to be opened in Chettinad.

> I am no doubt a Vysya—a Chetty, I can pride myself, like you. In Rangoon, when I stayed with Dr. Mehta, I familiarised myself with the details and customs of your domestic life. The Chettiars, who were counting money almost all day long in Rangoon, were pointed out to me by Dr. Mehta, saying, 'Do not think they are small moneylenders. Many are bigwigs.' Before knowing about your community in Rangoon, I had met a few Chettiars in South Africa. If you make up your minds, you can not only handle the khadi industry in Madras, but help to finance the khadi movement all over India.

Gandhiji strongly criticised the foreign furniture that the Chettinad bungalows were full of, restricting even free movement within, and the pictures and decorations on the walls which he found obscene, saying, "If I had been given the contract of decorating your houses, you would be spending one-tenth of what you have now spent, and I would have decorated your houses better." The result of Gandhiji's observations on Kanadukathan were seen in due course. Thereafter, wherever he went in Chettinad and stayed, the furniture used was seen to be minimal.

Temples of God

At the welcome by Nagarathars, Gandhiji shared a thought that would have been bitter for the Nagarathars.

> I know that you are contributing a lot of money for the establishment of temples. To assume that, merely by building a temple, God resides in it, is superstition. I believe that He resides in the houses of devadasis as much as he is found in temples. Some friends have given me money to build temples for untouchables. Unless I am able to find a man of pure heart, a good follower of 'dharma', I have said I will not use that money for such a temple to be built. … I know of several temples where God is found, as much as He is found in the houses of prostitutes.

This statement of Gandhiji drew strong opposition not only from orthodox Hindus in Madras but also from some others. For example, Nagaraja Sharma, a teacher in a government school in Madras, said,

> "It does not behove a person of Mahatma's stature to lose his sense of balance in making such statements. Let us assume that Miss Mayo [an American] had termed these temples as houses of prostitution. The Mahatma would have surely condemned her. He had written in the newspapers that the Nagarathars should continue to establish temples. Persons like Salem C. Vijayaraghavachariar had objected to this. They accepted no doubt that the devadasi system must be abolished. But, based on what Gandhiji had written, even Vijayaraghavachariar felt that it was wounding the sensibilities of the society.

Dharma

Gandhiji spoke about how charitable work should be done. "Alms must be given to those in genuine need," he said. "Let us assume that all of you got together to give charity to 50,000 villagers in India. This would be a huge burden. You can give food to the lame, deaf and dumb, but not to those who have the strength to work. Hence, helping the growth of khadi is today the best 'dharma.'"

23 September 1927, Amaravathi Pudur

As per the Indian calendar, Gandhiji's birthday fell on 23 September. Hence, in Karaikudi, 500 poor people were fed on that day. In the morning, Gandhiji left Kanadukathan, and reached Amaravathi Pudur (a village now in Sivaganga district, Tamil Nadu), via Pallathur, Kottaiyur and Karaikudi. Here Tirumathi Miraben[1] joined Gandhiji's group. At the Amaravathi Pudur meeting, he said that he had heard it was this place that had inspired people of the region to take up national service. "Do not consider what minimum you can give for khadi; rather how much you can. The meaning of Amaravathi is 'where God resides'. If, in your hearts and your surroundings, you practice purity, you can make this place truly the place where God lives."

Debate on untouchability

Vn. R. Ma. Venkatacha Chettiar ('V') of Amaravathi Pudur had a brief discussion with Gandhiji ('G') on whether or not untouchability was justified. Gandhiji's responses to his questions are relevant to this day.

V: Have not the Vedas and shastras justified untouchability?
G: They have not.
V: Can a chandala touch a God-fearing Brahmin when he is worshipping the idol of God? Is it correct?
G: Yes, he can. If I were to state it more clearly, the Brahmin must consider the chandala to be his brother.
V: Even though Nandanar belonged to a 'pariah' caste, he is supposed to have given up many of the harmful practices of his caste, and adopted a life of prayer. He got redemption only after a baptism of fire, is it not?
G: The severe penance undertaken by Nandanar reflects him with pride. However, it is not proper for the Brahmins to expect that all untouchables should go through the same rigour of penance.
V: Are there not noble and low varieties even in our crops? Do we not give more attention to the nobler produce? Should not the same be adopted by people in consideration of their practices and needs?
G: Let each caste decide on its own needs and observances. Others need not decide for them.

V: Can the servants of a master demand equal status with him? Will not such a demand affect their relationship?
G: A good master will consider his servant as his equal.
V: Can we go against the age-old tenets expounded by our Vedas and Agamas[2] on the matter of caste and ashrama?
G: If Hindu religion has to prosper, the duties of the four castes have to be well defined. The hypocrisy prevalent in this definition today must go.

Chettinad

Gandhiji stayed in Chettinad for four days. He treated Karaikudi (now a municipality in the Sivagangai district of Tamil Nadu) as the hub of the region, and returned to it every day after his tour of other places. He disliked the ostentatious weddings of the Nagarathars. The Nagarathars would frequently leave their wives at home for long periods, and go off to Burma, Malaya and Singapore on business—a practice that Gandhiji criticised. He also emphasised the need for clean drinking water, and cleanliness of the surroundings.

Gandhiji advised the Nagarathars on two things: instead of receiving proper education, children should not be closeted and made to become money-making instruments; and merely because they had wealth, the Nagarathars should not behave irresponsibly, but lead pure lives.

24 September 1927, Devakottai

At the women's meeting held the next day, in the bungalow in front of the Mahanombu Grounds, Gandhiji expounded on the objective of the Khadi Fund, and exhorted the women to hold Sita as their model for dealing with the troubles and sorrows in their lives. From the residence of Natesan Chettiar in Karaikudi, where he was staying, Gandhiji reached Devakottai in the evening.

In the large grounds opposite the Siva temple, Vendanpatti Chokkalingam Chettiar, an expert in spinning, had put up a small exhibition showing the different processes by which one could spin cotton into high quality yarn, which he showed Gandhiji. Praising the khadi cloth woven out of this beautiful, fine yarn at the public meeting, Gandhiji said he would allow it to be auctioned only if it fetched a minimum bid of Rs. 1000; otherwise, he would take it to the All India Charkha Sangam exhibition to be displayed there. As there were no bids beyond Rs. 1000, Gandhiji took it away. Only one Chatterji from Bengal was able to produce such fine cloth in India, Gandhiji said. He also praised the hand cloth spun and woven by one Srinivasa Iyengar. On behalf of the Devakottai Union Board, the town people, and Sri Meenakshi Vidyalaya High School, three welcome addresses were presented. The young zamindar of Devakottai, Ai. Ar. Rm. V. Somasundaram Chettiar presented a purse on behalf of the general public. A purse on behalf of the girl students of Suvarna Murthy Girls' School was also presented.

25 September 1927, Karaikudi

The next day, at a public meeting at Karaikudi, Gandhiji once again praised the fine cloth woven by Chokkalingam Chettiar, before talking about how the khadi movement was progressing. Then he said, "There are nine persons in the group which is in charge of this. The majority of them are non-Brahmins. The head of this group is also a non-Brahmin, whom the people wrongly address as the 'Mahatma.'" There was laughter from the crowd at this; no one could have here contested Gandhiji's statement about non-Brahmins in the khadi movement. He also cited a letter from a lady doctor, whose name was not revealed, to the effect that the undesirable practice of 'pottukkattal' (initiation ceremony of young girls as devadasis) was continuing because of some wealthy patrons in Chettinad, and that Gandhiji should speak to them to stop it. It is possible that the letter was from Dr Muthulakshmi Reddy.

Enthusiastic auction

In addition to the purses presented to Gandhiji at this meeting, there was substantial collection through auctions. Vai. Su. Shanmugam Chettiar announced at the meeting that he was prepared to take the khadi cloth at Rs 1000. Several rings were presented to Gandhiji, and there were many bidders for them. Gandhiji announced that there were more and more rings with him, as the rings were being bought, delighted that the auction was progressing so speedily, and said, "It appears that your town will almost equal Ahmednagar in the matter of auctions."

Farewell speech

The auction went on for an hour. After it was over, as an exception, on this occasion alone he made a farewell speech, and also gave his reasons for doing so.

> This sight [of the speedy auction] cannot be forgotten by me. It will remain one of the happiest memories in my life.
>
> I have spoken of many things in Chettinad that would have been unpleasant to you. You could have misunderstood me because of that. However, as stringent my words might have been, you have generously poured your affection on me. This is the reason for my great happiness. Not only have you given money, but it is only when you open your hearts to me that I can serve you.

On behalf of the public at the meeting, Chettiappa Chettiar read out the welcome address as president of the reception committee. Purses were presented on behalf of the Karaikudi general public, women and Adi Dravidar youngsters separately.

Meiyappa Chettiar

On this tour, Gandhiji was accompanied in Madurai, Ramanathapuram and Tirunelveli districts by Kamaraj. To some places in Chettinad, Meiyappa Chettiar went with Gandhiji, which Chettiar has written about—his diary entries of two days provide a picture of Gandhiji's visit.

27 September 1927, Jayankondapuram

"At 8 a.m., Mahatma, his wife, son, Desai, Rajagopalachariar, and Rajan arrived here and stopped for 3 minutes. Nachammai presented a khadi garland and gave Rs 100. Immediately, we, too, went with them to Karaikudi. Stay was at Sa. Na. Sa. Th. bungalow. In the afternoon, Nachammai and I, with children, went and took part in the welcome function at the Girls' School in Gandhinagar. Had lunch, and returned in the evening. Gandhiji made a speech at Gandhinagar at night. The next morning the Mahatma went to Devakottai and spoke at a meeting at night. We, too, went to Devakottai." 27-9-27

Baganeri route

"In the morning, we and Thi. Vu. went to Karaikudi in Thi's car, and joined the Mahatma's tour to Nachiapuram, Siravayal, and Tiruppatthur public meetings. The meeting at Merpadiyur Mission Hospital gave over. We reached Baganeri by 9 a.m. There was a public meeting there ... at which we bought a painting auctioned by the Mahatma for Rs. 81."

A day's fast

Sa. Ganesan narrates two curious events that he witnessed first-hand: "When Gandhiji came to Karaikudi in 1927, (his son) Devadas Gandhi had forgotten to lay out Gandhiji's shaving kit as per his morning routine, causing Gandhiji considerable disappointment. As an atonement for this dereliction of duty by Devadas Gandhi, the Mahatma decided to go on fast that day, and did not change his mind, despite the persuasion of several persons. Because of his decision, Kasturba, too, went on a day's fast. The 'roti' and spinach that she had prepared for Gandhiji that day were given to us."

Who is a teacher?

Under the auspices of the Money Traders' Association, approved by the government, 15 or 16 primary schools had been established. Pa. Jeevanandam (who later became a leader of the Communist Party), Kumbalingam, and some other school teachers and students came to meet Gandhiji, who gave them an interview of more than half an hour. Seeing the long hair of some students, Gandhiji asked the teachers, "Why are these students letting their hair grow so long?"

Jeevanandam replied, "They are all very poor, struggling even for their daily food. Hence they have no money for haircuts."

Gandhiji promptly retorted, "What is the meaning of a teacher?"

"One who educates," replied a teacher.

"Should he merely impart education? Is not the duty of a teacher to impart all knowledge that equips a student in his life? Is not providing such direction the duty of a teacher?"

All of them agreed, "Yes…Yes…"

"Then, cannot teachers themselves take on the haircutting needs of the students?"

Taken aback, the teachers half-heartedly replied, "Yes…it can be done."

Gandhiji said, "Oho! It appears that you look upon this chore as beneath your dignity. No matter, I shall myself undertake it," and turning to Devadas Gandhi, instructed him, "Devadas, bring me the scissors, etc."

Ashamed, the teachers said, "No, Bapu, we will ourselves do it for the students wholeheartedly."

Gandhiji accepted this response with satisfaction, and added, "It is not the man who teaches alone who is a good teacher; it is a man who sets an example by practising what he preaches."

26 September 1927, Wishes for Annie Besant

In his birthday greetings to Annie Besant on 26 September, sent through *New India*, Gandhiji acknowledged his debt to her: "I was first indebted to Besant in the year 1889–90. This has now multiplied several-fold. The unrelenting God has not given me enough strength to repay it."

27 September 1927, Baganeri

Via Nachiarpuram, Siravayal and Tiruppatthur, Gandhiji reached Madurai. He stayed at the residence of Chokkalingam Chettiar in Baganeri (now possibly the village of Paganeri in Sivagangai district of Tamil Nadu). On behalf of the Ashram at Siravayal, a welcome address was given to him. He lauded the work of the Ashram in running a gurukulam, a school for Harijan children, and working towards cleanliness. He criticised the skirts worn by the girls and said they looked obscene and affected their good looks.

Tiruppathur

At the welcome organised at Kala Mantapam, separate purses were presented on behalf of the general public, members of the Motor Union, Nattars (earlier, an administrative body in Tamil kingdoms), and teachers. While Gandhiji regretted that in the whole of Chettinad, the purse collected here was the lowest, the attendance of an equal number of women and men at the meeting pleased him. "Spinning gives women a livelihood opportunity," he said. He pleaded for the abhorrent custom of child marriages to stop.

Swedish Mission Eye Hospital

When Gandhiji visited the Swedish Mission Eye Hospital here, Dr Kukelberg enthusiastically welcomed him and introduced the doctors, nurses and other officials to him. Gandhiji had come here on the request of Dr Gurupadam, whom he had first met in Karaikudi in 1921. Not getting an appointment with Gandhiji, Dr Gurupadam had then sent him a note through Kasturba, whom he had seen coming down the stairs. Gandhiji had then invited him in, spoken to him for half an hour, and accepted his invitation to visit the Tiruppathur Eye Hospital. In 1927, he came as per his word. Someone brought to Gandhiji's notice a series of ten articles written by Dr Gurupadam in the British daily *The Guardian*, on 'The Food That is Good for Us,' which made Gandhiji desire to meet him. Dr Gurupadam's association with Gandhiji changed his life. The doctor gave up his lucrative medical practice in Chittoor, and set up an ashram devoted to agriculture, giving as much importance to agriculture as he had given to his meeting with Gandhiji. On his visit in 1927, Gandhiji spoke to Dr Gurupadam about the importance of khadi in the context of its non-acceptance at that time. When the Kasturba Gandhi Trust was established, Dr Gurupadam was one of the three doctors appointed on it, the other two being Dr. T. S. S. Rajan, and Dr Soundaram Ramachandran. Dr Gurupadam was also appointed on the higher education committee, along with Dr Savarirayan Yesudasan.

Ramana Maharishi and Gandhi

Gandhiji had heard of Ramana Maharishi (1879–1950) in a different context. Wanting to know the truth about him, Gandhiji wrote a letter to P. N. Sankaranarayanan, who was running the Madras Gokulam Colony, requested him to visit the Ramanashram and share his experience. Sankaranarayanan went there along with Dr Gurupadam. They stayed at the Ramanashram for three days and sent a report to Gandhiji. Although this report was confidential, it no doubt showed the greatness of Ramana Maharishi, because, later, some of Gandhiji's followers went with his permission to have a darshan of Bhagavan Ramana.

Rajendra Prasad came in 1938. While leaving Ramanashram, he asked, "I came here with Gandhiji's permission. ... Is there any message from Sri Ramanar that I should carry to him?" Ramanar replied, "A spiritual force in Gandhiji is driving him forward, and guiding him on his way…what more can I say?"

Devotees of Ramanar had asked him on several occasions about the various views of Gandhiji. Ramanar's vision was reflected in his replies. Gandhiji was often disturbed about the misdeeds of his ashramites, and felt personally responsible for those wrongs. When a devotee of Ramanar asked him about this, the Maharishi said, "Gandhiji has had to work hard for so many years to purify himself. Others, too, in time, will become so."

At one time, some Congress workers came to Sri Ramana and asked him, "Will we obtain freedom within the lifetime of Gandhiji?" Sri Ramanar replied: "Gandhiji has surrendered himself to God in his work. He does not have any self-interest, nor does he worry about the end result. He accepts the losses and gains that he gets at every juncture. A national worker's attitude should be like this."

A worker asked him, "Should we not examine whether our efforts are bearing fruit?" The Maharishi's reply was, "Follow the example of Gandhiji in working for the welfare of the nation. 'Surrender' is the right path."

Reading in the newspapers that Gandhiji was commencing a 21-day fast in Yerawada jail, a couple of youngsters asked Sri Ramanar, "Mahatma has started a 21-day fast. We, too, wish to rush to Yerawada jail and join this fast. We are in a hurry and seek your permission". It seemed to Sri Ramana that they were just waiting for his word to rush headlong into what they had resolved to do. Bhagavan smiled and said, "Your having such strong emotions is a good sign. But what can you do now? Get the strength that Gandhiji has already attained through his penance. You will then succeed."

Sri Ramanar was glad to read what Gandhiji had written about the miracles wrought by God. In a *Harijan* issue (11 March 1939), Gandhiji had written,

> What are God's miracles? My visit to Rajkot was surprising even to me. Why am I travelling? Where am I going, and for what? I never wondered about any of this. When God is showing me the path, what need I think about? Why should I think about it? My thoughts could act as a barrier for God to show me the way. The truth, however, is that I am unable to contain these thoughts. New thoughts do not appear. There are no intervals when thoughts do not arise. But what I am trying to say is that I have no concerns about my ultimate objective.

"What truthful utterances," remarked Bhagavan Ramana, as he re-emphasised every tenet contained in them. As an example, he quoted Thayumanavar (1705–42), a Tamil spiritual philosopher who famously said: "A man who suppresses his thoughts realises little." "Gandhiji has attained spiritual redemption by embracing the truth," said a devotee to Sri Ramanar, who replied, "What is the soul, but the truth? Truth is what is, and nothing more. Hence Gandhiji's truth is nothing other than the soul" (*Talks With Ramana*).

28 September 1927, Madurai

Gandhiji's arrival in Madurai was accompanied by rain, but fortunately, it stopped after a while. When he reached the house of George Joseph, where he was to stay, the Joseph couple welcomed him at the entrance. Nobody expected that Gandhiji would be staying with Joseph, not even Joseph himself, to start with, because he was opposed to the non-cooperation movement, and had stayed away from it.

Public meeting

Resting till the evening, Gandhiji proceeded to the Town Council Hall, received awelcome address of the Council president, R. S. Naidu, and went on to the public meeting. At this meeting held at Thazhukkam Grounds, welcome addresses were read on behalf of the Madurai general public, Students' Union, Nadars' Sangam, and the Hindi Prachar group. The Charkha Sangam read out its notice. The treasurer of the Madurai Khadi Fund, A. Vedarama Iyer, handed over those funds. On behalf of the students, book binders, and the Cuddalore general public, purses and silver cups were presented. Gandhiji replied to all these addresses of welcome together in his speech. The welcome addresses had highlighted the fact that Harijans were being appointed as teachers and staff in the Town Council establishments, Harijan boys and girls in great numbers were being admitted to the Town Council-run schools, and there was no discrimination practised in the Council in these matters. This pleased Gandhiji. As he was speaking, Gandhiji recalled his previous visit to Madurai, when he had first changed his attire, and recounted that story. He mentioned that, as he was travelling from village to village, this change in attire had occurred to him as being more and more important.

Welcome of Nadars

In some ways the welcome of the Nadars surprised Gandhiji. In their address they had said, "We have faith in the charkha, but not in your plan for allotment and distribution of funds therefrom. We are told that, due to mismanagement, there has been a loss of Rs. 1 lakh in the fund." (The reference was to an article in the *Tamil Nadu* paper of 16 January 1927, which said that for the growth of the khadi industry, a separate branch of the Madras Khadi Board, comprising 34 members, had been constituted, and that a sum of up to Rs. 1,10,000/- allotted remained uncollected.) "This is why we did not contribute to the fund," they said.

Gandhiji accepted that their not contributing to the fund, in the wake of information regarding the loss of Rs. 1 lakh, was justified, but assured them that no such mismanagement had taken place, and that there was no loss of Rs. 1 lakh. However, he said there can be no commerce without losses, and that no such example existed in the world. He declared that khadi merchandising was in fact being conducted better than any other commercial endeavour in the world.

Hindi

The two reasons given by students in their welcome address on why they did not study Hindi must have surprised Gandhiji—they said they had no time, and because Hindi was not made a compulsory subject. Generally, Gandhiji could never accept that there was no time for something. He said that students need not wait till Hindi was made compulsory, and could make use of the Madurai Hindi Prachar Institute and learn Hindi.

Slow auction

As feared by the Mahatma, a sorry feature of this meeting was the sluggishness in the auction. T. C. Selvam Iyer, who had met Gandhiji in the morning, presented him with attractive khadi cloths. Declaring these to be of excellent quality, he had asked for them to be put up for auction. However, there were no bidders for the price. The silver cups presented by the book binders (worth approximately Rs 20) fetched Rs 300 from A. Vaidyanatha Iyer. As there were no takers for the jewellery available with Gandhiji, the auction was stopped midway. In the days that Gandhiji stayed here, it was usual for him to take a walk in the sports grounds along with Rajaji. N. M. R. Subbaraman and N. S. Ramaswami also used to join them. Dr Soundaram Ramachandran came and played the veena at the place he was staying.

29 September 1927, Saurashtra Club

At a meeting held by the Saurashtrian community at the Saurashtra Club, opposite the Madurai Mariamman temple, a large number of people had come not only from Madurai, but from outstations, including Chettinad. On behalf of the Saurashtrian community, L. K. Thulasiram presented the welcome. On the way to this meeting, Gandhiji was presented with a purse by the shopkeepers in front of the Sri Meenakshi temple *sannidhi*. On this tour it was not known whether Gandhiji had considered any welcome address as especially attractive. He did so, though, in respect of the Saurashtra welcome address, and he gave his reasons for saying so; the Saurashtra language welcome had been written in the Devanagari script. It said that in the Madurai Saurashtra High School, Hindi was offered as an optional subject. Gandhiji went one step further and requested that Hindi be made a compulsory subject in the school.

Heavy responsibility

The welcome address stated that the Saurashtrians had migrated from the Saurashtra province a few centuries ago, and had close connections with Rajkot, where Gandhiji grew up. Gandhiji said: "I am delighted to hear this, but you must realise that to mention that you and I are connected is fraught with danger, because every work of mine then casts a heavy responsibility on you. What is the use of relatives who are of no help in danger?"

Agreeing with all the views expressed, Gandhiji mentioned one with which he differed. The Saurashtra Society members had suggested that, whatever be the source of the yarn, Gandhiji should approve hand weaving of the same. Gandhiji's response to this was:

> Many people were living off hand spinning. Spinning units had ruined their livelihood. If weaving was also taken up by these units, what will be your plight? What happened to spinning will also happen to weaving. At first, I, too, was weaving with yarn produced by spinning units. A thought occurred to me one day. If the weaving profession was also taken over by factories, I asked myself what will happen to thousands of weavers? Hence, to obtain hand-spun yarn, I found out a village with the help of one lady. Today, those who were weavers in Saurashshtra are working as scavengers in Bombay. Weavers in Punjab have joined the army. Some have set up scrap shops. Hence it is advisable to use your own spun yarn for the growth of the khadi movement.

As Gandhiji was speaking, it started to rain, and so he finished quickly. Muthuramalinga Asari presented a portrait of the Mahatma etched on a silver plate covered by glass. A European lady gave Gandhiji her necklace of gold studded with precious stones, which she had worn for 25 years. Many others presented jewels and purses. As usual, an auction was held.

30 September 1927, Women's meeting

The women's meeting held in the Victoria Edward Hall was attended by approximately 2,000 women. On behalf of the women, Tmt. Subbulakshmi ammal, wife of K. Sankararama Iyer, presented a purse. A few days before Gandhiji arrived in Madurai, some thieves had burgled a wealthy person's home and decamped with their child's jewels. Someone informed Gandhiji of this. Referring to it at this meeting, he said, "Women should not wear jewellery beyond the bare minimum. They should also not expose their children to such dangers by adorning them likewise."

Tirumangalam

As soon as this meeting ended, Gandhiji went by car to Tirumangalam (a town in Madurai district). A public meeting was arranged in the sprawling grounds opposite the District Magistrate's court. On behalf of the Union Board and the general public, welcome addresses and purses were presented. One of the addresses requested that, like Tiruppur, Tirumangalam should also be made another khadi capital. In reply, Gandhij said:

> The status Tiruppur has attained today is not as a result of my or the Indian Charkha Sangam's efforts. Already many workers had been engaged there in khadi work, which the Charkha Sangam made use of, that is all. The Tirumangalam Union Board can take up this important work—in fact, it must. When the meeting ended, Gandhiji got down from the car while returning, and walked for some distance.

Justice Party leaders

In Madurai, Gandhiji held discussions with the Justice Party leaders, and spoke about their objectives and working ethos. The press was excluded from these discussions. Still, a news item was put out that Gandhiji was displeased with the actions of the non-Brahmin leaders. He seemed to have warned them, "These actions, instead of bringing reform in Hindu religious ideology, would only serve to endanger religious fervour."

1 October 1927, Paramakudi

When Gandhiji and his group reached Paramakudi (a town in Ramanathapuram district) by train, he was welcomed by Ramaswami Iyengar and Rajaram Pandian. As the crowd was more than expected at the meeting venue near Melachathram, there was a lot of noise being made. To add to it, there was rain. Still, the meeting was held. On behalf of the Paramakudi general public, Cooperative Bank, Congress Committee and Charkha Sangam, welcome addresses were presented. Purses on behalf of the public, women, and the Cooperative Bank, were also given. The Mahatma began his speech touching on the importance of wearing khadi, eradication of untouchability, etc. The rain, though, did not abate, neither did the noise. Hence he stopped his speech abruptly, completed the auction, and returned to Madurai in the night by Rameswaram Express. Kasturba Gandhi, who had gone to Rameswaram, joined Gandhiji on this train.

2 October 1927, Virudhunagar

The next day, Gandhiji and his group took the morning train to Virudhunagar (53 km south of Madurai), his first visit. He inaugurated the Guest House for the poor that Pagalam K. Pazhanisamy Nadar had built in the name of his daughter, and his stay was arranged there itself. He said it was appropriate that, as a representative of the poor, he was staying at a guest house inaugurated by him. Rev. I. Himmel Strandt of the Usilampatti Swedish Mission Church met Gandhiji, who enquired about some specific doubts he had. Gandhiji stayed two days at Virudhunagar, of which one was his birthday, and the other his day of silence.

Gandhiji's belief in the caste system

In the evening, members of the non-Brahmin youth association met Gandhiji and requested for his responses to specific questions they had. Gandhiji patiently answered them, and explained to them the foundations of his belief in the caste system prevalent in India.

Q: What is your definition of the caste division that you mention?
Gandhiji: In Hindu religion, there are four castes defined: Brahmin, Kshatriya, Vysya and Shudra. Brahmacharyam, Grihasthashramam, Vanaprastham and Sanyasam are the four stages of life mentioned. ... The reason for the Indian traditions being maintained over centuries, when the Greek, Egyptian and Roman cultures collapsed, are due to the laws of caste division being intact in our country.
Q: Is there no caste division in the Christian and Mohammedan faiths?
Gandhiji: Caste division is as immutable as the force of gravity. Can we say that gravity did not exist before Newton discovered it? Similarly, it can be said that the Hindu religion can take pride in having given to the world the caste system.

Public meeting

The public meeting in the evening was held on the large grounds on Ramamurthi Road. Welcome addresses on behalf of Virudhunagar Municipality Association, the general public, Madurai Rail passengers' association, Kshathriya Vidyasala students, and Rao Bahadur Rathinasamy Nadar Library staff were presented. On behalf of the Virudhunagar general public, students, Bombay Nadar Merchants' clerks, and Melappatthi village folk purses were given.

Gandhiji lauded the good relations enjoyed between Hindus and Muslims here. P. N. A. Mohammed Ibrahim was the Town Council president. Though Muslims were in a minority in the town, Gandhiji was happy that a Muslim headed the Town Council. He also expressed happiness that the Nadar community was increasingly coming forward to take up important national work. He added that, more than primary education, a town council's first attention should be towards cleanliness of the surroundings. He emphasised that khadi lent a spiritual dimension to the commerce of a place.

4 October 1927, Rajapalayam

At all the small railway stations from Virudhunagar (here, the city; also a district) to Rajapalayam (now a city in Tamil Nadu), the general public and prominent people offered greetings to Gandhiji.

At Srivilliputhur station, on behalf of the Town Administration, a welcome was arranged. At Rajapalayam, Gandhiji and his group stayed at the residence of P. S. Kumarasami Raja, then a District Committee member (and future chief minister of the state).

Gandhiji proceeded to Nayakanpettai in the evening and inspected women at work on the spinning wheel. About 50 women were engaged in spinning there. Gandhiji approached them to inquire about the process they adopted, and the amount they earned. They told him they were able to earn Rs 4 per month. "Why are you not wearing khadi?" he asked them. The women replied, "Because of poverty. Besides, khadi is more difficult to obtain than mill cloth." Gandhiji then said, "If you could spin your own yarn, weave it, and buy it at a reduced price, would you wear khadi?" The women replied, "Yes, we would."

Women's meeting

After this, Gandhi went to a women's meeting at Pettharaja's house. Here, many women from rich families in purdah were present, wearing plenty of jewellery. It was no surprise that Gandhiji, who had just returned from observing poor women at the spinning wheel, was presented here with a picture in sharp contrast. A welcome and purse on behalf of women of the Andhra Kshatriya Raja community were presented. Pettharaja gave a purse on his own behalf. Mahatma's speech in Hindi was translated into Telugu.

After speaking on the importance of khadi, he spoke about the custom of purdah. "I do not understand why the Andhra Kshatriya women should be in purdah. If you just remain at home without seeing the outside world, how can you know what is happening?" He praised the khadi made in Rajapalayam to be of a high quality. Here, arrangements had been made to distribute 100 spinning wheels free of cost, which was done. Gandhiji presented a spinning wheel to the lady who had read out the welcome address. The remaining 99 spinning wheels were distributed to other women.

For the production and sale of khadi, the 'Gandhi Khadi Vastralayam' cooperative had been established here. After the women's meeting, Gandhiji went to the house of Kumarasamy Raja to attend the function there, at which the members of this Vastralayam had gathered. He advised that profit should not be their motive right at the start. He signed the visitors' book in Tamil.

Public meeting

In the evening, large crowds from Srivilliputhur and Sivakasi had massed at the Kanmai Grounds. Welcome speeches on behalf of the Rajapalayam general public, Rajapalayam Union Board, Khadi Vastralayam, Merchants' Association, Sivakasi Taluk Board and Srivilliputhur Town Administration were presented. Purses on behalf of the general public, Sethur Zamindar Sevakapandia Thevar, Sivakasi Taluk Board, Sivagiri general public, cardamom plantation owners and the Cooperative Supervisors' Association, were handed over.

In his address Gandhiji said: "The women of this town engaged in spinning tell me that they earn up to Rs. 4 per month. This is more than what their counterparts are earning in other centres. The reason for this is that the people here spin with better skill, alacrity and for longer hours." However, he also rebuked the women of more advantaged classes for wearing ostentatious ornamentation.

> Women in purdah, too, wear a great deal of jewellery, as if to show how wealthy they are… they should desist from doing so. Men must advise their women on the need for simple living. Without the help of men they cannot bring in such improvements. There is nothing better than khadi to make for simple living. That is why I say that khadi is the bridge between the rich and the poor.

Gandhiji also underlined the difference between the commercial aspects of khadi as compared to those of any other product.

> 'I am duty-bound to look after my welfare; those who buy from me can look after their own' is the byline of people selling products. But khadi does not work on that principle. I, who raise funds for khadi, consider myself a trustee of the sellers of khadi, those who go to villages to start khadi ventures, and those who spin khadi yarn. We are custodians of all spinners. (*The Hindu*, 6 October 1927)

Nadars and temples

About Nadars not being allowed into temples, Gandhiji said:

> I was speaking with some Nadar friends in Virudhunagar.
> They are intrepid and affluent businessmen. They are also
> religious-minded. They run successfully a high school, where
> boys, irrespective of caste, are given free education. As is their
> education, their temple, too, is open for all to enter. However,
> I am surprised and dismayed to hear that they, who live a life
> of such purity, are not allowed into any of the temples between
> Tirunelveli and Madurai. I feel ashamed that in my Hindu faith
> such discrimination is taking place. I have visited Madurai
> thrice so far, but have never so far entered the big temple. After
> hearing the plight of the Nadars, I feel in fact blessed not to have
> entered this temple. Hence you must all get together and work
> towards eradication of untouchability, and permission for all to
> enter temples.

From the time he arrived in Virudhunagar, he did not omit to
mention in every speech the ban placed on the entry of Nadars into
temples. It surprised him that this ban, which existed in Madurai,
Ramanathapuram and Tirunelveli districts, was not there in other
places of Madras State. "How can you deny entry into temples to a
community of such modern, progressive, businessmen?" was his
refrain at all the meetings.

5 October 1927, The old problem

Gandhiji was forced to address the Brahmin–non-Brahmin problem
again when he came to Kovilpatti. The welcome committee president
and the Kuruvikulam Zamindar, P. N. Kothandarayasamy Naidu and
others received Gandhiji at Nalatinputhur. In Srinivasapuram, Union
Board president, M. J. Ramaswami Iyer presented a welcome address.
Gandhiji's group stayed as guests of the Kurungulam Zamindar. In
the evening, at the public meeting near Senbagavalli Amman temple,
welcome addresses were read out on behalf of the Kovilpatti Congress
Committee, Khamma Mahajana Sangam, the Kovilpatti general public,
the Sankarankoil Taluk general public, Merchants' Association clerks
and Kovilpatti Southern Nadar Mahimaipettai. A 10-year-old girl,

Alamelu, who sang the National Song, was felicitated with a rose garland by Gandhiji at the end of the meeting.

One of the welcome addresses had mentioned the Brahmin–non-Brahmin problem. Hence, Gandhiji spoke about what decision he had come to regarding this issue.

> I have made efforts each time to understand this problem. I have allotted as much time as I could to discuss this issue with non-Brahmin leaders. I believe now that I have understood the problem. I will write about this in *Young India*, and attempt to dispel the differences between the two, and generate goodwill. There is nothing more that I can do, because I do not have the confidence that either group will act as per my advice. Leaders of both factions must meet and try to resolve their differences. Some of the complaints of non-Brahmins against Brahmins appear justified, but sometimes they magnify them beyond necessity. I will accept their justified complaints, but cannot countenance the hatred that they display towards Brahmins. I accept their criticism that Brahmins are not fulfilling their duties, but I cannot accept that all the ills are caused by Brahmins alone. Even if I do offer a solution, I doubt whether the Brahmins would give up the rights they have enjoyed for generations.

In the auction held here, it delighted Gandhiji that an exquisite, small palm leaf box went for Rs 50. All other articles put together fetched Rs 50, which brought a smile to his face.

6 October 1927, Thoothukudi

At Thoothukudi, Gandhiji stayed in the house of the Ceylon Legislative Assembly member, I. X. Pereira. That afternoon, he gave an interview to the Town Council president, Rose Victoria, I. X. Pereira, and Thoothukudi Bishop, Dr Tiburthin Roche's mother. In the evening, a public meeting was held at the Vattakkinaru Grounds. The girls of Tilak National School rendered the invocatory song. Welcome addresses and purses on behalf of the Thoothukudi general public, women, lawyers, Viswakarma Mahajana Sabha, lawyers' clerks, Bharath Mahajana Sangam, and Hindi students were presented. The Town Council's welcome was presented by its president, Rose Victoria. Gandhiji's speech here was first translated by Rajaji, and later by A. Masilamani Pillai into Tamil. The president of the meeting, I. X. Pereira, said that the people of Ceylon had eagerly awaited Gandhiji's visit.

National school

Gandhiji expressed happiness when he was told that, not only boys and girls, but adults, too, were learning Hindi here. He was also glad that a national school was being run in the name of Tilak. In their welcome address it had been requested that some amount out of the Khadi Fund be allotted to this school. Gandhiji declined, saying that it was not appropriate to divert funds received for some other purpose, and, instead, asked the affluent citizens of Thoothukudi to assist monetarily in the smooth functioning of the school.

Tamil and Gandhi

Gandhiji's insistence on learning Hindi, and on the use of khadi, everywhere he went gave rise to some misinterpretations. Many criticised him for not having any respect for Tamil. This reached his ears, and in Thoothukudi, he replied to this charge at length. From the translation of Gandhiji's speech in response, it appears that in one of the welcome addresses, the pride of Tamil and the greatness of *Tirukkural* had been mentioned.

> When I toured this state, I have heard people complaining that I have said nothing about the Tamil language, and the need to learn it. I cannot accept this accusation. Persons close to me will also concur that this charge has no substance. I have emphasised several times that before learning English you must learn Tamil. Years ago, from 1915, I have asked the people to learn Tamil in preference to English. From before 1917, I have said that education should be in the mother tongue, and that people should converse and read literature in their mother tongues.
>
> You have brought to my attention the treasure that is contained in the *Tirukkural*. I wish to tell you that it was with the intention of reading the *Tirukkural* that I started to learn Tamil 20 years ago. I am only sorry that God did not allow me enough time to learn this language fully. I am completely in favour of making mother tongue the medium of instruction. It must be given

more importance than English, more than any other language, in fact. In one place I was given a welcome in English instead of Tamil. I mildly chastised them. In all schools I would prefer Tamil to be given more prominence than English. Therefore, I hope that you will henceforward not fault me in this.

This speech on Tamil pleased all, and silenced those who held that Gandhiji did not respect Tamil. Thereafter, Thiru V. Kalyanasundara Mudaliar was given the task of bringing out the beauty and distinction of the *Tirukkural* on several occasions.

7 October 1927, Palayamkottai

T. S. Aram Valarthanata Pillai, C. Ramanathan and a couple of others involved in the production of khadi met Gandhiji at Palayamkottai (a locality in Tirunelveli city) and discussed their problems with him. They informed him that, as they were making individual efforts to propagate khadi, they would welcome technical help from the All India Charkha Sangam, wishing to have no connection with the Madras Charkha Sangam. Before they met him, the District Medical Officer, Dr. P. Eswaraiah, came, checked Gandhiji's blood pressure, pronounced that there were no alarming fluctuations, and said that it was all right for his age.

After this, Gandhiji went with Rajaji into the town and received the welcome of merchants and their clerks, who presented separate purses to him.

Public meeting

Gandhiji then proceeded to the public meeting at Karzan Grounds. Several welcome addresses and purses were presented. Orusal Veerabhadra Pillai presented a silver box. On behalf of the general public, Thirukoodasundaram Pillai handed over a purse. Welcome addresses were presented on behalf of Tirunelveli District Association, Tirunelveli Taluk Board and Tirunelveli-Palayamkottai Town Councils, by Dewan Bahadur S. Kumarasamy Reddiar, I. C. Eswaran Pillai, C. Azhagarsamy Naidu and K. S. Ponnusamy Pillai, and on behalf of the Palayamkottai Spinners' Sangam, the Youth National Congress members, the Kallidaikurichi South Tirupperai public, and

Tirunelveli District Indian Christian Association, by Daniel Thomas. Member of Legislative Council (MLC) Iyya Iyer of Cheramadevi presented a 150s count yarn spun by him and khadi cloth woven by school boys of Kulasekharapattinam (now a town in Thoothukudi district of Tamil Nadu) to Gandhiji.

The Christian welcome said that hitherto Christians had not considered themselves part of the national movement, but had now started getting involved in it. "All over South India, I am happy to see this involvement by Christians," Gandhiji said.

At this point, let us look at the relationship that people of other faiths had with Gandhiji.

Against religious conversion

Generally speaking, Gandhiji did not believe in religious conversions, and was opposed to the largely ignorant and innocent poor people and Harijans being misled and lured into conversion by other religions. He felt that Christians, Muslims and Buddhists sought to convert people to increase the numbers of their faiths. Gandhiji had clear differences of opinion in this matter even with his close friend C. F. Andrews. Once, in 1916, Andrews had asked Gandhiji, "If the natives of Tiruvangur (many of whom were educated at that time) had converted to Christianity voluntarily, is it not acceptable?" Gandhiji did not agree, saying, "A few of them could have been doctors or lawyers, but a majority of them are, like Harijans in other parts of India, backward."

All religions are equal

At the same meeting, Andrews had asked another question. "After much thought and prayer, a man comes to a conclusion that there is no redemption for him unless he becomes a Christian. What would you say to a man like that?" Gandhiji gave a straight reply to this direct question: "If a non-Christian (let us assume he is a Hindu) came to a Christian and said the same thing, that Christian should reply that, instead of changing your faith to obtain redemption, continue to be a good Hindu. A person of one faith can bring about improvements in the life of another of a different faith, but not seek to convert him to his."

Gandhiji was not in consonance with the pronouncement of Mohammed Ali that a Muslim, however faithless he may be to his own religion, and evil, is still higher than a Hindu. Gandhiji was not just of the view that a person of one religion should merely tolerate a person of another. It was more that he should believe that all religions are equal, and a person of one faith must respect people of other faiths. The underlying principle of all major world religions is equality.

Gandhiji was asked, "If there is one God, can there be so many religions?" His reply was: "The soul is one. But it is there in so many bodies. It is the root of the tree, but the tree itself has so many branches and leaves. In the same way, a true and pure religion is one, but when it is expressed through pure people, it becomes different religions, and is beyond all arguments."

Gandhiji's life exemplified his steadfast belief in the equality of all religions. In the ashram established by Gandhiji in South Africa, he had introduced books on all religions and common prayers. His famous tour of Noakhali (now in Bangladesh, during the large-scale riots and violence there in 1946), and his ultimate sacrifice and martyrdom were the high points of the extreme trial that he put himself to.

All Religions Movement

The leaders of the All Religions Movement had a close connection with Gandhiji. This was a movement that sought the coming together of all religions. There was a branch of it in Madras. Whether in the Indian movement or the one in Madras, A. A. Paul and Dr Khaitan (they were Americans, though originating from Madras), Dr Jesudasan, and Dr Gurupadam wielded influence in it. They did not hold the view that it was the Christian faith alone that offered man redemption. However, they had studied Christian doctrine in depth, and they believed that, should a non-Christian voluntarily seek to convert to Christanity because he felt it showed him the path to redemption, there was nothing wrong in converting him. Although they were close to Gandhiji, and many among them accepted 'Gandhi-ism', their stand on conversion was not acceptable to Gandhiji. "Religion is a matter of man's individual belief. It is between him and his God. Hence there is no place to casually treat the issue of religious conversion."

In 1928, when an all-religion conference was held at Sabarmati, there were two days of rigorous arguments that took place before the conference as to what the objective of the conference should be, but no agreement was reached. Gandhiji, who was invited to this conference, explained what, in his view, the objective of the conference could be. Those who believed that there should only be one religion in the world had no place here.

Christians issue a statement

After the Tiruvangur church entry, 14 prominent Christians from all over India—a majority of them belonging to Madras—welcomed that move, and issued a statement as to what the conduct of Christians should be in the matter of religious conversion. The warning contained in the words and views of this statement did not satisfy Gandhiji. Whilst on the one hand, it stated that the hardship suffered by the backward and depressed classes should not be used as a lever for conversion (the church castigated them for making this statement, and debarred them from attending the Christian conference), on the other, it said that if individuals and families came forward to get converted to Christianity as they believed it was the faith that embodied the spirit of God, such conversions could not be stopped. The duty of the Christian Church was to welcome people who came with faith in Jesus Christ and his truth, and to make them imbibe the doctrine.

Whichever religion they came from, the Christian religion had the right to welcome them. The Church would not forgo its right to fight against anti-Christian movements, and feed the religious hunger of those who sought it. This part of the statement was what Gandhiji took exception to. In his article in *Harijan* (3 April 1927) issue, he wrote, reprinting their advertising propaganda:

> The aim of this advertisement is not to condemn the conversion of depressed and innocent people, but to declare the right to spread the word of the Bible among crores of Harijans. Men and women are not rushing to join the church. Harijans and others are no better or worse. It is good if they have a genuine thirst for spiritualism, but this thirst is presently being quenched by our temples, however old these temples may be. When preachers

of another religion go to the public, they go as sellers in some market. Wherever they go, they do not have any high spiritualism to convey. They have with them material objects, and offer them as enticement to people to change over to their religion. Consider further ... in India, the duty of the Christian religion has become its right. When duty becomes right, there is no sense of duty left. Hence, the objective of this statement issued by them, which is to clear the confusion in people's minds and bring about peace, has not been served.

This statement of Gandhiji did not find favour with the Christians. Thereafter some bishops and important Christians met Gandhiji at Nagpur, and explained their views. "The conversion that took place in Andhra is the true conversion," they said. "No, it was not a true conversion. If you will take me there and prove to me that it was a true conversion, I will change my views," Gandhiji challenged. Dr Gurupadam was with him during this exchange.

Khaitan's closeness to Gandhiji

The view of all religions being equal held by Gandhiji provoked the displeasure of several Christian groups in Madras. Many Christians would fly into a rage if his name was even mentioned at meetings. However, some Christians, Madurai George Joseph, Dr. Pichaimuthu, Khaitan, Tiruppur Dr Jesudasan, Dr Patton, and Salem Dr. Gurupadam, remained his confidantes. It could even be said that Gandhiji's doctrine of the equality of all religions found favour with them. Particularly, Khaitan's closeness to Gandhiji could be attributed to this, as he had understood his constructive zeal. Gandhiji praised the work Khaitan did for the depressed classes. Dr Jesudasan and Dr Patton participated in the strike against liquor shops. When Dr Patton visited Madras, he was subject to police brutality even before participating in the strike. This became an all-India issue. Dr Gurupadam took part in national politics and administration, before becoming a minister in the Madras government.

The value of silence

From the age of 20, Gandhiji had enjoyed the friendship of Christians. As a result of this association, he had benefitted in great measure spiritually too. For example, when he was in South Africa, he learnt the value of silence when he visited a Trappist[3] monastery. After meeting the monks there, Gandhiji came away deeply impressed, and convinced that one had to be silent in order to hear soft voices; if we talk incessantly, these voices will not be heard.

Let us now come to Tirunelveli, where we last left Gandhiji.

Train students to spin

A few days before this meeting, Sir M. Visvesvaraya (1860–1962), eminent engineer and administrator, had decried the export of essential raw materials from India, thereby denying their availability for indigenous production, leading to widespread unemployment in the country. This was referred to by Gandhiji at this meeting.

> You grow cotton here. And there is good opportunity to convert it into cloth (praising the efforts of Aram Valartha Natha Pillai and Viswanatha Pillai, whom he was staying with, in training boys and girls in two schools in spinning). Just imagine the increase in production capacity of this nation if every school in India trained students for just a few hours in spinning. In every town, someone or the other comes up to me, gives me a dhoti, saying I should not auction it, but wear it myself. Here, too, one person has told me so. In this manner, there is a history attached to every apparel that I don. Through this profession, you can unite all the classes of people and religious groups in India.

Lack of faith

Continuing to address the public, Gandhiji now referred to the problem being discussed about Brahmins and non-Brahmins.

> These friends have great faith in khadi and its future, but not in the solution of the Brahmin–non-Brahmin problem. They say that, in the khadi work in Tamilnadu, more Brahmins are involved. Both of them sought an assurance from me. I can auction the khadi cloth that I have received from them at this meeting, but I should not use that money for the khadi related work in Tamilnadu. I have given them my assurance, and there is a reason for it. There is need for funds to carry on khadi work in

other places in India. At the same time I wish to say something
to you here. Even if there is without doubt a 'Brahmin air' in the
khadi administration of in Tamilnadu [*The Hindu,* 10 October
1927], the benefits of this movement are reaching the spinners
and weavers who are largely non-Brahmins. As the head of the
All India Charkha Sangam, I wish to give you an assurance. If,
based on my conditions, the technical experts who work with
me deny in any way the benefits accruing to the non-Brahmins,
I am willing to ask all the Brahmins to resign from the All
India Charkha Sangam. If the few Brahmins working under the
Charkha Sangam are asked to resign, I may tell you that they
would be earning much more than what they are earning here.
Such is the level of their expertise. The Charkha Sangam can in
no way match the salary they can earn elsewhere. Compared to
Rs. 1000 or 1100 outside, they are getting a paltry Rs. 100 from
the Charkha Sangam. Hence, if I were to pay them the higher
wages they deserve, I shall have to file a 'Pauper's Petition'.

Therefore, believe what I say. If any Brahmins have joined the
Charkha Sangam, they have come with a full understanding of
'Brahmin dharma'. If I were to get more number of such people in
India, I could solve all its problems. Brahmins are endowed with
good education and lack of self-interest. This is the fundamental
definition of a Brahmin. Not all Brahmins in India, though,
are so. There are some who are not. My efforts are to find such
[educated and selfless] people and use their services.

Aram Valartha Natha Pillai was an intense Brahmin opposer, and
supporter of non-Brahmins. How deeply their views had impacted
Gandhiji could be seen in the speech he delivered here. He said if
it weren't for the paucity of time, he would have spoken at greater
length on this subject. If one examines the basis of the Brahmin–
non-Brahmin divide, it is also a kind of untouchability, he said, and
if the snake of untouchability is killed, the Brahmin–non-Brahmin
conflict will automatically be rooted out. In a somewhat sarcastic
reference to the pollution of the Tambraparani river by effluents,
Gandhiji said: "On one hand, to prevent the spread of cholera, the
Town administrators are taking up a vaccination drive; on the other,
you are pouring 'medicine' into the Tambraparani."

Auction

When auction was taken up in this meeting, there was an odd incident. Auctioning the welcome address of the District committee, Gandhiji commented, "I hope the committee members themselves would bid for this." But neither the president nor members of the committee made any bid. A member of the public bought it for Rs 5, and handed over the money to Gandhiji. Mahatma offered it for auction again. Even then, none in the committee made any bid. Yet again, a member of the public bought it. Gandhiji put it up for auction a third time, and so it went on. Finally, C. Ramanathan of Kulasekharapatti (now a village in Tirunelveli district) bid Rs 8 for it and presented it to the District Committee president, ending the auction chain.

8 October 1927, Nagercoil

The next day Gandhiji and and his group reached Nagercoil. On behalf of the town people, Municipal Administration, and Scott Christian College, welcome addresses and purses were presented. Thereafter, Gandhiji left for Trivandrum. At the public meeting in Nagercoil, he condemned the practice of Harijans being asked not to see, and to stay away from caste Hindus. "It pains me that the temple priests who should be the true defenders of the Hindu faith are in fact destroying it, and this is the historical truth," he said.

15 and 16 October 1927, Meeting Sankarachariar

Having entered Tiruvangur princedom from Madras State on the 8 October, Gandhiji reached Coimbatore by car on the 16 October from Palghat. He met the Sankarachariar Swami in Palghat. The Kanchi Kamakoti Peethadhipathi, Sri Chandrasekharendra Saraswathi Swamigal's meeting with Gandhiji is a historic event. Although this meeting took place in the Nalli slum of Palghat, it is considered an event closely associated with the state now known as Tamil Nadu. In his book, *Sri Jagatguru Divya Charithram*, Ramachandrapuram S. Sambamoorthi Sastri wrote about this event.

The meeting

Having heard from *The Hindu* editor, A. Rangaswami Iyengar, S. Satyamurthi and others about the wisdom, compassion, and broadmindedness of the Sankarachariar, and his willingness to bless anyone, Gandhiji decided to make use of this opportunity to meet the Swamigal and speak with him. This historic meeting took place on 15 October 1927 in the cowshed at the rear of the Nalli slum residence where the Swamigal was staying. Only two or three persons were allowed in; no newspapermen were permitted. Gandhiji approached the Swamigal and paid his obeisance. Clad in khadi cloth of saffron, the Swamigal was seated on the ground, his aura immediately gripping the heart of Gandhiji. There was silence for some time. Thereafter, the Swamigal spoke a few words in Sanskrit. Gandhiji sat down, saying he was not practised in speaking Sanskrit, and requested he be permitted to speak in Hindi, though he could understand some amount of Sanskrit. As the Swamigal could understand Hindi, the arrangement was that he would speak in Sanskrit, and Gandhiji in Hindi. The Swamigal lauded Gandhiji's principles that governments should be established only on the basis of belief in God. Any government that is sought to be run ignoring spiritual values, and dictated by the strength of the people, was bound to result in ruin. The Swamigal added that there was a large majority of people who believed in our shastras and customs that prevented Harijans from entering temples. Any move to change this mindset would amount to oppression.

There was further discussion on the realities of life, reflecting the perspectives and experiences of both. There were no arguments or counter-arguments. Gandhiji only said what he felt genuinely about. He never bothered about whether people would accept him or not. Every word of his was steeped in inner truth, a quality which the Swamigal often praised. They spoke for about an hour. When he took leave of the seer, Gandhiji said that he considered the Swamigal's 'darshan' of great help to him, and assured him that he would bear in mind everything the Swamigal had said and try to implement them to the best of his ability.

Shanmugam Chettiar

In Coimbatore, Gandhiji stayed in the house of R. K. Shanmugam Chettiar (who later became the Finance Minister of Madras). Women arranged a rousing reception to the Gandhi couple at Victoria Town Hall. He was welcomed there by Tmts. Ramasamy Sivan, K. Cherian Jacob, and K. Meenakshiammal. On behalf of the Indian National Sangam, a purse and a silver plate on behalf of the Sisters' Association were handed over.

As there was a lot of noise at the meeting as usual, Gandhiji issued a warning at the outset that if it continued, he would be unable to deliver his speech. The commotion abated, and he started to speak. He said: "We all wish for a 'Rama Rajyam' [golden era] in India. Unless women like you live like Sitas, this cannot be attained. But many among you are wearing foreign clothes and distancing yourselves from this goal."

Travel plan

On this tour, it was in Gandhiji's plan to visit Gobichettipalayam (now a 'Selection grade municipality' in Tamil Nadu), Erode and Pudupalayam (now a panchayat town in Tamil Nadu). But owing to his frail health, he decided to cancel these visits. After a strenuous tour in Kerala, he was exhausted. Hence, he announced that he would rest in Coimbatore till till 21 October go to Tiruppur for three days and thereafter to Kallikkottai.

Coimbatore engagements

At the public meeting in Coronation Park (now known as Va. U. Si. or VOC Park), welcome addresses and purses were presented by the Coimbatore Town Council, District Congress Committee, Taluk Congress Committee, Adi Dravidars, and the Coimbatore general public. V. Mahalinga Iyer translated the Mahatma's speech into Tamil. As earlier, the welcome address of the Coimbatore Town Council reflected some differences in views. It expressed the opinion that the non-cooperation movement was of no avail, and that the caste division was the major cause of the high- and low-caste discrimination prevalent in the Hindu tradition; and that Gandhiji's 'solution' to this caste discrimination would only compound the existing problems and become a barrier to progress.

Gandhiji took up the Town Council's welcome first. He reiterated the arguments he had hitherto been making on those issues. He thanked them for raising these matters.

> From 1921, I have been carefully analysing the objections raised against the non-cooperation movement, but I have seen no need to change my views. Through peaceful non-cooperation, our country has reaped benefits that it has not seen for two generations. I believe that the objection today is based on the apprehension of the caste system. True caste division is a law of nature. I am increasingly convinced that it is because we are going against this caste division that more and more violence is being seen in India and in other parts of the world. The cracks in the Hindu religion are seen because of this.

Slums and liquor

In the welcome of the Adi Dravidars, one of the points mentioned pleased Gandhiji. "The government opens liquor shops very near our slums, and tempts us. If, instead, they opened factories, and if social workers befriend us rather than distillers, there is no doubt that we would progress very quickly. Hence we request you to ensure that factories in place of liquor shops are opened in our neighbourhood."

Reiterating their point in his own response, Gandhiji said: "I approve of this wholeheartedly. You, the people of Coimbatore, should agitate for this in support. You must establish training centres for Adi Dravidar boys and girls."

Khadi and nationalism

In the same manner, a problem arose out of the welcome address of the Congress. It asked the Mahatma to once again take up the leadership of the country. Gandhiji's response was: "A man who upholds ahimsa is in fact considered to be a leader fulfilling the mission objectives. Hence, as the head of the All India Charkha Sangam, I am indeed showing the way for the nation." He responded to each welcome address likewise. "All your welcome addresses raise important problems being faced. Therefore it is but right that I should respond to all the points to the best of my ability."

In the auction held here, the painting of Deshbandhu C. R. Das, by T. S. Ramachandra Rao was bought by the Trustee of P. S. G. and Sons, Ganga Naidu, for Rs 256. During the stay of Gandhiji in Coimbatore, Kondampatti Raghavendra Rao presented a purse on behalf of the public of Kinatthkkadavu (a suburb of Coimbatore). Gandhiji inspected the Khadi Vastralayam.

18 October 1927, Pollachi

Gandhiji left Coimbatore by car, and reached Pollachi (a town in Coimbatore district) in the evening, where he stayed at the residence of Ponnusamy Kalingarayar Gounder. It was planned to start the public meeting by 4.30 or 5 p.m. However, as there was an intermittent drizzle, Gandhiji arrived at the venue of the weekly *shandy* (a 'shandy market' is a trading place of local small traders on a specific day of the week), where the public meeting was to be held, at 5.30 p.m. Welcome addresses were presented on behalf of the Pollachi Town Council, Taluk Board, and Town High School. Purses were handed over on behalf of the Pollachi general public, Taluk Board, the general public of Erisanapatti (now a village in Tiruppur district), and the Town High School. Gandhiji's speech here was translated by R. K. Shanmugam Chettiar. As the public had been drenched by the rain, Gandhiji did not want to hold them up for long. Further, he himself was not so well. He finished his speech quickly.

22 October 1927, Gobichettipalayam

In response to the persuasion of the representatives of Gobichettipalayam, Gandhiji's tour programme had to be altered again; he gave up his plans to go to Tirupur (or Tiruppur) by train, and, instead, left for Gobichettipalayam by car, promising to come to Tiruppur in the same trip. He went from Coimbatore with K. Subramania Gounder. The public meeting was held in the grounds opposite Vellalar Colony. K. Subramania Gounder read out the welcome of the general public, while K. N. Nanjappa Gounder, the president of of the Taluk Board, read the Board's welcome. There was also a welcome by the Union Board. Here, the speech of Gandhiji was translated by a lawyer from Gobichettiplayam, G. R. Nageswara Iyer. At the end of the meeting, purses on behalf of the general public and Taluk Board were handed over by P. S. Muthuvel Gounder. Purses were also presented on behalf of Gobichettipalayam school students and Union Taluk Board. After this, Gandhiji left for Tiruppur via Uthukuli. In Uthukuli, he inspected the khadi unit run under the supervision of K. Subramaniam, known as Subri.

True to his word

To be true to one's word is a noble quality. Gandhiji's visits to Gobichettipalayam and Karur exemplified this. A week before he was to visit Karur, Ve. Ramalingam Pillai (1888–1972), the poet of Namakkal (now a 'special grade municipality' in Tamil Nadu), received a telegram to the effect that Karur had been dropped from Gandhiji's tour schedule. Having spent two–three months strenuously collecting money from people for the purse to be given to Gandhiji, he was hugely disappointed to learn this.

Likewise was the reaction in Gobichettipalayam when news was received that Gandhiji's visit was cancelled, and that he was proceeding directly to Kallikkottai. Gandhiji was then resting in R. K. Shanmugam Chettiar's house in Coimbatore. A friend from Gobichettipalayam met him, and burst out emotionally, "Can such an atrocity happen in front of your eyes?" Gandhiji wanted to know the truth, and Rajaji was summoned. "There is an accusation leveled against me. I must atone for it. Whatever the issue, a word is a word— it must be upheld," Gandhiji said in anguish (Akkoor Ananthachari, *The Way Shown by Gandhiji*). Rajaji accordingly changed the tour plan to re-include Gobichettipalayam and Karur.

Disappointment

While Gandhiji was en route to Tiruppur by car, the general public, who were unaware of the change in his plans, amassed at the Tiruppur railway station, anticipating his arrival. Not finding Gandhiji in the shuttle train from Coimbatore, they returned in dismay. It was only later that they got to know of his coming to Tiruppur by car. In the evening, Gandhiji inspected the Tiruppur Khadi Vastralayam. The manager of the Vastralayam, Narayana Iyengar, welcomed him, and also showed him round the dyeing unit run under the administration of Sharma.

Health check

Gandhiji stayed in a building named 'Mangala Vilas' in Tiruppur. Dr. T. S. S. Rajan examined him and cleared his state of health. Still, Gandhiji did not take part in any function this day, opting instead to rest fully. He received an invitation from Viceroy Irwin (Viceroy of India, 1926–31) to meet him, which Gandhiji accepted.

23 October 1927, *Gita* class

Lord Krishna expounded the *Bhagavad Gita* to Arjuna in Kurukshetra of ancient times. Early this morning, at 3.45 a.m. Gandhiji inaugurated the *Gita* class in the Tiruppur Town Council-run high school for students and teachers, and advised:

> Undertake the study of the *Gita* at 4 a.m. every morning. If you do not understand Sanskrit, study the Tamil translation, but not in English, because in the English translation, the essence of the *Gita* will be lost. The 3rd chapter of the *Gita* is most important. It teaches service. You must hold on to certain fundamental values in life. It is only then that you will be able to comprehend the inner meaning of the *Gita*. If you follow my advice on this, you will discover your own spirituality and soul.

Karur

He went to Karur on this day. The residents had for long been inviting Gandhiji to visit their town. He went there by car with S. Ramalingam, received their welcome and purses, and returned. Here, an individual who gave a purse of Rs 500 did not want his name to be revealed. On the way back to Tiruppur, on behalf of the spinners and weavers of an important khadi centre in Vellaikoil, Rangasamy Naicker presented a purse.

Caste division

In Tiruppur, Rao Sahib Vittal Das, Anand Seth, M. N. Sikkana Chettiar, T. Kandasamy Reddiar, T. S. Avinashalingam Chettiar, K. S. Ramasamy Gounder, P. T. Asher, and K. V. Venkatachalam Pillai sought interviews with Gandhiji to obtain his views on the tradition of caste division. Till then, his various clarifications on this matter had only served to increase the confusion among many. Hence, it was common for whoever met Gandhiji to seek clarity on this issue. Gandhiji's responses to the questions raised at Tiruppur were as follows:

Q: Are the present Brahmins true Brahmins? If not, why should they not be called non-Brahmins?

G: Most of the Brahmins these days are not true Brahmins. However, because they are Brahmins by birth, I will not call them non-Brahmins.

Q: Why cannot those who practise Brahminism in thought and deed also be called Brahmins?

G: I will not call them Brahmins, but those who are trying to be Brahmins, I believe that they would be born as Brahmins in their next birth.

Public meeting

In the public meeting held at Musabari, on behalf of the teachers and students of the Town Council High School, and etchers in khadi, welcome addresses were presented. Gandhiji was reminded that, when he had last visited Tiruppur, he had called the town the 'khadi capital', and that he himself was the 'king of khadi'. Tiruppur was truly the khadi capital. Compared to the rest of India, its khadi production was the highest even at that time.

> The quality of your khadi is also very high. But, in my opinion, this growth is not enough. You must be in a position to purchase all the cotton from neighbouring villages for spinning. It must be an incentive to all cotton growers to sell their produce to you. There should be no house in which a charkha does not work. If you have to legitimately take pride in your town being the khadi capital, you must do all these things, because you undertake this as a service and not for exploitation. You must appoint

yourselves as trustees of those starving villagers. Hence, if you obtain an honest profit, it must be shared [with] or returned to the villagers.

Before this, Gandhiji and Kasturba had gone with Rajaji to P. T. Asher and Company and received a purse from them. Gandhiji was told that a few weavers among them were addicted to liquor. He, therefore, advised them: "Khadi is a unit for the poorest of the poor. There is no place in it for alcoholics and gamblers. Weavers must at least not make their bodies impure by the consumption of alcohol. I hear that there are frequent murders in this area. Where there is alcoholism and gambling, the fundamental reason for murders must be examined closely, and avoided."

The spinning yagna

If there was to be one activity that would truly induce self-belief in crores of poor people in this era, as enunciated in the *Bhagavad Gita*, it would be spinning. If students wished to associate themselves genuinely in service to the poor, the spinning wheel was the only way, according to Gandhiji. Here, purses were handed over by P. T. Asher Seth, on behalf of the general public, by the principal, K. S. Krishnamurthi Iyer, on behalf of Town Council High School, by a Tiruppur khadi cloth etcher and a Vijayapuram khadi merchant.

In honour of Gandhiji's visit, 26 October 1927 was declared a holiday for all Town Council-run schools. In the early morning, Gandhiji left Tiruppur for Kallikkottai.

Satisfaction

After this tour, Gandhiji sent a communication about the gains and losses of his trip. Although he generally referred in it to South India, it was more specifically about the Madras tour. When he started from Mangalore, he released this communication: "I leave South India with a certain measure of satisfaction. Wherever I went, people welcomed me with much respect. Even those who did not accept my political ideology showed me great consideration. I saw genuine belief in the charkha wherever I went. Hence I leave with full confidence."

In this manner, khadi output, that had improved somewhat in 1921, earned his praises by 1927. The *Mail* editor asked Gandhiji what he himself thought about this tour. "In respect of khadi, I found widespread gain among the people, but it would be good if there could be more. This tour confirmed to me the fact that khadi has found good roots."

Temple and God

When told, "You have said that God resides in the house of a devadasi as much as He does in some temples. Many are disappointed with that remark," Gandhiji's reply was:

> I do not wish to change even one word in that statement. It is one hundred per cent true in one sense. God is everywhere, even in the caves of robbers. But we do not go searching for Him in those places, do we? Instead, we go to temples, because of the pure ambience in them, do we not? It is in that context only do I say that we cannot find Him in some temples. It is from my direct experience of some temples that I say this. That is the reason I made the statement that God resides as much in a devadasi's house as He does in temples. If this has hurt some Hindus, I deeply regret it, but merely to satisfy them I am not willing to take my statement back or change it.

Khadi Fund collection

The details of the Khadi Fund collection in Madras State (in rupees, annas, and paisas) are as given below.

Chettinad region: Rs 21,772-9-4
Madurai District: Rs 14,498-5-9
Coimbatore District: Rs 11,802-5-5
Tiruchi District: Rs 11,251-13-7
Tirunelveli District: Rs 10,467-7-9
Ramanathapuram District: Rs. 7,669-7-5
North Arcot District: Rs 6,870-12-3
South Arcot District: Rs 5,313-4-1
Chinglepet District: Rs 3,831-15-3
Salem District: Rs 3,112-1-7
Pudukkottai District: Rs 1,156-11-0

Delhi

From Mangalore, Gandhiji went to Delhi to meet the Viceroy. The Viceroy handed over to him a communiqué issued by the British government, that a committee had been formed within the existing laws (Simon Commission) to examine the Indian political system. This commission had been formed as per the Indian political establishment accord of 1919.

Ceylon

In November 1927, Gandhiji left Delhi for Bombay, and reached Ceylon by ship via Thoothukudi. As the ship had to unload cargo in Thoothukudi, Gandhiji realised that he would be unable to reach Ceylon on the appointed date; hence he changed ship and arrived in Ceylon on the night of 12 November 1927. His tour began on 13 November. The main reason for his visit was to garner funds for India's khadi programme.

Welcome by Nagarathars

In Ceylon, the first meeting he attended was a Tamil people's meeting—the Nagarathar's gathering. He asked for generous donations to the Khadi Fund, after expounding on the importance of khadi. He further said, "You must conduct yourselves honestly and with integrity among the Ceylon people. It is based on this that you will earn their respect. Wealth should not blind us. It should, instead, bestow responsibility."

In responding to the welcome of the Nagarathars, he referred to his recent visit to Chettinad, and how generously the Nagarathars there had donated for the Khadi Fund. "Indian businessmen in Ceylon must conduct themselves in such a manner as not to allow the Ceylonese people to find fault. Wealth should not lead you to greed. You must always remember who all have worked for you to earn such wealth, which should, then, be looked upon as a blessing," he said at the Colombo Tamil Sangam, which presented a purse. At the request of Sir P. Ramanathan in his welcome, Gandhiji explained the tenets of the Charkha Sangam, adding that, "A large part of the finances of the Charkha Sangam are being deployed in Madras as [most of] the spinning units are there."

30 November 1927, Dhanushkodi

After touring Ceylon for more than two weeks, Gandhiji returned to Dhanushkodi (now an abandoned place in Tamil Nadu after destruction during a cyclone in 1964) on 30 November 1927 by the ship *Hardinge*. Even before he left Delhi, he was aware of the institution of the Simon Commission, yet he left for Ceylon within a couple of days thereafter. He was unaware of what the views of Indian leaders were, or those of the Indian people, about this Commission.

Therefore, when he left Ceylon for India, and after his return, he informed the newspapers thus: "At the moment, my conscience is in the hands of the Congress president [then Srinivasa Iyengar]. After him, it will be with Dr. Ansari, who will take over from him."

Ramanathapuram

On the way from Dhanushkodi, he was welcomed in Ramanathapuram (now the name of a town and a district in Tamil Nadu) by Rajaram Pandian (brother of the Ramanathapuram king, who was later a leader of the working group at the Indian National Congress session at Madras in December 1927 under the presidentship of Dr M. A. Ansari). Kasturba did not attend this welcome. She, along with some others of Gandhiji's entourage, left by Boat Mail directly for Madras. There were intermittent showers, and the people were apprehensive that the public meeting might not be held. Gandhiji too had doubts, but the rain abated in a little while, and the meeting took place. Here, Gandhiji and his group stayed in the house of Rajaram Pandian.

Public meeting

The public meeting venue was Makara Nombu Grounds. On behalf of the Ramanathapuram public, Rajaram Pandian presented the welcome and purse. The students of Raja High School and S. P. G. Mission High School also accorded welcome addresses and gave purses. Before this, Gandhiji had been to a women's meeting. The women gathered there were mostly very poor. Despite this, when they gladly gave Gandhiji even the few coins they had saved, twisted into knots at the ends of their sari *pallu*s, he was deeply moved, and he mentioned this at the public meeting.

11 December 1927, To Orissa

From Ramanathapuram, Gandhiji reached Madras by train, and left by Calcutta Mail for Orissa (Kasturba took the Bombay Mail to Ahmedabad). Gandhiji's stay in Madras city on this occasion was only for a couple of hours.

Notes

1. Miraben, born Madeleine Slade (1892–1982), a British supporter of Indian independence, and close associate of Gandhi.

2. Agamas, a collection of Tantric literature and Hindu scriptures; the term *agama* means tradition or 'that which has come down'.

3. Trappists, a cloistered Catholic religious order, originating in France in the seventeenth century, that strongly discourages speech, except when strictly necessary.

23

MADRAS CONGRESS, 1927

After completing his Orissa tour, Gandhiji visited Madras again in 1927, the reason being that the Indian National Congress Conference, under the presidentship of Dr Ansari, was convened here in December. His slogan at that time was, "Freedom within the Empire, if possible. If not, freedom outside it." This conference was attended, with the exception of Motilal Nehru, by prominent leaders like M. A. Jinnah, Madan Mohan Malaviya, J. M. Sen Gupta (1885–1933) and Pandit Jawaharlal Nehru. Prior to Independence, Congress conferences had been held in Madras in 1887, 1894, 1898, 1903, 1908, 1914, and 1927. After Independence, the Avadi session (near Madras) of the Congress was held in 1955. Each Congress conference had its own special importance, and in the 1927 Congress conference in Madras the slogan, 'The objective of India [is] full freedom', was announced. Before 1927, the objective of the Congress had been limited to achieving 'Dominion Status'.

Gandhiji's health had not improved when he attended the 1927 Congress session. His blood pressure was still high. The doctors had advised him to reduce his workload as much as possible, and to take complete rest, with the result that Gandhiji could not speak much at the deliberations. It was announced that, as soon as the meetings of the main task force committees of the conference were over, he would return to Ahmedabad for rest. It was also decided that he would not participate in the discussions of these committees.

23 December 1927, Khadi exhibition

Arriving by Calcutta Mail, and with a view to avoiding crowds, Gandhiji got down at Basin Bridge (the station that now acts as the entry point to Chennai Central terminus) and went by car to Ranga Vilas building in Chetpet, where he stayed on this occasion. He inaugurated an All India Khadi Exhibition that had been put up in connection with the Congress conference. At the conference, men, under Rajaram Pandian, and women, under Kamaladevi Chattopadhyaya (1903–88), were responsible for crowd management. Leaders such as Rajendra Prasad, Shankarlal Bangar, Azad, and Rajaji had come for this conference. Gandhiji arrived along with Sarojini Naidu, S. Srinivasa Iyengar, Vallabhbhai Patel, and Dr Ansari. Owing to his ill health, Gandhiji had to curtail his speech.

He spoke of his coming to Madras directly from his Orissa tour, and his having met the impoverished general public there to emphasise the importance of khadi. He inaugurated the khadi and Hindi exhibitions here, deputising for Madan Mohan Malaviya, who did not come.

Request for Telugu translation

Rajaji translated Gandhiji's speech. A person from Andhra stood up in the middle of the speech, and requested a translation into Telugu, as there were a large number of Telugu-speaking people in the crowd. Earlier, Gandhiji had been asked on several occasions to have his speech translated into Telugu (from 1946 onwards, there was more insistence on this). Before the linguistic division of states, the people of Andhra had maintained that they had equal rights in Madras. Gandhiji might have felt that this request for Telugu translation could have been a political move in that direction, because he had never yielded to this demand, whenever raised. When, on this occasion, this request was made by one person in the gathering, Gandhiji said:

> I am going to speak very briefly. If it is to be translated into Telugu, I might be asked to have it translated in Hindustani, too, by certain sections who want so. It is desirable not to give a state colour to a national issue. I am shortly going to tour Andhra Pradesh, where I shall have arrangements made to get my speeches translated into Telugu.
>
> I am aware that there are many Andhras [i.e. people of Andhra] in Madras, and I request them to patiently hear out

my speech translated into Tamil. If Andhras and Tamils are to live in an environment of brotherhood, the Andhras should learn Tamil and the Tamils Telugu. ... We should all quickly learn Hindi and be prepared to conduct all matters in Hindi. If that happens, there will not be any embarrassment in using the language of another.

25 December 1927, Congress conference

The Congress conference began on the Spur Tank Road Grounds. First, the Congress workers entered in formation, followed by the leaders. Finally Gandhiji came in with Dr Ansari. As he entered, all stood up, and the air was rent with cries of "Mahatma Gandhi Ki Jai!"

At the time of this conference, there was increasing discord between Hindus and Mulims. The playing of Hindu temple instruments in front of mosques, and the severe objection by Hindus to cow slaughter practised by Muslims were the causes of resentment on either side. There were clashes in North India too on account of this. Hence, the Congress brought in a resolution to solve this problem, drafted by Gandhiji. This resolution requested that, to the extent possible, one side should not wound the sensitivities of the other. Pandit Malaviya, on behalf of the Hindus, and Mohammed Ali, on behalf of the Muslims, supported this resolution, which stated that religious conversion should not be done merely because of a change in thinking, nor should violence, enticement through money, or other unlawful means be employed for such religious conversion. Also, persons below 18 years of age must not submit to religious conversion without their parents' consent.

Gandhiji was of great help to the working committee to arrive at a consensus on this issue, as *The Hindu* reported (20 December 1927): "It is to the credit of Gandhiji to have solved this problem, and other such long-standing problems. His health did not permit him to indulge in long arguments. Yet, he was the cause of Hindu and Muslim leaders to realise the wisdom of his recommendations, and follow them."

28 December 1927, Health check-up

Dr Muthu, a leprosy expert, examined Gandhiji and pronounced:

> There is nothing wrong with his health. His blood pressure is slightly high, but he needs to worry more about his mind, as he gives it many hours of work daily.
>
> Even while he is eating, visitors come and talk with him, and, thus, he does not get enough rest and sleep. He must sleep for 7 hours.
>
> I have told him that he should rest for 2 hours every afternoon. Only if the public allows this would it be possible for him.

Departure

At night Gandhiji and his group left Madras for Bombay. From Bombay he planned to go to his ashram in Ahmedabad to take some rest. To avoid the crowds, he entrained at Basin Bridge railway station. He was largely satisfied with the Madras Congress. After reaching Bombay, Gandhiji said, "The Madras Congress was incomparable. It has laid the foundation for Hindu-Muslim unity."

24

IN THE MIDST OF THE ANDHRA TOUR

'Purna Swaraj'

In 1928, the boycott of the Simon Commission, and the Bardoli Satyagraha took place. In November, Lala Lajpat Rai succumbed to his injuries sustained in a police lathi charge. As the time period stipulated by the Calcutta Congress session (29 December 1929 to 1 January 1930), under the presidentship of Motilal Nehru, for the demand 'Dominion Status for India' had expired on 31 December 1929, the Congress objective from the next day itself became 'Purna Swaraj' or 'Complete Freedom', as declared by Gandhiji.

Burma tour

In 1929, Gandhiji was scheduled to visit Europe, but, in consideration of internal emergencies, he did not go. He toured the Sindh State, and came to Delhi to meet the Viceroy. On the way to Burma, he was arrested in Calcutta for having burnt foreign clothes in a public place. However, his arrest was stayed till his return from Burma. He started for Burma on 3 March.

In Burma, as he was raising money for the Khadi Fund, he sent out a circular requesting for generous donations. In it, he pointedly exhorted the Nagarathars not to ignore his request, adding that they should not forget that he too belonged to their community. "I am a Gujarati Chetty," he said. He mentioned that for Mandalay Indians it was a place of pilgrimage, as Tilak, Lala Lajpat Rai and Subhas Chandra Bose had been incarcerated there. He toured Burma for two weeks and returned on 24 March 1929.

It was only a few days after this, on 8 April 1929, that the revolutionaries Bhagat Singh (1907–31) and Shivaram Rajaguru (1908–31) attacked the Central Legislative Assembly in Delhi with grenades. Another freedom fighter, Jatindra Nath Das (1904–29), died on 13 September in a Lahore prison, after having undertaken a hunger strike for 63 days.

15 May 1929, Tiruttani

On 6 April 1929, Gandhiji began his Andhra tour. In the midst of that tour he visited Tiruttani. It is this Tiruttani visit that leads us to say that Gandhiji visited Madras State in 1929. Tiruttani, then, was part of Andhra within Madras State. It was after the linguistic division of states, and subsequent agitation that it came to be part of Madras (now in Tiruvallur district, Tamil Nadu). He came there the day he went to Tirupathi (15 May 1929). The funds garnered at Tiruttani during his visit were Rs 115-12-0.

25

THE VEDARANYAM WAR

Mass arrests

1930 was the year India's freedom struggle took on immediacy and vigour. It was also the year of the Salt Satyagraha, the Dandi March, and the anti-tax campaign. Strikes took place against foreign cloth being sold. More than a lakh satyagrahis were arrested. At the Round Table Conference called for by the Viceroy, the chairs to be occupied by the Congress were empty. As all the leaders were in jail, the Congress conference did not take place that year (the 1929 and 1931 sessions were held in Lahore and Karachi, respectively).

Opposition to laws

The protest started by Gandhiji involving opposition to laws found much participation from Madras. Before, during and after this protest, numerous public meetings and processions were organised. C. Rajagopalachari was in the forefront of arranging these protests. In April and May of 1930, the Vedaranyam (a town in Nagapattinam district) Salt Satyagraha took place.

Salt Satyagraha

The moral war for salt was a new concept for the world. It holds a pride of place in the annals of India's freedom struggle. In a letter to the Viceroy, Gandhiji wrote:

> The tax imposed by the British government on salt is highly unjust. I say this on behalf of the poor. The freedom struggle is mainly for those who are poor in India, and continue to be so.

Hence, it is with this opposition to the salt tax that our freedom struggle begins. There is no surprise in this. What is surprising is that we have for so long submitted to this authoritarian rule.

A bloodless war

The Salt Satyagraha forms a central part of the Gandhiji-led Indian freedom struggle that aimed to end British authoritarianism. K. Santhanam, in his book, *Vedaranyam*, writes that the election victory in 1934–35, the first Congress ministry, the developments of 1940–45, and Independence in 1947, can all be said to have been the results of the Salt Satyagraha. There is much truth in this. Sardar Vedarathinam has persuasively written:

> The humble salt has been introduced as the starting point for the freedom struggle of our great nation, unheard of anywhere in the world, to the extent that, from the children to the aged in India, the common people to the pandits, the very poor to the very wealthy, across divisions of religion, caste, community, and economic status, the salt satyagraha is the first general public uprising organised by Gandhiji towards the freedom struggle. Our resident poet has rightly sung, 'a swordless, bloodless war is coming'.

Pandit Motilal Nehru said in praise, "Gandhiji's salt army is akin to Rama's army that went to Lanka." To pan for and make salt, that is, wash and sift soil in a pan to find the mineral, as a protest against the British government's salt laws, Gandhiji led a small 'army' of followers, that included Tamils, to Dandi, a village on the coast of the Arabian Sea, now in Navsari district, Gujarat, from Sabarmati Ashram. The contribution of Tamils to the Salt Satyagraha did not end there.

Vedaranyam

A separate salt satyagraha under Rajaji took place in Madras. Of the several salt satyagrahas undertaken in various parts of the country, the next in importance to Gandhiji's Dandi March was the Vedaranyam Satyagraha led by Rajaji. This march to Vedaranyam happened a month after the Dandi March. It gave Madras a pride of place in the Gandhi-inspired freedom movement. One of the reasons was that it was led by Rajaji, known as the 'conscience' of Gandhiji. Another was the failure in quelling this revolt by the preventive measures undertaken by officials under the Collector of Thanjavur, Darren, I. C. S.

Rajaji said: "In 1930, it was Darren who discovered the baton which was used all over India as a weapon to beat the Congress workers into submission. Some were of the opinion that the 'credit' for this should go to some Indian officials working under Darren. I am not able to believe this, but, whatever it be, I am happy to give the entire credit to Darren." By adopting this practice of baton charging, Darren did what even Smuts in South Africa did not wish to do, added Rajaji.

Making salt, breaking the law

On 6 April 1930, at 8 a.m., Gandhiji panned for salt at Dandi. After that, he declared, "The Salt Act has now been officially opposed. Hence those who wish to pan [for] and sell salt can now do so." The week after this, on 13 April 1930, corresponding to the birth of the Tamil year, Putthaandu, the Tamil satyagraha army started its march from Dr T. S. S. Rajan's house in Trichy to Vedaranyam. Headed towards Uppalam (now a village in Thoothukudi district), this satyagraha army was welcomed and given send-offs by large numbers of people from various districts. Dr. Rajan's daughter, Tmt. Rajammal Sowmyanarayanan, applied *tilakam* on Rajaji's forehead and sent him on his way.

The army marches

In addition to the leader, there were 98 workers in this army. In spite of hundreds of people wanting to join the group, only 100 people were selected. The people who came forward were not ordinary people. Many among them had forsaken their comfortable lives to jump into the march of the freedom struggle. With truth as their foundation, they started from Tiruchirappalli, where Thayumanavar had received knowledge, to his birthplace, Thirumaraikkadu, also known as Vedaranyam. The following were allotted specific duties in the marching party.

Workers and groups

1. Leader: A. Duraiswami Iyer
2. Travellers group: T. Subbarao, etc.
3. Cooking group: Rangaswami Iyengar
4. Post matters: Dhanu Iyer
5. Workers' general head: Subramaniam
6. Publicity group: O. P. Ramasamy, K. V. Raman, T. R. Padmanabhan
7. Store: Srinivasan
8. Blowing of conch: Sivagurunathan
9. *Tanga* (horse-drawn cart): Ganapathi
10. Holding the national flag: Anand
11. Prayers: Subbaiah
12. Attendance and record: Krishnamurthi
13. Bell ringer: Mani
14. Treasury: K. Ramachari
15. Hindi teaching: Krishnaswami Konar

The people's spirit

Magistrate Darren was of the opinion that if this army was to be denied food and made to starve, they would not be able to reach Uppalam, and the protest would fail. Hence, he made it known throughout the district that those who provided a resting place or food for the marchers would be fined and imprisoned.

However, the wishes and spirit of the people were otherwise. Even those who were not directly in favour of this march began to ask, "While those who publicly burn the law of the land could justifiably be arrested, who is this authority who can put a stop to the camaraderie that exists among Indians for generations?" It was that spirit that prompted Kodiyalam Rangaswami Iyengar to render assistance to the marchers for successful completion of their march. "Should we just watch, while a person who has come from another country as their employee declares that our countrymen should not be fed?" Thus, moved by righteous anger, he stayed with the marchers from beginning to end. A large number of village folk on the way shared the same feeling. Consequently, wherever the satyagrahis went, there were welcomes and feasts awaiting them.

March route

The route followed by the marchers to Vedaranyam was via Srirangam, Tiruvanaikkaval, Tiruvalarcholai, Kallanai, Koviladi, Tirukkattuppalli, Agniswarankoil, Sathanur, Tiruvaiyyaru, Tirukkandiyur, Thanjavur, Nadar, Ayyampettai, Vazhudur, Nallur, Kumbakonam, Valangiman, Semmangudi, Alangudi, Narthangudi, Needamangalam, Poovalur, Rajappayyanchavadi, Mannargudi, Thattankoil, Adhicchapuram, Vilangudi, Tiruthuraippoondi, Melamarudur, Thagattur and Aayakaranpulam.

On reaching Vedaranyam, a satyagraha camp was established. During this march there were two places where untoward incidents took place. The march went on peacefully for the most part, and the satyagrahis reached Vedaranyam on 29 April 1930.

Vedaranyam is a holy place sanctified by the Vedas, the songs of religious gurus, the penance of great rishis like Nachiketa, and the nativity of enlightened preceptors like Paranjathi (army general of the Pallava king Narasimavarman I who ruled South India from 630–668 CE) and Thayumanavar. Here, Rajaji conducted another *yagna*. This army needed to stay in Vedaranyam and conduct its war, but not many were ready to give them accommodation.

In this situation, a young man of about 30 came forward, and not only arranged accommodation for them, but led the welcome group. This was Sardar Vedarathinam.

Rajaji arrested

Along with a selected 10 associates, Rajaji started in the early morning of 1 May 1930 to pan for salt (with local resident Rajagopala Iyer as guide) towards Agasthiampalli (under Nagapattinam district). He was arrested there after panning for salt. As the associates were not arrested, they returned. Rajaji was sentenced to six months' simple imprisonment.

It appeared that even Darren, who adopted repressive measures, was won over by ahimsa to some extent. When Rajaji, who was arrested in Vedaranyam, was being taken by train to Trichy, Darren boarded the train, entered Rajaji's compartment, shook his hand and conversed with him for a while. Not only that, he ordered his

subordinates to bring snacks and coffee for Rajaji, surprising everyone
present.

All arrested

After this, K. Santhanam was appointed group leader, and after
his arrest, Mattapparai Venkatarama Iyer, K. S. Subramaniam and
G. Ramachandran, in turn, were appointed group leaders. On 29
May 1930, when G. Ramachandran was functioning as the leader, all
the marchers were arrested, and there was no leader remaining to be
appointed. Dr Rajan, who had come to Vedaranyam on that day, was
also arrested.

The share of Madurai

At one point, as the number of workers in the satyagraha ashram
became too many to handle, it became necessary to separate them
and send them to different places. Hence, one group was sent to the
Vandal branch ashram under group leader, Chidambara Iyer, and
another to the Agasthiampalli branch ashram under Thanu Iyer. They
continued their protests from there.

Madurai A. Vaidyanatha Iyer and Tiruchi Dr Rajan came and
went during this march to Vedaranyam. When the police entered
the satyagraha ashram on 3 May 1930, and attempted to forcibly
remove the salt accumulated there, the ashramites surrounded the
salt, clasping each other's hands, preventing the police from doing
so. One among them was A. Vaidyanatha Iyer. Madurai associates,
K. A. Krishnamachari and Veerasamy, and Coimbatore associate,
Raju, lay down in front of this salt heap till the very end of this protest
and became unconscious.

On the next day, 4 May 1930, Mahatma Gandhi was arrested in
connection with the Dandi Satyagraha. On the same day, K. Santhanam
and Sardar Vedarathinam were arrested here. For defying the ban
order promulgated in Vedaranyam after this, A. Vaidyanatha Iyer.,
N. S. Varadachari and Madurai Pancharathinam were also arrested.

The first to receive police beatings were Vaidyanatha Iyer and
Varadachari. The first woman to be arrested in India in connection
with the Salt Satyagraha was Rukmini Lakshmipathi from Madras, it

must be said with Tamil pride. On the day she was arrested, 14 May 1930, Tiruvannamalai Na. Annamalai, too, was arrested. Harihara Sharma, who was involved in the Hindi Prachar Sabha movement, and Anand Theertha, who later participated in the Harijan movement, were arrested during this struggle.

Police repression

The cooperation of the public in this moral war was commendable. At every point and in every village en route, the marchers were welcomed and fed. The police, in anticipation of the possible places where the marchers could be lodged, tried to lock them up ahead of their arrival. For example, when the workers reached Agneeswarankoil, all the lodges and rest houses there were locked by the police, and the keys appropriated. When the workers entered Nadar village, they were informed that the police had forced the landowners to lock up their houses and go away. Still, the people did not allow the marchers to go without food. A little distance outside that village, people waited with buttermilk at a large temple entrance. The residents of Nadar had not really gone away, but waited for the marchers at a place called Thandangorai nearby and welcomed them there. In Mannargudi, it was almost a feast, with *laddus*, sweets, jack fruit, bananas, berries, potato *bajjis*, *vadai*, and *appalam*.

Equidistant from Ayakkaran Bridge and Vedaranyam, the marchers were greeted with tender coconuts by one person. At the same time though, when the C.I.D. officer, who was proceeding in front of the marchers asked for tender coconut, he was refused. In Vedaranyam and its surrounding villages, people ignored police orders not to extend support, and, from barbers to merchants and wealthy people, they extended all kinds of assistance to the marchers. The embarrassment caused to the authorities because of this was considerable.

Feast under the banyan tree

How eagerly and affectionately the people received the marchers has been described by Sardar Vedarathinam, with which we shall end this part of the history.

In the light of the restriction imposed on the satyagrahis, the government authorities did not want the people to get food and other comforts from anywhere, and went from village to village putting a ban on the people offering food to the marchers. But the satyagraha principle is based on the foundation of people's love. It is like a tree with firm roots in the ground. As large as a tree is, so deep are its roots. Hence, to make the government's efforts fail, the people thought up another plan. ... trees by the sides of roads are numbered. A man on the road would tell the marchers in passing, '42nd tree', signifying that food awaited them under the banyan tree number 42. The police were baffled. But we should be aware of a truth here. As the saying, 'inch by inch even the mortar stone can be moved', the enthusiasm of the people did decrease as time went on. As the repression of the government increased, the help offered by people to the satyagrahis dwindled. This is the reality. However, in the larger picture, ...the Vedaranyam 'war' was a great victory.

26

THE MARRIAGE OF
LAKSHMI AND DEVADAS

Madras–Gujarat

Through the marriage of Gandhiji's fourth and youngest son Devadas and Chakravarthi Rajagopalachari's daughter Lakshmi, Madras State and Gujarat became related. Incidentally, the brides of Gandhiji's three other sons were from his own community.

The test

Devadas and Lakshmi, who fell in love and wanted to marry, were subjected to a severe test by being separated for some years, before being allowed to wed. At first, both Gandhiji and Rajaji were reluctant to give their approval. "For some years there should not even be correspondence between you. If, after that, you both are of the same mind, I will give permission," declared Gandhiji.

After the stipulated period, Lakshmi stated, "I will marry only if I can marry Devadas." Devadas likewise declared, "If I am to marry, it would be only Lakshmi."

Hence, both the parents came to a favourable decision to get them married. However, before it could happen, the bridegroom, his mother, Kasturba, and his father were arrested. When they were released, and, after Gandhiji ended his 21-day fast in Parnakudi, this marriage took place.

Rajaji had written to Kasturba, "Babu [Devadas Gandhi] may be re-arrested at any time. I believe, therefore, that we should conduct the marriage between Lakshmi and him now. If you say 'yes', I will bring Lakshmi with me." With Kasturba's consent, he took his daughter there.

Mother-in-law

The wedding took place at Lady Thackersay's Palace in Parnakudi. This was an unexpected good fortune, Gandhiji remarked later. The bride wore a small gold necklace presented by Lady Thackersay, and a pair of gold bangles given by Kasturba. At the wedding, Kasturba, as always, conducted herself as a mother-in-law with full duty-consciousness. She had already received Gandhiji's approval to present four khadi saris to her daughter-in-law.

As per the shastras

This marriage was performed in adherence to the shastras. There are two kinds of marriages under the shastras, one of which is the 'anuloma' tradition (a boy from a higher caste marrying a girl from a lower caste). But the marriage of the non-Brahmin Devadas with the Brahmin Lakshmi was a 'pratiloma' (the reverse); this was against the normal practice and priests would not consent to perform such a marriage. But Acharya Kaka Kalelkar, a disciple of Gandhiji and an expert on the shastras, came forward and invited Lakshmana Sastri, a celebrated pandit of Sanskrit and principal of a Sanskrit college in Wai, Maharashtra, living a pure life, to conduct this marriage.

Same caste

Lakshmana Sastri had no objection to conducting the wedding. "Mahatma Gandhi and Rajaji lead the same kinds of lives, and, hence, can be considered to be of the same caste," he declared, but the moment he saw the bridegroom, he said it was essential that he should be wearing a 'poonal' (sacred thread). Thereafter, in consultation with Kaka Kalelkar, a 'poonal' ritual was first conducted for Devadas, after which the marriage took place.

The marriage, as described by Kalki

The marriage ritual commenced after the bhajan group, that sang during Gandhiji's fast, sang 'Raghupati Raghava Rajaram'. Kalki who was witness to this wedding, described it in *Ananda Vikatan* magazine for which he was working. Who, other than him, could have described it better? We reproduce verbatim what he wrote.

The pandal

"On the morning of 16 June 1933, we reached the portico of a compound in neighbouring Parnakudi. Under the bright sun in the compound, a small *pandal* had been erected, on four sides of which were tied plantain trees. Other than decorated mud pots, there was no other ornamentation. The bridal couple, clad in khadi, came and sat on the platform. The bed on which the Mahatma was reclining was brought out into the portico."

Exchange of garlands

"As a token of their acceptance to marry each other, garlands were exchanged to begin with. It need hardly be said that only cotton garlands were used. Thereafter, *punyavachanam* and *kanyadanam* were conducted. Having raised her as the light of his life on his own since the death of his wife, when Lakshmi was but a child, Achariar placed her palms in Devadas's. After the *mangalyadharanam*, and *sapthapadi homam* were gone through in traditional manner, the bhajan group sang 'Vaishnava Jana tho'.

"The couple, then, went up to the Mahatma to seek his blessings. After blessing them, he gave each of them a cloth garland, the *Bhagavad Gita*, bhajan books, and a coconut."

Advice to bride and groom

"Gandhiji tried to speak in order to give advice to the newly married couple. Because of intense exhaustion, coupled with emotion on his son's getting married, he could not. One minute stretched to five minutes. Not a word came from his lips. All around were greatly worried. Rajaji, standing next to him, fanned him. 'You need not speak as you are so tired,' he started to say, as Gandhiji began to speak. Gandhiji then pointed to Devadas and said:

> There has been no affront to dharma in the conduct of this marriage. Had there been, I would not given myself the opportunity to participate in it. You have received from Rajagopalachariar today an invaluable gift. You must be deserving of it. You must protect it. She is, in truth, Lakshmi. A treasure house of goodness, and, in beauty, like Goddess Lakshmi herself, you must keep her secure.

"Looking at Lakshmi, Gandhiji said,

> Through your marriage I desire that the affection and closeness
> between me and Rajagopalachariar should increase. It is because
> of the penance of you both that you have received our approval
> and blessings. Lead a God-fearing life at all times.
>
> If you will live as true Vaishnavites, as described by Narsinh
> Mehta [a Gujarati poet], the objections to this wedding would
> automatically fade. From a very early age, I have tried to
> understand the meaning of dharma, and have attempted to lead
> a life in conformity to it. In conducting this wedding I do not
> believe I have done anything against dharma. Had I believed
> so, I would neither have come to this wedding nor given my
> blessings.

No expense

"For the bride's father, there was no expense in this wedding, except
the train fare for her brothers and sisters. On Gandhiji's advice, the
marriage itself was performed with very little expense.

"In order to avoid crowds, Gandhiji sent back even the
ashramites who were with him. Somehow, prominent leaders like
Right Honourable Srinivasa Sastri, Aane, G. D. Birla, Sarojini Devi
and Bajaj managed to attend the wedding. Similarly, although it had
been specifically forbidden, many had sent gifts. Of these, Gandhiji
was forced to send a letter of thanks to one who had sent a simple
black bead necklace.

Birla's gift

"Birla gave as a gift a silk sari and an ordinary sari. Gandhiji insisted
that both be returned to him. After much persuasion, Gandhiji
accepted the ordinary sari. Pandit Jawaharlal Nehru and Sardar
Vallabhbhai Patel had sent wedding wishes from jail."

This marriage helped to strengthen the deep bond that Gandhiji
already had with Madras.

27

ABOLITION OF UNTOUCHABILITY

In the forefront

That Madras, the land where Nandanar was born, stood in the forefront of abolition of untouchability in India, is no surprise. In the Gandhian era, if there was one state where abolition of untouchability progressed at a fast pace, it was Madras. Compared to other states, this movement grew almost on a daily basis here, and if there was any one other movement that went even beyond this, it was khadi.

Reason

The reason for the rapid development in the untouchability eradication efforts in Madras State was the involvement of many Brahmins in this movement. They entered into the work of this movement, girding up their loins, almost as if in atonement of their sins in having been responsible earlier for such discrimination. "What law can be higher than the pronouncement of the Mahatma, the greatest among the great, on untouchabiliy eradication?" was their belief.

There were many examples of this. One such was that of T. R. Mahadeva Iyer of Dindigul, who gave up his law practice to work for Harijan service and khadi. He and his associates, Kuppuswami Iyer and Amrithalinga Iyer, declared, "If untouchability is not eradicated, the Hindu religion will be ruined."

While many Brahmins got down to the nitty-gritty of work on eradication of untouchability, it must be said that the non-Brahmins also toiled hard for this movement. Much good work was done by Sardar Vedarathinam Pillai, Suppanna Gounder, N. M. R. Subburaman, T. S. Avinashalingam, Somasundara Bharathi and Dr. Emberumal Naidu. Harijans also came forward to fight for their rights, though to a lesser extent. It was more the other classes who worked for their uplift. Through this, the race conflicts related to untouchability were avoided. If, today, the Harijans in Tamil Nadu have enjoyed this attitudinal change and have been able to move forward, the travails of Brahmins and non-Brahmins within their communities in espousing this cause cannot be so easily written about in this book.

Rajaji

The involvement of Rajaji, Bhashyam Iyengar, A. Vaidyanatha Iyer and Dr T. S. S. Rajan in the untouchability eradication work needs special mention. The value of their service had spread all over Madras.

When he was president of the Salem Municipal Administration, Rajaji appointed a Harijan for the work of opening the taps for water supply to the town, pursuant to which there was protest from the community of priests. It is now part of Tamil Nadu history. In Puduppalayam, as soon as Rajaji established the Gandhi Ashram, he housed Harijans in it. When Gandhiji was undertaking a fast in Poona, Rajaji found a compromise in the problems resulting from it, and saved Gandhiji a lot of trouble. After Gandhiji and Ambedkar reached an agreement, Rajaji worked tirelessly to convene meetings of Harijan and caste Hindu leaders to get them to accept the terms of this agreement.

Pioneers

In sum, therefore, the leaders who stood in the forefront of the Harijan uplift movement in Madras included V. Bhashyam Iyengar (Madras), Rajaji (Salem), T. S. Avinashalingam (Coimbatore), Suppana Gounder (Gobichettipalayam), Govindarao Gursale, Sahajanandar (South Arcot), Dr T. S. S. Rajan, L. N. Gopalaswami (Trichy), A. Vaidyanatha Iyer, N. M. R. Subburaman, P. K. Ramachari, K. Arunachalam (Madurai), P. R. Mahadeva Iyer (Dindigul), Munagal Pattabhiramayya (Chozhavandan), Narayanasamy Chettiar (Thevaram), Harijan Rangaswami Iyengar, Sivasubramaniam, his wife Kamala (Devakottai), P. S. Krishnaswami Iyengar, P. Gopalaswami (Manamadurai), S. P. Srinivasa Iyengar (Abhiramam, Ramnathapuram district), Yagneswara Sarma, Gomathisankara Dikshitar, K. R. Krishna

Iyer (Tirunelveli), Sardar A. Vedarathinam Pillai (Thanjavur) and Dr Emberumal Naidu (Nagercoil).

Harijan Seva Sangam

After the Poona fast, and his agreement with Dr Ambedkar, Gandhiji, with the efforts of caste Hindus, concentrated on the uplift of Harijans, abolition of untouchability, and temple entry for Harijans, for which he established the All India Harijan Seva Sangam. For this, a branch was opened in every Congress State. With Dr T. S. S. Rajan as president, the Madras Untouchability Abolition Sangam was established on 20 November 1932. The name of this organisation was changed the next year to Harijan Seva Sangam.

When Gandhiji fasted, the Tamil people were greatly disturbed. Harijans were permitted at many places to draw water from the same wells as caste Hindus. Some small temples were opened for Harijans to enter.

Mass conversions averted

On behalf of the Madras Harijan Seva Sangam, through education (specifically technical training in Kodambakkam, Kanchipuram and Devakottai), efforts were made to improve the lot of Harijans in several fields. On the other side, caste Hindus were encouraged to give up the practice of untouchability, and priests and Sanatanis persuaded to allow entry of Harijans into temples. Several small temples were built by the Harijan Seva Sangam especially for Harijans to worship in. At some places Harijans were granted interest-free loans.

In villages, Harijans living in desperately backward conditions were voluntarily converting en masse to Christian or Muslim faiths. The inhuman custom of untouchability prevailing in the Hindu faith was the main reason for this. Once, on hearing that 40,000 Harijans in the Cumbum area were planning to join the Muslim faith, the Harijan Seva Sangam leaders made an urgent tour of the area to talk them out of it and avert the mass conversions. Afterwards, through the efforts of N. M. R. Subburaman, P. K. Ramachari, and Ka. A. Annakamu, a Harijan Seva Institution was opened in Kokilapuram, near Utthamapalayam.

Madurai district

The Madras Harijan Seva Sangam opened a branch in every district. Although the work in all branches was carried out to the best of their ability, it is necessary to specially mention the work done in Madurai district which received praise on an all-India basis on several occasions. It was for the work done by A. Vaidyanatha Iyer and N. M. R. Subburaman, as two eyes of the district, that Madurai district gained a reputation in Harijan welfare. Apart from them, the service of S. Somasundara Bharathi, P. K. Ramachari and V. Krishnaswami Iyer must also be mentioned. The work of Harijan students, too, needs to be recognised. It was in Madurai that, for the first time in Madras, in 1934, a hostel, 'Sevalayam', was started. Its first warden, K. Arunachalam, in later years, became the vice-president of the All India Khadi Commission.

That history

There is a small story attached to K. Arunachalam's becoming the first warden of Sevalayam. At one time, when Gandhiji had come to Bangalore, he visited the brahmachari ashram run by Ramachandra Rao. Leaning on his stick outside the ashram, Gandhiji asked, "Are the 30 persons living in the ashram brahmacharis?" Ramachandra Rao replied in the affirmative. Being told that many among them were from Madras State, Gandhiji suggested, "The persons belonging to Madras can serve in Madras itself." Pursuant to this suggestion, he came to Madras and met Vaidyanatha Iyer and Subburaman; K. Arunachalam, on the advice of those two, served in the office of the Harijan Seva Sangam for a short while, and then became the warden of Sevalayam. Other than this, in Madurai district, S. Jagannathan, Ko. Venkatachalapathy, G. Ramachandran, Munagal Pattabhiramayya, Lakshmirathan Bharathi, Annakamu, Mahadeva Iyer, Ganesa Iyer and Kuppuswami Iyer were all actively involved in untouchability eradication work.

District-wise, the list of others involved in Harijan welfare work is given below.

Important persons

1. *Tirunelveli*: S. Kootha Nayinar Pillai, Shanmugasundaram Pillai, C. Veerabahu, V. Subbaiah, Gomathisankara Dikshitar, M. S. Narayanan;
2. *Ramanathapuram*: Rajaram Pandian, Sathaiah, Ra. Gurusamy, A. Rangaswami Iyengar, Lakshmirathan Bharathi;
3. *Madurai*: Sundaresa Iyer, Ramasamy Chettiar (Periakulam), S. C. Balakrishnan, P. Kakkan, P. A. Ramasamy Chettiar, S. A. Rangasamy Chettiar;
4. *Tiruchirappalli*: Dr T. V. Swaminatha Sastri, P. Sanglia Pillai, P. Rathinavelu Thevar, T. M. Narayanasamy Pillai, R. Ganapathy Reddiar, P. Ponnambala Gounder;
5. *Thanjavur*: Ramalingasamy, T. R. Venkatarama Iyer;
6. *Coimbatore*: T. S. Ramalinga Chettiar, R. K. Shanmugam Chettiar, Srikanta Ier (Gopi), Srinivasa Iyer, V. Rama Iyengar, Govindasamy Naidu, P. S. G. Ganga Naidu, V. Appavoo, Swami Gurubrahmanandar;
7. *Salem*: G. Ramachandra Naidu, Kandasamy Pillai, S. P. Adikesavulu Chettiar, A Rangachari;
8. *South Arcot*: Rajarathina Mudaliar, P. Thanikachalam, M. Devarajan, M. Arunachalam;
9. *North Arcot*: A. V. Gangadhara Sastri, A. Somasundara Iyer;
10. *Chinglepet*: M. Bhakthavatsalam, M. K. Reddy, Dr P. S. Srinivasan, Dr P. R. Raghuraman;
11. *Madras*: K. G. Sivaswami Iyer, R. T. Kesavulu, Dr Subbarayan, T. R. Venkatarama Sastri, M. C. Raja, R. Srinivasan; and
12. *Nilgiri*: A. Govindasamy Chettiar, G. Mahadevan, M. Govindarajulu, V. I. Munusamy Pillai.
13. *Others*: Maganpal Jain, J. Natarajan, Chandrasekhara Iyer, Marimuthu, Marudachalam and Vaidthilingam.

Institutions

Working in tandem with the Harijan Seva Sangam were Tiruchengode Gandhi Ashram, Tiruvennaiyanallur Kripa Ashram, Kallakurichi Khadi Ashram, Chidambaram Nandanar Educational Society, Madras Oppressed Classes Confederation, Indian Workers' Sangam, Mayanoor Village Improvement Society, Kovai Ramakrishna Vidyalayam, Tiruchirappalli General Public Workers' Sangam, Devendra Vellalar Sangam, Vellore International Welfare Sangam, Vellore Avvaiyar Educational Society, Madras Adi Dravidar Mahajana Sangam and North

Arcot District Equal Rights Society. In the Harijan uplift movement, great help was rendered by Ramakrishna Mutt. In Kallakurichi, the Harijan Welfare Sangam, run under the presidentship of retired Deputy Engineer, M. S. Narayanan, worked for the welfare and unity of Harijans in that Taluk. The Harijan Youth Sangam of Melur did much work to remove the drinking problem among Harijans.

Opposition and support

In Madras, some Harijan leaders did not support Gandhiji's movement. They demanded the total abolition of untouchability and conferment of equal rights to Harijans, and they did not believe that Gandhiji's movement could achieve this. Harijan leaders like Rao Bahadur Srinivasan and M. C. Raja could be included among them, although both were members of the Harijan Seva Committee and worked in it (among the leaders of the Adi Dravidar Mahajana Sabha, T. Chinnaiah alone opposed the Poona accord). Ultimately, a compromise agreement was reached between them.

However, even among the political adversaries of Gandhiji, there were many who supported this movement. T. A. V. Nathan, the editor of *Justice* (published by the Justice Party), wrote that the abolition of untouchability would purify the Hindu faith, and that the Justice Party supported this movement with enthusiasm and conviction.

At first, the programmes undertaken were the cleaning of slums, bathing of Harijan children, and sitting together with Harijans to eat. Thereafter, there was one important right remaining, upon the conferment of which the Harijans would enjoy equal status with other castes—that was temple entry.

Sri Meenakshi Temple

The Madurai Meenakshi temple is a renowned centre of pilgrimage. Hence, for the advocates of untouchability abolition, and even for Gandhiji himself, this temple held special attention. They believed that if they were successful in getting Meenakshi temple to open its doors to Harijans, other temples in Madras, and indeed in India, would follow. The Madurai public, too, were in favour of such temple entry.

One of the main reasons for this was the efforts of the Harijan Seva Sangam (Madurai branch), under the presidentship of A. Vaidyanatha Iyer, who, along with P. K. Ramachari, Halasyam Iyer, P. Varadarajulu Naidu, E. V. Ramasamy Periyar, S. Somasundara Bharathi and S. Krishnasamy Bharathi spoke strongly in favour of temple entry on various platforms. In 1932, there was a vote taken from the voters in the temple cities of Madurai, Kumbakonam, Kanchipuram and Srirangam.

Vote for temple entry

The votes showed that people were in favour of temple entry for Harijans. In Madurai, 4,746 out of 5,732 caste Hindus voted in favour of temple entry. Further, in the Madurai Devasthanam elections of January 1933, there was a big contest. A group led by N. Natesa Iyer, a lawyer, put up its candidate in opposition to temple entry. The group of nationalists put up their candidate in favour of entry. The number of votes polled in that election was 1,887, of which 1,498 votes were in favour of temple entry. Of the seven who contested for the Devasthanam Committee, six persons, who favoured temple entry, were elected.

Through this election, the Madurai public made it clear that they were in favour of Harijan temple entry. The nationalists started to prepare for the gradual entry of Harijans into the Madurai temple. Still, many years rolled by before it happened. It involved much hard work to overcome the opposition of priests, and remove other barriers, before implementing the will of the people. It required many public meetings, and door-to-door canvassing to convince the general public. N. Natesa Iyer continued to oppose the move. Being a leader in Sanatana circles all over India, he made strenuous efforts in Sanatana conferences held in other states to garner support for his cause. Opposing him in Madurai, and in favour of temple entry was his disciple, also a lawyer, A. Vaidyanatha Iyer.

A sight for sore eyes

A few weeks before the entry into the Madurai temple took place, a state conference of the Harijan Seva Sangam, led by Tmt. Rameswari

Nehru, was convened. Then chief minister of Madras State, C. Rajagopalachari, and Dr. T. S. S. Rajan, the Health minister, along with 800 delegates, participated in this conference, and helped in consolidating the favourable responses of the public for temple entry. In the public meeting held that day, when leaders called for the raising of hands in favour of temple entry, the near unanimous show of hands of those who had gathered was a sight to behold.

Temple entry for Harijans

Ultimately, on 8 July 1939, at 8.45 a.m., five Harijans, and a person belonging to the Nadar community, were taken into the Meenakshi temple under the leadership of A. Vaidyanatha Iyer.

That morning, Swami Muruganandam of Alampatti, Madurai District Committee member, P. Kakkan (later to become a Madras minister), Harijan Seva Sangam workers, Muthu, Madhicchiyam V. S. Chinaiah and Veeratipam P. R. Boovalingam, along with Virudhunagar Municipal administration member, S. S. Shanmuga Nadar, took off their shirts, liberally smeared *vibhuti* on themselves, and came to the entrance of the temple together with the Madras Harijan Seva Sangam president, A. Vaidyanatha Iyer, and secretary, L. N. Gopalasamy. The chief temple administrator, R. S. Naidu, welcomed them and escorted them into the temple.

They entered the *ardhamantapam*, hitherto only frequented by Brahmins, of the Sri Meenakshi Sundareswarar temple and obtained darshan of the Mother and the Lord. And thus, a great dream of Gandhiji and other social reformers was fulfilled. The Sanatanis had expected that the attendance in the temple as a consequence would dwindle, but it did not. The next day, upon the advice of the Trustees, the other famous temples in Madurai, Alayaman Koodalazhagar temple, and Sri Kallazhagar temple in Azhagarkoil were thrown open to all. In 1940, the notice of the All India Harijan Seva Sangam conference stated, "The most important work of the Sangam was arranging the temple entry in Madras State. As a result of this, not only Madurai Meenakshi temple, but the Palani temple and many others have been opened for Harijans."

Opposition of Sanatanis

Even though the Madurai temple entry went off peacefully, the Sanatanis did not stay quiet. They began to campaign that the temple was polluted by the entry of Harijans, and that Goddess Meenakshi had forsaken the temple. Led by Natesa Iyer, a small idol of Meenakshi was installed in his house, and opened for worship.

Thirty-six hours after the temple entry began, some priests of the temple were kidnapped, and the doors of the temple were shut and locked. The temple administrator, R. S. Naidu, Bar-at-Law was most helpful. On his authority, the lock was broken, and the poojas restarted as usual. Not finding the persons who normally performed the 'archanas', A. Vaidyanatha Iyer organised priests from outside Madurai to come and conduct the worship. After this, the attempts by the Sanatanis to stop the archanas in the temple and cause confusion among the people did not succeed.

The court case

Natesa Iyer and his supporters turned to the last resort available to them. They filed cases against A. Vaidyanatha Iyer, the temple administrator, R. S. Naidu, and the Harijans who had entered the temple during the official temple entry. The Congress ministry came forward to help. It promulgated the Madras Government Emergency Temple Entry Law and the Temple Entry Safety Law. The case went up to the High Court, where the supporters of temple entry triumphed.

Vaidyanatha Iyer's travails

After the temple entry issue was over, the hardship that Vaidyanatha Iyer faced at the hands of the Sanatanis grew intense. A friend brought this to the notice of Gandhiji. "The Sanatanis have tortured him," he wrote.

Consoling Vaidyanatha Iyer, Gandhiji him sent a long telegram: "Do not get upset by the words of people who wish to punish you. You, as a social reformer, must conduct yourself without being affected by opposition."

Iyer replied: "Through the grace of Sri Meenakshi and your blessings, I am keeping calm as usual, and continuing my work. I believe that other major temples will follow suit. Your love and blessings are my strength."

Gandhiji later wrote in the *Harijan*: "Among the workers involved in the eradication of untouchability movement, Vaidyanatha Iyer was one who conducted himself with humility and without fanfare. He is a true spiritualist."

When Iyer's father passed away, no Brahmin priest was willing to come to perform the funeral rites. Ultimately, *purohit*s from outside town had to be brought.

Major temples allow entry

After the Madurai temple entry, the Thanjavur temple too was opened to Harijans. Thereafter, Melur Taluk Valayapatti Sundararaja Perumal temple, Courtallam Tirukkattalainatha Swami temple, Tenkasi Viswanatha Swami temple, Udhagamandalam Mariamman temple, Hosur Chennakeswara Perumal temple and Karaikudi Siddhi Vinayakar temple permitted Harijans to enter.

To alleviate the problems faced by Harijans, Narayanan Nambiar, Dr Subbarayan, and M. C. Raja regularly brought bills to the legislature, but due to one barrier or another (or interference by those in power), they could not be made law. In 1937, the Congress established the government in Madras, led by Rajaji, allowed the right of temple entry for Harijans, and redressed their grievances through introduction of various bills. In India, the first state to pass a law on temple entry for Harijans was Madras.

New momentum

With the start of World War II (September 1939–September 1945), democratically elected governments were dissolved. The Harijan uplift and other government and social service work stagnated. The enthusiasm of the people, too, waned at that time. Still, in the 1946 elections, the Congress came back to power, and such work gained new momentum. From 1 January 1947, under the interim Indian government, Harijans entered the Tiruvarur Thyagesar temple led by Labour Minister, Jagjivan Ram. In the middle of that year, the Rameswaram temple was opened for Harijans. It could be said that temple entry for Harijans had now been allowed in all temples of Madras.

Bloodless protest

Gandhiji was aware that temple entry by Harijans and untouchability eradication measures that had progressed step by step could still be treated with contempt by the so called 'educated intellectual reformers'. Hence he warned, "Highly educated Harijans and others might look down upon these reforms as having come too late, but they should not forget that these great reforms came about without any blood being spilt. Nowhere else in the world has it happened so."

28

HARIJAN TOUR, 1933

1931

As with 1930, the year 1931 too became important in history. On 25 January of that year, Gandhiji and other leaders were released. On 5 March 1931, the Gandhi-Irwin Accord was signed. On 23 March 1931, Bhagat Singh, Rajaguru and Sukhdev were hanged. The Karachi Congress session was convened from 21 to 31 March 1931.

The tricolour that flutters today was accepted by the Congress Working Committee in that year. Gandhiji went to London for the Second Round Table Conference (September 1931–December 1931). On his way back to India, he met Mussolini. By the time he set foot in India, Jawaharlal Nehru and Abdul Ghaffar Khan (1890–1988) had been arrested. After his return, many other leaders were arrested. The Congress Working Committee authorised Gandhiji to begin his satyagraha again.

1932

Between 1928 and 1932, four great leaders—Maulana Mohammed Ali, Pandit Motilal Nehru, Annie Besant and Vitthalbhai Patel—passed away, leaving India bereft.

The year 1932 saw the historically famous Poona fast of Gandhiji, which almost took his life. The opposition to the 'divide and rule' scheme of the British government to allot a separate province for the backward people, ended successfully, with Ambedkar, on behalf of the backward people, signing the document. One of the leaders co-signing this was M. C. Raja[1] from Madras.

M. C. Raja was among the first to condemn the sinister move of the British government to allot a separate province for the backward castes, and to emphasise the importance of maintaining Gandhiji's health. When Gandhiji announced that he was going to undertake a fast, Congress and many other leaders and prominent nationalists got together in Bombay and decided that all efforts should be made to safeguard his life. M. C. Raja played an important role at that meeting. It is significant that, before agreeing to any decision on province allotment to the backward castes, Gandhiji desired to meet two Harijan leaders—one was Dr B. R. Ambedkar,[2] and the other was M. C. Raja. Through this landmark agreement, called the Poona Pact 1932, many benefits were sought to be given to Harijans, but the idea of a separate province and separate electorate for the depressed classes was given up.

Protests and fasts

When Gandhiji came to Madras on his 'Harijan tours' in 1933 and 1934, he still considered himself a prisoner of the government, on principle. He, therefore, did not discuss any political matters in his speeches. Having averted the threat of a separate province for the depressed classes, in February 1933 Gandhiji started the Harijan Seva Sangam. After this, as self-purification and for the cause of Harijans, he went on a 21-day fast, from 8 May to 29 May 1933. On his advice, the anti-law protests that were taking place were halted, and only protests by individuals continued. During the Dandi salt march, Gandhiji had pledged that he would not return to the Sabarmati Ashram without obtaining freedom. As pledged, he did not return to the ashram to stay, and, furthermore, he gave it up for the Harijan movement. He was arrested on 4 August, and as he began his fast in jail on 16 August 1933, his health weakened, and he was released unconditionally on 23 August 1933. He took a pledge that till the date of his scheduled release from imprisonment, as stipulated by the court, namely 3 August 1934, he would not participate in any protests against the laws.

The spread of swadeshi

After the Salt Satyagraha came to an end, Madras did not go into deep sleep. As per Gandhiji's advice, the protests against liquor shops went on spiritedly. Rajaji, who had been imprisoned consequent to the Salt Satyagraha, was released in October, and immediately the advocacy for swadeshi gained momentum. The Congress workers requested the public not to celebrate Deepavali.

Seeing Rajaji's influence among the workers and public, a bailable case was filed against him under I.P.C. Section 107. As he refused to pay bail, he was given one year's imprisonment, and lodged yet again in jail. On his request, S. Sathyamurthi became the Madras Congress president, and continued working to spread the swadeshi movement with zeal.

Oppressive measures

In 1931, a compromise arrived at between the Viceroy and Gandhiji brought relief to Madras. But later, on Gandhiji's return from the Round Table Conference, the protests intensified, and so did the oppressive measures of the government. After Gandhiji's arrest in the beginning of 1932, there were bans imposed even on the conduct of meetings. Emergency laws to ban protests and to ban unlicensed meetings and gatherings were promulgated. The government declared that the Congress was an illegal organisation. Hence, the Congress disbanded their committees, and in their place authorities were instituted. Even these were not allowed to function by the government.

In Madras State, the first of such authorities was Rajaji, and in Madras city, S. Satyamurthi. The government arrested both, and took over the Congress House. In spite of all this, the intensity and frequency of protests only increased. Clashes between the police and protestors turned ugly and violent in some places, dismaying the public. Post boxes were set on fire, bombs were burst. A violent protest in the name of Hindustan Socialist Republican Army was engineered. On 26 January 1933, when 'Freedom Day' was being observed, four workers entered the Legislature through the visitors' entrance, distributed leaflets, and burnt a small Union Jack. In 1932–33, in the face of rising govenment repression, such protests became the order of the day. In Madurai, efforts to ignite the no tax movement also took place. Madurai became a centre for revolutionary activities to gain freedom.

Kasturba's arrival

After Gandhiji began his fast in Poona, protests against the government decreased somewhat. In 1932, on her way to Guruvayur, Kasturba came to Madras. It was a time that Madras was deeply involved in the untouchability eradication movement. The All India Untouchability Abolition Day had been successfully celebrated. Several meetings giving support to this movement had been convened.

Swaraj Party

In 1933, during the period of Gandhiji's fast, there was a general strike all over Madras. Prisoners in Trichy jail, who had been arrested while protesting against the government, observed a day's fast. Moderates in the Congress got together under S. Satyamurthi and decided to establish the Swaraj Party within the Congress to attend to the work of elections and other developmental work. Thanjavur and South Arcot were ravaged by a cyclone that hit the Indian coast in December 1933, in which 168 persons lost their lives and 7,000 animals perished. It was in the midst of this that Gandhiji arrived.

Madras tour a big success

Stopping his tour to Andhra, Gandhi's three-day visit to Madras constituted his 1933 tour of the state. Although this tour was confined to Madras city alone, it was a success even beyond the expectations of Gandhiji. This time, since he had come with the single agenda of untouchability abolition, he faced strong opposition from the Sanatanis. It was a time when Madras State stood in the forefront of the movements against untouchability, protests against repressive laws, and for promoting swadeshi, khadi, and the salt satyagraha. Hence, despite their strenuous efforts, the opposition of the Sanatanis was ground to dust.

Wherever he went, Gandhiji was greeted by enthusiastic groups of people and given an overwhelming welcome. Gandhiji was not only delighted with the outcome of this visit, he was convinced that, if Madras took up a social cause, the rest of India would follow. Moreover, this visit was an important indicator to him of the response he could expect on his next visit to the state the following month. His visit was welcomed not only by the Congress and national press, but even newspapers normally known to be expressly critical of him. As K. M. Munshi, then at Bombay, said, this visit of Gandhiji felt like the coming of Buddha. Wherever he went there was great fervour, hope and excitement.

Wide support

In Madras, with the exception of the Sanatanis, there was broad acceptance by all other sections to Gandhiji's untouchability eradication programme. Even the *Mail*, which was normally not in consonance with Gandhiji's policies, came out in support of him through its editorial, and said: "Gandhiji's followers, who give more importance to politics, are not seen to be devoting as much interest to social service issues. Gandhiji has said that he has come here to undertake a programme of great human honour. As far as this work is concerned, everyone here would be in his support."

The *Swadesamithran* wrote in its editorial: "The Mahatma has had a longstanding connection with the south, particularly Madras. In his response to the welcome of the Corporation, he mentioned that it was to assuage the plight and hardship of Tamils in South Africa that he first developed the concept of spiritual opposition. Hence, he has a special place and gratitude for Madras."

The Hindu gave special importance to the work of untouchability abolition that formed the core of Gandhiji's visit on this occasion, and said: "More than in any other part of India, it is in Madras that untouchables live, mired in problems of economic and social discrimination, unable to breathe. It is here that barriers for removal of this social menace exist in large measure."

In an interview given to *The Hindu*'s special correspondent, Gandhiji said, "I have come in an effort to have clean water, and educational facilities provided for Harijans. Not only that, I am here to wean them away from liquor, and from their bad habit of eating the meat of dead animals. I am also trying to get public institutions opened for them to explain the tenets of Hindu religion."

However, Congress leaders and workers expressed disappointment with his tour. Gandhiji told *The Hindu* correspondent that according to Congressmen, by undertaking this tour at this point in time, he had diluted the civil disobedience movement against the unjust laws of the government, and the Congress demand for 'Purna Swaraj'. Gandhiji clarified that this was only a one-time exercise.

20 December 1933, A magnificent welcome

Those not in favour of Gandhiji's movement for the uplift of Harijans had printed posters with 'Gandhi Go Back' in bold letters, and pasted them on walls all over the city of Madras. Yet, he received a rousing, wholehearted public welcome on his arrival on the morning of 20 December, at Central station, Madras. He had travelled by Calcutta Mail from Bezawada, detrained at Basin Bridge, and was brought from there in a special saloon coach.

Thousands had gathered at the station with cries of 'Jai to Gandhiji'. Margaret Cousins[3] was among those who garlanded him on arrival. There was orderliness and peace at the station. Efficient transportation arrangements had been made by the Commissioner, G. M. M. Forbes. From Evening Bazaar to Moore market, massive crowds thronged the road. For half an hour, no buses or trams could be operated on the route near Central Station. The National Movietone people filmed the arrival of Gandhiji.

When the Harijan Seva Sangam sent Gandhiji the list of functions he was requested to attend in Madras, Gandhiji asked for the number to be cut down on account of his exhaustion after the Andhra tour. However, believing that all the events should be conducted to enable strong public cooperation, they still sent him the full agenda.

Corporation Council

At the Ripon Buildings, where the welcome was arranged, crowds were everywhere—inside the building, out in the courtyard, the gardens and on the walls, to the extent that the police and volunteers found them almost impossible to control. In honour of his visit, schools and offices under the Corporation had declared a holiday. W. W. Leyton, the Commissioner, and T. T. Warren welcomed Gandhiji. Replying to the Corporation Council's welcome, Gandhiji recalled the welcome that this Corporation had given him on a previous visit.

"I had spoken about the need for cleaning the surroundings during my last visit. This time I come with a request for a different cleansing drive: this is the work of cleaning up pertaining to religion," he said simply.

Swadeshi exhibition

At the Congress building on General Patter's Road, Gandhiji inaugurated the All India Swadeshi Exhibition. At the neighbouring Midland theatre, a special function was arranged. Here, at the welcome of the South Indian Merchant's Chamber, it was requested that national leaders should take up the task of charting the way for the country's economic progress. In his speech, Gandhiji, stating that he had undertaken this tour for the uplift of Harijans, said:

> You may ask me what this exhibition has to do with Harijan uplift. As far as Harijans are concerned, there is much importance for khadi. Several thousands of Harijans will benefit from hand spinning and weaving.
>
> I have myself directly seen the advantages to them through khadi. Hence I would want the khadi products made specifically by the Harijans to be exhibited here. Take the example of the leather profession. Had not the Harijans worked in it at the beginning, there would have been no leather industry in India.

In this exhibition, organised under the leadership of Sripada Sankar, 100 *kesam*s (strands) of yarn per hour were being spun. One Rajagopalan from Bangalore had invented a new type of spinning wheel, which also was exhibited. The National Movietone people filmed Gandhiji's visit to this exhibition. This film, along with the film on his arrival at Madras Central station, was shown in cinema theatres as a special feature.

The forewarning

Gandhiji spoke at a total of six meetings on 20 December 1933. However, he would not have expected that the warning he issued at the Indian Women's Association meeting, held on Pantheon Road, Egmore, would be borne out within a few weeks thereafter.

At that meeting, he had said: "I have never shied away from warning that untouchability will be the ruin of Hindu religion. God is very patient with us, but looking at the differences that are perpetrated in India between man and man, I feel constrained to say that even He would lose patience."

Just a few weeks after he said this, there was a massive earthquake in Bihar.

Muthulakshmi Reddy

Dr Muthulakshmi Reddy, who translated Gandhiji's speech at this meeting, handed over a purse of Rs 430 to him. Receiving it, Gandhiji remarked, "The purse is not heavy. Anyway, heavy or not heavy, it is going to be used for Harijan welfare."

Dr Reddy replied, "The women have given more for the Tilak Fund."

To this, Gandhiji jokingly retorted, "Is this a consolation? It seems you are equating yourselves with men!"

Women's meeting

After this, Gandhiji took part in a meeting arranged jointly by the Women's Association and Harijan women. Subhadramma welcomed him at this meeting, held at the Indian Workers' Sangam builing in Royapettah. The Women's Association consisted of caste Hindu women, some of whom were orthodox, as well as Harijan women.

Gandhiji outlined three ways in which Harijans should purify themselves: "Firstly, Harijans should keep their bodies clean. Secondly, they should not eat the meat of dead animals and beef. Thirdly, they should give up the liquor habit." Women should ensure that men followed these practices, he added.

Welcome by students

Students gathered in great numbers at Midland Theatre to welcome Gandhiji, and handed over a purse of Rs 1000. The event was very well organised by the secretaries, Bobby Needu and M. V. Sharma. In his speech, Gandhiji recalled the students' meeting that he had attended in 1896, and the rousing response he had received when he had said:

> Do not get drowned in words—get down to action. The orthodox priests who oppose untouchability eradication have not understood the essence of the Shastras. Neither do they have the authority to speak on behalf of the people. So, carry brooms and buckets and go to the slums and teach cleanliness to the people. You must spend a few of your leisure hours in this work.

The Mahatma said this is what he expected from all the students assembled here today, and in fact from everyone, and added: "If you realise what is good, I will expect that you work towards it. You agree that untouchability is evil, and that it should be eradicated. Keep that as your aim and work for it. Had you said through this welcome in what ways you are already rendering service, I would have been happier."

When the welcome address given to him was put up for auction, Thirumathy Lakshmi Swaminathan offered two bangles that she was wearing, and bought it.

Hindi

Seeing the thousand-strong students' gathering, Gandhiji felt he must also speak about Hindi.

> I have earlier talked about my disappointment with regard to students of this State. … They are not of Madras State alone, but Indian citizens. Therefore, how can they hold in contempt the Hindi language spoken by 22 crore people in India? [Pakistan was then part of India, and the country's total population was 35 crores.] Even if it is a fact that a few students are studying Hindi, it is not enough. You will realise what a major drawback it is when the burden of this country's responsibilities falls on your shoulders.

Gandhiji was later interviewed by A. Rangaswami Iyengar, K. Bhashyam, and the *Harijan* publication editor, R. V. Sastri.

A sea of humanity

A mammoth crowd had amassed for the public meeting on the beach front in Tiruvallikeni (or Triplicane, one of the oldest localities in Madras city). *The Hindu* reported that some two lakh people had gathered. The assembly proved beyond doubt that the posters all over town calling to boycott Gandhiji's visit had not had any effect whatsoever. People were eager to see Gandhiji and hear him speak. On the east was the ocean, on the west the Marina beach, the aquarium on the south—and then the vast sea of humanity.

People from Mylapore in the south, Roundtana in the west, and Georgetown in the north had started reaching the venue of the meeting in Tiruvallikeni from 4 p.m. onwards. Painstaking arrangements had been made for sound amplification, and for the smooth movement of crowds. The meeting was to have commenced at 6 p.m. Gandhiji arrived at the venue five minutes early.

Before Gandhiji's arrival, people were sitting quietly. But the moment he came, the crowds surrounded his car, wanting a closer view of him, and a huge uproar and pandemonium ensued. Gandhiji was deftly escorted to the dais, hot and sweating. As soon as he ascended the dais, he signalled for quiet with one hand, wiping the sweat off his brow with the other. Cries of 'Jai to Mahatma Gandhi' filled the air. There was a brief silence, and once again noise and confusion took over. Gandhiji's pleas for calm were in vain. Wanting to hear him clearly, the crowds surged towards the dais, made of bamboo poles, which started to shake, but somehow managed not to collapse. Forcing the people in front to sit down, the crowds at the rear began to throw sand on them, adding to the massive confusion.

'Gandhi thatha'

The women in the crowd, in particular, had a really trying time. Some of them handed over their children, including babes in arms, to those on the dais to protect them from harm. It was pathetic to see the children on stage holding on to Gandhiji's hands, crying, "*Thatha! Thatha!*" (grandfather). Some women, too, started wailing loudly from panic in the melee. Gandhiji had a few children on his lap and was seen trying his best to console them. A person seated on the dais, pointing to Gandhiji, asked a four-year-old: "Do you know who he is?" The child replied, "Yes, he is Gandhi."

After about half an hour, there was a temporary peace, and Gandhiji finally started to speak, but he spoke for barely seven minutes. In the meantime, P. Jagannath Das brought four policemen and a whole lot of workers to escort Gandhiji away from the dais. Tightly surrounded by them, Gandhiji got into his car and left. Many in the crowd were not aware that Gandhiji had left the stage, and so it took about an hour for the crowd to disperse. In all this chaos, Gopalammal, the daughter of a retired judge, had her 40-*pavun* gold waist ornament stolen. K. Bhashyam, one of the organisers, later apologised in a communication to Gandhiji and the public for the lack of adequate arrangements.

All are equal before God

Stressing on the urgency of abolishing untouchability from the land, Gandhiji once again emphasised that,

> God does not look kindly on the differences between man and man. Had He so designed, He would have created people with separate characteristics. If we do not eradicate untouchability from its roots, not just us, but Hindu religion will be destroyed, and we would be the cause of it. If, by the Grace of God, this realisation is ingrained in your heart, you will forget the distinction of high and low people.

This exhortation did find deep roots in the hearts of Tamils. This was the reason why, for Gandhiji, Madras stood in the forefront of the untouchability abolition movement. At this meeting, welcome addresses (unread) were presented on behalf of the Madras Mahajana Sabha, the Madras general public, the Harijan Divya Prabhandha Sabha, and Tiruvallikeni merchants. When Gandhiji visited the Khadi Bhandar in Tiruvallikeni, A. Rukmini Lakshmipathi and R. Parthasarathi welcomed him. A purse was also presented on behalf of the Khadi Bhandar directors.

Visit to the slums

Gandhiji knew that his work was far from over with delivering addresses at public meetings. He knew that speeches alone would not uplift the low-caste Kadayar community, or Harijans who were considered even lower than them, and lived like worms. Hence, on the second day, he set out to visit their slums himself. He visited about ten slums and spent not less than 10 minutes in each.

At 7.30 a.m., Gandhiji started from where he was staying, at Nageswara Rao Pantulu's 'Sribaug' mansion. Many workers followed him in a bus. Among the slums he visited was Pallakku Maniam slum, run by Swami Rudrendranath of Sri Ramakrishna Mutt, under the Harijan improvement scheme. Gandhiji warmly praised the social service being done by the Mutt there. Swami Rudrendranath, affectionately called Muthu Maharaj, later served in the Fiji Islands in the South Pacific.

The workers' association was in charge of two slums, Pallakku Maniam, near Luz Church Road, and The Garden. The president of the Madras Harijan Seva Sangam, V. Bhashyam Iyengar, welcomed Gandhiji at Pallaku Maniam slum. Swami Rudrendranath read out the welcome address. Surprised that it was so brief, Gandhiji remarked, "Has it finished so quickly?"

"I will add a few words," said the Swamiji. "Just a few?" Gandhiji retorted, laughing.

Later, in response to the welcome address, he said: "I am aware of the wonderful service being rendered by the Sri Ramakrishna Mutt. This is an institution that purifies the soul. Old and young people, men and women, should take part in their work."

Damodarapuram

In honour of Gandhiji's visit, 300 children were given new clothes. Gandhiji praised the work being done by the workers' association. After this, he went to Damodarapuram, near Adayaru, where Hilda Wood and members of the Brahmagnana Sabha were engaged in the work of rural reawakening, and he was told by them of the services being done there.

On the way there, children stood on both sides of the road singing the bhajan, 'Paahi mukham dehi Krishna,' which he listened to with emotion. At the Thiruvadhi Amman temple in Damodarapuram, Gandhiji circumambulated the shrine with hands folded in prayer. When the pot offered to the Goddess was brought to him, Gandhiji touched it with both hands and touched his hands to his eyes. This temple had been opened for Harijans just days before Gandhiji's visit.

When he visited the Montessori school nearby, he went up to a Harijan boy picking his nose, chucked him gently under his chin and told him that he should clear his nose properly. Then he said, "Children, boys and girls, let me tell you something. You all have a duty in this purification work. Hence you must be good children. You must think of God whenever you are troubled."

Bharatha Sabha

At the Narayanasamy Chettiar Park in Teynampet, at the meeting with slum dwellers, he was offered welcome addresses on behalf of the Bharatha Sabha, and the people of that locality. The Bharatha Sabha welcome was read out by T. S. Swaminathan. A purse of one rupee eleven annas, collected from Harijans, was handed over to Gandhiji. As there was a large crowd, Gandhiji used his car as a stage and spoke from there. He invited some girl children, who were standing on one side of him, to sing. After they sang for a while, he stopped them, saying in Tamil, "*Podhum, podhum*" (Enough, enough). The welcome address copy of Bharatha Sabha was auctioned at three rupees. The manuscript of the welcome by slum residents went for two rupees.

At all the slums Gandhiji visited that day, he exhorted Harijans to do their duty in purifying the Hindu religion. He also spoke at several workers' meetings. In the evening, he went to Perambur and received the welcome of the M. S. M. Railway Workers' Sangam at Unity House. The people of Perambur and Sembium (part of Chinglepet district) gathered at the Perambur Tank ground for the public meeting, where he was presented a welcome address. Gandhiji was then on fast. He was taken to visit the Sundara Vinayakar temple opened for Harijans, and the free dispensary run by the ascetic Balagurusamy at his mutt. A large crowd enthusiastically welcomed Gandhiji at Rayavaram Robinson Park.

"Men and women are [both] required for this great spiritual movement. Casting away all your bad habits, educate your children," he advised them. His speech there was translated by T. Adhikesavulu Naicker.

Kannappar Reading Room

Of those who garlanded him at Robinson Park was Ma. Po. Sivagnana Gramani, as secretary of the North Madras Welcome Committee. There had been correspondence between Gandhiji and the Kannappar Reading Room in Rayavaram Rama Naicken Street. Through their secretary, M. K. Arumugam, they had expressed that they wanted a building for the school being run under its aegis, and required financial assistance. This was sent to the editor of *Swarajya*, T. Prakasam (later, chief minister of Madras), who then asked Gandhiji whether any help could be given. Within days of this letter being sent, on 21 December 1933, Gandhiji manifested himself—yes, that is what must be said—at the Reading Room!

Lifted on a chair!

When Gandhiji arrived at the Kannappar Reading Room, the crowd waiting to see him was so dense that it was impossible for him to enter. Hence, a bold decision was taken. A chair tied to a rope was lowered, Gandhiji was made to sit on it, and lifted to the upper floor! The people who had gathered below thus managed to get a good view of Gandhiji. Responding to the welcome address of the Reading Room officials, Gandhiji said, "This school will grow strong with the blessings of the Almighty." He also promised help from the Harijan Fund.

Varadarajapuram

Varadarajapuram, or Nariyangadu, as it was known, was a slum in Puduppettai of Egmore. Jagadeesan, an important representative of the slum people, welcomed Gandhiji. Some children from this slum had painstakingly saved up coin by coin to give Gandhiji a rupee each. A seven-year old boy had purchased a garland for two annas, which he now put on Gandhiji. Gandhiji praised the service being rendered at this slum by the Kumara Bhaktha Jana Sabha.

Periamet

Next, Gandhiji visited the large Periamet slum, where Anglo-Indians, and a few higher-caste people also lived. He was welcomed there by the trustees of Ellamman temple. Gandhiji put a few queries about the temple to C. Venkatarama Naidu ('V').

G: Are Adi Dravidars allowed into this temple?
V: Yes, for a long time. What is special is that some of the Trustees are themselves Adi Dravidars.
G: Do caste Hindus also come to the temple?
V: Yes.
G: (Pleased) Who is the priest here?
V: A. Pandaram.

V. Bhashyam told Gandhiji that A. Pandaram was a caste Hindu. At this point, A. Pandaram came up to garland Gandhiji, and performed other temple formalities in his presence. After this, C. Venkatarama Naidu and Janab Shafi Mohammed took him to Kadappai Rangaiah Chetty street, and presented a welcome there on behalf of the Ramakrishna Bhaktha Samajam, read out by Sarangapani. In his reply, Gandhiji blessed the association, and exhorted them to stay united.

From here he proceeded to Arundhatipuram in Perambur, and inspected the students' hostel there. P. R. Ramachandraiah welcomed him and explained that the hostel for 22 students was being run with the help of workers. In token of Gandhiji's visit, 400 boys and girls were given free khadi dress. The boys and girls here sang his favourite 'Vaishnava Jana tho' hymn, which he listened to with rapt attention from his car.

Perambur

The last meeting for the day was held under the auspices of the Madras Workers' Association at Perambur Wadia Park, and attended by huge crowds. Gandhiji was to have unveiled a portrait of the late Annie Besant at this meeting. Scheduled to arrive at 6.30 p.m. for this meeting, he had not reached there till 8 p.m., owing to the chain of delays caused by the earlier meetings, with the result that the crowds had swelled even further, and seemed to be at bursting point. Many in the crowd, unable to handle the suffocating atmosphere, returned home. When Gandhiji did finally arrive, he was unable to go through the crowd to reach the dais. So he remained in the car, called for Annie Besant's portrait to be brought to him, and unveiled it there itself. In the meantime, unable to get a glimpse of Gandhiji, a section of the crowd had ascended the dais, which collapsed from the weight.

At the Choolai Gandhi grounds, Gandhiji was only able to give a 'darshan' of himself to the crowds. But the crowd here was patient enough to allow him to get up on the dais to be seen by all. It was 9.30 p.m. when that meeting ended. Right Honourable Srinivasa Sastri, T. R. Venkatarama Sastri, Dewan Bahadur V. Bhashyam Iyengar, Dr A. Lakshmipathi, Dr Kumarappa and Krishnabai were granted interviews by Gandhiji.

22 December 1933, He ran and he flew!

On the third and last day of his tour, Dr S. Rangachari did a health check-up on Gandhiji. On the afternoon of the first day, Dr Muthu had examined him. Both doctors gave him a clean chit of health. Dr Muthu remarked, "From the time I examined him at the Round Table Conference, Gandhiji's health is better now." On the third day, one could not say that Gandhiji walked—he virtually ran and he flew. In the morning, he attended four functions and received welcomes and purses. There were massive crowds at all places.

Harijan Seva Sangam

First, he went to George Town, St Xavier's Street Harijan Seva Sangam, where he received the welcome and purses from various associated organisations. As he was late by an hour at this function, a large crowd had assembled inside and outside. He was received with the traditional *purna kumbham* by K. Nageswara Rao Panthulu, Dr P. Varadarajulu Naidu, V. Sarkkarai Chettiar and the Association president, M. S. Koteeswaran. Gandhiji ascended a high dais erected for him for all to see him. An amusing thing happened.

A woman named Saraswathiamma wished to garland him, but he was at a higher level. How could she do it? Two persons rushed up with a table, standing on which she was able to garland Gandhiji. People introduced the woman to Gandhiji. "The lady is a satyagrahi. She has gone to jail twice, protesting along with her husband against the repressive laws of the government," they said.

The charkha of fortune

On behalf of this branch of the association, G. Rangaiah Naidu, in his welcome speech, said, "A majority of the backward community are not happy with the name 'Harijan' that you have so generously given them." This welcome address was translated into both Hindi and Tamil. M. S. Koteeswaran read out the Tamil version on behalf of Harijan Seva Sangam, Cinema Central, Pachaiyappan High School teachers, students, and George Town Hindi Vidyalayam; purses and gifts were presented. One person gave a silver cup filled with peanuts!

Finally, Gandhiji rose to speak. "Dear friends, we have not bargained till now. Hence, before I speak, I must bargain a little." This evoked laughter from the crowd. Thereafter, he auctioned the articles received by him. He held up a charkha and said, "This beautiful charkha is the handiwork of a school student. The girls can give their bangles to purchase it, can they not?" With each one bidding, the bid reached thirty rupees. "*Seegharam! Seegharam!*" (Quick! Quick!) he urged the people in Tamil, again causing amusement. "This is a beautiful charkha. The one who buys it will be rewarded with good fortune," he urged. Ultimately, Cinema Central owner, M. P. Rajan, bought it for Rs 40. Gandhiji blessed him, saying, "It will bring you good fortune."

Jewels gifted

At the next auction here, however, Gandhiji's urgings were of no avail. He started the auction at a price of Rs 75 for Rangaiah Naidu's diamond ring. "Ladies can buy it by donating their bangles," he said. As no one bid for it, he kept it aside and began to auction other articles. V. Sarkkarai Chettiar bought the peanut-filled silver cup. Thereafter, women gave their jewels eagerly. Gandhiji's secretaries were hard put to note all of it down.

Rangaiah Naidu's little daughter came up to Gandhiji and gave him her jewels. "Will you give me your gold chain too?" Gandhiji asked her. She glanced at her father, and, at his nod, she replied, "Yes." Gandhiji took the chain from her and asked, "Does anyone want to bid for this?" As again, nobody came forward with a bid, he put it back into the bag.

He also explained why he had given the name 'Harijan' to the people of backward communities. (This is mentioned a little later in this chapter.)

'I come to dig into your riches'

Ramnath Goenka conducted the meeting arranged by Gujaratis, Sindhis and Marwaris at the Thanga Salai Jain temple. Gandhiji opened his speech with, "For long you have dug into the riches of the people, and made money; I now come to dig into yours," evoking laughter, and began the auction. The articles here went for high prices. "I am now undertaking God's work. I am convinced it is the way of truth," he declared. After this, he took part in the meeting of Gujarati, Sindhi and Marwari women on the upper floor of this building.

Many women gave him their jewels. When he went to the meeting of the Madras Vysya Sangam on Govindappa Naicken Street, public transport had to be temporarily suspended to manage the crowds, and a large number of policemen deployed. Here, too, the 'Vysya' Mahatma impressed upon the Vysya community the need to work towards the eradication of untouchability. The welcome here was read out by Swami Venkatachalam Chetty.

A pen, with the words, 'Remove the differences between high and low: M. K. Gandhi' was presented to him by someone. When this pen was auctioned, a person bought it for Rs 250. When Gandhiji spoke later, he said: "This fountain pen has written [on it] the same objective with which I have come. It is wrong to say that only the higher castes can study the Shastras, and the lower castes should not. It is this feeling of high and low that is the cause of much of our troubles."

Satyagraha in front of Gandhiji

An unexpected incident took place, of a person doing satyagraha in front of Gandhiji, on Govindappa Naicken street. The George Town Dharma Hindi Charkha School authorities had planned to present him with a gold charkha. This was an unscheduled event on Gandhiji's agenda. As he came out of the Vysya Sangam and got into his car, a person belonging to the above school stood in front of the car, in an attitude of satyagraha. His demand was that Gandhiji should attend the meeting arranged by them. A police official intervened and dragged the man away, allowing Gandhiji's car to proceed. Notably, in his interview to the press, Gandhiji expressed his gratitude for the alertness and assistance of this police official. For the meeting arranged by that person, without prior permission, tickets for admission had already been sold. When those who had bought tickets sought refund, there was much confusion.

Proceeding to Godown Street, Gandhiji unveiled a portrait of K. Nageswara Rao Panthulu (1867–1938), journalist, nationalist, politician and businessman, and staunch supporter of khadi. "I know of a special virtue in Panthulu. He will go out of his way to help anyone who comes to him," he said in praise.

Marriage Hall

Gandhiji went to the Marriage Hall (built by Nelson and Company) in Tiruvallikkeni Main Road, and received the welcome and purses from the Marwaris there and Manikka Mudaliar. In Krishnampettai Sakkilipalayam, Adi Dravidar youths accorded him a welcome. At the Gokulam run by P. Sankaranarayana Iyer (who had, on Gandhiji's request, gone to Ramanashram) and his wife Visalakshiammal, a bottle of honey prepared by the people was presented to Gandhiji. In honour of his visit, a coconut sapling was planted there by him. Thereafter he visited several slums.

Convocation

After granting interviews to leaders of the backward classes, Gandhiji proceeded to the Dakshin Bharat Hindi Prachar Sabha's third convocation—one of his most important engagements on the third day of his tour. Pandit Ram Naresh Tripathi of Allahabad addressed the convocation. Khadi shawls were given as diplomas to the students passing out. Praising this, Gandhiji said in consternation, "Oh, are you going to adorn me with this too? Do not forget that I will be auctioning it at the end of the meeting." In the Gokhale Hall, he explained how the national language was intrinsically woven into the uplift of the backward classes.

Gandhiji accepted it was difficult to learn Hindi in the south of India, but exhorted the students to master it with strenuous efforts. Instead of looking to North India, the Dakshin Bharat Hindi Prachar Sabha must endeavour to raise its finances from South India, he said.

> You accept that you belong to one part of India. If so, how can you ignore the national language? Now I am deeply involved in the movement of untouchability eradication. If you wish to be part of this movement all over India, you must become aware of the need to learn Hindustani. If you do not know Hindustani, your service will become very difficult.

He auctioned the gown he was wearing for Rs 100, and gave it to the Harijan Fund. The person who bought it did not want his name revealed.

Harijan leaders meet Gandhiji

In the evening, the Madras City Backward Classes Association managing committee members interviewed Gandhiji. Rao Bahadur Srinivasan was one among them. He was known to Gandhiji from his days in South Africa. Later, as a representative of the backward classes, he had argued against Gandhiji at the Round Table Conference in London. He was one of the main leaders who prepared the Poona agreement in 1932, while in Yerawada jail, during Gandhiji's fast. He, along with Rao Sahib V. Dharmalingam Pillai, Swami Sahajananda, P. V. Rajagopal Pillai, V. K. Pushparaj, H. M. Jagannathan and some others met and discussed with Gandhiji on this occasion. On behalf of all of them, Rao Bahadur Srinivasan submitted a memorandum to Gandhiji, which stated: "The Poona accord must be faithfully implemented. The backward class representatives who are put up for elections must truly belong to the backward classes. The Harijan Seva Sangam must cooperate to properly implement the laws introduced by the government for Harijans' progress."

Respect for Gandhiji

Though many people had differences of opinion with Gandhiji, politically and otherwise, their enduring personal respect for him becomes clear from the following incident. Gandhiji had just finished his evening meal, when the Harijan leaders led by Rao Bahadur Srinivasan approached him. "Come, Rao Bahadur," Gandhiji invited him with a smile and said, "Shall I ask for a chair to be placed for you?"

Srinivasan expressed his preference to squat on the mat on which the others were seated. Swami Sahajananda and Pushparaj prostrated themselves full length at Gandhiji's feet, while others touched his feet in respect. They then told him, "When you started referring to the backward classes as 'Harijans', you had not sought their approval. Some of them are, therefore, aggrieved by this."

Why the name 'Harijan'

Gandhiji's reply illustrates how the phrase 'God is my companion' had touched his heart. "You say that I had not consulted the backward classes. But they consulted me, that is what is important." This brought smiles to their faces. Gandhiji continued:

> 'Do not refer to us in a way that keeps us mired as a lower-class people. It is a phrase that makes us slaves,' an 'untouchable' said to me once, and he was right. I could not think of any other name, and so I asked him to suggest one. It was then that he suggested the name, 'Harijan'. Narsinh Mehta, the Gujarati poet, had also referred to untouchables by this name. Hence, it immediately struck me as appropriate. I am aware of the Tamil saying, 'For the directionless, God is the companion.' Is not the term 'Harijan' the core meaning of this saying? Those who have been discarded and held in contempt are in fact God's favourite children. When we refer to the depressed classes as 'Harijans', it is this concept that is being reflected.

Temple entry

Regarding temple entry, the Harijan leaders' memorandum said: "We do not oppose temple entry, but when we look at the experience in Nasik and other places, we feel that to take part strongly in this movement is not desirable. If the temples are opened for us, we will enter them whenever we want and when convenient."

Gandhiji accepted this. "I am not asking Harijans to take part in this movement. They have as much right in a temple as caste Hindus have. It is important that this right should be established. You may accept it or not."

The drinking habit

One of the other points raised in the memorandum was: "There are several drunkards in all castes; it is not correct to say that drunkards are found only among the lower castes." Gandhiji's response was:

> I know that the drinking habit exists in other classes, too. But, for Harijans, who have to progress under circumstances of severe hardship, this habit affects their economy. Hence the need to come out of the liquor habit is more essential for them. I have toiled for several years to remove this scourge from their lives. Please do not fence in my liberty in this matter. I will not say a word to hurt the feelings of anyone. Untouchability is at death's door. As it is a demon, it continues to gasp for its last breath, but it is going to be indeed its final breath.

Gandhiji's faith in the future

The three days that he spent in Madras city confirmed his belief, from all that he and heard, that the demon of untouchability was in fact dying. Before leaving Madras, Gandhiji told the press:

> Wherever I went, the people showered on me their deep love and respect. However, on the beach in Madras and at meetings in workers' sections, I can say that I had never anticipated the gathering of as many people as I witnessed. I firmly believe that these people who have accepted me have fully understood why I have come, and what my principles are. If their religious beliefs had stood against untouchability eradication, would they have accorded me such enthusiastic welcome? I will never completely lose their respect, as otherwise their welcome would have been muted. I am in the habit of recognising the working of people's minds from the looks on their faces.
>
> I have not seen an iota of opposition from people to my work towards abolition of untouchability. Their generous donations strengthen my conviction. I have, therefore, full faith in the future. I see in Madras, too, that untouchability is being pulled out by its roots.
>
> I would like to assure my friends that I never have the intention to wound their feelings. I like to work with the similarity they have with my views. There are many. The differences are only a few. Even if we do not find common ground in these differences,

I will have patience, a virtue, I believe, I possess. In time conformity will take place.

Opposition of Sanatanis

When Gandhiji arrived in Madras city, K. M. Munshi (1887–1971), Indian independence activist, writer and educationist, who had come with his wife, was astounded at the overwhelming reception accorded to Gandhiji by the common people, because Madras was a stronghold of orthodox Brahmins, where the Sanatani opposition to the abolition of untouchability continued to be aggressive.

At the time of Gandhiji's visit, a memorandum was issued by 'Bhasyha Bhavagna' Vaidyanatha Sastriar (including those from Sengalipuram), and other Sanatanis. The memorandum stated that it would have been all right if Gandhiji had asked foreign philosophers to follow his principle of untouchability eradication, but to point out Sanatana dharma as an example was most shocking. They also said that Gandhiji should meet and discuss this with Jagadguru Sri Sankaracharya Swami, Bharathi Krishna Theerthaji, who had come to Madras on their invitation the same day. M. K. Acharya wrote that 95 out of 100 persons even among the backward classes would not accept "the Gandhian principle".

"What is the Gandhian principle?" asked Gandhiji in return. "I myself do not know! How could the Acharya have known?" The Acharya's reply in the *Mail* indicated that he had little idea of what the Gandhian principle was. "Caste Hindus are all sinners. The backward classes are Harijans. This is what I believe to be the Gandhian principle" is what he wrote. The Acharya, however, added that he was willing to accept the abolition of untouchability within the constraints of the Sanatana doctrine. At the same time, his other notice to Gandhiji was one that seemed contrary.

He said: "In Valmiki's *Ramayana*, Ravana declared that taking away of another's wife was part of his dharma. I want that Gandhiji must be careful, as even good intentions can lead to disaster and hell. … Only a great sage can purify Hindu religion, or any other religion for that matter. Does Gandhiji consider himself a great sage?" His last two sentences reveal on what balancing scale the Acharya weighed the Mahatma.

Regardless of what M. K. Acharya, other Sanatanis or any other leader, spiritual or political, said, the common people saw Gandhiji as a sage, and even beyond one. In their minds, eradicating untouchability would cause some strife and bitterness in the early stages, but there was no confusion about it once Gandhiji had pronounced his decision.

The Indian nation

A few believed that Gandhiji's untouchability eradication campaign had a political basis. However much he emphasised that it was a spiritual movement, and that he had no intention to use it for any political objective, not everyone would see it that way. Nevertheless, Gandhiji made a vital and categorical statement, which is as relevant for us today, if not more, as it was then: "I do not say that the Indian nation and Hindu religion are one and the same, as the Hindu Mahasabha believes. The Indian nation is a conglomeration of Hindus, Christians, Muslims and people of other faiths."

The *Mail* notably wrote on 22 December 1933: "Only one Gandhi stands between the movement and its misuse. Those who follow him will not be so concerned with examining the nuances of different opinions expressed, and will not hesitate to boycott those who are against this movement."

Jewellery auction

One newspaper carried an article condemning the auction of jewellery given by women to Gandhiji, and other articles given to him for the Harijan Fund, at higher prices than they were valued at. Gandhiji responded to this in the 22 December issue of *Harijan*.

> In truth, I would prefer if the women who attend my meetings give me all the jewellery they are wearing. In a country where 80% of people are starving, the sight of a few wearing jewellery offends my eyes. Much capital is confined with a few. Hence, women offering their jewels will certainly benefit society. Those who offer these jewels to me do so happily, and I accept them on condition that they do not wear other jewellery instead. Moreover, those who buy these articles on auction at higher prices do not do so merely to satisfy me. Is not the value of an article the price a person happily pays for it?

Departure

Completing his tour successfully, Gandhiji left Madras on the night of 22 December 1933. Those who had come with him, like Miraben, boarded Calcutta Mail at Central station for Tenali (a city in Andhra Pradesh). To avoid the crowds, Gandhiji alone went up to Ennore (in Madras city) and joined them there; as the train did not normally stop at Ennore, special arrangements were made for it to stop there to allow him to board. From the house of K. Nageswara Rao, at 7.40 p.m., Gandhiji started by car at 7.40 p.m., along with V. Bhashyam Iyengar, and K. Nageswara Rao Panthulu, They waited for five minutes at Ennore station. Although this had been kept a secret, somehow a few people did manage to come to the station, and Gandhiji was even able to collect some money for the Harijan Fund there. "This is the first time I am boarding a train without difficulty," he remarked happily as he left Ennore.

Notes

1. Mylai Chinna Thambi Pillai Rajah (1883–1943) was a Tamil politician, educationist, social activist, and the most prominent leader of the Scheduled Classes in pre-independence India who organised them at the national level.

2. 'Babasaheb' Bhimrao Ramji Ambedkar (1891–1956) was an Indian jurist, economist, social reformer, political leader and freedom activist who headed the committee drafting the Constitution of India, and served as independent India's first Law and Justice minister. He advocated against untouchability and for political and social rights for Dalits, and inspired the Dalit Buddhist movement after renouncing Hinduism.

3. Margaret Cousins (1878–1954) was an Irish-Indian educationist, suffragist, theosophist and founder of the All India Women's Conference in 1927.

29

HARIJAN TOUR, 1934

A month later

One month after Gandhiji left Madras, he re-entered the state. The tour from Madras to Andhra, then on to Mysore, Tiruvangur Principality via Malabar, and from there to Nagercoil, had taken one month. Nagercoil, in those days, was under the rule of the Tiruvangur prince.

Bihar earthquake

In this one month, a tragedy of unimaginable proportions struck North India. On 15 January 1934, a major earthquake shook Bihar, making villagers there believe that the end of the world was at hand. In the three minutes that the earth heaved, it seemed that entire north Bihar would be destroyed. This shock was experienced even a thousand miles away. Buildings were razed to the ground, lakhs of villagers lost their homes, lands and occupations, leaving them completely helpless. The earthquake, which wreaked devastation across 30,000 square miles, affected one and a half lakh people (causing more than 7,000 deaths in Bihar), and damaged 900 miles of railway tracks. Gandhiji was then at Tiruvangur Principality.

Gandhiji's grief

In the belief that this disastrous situation needed leaders of stature to help people withstand the colossal tragedy, Rajendra Prasad was released from jail within two days of the earthquake. He immediately reviewed the situation and sent a telegram to Gandhiji, who, in his grief-laden reply, wrote: "I feel that I have been shattered into small pieces, and am consumed by these thoughts all 24 hours. However, I feel that suspending the work I have started here is unjust. Even were I to come there, what could I do?"

The journey begins

The conviction Gandhiji had on untouchability abolition could not be shaken even by the Bihar earthquake. With all the compassion that he must have experienced following this tragedy, he entered Madras State with determination. It was in Tirunelveli that he first made the fervent appeal to donate liberally for the Bihar Relief Fund. Thereafter, no meeting took place without his referring to the Bihar earthquake.

Gandhiji's Madras tour began with his entry into Nagercoil from the Tiruvangur Principality, although in those days, Nagercoil was within Tiruvangur; he reached Nagercoil on 22 January 1934. This visit to Madras, during which he traversed almost the entire state, was considered by leaders and the public as the most important of all the tours made so far by Gandhiji. Many books have been written on it.

Victory

This tour of Gandhiji could be hailed as a great victory. Indian society, that had thought untouchability would never be eradicated, was witness to its being ground to dust in front of people's eyes during this visit. At the end of the tour, two things were apparent. One was that, whatever their financial constraints, people gave liberally to the Harijan Fund, and the other was that, in spite of warnings issued by the Sanatanis, men and women attended the public meetings in thousands. Even simple village folk contributed money and gifts within their capacities.

To ascertain whether people had truly understood the objective of his tour, Gandhiji would ask, "Why are you giving me all this?" He would be delighted with their answer: "For Harijans."

That it overcame the consistent strong opposition of the Sanatanis was one of the great successes of this tour. Throughout the tour, the Sanatanis had been writing letters to the *Mail*, that Gandhiji was continuing to fleece the people, and interfering in their religious rights.

Miraben's service

Miraben evinced true bhakti for Gandhiji. T. Govindasamy, who oversaw the welcome arrangements when Gandhiji arrived at the Vadapathimangalam bungalow in Vijayapuram of Tiruvarur, said: "Before Gandhiji arrived, Miraben came and supervised all the arrangements. The attention she bestowed on cleaning the utensils to be used by Gandhiji for his food, with soap and *shikakai* powder, was praiseworthy. She carefully examined what was available ... for his food, in the light of his own preferences."

Demanding schedule

When Gandhiji undertook this tour, he was 64. He was nevertheless able to withstand such a demanding schedule. He had come to Madras in the midst of a lengthy all-India tour. British social reformer and pacifist Muriel Lester (1885–1968) wrote:

> For months we were travelling from one place to another. There were upto seven public meetings a day at some places. Collections would be made after his long speeches. Thereafter, people would stand in line to offer gifts and jewellery, which he would then auction. He would never stop until even a small article fetched the price it deserved. This was a long, arduous and exhausting task. After this, he would have to travel at night, and would be met by seas of people at railway stations, where he would have to address them from erected platforms. Many would hang on to train windows and drag themselves for many miles. Most of us would be exhausted, but Gandhiji—never.

Car journey

When Gandhiji came to Coimbatore district, T. S. Avinashalingam, who toured with him in the district throughout, has written about the car journey experiences.

> He would ask the [driver] to proceed slowly wherever there were large crowds. On empty roads he would not bother how fast the car was driven. If he wanted to reach somewhere quickly, he would even ask for the car to be driven faster. 'What speed are

you driving at?,' he would ask. The driver, in some nervousness, would reply, 'At 50 miles.' 'That's all? Could you not drive faster than this?' Enthusiastically, the driver would reply, '55 miles.' 'Not more, 60–65?' Even then, he would declare, 'That's all?' with a smile. The driver would own up to his inability.

22 January 1934, Nagercoil

After Gandhiji left Andhra, the largest crowd that attended his meeting was at Nagercoil. On seeing this crowd, he remarked, "We have reached Madras—this crowd is proof of it." At the meeting held at Jawaharlal Maidan, the crowd was not less than 20,000. The number of women too was large.

In spite of the Tiruvangur Principality promulgating an order that welcome addresses should not be presented to Gandhiji, the Nagercoil Town Council president or its members did not heed it. Not content with this, the Principality had sent out a circular to its employees that the public should neither attend the meeting nor contribute to the funds Gandhiji was raising. Separate welcome addresses were read out and purses presented on behalf of the general public of Nagerkcoil, Harijans and Hindi Prachar Sabha at the meeting.

23 January 1934, Kanyakumari

That night he reached Kanyakumari and stayed at Arunachala Pandaram Choultry. The next day was his day of silence. He bathed in the sea, and, in the evening, strolled on the beach, followed by a crowd of villagers.

Dr Rajan, then the president of the Madras Harijan Seva Sangam, came to Nagercoil to escort Gandhiji into Madras. On this tour, the Harijan Seva Sangam had already decided, when Gandhiji had last come to Madras, that they would arrange a car for him in which he could lie down and rest, stand, give darshan to people and sit comfortably to avoid tiredness. Accordingly, a second-hand car was bought, and the above facilities incorporated in it. Harihara Sharma brought that car to Kanyakumari.

'The bad penny'

When Dr Rajan went to the Arunachala Pandaram Choultry, where Gandhiji was staying, to inform him of his arrival, the Mahatma greeted him jocularly with, "So, you have returned like the bad penny." It was quite usual for Gandhiji to refer to people who came to see him regularly as 'bad pennies'. After all, in a box containing a thousand good rupee notes, does not the one bad note often hit the eye?

Departure

In the quickly darkening evening, Gandhiji left Kanyakumari for Tirunelveli. Including a German journalist named Peutto, there were 20 people in Gandhiji's entourage. To enable Gandhiji to travel comfortably, it was the practice to send members of his party separately to places ahead. For example, Miraben would proceed ahead to ensure that the arrangements for his visit to any place were proper. In this case, Miraben was sent from Kanyakumari one hour in advance, while Dr Rajan set off with Gandhiji. Noticing the carefully made arrangements for his comfort in the car, Gandhiji remarked as he got into it, "I had thought you would have arranged an ordinary car for me. Instead you have brought a 'pucca Mahatma' car."

Valliyur

On the way from Kanyakumari to Nanguneri, there is a small village, Valliyur. Legend has it that Sri Valli (a consort of Muruga, son of Siva and Parvathi) was born in this village. The people here were keen that they should welcome Gandhiji as he passed through their village. Arrangements were made under the leadership of a grocery merchant. On both sides of the road, Petromax[1] lights were hung, a welcome arch of flowers strung up, garlands and a purse of money kept ready on a bench, with the merchant waiting in readiness. On either side of the road, about 2,000 people were lined up. As soon as Gandhiji's car stopped there, it was immediately surrounded by the crowd. In the confusion, no one knew where the merchant was, nor where the garland and purse. Fortunately, the merchant was able to locate them and hand them over to Dr Rajan.

Nanguneri

In Nanguneri, the crowd was so large as to make it impossible for Gandhiji's car to approach the dais. It was raining. As there was not an iota of space at the meeting venue, behind the temple, the crowds had blocked the shopping areas also. The welcoming party, though, stood on the dais, attractive welcome addresses in hand. As even after 15 minutes Gandhiji could not reach the dais, the welcome addresses and purses were brought to his car. A welcome address on behalf of the Union Board and another on behalf of the people were handed over to Gandhiji. His reply lasted just two minutes. Thereafter, he got into the car under an umbrella to enable the crowds to see him. The car somehow drove out of the crowd with police assistance, and, at about 9 p.m., reached Chavadi Ilam, the residence of Kootha Nayinar Pillai in Tirunelveli, where Gandhiji's stay had been arranged.

24 January 1934, Tirunelveli

The speech that Gandhiji made at the Tirunelveli public meeting became the starting point for an intense and historic debate. The meeting was held at the Town Council market. On behalf of Tirunelveli Town Council, its vice president Janab V. M. S. Mohammed Mustafa, on behalf of Palayamkottai Town Council, Rao Bahadur K. S. Ponnusamy, and on behalf of Tiruneveli District Committee, its president I. C. Eswaram Pillai handed over welcome addresses, without reading them out. Purses were presented on behalf of the general public, the Mukkootal public, the Palayamkottai Saurashtra community, and Tirunelveli Town Council members.

In this meeting, attended by some 20,000 people, Gandhiji emphasised the need to donate for the Bihar Earthquake Relief Fund. Before he had started out on his tour, the Madras State government had issued a circular that government servants should not contribute to his Harijan Fund, which Gandhiji referred to here.

> The government servants have been prevented from contributing to the Harijan Fund under any circumstances. The priests, too, have refused to come forward to donate money to this fund, as I am believed to have not only offended them, but committed some crime against God. I do not expect either that non-Hindus

will freely contribute to this fund. However, there can be no
hesitation to donate for the Bihar Relief Fund. Hence, I appeal
to all communities, political parties, religious groups, those in
authority or otherwise to generously donate to it.

There was no opposition to this appeal.

Bihar quake a divine punishment

It was, however, Gandhiji's statement, that there was a divine link
between the Bihar earthquake and untouchability, that triggered
vehement opposition, not only in Madras, but across the country.

Gandhiji declared: "I say that there is a close connection between
the Bihar earthquake and the untouchability movement. You must
understand that there is some divine reason for such a massive
tragedy to happen. The Bihar earthquake happened without warning,
but it shows what our situation is, and that of God."

Many discarded this view expressed by Gandhiji as 'dangerous'.
The *Madras Mail* condemned Gandhiji's statement and wrote an
editorial. But Gandhiji was not without support. In the same *Mail*,
a 'friend' wrote that Gandhiji's view that the earthquake was God's
punishment for the sins of mankind is only a reiteration of what our
ancestors have said in ancient times, also quoting passages from the
Bible in support. The debate on this speech soon moved up to the
higher echelons.

Gandhiji re-emphasised and categorically defended his statement
and his belief through an essay in the *Harijan* issue of 2 February
1934, in which he wrote:

> The developed and underdeveloped world alike believe that
> disasters, like the earthquake in Bihar, are punishment for man's
> sins. I, too, accept this. When people wholeheartedly realise
> this, they pray to God, repenting for their sins. They, then, take
> steps to purify themselves. I say that untouchability is a grave
> sin that attracts the punishment of God. You may ask, 'Why
> the punishment now for the sin that has been committed for
> generations? Why Bihar alone should be punished and not the
> south of India? Why only an earthquake, and not any other kind
> of punishment?' All these questions do not alter my conviction.
> My reply to them is this:

I am not God. I understand God's will only in my limited way. Just as the planets are governed by certain laws, so also God or Nature's work is never random, but within given laws. We cannot know the laws under which these incidents happen, and hence we term them disasters or problems. We can only guess as to why they happen, but in our lives there is some necessity for such guesses. I will not say that this catastrophe is a punishment for the sin of untouchability alone. If others are of the opinion that this is retribution for the many sins we have committed, I will not question it.

Tagore's opposition

Rabindranath Tagore deeply admired and respected Gandhiji. But he was not in the habit of accepting anyone's point of view without due analysis, and unless he was fully convinced. He believed that Gandhiji was wrong in this matter, and he wrote to him, honestly expressing his views. The newspapers had a field day publishing Gandhi and Tagore's arguments and counter-arguments.

Sacred thread

There was never any paucity of work wherever Gandhiji went. Spin like a top, as he did, work, like a serpent's tail, never seemed to end. It was the same that day in Tirunelveli. Among his numerous tasks on the morning of 24 January 1934 was an interview that he gave the Tirunelveli welcome group member, Aram Valartha Natha Pillai of Kulasekarapattinam, who was a cousin of Kootha Nayinar Pillai,[2] president of the Tirunelveli Congress Committee. It was at the latter's residence, at Chavadi Ilam, that Gandhiji stayed in Tirunelveli.

One Sharma had been stationed to issue passes to those who wished to meet Gandhiji on the first floor. When A. V. N. Pillai arrived for the interview, he was at first stopped by Sharma at the entrance, but sent up when he showed the permission granted to Kootha Nayinar Pillai for the interview. When A. V. N. Pillai entered, Gandhiji asked him, "When you had met me the last time, you had pointed out certain faults. Do you have any this time?"

A. V. N. Pillai replied, "Yes, why are you the guest of my brother? I was blocked at the entrance itself by a Brahmin. In this state,

3 per cent of Brahmins are exercising authority over 97 per cent non-Brahmins. Hence, when you next speak at a public meeting, please ask the Brahmins to take off their sacred threads and throw them away!"

Gandhiji replied in some mirth, "Instead of asking the Brahmins to do so, why don't you ask the non-Brahmins to wear it?" (Interview by Chavadi Kootha Nayinar, Tirunelveli)

Cheramadevi Gurukulam

After this, the administrator of the Cheramadevi Gurukulam, T. R. Mahadeva Iyer, handed over the documents concerning the land, buildings, library, etc. to Gandhiji, declaring that he might use the property for any social work that he might desire. Thus, the long and chequered history of the Cheramadevi Gurukulam came to an end.

Pettai

As it had rained a lot on the first day, the roads in Tirunelveli were slushy. Having inspected the khadi exhibition, proceeding to the neighbourhood of the Kurundi canal and enquiring after the welfare of the scavengers at their houses there, Gandhiji accepted the purse presented to him at Pettai (an industrial suburb of Tirunelveli city). Thereafter he attended a public meeting at Viswanatha Town Hall market on Courtallam Road, where he made a historic speech, even as it rained.

Tenkasi

When the meeting ended, Gandhiji started for Tenkasi (now a town, and also a district, in Tamil Nadu). At the public meeting held on Tenkasi Board High School grounds, welcome addresses and purses were presented on behalf of the Panchayat Board, Tiruvallur Society, Harijan Seva Sangam, and Students' Association. There seemed to be more women than men at this meeting.

"Untouchability is a grave sin. It is the duty of caste Hindus to remove this scourge" was the substance of Gandhiji's speech. After auctioning the articles presented to him at Tirunelveli here, he set forth for Courtallam (a panchayat town in Tenkasi district, at the foothills of the Western Ghats), where a major problem awaited him.

Courtallam waterfalls

To reach the Courtallam waterfalls, one had to walk past the front gate of the temple of Courtallanathar, the presiding deity. The Sanatanis had prohibited Harijans from passing through that route. This was a cunning method devised by caste Hindus to prevent Harijans from bathing in the waterfalls, their contention being that they had no objection to Harijans bathing in the falls—only to their walking across the entrance to the temple. More than the general public, it was the temple authorities who were posing this problem. A group led by Taluk Board member Kumaravelu Kudumbar had met Gandhiji, and apprised him of this situation before his arrival in Courtallam. Gandhiji promised them that he would study the documents of the temple and take needful action.

In the approximately three hours that Gandhiji stayed in Courtallam, having rested at Iyyasamy Pillai's bungalow, much of the time was spent investigating who were the barriers for Harijans to bathe in the waterfall. On inquiring about the Waterfall Committee formation, he concluded that this committee was not the barrier for the Harijans, but rather the temple authorities. At 3 p.m. that afternoon, Gandhiji went to see the waterfalls, but declined to take a bath in it. "On the day my Harijan brothers are allowed, like all others, to bathe in these falls, I will do so," he asserted. In his speech at Courtallam, he said in grief, "Only if the cancer of untouchability is eradicated will our religion grow. If not, its ruin is definite."

In the evening, via Srivaikuntam, he proceeded to Thoothukudi. On the way, Tirunelveli Hindu College students handed over a purse to him.

Speeding through Srivaikuntam

When the car reached Srivaikuntam (now a panchayat town in Thoothukudi district), it was already close to 6 p.m., though as per the schedule, Gandhiji should have reached by 5 p.m. The driver was thus repeatedly urged to drive fast. The schedule did not provide for a stop at Srivaikuntam, despite which the local people waited to welcome him on Srivaikuntam Temple Street, lined with arches made of mango leaves. It had been advertised that Gandhiji would reach that point by

2.30 p.m., so people from Tiruchendur and surrounding villages had gathered there. As Gandhiji had not reached by 4.30 p.m., and being informed by Kootha Nayinar Pillai, who passed that way by car, that Gandhiji had already reached Thoothukudi, the leaders and most of the crowd dispersed.

A crash, and a narrow escape

Gandhiji's car took a wrong route via Murappanadu Road, and landed up at the bank of the Tambrabarani river, which then had no bridge across it. Retracing its route after enquiries, it drove towards Srivaikuntam. Seeing crowds in the distance blocking the way, and apprehending further delays, Dr Rajan stood up in the car and waved to them to give way. Because the car was moving at some speed, the crowds yielded way, but the car crashed into a bench, and round boulders placed in the middle of the road were lifted and thrown 10–12 feet away. Even so, the driver did not stop but moved on without slowing down. Had the car turned turtle that day, the lives of Gandhiji and the others might have been jeopardised. Fortunately, no one was hurt. Gandhiji, who, till then, was sleeping, was jolted awake.

The people of Srivaikuntam went away disappointed that Gandhiji did not stop at their town and receive their welcome. To compensate for this loss, the presidents of the Taluk Board and Union Board, Kumaraguruparan Pillai and Basha Sahib respectively, went to Thoothukudi and handed over their welcome addresses and purses to Gandhiji.

One man's achievement

However, what the town people did not achieve as a whole, one man did—and this is an interesting side issue. There is a small Muslim village just beyond Srivaikuntam. The people of this village wished to stop Gandhiji's car and present a welcome. They somehow managed to stop his car. After handing over the purse, one person stood up on the car's footboard and began to read out the welcome. Those in the car requested him not to read but hand over the welcome. The man did not heed them, and the car was directed to keep moving. Still that person did not get down, holding on to the car with one hand, and continuing to read. It was only after a mile that he finished reading the welcome, handed it to Gandhiji, descended from the car and returned to his village.

Thoothukudi

Thoothukudi had prepared itself to welcome Gandhiji. In descending darkness, when Gandhiji reached Thoothukudi, from a mile to the town, crowds had lined up to greet him, allowing little space for the car to move.

On 10 December 1933, one and a half months before Gandhiji's arrival scheduled for 24 January 1934, a large public meeting had been convened by 'Kappalottiya Tamizhan' V. O. Chidambaram Pillai in Sivan Koil Street. "Because of the great penance undertaken by the people of this town, Gandhiji is to visit us. When you meet him, you must give up your prejudices and chase away the devil of untouchability," he had then exhorted his audience.

In 1933, when Gandhiji had undertaken his 21-day fast, some temples had been opened for the entry of Harijans. Among those was the Thoothukudi Sri Prasanna Vinayakar temple. When he came in 1934, Gandhiji was first taken there, received with *purna kumbham*, and witnessed the *deepa aradhanai* (evening prayers) to the deity. Gandhiji's car had to briefly halt there, and was immediately surrounded by a crowd. A small workforce under the leadership of Masilamani Pillai controlled and managed the crowd. Gandhiji was then taken to the newly-built house of nationalist, lawyer and politician M. C. Veerabahu Pillai (1903–1976) for a brief rest, after which he went to the public meeting.

Public meeting

The arrangements for the public meeting and stage decorations were made efficiently. There was a bamboo barricaded space between the public and the stage to allow two cars to move, and Gandhiji's car was able to reach the dais without any difficulty. Before his arrival, one Ayya Pillai and some Harijan children regaled the crowd with songs. As soon as Gandhiji climbed on to the dais, pandemonium ensued as people jostled one another to get a view of him. When Gandhiji pleaded for peace, they quietened down, and the meeting could begin.

Who paid for the lighting?

The public meeting was held at the Tharuvai grounds on the beach, attended by a crowd of some 30,000. The lighting for this meeting was well organised, almost turning night into day. This saddened Gandhiji. He drew Dr Rajan to him and asked, "At whose cost has so much illumination been provided? Till I know this, I will not start the meeting." It was clarified that not a paisa of Harijan funds had been spent for this lighting. A town contractor had come forward on his own to provide these facilities, Gandhiji was told by Dr Rajan.

Gandhiji was not satisfied. "Unless what you tell me gives me full satisfaction, I will not allow this meeting to start," he declared. Dr Rajan sent for the members of the committee of this function and requested them to speak to Gandhiji. They confirmed that what Dr Rajan had said was true.

Yet Gandhiji remained dissatisfied. "Is that contractor here? If so, ask him to come," he said. The contractor came and confirmed that he had arranged for all the lighting, and that he did not expect to be compensated for it. It is only after this that Gandhiji started the meeting.

For Dr Rajan, this came as a wake-up call. He sent out a circular that in no place should the funds collected for Harijan welfare be used for functions being arranged for Gandhiji. Further, transparent accounts must be maintained of the funds collected, and submitted to Gandhiji before he left that town. He went on to say that in no other tour of Gandhiji had he been as particular about money matters as in this tour.

L. V. Rose Victoria presented the welcome address on behalf of the Town Council. Thereafter, welcome orations on behalf of the Indian Merchants' Association, Iron Merchants' Association, Money Changers' Association and Harijan Seva Sangam were read out. The Money Changers' Association presented a gold lemon, while Kothandapani Naidu gave a water pot and a eulogy containing songs of Azhwar Tirunagari Raghavendra Narayana Rao.

"Harijans are God's own people—they should not be demeaned," Gandhiji said in his speech. After the meeting, he went to Veerabahu Pillai's residence for his overnight stay.

How much to spend

In spite of the welcome extended at Thoothukudi being a success, the issue of the elaborate arrangements for illumination made at the meeting rankled in Gandhiji's mind. He sent for Dr Rajan that night, and said, "I need to see the accounts of the secretary. Till I see it, I shall not be able to sleep," he said. Immediately, an approximate statement of accounts was prepared and shown to Gandhiji.

The total collections were Rs 2,600, expenses were Rs 500, and the balance amount was given as a purse to Gandhiji, it stated. On examining it, Gandhiji remarked, "Spending one-fifth of the collections is not proper. Expenses should only be one-twentieth of collections." He then harangued for an hour, giving advice to Dr Rajan on how to raise public money and how to judiciously spend it.

25 January 1934, Whirlwind tour

From Thoothukudi, via Virudhunagar, and Tirumangalam to Madurai in a single day was indeed a whirlwind tour. Perhaps because the weather gods were happy, there was rain all through Gandhiji's tour! There was incessant rain at Thoothukudi at night, and it did not let up when he left in the morning.

Gandhiji visited the Sevanthakulam slum, where Vadivel Nadar read out an artistically drafted welcome. Thereafter, Gandhiji and party had a darshan at Sri Prasanna Vinayakar temple, and proceeded to Rajapalayam via Ettaiyapuram and Kovilpatti. A heartfelt welcome was accorded at Ettaiyapuram, birthplace of India's great son, Subramania Bharathi. He accepted the welcome and purse, and went on to Kovilpatti, where a large crowd at the Swarajya Ashrama Grounds gave him a rousing welcome and presented a purse. A welcome address on behalf of the people of Mandhithopu village was read out on this occasion. Gandhiji thanked them and started for the next town. At Kovilpatti, Kazhugumalai, and Sankarankoil he received the welcome from his car and responded from there. A silver statuette (*velli padhumai*) was presented to him at Sankarankoil.

Rajapalayam

Even after proceeding at speed, Gandhiji was half an hour late at Rajapalayam. Arrangements had been made for his stay at Kumarasamy Raja's residence. At the public meeting, welcome addresses were read out on behalf of the Gandhi Welcome Committee, Srivilliputhur Taluk Board, Khadi weavers, Shroff Merchants' Association and the Panchayat Committee, to which Gandhiji responded. "Untouchability must be eradicated from your hearts. Otherwise, your welcomes and purses will give me no satisfaction whatsoever. The untouchability that we are practising now has no basis in our shastras."

From here, Gandhiji went to the Bhoopathy Cooperative Society building, and received a welcome organised by women. Although the women belonging to the princely order in Rajapalayam were in seclusion, they allowed Gandhiji and those accompanying him to come to this meeting. It was noon by the time he finished with this meeting and reached the residence of Kumarasamy Raja. When they finished their bath and lunch, it was still pouring. Kumarasamy Kamaraj (1903–1975) and another noted nationalist, Muthusamy, came and interviewed Gandhiji, and formally invited him to Virudhunagar. As per the schedule, Gandhiji was to leave Rajapalayam at 3 p.m. As it was raining heavily, and the car could not be driven fast, Gandhiji cut down his rest time and started earlier.

In the hired car sent from Madurai, Gandhiji reclined in the rear seat, while Dr Rajan and Kumarasamy Raja shared the front seat with the driver. There was no let-up in the torrential rain, strong winds blew, and visibility was poor. There were curtains on the side of the car to protect Gandhiji from the rain. As there was no such protection for the front seat, Dr Rajan and Kumarasamy Raja used their towels to shield themselves. The car was crawling at 10 miles an hour because of the rain and poor visibility. They were followed in another car by Ko. Venkatachalapathy and others, and by Kamaraj and Muthusamy in a third. Gandhiji was sound asleep. They reached Sivakasi in two hours, where more trouble awaited them.

Car damaged

In Sivakasi, arrangements had been made in a school ground for the meeting to be held. A decorated pandal had been erected for Gandhiji's car to halt. The rain had not ceased when he arrived here. Were one to get down, a one-foot deep slush had to be negotiated. Even in that rain and cold, some 4,000 people had gathered, soaking wet. Gandhiji's car got stuck in the mud 20 feet from the pandal. Thousands rushed to surround Gandhiji's car the moment they realised that he had arrived. In that commotion, the roof of the car flew off into the air! On the one hand were shouts of 'Jai to Gandhiji', and on the other the screams of the driver that his car had been damaged.

A stick fight demonstration

It became necessary under these circumstances not only to save the car from damage but to rescue Gandhiji from the mob, which was mindlessly swarming around the car. Fortunately, even in this melee, the person who had the purse to be presented to Gandhiji managed to reach Dr Rajan and handed it over to him, specifying the amount of money it contained. Within a few minutes, the pandal collapsed. Luckily the car had got stuck ahead of this pandal, thereby preventing grievous injury. Despite several pleas by Gandhiji, the crowd did not give way. It was 5 p.m. by then, and he continued to sit patiently in the car.

In this situation, Kumarasamy Raja jumped out of the car, picked up a roughly 5-feet long pole from the collapsed pandal, and began to twirl it in the manner of a professional stick fighter. Some others followed suit. Whether this caused injuries to people in the crowd or not, a couple of the stick wielders did get hurt. Kumarasamy Raja's diamond ring slipped from his fingers, and was lost. There was damage on all sides of the car, but Raja's action yielded success. As the crowd parted in this stick-wielding exhibition, the driver started the car and drove away. Kamaraj had already left for Virudhunagar to review the arrangements there.

Kamaraj's presence of mind

Gandhiji's car stopped two miles from Sivakasi. Everybody took the opportunity to squeeze their clothes dry before proceeding. Because of heavy rain, they had to take a detour of 15 miles. The police official who was following Gandhiji in a separate car, noticing Gandhiji's predicament, offered his own car for him to travel in; Gandhiji declined. When the car was two miles from Virudhunagar, Kamaraj met them in another car; he had, with considerable forethought, come to meet them to avoid a repetition of what happened at Sivakasi.

"From 50 villages around Virudhunagar, several thousands of people have assembled in Virudhunagar, and are waiting since 1 p.m. There is no way by which the car can go through the streets of the town. Please stay here and dry your clothes in this place. We will go, disperse the crowd, and return with the purses to be given to you. You need not halt at Virudhunagar, but proceed onwards," Kamaraj advised. Accordingly, Gandhiji and his entourage halted at a small bungalow in Soolakkarai village. He had his evening meal there, and finished his prayers. Thereafter, he went for a stroll outside for about half an hour.

Kumarasamy Kamaraj later went on to become the All India Congress president, and chief minister of Madras State (1954–1963), and was responsible for several milestones in Indian politics.

Soolakkarai

After making arrangements for Gandhij and the others at Soolakkarai, it took a long time for Kamaraj to return. While they were waiting, Ko. Venkatachalapathy recounts an interesting incident:

> At Soolakkarai, only a few of us had the good fortune to stay with Gandhiji in peace and quiet. Kumarasamy Raja had introduced me to Gandhiji as an 'Establishment worker'. I was at that time the principal of a school in Gopinayakanpatti. I had brought with me the welcome address that I was to read at the meeting on behalf of the school. I read out that welcome slowly and clearly, and handed it over to Gandhiji. Humorously, Dr Rajan remarked to Gandhiji, 'Bapuji, have you ever heard a welcome address read with such deliberation?'
>
> At this time, Miraben served goat milk curd, sweet lime and orange fruits along with Gandhiji's meal. Gandhiji peeled the oranges, savoured each slice, and carefully spat out the fibres on to a paper. He told me to put it all in the trash. I took out my

handkerchief to tie them in. My thought was to preserve these fibres discarded by Gandhiji, but somehow he noticed this. In some anger, he said:

'Look here, Kumarasamy Raja introduced you as an 'establishment worker', but here you want to tie up what I had spat out in your handkerchief. Is this what you have learnt of cleanliness?' Immediately I took them out to trash.

There was prayer after this. Gandhiji went out for a stroll after the prayer. As his clothes, and those of his entourage of prominent people, had got wet, Kamaraj had tried to buy fresh khadi clothes for all of them to wear. The manager of the khadi vastralayam, though, had closed shop and gone to attend the public meeting, where there was a sea of people. How could one find him there? But somehow, Kamaraj located him, and returned to Soolakkarai with fresh clothes. In the meantime, R. T. P. Subramania Nadar and a couple of other prominent Virudhunagar people (of the welcome group) landed up where Gandhiji had halted.

Police officials also arrived there. "The crowd has largely dispersed. If you come now, the meeting could be held without much difficulty, and the purses could also be handed over there," they said. Dr Rajan did not agree at first. Seeing them arguing, Gandhiji asked, "What is the issue?" Dr Rajan replied, "They are bargaining for time."

Thereafter, at about 8 p.m. they reached Virudhunagar. Even at that hour, some 10,000 people were waiting there. Although a separate women's meeting had been arranged, it did not take place. Their welcome speeches and purses were handed over to him the next day at Madurai.

Tirumangalam

While Gandhiji was in Virudhunagar, thousands of people in Madurai, and villagers on the Virudhunagar–Madurai road were eagerly anticipating his arrival. Of these, the yearning of two souls was realised. In the meeting at Tirumangalam, Gandhiji called them to his side and spoke affectionately to them. He also blessed the daughter of George Joseph.

In Tirumangalam, a beautiful, new-design 'suitcase' spinning wheel, specially made by Thazhai Muthu Achariar, was presented to Gandhiji. A noted nationalist of Tirumangalam, Nithyanandam Adigal, presented to him a packet containing historic salt panned from Veeramgam, Madras, Dandi and Sholinganallur. In his speech Gandhiji exhorted men and women to abjure the distinctions of caste.

Kallikudi

On way to Tirumangalam, it was after 9 p.m. by the time they reached Kallikudi. The thousands who had waited patiently had to go away disappointed. Still, the crowd that had not dispersed by then welcomed Gandhiji enthusiastically when he reached. Tirumangalam Taluk Board President and Madurai District Committee member, A. K. A. Ramachandra Reddiar, read out the welcome address and handed over a purse. On behalf of the women, Kumari Rajam Ramachandran and others presented a separate welcome and purse.

Vaidyanatha Iyer

As soon as Gandhiji and his group had crossed Tirumangalam, Vaidyanatha Iyer came from the opposite side with a bronze boat. Having waited for Gandhiji's arrival in Madurai for a long time, Iyer assumed that they had been held up in the blinding rain. He had, therefore, dispersed the Madurai crowd gathered for the meeting, and come searching for them. He met Gandhiji's car some ten miles from Madurai, and declared that he had cancelled the Madurai public meeting and announced it for the next day. Almost 20,000 people had been waiting there from 4 p.m. till 10 p.m., not knowing where Gandhiji was or when he would arrive.

Thereafter, Gandhiji reached the bungalow of another noted Tamil nationalist, N. M. R. Subburaman (1905–1983), in Madurai by 11.15 p.m. Thousands had gathered there to see Gandhiji. It was only after he offered darshan from the verandah of the first floor that the crowd dispersed.

26 January 1934, Change in programme

Due to the difficulties caused by rain in travel, and the late arrival in Madurai, drastic changes were made in Gandhiji's tour programme. It was decided to postpone his visits to Bodi and Cumbum till after he returned from rest at Coonoor. In addition, Dr Rajan announced that the visits to Dindigul and Coimbatore Districts were temporarily suspended.

The cleanest slums in Madurai

Gandhiji inspected the slums of Melvasal, Therkuvasal and Madhucchiyam. Even though they were considered the cleanest slums in Madurai, they did not satisfy Gandhiji. One reason was that the rainwater, because of inadequate drainage, remained at ankle level. After inspecting the cages that passed for houses in these slums, this old man spent some time talking and laughing with some old women there.

Merchants' welcome

In the morning, town criers banging their 'tom-toms' announced the news all over town that Gandhiji had arrived. Hence, when Gandhiji reached the Victoria Edward Hall for the welcome arranged by merchants, a large crowd had gathered to see him at the entrance itself. The Madurai-Ramanathapuram Merchants' Association and the Bombay Hindu merchants had jointly organised the welcome. In addition, the brass merchants presented a purse at this meeting.

Gandhiji began his address fondly with, "My brother Baniyas," and said, "You have spoken of the national language and charkha. If what you say is wholehearted, I expect that you must know to speak Hindi and wear khadi."

Municipality welcome

Gandhiji next went to receive the welcome of the Municipality. In his response, translated into Tamil by Vaidyanatha Iyer, he mentioned the poor condition of the slums. The Municipality president, V. S. K. Muthurama Iyer read out the welcome. One Thayammal presented a silver plate and cup. Gandhiji appreciated the enthusiasm this municipality had shown in hand spinning and the propagation of Hindi, and said: "I offer my heartfelt congratulations that there are no problems between Hindus and Muslims here. I desire that all of India should follow your example in this matter of Hindu-Muslim unity." This observation gladdened everyone, but his remarks on slum conditions did not. Referring to his visits that morning to three slums, he said, "This municipality has not done anything useful there— forgive me for saying so."

Students' welcome

The students of Sethupathi High School accorded a special welcome to Gandhiji. Two separate welcome addresses were read, one on behalf of all town students, and one specifically for Sethupathi High School students. Gandhiji explained that there was an education beyond what is available in schools. "You must go into the slums in large numbers at least once a week on Sundays. If you find that the clothes of Harijans are dirty, take buckets of water and soap to wash their clothes with. This education is much higher than what is imparted in schools."

Adorned with kumkum

When Gandhiji began to auction the articles received here, one girl student (George Joseph's daughter) came up to him and asked for an autograph. "This girl is giving me a bangle to receive my signature. Likewise, I request boys and girls to offer me their rings," he appealed. Many students came up to the dais and gave him gifts. One presented a circular silver box. On opening it, it was found to contain kumkum. Gandhiji began to adorn the Harijan children who stood in line on the dais with this kumkum.

Meeting with workers

The workers involved in Harijan welfare met Gandhiji in the afternoon where he was staying, and sought his advice on various matters. When Dr Rajan, G. Ramchandran and others pointed out problems in the issue of temple entry, Gandhiji offered them his advice. The workers were introduced to Gandhiji. One of them was the future minister of Madras, P. Kakkan, at that time a student. A. Vaidyanatha Iyer and P. N. Ramasubramaniam spoke to Gandhiji separately on an important, confidential matter. On the basis of a letter written by

Gandhiji, the noted Saurashtra poet and nationalist, T. R. Padmanabha Iyer also met him.

Women's meeting

This meeting was held in Melmasi Street, at the hall where Chandra Talkies later stood. In the hall, designed to accommodate some 3,000 persons, more than 5,000 women and children had congregated. One could imagine the level of noise and the jostling. It became an effort for Gandhiji to even reach the dais. As Gandhiji's soft voice was drowned out by the noise from the women and children, nobody could hear what he had to say. His speech was translated into Tamil by A. Vaidyanatha Iyer in his stentorian voice, but even that went unheeded in the din. The welcome formalities were somehow conducted. Welcome addresses were read out on behalf of Bharat Sevika Samithi, the Sisters' Association and the Housewives' Association.

"If you have attended this meeting in such large numbers solely out of the respect you have for me, I will not be happy. I will be satisfied only if you have come out with the support you wish to give to my objectives. You must show this respect for me by working to realise my aim of untouchability eradication," he said.

Miraben's collection

As he had to leave this meeting early, he advised his audience to hand over their contributions or jewels to Miraben. It was common for Gandhiji to request to Miraben to stay back at such women's meetings for collection, and for Miraben to return more or less empty-handed. But on that day, she managed to receive a large amount of jewellery. Tirumathi C. M. V. Krishnamachari gave a costly gold necklace, in which the weight of the gold alone must have been about 20 *pavun* (160 grams).

Hindi Prachar Sabha

The welcome of the Hindi Prachar Sabha, dear to Gandhiji's heart, was held at Victoria Edward Hall. He distributed awards and certificates to meritorious students. The welcome address in Hindi was read out by a student, Rajathi. When Gandhiji unwrapped the prize of books received by a girl and asked her, "Come, read the Hindi that is written in this book, let me see," the girl blinked, reducing him and others in the meeting to laughter.

Public meeting

The public meeting held that day at Madurai's sand bank was impressive. The dais was at a great height to enable all to easily see Gandhiji. A total of about 50,000 persons had gathered, and about one-third of those were women. That such a huge crowd waited patiently till then is worthy of mention. Here, too, the responsibility of translation into Tamil was given by Dr Rajan to Vaidyanatha Iyer. Hence there was no complaint from anyone in the crowd that the speech could not be heard. The meeting finished soon, starting at about 5.45 p.m., and ending by 7 p.m. Separate welcome speeches and purses were presented on behalf of the Madurai public, workers of Sri Meenakshi temple, Lajpati Institutution, Babukanu Library, Vysya Youth association, Ramanathapuram Street Youth Association, Bharat Sevika Samithi, and Sokkampatti Harijans. N. M. R. Subburaman gave four gold bangles and a gold chain. The Jothi Krishna Organisation gave an all-India travel pass as their contribution.

To enable everyone to have a good view, Gandhiji spoke while standing throughout. Referring to the hardworking Harijans in Madurai city, he said:

> They spin all day long to earn small sums of money. Jealous of even this, some are buying and spinning heavier counts of yarn and passing them off as khadi. By doing so they deny even the little money the Harijans earn from their spinning. I do not have any objection to their weaving cloth from such yarn, but they should not call it khadi. I also appeal to the public to examine whether in fact they are buying khadi at the time of purchase.

Workers' meeting 'A-1'

If there was one public meeting that Gandhiji termed as "A-1", for maintaining peace and order, it was the workers' meeting held at the Ponnagaram Municipality sports ground in Madurai. Arrangements

had been made for the 5,000-odd workers to have a clear view of
Gandhiji. There was complete silence throughout the meeting. On
behalf of the Madurai Labour Union, its secretary, S. R. Varadarajulu
Naidu, read out the welcome address. When Gandhiji undertook his
fast in Yerawada jail on the issue of untouchability, the first people to
offer sympathies by telegram were the workers of Madurai temple.

At this meeting Gandhiji recounted the close connection he had
with Balasundaram in South Africa. "After this meeting I began to
live as a co-worker to all workers. I know the travails of workers, but
workers must work, keeping in mind that the place of their labour is
their own."

As it was night, and because the workers assembled had wished
to see Gandhiji at close quarters, he walked in their midst for a while
after the meeting was over. Even after returning to his place of stay,
there was no respite for Gandhiji. He offered advice to the workers
assembled there, and said:

> You must conduct yourselves with one another with true
> affection. When you serve other people, you must not consider
> yourselves as employers. I, too, am rendering service to the
> common people. It is not such an easy task to serve them—it
> needs astuteness and attention. If your service has to yield fruit,
> you must lead a pure life.

A Nadar lady in Madurai gave Gandhiji a gold necklace worth Rs 500.
The traffic arrangements made for Gandhiji's visit to Madurai by Asst.
Superintendent of police, Rao Bahadur M. Ananthachariar, and his
team were commendable.

Interviews

Gandhiji gave a detailed interview of some two hours to
N. M. R. Subburaman during this stay. Subburaman said: "Gandhiji
advised me on how I should lead my life, quoting several slokas from
the *Bhagavad Gita*. I had with me then a book of the *Tirukkural*,
which I gave to him to bless. He took it and wrote in English, 'May
God give you light.'"

The Municipal president, V. S. K. Muthurama Iyer interviewed
Gandhiji, and suggested that spinning on several light spinning

wheels could make spinning a profitable venture. Gandhiji, however, did not accept this suggestion. "Doing so would be akin to opening small mills. My aim is that every household should have a charkha spinning, to earn income from it. If one were to accept your suggestion, incomes would be limited to 5 per cent of the population, 95 per cent going hungry."

Muthurama Iyer further suggested, "This is an age of growth in mechanisation. Hence, if you desire that khadi must survive in this competition, there is only one way—those wearing mill-woven clothes should wear khadi." This, too, Gandhiji did not accept, declaring that khadi is completely practicable.

In honour of Gandhiji's visit to Madurai district, Madhicchiyam Mamta Konar opened his temple to Harijans. In Mavudamarudhur (sometimes called Ambattanpatti), 15 miles from Madurai, too the temple was opened to Harijans.

27 January 1934, Amaravathi Pudur

Gandhiji rested in Madurai. After lunch, when he set off for Chettinad, it was 2.30 p.m. At a visit he should have made the previous day, he was given welcomes and purses in South Street and Melur. When he reached Amaravathi Pudur by about 5 p.m., Rai Chokkalingam had arranged a lavish banquet for Gandhiji and his entourage.

Dr Rajan reports an interesting incident.

> As the Mahatma sat down for the feast, I told him that a palmist was outside, wanting to meet him along with testimonials, and that I had asked him to wait. The Mahatma replied, 'Tell him, if he is willing to give me a thousand rupees, I will allow him to read my palm.' When I conveyed this to the palmist, he retorted, 'Ayya! I am myself a beggar, and don't even have a paisa. Still, I am obsessed with the thought of wanting to read the palm of the Mahatma. Tell him I will not budge from here,' and he sat down.
>
> I went in again and told the Mahatma this. He said, 'I am also obsessed with his having to give me a thousand rupees—tell him that.' The palmist, on being told this, decided that in the face of Gandhiji's obsession, his own would not stand, and left with his things.

'A child of Tamil'

As an illustration of how closely Gandhiji's life was aligned with the *Kural*, the 'Tamil Ocean', Rai Chokkalingam sang a song encapsulating 125 kurals. The 'Gandhi Pillai Tamil' song was printed and handed over to Gandhiji personally by Rajaji at the Belgaum Congress, much to the delight of Rai Chokkalingam. The gist of the song, which praises Gandhiji as a 'child of Tamil', is as follows:

> *Just as his mother's heart was cooled by his birth*
> *Just as Kasturba's heart was cooled by being his wife*
> *Just as the waters of Sabarmati Ashram were cooled by his residence*
> *Just as Yerawada jail was cooled by his presence*
> *This poet's heart, too, is cooled by thoughts of the Mahatma*

Karaikudi

After the meal taken at Amaravathi Pudur, Gandhiji reached Karaikudi at about 6 p.m. to receive the welcome of the Town Council and the purse presented by Dewan Bahadur Chidambaram Chettiar. The Harijan employees of the Town Council gave a small purse. Gandhiji thanked the luminary who donated Rs 10,000 to the Harijan Fund. Although Gandhiji did not name this person (on that person's request), it later became known on enquiry that it was 'Inba Nilayam' Vai Su. Shanmugam Chettiar.

Public meeting

Thereafter, Gandhiji received the welcome and purse of the 15,000-strong Karaikudi public at the meeting held on Maha Nombu grounds. Next to Thoothukudi, this place had the most number of electric lights. On behalf of Karaikudi Welfare Society, Aru. Al. Rama. Chokkalingam Chettiar read out a welcome and presented it in a silver casket.

Dr Govindarajulu presented a purse on behalf of Karaikudi Tagore Library. A silver charkha presented to Gandhiji was bought through auction by noted Harijan representative and nationalist, the lawyer from Devakottai, Mukundraj Iyengar.

"God has bestowed you in Chettinad with wealth. He has also endowed you with the wisdom to understand the plight of Harijans.

I, therefore, request you to use both your wisdom and wealth in uplifting the status of Harijans," Gandhiji said.

The Tagore Library and Yuvabharat Society presented welcomes addresses. When Gandhiji auctioned the articles received, there was brisk bidding and sale.

Devakottai

Arriving in Devakottai from Karaikudi, Gandhiji received the mandatory welcome and purses. A pomegranate-shaped silver casket offered by Nataraj Asari at the meeting stood out. The Gandhi welcome group leader, Narayanan Chettiar handed over a purse of Rs 2,600. Gandhiji, however, said, "As your old friend, I had expected an even larger contribution by you. But since I am going to be staying overnight here, I do believe you will fulfil my desire. This is your duty."

At this meeting held at Devakottai Muniappa temple grounds, he named a girl child Savithri, wrote her name in Tamil on her photograph, and signed it. The girl's mother, Sivagami, came up to the dais and presented a silver plate and one pavun of gold to Gandhiji, as a mark of gratitude and respect.

Auction of a handkerchief

Auctioning a handkerchief at the Devakottai meeting, Gandhiji exhibited all his marketing skills. "Here, this cloth has been woven from the most delicate yarn," he began, stroking the handkerchief with his palms. "My friend, Chokkalingam, is an expert in spinning. (When Gandhiji had come in 1927, he had observed Chokkalingam's spinning expertise, and praised him as a 'charkha poet'.) He had presented to me a lengthy khadi cloth at that time. You can yourself see its quality. Hence, bid for it—bid the highest prices," he added, as he put up the handkerchief for auction. He would not concede defeat. Ultimately, the kerchief was taken at Rs 25!

28 January 1934, Ram Nagar

After the public meeting, Gandhiji and his entourage stayed overnight at the residence of Rangaswami Iyengar. The first thing the next morning, Gandhiji laid the foundation stone for a government school. Proceeding to the Sitthanar slum, the area of much past conflict between Nattars and Harijans, he still did not miss out on the opportunity to collect funds—seven and a quarter annas!

Meeting with Sanatanis deferred

Rangaswami Iyengar was an advocate. He had written a letter to right-thinking Sanatani co-advocates, saying that if they wished to discuss the temple entry issue with Gandhiji, they could come between 10.30 and 11 a.m. However, no Sanatani members turned up. After 12.30 p.m., Gandhiji was scheduled to meet the Nattars, visit other places in Chettinad, and board the train at Manamadurai for Coonoor.

After 12 noon, a Sanatani lawyer arrived to meet Gandhiji with a letter from the Hindu Society secretary. It said: "The Sankaracharya of Puri is in town. He has researched the shastras extensively. The invitation from Rangaswami Iyengar reached us late, at which time the swamigal was in pooja. After his pooja we asked him if he would like to discuss with you about whether there is any authority in our shastras for untouchability. He agreed. Hence, we have come to ask if you could spare half an hour for this discussion with him."

Gandhiji, however, was particular about adhering to the schedules drawn up for him. He told the lawyer, "I, too, am interested in having such a discussion, but the Nattars have already come to meet me at the appointed time, after which my journey continues. Therefore, I cannot have this discussion here and now. I am going directly to Coonoor, where I plan to stay for eight days. If the Acharya Swami is willing, we could fix a date and time for us to meet there."

Asking Rangaswami Iyengar to send this reply in writing to the Devakottai Central Hindu Society secretary, Gandhiji resumed his journey. The Sanatanis, though, did not let this matter go easily. They issued a circular alleging that Gandhiji had reneged on his assurance to meet the Sankaracharya.

The Nattar-Harijan issue

The Nattar-Harijan problem that was sought be resolved by Gandhiji on that day became aggravated. Most of the villages there were considered the strongholds and jurisdiction of the Nattars. The

Nattars were a branch of the Mukkulatthor community. In the Nattar areas there were restrictive parameters established for Harijans. There was untouchability practised to the extent of dictating the kind of clothes Harijans should not wear. Men were not allowed to wear cloth above the full cloth at the waist; no upper body cloth or shirts were permitted. Women were not allowed to wear blouses. The Nattars were in the habit of checking during festivals whether the Harijans were conforming to these dress regulations. As a result, for a couple of years, there had been skirmishes between the Nattars and Harijans here and there.

Gandhiji went to meet the heads of the Nattars to persuade them to discard these practices related to untouchability. Compromise talks were held at Sitthanur. These talks had been arranged by advocate Mukunda Raja Iyengar, who was involved in the untouchability eradication movement, and Re. Rangaswami Iyengar, respectfully referred to as 'Harijan Ranganna.' About a hundred to a hundred and fifty Nattar representatives attended this meeting, and stood up as Gandhiji entered the pandal.

As Gandhiji sat down, the others followed suit. The interpreter indicated that if the Nattars had any questions for Gandhiji, he was ready to answer them. The Nattar representative, however, an old man, leaning on a heavy stick, said, "Let Gandhiji express his views first. We shall then share our concerns with him."

Gandhiji began his persuasive speech. According to those who had accompanied Gandhiji, the advice he gave to the Devakottai Nattars was the first of its kind. His 45-minute speech on behalf of Harijans was imbued not only with the beauty of words, but with awareness of self, compassion, truth and sense of duty, all expressed in the simplest of ways that would have attracted even small children. Yet, despite such a fervent plea, the Nattars remained unmoved, firm in their stand that they could not disregard established practice. The compromise talks failed.

Before the meeting concluded, Gandhiji summarised his views again: "To say that you are higher in status than the Harijans, and can stipulate what they can wear or not, is wrong. This can only result in ill-feeling. Under the guise of established practice, you cannot prevent them from doing what they want. If one has the opportunity to do good, one must grasp it."

Gandhiji also did not lose the opportunity to raise money for the Bihar Earthquake Relief Fund. Some who had come made a few donations. The Nattar representative promised to collect and send money from his community.

Efforts for a resolution

Before Gandhiji spoke to the Nattars in January 1934, a conference had been held on 25 June 1933 under the chairmanship of Rajaram Pandian to discuss a compromise between Nattars and Harijans. There was no great shift in the stance of the Nattars, but men like Mukunda Raja Iyengar, Rangaswami Iyengar and Lakshmiratan Bharathi did not discontinue their efforts. At the beginning of 1936, Dr Rajan, Dewan Bahadur V. Bhashyam Iyengar, and Rao Bahadur M. C. Raja toured this area, met Nattar leaders, and offered consolation to Harijans.

After this, the Revenue Divisional Officer, R. S. Malayappan, in his tenure from November 1937 to August 1938 and till his retirement, involved himself in efforts to achieve a compromise between the Nattars and Harijans. The Congress government had taken over in Madras State at that time. Together with the Harijan Seva Sangam leaders, Malayappan strove to successfully reach a compromise in 1938, thus resolving this longstanding problem.

Tiruppathur

After completing his work at Devakottai, Gandhiji started for Manamadurai (now a town in Sivaganga district of Tamil Nadu) via Tiruppathur and Baganeri. At the public meeting in Tiruppathur, a few white men came up to the stage and greeted Gandhiji. An attractive shield, with Gandhiji's face embossed on a silver plate, embedded in a wooden frame, was presented to him. Gandhiji said, unless a high price was bid for this, he would not put it up for auction. As no one bid a high enough price for it at the meeting, Gandhiji did not sell it. However, a young man seated on the dais at Baganeri, bought it for Rs 100.

Manamadurai

The only place in this region where the meeting was held amidst noise and chaos was Sivaganga, where the crowd was much more than the numbers expected, and could not be controlled. The Mahatma's voice inaudible in the din.

In sharp contrast, the crowd at Manamadurai was a picture of order and quiet. Held in pleasant moonlight at about 7 p.m., the crowd conduct was indeed praiseworthy. There was just enough space for Gandhiji's car to come and stop, and the dais was not very high. Despite this, not one of those gathered moved from their place, nor did they indulge in any shouting or rowdy behaviour. There was unanimous praise for advocate Krishnaswami Iyengar, who had made the arrangements. Gandhiji's heart shone, as the silvery moonlight did over this gathering. To avoid the large crowd anticipated at the Manamadurai railway station, he detrained at the railway gate ahead of it. When he was interviewed by newsmen at Madurai, en route to Coonoor, Gandhiji spoke about the discussions he had with the Nattars.

> I met the Nattar leaders and spoke with them for an hour. I believe that this discussion would lead to fruitful results. The Nattars listened to me fully without interruption, giving me the impression that some among them did realise the need for reform. I also think that the Harijans will be alert to claim their rights in the matter. There is no doubt in my mind that the issue of untouchability, that has so far been in the background of our consciousness, has acquired a new impetus now, awakening even the remote villages.

Hearing that Gandhiji was to pass by Dindigul, a large crowd waited for him at the railway station, but they did not get the chance to meet him. Gandhiji was asleep when the train reached Dindigul. It was considerate of that crowd to leave the station without disturbing his sleep.

29 January 1934, Pazhani–Udumalaipettai

When the train reached Pazhani (or Palani, now a town in Dindigul district, 67 km from Kodaikanal), Udumalaipettai (a town in

Tiruppur district) and Pollachi (a town in Coimbatore district), it was early morning. Gandhiji finished his normal Monday prayers that morning at Pazhani. It was his day of silence. At Chettipalayam (a suburb of Coimbatore city), the Panchayat Committee president, M. K. Manikkam, along with a large crowd, welcomed him. A Chettipalayam merchant, Na. Pa. Ra. Vengudusamy Chettiar presented a purse.

Coonoor

To avoid the crowds at Pothanur (a panchayat town in Namakkal district) railway station, it was arranged for Gandhiji to get down at the railway gate, but he and his group were outwitted in this manoeuvre. Directions given to the guard at Pothanur railway station to proceed to the railway gate to await Gandhiji's travel to the Nilgiris somehow got transmitted to the workers and police personnel, who thronged the gate. From there, with brief halts at Periyanaickenpalayam, Karamadai, and Mettupalayam to receive welcome addresses, Gandhiji reached Coonoor by car. The ornate arrangements at Mettupalayam were some of the most exquisite decorations seen anywhere in Madras. Dr Rajan briefly spoke on Gandhiji's behalf at a few places. Acknowledging the welcome of the crowds on both sides of the Coonoor road, Gandhiji reached the bungalow of the nationalist, Nageswara Rao, on Anand Hill, where the Nageswara Rao couple welcomed him. As the bungalow was on top of the hill, Gandhiji enjoyed the panoramic views of the Nilgiris in his spare time in the evenings.

The benefits of rest

The arrangements made for Gandhiji to rest at Coonoor for eight days proved beneficial in many ways. Because of this, Gandhiji's Madras tour schedule was also extended by that period. As they came to know this, people from various places started sending him invitations to set his holy feet in their towns. After carefully perusing these invitations and telegrams, a schedule was drawn up to accommodate such requests to the extent possible, without causing disappointments.

Change of guard

The getting down at Pothanur signaled the first 'change of guard'. Till then, Dr Rajan, as the president of the Madras Seva Sangam, had undertaken the responsibility of arranging for Gandhiji's tour of Kanyakumari, Tirunelveli and Madurai districts. From Pothanur onwards, Avinashalingam took up the responsibility for Coimbatore district. A vibrant, enthusiastic young man in 1934, T. S. Avinashalingam (1903–1991), who had started the Ramakrishna Vidyalayam at the time, later went on to become the Education Minister of Madras Presidency (1946–1949).

Dr Rajan has written praising the efficiency with which he had arranged for Gandhiji's welcome: "T. S. Avinashalingam determined that Coimbatore must be ahead of all other districts in the collection of funds and the scale of welcome. He succeeded. Coimbatore alone was responsible for a quarter of total Madras collections. Limitless enthusiasm, unbounded emotion, infinite devotion to Gandhiji—all these were seen in Coimbatore."

Injunctions to the public

After altering Gandhiji's tour plans from Coonoor onwards, Dr Rajan issued a circular to the public, which said that if the people had adhered to a certain discipline during Gandhiji's tours in Ramanathapuram, Tirunelveli and Madurai, it would have helped to make them more successful. Some of Dr Rajan's observations and injunctions to the public were:

> Do not fall at the Mahatma's feet or touch them in reverence as he walks. Shouting 'Jai to Mahatma' from close quarters hurts him. Only simple food should be prepared for the Mahatma's group. The Mahatma needs goat's milk thrice a day, fresh vegetables, oranges, and tomato slices. Public money should not be spent on garlands or stage decorations. Gandhiji is prepared to speak from the tops of buses or from the balconies of houses.

Work or rest?

What is full-time work for ordinary mortals constituted rest for Gandhiji. That Gandhiji rested for a week at Coonoor implies that there was no whirlwind touring as before and after his stay here. The place where he stayed abounded in natural beauty, but there was little time for him to savour all this. Shorn of a personal life, from the time he went to South Africa his life was devoted to the public cause. In Coonoor, people from various organisations, people from Mysore, Pondicherry and Ahmedabad, and Congress workers kept coming to meet him on one pretext or another, or to invite him to visit their towns. He also set about replying to the mountain of letters that were received.

Further, he made trips to Ootacamund and Kothagiri to meet the Adivasis and other communities settled there. In addition, he continued to write articles for the *Harijan* publication. He appealed to many friends to donate for the Bihar Earthquake Relief Fund. The salubrious climate of Coonoor and the tranquil atmosphere to go about one's work with peace of mind were a boon to him.

Deplorable

On the day Gandhiji arrived in Coonoor, an incident took place that forced people to seek his forgiveness. After their meals, the servants picked up the used plantain leaves and carelessly threw them near the bungalow itself. When the Mahatma walked around the building in the evening, he noticed this. Then, true to his own modest nature, he started to clean the place himself, not wishing to trouble anybody. Those who saw this were filled with dismay, and rushed to ask for his pardon. Thereafter, they all got together to clean that area.

1 February 1934, Adi Dravidar Janasabha

On 1 February, a representative group of the Adi Dravidar Janasabha (ADJ) met Gandhiji and informed him of the main problems being faced by Harijans in those areas. There were 12 representatives of this group, led by the Madras State Board member, R. T. Kesavulu, and Town Council member, R. T. Manickam. The problems they discussed with Gandhiji were general ones, faced in other areas, too. Their exchange with him is given here in brief:

ADJ: There is rampant unemployment. Hence, to provide employment to Harijans, a leather factory may be established here.

Gandhiji: By starting such a factory, a whole lot of Harijans are not going to get work, only a few ... who have traditionally worked in this field. I need to look at the statistics of those who are unemployed in various other trades also.

ADJ: A separate publication is required to highlight the plight of Harijans. The Central Board must help with finances for this.

G: Not necessary ... There are more important matters requiring money. Moreover, there are already important Tamil and English papers being published. They cannot refuse to include the problems of Harijans in their articles. You must use those publications judiciously.

ADJ: Do you find in this tour of yours that there is change of heart among caste Hindus?

G: I am strongly convinced that it is happening, in fact more than I expected.

ADJ: But Mahatmaji, we read in the papers that, in spite of your persuasion, the Nattars are stubborn in their stand that they will not change established practices?

G: I do not know what the papers have written, but I do know that the Nattars fully understood what that old man among them spoke. That more than a hundred Nattars listened to what I had to say without interruption is what is important. I can say with conviction that there are Nattars among them who are willing to accept what I said, and help their members to follow. Fear not—the reform we desire will definitely happen.

2 February 1934, Badaga meeting, Kothagiri

The next day, on way to Kothagiri, near Crown Bakery on Mount Road, one Shamsuddeen (one of the oldest persons in the area), stopped Gandhiji's car, and garlanded him on behalf of Muslims. Gandhiji halted briefly at Pandicholai, Ettappalli and Koottapottu, en route, and received welcome addresses of the people.

At the Fort Maidan in Kothagiri, some 1,000 people, most of them from the Badaga community, had gathered. After receiving their welcome and purse, Gandhiji said:

> Untouchability in the hills is not as severe as seen in the plains. However, until distinctions of high and low among you persist,

it cannot be said that untouchability has been erased from our country.

Yesterday, I heard that two of you got into a fight, in which one person died and the other is in hospital. The movement that I have started is for purification of your soul, and I appeal that you give up alcohol consumption. The man addicted to liquor does dishonour to his mother and wife.

Here, as requested by a Tamil pundit, A. Krishnaswami Naidu, and his wife, the Mahatma named their six-month old child 'Gandhiappan'.

3 February 1934, Ottupparai

There was much official business to be completed by Gandhiji. He visited the Sakkiliar settlement in Ottupparai. At the meeting held in front of the Kali temple there, Gandhiji said: "By closely mixing with Harijans, caste Hindus must seek to purify themselves. The Harijans, too, should not believe that they will obtain the blessings of Kali by sacrificing buffaloes."

When he went to the Dandakaran slum, where the scavengers of the Town Council lived, the crowd was so large and eager to approach him that he could not sit in a chair, but spoke standing up near the table. Here, Gandhiji emphasised the importance of cleanliness.

Azhwarpettai

Moving on to a public meeting attended by more than 800 people in Azhwarpettai Grounds, Gandhiji spoke about how untouchability affected not just the poor Harijans and Adi Dravidars, but all communities throughout India. "All religious factions—Christians, Muslims, Parsees, Jews and Hindus consider each other as untouchable," he said.

4 February 1934, An orange for dinner

The representatives from Coimbatore, led by R. Virayan, who advertised themselves as 'appointed by capability' approved by Gandhiji himself, provided the lunch the next day. They introduced themselves as representing original Hindus from different districts of Madras. An aged Harijan lady had come with this group. She garlanded him and offered an orange. Gandhiji invited her to sit beside him and said, "Both of us are old. I will receive your blessings, and will keep this orange for my dinner."

Ootacamund

As Coonoor was bathed in the cool sun's rays, the welcome group, led by Abdul Majid in a car in front, was followed by his 'family'. Thakkar Bapa (Amritlal Vithaldas Thakkar), Ramachandran, R. T. Kesavulu, R. T. Manickam, S. R. Narayana Iyer, A. Govindasamy, Dr C. N. Narayanan, Bajaj's daughter and two ladies from Hungary (Sanbrun and her daughter, who had come to draw a portrait of Gandhiji), were in the vanguard, as Gandhiji reached Ootacamund.

On the way, at Wellington and Ketti, crowds had gathered to see Gandhiji. At the public meeting in the Town Council Grounds, three welcome speeches were read out on behalf of the town people, Adi Dravidars and Marwaris. Gandhiji said: "I do not look for superficial change. If untouchability in any form has to be eradicated, there must be an integral and wholehearted change in the crores of caste Hindus."

Ramakrishna Mutt

Thereafter, Swami Sidbhavananda, who met Gandhiji at Coonoor, escorted him around the Ramakrishna Mutt. The Swami later recounted his exchange with the Mahatma.

> I had written seeking an interview with Gandhiji on the interpretation of a couple of slokas in the *Bhagavad Gita*. I was then residing at the Ramakrishna Mutt in Ootacamund. I received a reply that I could get 10 minutes at 4 p.m.
>
> Accordingly, at 4 p.m., I entered the room, as Gandhiji came through another door. As he plied his charkha, he asked me, 'Swamiji, what is the matter you wish to discuss with me?' I replied, 'Mahatmaji, it is my belief that in the same family of four brothers, it is possible that one can be a Brahmin, another a Kshatriya, a third a Vysya and the fourth a Shudra. Do you agree with this?"
>
> *Mahatma*: No, I do not agree.
> *Swami*: Does not the *Gita* base the caste differences on virtue and duty?

M: It is true. By caste I am a Vysya. This is a societal distinction which I cannot change. My children, too, are Vysyas. My children and I must follow the customs and rituals of the Vysyas.

S: The Brahmins, who are expected to follow a spiritual path, are today pursuing a materialistic existence. Do you accept them as Brahmins?

M: As per the societal division they are Brahmins. If they go against their dharma, they become sinners, not members of another community.

S: Then, is it your belief that caste is related to birth?

M: You cannot condemn birth. Sinners within castes must work towards restoring their original virtue. I do not wish to debate this any further.

S: The youngsters of today must be educated on the Brahmin, Kshatriya, Vysya and Shudra dharmas together. This is my view. What is your opinion about this?

Gandhiji considered this deeply for a couple of minutes, and agreed.

Invitation to the Mutt

Swami Sidbhavananda invited Gandhiji to the Mutt in Ootacamund, saying that Harijan boys and girls sang bhajans there, and that if he went around the Mutt, they would feel happy. Gandhiji accepted this invitation. The Swami also had two more requests to make of Gandhiji. The first was: "A Harijan elder has established a mutt in a place called Kanthal in Ootacamund. I would like you to see the benefits being received by the inmates there." His second request was: "The authorities of the Ganesa temple of Kodambatthu in Ootacamund have said that if you inaugurate the Harijan entry into that temple, they would accept it as divine authority, and continue to permit the worship of Harijans in it. Would you inaugurate this holy work?"

Gandhiji happily consented to both requests of the Swami. Subsequently it was arranged that Gandhiji would finish addressing a public meeting at the Ooty race course grounds by 5.45 p.m., and would thereafter be escorted to the three places mentioned, and complete those functions by 7.30 p.m.

The promised visit

Swami Sidbhavananda has recounted in detail Gandhiji's visit to the mutts.

> As promised, Gandhiji came out of the public meeting in Ootacamund. When we entered the ashram, women were fully seated there. Mahatmaji happily sat on a platform that we had provided for him. A plate of fruits that had been offered in prayer was placed before him, which he partook of at intervals. This was unusual, as he was not known to eat anything outside of his normal eating hours.
>
> *Kanthal Mutt*
> When we went from Ramakrishna Mutt to Kanthal Mutt, I was sitting beside the Mahatma, and telling him about the history and establishment of that mutt by Adimoola Swamigal, which he listened to attentively. As we entered the Kanthal Mutt, Gandhiji was escorted to the samadhi of Adimoola Swami. He inquired about the two samadhis placed side by side.
> The wife of Adimoola Swami, not willing to live on after the Swami's passing, went into deep penance and renounced her own life on the fifth day after he had attained 'samadhi'—hence her samadhi by the side, I explained. 'A matter of surprise,' the Mahatma remarked, as he stood in meditation for a while. The visit to Kanthal Mutt greatly pleased the Mahatma.
>
> *Kodambatthu Ganesa Temple*
> Finally, we reached the Kodambatthu Ganesa temple. The key of the locked temple was handed over to the Mahatma. Taking the Harijans with him, he entered the temple, where, after the *deepa aradhanai* to the Lord, *prasadam* was distributed to all, without any discrimination. The Mahatma blessed everyone, declaring that the common love shown to Ganesa by all is most elevating, and that the temple had now acquired a new divinity. He took leave from there at 8 p.m. and returned directly to Coonoor.

Gandhiji speaks, in Subri's voice

During his stay in the Nilgiris, all the speeches of Gandhiji were translated by Subri, as K. Subramaniam was affectionately known. He translated them in his stentorian voice that could easily be heard by the crowds. One day, Gandhiji asked Subri, "How did you come to be endowed with such a good voice?" to which Subri replied, "Through God's grace and your blessings." Gandhiji responded, "Definitely through God's grace alone."

6 February 1934, Mettupalayam

The Mettupalayam public did not let him go once he descended from Coonoor after his rest. When he had passed through on his way to the hills, it was his day of silence; decorations had been made at Mettupalayam to receive him. Hence they had sent a request to stop on his way back and address a meeting.

Sokkampalayam

Sokkampalayam is a small village. Even so, a purse of Rs 1001 was presented here. In the meeting held on open grounds, where more than 4,000 women had assembled, it can be imagined what the attendance of men must have been. A. A. Subbaiah Naidu of Punjai Puliampatti presented a penciled drawing of Gandhiji to him. Welcome addresses were read out by Ranga Chettiar on behalf of the village folk, and by Madatthupalyam Pazhani Gounder on behalf of the Taluk Board. "I laud the work you have done for khadi, untouchability eradication, and prohibition," Gandhiji said in his speech, dwelling on the importance of untouchability eradication particularly. The meeting was over in half an hour.

Tiruppur

Nearing Tiruppur, Gandhiji was welcomed at three places— at Karuvalur village, about five miles from Sokkampalayam, Tirumuruganpoondi, near Avinashi, and Anuppapalayam. The route from Mettupalayam to Tiruppur was lined all the way by seas of people. The arrangements for Gandhiji's welcome in Tiruppur had been made by P. T. Asher, and the secretary of the Madras Sarvodaya Sangam, A. Ayyamuthu. At Tiruppur, the Mahatma was taken to the newly built house of Ponnusamy Gounder of Duraisamipuram, where Gounder gave Rs 750 for the Harijan Fund. After receiving this, Gandhiji proceeded to receive the welcome of the public at the grounds next to the Town Council Musabari bungalow.

Rajaji

Chakravarthi Rajagopalachariar, who had been sentenced to six months' imprisonment in the Coimbatore jail for his role in the Tiruchengode Satyagraha, was released on that day, after serving his term. Knowing that Gandhiji was in Tiruppur, together with his friend, E. V. Ramasamy Naicker in his car, and Dr Rajan, he reached Tiruppur. When Gandhiji descended from the dais, the two of them had a discussion. Gandhiji had stayed at the residence of Muriel Lester in London, when he had gone for the Round Table Conference. This lady, along with her elder brother's daughter, Ms Hock, had come to Tiruppur to meet Gandhiji.

The Town Council welcome was read out by its president, K. R. Royappa Gounder. Another welcome was given by the khadi employees and Khadi Sangam. The purse on behalf of the general public was presented by P. T. Asher. Separate purses were presented by khadi employees, Ramakrishna Lunch Home, Chinnuswami Iyer and students. Gandhiji praised the service being rendered by Tiruppur Town administration for Harijan welfare. Tiruppur brings to mind khadi, hence Gandhiji's speech on khadi here acquired special significance.

> We must warn the people not to buy khadi that does not bear the stamp of the All India Spinners' Sangam. There is a rumour floating around that I have changed my views on the importance of khadi. This is untrue. I wish to firmly declare that there is no such change. In fact, my belief in khadi has only become stronger. I believe that khadi is the only way to assuage the misery of the 'untouchables'.

Interview with khadi merchants

After Gandhiji went to the house of P. T. Asher, had his meal and rested, the khadi merchants of Tiruppur sought an interview with him, at which the subject of 'imitation' khadi came up. They complained that for some years khadi sales were down, and that stocks had piled up in their godowns, leading to tying up of capital, and weavers not being able to get work all through the year. They added that, hitherto, the All India Charkha Sangam had been lifting these stocks, which practice had now been discontinued, and unless Gandhiji found a way out, khadi production would be in grave danger. Gandhiji's response to them provides much food for thought.

> The first State in India to enter into khadi production was Madras. Tiruppur took the lead and became the source of khadi for other parts of the country. Because of the increase in buyers of khadi, many unscrupulous merchants, with a view to making quick money, resorted to unbusinesslike practices. They sold inferior goods and brought a bad name to Tiruppur. They raised many problems for the All India Charkha Sangam, too, by opposing it in various matters. Ultimately, they fell in line with the regulations of the Charkha Sangam. In the meantime, here and there in some States, as khadi production under the aegis of Charkha Sangam was started, the takers for Tiruppur khadi dwindled.

> The Charkha Sangam, on its part, did its best to lift the piled up stocks for sale. Moreover, there were no varieties in Tiruppur khadi, whereas other regions produced khadi varieties required by the consumer, capturing the market, depriving Tiruppur merchants. You must go and see how the other regions are working. How long can the Charkha Sangam support you? If, after 10 years of support by it, you have not found a way to make your business profitable, I can only say that you are not equipped to do business. You must produce and sell products after studying the changing needs of the times.

> Your duty is to produce cloth that attracts people to wear them. If you do so, with integrity and compassion, not expecting runaway profits, adhering to the principles of the khadi movement in merchandising, your business will never suffer.

A silver-framed portrait of Gandhiji, presented by P. T. Asher, was bought on behalf of cotton merchants by M. K. K. Kumarasamy Chettiar in the auction, who declared that they were going to present it to Padmavathi Asher. She was not in Tiruppur when Gandhiji visited. The women of Kumarasamy Gounder's family donated their jewellery to Gandhiji. A. R. Gurumurthy Naidu's daughter, Kumari Sarada, gave an expensive pair of earrings.

Tiruppur

Tiruppur bore a festive atmosphere. A holiday was declared for government schools and offices. However, a small incident took place that saddened Gandhiji. Mrs. Abdus Salam of Sabarmati Ashram, one of the members of Gandhiji's entourage, was afflicted by fever even before coming here. In Tiruppur, her fever worsened. She was left behind by Gandhiji at P. T. Asher's house under the care of K. K. Padmavathiammal and K. K. Narayaniammal of Ottapalayam. Coming to Coimbatore, via Palladam, crowds, disregarding the heat, gathered in large numbers at Palladam and Sulur. As usual, welcome addresses and purses were presented.

Coimbatore

Before going to Coimbatore, Gandhiji went to inspect the YMCA Village Reconstruction Institute in Ramanathapuram, an area in the vicinity of Coimbatore. Its secretary, Jayakaran, welcomed him and took him around the facilities. Gandhiji spent a lot of time observing the bee keeping section. Jayakaran's child presented Gandhiji a silver jug containing honey extracted at this centre, and a silver plate with Rs 50.

Women's meeting

After these largely peaceful events and exchanges, when Gandhiji arrived at the women's meeting in Coimbatore, held at the YMCA building, the situation was in direct contrast. As usual, there was a large number of women, and noise and confusion abounded. Gandhiji called out several times for quiet, but to no avail. He left the meeting in 15 minutes.

Arriving at the Harijan Students' Hostel next, Gandhiji enquired in detail if they were getting good food and proper attention. Then he went to the Gujaratis' meeting, received their welcome and purse, returned to where he was staying, and gave an interview to Harijan leaders.

Public meeting

On this tour, a public meeting that could be said to equal the one at Madurai was organised at Coimbatore. There was a new arrangement here, not seen elsewhere. Before Gandhiji began his speech, a separate platform had been erected right in the middle of the crowd to provide a good view for the public. It was on this platform that welcome addresses were read, purses and gifts presented. Thereafter, Gandhiji was escorted to the dais from which he would speak. The crowd remained disciplined throughout.

On behalf of the Town Administration, its vice-president, R. K. Venkatachalam, presented the welcome address in a silver casket. On behalf of the Coimbatore District Association, V. C. Vellingiri Gounder presented a welcome address, as did the Coimbatore Taluk Harijan Seva Sangam members. Gandhiji emphasised at this meeting the importance of the leaders' role in untouchability eradication.

"If untouchability is not completely eradicated, it is the people's fault, the failure of the leaders and the workers. Harijans in villages within a three or four-mile radius of Coimbatore are being oppressed by caste Hindus. I hear that caste Hindus are denying them even their legitimate wages," said Gandhiji with severity. He suggested that some leaders from Coimbatore should visit these villages and attempt a compromise between Harijans and caste Hindus. Before concluding, he offered condolences on the demise of *The Hindu* newspaper chairman, A. Rangaswami Iyengar. "Whether as the head of a newspaper or as a national worker, one cannot find another like him. His hard work and wisdom have helped the Congress at crucial times," he added in praise.

Peelamedu

After this meeting, Gandhiji went to the P. S. G. Industrial Institute in Peelamedu, and received a purse from Rao Bahadur P. S. G. Rangasamy Naidu. A five-rupee currency note was proffered to Gandhiji for his signature, but Gandhiji was not taken in. "What is this five rupees? It is not for the receipt towards your Rs 500, is it?" he jokingly remarked, remaining seated in his car. "Kindly get down and see around our factory," requested Rangasamy Naidu. "Oh, should I get down? Then you have to pay me," Gandhiji promptly replied. Naidu said, "I will give Rs 25." Gandhiji replied, "You are a miser," and did not get down from the car. Ultimately, a compromise was reached, and on being given Rs 50, Gandhiji was escorted into the factory.

When an old lady, a relative of the factory owner, met him, Gandhiji patted her back and asked, "What have you brought for me?" The old lady bent down and touched Gandhiji's feet. When she rose, Gandhiji fondly cupped her chin in his hands and chuckled aloud. Thereafter, he proceeded to watch a play.

He consents to watch *Nandanar*

Having seen one historical play, *Harishchandra*, Gandhiji had rarely ever agreed to watch any other play or film later in life. On strong persuasion, he would on occasion agree to see plays based on bhakti. He consented to come and watch *Nandanar*, being staged by Madurai Devi Balavinodha Sabha in Coimbatore, but on certain conditions.

He had received an invitation to witness this play even while he was resting in Coonoor. At first he did not accept, but on being told that it was being performed by the renowned 'Nawab' Rajamanikkam Pillai troupe, and that the playwright was Rajaram Bhagavathar, known as 'Gandhi Bhagavathar' because of his reverence for Gandhiji, he agreed to come to this play in Coimbatore—but just for five minutes. Another condition was that the producers of the play should donate the entire collections of that day to the Harijan Fund. "What collections do you expect?" he asked. "Approximately Rs 2000," they said. Gandhiji then demanded that Rs 1500 must be kept aside in advance for the Harijan Fund, and Rs 500 for the Bihar Earthquake Relief Fund.

The collections for the play that day were expected to be spectacular, but they were not. Some may have thought that, having seen Gandhiji at the public meeting, they could go home, and there was no need to see him again at the play. But the route through which Gandhiji had to drive was so choked with crowds that the police had to resort to lathi charge to clear the way, because of which many in the crowd possibly could not reach the venue of the play. Consequently, the collections that day were a mere Rs 150. The play began only after

Gandhiji arrived. However, he stayed considerably longer than he had said—about 20–25 minutes. His seat was specially arranged on the stage itself.

The little buffoon's fun

There was a largely unconnected buffoon's role in the play, enacted by a small boy, who would appear at intervals and do some funny antics. He wore a lensless frame over his eyes, which, to the viewers below, looked like a normal pair of spectacles. Gandhiji gestured to the boy to come and sit beside him. Then he put his fingers inside the spectacle frames to check whether it was a real pair or not. Everybody laughed. Unnoticed by anyone, stuck on the boy's chest was Gandhiji's portrait, above which was the tricolour in khadi. Baring his chest proudly, the young boy said, "You are always in our hearts, Mahatma." At this Gandhiji laughed aloud in delight, to applause that reverberated through the auditorium.

The leader of the theatre troupe presented a welcome to Gandhiji. In addition to the purse, the artist of the company, a disciple of Ravi Varma, Devaraja Iyer, presented him his portrait drawn by him. Nawab Rajamanikkam presented a *navaratna* (nine-gem) ring. Gandhiji wrote a note to the drama company before leaving, signing it in Tamil and Gujarati: "I hope that this Sabha's activities prove beneficial to the nation." (Based on the interview of Nawab Rajamanikkam.)

Car accident

There was an accident at the railway gate en route from Coimbatore to Ramakrishna Vidyalayam in Pothanur. From Pothanur railway station the Vidyalayam was about a mile away. The road ran along the railway line for half a mile, before crossing the tracks to reach the other side. As there was a deep curve on the road before the railway gate at Pothanur, it was not easily visible. The driver of Gandhiji's car, named Kaimal, was clever, having been specially recruited from Madras. T. S. Avinashalingam was seated beside the driver giving directions. Inside the car were Thakkar Bapa, Muriel Lester, Mrs Hock, and Gandhiji. Kaimal was new to those parts, and was driving at about 40 mph.

As Avinashalingam had turned around to speak to Gandhiji seated behind, he did not see the railway gate coming up. When the car suddenly negotiated the curve, Kaimal did not see the gate in time either, and so could not apply his brakes timely. The car rammed into the iron railway gate. In the impact, the lantern hanging as a warning on the gate flew up and landed on the front seat of the car, between Kaimal and Avinashalingam. The gate itself was twisted and leaned towards the railway track.

Providential escape

Avinashalingam was apprehensive of what Gandhiji would say. But Gandhiji laughed and said, "Avinashi, what happened?" He was not hurt, nor did he raise his voice against anybody. He got down immediately and started walking towards the Vidyalayam. As there was much dust being raised by Gandhiji's car, the car in which Dr Rajan was travelling was some distance behind. They noticed Gandhiji walking beyond the gate as they reached the Vidyalayam. Seeing Dr Rajan, Kaimal swooned, and was revived with water spray. It was the same car that had been arranged for Gandhiji to travel from Madras to Kanyakumari. Gandhiji's escaping unharmed that day could only be attributed to providence and the good condition of the car.

Day not yet done

After visits to so many places and functions that day, and then the accident, when he reached the Sri Ramakrishna Vidyalayam in the evening, Gandhiji could not sigh in relief and say, "Today's work is done!" Students of the Vidyalayam had been waiting sleeplessly for his arrival with great expectation, and greeted him excitedly. After spending some time talking with them, Gandhiji read the letters received in the mail, and verified the accounts of the collections made on the day. Only then did he retire for the day.

7 February 1934, Sri Ramakrishna Vidyalayam

The foundation stone-laying ceremony for the new building of Sri Ramakrishna Vidyalayam was held the next morning. Before

Gandhiji left for the function, a teacher of the school came with a portrait that he had drawn of Gandhiji, requesting that he sign on it. Gandhiji wrote: "I hope the boys of the Vidyalayam will be strong in truth and faithful to God," signed in Tamil and Gujarati, and then left for the function.

Sri Ramakrishna Vidyalayam, encompassing several colleges like a banyan tree, stood majestically a few miles outside Coimbatore in Periyanaickenpalayam. It had started as an orphanage with just one Harijan boy. When Gandhiji had come to Pothanur, there were 60 students, and the institution was functioning out of rented premises. T. S. Avinashalingam, who established the Vidyalayam, worked tirelessly day and night to bring it to the status it then enjoyed, but did not have a permanent site for it. Near the Vidyalayam, in Pothanur, his brother, T. S. Kalyanasundaram had four acres of land, and it was decided that Gandhiji would be asked to lay the foundation stone for the new building there. It was on this land on Kurichi Road that the function was organised.

Gandhiji started from Sri Ramakrishna Vidyalayam, laid the foundation stone for the new building, and continued on his tour. "I believe that this Vidyalayam would become a place of pilgrimage for national workers, and that the students who pass out of this institution will turn out to be brave upholders of truth, God-fearing, and of service to humanity," he said, as he laid the foundation stone.

Gandhiji did not have an opportunity to visit this Vidyalayam in future years, but he never failed to enquire about its progress from Avinashalingam whenever he met him.

Pollachi

The train that started on time from Pothanur took 45 minutes to reach Pollachi, after stopping at Kinattrukadavu (now a suburb of Coimbatore city) and Nallattipalayam (now a village in Pollachi taluka of Coimbatore district) for Gandhiji to receive the welcome speeches and purses of the public at these stations.

In a public meeting, attended by more than 20,000 people, welcome addresses and purses were presented on behalf of the Municipality, the Taluk Board and the general public. The Viswakarma Sangam presented a spinning wheel made of silver.

"From the crowd here, it can be seen that you are ready to uproot untouchability," he said in praise. As he was already delayed coming here, Gandhiji did not conduct the auction and left for Udumalaipettai.

Udumalaipettai

En route to Udumalaipettai, a thousand-strong crowd waited at Komangalam, led by District Taluk Board member, Ramasamy Naidu, to present a welcome and purse to Gandhiji. When he reached Udumalaipettai in mid-afternoon, there was no lack of enthusiasm in the gathering.

In the public meeting held on the open grounds in Pazhani Andavar compound, welcome speeches and purses were presented on behalf of the Town Council by K. Chellamuthu, on behalf of the Taluk Board by R. V. Gurusamy Naidu, on behalf of the general public by Appavoo Pillai, and on behalf of women by Savithriammal. Gandhiji was a guest here of Rajaram Pillai, had lunch at his residence and rested. When Gandhiji was auctioning a silver jug at the public meeting, a girl came up to offer him her two bangles. Somebody had informed Gandhiji that she was giving the bangles against the wishes of her father.

"I will then become the cause of a fight between you and your father," said Gandhiji.

"No, Mahatma, I am giving these to you of my own free will. Please accept them," the girl replied.

Gandhiji then asked her, "Have you reached puberty?"

She replied, "I am 12 years old."

Seeing this protracted discussion on the dais, the girl's father came up and said that he had no objection to her offering the bangles. But Gandhiji was not one to let it go at that, and said, "Now that I know your status, you must give me more."

He named a boy 'Raman' at this meeting.

Vanneer Valasu

On the way from Udumalaipettai to Pazhani, Gandhiji took a detour of two miles to the north to inspect the settlement of Harijans at Vanneer Valasu—and therein lies a tale, as narrated by Dr Rajan.

In a village called Vanneer Valasu, Sri Appavoo, deciding to serve the Harijans, settled down with a friend of his, obtaining the respect of the Harijans living there.

Appavoo made up his mind to somehow get Gandhiji to visit this village, and took steps towards this in full earnest. In Trichy, once, and in Coonoor, again, he met Gandhiji, and ultimately got him to [agree] to visit his village.

There was no proper road to the village. If Gandhiji were to visit [it], a road for his car to go through was required. Appavoo did not consider this to be an impediment. Together with his friends and the village folk, he began the work of building the road. Within 10 days, a two-mile stretch of road was laid, they named it Gandhi Road, and hung that name painted on a wooden board like a signpost from a tree. To a village, hitherto unreachable by car, we went within ten minutes.

Immensely pleased with the slum conditions, Gandhiji assured [the residents] that he would do what he could for its development. 'I am also very happy to learn that these slum dwellers have mostly given up the bad habits they had, owing to your persevering efforts,' Gandhiji said, as he took leave.

Pazhani

In the evening Gandhiji arrived in Pazhani and spoke at the large public meeting held at the foot of the Pazhani hills. He spoke most movingly: "We are now congregated at the foot of the holy Pazhani hills, but we continue to hear that Harijans are still not permitted to enter the temple. Why should such permission be denied? It is my belief that God cannot exist in a temple that does not allow these people. We refer to God as 'our Help in danger' [and] 'Protector of orphans'—how could He be so hard-hearted?"

The prasadam of the Lord was offered to Gandhiji.

Dindigul

Dindigul turned out to be another Thoothukudi. In the open Fort grounds, a high dais was erected, and the whole area was brilliantly illuminated with electric lights. As with Thoothukudi, during which journey they had lost their way and reached Tambrabarani river, having to retrace their route, so also did they miss the route from Pazhani to Dindigul, consequently being delayed by three hours.

At the Dindigul meeting, M. S. P. Solai Nadar read out the welcome address on behalf of the Town Administration. The National Youth League and Self-Respect Society read their separate welcome speeches. There is a saying that even at night, parasols were held over kings. Likewise, when Gandhiji spoke here at night, the National Youth League held up an umbrella, bearing their name in English. Several Europeans had come to the meeting, and were seated on the dais.

In his speech, Gandhiji said, "Why should we torment some people all through their lives, merely because of their birth? The sooner we erase the stain of untouchability, the better it will be for us."

Prayer meeting

Completing this meeting quickly, Gandhiji and his party came to Baluswami Choultry to stay the night. After the prayer meeting concluded, Kuppuswami Iyer's wife came up to Gandhiji and offered him two bangles, one diamond ring, one watch chain and Rs 101. The next morning, Gandhiji left for the areas of Cumbum and Periakulam (now, both are towns and municipalities in Theni District of Tamil Nadu).

8 February 1934, Cumbum

In those days, Dindigul was a separate Congress district in which Cumbum and Uthamapalyam were included. The Cumbum area, between the Eastern and Western Ghats, was marked by natural beauty, giving much sightseeing pleasure to tourists. Since it was in rather a remote corner, there was initial reluctance to include it as part of Gandhiji's itinerary. However, thanks to the untiring efforts of two persons, the people of this region had the good fortune of seeing Gandhiji. One of them was Bodinayakanur Nithyanandam. The other was Narayanasamy Chettiar, the owner of *Bharati* newspaper, and a nationalist who had gone to jail during the Salt Satyagraha.

"If you grace our region, we will collect Rs 5,000 from our Taluka alone," they had said. Hence, Gandhiji extended his tour by a day to accommodate a visit to this area. Because of rain in Madurai, and the resultant extension of the Madras tour by 10 days, the money collection from the Thevaram region took place over two days. Consequent to this good fortune, Nithyanada Swami's Bodinayakanur could be included in the tour. But ten days before going there, the area was affected by plague, and Gandhiji did not proceed beyond the Bodi limits.

Vathalagundu

From Dindigul, Gandhiji went to Ottuppatti village near Vathalagundu. Here, in the meeting arranged by Harijans, led by Sankara Iyer, he received their welcome. In front of the Vathalagundu Panchayat office, its president, Arockiasamy, read out his welcome. The Vadugapatti public and Harijans read out their separate welcome speeches, and presented purses, after which Gandhiji reached Periakulam.

Gandhiji praised the munificent donation given by Vathalagundu Muslims, particularly that of K. S. Abdul Khader Rawthar. "The basis of untouchability is the distinction of high and low. Remove it, and it will lead to unity, not only among people of different religions, but also among Muslims themselves."

The handwritten welcome address of the Harijans of Vadakkapatti drew praise from Gandhiji. "Printing of welcome addresses is a waste of money. If they are given to me unframed, it would please me even more," he said.

Periakulam-Theni

A pleasant news was waiting for him at the public meeting organised at the market place of Periakulam. Welcome addresses and purses were presented by Periakulam Harijan Seva Sangam and Hindi Prachar Sabha.

"I am delighted to learn that so many people in Periakulam know Hindi!" he lauded. He went on to say that that, although good work was being done here in favour of Harijans, not only Hindus but members of other religions must bestow more care on their progress. At the end of the meeting, he went to A. Ramasamy Chettiar's house, rested for about two hours, and continued his tour.

On the way, he received the welcome of Puduppatti, and reached Theni, where his car was stopped by the Theni public, who presented their welcome, as also the welcome of the Kandamanayakanur Zamindar.

Subsequently, after receiving the welcome of Pazhani, Chettippatti and Veerandi, Gandhiji reached Chinnamanoor (now a town and municipality in Theni district of Tamil Nadu). The welcome speeches on behalf of the Chinnamanoor and Karungattakulam people were offered by the Panchayat president, Chokkalingam Pillai.

Uthamapalayam

In Uthamapalayam, a discovery at the meeting that took place in the elder Syed Rawther's tamarind orchard caused Gandhiji much distress. Here, the Hindu Harijans and the Christian Harijans jointly presented a welcome address to Gandhiji. Realising then that there were Harijans even among Christians upset Gandhiji to such an extent that he hastily finished the Uthamapalayam meeting, and, on reaching Cumbum, talked only about this.

Cumbum

His speech at Cumbum was hard-hitting. "The fact that there are Harijans among Hindus is itself a matter of shame, but Harijans even among Christians? I find this very difficult to understand," he began, and went on to say:

> Among Christian intellectuals or the uneducated, I have never heard anyone say there is any place for untouchability. I guess that it is from the Hindu religion that this worm has crept into Christianity. At the same time, if I work towards eradication of untouchability among Christians, I would be exceeding my limits. Hence, Christians must realise the movement that is happening in India, and exhort their constituents to remove this scourge. Hindus, too, could be of help in this. If we remove untouchability among the Hindus, it would not only benefit the Hindus, but bring unity in humanity throughout the world.

The meeting took place at the Union Board building. The welcome of the Panchayat was read out by M. S. Shahul Hameed, and that of United Institute Library by Rajamanikkam Pillai.

As Bharati Narayanasamy Chettiar had said, in that single day, the amount donated to the Harijan Fund was Rs 3,500. Hindus, Christians and Muslims got together to accord a cordial welcome to Gandhiji, who stayed here in the house of a Muslim. The next morning, the purse of the people of Kamaya Gounder Patti was presented.

9 February 1934, Kombai

Starting from Cumbum in the morning, almost as if to remind Gandhiji that he was travelling towards the cardamom plantations, the V. S. R. and Brothers organisation presented him with a sack of cardamom, as he reached Kombai (a panchayat town in Theni district). The Vysyas too presented a purse, but what pleased Gandhiji the most was the appeal that was contained in the handwritten welcome given to him by the Muslims of that area.

It said: "Although our immediate participation may not be required for the work being undertaken by you at present, we are inspired by the message you are spreading that all men are equal. Hence we request that this humble contribution of Rs 20 from 30 families may please be accepted for the Harijan Fund."

Gandhiji praised them. "Your help is truly very significant. In my work I am always ready to accept the help from people of other religions."

Thevaram

All the way to Thevaram, workers wearing khadi caps were seen controlling the crowds. As Gandhiji was impressed by these workers and by the natural beauty of the place, Gandhiji's speech devoted time to praise them and talk about the loveliness of the area.

As soon as Gandhiji sat on the dais, Bharati Narayanasamy Chettiar honoured him with a garland of cardamom. Welcomes were read on behalf of the Thevaram Panchayat Board, Thevaram general public, Vivekananda School students and Harijans. Gandhiji gave a long speech here, starting from how he came to tour this area.

Workers' army

It is only after much effort that Thevaram got included in my tour schedule, but I am happy that I have been able to come to this beautiful area. All along the way to Kombai, workers were busy controlling the crowds and traffic. The help of these workers must be utilised for maintaining and improving the beauty of this place. To lay a road to Vanneer Valasu, Harijan workers, whose numbers could be counted on one's fingers, had toiled for two months. The number of workers here is much more. Hence they should be used to lay a good road between Kombai and Thevaram. Taluk Boards and Disrict Boards are in fact laying roads for free, are they not? If you put in your complementary efforts, you could even eradicate malaria. But, until untouchability is eradicated, you cannot effectively carry out these health practices.

Women's meeting

After speaking thus about untouchability in the local context, Gandhiji proceeded to the mansion of the Zamorin, where he was welcomed by women. (The Samoothiri, anglicised as Zamorin, was once the hereditary Nair monarch and ruler of the Kingdom of Kozhikode or Calicut in the South Malabar region.) Receiving their donation of jewels, he emphasised that women at least must realise the need for eradication of untouchability, and remove such thoughts from their minds. In the few hours he stayed at Thevaram, Gandhiji was the guest of C. Gurusamy Pillai.

The Bodi welcome

As already decided, it was not possible to visit Bodi, owing to the plague in that area. Hence, at a place some eight miles from there, in a village called Bodivilakku, Gandhiji was accorded a welcome. Welcome and purse were presented on behalf of the Bodi people. After the meeting, he rested at the Arya Vysya Bank building in Theni for a while, waiting for the train, which took him to Chekkanoorani (in Madurai district).

Usilampatti

There was a large crowd at Andipatti railway station. Welcome speeches and purses on behalf of the people were presented there. Gandhiji got up on a bench and spoke about the eradication of untouchability. There was a similar crowd at Doddappanayakanur (also in Madurai district) railway station. At Usilampatti too the railway station could barely hold the crowd that had assembled. Gandhiji received the purse presented there through the window of his compartment.

Chozhavandan

Alighting at Chekkanoorani station, Gandhiji and party proceeded to Chozhavandan by car. Mungala Pattabhiramayya (he had been released from jail a few days back), Mattapparai Venkataramayya, Dr Gopalasamy, and Shanmugavelu Mudaliar received Gandhiji at Chekkanoorani. On the way to Chozhavandan, from Kocchadai to Melakkal, noticing the coconut trees beautifying the road on either side, Gandhij remarked in pleasant surprise, "This truly looks like an avenue."

At the public meeting held on the 'shandy' grounds, separate welcome addresses and purses were presented on behalf of the Chozhavandan general public, Union Panchayat Committee, Mudaliars of Chozhavandan, Arasan Shanmuganar Spinning Mills and the South Street public.

The welcome of the Mudaliars was read out by Shanmugavelu. The welcome and purse of the general public was presented by Munagal Pattabhiramayya. On behalf of Chozhavandan students, a silver cup was presented. Gandhiji praised the crowd that conducted itself with silence and discipline.

Students

If the workers were the heroes in Gandhiji's talk in Thevaram, it was the students who took the pride of place in Chozhavandan. His speech was largely filled with advice for students, who had presented him a silver cup without any cash. "You have given me an empty silver cup, whereas in many other places students have given a sizeable amount of money. With a little more effort, you could have filled this cup with money!"

Unknown to many, a land donation or *bhoodan* took place here. Vilampatti Duraisamy promised to donate about 300 square feet (2 *kuzhi*s) of *punjai* or dry land to Gandhiji. Thereafter Gandhiji went to Gopalaswami Iyer's clinic, and lay down on the floor to rest without even spreading a mat, taking everyone by surprise. After a bit of rest, he took the Shencottah (now a town in the Tenkasi district of Tamil Nadu) Passenger train at night to Tiruchirappalli (based on the interview of Munagala Pattabhiramayya).

10 February 1934, Tiruchi

It was 3.50 a.m. when Gandhiji reached Tiruchi. Yet, the platform was filled with people waiting to receive him. The arrangements had been made by the prominent Sanatani and advocate, Srinivasa Iyer, as president of the welcome committee. On the way from the station could be seen some posters on walls, which said, "Gandhiji Go Back". In front of Gandhiji's car, two Sanatanis, clad in khadi and smeared with vibhuti or sacred ash scattered leaflets—provided by the Hindu Central Committee, Srirangam—with "vulgar words about Gandhiji" (an expression used by Dr Rajan) along the road. A few youngsters en route held black flags.

Srirangam

As there were many establishments in Tiruchi, Gandhiji and his party started five minutes before time from the Cantonment where they were staying. Rajaji joined them from Madras. First proceeding to Peerthan Juhurmal Bank in Thennur, Gandhiji received welcome addresses and purses from the Director of the Bank, Lum Sant Seth, on his own behalf, and on behalf of the Gujaratis of Tiruchi, Multanis, Marwaris, Jains and Sindhi merchants.

He went on to Srirangam after this. It was sad to see a few Sanatanis in this holy pilgrimage centre, sanctified by Sri Ramanuja who lived there some 800 years ago, opposing Gandhiji's campaign against untouchability. A black flag was flying on the Raja Gopuram in Srirangam temple when he arrived.

Yet, Srinivasa Iyengar, the younger brother of Kodiyalam Rangaswami Iyengar, said in his welcome to Gandhiji, "We believe that you are a true Sanatani." This pleased Gandhiji, who thanked him, saying that he accepted what was said of him with humility, and that from the time of his youth he had always endeavoured to live according to the shastras. "I can only promise one thing to my friends who oppose temple entry of Harijans. Had the public objected, Harijans would not have gone against them and violently entered the temple. It should not happen merely because I say so. Likewise, merely because a particular person is against it, it cannot be stopped."

Thus, Gandhiji appealed to the people to move with the times and accept the entry of Harijans into temples. "I invite the Sanatani who strongly opposes this to meet me. After all, this is only a friendly debate" (as reported by Sangilia Pillai).

'Praise' for the black flags

Gandhiji praised the welcome committee for not wasting money on needless decorations, as also those who held black flags. He praised the Sanatanis for merely putting up anti-Gandhi posters and holding black flags, and not resorting to vocal and vulgar abuse during the meeting! At some places, children holding black flags were also shouting 'Jai to Gandhiji', which was quite funny, he added.

Which Rangaswami?

At the beginning of his speech, Gandhiji paid a condolence tribute to the late nationalist, Kodiyalam Rangaswami Iyengar. Instead of adding the name 'Kodiyalam', Gandhiji merely said, "It is a personal loss for me that Rangaswami is no longer by my side." People were unsure whether he was referring to Rangaswami Iyengar, chief editor of *The Hindu* (from 1928 till his death in 1934), or to Kodiyalam Rangaswami. A member of the audience even asked him to clarify this. Just a few days prior to this, Gandhiji had mentioned the passing away of *The Hindu*'s Rangaswami Iyengar in Coimbatore. So Gandhiji promptly responded, "I have spoken of the demise of 'Hindu' Rangaswami Iyengar at an earlier meeting. I am now referring to K. V. Rangaswami, which is why I did not use the word 'Iyengar'. This illustrates his close attention to the use of words.

Has it not been said in the *Tirukkural*: 'Speak what is useful, and speak not useless words'?

Manachanallur

When Gandhiji left Srirangam by car for Manachanallur, Sanatanis in a car in front continued to scatter anti-Gandhi leaflets on the road. As the car passed Bhikshandarkoil, a few school students waved black flags. In Manachanallur, a noted centre of commerce, Panchayat president S. N. Nambiappa Chettiar presented a welcome at the public meeting on behalf of the Panchayat. Primary school children here enthusiastically collected money and gave it to Gandhiji with great affection.

After this, through a short cut, Gandhiji's party reached Samayapuram, famous for its holy Mariamman temple. After the usual presentation of welcome and purses, Gandhiji advised, "All this welcome is meaningless unless you involve yourselves wholeheartedly in untouchability eradication."

Workers' meeting

On the way back, he went to Chintamani on the banks of the Kaveri, accepted the welcome of T. V. Narasu Pillai, and went to inspect a slum nearby. The next function Gandhiji attended was the workers' meeting at the Harijan Seva Sangam State headquarters. There was discussion at this meeting about permitting Harijans into eating houses and hostels. In the afternoon, Gandhiji gave interviews to the representatives of Sanatanis and Harijans at Dr Rajan's bungalow. Thereafter, he went to Devanga Sabha, via Uraiyur (a locality in Trichy), to receive their welcome. Coming to Tiruchirapalli, he accepted the welcome of the Taluk Board, read by its president, K. Singam Iyengar, and lauded them for giving employment to two Harijan members in their office.

The women's meeting in Tiruchirapalli was drowned in noise and confusion. Dr Sastri's wife, Kalyani, presented the welcome address. The money collected was due to the untiring efforts of Kalyaniammal and Padmavatiammal. It seemed unlikely that Gandhiji would be able to speak amidst all the din generated, so he collected the money and jewellery, and went on to National College.

Students' service

Seeing the number of students in the college, Gandhiji felt that the amount collected was insufficient. Professor Saranathan read out the welcome speech and handed over the purse. "Although your collection of money is small, if you have given it wholeheartedly, it is enough," Gandhiji told the students, adding that, "You can form yourselves into small groups. Each group can have its appointed day or week to render service to Harijans."

Public meeting at Puthur

In the history of Tiruchi there was not a public meeting to match the one held that evening at Puthur grounds. The name of Sarvodayavadi Sangilia Pillai of Tiruchi needs special mention for the welcome arrangements made, not just for the crowds present. Gandhiji's speech was replete with spiritual and thought-provoking words. The Tiruchi Town Council's welcome address was read out by S. N. Paramasivan Pillai. On behalf of the general public, Srinivasa Iyer read out the welcome. The social service sangam of Kallar Street also extended a welcome.

The welcome address of the Muslims, however, created a problem. "We believe that a time will come when service for the progress of just one section of people will be replaced by service to humanity as a whole," it said. Gandhiji responded to this.

> This movement may appear to favour one set of people, but its aim is not that. If one group of people is treated with contempt by others, it brings a bad name to humanity as a whole. In India, because of living alongside Hindus, other religious groups are also being affected by caste differences in their own ways. If such discrimination is eradicated, there will be equality, brotherly love and benefit in every community. I earnestly request people of all faiths to join with me in this endeavour.

As in the Devakottai area, where there had been problems between Nattars and Harijans, near Tiruchi, at a place called Mel Arasur, there was a conflict between caste Hindus and Harijans; the former did not permit Harijans to draw water from the same well, and tormented those Harijans who defied this diktat. As this was brought to Gandhiji's attention at this meeting, he chose to mention it in his speech.

11 February 1934, Farewell

The roads were full of crowds even in the early morning when Gandhiji visited the Varaganeri slum settlement. He got down and walked, street by street, through the settlement, entering five or six houses in the process. Thereafter, he and his group left by train for Karur.

He received a moving farewell at Tiruchirapalli railway station. "The son of a doctor wishes to say farewell to you," someone said. "Without charge? This is not good practice," quipped Gandhiji. The train started. There were many familiar faces among those who had come to bid him farewell. "I will not be able to see you for some years, I think," Gandhiji said sadly, as the train left the platform.

Kulithalai

En route to Karur, every station witnessed large crowds. At Muttharasanallur (a village in Trichy district), a dais had been erected on the railway platform for Gandhiji to sit, and a purse presented. There were massive crowds at Kulithalai (now a municipality and suburb of Tiruchirapally city) station. On behalf of the Kulithalai Union Panchayat Board and Taluk Board, welcome orations were read and purses presented. The prominent people of Kulithalai were introduced to Gandhiji by a nationalist of that town, Govindasamy Mudaliar. It was to be expected that the people here would find fault with Gandhiji's tour arrangements, despite all the troubles taken. To express his disappointment at Gandhiji not getting down at Kulithalai, Govindasamy Mudaliar went on fast, and declared that he would not break his fast till Gandhiji left the boundary of Tiruchi district. So a notice persuading Gandhiji to clear the Tiruchi boundary quickly was also issued.

At Mayanur railway station, a purse was presented on behalf of the Indian Workers' Sangam, a society for village improvement.

Karur

It was mid-afternoon when they reached Karur (now a city in Tamil Nadu). Shops had been closed in order to give an enthusiastic welcome to Gandhiji. At the public meeting held here in the afternoon, one Bhaskar read out the welcome address on behalf of the town administration, the general public and Samarasa Sangam. In his address, Gandhiji said:

> Some Sanatanis have written that they should yield to Harijans the right of temple entry. I commend this. I am told that a few among them have also contributed to the Harijan Fund. However, I do not accept it when they say that the conditions inposed by Harijans should be given up. I, too, am a Sanatani, like them. The right that caste Hindus have to enter a temple must be the same for Harijans.

A stage actress and singer, K. B. Sundarambal, presented a gold plated tumbler, which Gandhiji auctioned.

Kodumudi

As Gandhiji left Karur, and was nearing Erode, his car suffered a tyre puncture some 10 miles from Karur. He got into Dr Rajan's car and proceeded, with the result that the others were a little delayed. When he reached Kodumudi, the car stopped in the midst of the crowds, and Gandhiji got up on it for all to see him. As there was no one there to translate his speech, Dr Rajan's driver did the honours! Magudapathi read out the welcome address on behalf of the general public. Subramaniam, an eight-year-old boy belonging to the Sakkiliar community, read out another welcome speech. A welcome was also presented on behalf of the Harijan school students. This handwritten welcome was praised by Gandhiji, who said, "I have only one sentence to speak: Abolish untouchability."

Erode

At Erode, he rested for a bit at a lodge on Eswaran Koil Street. A welcome was given to him at Peoples' Garden. Khan Bahadur Janab K. A. Sheikh Dawood, president of the Town Council, presented its welcome. The welcome of the Taluk Board was presented by the president, V. S. Raja Gounder. Welcome addresses were also presented on behalf of the Merchants' Association, Swadeshi Cloth Merchants' Sangam, Harijan Seva Sangam and Shroff Commercial Association. The trainees of London Mission General Training Institute presented a small woven mat.

"I hope to bring about a change in the mindset of all Sanatanis that I have met on this tour," Gandhij declared. Owing to the uproar of the unruly crowd, he could not speak for long.

That evening, a protest march was organised by youngsters of the Self-Respect Sangam opposing the visit of Gandhiji, putting up black flags on main thoroughfares, at E. V. Ramasamy Periyar's house and at the People's Park.

Bhavani

Gandhiji auctioned a pretty, flower-patterned embroidered cloth at Bhavani. Separate welcome speeches were presented at the meeting on behalf of the Adi Hindu Seva Sangam and the general public. A small Harijan girl was lifted on to the dais to garland Gandhiji. He stretched out his hand to receive this garland, but the little girl insisted she would put it round his neck. "You are stubborn; so, I, too, should be stubborn," he said, smiling, and as the girl was getting down from the dais, Gandhiji threw a chrysanthemum garland, which landed neatly around her neck.

One person presented a fake khadi cloth to Gandhiji, while another man attempted to give him a cigarette packet. "What is this?" Gandhiji asked in surprise. "We do not want whiskey or cigarettes," Rajaji angrily told the man, who quietly sat down.

Tiruchengode

Gandhiji proceeded on to Tiruchengode, halting on the way at Kumarapalayam to receive a purse. By the time he reached Tiruchengode (now a city in Namakkal district of Tamil Nadu), Gandhiji was exhausted. The trip was made more strenuous because of the hot sun. It was not an easy journey from Tiruchirapalli to Karur by train, thereafter 79 miles by car to the Gandhi Ashram at

Tiruchengode. As he had to address several meetings en route, he reached Tiruchengode only by about 10 p.m.

He began his speech at the Board High School by saying, "I am very tired." Welcome addresses were presented on behalf of the Taluk Board, Union Board, Taluk Cooperators, Samarasa Sanmarga Sangam and Adi Dravidar Mahajana Sangam.

"Untouchabilility is created by man. If Hindus and the Hindu religion have to flourish, this must be eradicated," he declared. After completing an arduous tour, and visiting so many organisations, Gandhiji began his 24-hour silence when he reached Pudupalayam.

12 February 1934, Pudupalayam

The Tiruchengode ashram, established by Rajaji, was located seven miles from the city in a small village called Pudupalyam. The day after Gandhiji arrived there was celebrated as a special festival day. Following Gandhiji, about 100 guests came to the ashram separately over a period of time. As the first day here was his day of silence, many of these visitors went back. Rajaji had issued a communication before Gandhiji arrived that he was here for rest, and that those with business with him should refrain from disturbing him. On the first day, Gandhiji, accompanied by a few workers, inspected the surroundings of the ashram and a nearby slum.

13 February 1934, Ashram meeting

On the next day, at the meeting on the Ashram Pavate grounds, Gandhiji gave some advice, after receiving the purses presented on behalf of khadi workers of the Gandhi ashram, and Pudupalayam villagers. "It must be examined to what extent the minds of caste Hindus in a village like Pudupalyam have changed, owing to the work done by some constituents in this ashram, who do not carry the taint of untouchability in their hearts," he said.

'I miss the love of Hindi'

A. Krishnan, who earlier served in the ashram kitchen, and was then working in the Khadi Vastralayam, has said that Gandhiji used to come and inspect the kitchen twice daily when he stayed at the ashram, to ensure that the kitchen was tidily maintained. On the occasion of this visit, he stayed at the residence of C. Rajagopalachariar. This was a small house, hence Gandhiji's meetings were held in its front compound. A platform was made for Gandhiji to sit on. He wrote thus in the ashram visitors' book. "I miss the love, enough use of Hindi, and knowledge of Sanskrit to understand *Gita*, more so because everything else is so good." He signed as 'Bapu' in Tamil and Hindi, dated 13 February 1934. At the ashram, as always, he read the *Gita* at prayer meetings.

It was usual for one person at these meetings to recite the slokas for those gathered to repeat, but, as those in the meeting were not familiar with Sanskrit, they were not able to repeat it uniformly. Further, in the two days he stayed at the ashram, Gandhiji realised that the ashram inhabitants did not know Hindi. This was why he wrote so in the visitors' book.

Smt. Abdus Salam

Smt. Abdus Salam[3] of Gandhiji's entourage had fever, and was asked to stay on at the ashram to convalesce. Before continuing on his tour, Gandhiji left her in the care of Lakshmiammal, the wife of M. K. Venkataraman. Gandhiji explained in detail the kind of food Mrs Salam was to be given, and that she should receive the care that he himself would have got. His final question was moving: "Will you treat her like your own mother?" Lakshmi ammal replied, "I will do so, Mahatmaji," only after hearing which did Gandhiji proceed on his tour. That he entrusted Dr Ranganathan with the responsibility of Smt. Abdus Salam's medical treatment showed Gandhiji's concern for her wellbeing.

"Doctor, give Smt. Abdus Salam whatever medicines you consider appropriate, or even kill her, I will not question your methods. But in the matter of food, my suggestions must be followed. Till her fever subsides you must give her orange juice, water and honey, and similar nourishment only." Gandhiji took a pair of scissors and cut the convalescing lady's hair himself. Later, he sent a letter expressing his happiness to the doctor. After two such days of rest, Gandhiji continued his tour.

14 February 1934, Namakkal

On the way from Pudupalayam to Salem, Gandhiji visited for the first time the birthplace of poet Ramalingam Pillai in Namakkal. The public meeting here was near the temple, on the square opposite the Kamalalayam hills. The arrangements jointly made by Mittadar Venkatachala Chettiar and advocate Nagaraja Iyer were efficient. The orderliness of the crowd, natural beauty of the place, and the timing were all almost unmatched, eliciting high praise even from Gandhiji, who said: "You have brought me to one of the most beautiful locations in India, a place most suitable for such meetings."

There were some 15,000 people, more than a quarter of whom were women. The Congress workers and policemen had made satisfactory arrangements to maintain order among the crowd. The Taluk Board president read out the welcome of the Board. Welcome speeches were read on behalf of Union Board and Harijans. The zamindar of Kooduthurai, K. Venkatachala Reddiar, presented a purse. A copper idol was presented to Gandhiji.

In their welcome address the Harijans said that through the munificence of some, money had been collected to build a temple, which, however, remained unfinished. They requested financial help to complete this work. Gandhiji referred to this and appealed to leaders in Namakkal to come forward with help. More than the purse presented at Senthamangalam by elders, Gandhiji was touched by the Rs 4 presented by children.

After receiving the welcome addresses at Kalappanaickenpatti and Belukurichi, he reached Rasipuram, where these were read out on behalf of Panchayat Board and Adi Dravidars. The purse collected by the employees of the District Urban Bank at Thoppampatti was handed over here.

Salem

In honour of Gandhiji's visit, a holiday was declared for all Municipal establishments in Salem. Attractive decorations were made at Gandhiji Tiffin House, and in front of Vysya Literary Society. On reaching Salem, Gandhiji went to Natesa Pandaram's house in Kumarasamipettai for rest till 3 p.m. Where he stayed was opposite the Salem College, later a post office building. While he was there, G. Ramachandra Naidu, P. Kandasamy Pillai, C. Ananthachariar, and S. C. Venkatappa Chettiar, along with some others who were engaged in service to Harijans, sought an interview. Many Harijans too visited him. Gandhiji named a Harijan Kandasamy Vadhiyar's daughter as 'Radha' and Sevappettai Sithalingam's son as 'Yogidas'. C. Vijayaraghavachariar met Gandhiji and had discussions with him. After the women's meeting, Gandhiji went to Vijayaraghavachariar's house at around 4 p.m. for some discussions. The *thinnai* (outer sitting platform) of that house, even after several modifications made to the house, long remained exactly as it was then. It became known as 'Gandhi Thinnai'. "He had peanuts and grapes when he came here. He placed a child of the house on his lap and talked with her," Smt. Vijayaraghavachariar told the author of this book with great joy.

Women's meeting

After resting in the afternoon, Gandhiji attended the women's meeting held in the hall on the upper floor of the college. Madhavi ammal garlanded him, and presented him a chain in which was inscribed, 'The greatest Harijan, M. K. Gandhi'. A purse was presented by Kamakshi ammal. Lalithambal read out a welcome in Hindi. Thereafter he visited a Harijan hostel in Mullavadi, and a few slums. In Kicchipalayam, the Harijan Workers' Sangam read out a welcome speech for him. He also inspected the school run by that sangam. On the way back he went to Subbaier Tiffin House, where there was something special.

'Gandhi Iyer' hotel

Subbaier had allowed Harijans to enter his canteen and to eat along with caste Hindus. Consequently, at first, no one patronised his tiffin house, and he suffered big losses. He, however, was firm in his conviction and had complete belief in the Mahatma. Success finally came to him, as, slowly, caste Hindus started coming to his hotel. Because of this, in some time, his hotel acquired much fame, and attracted a large number of customers.

Local people began to refer to him as 'Gandhi Iyer'. Hearing that the Mahatma was going to visit the 'Gandhi Iyer' hotel, people in Salem gathered in large numbers. When Gandhiji arrived at 3.30 p.m., neither his car could enter because of the crowd, nor could he get down and walk. Hence, the welcome address, garland and purse were handed over to him in the car itself. Thereafter, he went to the Vysya Literary Sangam and received their purse. Here, A. V. Ramachandra Chettiar presented him with a silver casket displaying intricate workmanship. On this casket were embossed the faces of Gandhiji and other national leaders. In Salem, the Grocery Merchants' Association and Shroff Merchants' Association handed over purses. Anjaneya Body Building Sangam also presented a welcome and purse.

After addressing a college assembly, Gandhiji was met by a five-year-old girl, who presented him with a silver plate, receiving an orange from him in return, as a token of his satisfaction.

Public meeting

At the public meeting held in the large grounds behind the college, more than 50,000 people attended. As the grounds were overflowing, the crowds had spilled on to the public thoroughfares adjacent to them. Welcome speeches and purses were presented on behalf of the Municipality, Taluk Board, the Salem public, District Board, Taluk Board Leaders' Association, Saurashtra Youth Association, Anjaneya Body Building Association, Bhagat Singh Youth Association, Vysya Literary Association, Kerala Samajam, Adi Dravidar Mahajana Sangam and the Town Council College Students.

The District Board president Dewan Bahadur S. Ellappa Chettiar, the Town Council president T. M. Chinnaiah Pillai, and the Taluk Board president S. P. Rajamanikka Pandaram read out welcome addresses on behalf of these institutions. As Gandhiji had to catch a train, he finished his speech quickly.

> I will say it in one sentence. All castes must have equal rights. If we believe that we are all creations of God, will there be any place for untouchability? We are all Harijans. It is caste Hindus who cannot go near God, because it is they who do not do their duty towards Harijans. To obtain the blessings of the Lord, we must uplift the status of Harijans.

Then he left for where he was staying, had his meal, and started for the railway station.

15 February 1934, Thanjavur

Leaving from Salem by Shencottah Passenger, via Tiruchi, Gandhiji reached Thanjavur early in the morning. The train was halted a furlong ahead of the station with the help of the railway authorities, and Gandhiji was taken from there to the Roman Catholic High School grounds, where the public meeting was to be held. As he was coming to this meeting, the sun was just rising, bathing the atmosphere in its cool rays. Gandhiji used this as a topic for his speech.

> Caste Hindus say that they accept all the reforms related to the eradication of untouchability, but desire that I give up just the matter of temple entry. They do not realise that this is the core of my movement.
>
> Now, I passed by the Thanjavur Big Temple. I saw the temple once, as in a few moments the sun rose, which, too, I saw. I asked myself whether the sun rises only for the caste Hindus, or also for Harijans. The sun does not differentiate. If the temple of God itself has been opened for Harijans, should not the temple built by man be opened to them? But the Sanatanis, who claim they are supporting all the reforms, refuse to lift a finger when it comes to this temple entry issue. Let them at least show that they consider the Harijans equal in all other matters.

Welcome addresses were read and presented on behalf of the Municipality, District Association, and Taluk Board. The purse on behalf of the Thanjavur public was presented through the Harijan Seva Sangam. A wax image of Gandhiji made by Sri Krishna Company of Thanjavur, and a beautiful silver plated brass plaque were presented by the Viswakarma Society.

Viswakarmas' handiwork

The plaque with delicate workmanship presented by the Viswakarma Society pleased Gandhiji. With figures of goddesses gilded in silver, on the back of this plate was etched: 'God is truth—a gift to Mahatma Gandhi from the Viswakarma Society, Thanjavur.' Gandhiji was keen to auction it at a good price. Hence, without referring to its price elsewhere, he took it to Belgaum (now a city in Karnataka, also a district) to be auctioned, but even there its bid started at Rs 5 and went up only to Rs 60. As he was unwilling to give away this attractive plate for Rs 60, Gandhiji put it up for auction again in Mysore at the commercial centre of Nipani (now in Belgaum District), noted for growing high-quality tobacco.

Gandhiji started the auction with a strong pitch, saying,

> This plate has been presented by the Viswakarmas of Thanjavur, with very intricate workmanship. I had thought to auction this only in Belgaum or here, but there was no attractive bid in Belgaum for it. I want at least the cost price of this plate, and trust that the Nipani people will not disappoint me. Now, who is there to offer me more than Rs 75?

Immediately, a bid of Rs 76 was received on behalf of an association. The attar, incense sticks, perfume products and other handworked articles from Thanjavur were also offered for auction here. After this, the Union Board in Ayyampettai gave him a formal welcome. The people of Mangudi stood on the road and offered him a purse. In Papanasam, at the Panchayat Board office, a welcome address written on palm leaf was read out on behalf of the Taluk Khadi Improvement Sangam by its vice-president. The welcome words in English of the Taluk Board and Panchayat Board were also presented without being read.

Kumbakonam

The first persons to be fortunate to welcome Gandhiji in Kumbakonam were the Viswakarma brass workers. At the corner of Kumbeswaran South and West streets, a welcome by brass workers other than Viswakarmas was also given.

There were many problems and tussles to welcome Gandhiji in Kumbakonam. From the time Gandhiji's arrival schedule was made known, a competition began. Unlike in any other place, the Town Council declared that they could not present their welcome at a public meeting, but only in their own headquarters. Gandhiji consented to receive their welcome there, and went to their Patel Nagar building to have their welcome address read out by Rao Bahadur N. Thiruvengadathu Iyengar. On the way there, Sanatanis showed black flags on Maheswaram Thirumanjana Street and Madathu street. They had been propagating strenuously from the day previous to his arrival that people should not attend his functions. All along Madathu Street were posters that said 'Gandhi go back'. Gandhiji smilingly passed by these posters as he went to the Town Council's welcome, almost as if he was endorsing these protests!

The welcome address said, "One should not go against traditions followed in temples, matters of society and religion, and further split the nation. It should be left to the improvement in economic conditions, and gradual change in the mindsets of people for such changes to happen. Hence, we hope that you will show us the way for the entire country to follow you, without giving any cause for such fighting and differences."

Thus, while receiving Gandhiji wholeheartedly, the welcome address clearly stated that the local people were against his movement for the temple entry of Harijans. Gandhiji responded to this welcome calmly, yet firmly.

> I greatly respect this welcome that you have given me, emphasising your strong concerns. Even after hearing your views, I am determined to carry on with my movement. It is only to provide full justice to the Harijans among the thinking of the general public that I have embarked on this tour. Wherever I have had temples opened to Harijans, thousands of caste Hindus have welcomed it. Their views are in support of temple entry for Harijans.

He left for the public meeting from there, but there, too, was a conflict of views, not on temple entry, but on who should have the authority to welcome Gandhiji!

Another conflict

The responsibility of welcoming Gandhiji in Kumbakonam town had been given to one Dr Sambasivan. That he had not gone to jail in the cause of the nation was held as a major fault against him. Further, it was argued that he had not included in this welcoming committee some martyrs who had gone to jail; and so a parallel welcome committee was formed, of which a doctor was the president. This led to a great deal of confusion. As soon as Gandhiji reached the venue of the public meeting at Town High School grounds, the question arose as to who should be the first to read the welcome speech.

Meanwhile, the Sanatanis were peacefully demonstrating with black flags opposite the meeting venue. Dr Sambasiva Iyer magnanimously yielded ground. Although the purse presented by Dr Venkatachari of the parallel welcome group was less than that of Dr Sambasiva Iyer, the welcome was given by him. Next, on behalf the Harijan Seva Sangam, Dr M. K. Sambasivam read out the words of welcome. Stating that he had received an anonymous telegram that the welcome of Dr Sambasivan's group should not be accepted, Gandhiji said:

> For [a person like] me, who is involved in Harijan welfare work, there is no difference between a Congressman or non-Congressman. If a non-Congressman becomes the friend of a Harijan, if he has faith in religion, passion to work, it is a Congressman's duty to follow his directives. If Congressmen feel that Harijan uplift work is by right only theirs, and that non-Congressman should stay away, untouchability will never be eradicated from our religion. There is no political motive in this issue.

Interviews

From here, Gandhiji went to Gopal Das's house on Big Street, received the purse handed over by women, and proceeded to Arogya Ashram for rest. Before that, there was a graduation ceremony for Hindi students, at which he awarded books and stationery materials to the successful students. The Hindi Prachar Sabha offered a welcome to him with a purse. Gandhiji also gave an interview to the Self-Respect Group of the town, while the local Gujaratis presented a purse. The wife of Dr M. K. Sambasivan, Thangam Ammal, donated a gold necklace. Raghava Sastri's daughter gave four bangles, one of which Gandhiji himself helped to remove from her wrist. Some Harijans met him and requested that the school that was being run in the nearby village of Koranattu Karpur, which had been shut by the Taluk

Board, may be reopened. Gandhiji replied that he would get the school reopened, and that the Harijan Seva Sangam would oversee the running of that school. He said he would like to allot half an hour to discuss the issue of untouchability and dharma with the Sanatanis of Kumbakonam, but the Brahmin Mahasabha refused to accept this invitation. Their condition was that Gandhiji should agree to the view that the shastras were the final word on the matter, and then come for discussion. Further, half an hour was inadequate for such discussion, they said.

Another 'Sivakasi' at Koratacheri

Although the sun was beating down in Kumbakonam when he started, he was forced to travel in an open car to enable the public to see him. Starting at 2.30 p.m, it was 5 p.m. when he reached Tiruvarur, because another 'Sivakasi' happened en route. Nachiarkoil, Tiruchirai and Kodavasal did not take up too much of his time. He was presented a purse on behalf of Ammayappan village. It was Koratacheri that became another 'Sivakasi'. There was a sand bank below the road he travelled, where the meeting was held. There was a quarter mile between the road and this point, half of which could not be negotiated by car. The Mahatma had to walk on thorny sands beyond that. There were no arrangements either to control the crowd or to safely escort Gandhiji and his team to the dais, and they got caught in the crowd. There was no way out of this, and the sands were hot underfoot as the sun beat down mercilessly. The swirling sand dust made breathing difficult, and there was still a furlong left to walk to reach the dais. But somehow Gandhiji managed to do it.

An old man attempted to sing a poem that he had composed on Gandhiji, but not allowing this, Gandhiji tried to get down from the stage quickly, after receiving the welcome speeches and purses. The tumult on his return had increased severalfold, compared to when he arrived, and the prominent leaders in his entourage got scattered in the melee that resulted. In this confusion, C. Rajagopalachariar managed to get the car to reach Gandhiji, got him into it, and reached the road.

"The trouble taken on the sands today is no less than the disruption caused by the rain at Sivakasi. There were five minutes allotted for this meeting, but it took one and a half hours," said Dr. Rajan.

Four welcome addresses were presented on behalf of Nannilam Taluk Board, the Korattacheri Koothanallur region public, Nannilam Taluk Harijan Seva Sangam, and Iluppur General Public Seva Sangam. An 'ashtothram' (poem in praise) composed by Duraisamy Pillai of this village, containing 108 names depicting Gandhiji's life story, and the various services rendered by him, was presented to him on this occasion.

Tiruvarur

At the Tiruvarur welcome, Ramanuja Mudaliar, on his and the public's behalf, presented two purses. The welcome of the Town Council was read out by its vice-president, T. N. Sabapathy Mudaliar. Gandhiji warned, "Till untouchability remains as a sore in Hindu society, India cannot achieve a predominant place in the world."

After having his dinner at the house of the senior Mudaliar of the Vadapathimangalam Estate, Gandhiji and party left for Nagapattinam.

Nagapattinam

He reached Nagapattinam after receiving purses at Manakollai and Manjakollai. At the public meeting held on the large grounds in front of the Government Office building, Gandhiji received the welcome speeches of the Town Council, Nagapattinam Taluk Board, Charkha Sangam, Harijan Seva Sangam, Hindi students, Vaduvur village folk and several others.

The Town Council welcome address was read out by Ramanatha Mudaliar and the Taluk Board welcome by Manaithuna Natha Desagar. There was a moving sight as an elderly lady came up to Gandhiji in tears, presented a silver cup, and touched his feet. Gandhiji's speech that day reflected his far-sighted vision.

"It might appear that my appeal has been only to caste Hindus, but it is in fact an appeal to all of humanity. If I am able to convince the caste Hindus to give up untouchability, it will go a long way to promote brotherhood among all Hindus. The world today is yearning for a spirit of brotherhood, is it not?" he asked. Even today, the world is longing for this brotherhood.

The Self-Respect Group waved black flags against Gandhiji. In honour of his visit, the Gandhi Samaj arranged a feast. That night Gandhiji and his group stayed as guests of C. Rajam at 'Ahmad Villa' at Kadambadi, and left in the morning for Nagore.

Although there had been several engagements the previous day, it was the ordeal at Korattacheri on the sands that had exhausted Gandhiji. Hence, against the schedule of a 6 a.m. departure from Kadambadi, Gandhiji left only at 7 a.m.

16 February 1934, Karaikal

From early in the morning huge swarms of crowds had gathered at the Karaikal (now a town in the Union Territory of Puducherry) beach front. At Nagore (now a town in Nagapattinam district), Sri Tilakar Library's president Ma. Thi. Muthuvelu Chettiar presented a purse on behalf of the citizens, and a welcome of the library. In Karaikal, on behalf of the Harijan Seva Sangam, Ilayathangudi Rangasamy Naidu, the Tirunaniyar Commune Mayor, read out a welcome. Consul General, vice-president Thyagaraja Pillai presented a purse.

It was the second time that Gandhiji visited a French province (in India) during this tour. In Kerala, as part of his tour, he had been to Mahe (now a town in Puducherry). As it was an Indo-French region, Gandhiji referred to the French traditions and emphasised the connection with untouchability eradication. "It was France that gave the world the slogan 'Liberty, Equality and Fraternity'. But there have been very few who have actually put this into practice. The people who are most guilty of not implementing this are the Hindus. They quote God's name to perpetrate untouchability."

At the end of the meeting, a purse was presented on behalf of students.

Tharangambadi

A public holiday had been declared in Tharangambadi, Poraiyaru and nearby places, and all the shops were closed. The entire population had gathered at Tharangambadi Fort entrance to see Gandhiji at the public meeting arranged there. Welcome addresses and purses were presented on behalf of the people of Tharangambadi, Poraiyaru and its surrounding area, and Thillaiyadi.

Mayavaram

Here, too, a holiday had been declared for the Town Council schools in honour of Gandhiji's visit. Even as Gandhiji's car entered the southern end of Mahadana Street in Mayavaram, the merchants of Chinnakadai Street presented him a purse towards the Harijan Fund. The public meeting was held in Rajan Park grounds. Welcome addresses were presented on behalf of the Town Council and Taluk Board. The Taluk Board welcome speech was read by N. Somasundaram Pillai. A purse encased in a silver casket was presented on behalf of the public by Town Council president, P. Nagalingam Pillai; it contained Rs 101.

"I cannot express thanks for the purse that you have given me, because I know Mayavaram very well. I expected a much higher contribution from you," he said with some disappointment. "The last time I visited, many who had attended the meeting then have not come today. I can only surmise that they do not have wholehearted interest in Harijan welfare."

Gandhiji made some prior arrangements before reaching Sirkazhi (or Sikali, now in Mayiladuthurai district of Tamil Nadu). Some time ago a devastating cyclone had ravaged that area, leaving widespread destruction in its wake. The travails of Harijans in this disaster were more than those of others. Hence, even as he started from Nagapattinam early in the morning, he sent Thakkar Bapa, and Madras Seva Sangam secretary, G. Ramachandran ahead to Sirkazhi to assess the damages caused in the villages in the region, and report to him. They, along with Cyclone Relief Group leader A. Subbaraya Mudaliar, went there, and joined Gandhiji at the public meeting in Sirkazhi.

Sirkazhi

Festoons decorated the route taken by Gandhiji in Sirkazhi. There were large crowds on the street to catch a glimpse of this 'Man of God'. At the meeting arranged in an attractive pandal put up in

Oozhiyakkaran Gardens, Gandhiji was greeted by the welcome group president, S. Vedagiri Mudaliar and the secretary, C. S. Saminatha Chettiar. On behalf of Sirkazhi general public and Taluk Board, welcome speeches and purses were offered. Idamanal Balakrishna Naidu not only read out a welcome address, but, in a humorous vein, presented a basket of grapes plus Rs 5 for Gandhiji's tiffin.

A picture of Sri Ramakrishna was given to Gandhiji, who delivered a moving speech. He started by saying that owing to the great losses caused by the cyclone, he had not expected any purses to be given at Sirkazhi. Still, receiving money separately for the Sirkazhi Harijan Fund and Bihar earthquake relief was most praiseworthy.

"75 per cent of what I collect for the Harijan Fund is spent for the welfare of Harijans in that region itself. I would like to say this to the Harijans and Harijan workers who have been affected by the cyclone here," he said, as he consoled them.

'I am not a plaything'

At the meeting, there were some who held black flags in front. During his speech they stood quietly with the flags in hand. Noticing this, Gandhiji remarked,

> Even though they are holding black flags, I appreciate the respect and orderliness with which they are doing so. They have full right to display their emotion in this way. They perhaps feel that the money collected here may not be utilised for the purpose of its collection. The people behind this black flag demonstration believe that I am a plaything of owners and wealthy people. I would like to promise them just one thing—*I am not a plaything of anyone but God.*

Gandhiji also spoke of his discussions with members of the Self-Respect Group.

> I had said yesterday that there is much in common between me and the Self-Respect Group. They say that there is no person like God, and if there is one, it is the human race. I do admit that I am superstitious enough to believe that there is a God, but I am not ready to enter into an argument with them on words. If they prefer to use the term 'human race', I am willing to go along

with them and refer to God as such. They claim that love and human compassion are their objectives. I have told them that I appreciate that, and that I am 100 per cent with them. They say that wealth should be spread evenly. As an objective this is fine. However, when they are saying all this in mere words, I, on my part, am actually approaching people of means with love to collect money for the Harijan movement, Bihar earthquake relief, or for the poor and needy people, thereby reducing the wealth of those donors—this I explained to them.

In this manner thousands of people have shared their wealth with poor people. I do not see how else the divide between the poor and the rich can be bridged. I said all this from my 50 years experience in public life. This divide will take some time to bridge.

At the end, Gandhiji appealed to the Self-Respect Group members to support his movement.

A boy faints

As Gandhiji's speech was in progress, cries from the crowd of "Soda! Soda!" rent the air. Gandhiji realised that in the heat of the sun and suffocation of the crowd, a small boy had fainted. Gandhiji's presence of mind, not just on major issues, but even small incidents like these, was in evidence here as he summoned Dr Rajan and said, "Rajan, there is a first-aid kit in my bag, please go and immediately attend to the boy." The boy was revived before Gandhiji finished his speech. Thereafter, Gandhiji went to the Sirkazhi Panchayat Board office building, had lunch, rested for about two hours, then went to K. Chidambaranatha Mudaliar's house and collected a purse for the Bihar Earthquake Relief Fund. While he was having lunch, the principal of Parangippettai National Christian School, Annie-Marie Peterson, came to meet him, along with her students.

An interruption

As per schedule, Gandhiji was to have reached Chidambaram by 11 a.m., but, due to unavoidable circumstances, he and his party could reach only about 3.35 p.m. As a result, he had to complete a lot of schedules in the limited time available. He could fulfil these engagements only if the car speeded up, but because of the crowds gathered everywhere to see Gandhiji, the car could not be driven fast.

There was yet another impediment to the car accelerating. An unscheduled event had been arranged by one Kunjithapadam. On the way from the railway station, a large, decorated pandal was erected at the bend of the road by this person, and he almost compelled Gandhiji to get down from the car, enter the building and receive the welcome. Since this was unplanned, Gandhiji wanted this welcome to be conducted at the car itself, but Kunjithapadam was adamant, and insisted that Gandhiji get down and come to the building. Gandhiji did not like this, and asked the driver to move the car. Instantly, Kunjithapadam lay prostrate in front of the car in a kind of satyagraha. "Oh, have you begun to show your satyagraha to me?" remarked Gandhiji, preparing to get down from the car. Meanwhile, people removed Kunjithapadam from the way and allowed the car to pass.

On the way to the Taluk office, Gandhiji received the welcome and purse from the Thillai Samarasa Sanmargam members. At the Taluk Board headquarters, the welcome addresses in English and Tamil were read out by T. S. Kanakasabapathy Pillai, and a purse was presented. It was requested in the welcome that the collections made in Chidambaram be given to the Nandanar Education Society there.

Swami Sahajananda

Brahmachari Swami Sahajananda had established several institutions for Harijan uplift—the Nandanar Mutt, temple, school and hostel. Born into a Harijan family, Swami Sahajananda, a Tamilian not versed in English, had studied Tamil and Sanskrit at a young age, equipped himself with knowledge of the shastras, and had dedicated himself to the work of amelioration of the Harijans' condition. Because of his devoted service to the Nandanar Education Society and its associated establishments, he had to encounter extreme societal opposition and boycott in that town.

Hearing that Gandhiji was coming, Swami Sahajananda wrote him a letter inviting him to Chidambaram, and to stay at the Nandanar Mutt. On receiving the letter, Gandhiji instructed Dr Rajan that, should Chidambaram be included on his tour schedule, he would stay only at the Nandanar Mutt. Dr Rajan, in his journal, wrote that, although many changes were made in Gandhiji's schedule later, his visit to Chidambaram was not dropped.

A donor's desire

Despite the affection he may have for anyone, that Gandhiji would not cross limits or change his principles for anyone was made clear in his response to Kanakasabapathy Pillai's suggestion. "Your suggestion to give your donation to the Nandanar Education Society gives me pleasure. The donor's desire is indeed important, but the collection now is only for the Harijan Fund, and it can be used only for work related to the welfare of Harijans. The Nandanar Education Society's requirement will also be separately considered by the donor," he said.

Charkha Sangam

Thereafter, Gandhiji proceeded to the khadi shop of the All India Charkha Sangam. The shop manager, A. Balakrishna Pillai, received from Gandhiji's hand the shield the shop had been awarded for record sales. A purse was also presented to Gandhiji at the shop. Then he went to the Nandanar School for inspection, and complimented the students who came there from Salem to study. Proceeding with his group to Nandanar Mutt from there, he had lunch, rested for a while, and went to attend meetings.

Kunjithapadam

The first programme was at Annamalai Nagar, followed by the public meeting. But, here again, Kunjithapadam did not let go, and used all his wiles to force Gandhiji to come to the pandal in Senguzhuvarai Street. What happened thereafter has been described by Dr. Rajan:

> When we left Nandanar Mutt by car (arranged by the Chidambaram committee), there was a car in front of ours, as though it was showing the way. There were four friends in it driving slowly in such a manner as to not allow our car to pass. In spite of us asking our driver to speed up, he was not in a position to do so. Neither was there any way to take a different

route to avoid the vehicle in front. Even when we tried to find an alternate route, the car in front managed to come around and continue to block the road in front. Ultimately we stopped near the railway gate where Kunjithapadam had done his satyagraha. Kunjithapadam held a purse in his hand and came and stood in front of the car, forcing the Mahatma to get down and come to his mutt. In spite of Gandhiji saying no firmly, Kunjithapadam did not yield. The crowd there was also massive.

When we asked the driver to drive on, he could not. Seeing all this, Gandhiji suddenly got out of the car, and started walking away from the pandal. Immediately we in the car got down to follow him, twining our hands around him to ensure that he was not hurt by the surging crowds.

There was another corollary to this incident. Kunjithapadam filed a case that, when he had lain prostrate on the road in front of Gandhiji's car, Dr Rajan had kicked him. Not just that, he even summoned Gandhiji as a witness. However, upon the intervention of several prominent people, he withdrew his plaint.

Excess of affection

Gandhiji and his group walked for a furlong and reached the venue of the public meeting an hour ahead. As there were already huge crowds at the venue, they conducted the meeting, and proceeded to Annamalai University, in Chidambaram. At the meeting, the Mahatma said: "Out of an excess of affection, the trouble caused by some friends needs to be mentioned by me. In my tours, time adherence is of great importance. Without that, functions cannot be organised and conducted. Friends must understand this. I should not be prevented from moving merely out of boundless affection." He also said that Kunjithapadam's insistence on attending his welcome had put Gandhiji and his group in grave danger because of the constantly surging crowds surrounding them.

A welcome address on behalf of the South Arcot Harijan Seva Sangam was read out at this public meeting held at Annamalai Nagar Hall grounds. The Chidambaram public, and Hindi Premi Mandal presented purses.

Peace at Annamalai Nagar

The atmosphere was peaceful at Annamalai Nagar. Led by the Vice Chancellor, S. A. Rangarajan, and Professor S. Somasundara Bharathi, the professors and students welcomed Gandhiji. Under the aegis of Srimushnam (a town panchayat in Cuddalore district) Mirasdar Sangam, Sundararamier presented a purse. A welcome address was also presented by Annamalai University Improvement Society. It stated that students were involved in conducting a night school for the education of Harijans. Gandhiji referred to this and said, "More than adults, it is the students who can render such useful service." Gandhiji also remarked that his friend V. S. Srinivasa Sastri, as the former Vice Chancellor of this university, had devoted much care to its growth.

Gandhiji went to the railway station directly from this meeting and left for Cuddalore. En route, at Killai and Parangippettai stations, purses were presented to him on the platform. The purse at Parangippettai was from Thyagu Memorial Sangam.

Temple doors closed

There was an incident at Chidambaram that was farcical, but could have turned ugly. Apprehending that, taking advantage of Gandhiji's visit, the Harijans would cause a stampede and force an entry into the temple, all the temple doors were closed. Because of this, the people inside the temple also could not get out, and, hence, could not meet Gandhiji that day. Further, the Sanatanis of the town had distributed leaflets saying, "Go back Gandhi! The one who forcibly collects money from town to town—go back!"

Left in the dark

There was no adequate lighting at railway stations in those days. Hence, it was a problem whenever Gandhiji arrived at night. Everyone would surround him, making it difficult for those who had come to welcome him to see their way and to lead him out of the station. That night, when Gandhiji arrived in Cuddalore at 9 p.m., he adroitly solved the problem on his own. He somehow found a way through the crowd and managed to reach his car.

However, the people were not fooled. They came straight to the car and gave him their welcome write-ups and purses on behalf of the people of Nellikkuppam (now a municipality in the Cuddalore city corporation), Cuddalore O. T. Youth Association, Cuddalore N. T. Association, Dhana Sangam, the Workers' Association, and women. As Gandhi got down from the train, a traditional welcome with garlands was offered by the Town Council president, P. Govindasamy Chettiar, and the Gandhi Welcome Committee's R. A. Sivananda Mudaliar. Welcome speeches were also given on behalf of the Town administration and the District Committee at District Committee headquarters in Devanampattinam Street. The president of the Town Council read out the welcome address in Tamil, and the District Committee president, T. M. Jambulingam Mudaliar, in English.

District Committee

In its welcome, the District Committee said that it had been helping the Harijan students' hostel in Nandanar school with financial aid. It added that an Adi Dravidar representative had been elected from the reserved constituency of Ammavatta Society. This earned Gandhiji's praise. He said, "However, you must not be satisfied with this. Untouchability must be eradicated from its roots."

The MLC of that area, K. M. Duraisamy Mudaliar, gave a diamond ring to Gandhiji. Thereafter, together with Omandur Ramasamy Reddiar (noted Gandhian and later, chief minister of Madras State), Gandhiji left for the public meeting at Manjakuppam (one of the three large divisions of Cuddalore city). On the way, at Cuddalore Taluk Board office, A. Lakshminarayana Reddiar gave a welcome oration in Tamil, and presented a purse for the Harijan Fund and Bihar Earthquake Relief Fund. These were handed over by his four-year-old daughter. The Cuddalore Body Builders' Association also handed over a purse.

Public meeting

At the public meeting, P. Thanickachalam Pillai read out a welcome speech in Hindi. A purse was presented on behalf of the citizens. Gandhiji apologised for the delay in arriving at this meeting; it was almost midnight. He explained that at the last moment he had had to accept the invitation of Pondicherry friends, leading to this delay and the necessity of holding this meeting so late. The welcome group at Pondicherry was led by advocate Swaminatha Mudaliar, which was opposed by Sellanna Naicker and Bharathi Dasan Mudaliar. The Pondicherry visit, originally cancelled, was reinstated, based on the persuasion of V. Subbiah and others, who had gone to meet Gandhiji.

"You could have given more," said Gandhiji. "Your contribution to the Harijan Fund will go towards abolition of untouchability and inspire confidence in them. Never consider Harijans as inferior to you."

Gandhiji stayed that day at the bungalow of Dewan Bahadur P. Subbarayulu Reddiar in Devanampattinam Street.

17 February 1934, Pondicherry

At Pondicherry (renamed Puducherry in 2006), sitting on a table at the public meeting grounds in the morning, Gandhiji said: "My efforts now are to shatter the stony hearts of people. They should understand that divinity can be achieved not through subjugation of people, but the yielding of equal rights. I trust there is no untouchability in Pondicherry. If it is there, eradicate it."

The president of the Pondicherry Harijan Seva Sangam, J. Sourinathan, read the welcome address. Welcome was also accorded on behalf of Pondicherry Harijans, and Kurukapathy Sri Sathyananda Sanmarga Education Society. The issue of unification of Pondicherry territory with India after freedom had been taken up with Gandhiji in Delhi by S. R. Subramaniam, R. Purushottama Reddiar, and Ku. Sivaprakasam Mudaliar. Gandhiji was fully seized of the problem, and had arranged for them to meet Prime Minister Jawaharlal Nehru to discuss the matter. When Subramaniam requested that this unification move should have the blessings of Gandhiji, he readily agreed.

Sanatanis' conference

As Gandhiji was touring the northern part of Madras State, a conference of Sanatanis of Tamil districts took place in the south at Madurai. With the Sankaracharya of Puri being the president of this conference, and Rao Sahib N. Natesa Iyer, the welcome committee president, the condemnation that was heaped upon Gandhiji did not come as a surprise. Outlining the objectives of this Sanatani conference, Natesa Iyer scornfully said, "Our aim is not to forcibly collect a crore of rupees from unsuspecting girls and boys and reluctant merchants through donations of rings, bangles, gold chains and cash."

The Sankaracharya of Puri added that issues arising out of established traditions of our ancestors should not be put to vote by people for change, and went on to say that, "Gandhi is neither a Sanatani, nor a person who follows the established tradition of caste. He does not have belief in the Vedas or our temples." In this conference, resolutions were passed against temple entry and untouchability eradication movements.

Despite all of this, Gandhiji never wavered from his resolve.

Bhoodanam

Going to Panruti from Pondicherry, Gandhiji went on to visit the Gandhi Kuppam slum at Tiruvennainallur (a taluk in Viluppuram district). At Panruti, he received a welcome address read by S. K. Chettiar of the Union Board, and accepted the welcome and purses on behalf of the citizens, and the association of commercial clerks. In Gandhi Kuppam, one person donated land to Gandhiji (a person from Chozhavandan had already made a similar donation). Gandhiji's spiritual heir Vinobaji had taken up Bhoodan as a movement, and had defined its guiding principles.

The donation of Kadaya Gounder of Thakkai village on that day satisfied the broad conditions of bhoodan. Gounder was introduced to Gandhiji by a teacher, Govindarao Gurzali, who had established the 'Kripashramam' at Gandhi Kuppam for service to Harijans. Kadaya Gounder declared that he was donating 1 acre and 78 cents of land to Kripashramam for construction of a building. Gandhiji was touched by this gesture; and blessed Gounder. Thereafter, Gandhiji and his party went to Kripashramam for lunch. Inside the ashram, welcome and purses were presented on behalf of Villupuram Women's Association, Jains' association, Thathva Gnana Sabha, Tiruvennainallur public, as well as Tindivanam Taluk and Villupuram Taluk residents.

Tiruvannamalai

On the way to Tiruvannamalai, Ramakrisnaier, Venkatesa Mudaliar and Ramasamy Naicker welcomed Gandhiji at Tirukoilur with garlands. At a meeting of some 20,000 people, purses were presented by the Harijan Seva Fund Committee, and Temple Tamil Sangam. At a place called Vandimodu opposite the Ramana ashram, more than 30,000 people had gathered. Gandhiji was welcomed on behalf of the welcome committee by P. S. M. Thirthagiri Chettiar, and on behalf of Chengam Taluk Board by Em. Mi. Rangasamy Chettiar. A welcome and purse were presented on behalf of the Town administration. One person presented a book, *Ramana Sanctum Tradition*, to Gandhiji, who advised, "Just as you are sitting now without any distinction of caste, you must always live likewise."

As he spoke, the noise and confusion increased, and he descended from the dais to go to the railway station. The train was half an hour late. Thinking about how he could profitably spend that half hour in the station, Gandhiji decided to conduct an auction from his car itself of articles received. He collected some money for the Earthquake Relief Fund also. As he was involved in this work, the Tiruvannamalai Adi Dravidar Movement Sangam's welcome was read and presented by R. Arumuga Pillai.

A German youth

The train that brought Gandhiji from Tiruvannamalai reached Vellore at 9.30 p.m. There was a crowd of 10,000 waiting for him at the railway station. Wading through this crowd, Gandhiji was led forward by Peutto, a German youth. Either jostled by the crowd, or because he tripped, Peutto fell down, and was trampled by that undisciplined mass of people, becoming unconscious. Getting into the car, Gandhiji said, "Rajan, stop the engine, go and check. I think Peutto has fallen down and been trampled on."

Owing to the pressure of the crowd, electric posts were bent and the lights went off, plunging the area into darkness. Dr Rajan discovered that Peutto had indeed fallen down. He lifted him into the car, drove to MLC Ramasamy Mudaliar's house, where Gandhiji was to stay, and attended to Peutto. Gandhiji sat beside him for an hour, and only after he partially recovered consciousness did he go for his prayers. Peutto recovered full consciousness only the next morning.

18 February 1934, Harijan school

There were many people who joined the prayer meeting early next morning. After that, Gandhiji inspected the Harijan school in the paper workshop, and proceeded to the town, where he received the welcome of the citizens, as also the purse given by the villagers who had gathered. He went into the slum and enquired after the conditions there with much concern. Here, the Adi Dravidar Improvement Society read out a welcome speech.

'I will not leave without the Harijan fund'

Gandhiji who invented satyagraha had to himself stage a satyagraha of sorts in Vellore. At the Town Council headquarters, holding out a silver plate of cash, he eagerly asked the Council president, "Is this plate for you or for Harijans?" "For you," replied the president, V. T. Rangaswami Iyengar. Gandhiji took the welcome address and purse given here, and left, without giving a speech, for the District Association to accept their welcome. There, the North Arcot District Association president, Janab C. Abdul Hakim, welcomed him. The vice-president V. M. Ramasamy Mudaliar read the welcome address.

Noting that no purse was presented by the District Association, Gandhiji then firmly asked, "Where is the Harijan fund? I will not leave without it," and sat back in his chair, adding that, "A small Town Council gave Rs 200, whereas you have given nothing!" The president C. Abdul Hakim offered to give Rs 200. But Gandhiji was not prepared to accept his personal donation alone, and said: "If I were to receive your money, I could receive it even after going back to Madras. What has happened to your colleagues in the committee?" Thereafter, Rs 50 from the other members was added to the Rs 200 from the president and Rs 250 was handed over. A Harijan member gave one rupee. Receiving the money, Gandhiji left for the public meeting, at which purses were presented on behalf of the general public, Vellore Sri Mahant High school, Cooperative Society, Voorhees College (in Vellore), Salamanattham village, and Calamur.

The following incident is an extract from the book *The Way Shown by Gandhi*, written by Akkoor Ananthachari.

> A Harijan boy had come to the meeting, carrying a large garland that he himself had strung for Gandhiji, who enquired about the boy, and, after being told, put the garland around the boy's neck. Not only that, he made him sit beside him on the dais. The name of that boy was R. Subramanian, and till his last breath, he worked truly and untiringly for Harijan uplift.

Public meetings

At the public meeting in Katpadi, Kannappa Mudaliar presented a purse on behalf of the public. The sands of Gudiyatham (a municipality in Vellore district) were burning under the sun, yet some 7,000 people gathered there to welcome Gandhiji. Welcome and purses were presented on behalf of the Town Council, Taluk Board, Harijan Seva Sangam and Youth Association. Thereafter, Gandhiji left for Ambur, receiving en route the welcome on behalf of the public at a place called Pallikondan. At the public meeting in Ambur, Thangavelu and Kasi gave a purse on behalf of the public. There were some Christian padres at Ambur, such as Arch Gould, who had also attended the welcome. At Periankuppam, too, a welcome address and purse were presented.

'A car programme'

Gandhiji went to Vaniyambadi after this, and, from there, to Nattrampalli village, where, under the aegis of Sri Ramakrishna Mutt and Swami Sarva Gnanada's leadership, village improvement works were being successfully undertaken. Gandhiji walked around the Sri Ramakrishna Mutt and accepted the purse presented by the general public. Akkoor Ananthachari has written about this visit in *The Way Shown by Gandhi* in the following words:

> At the time Gandhiji undertook his tour to North Arcot district, a request was made that he visit the village of Nattrampalli. This invitation was sent by the head of the Sri Ramakrishna Mutt in that village, Sarva Gnanada. As this request was made after the tour itinerary was finalised, this village had not been included in it.

However, Gandhiji decided at the last minute that he would visit that village. He, therefore, had to alter his schedule and travel five miles extra to reach it. This change was not liked by Dr Rajan and Ranipet Kalyanaramaier, bearing in mind Gandhiji's health. Still, not wanting to go against Gandhiji's wish, Dr Rajan termed this visit a 'car programme', indicating that, at Nattrampalli, Gandhiji would address the people from the car itself.

As soon as Gandhiji's car reached Sri Ramakrishna Mutt, Dr Rajan sent for the Swamiji. The people of the village were not aware that Gandhiji was coming, and hence, there was no crowd. The Swamiji came up to the car, and was absolutely overcome to see Gandhiji, inviting him into the ashram.

Gandhiji, too, in deference to the Swamiji's request, got down from the car and went into the ashram. Prayers were offered. Gandhiji stayed till the end, received the vibhuti, returned to the car, and asked the Swamiji, 'I hope you are satisfied?' The Swamiji, engulfed in a flood of happiness, stammered a reply. Observing this, Gandhiji's face brightened. It could be clearly seen from this the reverence Gandhiji had for Sri Ramakrishna Paramahamsa, and the service being rendered by his institution.

Idgah meeting, Tiruppathur

At Tiruppathur, 15,000 people awaited Gandhiji at the public meeting on the Idgah grounds. The Tiruppathur Town Council welcome was presented by its president, M. Viswanatha Mudaliar, and that of the Taluk Board by Ka. Shanmuga Mudaliar. Welcome addresses on behalf of the general public, the Ramakrishna Mutt, and the Hindi Prachar Sabha were handed over without being read. Purses, too, were presented. Gandhiji responded to all the welcome speeches together. By then he and his entourage were exhausted after such strenuous touring. With no sign of the noise in the crowd abating, Gandhiji spoke briefly. "It is a sin to term even one person as untouchable," he said, and left for the Christ Society ashram.

Christian ashram

There is a story behind Gandhiji's visit to this Christian ashram, which was being run on the tenets of promoting oneness and national feeling, and not forcing Hindus to convert to Christianity. A European named Patton, and a Tamilian, Jesudasan, were two double-degree holding doctorates, bachelors, who ran this ashram very much on the pattern of Hindu institutions. In 1928, when Dr Jesudasan had been to the Sabarmati Ashram, when attending the International Goodwill Conference, he had invited Gandhiji to visit the Christian family ashram. So, when the Madras tour was being finalised, Gandhiji told Dr Rajan that this ashram visit should be included in the itinerary.

'Like coming home'

When Gandhiji came to the dais at this public meeting, Dr Jesudasan sat next to him to translate his speech. The Mahatma, however, remained silent. After some time Dr Jesudasan asked, "Bapu, are you not going to speak?" Gandhiji replied, "What speech? Should you not first introduce me to the audience?" Dr Jesudasan said, "Do you need to be introduced at all?" to which Gandhiji retorted with a laugh, "I am only trying to confuse you!" The truth was that Gandhiji was exhausted after such a demanding tour.

Many of Gandhiji's followers had been trained in this Christian ashram. Still, in 1934, on learning that Gandhiji was going to visit this ashram, some people met him at Vellore to dissuade him from visiting it as they felt that this ashram was engaged in secret conversions of people to Christianity. Speaking at the public meeting on the ashram premises, Gandhiji said:

> Coming here feels like coming home. For many years I have been wanting to come here. It is not enough if caste Hindus merely touch the Harijans physically; they must touch them with their hearts. Anyone considering the other of inferior status to him is only at a loss himself. If you look at it in this context, not only Hindus but people of all faiths and religions in the world must seek to establish brotherhood—that is the aim of this movement.
>
> Alcoholic substances make a person mad and destroy his body and spirit. In that way, an alcoholic is similar to a man who contemplates suicide. Therefore, Harijans who are addicted to alcohol must give up this addiction. Some Harijans say that till the caste Hindu gives up alcohol consumption, they should not

ask this of them. Should one lie merely because another speaks untruth?

Krishna

After the public meeting, a boy ran up to Gandhiji and requested, "Sir, please give me a name." Gandhiji looked at him and, noticing his dark complexion, named him, "Krishna," after the blue-complexioned god. Some people came and fell at Gandhiji's feet, prompting him to say, "This is not a greeting, but an obstacle in my path."

Thereafter he went to the private meeting arranged for the workers of the Christian ashram. He advised them on the ways in which service was to be rendered, before proceeding to the chapel in the ashram and taking part in their prayers. When hymns on Jesus were sung in the solemn atmosphere of the chapel, Gandhiji's heart was filled with joy.

On the way from Jolarpettai to Madras, at a place called Kothandapatti, he gave the wife of Tha. Aa. Amutha Iyengar a Tamil–Hindi primer, and asked her to learn Hindi.

19 February 1934, Day of silence

Of the two days that Gandhiji spent in Madras, 19 and 20 February, the Maharani of Vizianagaram, Vidyavati, and Ambujammal visited him on the first day, which was his day of silence. The next day, he did not have as many engagements as he'd had on his previous visit. The main reason for Gandhiji to stay for two days in Madras was to review the Harijan service taken up by the nationalist S. Ganesan, and render whatever help necessary. Moreover, the Madras Harijan Seva Sangam meeting was to be held here. A merchant of Tiruvallikkeni, Prathap Roopchand, received Gandhiji as his train arrived in Perambur early in the morning. It was at his residence in Kodambakkam that Gandhiji was to stay.

20 February 1934, Harijan Seva Sangam

On the second day, the meeting of the Harijan Seva Sangam took place. Gandhiji agreed to speak for half an hour at this meeting. "Temple entry as such is no doubt important, but there is nothing that we need to do about it immediately. We must persuade caste Hindus to open the temples to Harijans. That is what is to be done now," he urged. In response to this, Bhashyam Iyengar said, "Some say that Harijans can be allowed to enter after they purify themselves. What is your view on that?"

Gandhiji: I do not believe that is necessary. They must be clean. I have been saying that they should desist from eating the meat of dead animals or cows.

Iyengar: If a movement to purify Harijans is started, would you support it?

Gandhiji: If the Harijans oppose it, I will support them.

Gandhiji further declared that 75 per cent of the collections made on this tour should be allotted to the Madras State Harijan Seva Sangam, and that amount should be spent on useful programmes. After speaking for half an hour, Gandhiji checked the watch at his waist, and got up from the meeting.

Public meeting, Puliyur

At the public meeting arranged in Puliyur, Gandhiji's car was driven right to the centre of the crowd that had assembled. As there was no proper dais from which Gandhiji could speak, he spoke standing on the car! Harihara Sharma translated his Hindi speech into Tamil. "If the objectives of the Harijan movement are realised, it would form the foundation for brotherhood in society. Students must involve themselves in this work and do whatever service they can for Harijans," Gandhiji urged.

A poor man, unable to offer anything of value, gave Gandhiji three shell buttons from his shirt. Gandhiji was surprised that these fetched one rupee in the auction.

In the evening, he visited the home of the late A. Rangaswami Iyengar, chief editor of *The Hindu*, and offered condolences to his wife and children. "In the world of newspapers, people have praise for the abilities of Rangaswami Iyengar. But there are many other virtues he had that I have absorbed," he said on that occasion. As he came out of Rangaswami Iyengar's house, the grandson of S. Srinivasa Iyengar gave him a letter, which he read, and went directly to Srinivasa Iyengar's residence for an hour's discussion with him.

21 February 1934, Kanchipuram

Gandhiji took the train from Tambaram in the morning and reached Kanchipuram. Perhaps anticipating violence from the Sanatanis, no one except the reception committee was allowed anywhere near his car at the railway station. There were policemen stationed every ten feet on his route from the station. However, there was no untoward incident caused by the Sanatana Dharma Sangam. The Self-Respect Group members, though, stood in the corner at the public meeting, holding placards that said, 'Gandhi Go Back,' waving black flags. As in Chidambaram, fearing that Harijans would storm into the temple along with Gandhiji, the silver doors of the Sri Yathokthaswami sanctum and the two entrance gates of Sri Varadarajaswami temple were locked. It was almost noon, and the sun was beating down, but there were more than 20,000 people gathered at the Sankoosappettai grounds for the public meeting.

Welcome addresses were presented on behalf of the Kanchipuram Town Council by its president M. Swaminatha Mudaliar, of the Chinglepet Harijan Seva Sangam by its president Dewan Bahadur M. K. Reddiar, of the Small Kanchipuram Hindi Vidyalayam by M. T. Vedantham, of Samarasa Sanmarga Sabha by Va. Pe. Ekambaram Chettiar, and of Kanchipuram Harijan Seva Sangam by Ne. Sa. Rajarathina Mudaliar. A sum of Rs 2,000 was given as a purse for the Harijan Fund. On behalf of Marwari merchants and Small Kanchipuram Asti Giri Street Viswa Brahmins, a purse and a silver charkha were presented.

'Open your doors to Harijans'

At this meeting Gandhiji referred to the ancient heritage of Kanchi, saying:

> Kanchipuram is famous for its education in Sanskrit shastras. Unfortunately, however, those who have studied these shastras are using them against Harijans today. The doors of your temples

are still closed to Harijans. God, who is the embodiment of truth and justice, will not reside in a temple that denies entry to Harijans. This sin will visit not only on the scholars of Sanskrit, but those who call themselves caste Hindus, like you and me. Caste Hindus must work towards opening the temple doors to Harijans.

Gandhiji stayed at the house of C. Rajagopalachariar in Small Kanchipuram (now Little Kanchipuram). While he was spinning the charkha here, the administrator of the Kanchipuram Hindu Girls' School, M. K. Ramanatha Sharma, sought an interview with him. "Admit Harijans in your school, or else, shut it down," Gandhiji advised him.

When the assistant editor of *Iyaparadhi* magazine, P. S. Venkata Arya, met him, he was told, "The orthodox people of Madras must see to it that the scourge of untouchability is removed and the temples are opened to Harijans."

The Harijans of Cheyyur village met him and said, "We started building a temple in our slum, but it is now half finished. You must help us with the finance to complete it." The Mahatma replied, "I do not encourage building of temples in slums."

On the way to Arni, via Ranipet, purses were presented to Gandhiji on behalf of the Kaveripakkam public, Walajapet Harijans and students at the small villages of Velam and Ammur, the public of Ranipet, the Arcot public and Merchants' Association. At the Walajah Town grounds, where about 10,000 people had gathered for the public meeting, Sundaravadanam and Subbu Chettiar presented a welcome address prepared in silver on palm leaf. At Ranipet, Rangasamy and Manikkam presented a welcome address and purse. In Arcot, the news spread that, as E. Janakiram Mudaliar could not have a good view of Gandhiji, he got very angry, blocked Gandhiji's car and beat up the driver.

'Cleanse your hearts'

At Arni, welcome addresses were given on behalf of the people and Harijan Seva Sangam. In his speech here, translated by Tiruchi Halasyam, Gandhiji said: "At this point, as I am leaving Madras, I ask that each one of you must remove this pollution of untouchability from your hearts. Harijans must enjoy all the rights that other castes do."

Gandhiji stayed here at the residence of Seshachalam Chettiar. When Seshachalam's mother offered Rs 10 as a gift to Gandhiji, he remarked laughingly, "My stomach is large, amma," and called Chettiar to ask, "Does a national school function here?" Chettiar replied that he would start one in six months, failing which, he would give Gandhiji Rs 10,000.

The Arni Union Board and Taluk Board did not give Gandhiji any welcome. At Sholingapuram, more than 7,000 people welcomed him, and purses were presented. En route, he accepted purses from the people at Paranchali and Gururajappettai.

The last town, Arakkonam

Arakkonam (now a suburb of Chennai) was the last town on this extended tour of Gandhiji. Purses were presented here on behalf of the general public, Marwaris, and the Union Board. With a sense of fulfilment, the Mahatma said, "Tonight, at this place, my tour of Madras successfully concludes." He thanked the police and railway authorities for the facilities provided by them throughout this tour, adding that, "The police functioned as friends of the people, much like the police in London."

"Workers must always keep in mind our high objectives in the eradication of untouchability. We must work towards the brotherhood of all humanity. We may not be able to atone for the maltreatment of Harijans over hundreds of years, but we can change our minds today and adopt this noble objective. May the Lord bless you all."

Thus, Gandhiji took his leave. The tour that had begun on 22 January 1934 at 4.30 p.m., ended smoothly at 10.30 p.m. on 21 February 1934. As 'Kalki' wrote, after this fruitful visit, the total collections towards the Harijan Fund in Madras State were as under:

1. *Coimbatore District*: Rs 23,658-4-8 (excluding jewels)
2. *Madurai District*: Rs 13,809-0-6 (including jewels)
3. *Dindigul (Congress) District*: Rs 10,972-1-2 (excluding jewels)
4. *Karaikudi District*: Rs 11,152-3-9 (including jewels)
5. *Tiruchirapalli District*: Rs 7,438-11-5 (excluding jewels)
6. *Tirunelveli District*: Rs 7,052-4-10 (including jewels)

7. *Nilgiri District*: Rs 4,023-13-5 (including jewels)

8. *Ramanathapuram District*: Rs 3,103-1-6 (including jewels)

Notes

1. A paraffin lamp, first made by Max Graetz (1851–1937) in Germany in 1910, the name is derived from Petro(leum) + Max (Graetz). The design was so successful, it is used even today.

2. It is said that Kootha Nayinar Pillai had donated land, now on Vadambokku Street in Tirunelveli, to the British government in order to procure permission for Gandhiji's visit to Tirunelveli, and also gone to jail for Gandhiji.

3. Wife of the scientist and physics Nobel laureate Dr Abdus Salam (1926–1996).

30

ON THE WAY TO NANDI HILLS, AND BACK, 1936

9 May 1936, Basin Bridge

In 1936, on the way up to Nandi Hills near Mysore for rest, and on the way down, that is twice, Gandhiji visited Madras. On 9 May 1936, Gandhiji and Kasturba arrived by Grand Trunk Express, alighted at Basin Bridge junction, and drove to Madras. Putting up at the residence of K. Bhashyam that morning, they returned to Basin Bridge to board the Bangalore Mail. The crowds at Central station in Madras, eagerly awaiting Gandhiji's arrival were, however, not disappointed as his car had to pass through Central station from Basin Bridge. They made the car stop for a minute to have a glimpse of Gandhiji, before letting it proceed.

No politics, please

S. Srinivasa Iyengar, his wife, R. Alladi Krishnaswami Iyer, Tmt. Rukmini Lakshmipathy, G. A. Natesan, N. S. Varadachari and Pandit Harihara Sharma met Gandhiji for discussions. Gandhiji did not speak about politics to the press that day as at that time he had dissociated himself from it. When they approached him, he remarked, "I am now like a cow dried of milk." To one of them, he said, "Talk to me about flowers, about time, but not politics. When I have distanced myself from politics, it is not proper that I comment about it or politicians."

Hindi Prachar Sabha

It was at that time that preliminary work had been started for the construction of the impressive building of the Hindi Prachar Sabha in Thyagaraya Nagar, Madras. Gandhiji went with Bhashyam to inspect the work. Somehow getting wind of his visit there, thousands of people gathered to see him. Gandhiji could not even get down from the car. Thereafter, he proceeded to inspect the Harijan Training School and Harijan Welfare Centre in Kodambakkam. Along with Kasturba, he took part in the traditional meeting there. Among those who sang prayer songs at this meeting was the noted Tamil novelist, V. M. Kothainayaki Ammal.

13 June 1936, On the way back

Staying one month at the Mysore Samasthanam (Principality), Gandhiji's health showed much improvement, after which he was to go to Wardha via Madras. Alighting from the Bangalore Mail at Basin Bridge on 13 June, he went to inspect the progress of work at the Hindi Prachar Sabha building in Mambalam. On that day the building construction was to commence. He spent some time discussing with the persons responsible for this construction and officials of the Hindi Prachar Sabha, and went on to Tiruvallikeni for breakfast, along with his entourage.

Departure

Breakfast had been arranged at Nelson Manikka Mudaliar Kalyana Mandapam, Tiruvallikeni, by the treasurer of the Kodambakkam Harijan Training Centre, Roopchand Pratapmull. After his bath, breakfast and giving interviews to a few people, Gandhiji went to the house of S. Srinivasa Iyengar for some discussions, before leaving for Basin Bridge station to board the train.

Kasturba Gandhi and Tmt. Brijlal Nehru stayed as guests of Hem Chand Shah. As Gandhiji and party had reached the station some 15 minutes before the train's arrival, they sat on chairs arranged by the railway authorities on the platform. This gave an opportunity for some who had gathered there to speak with Gandhiji and Kasturba.

31

TEMPLE TRADITION, 1937

Withdrawal from Congress

Gandhiji's withdrawal and resignation from the Congress membership in 1934 was an important watershed in the history of the Indian National Congress. That he wrote not a word on it in the *Harijan* magazine tells us the extent to which he had distanced himself from the Congress and politics. As he had decided to now devote himself fully to village reconstruction and welfare work, letters to Gandhiji requiring his attention on other matters fast piled up.

In Madras, Gandhiji's withdrawal from the Congress was received with relief by other all-India organisations, and by the British administration. The Madras government wrote to the Central government: "Moderates in politics and some Congressmen secretly believe that Gandhiji's withdrawal from politics is beneficial in a way. They believe that, without his great influence, the work of the Congress would suffer."

Sevagram

In 1934, Gandhiji settled in Satyagraha Ashram in Wardha (now a city in Maharashtra). Mid-1936 witnessed Gandhiji's new thrust towards the village reconstruction movement. Village resurgence, village economy, village handicrafts and traditional, local and indigenous professions and crafts received his full and wholehearted attention at this time. And Wardha became the veritable holy 'Kasi' of the village movement.

On 30 April 1936, in consonance with his call to "Go to villages," Gandhiji visited a village called Shegaon, five miles from Wardha, which he later renamed as Sevagram, which means 'Village of Service'.

To reach this village, Gandhiji walked four miles and then rode a bullock cart for the last mile. He said those who wished to meet him at Sevagram must walk the distance, not expecting to be transported by any vehicle.

Worsening health

In 1935 December, Gandhiji's health deteriorated, and his blood pressure rose. Noted industrialist Jamnalal Bajaj (1889–1942) stood in devoted attendance over him during this period, and kept visitors strictly away. In mid-1936, going against the advice of doctors and well-wishers, Margaret Sanger[1] (1879–1966), was granted an interview with him. His health, still frail, worsened as a result. He had to be taken to Bombay, have all his teeth removed, and brought to Gujarat Vidya Peeth in Ahmedabad for rest and recuperation. For two months thereafter, he was too weak even to write for the *Harijan* magazine.

First elections

The first elections that the Congress officially participated in were in 1937. As a preparation for this, the Congress Committee met in August 1936 in Bombay to finalise its publicity programme. Thereafter, Gandhiji travelled to Kasi, Rajkot, Nadiad, Ahmedabad and Sabarmati, before returning to Sevagram in November 1936. Gandhiji did not take part in the election campaign, confining himself to administration work. Likewise, even in *Harijan*, he only wrote about his work relating to administration.

New party

With the dawn of 1935, a new all-India party was born in Madras. Under the patronage of Mrs Besant's followers and the leadership of Dr G. S. Arundale (1878–1945), English theosophist, supporter of the Indian freedom movement and Catholic bishop, the Indian National League came into existence. Although its objective was to secure swaraj, it also desired that, in time, India should get equal status in the British Commonwealth.

Congress rejects socialism

In 1935, nationalistic fervour was seen in full measure all over Madras. Public meetings under the aegis of the Congress were held in many places. It seemed that no meetings could be held in opposition to the Congress. In 1936, when a meeting of the moderates under P. S. Sivaswami Iyer was held, it was stated by V. S. Srinivasa Sastri that the Congress would be victorious in the forthcoming general elections.

In a speech given at the European Society meeting in Annamalai in May 1936, S. Satyamurthi declared: "The Congress has not accepted socialism. There are bound to be harmful effects in socialism. The Congress believes in non-violence and right to private property. However, major industries will be nationalised. The rich will be taxed to benefit the poor."

Election propaganda

On 5 October 1936, Jawaharlal Nehru undertook a whirlwind tour of Madras in connection with election propaganda. In December end, Sardar Vallabhbhai Patel toured the state for two weeks. On hearing that the Congress would put up backward class candidates in the elections, leaders like Dewan Bahadur R. Srinivasan from the backward classes were unhappy. Having established the Madras Province Backward Classes Party, they sent a telegram to Gandhiji that S. Satyamurthi should desist from appointing such candidates in the elections. Gandhiji's reply was, "Harijans are on their own coming forward, requesting some political parties to show them the way. How can I interfere in that?"

Electioneering was hotting up in Madras city and in the state, Rajaji, who had withdrawn from public life for a time, re-entered the arena and became an important part of Congress public meetings. It was in such a situation that Gandhiji went to Trivandrum via Madras.

Welcome in Tiruvangur

In Tiruvangur Principality, on the advice of the Dewan to the Prince, Sir C. P. Ramaswami Iyer, temples were opened to Harijans. Gandhiji started for Tiruvangur Principality from Sevagram in mid-January

1937 to worship in these temples, announcing, "My Tiruvangur trip is a pilgrimage." By then Nagercoil, Kanyakumari and Suchindram, originally in Tiruvangur Principality, had become part of Madras. Hence, Gandhiji's visit could be considered as one not just to Tiruvangur, but to Madras State as well.

The anger of Sanatanis

The Sanatanis in Madras could not tolerate even the temple entry that was introduced in Tiruvangur. They expressed their grievance that the tenets of the Sanatana dharma had been breached, and the rights of caste Hindus forfeited. They convened a public meeting under the aegis of the Madras caste-based Swarajya Sangam to consider future action to further their opposition to the temple entry proclamation.

11 January 1937, Madras

To meet Gandhiji, who was travelling by the Bombay Express, V. K. Satagopachariar and O. Duraisamy Chettiar had made arrangements at Tiruttani railway station, with a crowd of 2,000 people that had gathered. Gandhiji reached out of his railway compartment to receive collections for the Harijan Fund.

The train reached Madras on the evening of 11 January 1937. At first, mistaking the Grand Trunk Express from Delhi, that arrived earlier, for Gandhiji's train, the crowd surged forward with cries of 'Mahatma Gandhi ki Jai'. They were disappointed in not finding him on that train. When Gandhiji's train did arrive, it became a huge problem for the police and railway officials to escort him through the crowd to his car.

Hindi Prachar Sabha

Gandhiji went first to the Hindi Prachar Sabha office. His secretaries, Mahadev Desai and Pyarelal, were with him. This was the first time he was visiting the Hindi Prachar Sabha building after completion of construction. Together with Rajaji, Gandhiji went to the house of Harihara Sharma who lived in the same compound. There he held discussions with Dewan Bahadur V. Bhashyam Iyengar, Madurai A. Vaidyanatha Iyer, K. Srinivasan, H. S. L. Pollock, K. Santhanam,

P. Jagannath Das, Tmt. S. Srinivasa Iyengar and Tmt. Swaminathan. Having bathed at Sharma's house, he partook of orange and jujube fruits. Goat's milk was offered, but he commented, "It is better to eat less during tours." When someone asked him, "Is it all right then *not* to eat less at other times?" his reply was, "It is applicable at other times, too, but more so when travelling."

Autograph hunting

In this interval, autograph hunters, mostly women, had somehow managed to gather, and surrounded Gandhiji. Thrusting an autograph book forward, a woman asked, "Please write your name on this." Gandhiji replied with a chuckle, "Without any money?"

Woman: I have brought one rupee.
Gandhiji: Not enough. The price of my signature is five rupees.
W: I am not such a rich person. Please accept this amount and sign.
     But Gandhiji was not one to let it go.
G: Do you not know that I am a big 'baniya'? I must get the price I am asking for.
     The woman borrowed four rupees from another woman standing by her side and placed the money at Gandhiji's feet, requesting him again to sign.
W: Please sign in English.
G: Why, do I not write legibly in Tamil?
W: You write your name well enough, but why don't you speak in Tamil?
G: I do wish I could. I am not able to find anyone who has the ability to teach me to speak. Will you be my adopted daughter and teach me? I will allot half an hour each day for this.
     Everybody laughed at this exchange. The woman was content having received the autograph. All those autograph seekers, then, gave five rupees each to get Gandhiji's signature.

Prayer meeting

Thereafter, Gandhiji arrived at the prayer meeting. The employees of Dakshina Bharat Hindi Prachar Sabha read out a welcome to their leader, Mahatma Gandhi. "The seed you sowed some 18 years ago has now grown into a large tree. It is all your blessing," said the welcome address of the Sabha, referring to its growth. As there was no time for Gandhiji to respond to the welcome, he lifted his arms in thanks, blessed the gathering, and left for Tambaram railway station with Rajaji, Mahadev Desai and others. He got down from the car some two miles before the station, and walked there along with Rajaji and Mahadev Desai. Jamal Muhammad Sahib also walked with them for some distance.

A basket of fruits

Observing that there were some children among the crowd that had come to the station, a thought occurred to Gandhiji. Tmt. R. V. Sastri had brought for him a basketful of fruits, which he distributed among the children. When the Trivandrum Express arrived, he got into the third class compartment that had been reserved for him and his group. The Railway Transport Superintendent, Poornaiah, made sure that Gandhiji was comfortably entrained.

12 January 1937, Madurai station

On 12 January 1937, the number of platform tickets sold at Madurai station exceeded anything that had been witnessed earlier. Gandhiji was garlanded on arrival at the station by N. M. R. Subburaman, George Joseph, Krishnaswami Bharathi, P. K. Ramachari, Akhilandammal, Vaidyanatha Iyer and Parvathavardhini Subburaman. Gandhiji started collecting for the Harijan Seva Fund there itself. The speech he gave in front of his railway compartment in Hindi was translated by N. M. R. Subburaman into Tamil.

"I am going on a pilgrimage to Trivandrum. The Prince has ordered the opening of all temples there for Harijans. Public opinion must also be mobilised for the opening of Sri Meenakshi temple in Madurai likewise. All good-minded people must work towards this."

N. M. R. Subburaman and L. Krishnaswami Bharathi went with Gandhiji up to Virudhunagar, and sent him on his way.

Other railway stations

There were large crowds at Dindigul, Chozhavandan and Tirumangalam, too. At Kodaikanal Road station, Kombai Human Respect Sangam secretary Shahul Hamid, C. P. Ramachandran and G. Krishnamurthi Iyer welcomed him with garlands.

At Tenkasi railway station, welcome addresses were presented on behalf of the Peoples' Rights Association and Hindi Youth Association. The Shencottah Town Council president, N. K. S. Krishnasamy Karaiyalar garlanded Gandhiji. Akkoor Ananthachariar offered a garland on behalf of the Kittappa Sports Association. Led by Subbaiah, many Harijans had come to greet Gandhiji with fruits and flowers. From Trivandrum, Gandhiji toured Nagercoil and Kanyakumari, returning thereafter to the internal regions of Tiruvangur Principality.

14 January 1937, Nagercoil

It was evening when Gandhiji reached Nagercoil. He went to Musabari bungalow and rested for an hour. Nagercoil Harijan Seva Sangam president Dr Naidu, and Town Council President Sankaran Pillai, together with some other prominent people, welcomed Gandhiji with garlands. Gandhiji spent some time in discussion with Harijan leaders, after which he accompanied Dr Naidu and G. Ramachandran to the Nagarajaswami temple. The Suchindram Devasthanam Trustee Mahadeva Iyer, and other dignitaries welcomed Gandhiji.

Nagercoil meeting

In Nagercoil, the public meeting was held in the vast expanse of the S. L. P. Government English High School grounds. District officials and some Europeans attended this meeting. The biggest surprise was that there was pin-drop silence throughout Gandhiji's speech. The loudspeaker did not function satisfactorily, the translation was terse, yet the crowd was on its best behaviour. On behalf of the Town Council, its member Dr. Vaidyanatha Iyer read out the welcome speech. Another member Krishnaswami offered a khadi garland. When fruits were offered on a silver platter, Gandhiji directed that they be distributed among the Harijans. Gandhiji was surprised at the Hindi Prachar Sabha and Hindi Premi Sabha giving separate receptions, which he mentioned at the meeting. Upon enquiring through the *Mail*, it was learnt that one represented a Tamil group, and the other Malayalis. When the representative group of the Hindi Premi Sabha led by M. Sivathanu Pillai sought an interview with Gandhiji, they said that they were not in competition with any other Hindi group. Nanjil Nadu Sambargal Sangam also presented a welcome, almost as if to say, "We are not inferior."

Hindu religion

Gandhiji began his speech on 14 January with the Prince's proclamation, praising it by saying that it had pulled out the scourge of untouchability by the roots. "I was hitherto not entering temples because Harijans were prevented, but now, I have no other work than going to temples from the time I have set foot in Tiruvangur. This proclamation is, in a sense, the purification of Hindu religion." He emphasised in every meeting thereafter that caste Hindus must now educate Harijans in the ways of temple traditions.

From Nagercoil he went to Kanyakumari and rested there. Other than his secretaries, prominent among those accompanying him on this tour included Rajkumari Amrit Kaur (1887–1964, independence activist and politician), Kerala Harijan Seva Sangam president Changanacheri K. Parameswaran Pillai and its secretary G. Ramachandran.

15 January 1937, The tradition of Amman

There was a cool breeze in Kanyakumari on that day, and Gandhiji slept well. Rising early, he completed his morning routines and went for a stroll on the beach. It seemed that the fatigue of the journey had vanished. With a group of the Nagercoil Harijan Seva Sangam leading the way with bhajans, and Gandhiji following with a large crowd behind him, he went into the temple for its rituals. Singing bhajans himself, he, together with everybody, went around the outer *prakaram* (surrounding courtyard) of the temple, before entering it through its main doorway.

During his previous visit, Gandhiji had not been allowed to enter this temple, causing him distress. On this occasion, though, the assistant trustee of the temple, Mahadeva Iyer, other officials and priests received Gandhiji with full temple honours. 'Amman', the residing goddess of the temple, was adorned beautifully, and the temple itself shone brilliantly, lit with a myriad lamps. Gandhiji went in up to the point that Brahmins could enter. At this point, a doubt arose in his mind. He did not know who were the Harijans who had come in with him. "Is there any Harijan here?" he asked the crowd. A person from the bhajan group answered, "We are all Harijans," which pleased Gandhiji.

After visiting the other shrines in the temple, he was shown the beautiful *kolams*, geometric floor drawings created using rice flour or chalk powder, they symbolise auspiciousness and divinity. He then went to the library, inspected the books kept there, and praised the efforts evident in obtaining and preserving the texts efficiently.

By this time it was 8 a.m., and Gandhiji's day of silence began, which ended at 5 p.m. Thereafter, Gandhiji and party left via Suchindram to Kottarakkara (a town in the Kollam district of Kerala). This was the last time Gandhiji visited the tip of the three seas and oceans in Kanyakumari to meditate. On the way, the villagers of Tamaraikkadu and its surrounding areas welcomed him with garlands at a place called Eethan Kadu.

Suchindram

When he reached Suchindram, enthusiastic crowds blocked his car in front of the English school there. The administrator of the school, Subramania Pillai, received him with garlands. Gandhiji wrote his congratulatory comments in the school's visitors' book. It was in Suchindram that, some years ago, it became necessary to conduct a religious war, not only against the ban on temple entry for Harijans, but even for them to enter certain streets. Today, however, Gandhiji went into the temple with the bhajan group. The temple authorities received him and showed him some of the exquisite temple sculptures. Gandhiji viewed them in awe. Thereafter, when he left for Trivandrum via Nagercoil, it was 7.30 p.m.

21 January 1937, The journey ends

He completed his Tiruvangur tour and returned to Kottarakkara on the night of 20 January 1937. There, the next day, he formally opened to Harijans the Tirukkannamanaikkal Vishnu temple belonging to Kadal Manaikkal Murthy Narayana Namboodirippad. He thanked the Prince and the Rani of Tiruvangur, as also the Dewan for their invitation, and boarded the train to Madras.

None equal to Tamils

On the way to Madras, as always, there were large crowds at every station, more so in Virudhunagar, Madurai and Dindigul stations. Mahadev Desai described the crowd at Tirumangalam in the *Harijan* issue of 13 February 1937 as follows.

> There is no crowd anywhere in India that matches the disorderliness and noise of the crowds in Tamilnadu. 'Why is there so much indiscipline?' I asked the crowd at a railway station. Without understanding my question they shouted, 'We are supporters of Rajaji, the Mahatma must give darshan.'
>
> At another station the crowd shouted, 'He must get up. Even if we come a hundred times, he must give us darshan.' There was no doubt, however, that their intention was honourable. At a small railway station (Desai refers here to Tirumangalam), a person in the crowd gave one paisa towards Gandhiji's collection drive. 'Who gave this one paisa?' they shouted, and in the auction that took place thereafter, it fetched Rs 5. There was, likewise, another paisa. That went only for Re 1.
>
> At Tirumangalam, as the crowds filled the air with noise. I noticed a European lady, with a child on either arm, trying to force her way through the crowd. Assuming that she was a passenger intending to board the train, I requested the crowd to make way for her, but they would not. Even were they willing, there was not an inch of space she could squeeze through. As she was so struggling to move, the children were crying aloud. 'I need to enter, please take my children,' the lady pleaded, as she neared our compartment. Gandhiji took the two children into his arms, and we opened the door of our compartment to allow the lady in. Till the train started we did not realise that the lady was a friend of Gandhiji, who had come to see him. When we

began to converse with each other after the train had started, the lady introduced herself as the wife of Khaitan. Sri Khaitan had been with the American mission a few years ago, and had got into trouble because of his independent views. He was still facing problems.

Gandhiji welcomed the lady with affection, as her four-year-old elder daughter engaged playfully with him. However, the attention of both children were focused on the coins that had been spread out in front of them. The boy, who was younger, began to play with the money. Immediately the lady took out two rupees from her purse and asked the children to put the coins in the heap before them, which they did with delight.

The young girl then started to pepper us with questions... 'Why have all of them come to the railway station? ...Why such a large crowd?' and so on. We in turn asked them, 'Why have you come?'

The child replied, 'To see Gandhiji'. The lady added, 'They, too, have indeed come to see Gandhiji. They are his friends'.

'But why have they given money to Gandhiji', we asked. 'Why did you give me money?', Gandhiji asked the child.

'We have given it for the poor', was the reply, 'That is what others have done.'

A small but thoughtful change

Some, who were unsure whether they could see Gandhiji in the crowd at Madurai station, gathered at Tirupparankundram (a town in Madurai District) station. Together with the Madurai leaders, thousands of people massed at Tirupparankundram.

An example of how a small but thoughtful change executed carefully could benefit many was witnessed in the work of the Madurai railway station Chief Superintendent, Wheeler. In those days, it was not usual for the Trivandrum Express to stop on Platform No. 1. But, so as not to inconvenience the crowd by climbing up and down the pedestrian bridge, it was arranged for the train to stop at Platform No. 1, and Gandhiji's compartment was halted at an open space for the crowds to gather and see him. A few students who were introduced to Gandhiji here offered him fruits.

22 January 1937, Madurantakam

At Madurantakam railway station, the Nehru Youth Association members came in procession to see Gandhiji. On behalf of the public, Pisirilal Sarkar handed over a purse for the Harijan Fund. District Committee member V. A. Munusamy Reddiar offered a khadi garland.

The moment the train reached Madras, the difference between Tiruvangur and Tamilnadu became clear to Gandhiji. "I spoke at many meetings in Tiruvangur. There was a divine peace at those meetings, but even in the small crowd here, I do not find this," he remarked at the evening prayer meeting in Kodambakkam. He stayed at the Kodambakkam Harijan Industrial Training School. At the meeting held in front of this school, he emphasised the importance of prayer. "If you continuously and wholeheartedly pray over a period of time, you will discover the kind of truth that I have. You will realise that you can stay without nourishment for the body for some time, but never without nourishment for your soul."

Satyamurthi's daughter

At the end of this meeting, when Gandhiji requested the public to donate generously to this Harijan Training Centre, as it had been rendering useful service, people in the crowd gave money, jewels, watches, fountain pens, and anything of value they possessed. The daughter of S. Sathyamurthi, who was sitting beside Gandhiji, was asked in a light vein by him, "What are you going to give me?" The lady immediately removed her two bangles and offered them to him.

Kodambakkam

Gandhiji, Rajaji and Sathyamurti met first at the Kodambakkam Harijan Handicrafts School for discussions. The conversions practised by Christians, and the need for Indian Christians to follow the proclamation issued by the Tiruvangur prince were subjects that were discussed with him by A. A. Paul, Sudarsanam, and other prominent Christians. When Gandhiji made known his views on religious conversion, he also stressed the fact that people should respect all religions, and believe in the tenet that we are all one world and one family.

Rt. Hon'ble Srinivasa Sastri, who had just then returned from a tour of Malaya, met Gandhiji in the afternoon to report on his travels. Sita Devadas, K. Srinivasan, Jamal Mohammed, C. R. Srinivasan, T. R. Venkatarama Sastri and G. A. Natesan also met and spoke with Gandhiji.

On the way from Tambaram to Kodambakkam, Gandhiji visited Nageswara Rao Panthulu's home in Pallavaram, where, for some time, he was in discussion with him. Receiving the fruits offered to him with a smile, he said, "Let the fruits be—where are the 'notes'?"

Kasturba's signature

While Gandhiji was walking round the Harijan Training School premises, his sharp eyes did not miss the cobwebs hanging from the ceilings. He also observed pitting on the floor. That evening, when he addressed the students, his entire speech revolved around cleanliness. "Your intelligence can be gleaned from how clean you maintain your surroundings," he said. He also pointed out the absence of spinning or weaving in the school, and emphasised that they should acquire these skills.

A girl named Jayanthi Bai gave him five rupees and sought Gandhiji's autograph in her book. He took the book from her, and was pleasantly surprised to discover Kasturba's signature in it. "My signature after my wife's? It is a matter of pride for me, but your five rupees is not enough for this—you have to give me ten rupees." The girl promptly gave him an additional five rupees and obtained his autograph.

The students of Dakshin Bharat Hindi Prachar Sabha read out a welcome to him. He had no time to respond to it, hence he merely blessed them and left for the prayer meeting, after which he hurried to the station.

Departure

Completing his holy tour, the Mahatma went on to carry forward his usual tasks. A *karmayogi*, one dedicated to work with a religious zeal whose service goal was to wipe the tears from the eyes of the downtrodden, his focus at that time was the Guntur province (now in

Andhra Pradesh) ravaged by a recent cyclone. To inspect the cyclone-affected areas, he started from Central Station in Madras in a third-class compartment. As usual, leaders and thousands of people had come to bid him farewell. Cries of 'Gandhiji ki Jai' reverberated, as people reluctantly saw him leave, for Sevagram via Guntur.

Note

1. Margaret Sanger (1879–1966), pioneering American birth control activist and lifelong advocate of women's reproductive rights.

32

THE HINDI SAMMELAN, 1937

Election results

The results of the General Elections were declared in February 1937. In the 11 states of then undivided India, the Congress won a majority in six. Of these six, the victory in Madras deserves special mention. The Justice Party, that had been in the majority in the Assembly since 1922, managed to secure only 21 Assembly seats against 159 of the Congress, as seen below.

Indian National Congress: 159
Justice Party: 21
Independents: 15
Muslim League: 9
Europeans/Anglo-Indians: 9
Muslim Progressive Party: 1
People's Party: 1
Total: 215

The compromise

Gandhiji duly participated in the Congress Committee meeting held at Wardha to review the election results, and to decide what objectives the Congress was to follow in the Assemblies. However, despite this, he still did not write about it in the *Harijan* newsletter. The All India Congress Committee, at its meeting in Delhi in the third week of March, decided that, if the leader of the Congress Party in the Assembly was convinced that the Governor would not exercise his veto powers, it would go by the compromise plan brought forth

by Gandhiji to assume power in the states in which it had secured a
majority.

During the following week, Gandhiji came to Madras to attend
the Hindi Sahitya Sammelan. This was the first such Sammelan held
in Madras.

26 March 1937, Back in Madras

The Madras public that had mounted a vigil at Central station
for Gandhiji's arrival felt let down. An ornate pandal had been
erected at the car park outside the station with welcome placards.
Sir C. V. Raman's[1] wife Lady Raman, Ambujammal, Madras Mayor
K. Sriramulu Naidu, and workers were waiting with khadi and flower
garlands for Gandhiji's arrival. But, a few minutes before the Grand
Trunk Express by which he was travelling was to arrive at Central
station, a railway official informed them that Gandhiji had detrained
at Ponneri. As an overflowing crowd was anticipated at Central
station, Rajaji had gone up to Ponneri to receive Gandhiji, although,
even at Ponneri, there was such a crowd that it was difficult for Rajaji
to reach Gandhiji's compartment.

There was just one policeman on duty at Ponneri station, and he
was helpless in controlling the crowd. Finally, by the time Rajaji did
manage to reach Gandhiji's compartment, get in, carry his luggage and
come to the door, the train started. Rajaji frantically waved his hands
for the train to stop. When it did, Gandhiji alighted with Rajaji, khadi
bag in hand, and got into the car waiting outside to go to Mambalam,
where V. Bhashyam Iyengar, Pandit Harihara Sharma, T. Prakasam
and K. K. Bhashyam welcomed him.

Welcome to 'Ba'

Kasturba Gandhi (affectionately known as 'Ba') and Jamnalal Bajaj,
who got down at Central station, received the welcome organised
for Gandhiji in his stead. They were taken for some distance in a
decorated car, and thereafter to Mambalam.

The purpose of Gandhiji's visit to Madras was the convocation
of the Hindi Prachar Sabha in Mambalam that evening, and the
Hindi Sahitya Sammelan. It was the first time that a Hindi Sahitya

Sammelan was being held among non-Hindi-speaking people. As Lady Raman had been appointed president of the Sammelan's welcome committee, she had come down to Madras from Bangalore. In addition, the Bharatiya Sahitya Parishad meeting, and a women's conference under the leadership of Kasturba Gandhi were also held at this time. An exhibition of important magazines, newspapers, books and manuscripts was organised. With all this activity, Madras city buzzed with activity during the four or five days of Gandhiji's stay.

Gandhiji's ire

At the convocation programme, before he began his speech, the nuisance caused by press photographers seated in front angered Gandhiji. Witnessing his anger, people might have been reminded of the adage: When the saint rages, even the forest bursts into flames.

"You have all misunderstood my tenet of ahimsa. Without exception, all photographers must leave this place immediately," he remonstrated. The convocation was conducted in the pandal erected in front of the Hindi Prachar Sabha for the All India Hindi Sahitya Sammelan.

Victim of mockery

The first victim of Gandhiji's mockery was G. A. Natesan. Gandhiji spoke in Hindi. Before starting his speech, he said, "Those who can understand my Hindi may please raise their hands." Many hands went up. He then asked those who could not understand him to raise their hands. A few did. Gandhiji looked at each of them individually; G. A. Natesan was one of them. Till Gandhiji noticed him, he did not lower his hand. "It is a shame," remarked Gandhiji, as Natesan stood up and acknowledged the rebuke. Later, in his address, Gandhiji said, "Do you know who I was referring to when I said 'It is a shame?' It was my friend G. A. Natesan." The next victims of Gandhiji's mockery were the Hindi degree holders.

The need for Hindi

Gandhiji first emphasised the need for Hindi, in the process, also responding to the strong opposition that had been expressed to it from various quarters. He said: "The view of some that the learning of Hindi will affect the learning of the local language is wrong, because local languages are the foundations for learning the national language. The national language cannot grow by destroying local languages. I examined whether any language, other than Hindi, could be our national language, and came to the conclusion that no language but Hindi has that right."

Why Tamil has not spread

He then went on to say how he had attempted to learn Tamil, and failed.

> I am partly the reason for this failure. Nobody came forward to ensure that I did not forget even the little Tamil that I had learnt. Why, my daughter-in-law herself did not come forward. I learnt only a few days back that Lakshmi had not even taught her husband Tamil. It is because Tamil women themselves have failed to do their duty in this matter that the Tamil language has not spread.

27 March 1937, A most important day

After the first Bharatiya Sahitya Parishad's meeting in Nagpur, this was its second meeting at Madras. As Gandhiji said, it was the objective of the Parishad to select a treasury of writings from all languages and spread them through Hindi all over India.

In Madras, most appropriately, Mahamahopadhyaya U. Ve. Swaminatha Iyer, who is hailed as 'Tamil thatha' (grandfather of Tamil), was the president of the welcome committee. At the Parishad meeting the next day, he said of 'Gandhi Thatha' (Grandfather Gandhi): "I consider this day a most important day in my life, when I have been given the opportunity to participate in this significant meeting, enveloped in the love of the man who is praised by the intellectuals of the world, and one who lives not for himself, but for others—Mahatma Gandhi." Iyer's welcome address was entirely in Tamil, but he referred to Hindi, saying, "We have accepted Hindi as our common language. Among the many languages in India, this does belong to India as a whole, as its name itself suggests."

A common script for all

Gandhiji's speech was in Hindi, in which he stressed on a revolutionary view. He said that there should be a common script for all the languages of India, and that the most suitable script according to him is "Nagari", adding that this would aid mass nationwide literacy. Taking Madras as an example, he said: "In Madras, 93 out of 100 people are illiterate, and only 7 can read. Hence, if the 93 can be taught to read through 'Nagari' script, there should be no difficulty." Gandhiji, however, warned that it should not be concluded thereby that he had a passion for Hindi, or a hatred for Tamil. He only felt that the Devanagari script should be given an opportunity and tried along with the Tamil script.

Lady Raman's response

Lady Raman's views on Hindi were clear. In her address as president of the Hindi Sahitya Sammelan welcome committee, she said: "Some knowledgeable people say that English fulfils our need for a common language, and there is no need for Hindi. But they forget that India lives not in a few, but innumerable villages," she said. However, she was also equally unambiguous in her response to Gandhiji's proposal of Devanagari as a common script for all Indian languages.

> There could be a common script for Indo-Aryan languages, but it need not be extended to Dravidian languages. One cannot write the Tamil alphabet in the 'Nagari' script. This could have some success with Telugu and Kannada scripts, but will not succeed with Tamil. Moreover, as far as I am concerned, I have doubts whether such an exercise would be useful. My personal view is that we should not forsake our own alphabet and script.

Gandhiji was on the dais when she said this, with Jamnalal Bajaj presiding.

Spread Hindi in Madras

That evening, the Congress members of the Assembly, Upper House members, some 30 of them, met Gandhiji to seek his advice on what could be done to spread Hindi in the State of Madras. Rajaji and

Prakasam were present at this meeting. On that day, all of Gandhiji's work was confined within the Hindi Prachar Sabha building. He did not leave the premises. After finishing his prayer and routine work in the morning, representatives and several others came to meet him. He took part in the Parishad meeting till 10 a.m.

When Gandhiji returned to where he was staying, many had come to see him, and it took half an hour for them to leave. He then had his lunch, and, as he was going for his rest, Rajaji came with some important work. They spent about 20 minutes discussing matters, and went immediately to the meeting of Hindi Sahitya Sammelan, returning only by 3 p.m.

Advice to women

People belonging to the Gokulam Harijan settlement led by P. N. Sankaranarayana Iyer, met Gandhiji and informed him that several in their settlement were going to villages and involving themselves in village improvement work, for which certain villages had been chosen. This delighted Gandhiji. At the same time, he noticed some women belonging to this group wearing jewellery. "Rather than beauty from such adornment, look towards the beautification of your soul," he remarked.

Kasturba speaks

In the afternoon, a women's conference under the aegis of the Hindi Sammelan was held, with Kasturba Gandhi presiding. Ambujammal and Leelavathi spoke at this conference. In her presidential address, Kasturba said, "I had thought till now that in Madras State, people would be more attracted to English. I realise that I was mistaken."

Harijan school, Kodambakkam

Early the next morning, Gandhiji walked from the Hindi Prachar Sabha in Thyagarayanagar to the Harijan Handicrafts Training School in Kodambakkam, a distance he covered in 40 minutes. Dewan Bahadur Bhashyam Iyengar, P. Jagannath Das and M. Papineedu accompanied him. Gandhiji's visit here was kept a closely guarded secret, despite which, when he reached the place, hundreds of people were waiting for him at the gate of the Training School. Gandhiji asked them to donate some money to the school, and collected about Rs 25.

He inspected the work of the students. Having seen their tailoring, cane and metal work, he asked them if they had any complaints. Some students did, and said that they should be given annual leave. Gandhiji responded by telling them that this was also their home, and that they should "finish learning everything before wanting to leave". After this, the boys and girls of Gokulam sang bhajans. The students of Perambur Harijan settlement, who had come to see Gandhiji, were introduced.

When he returned from Kodambakkam to where he was staying, he gave an interview to Ramalingam, a worker from Ramanathapuram District.

Resolutions for Hindi

In the Hindi Sahitya Sammelan meeting that day, Rajaji brought a historic resolution with Gandhiji's approval that, henceforth, the Congress Committee meetings should be conducted only in Hindi-Hindustani. The resolution was adopted.

As the next day was Gandhiji's day of silence, he stayed awake till late night and met the leaders and members of the Dakshin Bharat Hindi Prachar Sabha. The Sabha meeting began at 9.30 p.m. and went on till 11.30 p.m. A few Europeans too met Gandhiji for discussions. A resolution was adopted in the Hindi Prachar Sabha meeting that the salary of Hindi teachers, which had been fixed at Rs 20 per month by the government, should be brought on par with those of other teachers.

Gandhiji's clarification

That night, after the prayer meeting, when Gandhiji gave an interview to the press, he clarified, "When I said that there should be a common script for all languages, it was not my intention to discourage the growth of any language."

His observation that, on the one hand, the interest in khadi appeared to be waning, yet, on the other, sales of khadi were increasing—a fact Gandhiji was reluctant to admit—came as a surprise to many. A casual comment made by Gandhiji during this interview also caused some confusion among the press. He said: "Till now, I have taken medicine only twice."

30 March 1937, Back in politics

Although Gandhiji had determined not to involve himself directly in politics, he needed to, and right here in Madras. It was a time of much debate as to whether the government should interfere in matters of administration or not. As a result, he could not keep quiet. There were three cables from London asking for his views on this, and Gandhiji decided that there was no virtue in delaying any further. On 30 March, when he left Madras, he issued this notification, which stated:

> The Resolution of the Congress in accepting to take up office in consonance with the principle of non-violence was intended to give the authority to the people and strengthen the Congress. This objective cannot be attained if the people's interests are not reflected, which is what the Congress is setting out to achieve. Hence, as long as Ministers are functioning within the ambit of law, there should be a tacit understanding that Governors will not use their authority, without which the objectives are unattainable. If such an understanding is not reached, it would become a barrier to the satisfactory functioning of those who have been elected to office. I believe that such an understanding is critical for the benefit of both parties and for the conduct of Governors within the realms of propriety. They should declare that they would not use their authority against ministers who are functioning within the parameters of law. There is nothing beyond law in politics. A Party that has taken on people's welfare as its credo should not be interfered with by Governors. This is dangerous.

With this declaration by Gandhiji, even the few who may have had doubts about whether the governors could have a point found clarity. The newspapers began to write forceful articles on these observations. "At this time, a communication sent by the Madras government to the Central government said [that the] major event that took place in Madras in these last two weeks was the refusal of Rajaji to form the government. The stand of the Congress is unanimously accepted by the Congress newspapers."

The Hindu which, for had some time voiced moderate views, now began to write stridently. In their editorial titled 'Gandhiji's declaration' (30 March 1937), it wrote: "The declaration of Gandhiji relating to the failure of the talks to establish a Congress government must have opened the eyes of those in authority as to how unwisely they have approached this problem."

Reading it today, one feels the vehemence behind that editorial, but despite several newspapers carrying similar views, it all fell on deaf ears of the government. This impasse went on for several months before being resolved.

Rajaji elected leader

As the Congress had achieved a majority, Rajaji, elected as leader of the Party in the Assembly, held talks with the Governor on the formation of his ministry. During Gandhiji's second visit to Madras in 1937, these talks were ongoing. As the Governor was unwilling to forgo his 'veto' power, there were problems and delay in the matter. Gandhiji's presence in Madras at this time was of great assistance to Rajaji, who consulted him on all important matters. However, as the Governor was adamant, it was not possible to form the government at that time. It was only in mid-July that the Congress ministry could be formed. Those in this ministry were:

1. C. Rajagopalchariar: Chief Minister, General, Finance
2. T. Prakasam: Land Revenue
3. Yakub Hassan: Rehabilitation
4. Dr P. Subbarayan: Education, Law
5. Dr T. S. S. Rajan: Public Health
6. V. J. Munusamy Pillai: Agriculture, Village Improvement
7. V. V. Giri: Labour, Workers' Welfare
8. S. Ramanathan: Administration, Public Relations
9. K. Rama Menon: Courts, Prisons
10. B. Gopal Reddy: Establishment

Exhibition

29 March was Gandhiji's day of silence. It was a kind of rest for him in the midst of a busy day. On the next day he left by Grand Trunk Express for Wardha, along with Kasturba. Before leaving, he inspected

an exhibition arranged by Hindi Prachar Sabha in connection with the Sammelan. What fascinated him most at this exhibition was Mahamahopadhyaya U. Ve. Swaminatha Iyer's compilation of the original palm leaf Tamil manuscript of *Tholkkappiyam*.

As always, large crowds bid Gandhiji farewell at the railway station.

Note

1. Sir Chandrasekhara Venkata Raman (1888–1970), born in Tiruchirapally, received the 1930 Nobel Prize in Physics for his groundbreaking work in light scattering.

33

THE 'TAMIL' GANDHI

The lure of Tamil

That, among languages, Tamil, through its classicism and purity, captured the heart of the Mahatma, who was himself held as a symbol of purity and reverence, was not surprising. The fact that he started learning Tamil when he was 36, and while in South Africa, and continued to be its student even at an advanced age, must make every Tamilian's heart swell with pride. In the midst of his unrelenting workload, and the innumerable problems that he had to encounter, he did not give up his efforts to learn Tamil—something that reflects the sweetness of this tongue and its ability to enthrall people.

The Tamil language has long fascinated scholars and intellectuals from other parts of the world, such as German-born philologist and Orientalist Friedrich Max Müller (1823–1900), George Uglow Pope (1820–1908), an Anglican Christian missionary and Tamil scholar who spent 40 years in Tamil Nadu and translated many Tamil texts into English, and Constantine Joseph Beschi (1680–1747), an Italian Jesuit priest, also known by his Tamil name of Viramamunivar. It was thus perhaps natural that it should attract the Mahatma. "In the ashram, we might have at times done work without Tamilians, but never without Tamil songs being sung," Kaka Kalelkar said. Gandhiji's reverence and love for the Tamil language was considerable.

What were his reasons?

Why had Gandhiji started learning Tamil? There are two views on this. One was that it was his way of showing his gratitude to the Tamils who had worked with him in South Africa. The other was that he wished to study the *Tirukkural*. Both were true, because Gandhiji has himself said so, and it mattered not which preceded the other.

In the struggle in South Africa, no community made as many sacrifices as the Tamils—making light of their lives, losing all their wordly possessions, consenting to go to jail as to some banquet, and suffering untold tortures. Gandhiji wished to show them his deep gratitude. He believed that learning the mother tongue of the Tamils and conversing with them in their own language was the best way in which he could repay their selfless service. He said:

> If not for any other reason, for my peace of mind and to express my undying gratitude, I am learning Tamil. As I keep studying it, I am appreciating its attraction more and more. It is a language of great beauty and sweetness. As I read on, I realise from its structure and content how it has shaped the wisdom and intellectual ability of so many Tamils over the years.

Gandhiji also said that, in later years, when he came to Thoothukudi to address meetings, he had stayed at the Seva Gram of Pandit Natesanar of Madras, and that he had wanted to be introduced to the study of the *Tirukkural*. Hence, it would be fair to conclude, looking at both these reasons, that Gandhiji had begun to learn Tamil in gratitude to the Tamils, and then, charmed by the language, wished to explore the treasures of the *Tirukkural*. Mahatma Gandhi, the 'twentieth-century Valluvar', being moved by the original Valluvar was quite natural.

Learning the language

Gandhiji started learning Tamil when he was in South Africa. Some Tamil books had been made available to him then. He also made considerable efforts to obtain G. U. Pope's English translations of Tamil texts and his works in Tamil, and tried to study them. In South Africa, with his time divided between his work as a lawyer and public service, there was hardly any leisure, but that he could still devote some time to the study of Tamil showed his keen desire to learn, and his gratitude to the Tamils. This little time he spent on learning Tamil often came in the way of his writing for the *Indian Opinion*, despite which he did not discontinue his study. When Gandhiji went to London in 1906 with H. O. Ali, he had learnt the rudiments of Tamil.

In 1908, when he was jailed for the first time, he took some Tamil books with him, and studied them diligently in jail.

At the end of 1913, when he was incarcerated in Bloemfontein prison, he continued to study Tamil after attending to the jail duties given to him. "In Bloemfontein prison, I devote 8 hours to read and write, much of which time I [spend] in studying Tamil," he had written to his son Manilal Gandhi in a letter.

Tamil teacher required

Gandhiji's consistent keenness to learn Tamil was indeed remarkable. After he returned to India, he asked Srinivasa Sastri to select and send him a good Tamil teacher, and reminded him of that in his letter dated 16 July 1915. Further, the trouble he took to appoint a Tamil teacher in his ashram was seen in a letter to Maganlal Gandhi, who had come to Madras in 1915 with his wife, specifically to learn Tamil. He wrote: "See whether you could send a Tamil teacher here. We could pay him the requisite salary. We should have no objection even if he wishes to stay outside the ashram. He must be simple in his habits and behaviour."

Learning Tamil through mail

In later years, after his return to India, Gandhiji learnt Tamil from V. A. Sundaram and whoever else was near him at any given time. Those who have read this book would have known that it was his usual practice to buy Tamil books on his visits to Madras, or write to close friends like G. A. Natesan to send them. In addition to all this, he learnt Tamil through mail. For this his teacher was Rajagopalachariar. The following correspondence between them on Tamil words is interesting.

> Dear C.R.,
>
> Received your affectionate letter. The Tamil lesson that you had sent was very good. I do not think I will forget the words, 'anbu' (love) and 'ambu' (arrow). Does not the word 'ambu' also have the meaning of lotus? What is the meaning of 'anbudan'? Is the last syllable 'n'?
>
> With rombu affection,
> Bapu

Rajaji later corrected the 'rombu' as 'romba', meaning 'much'.

Gandhiji also felt that, in general, Tamilians were not too attached to their language. He had written about this on 20 October 1917.

> It was only a few years ago that Madras began to recognise the need for education in the mother tongue. More than the Tamils, the Telugu-speaking people are more keen about this. As the Tamils are fluent in English, they do not care to devote enough attention to make Tamil the language of instruction. In Telugu-speaking areas, education in English has not taken on as much. Hence, in those parts, they use their mother tongue more than the Tamils.

Favourite Tamil texts

We know that the *Tirukkural* was a favourite of Gandhiji, and he was fond of this *kural*: "Let a man learn thoroughly whatever he may learn, and let his conduct be worthy of his learning." A Tamil proverb that he most frequently quoted in his speeches and writings, that strengthened his steely resolve and influenced him greatly is: "For those who have lost their direction, God is their companion." He has said with much emotion: "In all my Tamil lessons, there has been a proverb that has been embedded in my heart, that is, 'For the man who has lost direction, God is his companion.' The essence of satyagraha lies in one's innate belief in its truth."

Gandhiji was fond of repeating this whenever the satyagrahis would begin to lose faith in satyagraha (Gandhi, English book, chapter 26, page 158). Next to *Tirukkural*, among the bhakti books that had secured an abiding place in his heart was Manickavasagar's *Tiruvasagam*. The gist of the *Tiruvasagam* verse that appealed to his heart was: "I have lived, O God, among ignorant men, and have imbibed their foolish ways. You have forgiven all my sins and led me to the path of knowledge and redemption." He would have this song sung daily at Sevagram and Sabarmati Ashram, and took great joy in listening to it.

Why not in Tamil?

It was difficult to find someone with a greater attachment to the mother tongue than Gandhiji. His conviction was that a person should learn his own mother tongue and write to others in it. He would barely tolerate a father, who was himself working for the growth of his mother tongue, writing to his son in a foreign language. Therefore, when he learnt that Rajaji had written a letter to his son in English, he was pained. Consequently, Gandhiji awoke at 3.30 a.m. and wrote a moving letter to Rajaji:

> It is now just after 3.30 am. I could not sleep after midnight, one of the causes being you. I was talking to your son last night. By chance I asked him the language in which both of you were corresponding with each other, English or Tamil. When he told me English, I felt my heart shattering. We debated about what all could be written in Tamil. The young Ramaswami said that Tamil could not be used to convey complex scientific ideas. Thereafter, my brain began working—it is doing so even at this moment.
>
> You are one of my most trustworthy associates. Hence, why this great defect? If your own children do not respect you, what can you expect from the common Tamil people? As a worker in the midst of common folk, what future can there be for Ramaswami? Please clarify this to me, or else, write to that young man in your celebrated Tamil and convince him.

We could cite many such instances as evidence of Gandhiji's high regard and love for Tamil. As one example, it was the garland of praise he offered at the Madurai meeting (26 March 1919): "I know a little of the Tamil language. It is full of beauty." Of the four languages taught at his ashram, Tamil was one (the other three being Sanskrit, Gujarati and Hindi). To learn Tamil, and for training in handicraft, Gandhiji had sent his son, Manilal Gandhi, to Madras in 1915. Before this, Devadas had been learning Tamil. At Nagpur, in 1936, Gandhiji said: "Some of us know the name of Tiruvalluvar. North Indians remain unaware of that great saint's name. There are very few who have encapsulated in such brevity the treasury of wisdom."

Kambar and Avvaiyar

Gandhiji held in high esteem the work of the noblest of poets, Kambar, and that of Tamil's own daughter, Avvaiyar. He had read about Kambar. In a letter written from Bardoli to Rajaji, who was in jail, Gandhiji had said:

> I am envious that you have both the spinning wheel and the *Ramayana*. I believe it would not be an unsatisfactory translation of Valmiki's *Ramayana*, but that of Kambar. In [G. U.] Pope's Tamil book, I have read a lot about *Kamba Ramayana*. I realise every moment that it is not easy to be venerated as a respected old woman like Mother Avvai [as he referred to Avvaiyar].

On one occasion, a Vaishnava dignitary took objection to Gandhiji's reference to Rama without the honorific, and said that Rama must always be addressed as 'Sri Ramachandra Prabhu.' In response, Gandhiji wrote in *Navajivan* (5 September 1924) that, addressing Rama without the honorific brings him nearer to the people, which is desirable, and he gave the example of Avvaiyar.

> There was a saint in Madras called Avvaiyar. Like, Mirabai, she had great devotion to the Lord. It was her habit to stay day-long at the Vishnu temple. At times she was seen to sit with her back to Vishnu's idol, and sometimes even with her legs stretched in front of him. On one occasion, a young devotee happened to come there. He was not aware of the closeness of Avvai to the Lord, so his eyes reddened with anger at seeing Avvaiyar thus seated, and roundly abused her. Avvai, on hearing this tirade, collapsed in laughter that echoed everywhere. Ignoring his aggressive outburst, she told him:
>
> 'My dear son, come and sit here. To which place do you belong, my precious fellow? You spoke harshly to me, but I ask you one thing, will you answer? In my long life I have not come across a place where God is not present. Wherever I stretch my legs, He is there. If you can show me a place where He is absent, I shall stretch my legs out in that direction.'
>
> That young devotee was abashed. It was because of his ignorance that he had not understood the venerable Avvaiyar, and he was filled with apprehension. Pearl-like tears rolled down from his eyes and fell at Avaiyyar's feet. When she began to fold her legs, he grasped them with both his hands and cried, "Mother, I have done grievous wrong, please forgive and protect me."
>
> She took him by the hand, kissed him and said with a smile, 'Chhee...What is there to forgive? Don't you know you are like

one of my sons. I have many sons like you. You are a good boy, because the moment you had a doubt, you told me. Go, Sri Ranganathar will protect you. But, my son, do remember this mother some time.'

Seeing the kind of appreciation and reverence Gandhiji had for Valluvar, Manickavasagar and Avvaiyar fills one's heart with rapture.

Language of choice

On one occasion, in 1905, Gandhiji received an important letter from Ceylon. The Tamils from South Africa had met and started a matriculation and arts school in London University, and requested Gandhiji to write to the Registrar of the university to include Tamil as a preferred subject in the syllabus. Gandhiji brought this letter to the attention of the Tamils, and asked them to formulate such a request to the Registrar. Not satisfied with that, he wrote a well-considered article in *Indian Opinion* in which he said: "Among Dravidian languages, Tamil is one that boasts of a great literary heritage. As the Italian language is to Europe, Tamil is to India. Whichever way you look at it, it is fit to be offered as a language of choice in London university."

When he learnt that London University did not heed the legitimate request of the Tamils, he spurred them on not to give up their efforts. "It is very difficult to change the mindset of an old establishment like London University, but with concerted efforts of the Tamils, their language, that contains treasures of literature, the 'Italian' among Indian languages, will definitely be accepted ultimately by London University."

Tamil in South African schools

In the provinces of South Africa, where there were large numbers of Tamils, Gandhiji had insisted that, in schools having a large Tamil student strength, Tamil must be taught. At a government school started in Johannesburg, when he came to know that no arrangements had been made to teach Tamil, Gandhiji criticised the government. His stinging article appeared in an essay titled 'Johannesburg School'.

> I understand that problems have already started to surface in this school started recently. It was expected that Tamil and

Gujarati would be taught during school hours, but we hear now that Tamil would be taught only outside school hours. It only means that Tamil will not be taught in this school. This is [a] grave injustice by the government. Tamil is an important Indian language, and there are a large number of students in this school who know it. It is the duty of the government to teach that language to a reasonable extent.

India must learn Tamil

Gandhiji had written often, and as early as 1909, that, as Bharat is one country and an ancient civilisation, people outside Madras State must also learn Tamil, and, like Ravji-bhai Patel, be able to speak with Tamils in their own language. No praise is high enough for such a desire on his part, to the extent that he encouraged his own family members to learn Tamil. The spread he envisaged in this context needs to be examined carefully. When he declared that people outside Madras State should learn Tamil, it must be understood that Madras State encompassed at that time Andhra, Malabar, and a part of Mysore (now Karnataka).

There are many who have extolled the divine son of the divine mother Tamil, that is Mahatma Gandhi. Among them are Thiru Vi. Kalyanasundara Mudaliar, Chakravarthi Rajagopalachari, Va. O. Chidambaranar, Po. Thirukooda Sundaram Pillai, Sangu Subramaniam, Sangu Ganesan, 'Dinasari' T. S. Chokkalingam, 'Dinamani' A. N. Sivaraman, 'Kalki' Krishnamurthi, Dr T. S. S. Rajan, Swaminatha Sarma, Thi Ja. Ranganathan, C. R. Srinivasan and T. S. Avinashalingam.

It would also be appropriate to mention here the names of Ra. Venkatarajulu, Jayamani Subramaniam, Dr Mu. Varadarajanar, and A. K. Chettiar. Prominent among these names was that of Thiru Vi. Kalyanasundara Mudaliar (1883–1953), whom Gandhiji met for the first time when he arrived at Central station in Madras, in 1919.

A follower of the ethical poems of Tiruvalluvar, and leading a life advocated by Gandhiji, Kalyanasundaranar, through his substantial editorial writings, essays, and books had highlighted the principles and practices promoted by Gandhiji to the educated and informed Tamil reading public. There could hardly have been any Tamilian who had not read his book *Humanity and Gandhiji* (*Manitha vazhkkaiyum Gandhi Adigalum*) at the time, such was its spread and reach. The close bond between Kalyanasundaranar and Gandhiji has also been mentioned in his autobiography, and other books. Written by anyone else, it would not have had the same flavour.

Poets

Tamilians who have showered encomiums on Gandhiji in poems include Bharathiyar, Namakkal Kavignar, Desika Vinayagam Pillai, Muruganar (Tiruvannamalai Ashram), Rai, Anjalai Ammaiyar, Suddhananda Bharathiyar, Surabira, Ayyasamy and Kothamangalam Subbu. Tamil publications that propagated the Mahatma's greatness were *Desabhakthan, Navasakthi, Vimochanam, Suthanthira Sangu* and *Gandhi*. Tamil newspapers and magazines of the time have written reverentially about Gandhiji.

"In Tamil literature, Appar [570–650, Tamil Saiva poet-saint] could be compared to Gandhiji in his approach to religion. Both believed that service was a debt to society, and had received the Grace of God in that endeavour," said Professor Swaminathan.

Two Tamilians

Before ending this chapter we must mention two Tamilians who were blessed to personally serve Gandhiji. One was Sankaran, who was a worker in the Basic Education Sangam, and a member of Sevagram, from where he functioned. A couple of days before Gandhiji's death, Gandhiji had sent a condolence message to Sankaran on the passing away of his daughter. This was one of the last letters written by Gandhiji.

The other was Parasuram, a shorthand writer, who accompanied Gandhiji on his tours of Noakhali. When Gandhiji had visited Srirampur in Noakhali, he did not wish that anyone else other than Parasuram go with him.

Gandhiji declared that each person should work towards peace at the place they had been chosen to do so. However, he permitted just two persons to accompany him wherever he went, one of them being Parasuram. He described him as "a man who is devoted to me, without self-interest and ulterior motive."

34

HINDI AND GANDHI

A common language essential

Gandhiji, in his national endeavour, had one eye trained on the freedom of India, and the other on its unity and progress. He believed that the plethora of languages in the country had in the past contributed to its lack of cohesiveness and consequent state of subjugation, having the potential to subvert the unity of the country in the future too. He, therefore, toiled for the pursuit of a common goal, not only in the present, but for the future of India. It was his belief that a common language would be like having a single heart for the nation.

In his search for a national language, he did not care for what would be easy for administration purposes. Not concerned with the advantage a few in authority would gain, he was more interested in what would be beneficial to crores of citizens. Consequently, he came to the conclusion that Hindi, being spoken by a majority of the population, should become the national language.

Two states

Gandhiji was aware that two states in India would not welcome this move. The people of Bengal, convinced that no other language could match their own, would not be happy at being forced to learn Hindi. As there was no similarity between the Dravidian language and Hindi, Gandhiji also knew that the Dravidian people would find the learning of Hindi difficult and resist it. He, therefore, came to the considered conclusion that, if Hindi was to become the national language, the people of Madras State must be made to accept it first.

Devadas Gandhi

His efforts to make the people speaking Dravidian tongues, particularly in Madras, to learn Hindi were indeed Herculean. As in days of yore Emperor Ashoka sent his children and close relatives to other countries to spread Buddhism, so Gandhiji sent his son, Devadas, to teach Hindi to the Tamils.

Devadas Gandhi came to Madras, stayed in the house of Ramji Kalyanji, and taught Hindi under the auspices of the Indian Service League. From 1919 to 1923, Pratap Narayan Vajpayee, belonging to Bihar, conducted intense teaching of Hindi in Tiruchi. He had been well trained as part of the Hindi Prachar group from North India to make Hindi learning easy, so he made available a small book, *Quintessence of Hindi*, published by the Sabha. The other person who rendered service for the propagation of Hindi was Swami Satyadev, who had been sent by Gandhiji to assist Devadas. He brought out a book for adults to learn Hindi.

It was never Gandhiji's wish that teaching Hindi to Tamils should be a one-way process. He desired that, through Hindi, the learning of other languages should also be facilitated. His advice to Devadas was, "Teach Hindi, and return having learnt Tamil." Devadas did just that.

Harihara Sharma

Gandhiji did not believe that Hindi would be spread state-wide merely by one person teaching Hindi in Madras city. He realised it was therefore imperative for the language to reach the interiors. He made arrangements for Harihara Sharma and some others to go to North India and return after learning Hindi. Accordingly, going to Prayag with a few students, Harihara Sharma returned in 1919 after completing Sahitya Visharad, took over the responsibility from Devadas Gandhi, and became the secretary of the Hindi Prachar Sabha (known as the Hindi Sahitya Sammelan Prachar Office till 1926). He served as secretary till 1936, after which Satyanarayana took over from him.

Hindi Prachar Sabha

As a result of commendable work done by the Hindi Sahitya Sammelan, Dakshin Bharat Hindi Prachar Sabha was established in Madras to serve the states of Madras, Andhra, Kerala and Mysore. It trained several thousands of teachers and sent them out to these states. For some time, much of the funds for this Sabha were forthcoming from North India, but, after 1927, it became financially self-sufficient.

Individual efforts

If the services of the Hindi Prachar Sabha were laudable, efforts made by some individuals for the propagation of Hindi were equally praiseworthy. Even if Hindi teaching commenced in Madras city in 1918, much service was rendered by people from Tirunelveli. Harihara Sharma hailed from that district. Closely involved with the spread of Hindi through the Hindi Prachar Sabha was K. R. Krishna Iyer—a majority of people in Kallidaikurichi (now a town in Tirunelveli district) learnt Hindi from him—and Sakthi Iyer of the same district. Giving up his government job, Kodaikanal Kalyana Sundaram was another among those in the forefront of Hindi propagation. Mahadeva Iyer ran a Hindi school from his own house in Dindigul. Dindigul Narayanaswami Iyer was of great assistance to Devadas in this work. Dindigul K. Ganesa Iyer, with a view to spreading Hindi among women, set up a training school for female teachers. The Madurai nationalist, Vaidyanatha Iyer, did good work in this direction in Madurai.

Other than these, in many places, followers of Gandhiji did similar work. Many educated persons in Madras city gave their support to these ventures. Several senior judges, like Venkatarama Sastri, K. Bhashyam, Sadasiva Iyer and N. Sundaram Iyer, met Devadas Gandhi in the Hindi classes that he conducted at Mylapore Club.

Justice Seshadri Iyer, Ramadas Panthulu, Srinivasa Iyengar, A. Rangaswami Iyer and Justice Sankaran Nair learnt Hindi by appointing private tutors. Their encouragement for Hindi learning was what made such propagation possible, admitted Gandhiji.

Opposition to Hindi

However, it was only after Rajaji established the Congress ministry in Madras that the first strong opposition to Hindi—compulsory Hindi—surfaced. The Self-Respect Party, Justice Party, Muslim League, Depressed Classes Sammelan, among others, opposed this measure for the spread of Hindi, and they were led by Periyar E. V. Ramasamy. He, and more than a thousand workers, were arrested in this protest. The protests, however, continued. It was in 1939, when the Congress ministry was dissolved, that these protests stopped.

On the opposition to Hindi, Thiru Vi. Ka. put it succinctly in his book *Humanity and Gandhi* as few could have said better:

> In the Congress rule, there were efforts to make Hindi the common language. There were different approaches in each province. It caused a big upheaval in Madras, where the protest was that Hindi should be made only an optional language, and not compulsory.
>
> The then Congress ministry lent a deaf ear to this protest. Approximately 1000 protestors were sent to jail. There had been no protest when Hindi was being talked about as a common language. It was under Congress rule, when Hindi was sought to be made the common language, that protests erupted. It was not possible to declare conclusively what the common language of India was, except to say that it was what the country naturally adopted.

Gandhiji's support

Those who opposed Hindi were not against its introduction as an optional language. But the Congress government felt that making Hindi compulsory was the only way to propagate it, and had Gandhiji's blessings on this. Then, in a press announcement, the Madras State government declared: "If our State has to be given its appropriate place in national life, it is necessary for our people to have some knowledge of the language spoken by the majority of people in the country, which is why our State has introduced Hindustani in the syllabus of the schools."

Gandhiji then wrote an essay in *Harijan* (10 September 1938), titled 'Congressmen Beware,' in which he clarified two issues. To the question, "Can we make Hindustani a compulsory subject?" he answered, "If our intention to make Hindustani a common language or 'Rashtrabhasha' were true, there is nothing wrong in making some knowledge of the language compulsory. In English schools, Latin is a compulsory subject even today, as I understand. That study does not affect English. On the contrary, that celebrated language only improves one's study of English."

Responding to those who wrote, 'Danger to Mother Tongue,' he firmly said: "Proclaiming so reflects the ignorance of such people, or pretence. Is India one country or several? Those who consider India as one nation must give their full support to Rajaji."

This dispute, however, did not continue for very long. When World War II began (in September 1939), as Rajagopalachari's ministry had to step down, the Governor, who took over, along with his advisers, removed the stipulation that Hindi should be a compulsory subject, and made it an elective one.

In the meantime

In all matters, Gandhiji preferred swadeshi—in apparel, products, and so on, and so he emphasised this in the matter of language too. His firm conviction was that English could on no account take the place of Hindustani in India or be the spoken tongue in the homes of crores of people and their families.

"If that was his belief, why did he run an English language paper?" some people asked. Others felt that perhaps it was because Englishmen needed to read what Gandhiji wrote. But Gandhiji said that he was doing so for the people in Madras. In an article for 'Readers and Journalists' in 1918, he wrote:

> I openly admit that I am not happy to publish a journal in English. I am aware that, by doing so, I am not spending my time in the best possible way. If not for Madras, I could well give up the editorship of *Young India*. It is necessary that I must keep the government informed of problems in current events, but, I do not have to run a journal only for that.

Hindi in every village

Hindi spread through Madras in stages. That many people voluntarily came forward to learn Hindi with proper diction pleased Gandhiji. During his final visits to Madras in 1946, he was satisfied to some extent in this matter. At the Silver Jubilee celebrations of the Sabha (25 January 1946), he said in his speech: "The Sabha is doing good work. It is only after 27 years of hard work that we have reached a stage when the South Indian people gathered in front of me have begun to understand to an extent what I am saying in Hindustani."

At what stage would Gandhiji be completely satisfied, he was asked. Addressing the Tamil people through Pandit Harihara Sharma, Gandhiji said on 17 June 1933: "I will be truly happy only after Hindi has spread through every village."

The proceedings of the Congress and its conferences continued to be conducted in English. The readers of this book should be aware that a resolution to conduct all this in Hindi was passed at the Sahitya Sammelan in Madras. When it came up for the consideration of the committee, Rajaji responded to all the strong objections to it, before getting the resolution passed.

Mother tongue comes first

To the repeated question, "Will not the mother tongues of people be jeopardised by the spread of Hindi?" Gandhiji responded at length several times. He did not wish Hindi to grow at the expense of the local language, and he was confident that such would not be the case. If Hindi was to grow, it had to be alongside the local languages. He gave pride of place to the mother tongue. The importance of a common language came after that. The mother tongue and the common language are like the two eyes, and he believed that improving the vision of one would aid the other.

35

THE FINAL TRAIL

In the interim

The control Gandhiji had imposed upon himself not to write about politics in *Harijan* was lifted by him on 17 July 1937, when he began to write articles, giving advice to the Congress ministers who had taken up office, and to members of the Assembly.

On 22 October 1937, at the Education Conference in Wardha under his presidentship, Dr Zakir Hussain, Ariyanayakam, ministers of several states, and prominent personalities participated, and laid out the tenets of Gandhiji's 'Basic Education' or *Nayi Talim*.

1939

In February 1938, at the Haripura (village in Surat district, Gujarat) All India Village Handicrafts and Khadi exhibition under the leadership of Subhas Chandra Bose, Bose subtly outlined the differences of opinion he and Gandhiji had in the matter of industry. The year 1939 was a significant year for the Congress presidential elections. That year, Subhas Chandra Bose stood against Pattabhi Seetharamayya, and won by a wide margin—despite leaders like Maulana Abdul Kalam Azad, Jawaharlal Nehru, Rajendra Prasad, Bhulabhai Desai, J. B. Kripalani (1888–1982), Sardar Vallabhbhai Patel, and Gandhiji himself backing Seetharamayya. "It is not Dr Pattabhi's loss, but mine. It is clear that whatever principles I uphold are not supported by the Congress," said Gandhiji.

Subhas Bose expressed his regret at Gandhiji referring to this as a personal defeat, and wrote: "I will always make efforts to win Gandhiji's trust. In spite of obtaining the trust of others, if I am unable to garner the trust of the greatest man in India, it is my loss."

At the Congress annual session in Tripuri (near Jabalpur in Madhya Pradesh) in March 1939, Subhas Bose was the elected Congress president. However, a 'confidence motion' was passed in favour of Gandhiji and his followers, and ultimately, Bose was forced to step down from the post. In May 1939, at the All India Congress Committee meeting in Calcutta, as Bose stepped down from the party presidentship, Dr Rajendra Prasad was elected interim president for the remaining term.

India joins the War

England declared war against Germany, after Hitler's invasion of Poland on 1 September 1939. On the same day, without consulting the Indian leaders, the Viceroy announced that India would join the War (World War II, 1939–1945). At the end of March 1940, at the Muslim League conference held in Lahore, the resolution to form Pakistan was adopted. As per Gandhiji's plan, Acharya Vinoba Bhave, the first satyagrahi, began his individual satyagraha on 17 October 1940 at his ashram in Bhaunar village, in Bihar.

Chosen as the second satyagrahi, Jawaharlal Nehru, however, got arrested even before he could start his satyagraha, and was sentenced to four years in jail. Thereafter, by turns, prominent leaders started getting arrested. Around April 1940, almost all the leaders and satyagrahis, about 20,000 in number, had been jailed.

Cripps' mission

In mid-June, 1940, as Germany invaded Russia, there was a change in the global political arena. Britain introduced some modifications in the Central government administration in India. These were not acceptable to Gandhiji. On 11 February 1942, Jamnalal Bajaj passed away. On 22 March, Sir Stafford Cripps, sent by British Prime Minister Churchill, arrived on a 'mission' to negotiate with Indian leaders. After listening to his proposal, Gandhiji termed it a "post-dated cheque on a crashing bank," and, without any attempt at diplomacy, said to Cripps: "If this is your plan, why did you come this far? Take the first flight back home."

Rajaji and Gandhi

Among his associates, Gandhiji held Rajaji in the highest esteem, and he wrote so in the *Harijan*. He also did not avoid mentioning it whenever there was a difference of views between them. 1942 was the year in which the movement not to give in to the idea of a separate Pakistan was strongly in force. Rajaji was broadly in favour of such a division, but not Gandhiji.

Gandhiji declared that if the Muslims had made up their minds, unless the people were prepared to strongly and firmly oppose it, there was no way this eventuality could be prevented. Rajaji maintained that this view of Gandhiji was in consonance with his. Many brought this to Gandhiji's notice. It was only when he wrote in the *Harijan* that Gandhiji made it clear that on this issue his views and those of Rajaji were as different as butter and lime.

However, Gandhiji appealed to the people not to make too much of this difference of views between him and Rajaji, adding that the freedom and courage to offer opposing views was useful in shaping public opinion, and praised Rajaji in voicing his considered opinion. This conflict of views, though, led to confusion and violence at Rajaji's meetings, which Gandhiji never failed to condemn. Neither did he miss an opportunity to assert that this or that view of Rajaji was wrong. He declared that, till the British left India, such talk of the division of India and Pakistan was baseless. Later, he said, "Henceforward I shall not be talking about the difference of views on this matter between Rajaji and myself openly in front of the public. It offends me to do so."

August 1942 declaration

On 8 August 1942, the All India Congress Committee meeting in Bombay made the declaration to the British government: "Quit India!" Gandhiji was the prime mover of this affirmation, and he was vested with the full authority to initiate and conduct this protest. Accepting this responsibility, Gandhiji addressed the people of India with the clarion call: "Do or Die!" The next day, with Gandhiji, Mahadev Desai, and later, Kasturba and other leaders being arrested, violence erupted in several parts of the country. Till these protests died down, it was decided that the *Harijan* publication would be suspended. A week after this, on the morning of 15 August 1942, Mahadev Desai passed away in jail.

Kasturba no more

In 1943, lakhs of people died in the Bengal famine. In February 1943, after a protracted correspondence between the Viceroy and Indian ministers, Gandhiji went on a three-week fast. As an echo to this, Sir C. P. Mody, N. R. Sarkar and M. S. Aney in the Viceroy's administration stepped down from their posts. On 22 February 1944, Kasturba passed away in prison. In April of that year, Gandhiji was afflicted with malaria. He and his associates were released from prison on 5 May 1944.

Kasturba Fund

Upon the passing away of Kasturba, a fund was set up in her name. The collection far exceeded what was aimed at, and Gandhiji desired that it be used for the progress of Indian women. Hence, it was deployed for the training of women working in villages. In Madras, such training was being given in Gandhi Gramam, near Madurai. A close associate of Gandhiji, G. Ramachandran, and his wife, Soundaram Ramachandran, had established the Gandhi Gramam, and were in charge of its administration. For years, the Kasturba Fund was administered by Soundaram Ramachandran.

Case against INA

A dialogue between Gandhiji and Jinnah began on 9 September 1944, and went on for 17 days, before it failed. In November 1945, the case against the Indian National Army (I.N.A.) heroes was heard at the Red Fort. Along with Bhulabhai Desai was Jawaharlal Nehru, who argued for them. Thereafter, Gandhiji toured Assam, Orissa and Bengal, before coming to Madras.

Madras elections

Several important events had taken place in Madras meanwhile. In the Town Council elections of April 1939 in Madras, the Congress had won with a large majority. In the District Council elections, too, the Congress had emerged victorious by a huge margin. A Bill introduced by M. C. Raja in the Madras Legislature, on the 'Removal of Housing Restrictions for Harijans', was passed. Prohibition was brought into force in the North Arcot district. Leaders and workers of the Harijan temple entry movement gave it much importance, applied themselves assiduously to it, and achieved good results. On 8 July 1939, the Meenakshi temple in Madurai opened its doors to Harijans.

Temple entry lauded

Gandhiji lauded the temple entry in the Madurai Meenakshi temple and wrote in the *Harijan*: "For working tirelessly in shaping the views of people, Sri Vaidyanatha Iyer and his associates deserve all our praise." When Rajaram Raja Sahib of the Thanjavur palace opened the associated temples to Harijans, too, Gandhiji was quick to applaud. The Trustee and Harijan Seva Sangam president were likewise lauded when the Courtallam temple similarly opened its doors.

'Temples should not have wealth'

Some people were, however, surprised when Gandhiji, who had wholeheartedly worked towards temple entry, declared that no funds should be collected for building temples. This issue arose when O. P. Ramasamy Reddiar was the chief minister. Reddiar later said:

> When I was Chief Minister in 1947, Gandhiji wrote in *Harijan* that funds should not be collected for temples. I had been to Delhi at that time. I said that I was not in favour of destroying temples and mutts. Perhaps I spoke too vehemently. At the end, Gandhiji asked me, 'How did temples come about?' I replied, 'Through bhakti.' He said, 'I accept what you say. If temples came about because of bhakti, it is harmful for a temple to have money. … Bhakti cannot grow if there is money; it is only when there is no money that bhakti will grow. Devotees will come on their own to temples, give money, and perform whatever is necessary in the temple. Wealth only leads to disputes. Hence temples and mutts should not have wealth.

Dissolution of ministry

The Madras Legislature passed a resolution to the effect that India had been dragged into World War II without its express approval, hence the Madras ministry would step down. As no other party had the strength to form the ministry, Governor's Rule was announced, with IAS officials as advisors.

Opposition to laws

In the beginning of 1941, Madras witnessed many protests against imposed laws. The Madras Congress considered itself a satyagraha group and took on members. Its first act of protest was condemnation of the arrest of the first individual satyagrahi, Vinoba Bhave, and the postponement of the meeting of the Madurai District Committee. All over India, thousands were arrested and sent to jails. The clamour for a common national government in India grew. The statement of Rajaji that the Muslim demand for creation of Pakistan be met was the subject of fierce debate.

Hearing that the Congress Committee was considering a no-confidence motion against him, Rajaji resigned both as a Congress Party member and as a legislator in Madras State. Following this, Assembly leaders P. Sambamurthi, Dr T. S. S. Rajan and Ramanathan, too, stepped down as members of the legislature, leading to a difficult situation within the Congress. However, those remaining in the Congress leadership conducted meetings in several parts of the state without losing heart, and exhorted people to follow the leadership of Gandhiji, and act as per the decisions of the All India Congress Committee at all times, thus defusing the situation.

Lakshmi K. Bharathi

A Madurai nationalist, L. Krishnaswamy Bharathi led an independent satyagraha, and was jailed in November 1940. His wife, Lakshmi Krishnaswamy Bharathi was also determined to be involved in this moral war and go to prison. However, as she was suffering from a heart condition, she was counselled by her family and friends that it would not be advisable for her to go to jail. The doctor attending on her also warned her that, should she go to jail, she might not return alive. The lady, though, was determined, come what may, to go to jail. In this situation, G. Ramachandran devised a method to keep her out of jail. (Ramchandran was, then, staying at Krishnaswamy Bharathi's house in Madurai). He wrote a letter to Gandhiji, explaining the situation, to which Gandhiji responded in his own handwriting to Lakshmi:

> Dear sister,
>
> Owing to your health condition, it is not necessary for you to take part in the war against laws.
>
> Yours, Bapu

Yet, overriding Gandhiji's advice, Lakshmi took part in the protests and went to jail. Hearing this, Krishnaswamy Bharathi wrote to Gandhiji, regretting that his wife had gone against his advice. Gandhiji's reply to this letter was moving, reflecting his generous nature: "It is proper for a Hindu lady to follow [in] the footsteps of her husband. That is what your wife has done. You say that she has gone against my order. But she has answered a much higher call, that of the nation. Shortly her health will improve, do not worry."

Lakshmi Bharathi, who was afflicted by a serious ailment, recovered and came out of jail. The truth of Gandhiji's statement was borne out. There was another occasion when such a surprising occurrence was witnessed in Madras.

Fenner Brockway

When Gandhiji came to Madras, he heard that the British Labour leader, Fenner Brockway,[1] was in hospital. Gandhiji went to see him and enquire about his health.

"I am unable to sleep. If I could, I should get well," said Brockway.

"Yes, what you say is correct. There is much virtue in sleep. It changes the chemical balance in your body, and I have found great relief in it," said Gandhiji. He placed his palm on Brockway's forehead, closed his eyes, and stood silently for a while. Opening his eyes and looking at Brockway, he said, "Now you will sleep peacefully, and thereby get fully cured."

Before Gandhiji left the room, Brockway had fallen into a deep sleep. His health improved soon after.

August protests

The echoes of the arrests of prominent leaders following the August demonstrations were felt strongly in Madras. There were processions and protest marches everywhere. The police went on a rampage, and many people lost their lives. Acid was thrown at a police official in Sri Meenakshi temple, Madurai. A certain peace that had descended for some time was broken in 1943 February; Gandhiji went on fast in jail. In the protests that took place in Madras then, students took the larger part. Many in the Congress movement went underground.

In 1945, after release from prison, Bhakthavatsalam, Obaidullah, and Venkatachalapathy went to meet Gandhiji in Sevagram, and sought his advice on administration in Madras, in the light of the Congress having been banned.

Opposition to Rajaji

When Rajaji rejoined the Congress in 1945, many in the party did not welcome it, and he faced open opposition. Examining the differences of opinion with a view to removing misconceptions, the efforts of noted lawyer and freedom fighter Asaf Ali (1888–1953) did succeed temporarily, but a permanent reconciliation proved elusive.

Justice Party Conference

Between 1939 and 1945, at the time the Congress was making strenuous efforts to achieve freedom, some other parties cooperated with the government to strengthen its position. Periyar E. V. Ramasamy held a conference of the Justice Party in Kanchipuram, and presented a map of a separate Dravida Nadu, comprising those provinces where Tamil, Telugu, Kannada or Malayalam was spoken. Thereafter, a party by the name of Dravida Kazhagam under his leadership was formed. Many from the Justice Party joined it. Subsequently, arising out of a dispute in policy with Periyar, C. N. Annadurai (later chief minister of Tamil Nadu) left the party and established the Dravida Munnetra Kazhagam (DMK).

Dravida Nadu

Division of the country was against Gandhiji's principles. He had opposed the formation of Pakistan. He had written and spoken about the demand to create a separate Dravida Nadu based on the Tamil, Telugu, Kannada and Malayalam speaking linguistic provinces. He said in 1947:

> Why should these four language-based areas [form a separate region in] India? Have not these languages been inspired by Sanskrit? I have toured these four, and have not experienced them to be any different from other states. It is a fantasy to say that those below the Vindhyas are not Aryans, and those above it are. We have no idea what it was in times past, but today both groups of people are one. From Kashmir to Kanyakumari, they have become one.

His last visit, in 1946

It was in 1946 that Gandhiji's feet graced the soil of Madras (now Tamil Nadu) for the very last time. When he had come here for the first time, in 1896, he had come as a leader, and it was as a leader that he made his final visit 50 years later. But in that half century, a small seed had grown into an enormous tree.

It was only after his first visit to Madras that the people here knew who he was, but by the time of his final visit, extra buses and trains had to be organised to meet the demands of the crowds that came to see him. On this occasion, he had come for the Silver Jubilee of the Hindi Prachar Sabha, and the temple entry of Harijans into the Madurai Sri Meenakshi temple and the Pazhani temple. The Silver Jubilee celebrations of the Hindi Prachar Sabha ought to have taken place two years earlier, but they had waited for Gandhiji's visit.

Mambalam, where the Sabha was located, shone like a new town that day. Three beautifully decorated arches, courtesy of S. S. Vasan, the owner of 'Ananda Vikatan', surrounding the Sabha were named 'Kasturba Gate', 'Bajaj Gate' and 'Hindustani Gate'. The Kasturba Gate was opened by Tmt. Jamnalal Bajaj, the Bajaj Gate by C. Rajagopalachariar and the Hindustani Gate by Kaka Kalelkar. These gates depicted beautiful examples of ancient Tamil art, and vignettes of Gandhiji's life. Not only Tamils, but men and women from Andhra, Mysore and Kerala had come to attend this function. At the time of Gandhiji's visit, the Hindi Prachar Sabha area was named Gandhi Nagar, and its exhibition area, Hindustani Nagar. The function itself was a success, and a cloth merchant, Sri Ramulu Chettiar, gave a large donation. Tmt. Apte and Tmt. Ambujammal looked after the work of women volunteers, while the male volunteers were overseen by C. R. Pattabhiramayya.

21 January 1946, Arriving early

Gandhiji was scheduled to arrive in Madras on 23 January. On 22 January every year, he observed the death anniversary of Kasturba. Hence he left Calcutta ahead of schedule and announced his earlier arrival in Madras.

On Monday, 21 January evening, he reached Ambattur railway station. To avoid the crowds, his compartment was detached from the Calcutta line and diverted to the Bombay line, to allow him to detrain. Rajaji, Gopalaswami, the Madras Congress president, K. Kamaraj, M. Satyanarayana, Kamal Nayan Bajaj and Dr P. Subbarayan welcomed him at Ambattur railway station. Gandhiji got down with arms folded in greeting, and wearing only a dhoti. As his day of silence had not yet ended, he did not speak a word. The watch dangling from his side showed the time as 4.15 p.m. Kamaraj garlanded him.

Gandhiji's arrival had been kept secret even from Rajaji. Arrangements were made accordingly by the Railway District Superintendent of Police, who privately visited and invited Satyanarayana, Rajaji and N. Gopalaswami Iyengar to the Ambattur station. Others came to know of this somehow, and on the way, the train was forcibly stopped at Ponneri for the crowds to get a glimpse of Gandhiji, and to present a purse.

Tamil and Telugu

At 4.50 p.m., Gandhiji reached the Hindi Prachar Sabha, where the crowd conducted itself peacefully. There were many women at the entrance to offer *aarathi* to him. On this visit, he took a stand regarding Tamil and Telugu, and the raging question of the time: 'For whom is Madras? For Andhras or for Tamils?' When a lady at the women's meeting asked him to speak a few words in Tamil, he laughed aloud and replied, "*Enna, tamizha theriyume!*" (What, I know Tamil!). An Andhra lady promptly asked him to say something in Telugu, to which he replied in Hindustani, "I know Telugu, but all of you must learn Hindustani" (*Swadesamithran*, 22–23 January issue).

22 January 1946, Meeting friends

Early morning the next day, Gandhiji and his entourage read the *Gita* in full, to mark Kasturba Day. He did not schedule any official engagements, but many people visited him where he was staying. When S. Satyamurthi's wife and daughter met him, he enquired fondly after their welfare. In connection with the election of Harijan representatives to the legislature, there had been a written agreement in 1936 between their leaders and Satyamurthi. A Harijan leader, J. Sivashanmugam Pillai (later the leader of the Madras Assembly), met Gandhiji to stress that this agreement must continue to be operative, and desired to know if there was any major change in the Congress thinking on the matter. Gandhiji assured him that the agreement would continue to hold.

Prayer meeting

A snap decision was taken to conduct a prayer meeting on this day, at which the public could participate. It took place at 5 p.m. Though no prior information had been given, about 12,000 people attended, giving an idea of how at any given time thousands of people were desirous of seeing Gandhiji. H. D. Raja and the Pethapuram prince had made good arrangements for this meeting. Agatha Harrison, an associate of the Mahatma, was also present. Gandhiji's speech in Hindustani was translated by G. Subramaniam of the Hindi Prachar Sabha into Tamil.

Visit to V. S. Srinivasa Sastri

The Rt. Hon'ble V. S. Srinivasa Sastri's health had deteriorated at this time, and he was admitted into the Government General Hospital. Gandhiji met him thrice, twice in the hospital, and once at his house, to enquire after his health. These were poignant meetings, and were written about in detail by Tmt. Sushila Nayyar in the *Harijan* after Sastri's demise.

Gandhiji met Sastri for the first visit on 22 January 1946. Sastri's doctor, Dr Srinivasan, escorted Gandhiji to the hospital, where he was welcomed by the Hospital Superintendent, M. A. Sheppard, the R.M.O., and V. K. Venkataraman. As he left the hospital after visiting Sastri, Gandhiji was seen off by officials and employees of the hospital. On his way out, Gandhiji entered a ward and enquired after the health of the inmates there.

Mutual affection and regard

From the time that Srinivasa Sastri had proclaimed Gopal Krishna Gokhale to be his political mentor, during his visit to South Africa, Gandhiji had developed much affection and respect for him. Sastri was considered a moderate in Indian politics. After Gokhale's demise, he became the president of the Indian Workers' Association. Involved in proofreading and correcting the English translation of Gandhiji's book, *Sathya Sodhanai* (*My Experiments With Truth*), he was considered to be an expert in Sanskrit and English, and a celebrated public speaker.

Sastri met Gandhiji for the first time on 9 January 1915, and wrote about Gandhiji's views to his brother. In it he had said that Gandhiji's speech and his humility reminded him of his close friend Krishnaswami Iyer. The views of Gandhiji and Sastri were often in opposition on many political issues. Yet, their friendship blossomed by the day, and their mutual respect grew over the years. As Gandhiji said, they were like brothers borne by the same mother. Sastri was convinced that Gandhiji was the greatest person living on earth.

Conscience keeper

The quality of Sastri that Gandhiji admired most was his sense of truth. If Sastri raised any issues, Gandhiji had no doubt whatsoever that he was being true to his conscience, which is why he once wrote to Sastri: "When you speak publicly about me, it gives me satisfaction. It is only when you do not, that it makes me anxious." From this, it seems apparent that, like Rajaji, Sastri, too, was Gandhiji's conscience keeper.

Sastri is no more

A few weeks after Gandhiji's final visit to Madras, V. S. Srinivasa passed away. This news reached the ashram late at night, when Gandhiji was fast asleep. Hence it was conveyed to him after the morning routine the next day. Gandhiji's grief was boundless. In that week's *Young India*, he wrote an obituary which read, in part: "The demise of one of India's favourite sons has snatched him from us, why, the world. His patriotism was no less than anyone's. His body may be turned to ashes, but Sastri, the man, will live on."

Sastri, the teacher

When Gandhiji came to see his dear friend at the hospital, Sastri, in his enthusiasm, went on speaking, to the extent that the doctor was concerned. He said something in Tamil, and Sastri responded with a smile, saying, "Yes, you are right. The expert on oratory should indeed spend more time listening, but they say that 'a teacher at five is a teacher at 50,' hence I tend to go on speaking." Speaking thus for a while longer, Sastri was still not done when Gandhiji was about to take his leave.

"I had thought of telling you something," he started again, and as he was speaking, tears filled his eyes. "Another opportunity for peace has gone by, and now they are conducting a peace conference. Who is there but you to talk about this on behalf of humanity? I fear that India has failed to do its duty," he said. And this was not the only time he said this. From the time that Gandhiji had been released from prison, Sastri had been emphasising this point in his letters. On this occasion, these great men had an interesting discussion on the peace conference and the state of Indian politics.

"If only the doctor assures me that my visiting you has not worsened your health will I come again," declared Gandhiji, as he took his leave of Sastri.

23 January 1946, In-camera meeting

The Parliamentary Mediation Committee from Britain, set up to discuss India's freedom with the leaders, met Gandhiji in Madras, and held talks over two days. On the first day, that is, 23 January night, they had an in-camera meeting for two hours with Gandhiji, at which even Gandhiji's secretary, Pyarelal, was not present. On Gandhiji's advice, this committee later met the Kumarappa brothers, J. C. Kumarappa and Bharathan Kumarappa, and discussed matters of the economy and social problems.

Views on India's freedom

On 24 January 1946, this parliamentary committee met Gandhiji again to discuss India's freedom and all the issues arising out of it. During these talks, Gandhiji shared his views on how the future political establishment of India should be. "Our meeting with Gandhiji was a good forerunner for the future, not only of India and Britain, but of the world," declared one of the members of this committee, Bottomley, and it was an appropriate statement.

Speak in Hindi

On the third day, a leader of the Harijans, V. I. Munusamy Pillai, met Gandhiji and told him that he could see some small change in the attitude of caste Hindus in Madras towards Harijans. Gandhiji said that his experience was likewise.

When the daughter of former Madras High Court judge, Sir T. Sadasiva Iyer, went to see Gandhiji, she spoke to him in English. Gandhiji interrupted her and asked her to speak in Hindi. She admitted that though she had learnt the *Bhagavad Gita* by heart, she regretted she had not studied Hindi. Gandhiji then recounted to her that when his son Devadas had started Tamil classes in Madras, T. Sadasiva Iyer was among the first to learn Hindi. His daughter, thereafter, promised to learn Hindi in the shortest possible time, and took his leave. Gandhiji was also met by Madurai N. M. R. Subburaman, Kovai T. S. Avinashalingam, V. K. Palanisamy Gounder, Vedaranyam Vedaratthinam Pillai, the London priest Hickman Johnson, V. V. Giri (later the President of India), and P. S. Murthy.

Prayer meeting

When Gandhiji announced his prayer meeting, the crowds that gathered threatened to go out of control. There was a sea of people between Venkatanarayana Road and Boag Road. The meeting began with Kumari Sarojini Mahadevan singing an invocation to Kapaliswarar by Carnatic composer and singer Papanasam Sivan (1890–1973). Gandhiji referred to this song in his speech and said that it reminded him of a composition of Gurudev Tagore sung at Jyothipuri. "In that song, a devotee prays to God that, in his weak state, God must come as 'Rudra' and fill him with strength. A somewhat similar emotion is conveyed in this song," he said.

There was noise and confusion at the start and end of this meeting. Hence Gandhiji kept standing for the entire duration of his speech.

'I shall speak only Hindustani'

At the Workers' Conference inaugurated by Gandhiji, Krishna Das Jaju of the All India Charkha Sangam presided. About 200 workers from Kerala, Mysore, Andhra and Madras attended. Gandhiji criticised the invitation for this conference being printed in English, saying it should either have been in Tamil or in Hindi. He faulted the workers in his speech for not learning Hindi. "Gone are the days when I need to entertain you with speeches in English. I will speak in English now only with Englishmen and foreigners. As far as you are concerned, I have decided to speak only in Hindustani."

When asked "What is your view on economic equality?" Gandhiji replied: Hundred per cent equality is not possible. Some may require more food; others more warm clothes for the cold. It becomes necessary to meet each one's requirement. In such an economy it cannot be that the poor become poorer and the rich richer."

The translation of Gandhiji's responses to the queries went on till 4.30 p.m. Some 300 people participated in the spinning.

Thyagaraja

Gandhiji referred to the Thyagaraja Krithi sung at the prayer meeting, and said that he was aware of the greatness of Thyagaraja in South India.

Wherever I have travelled, in Madras, Mysore, Andhra and Kerala, I have heard the beautiful strains of Thyagaraja's compositions being sung. The melody is transmitted from the singer directly to one's heart. The discord we see between States today is diametrically opposite to the unifying music of Thyagaraja.

"Some say they want only Tamil. There is also a feeling of difference between North and South India. In a balance, if Rama's qualities are placed on one pan and his various names on the other, how much heavier the latter would be? Likewise is the conflict between Madras and Andhra, Gujarat and Bombay Presidency. If these are put aside and only the greatness of Hindustan is considered, how proud we should be. There are just two syllables in the name 'Rama' but there is no limit to its power. Similarly, 'Hind'—it has a special strength.

Interview

Some major industrialists of Coimbatore, P. S. G. Ganga Naidu and others, met Gandhiji, and requested him to visit Coimbatore. A purse for the Harijan Fund was presented. The president of the Madras Harijan Seva Sangam V. Bhashyam Iyengar and K. Bhashyam met Gandhiji and discussed with him the issues pertaining to the Kodambakkam Harijan Training School's future.

25 January 1946, Madras

When he inaugurated the Silver Jubilee of the Madras Hindi Prachar Sabha, Gandhiji poured his heart out in his speech. Asking for a chair to sit on to enable people to see him clearly, he said, "It was in Madras that I started this movement for the underprivileged. Prominent, educated people of this city welcomed me at that time." *The Hindu* (26 January 1946) had written elaborately about how Madras was involved in political work.

The people who had been involved from the start in Hindi Prachar work (all Pandits) Rishi K. Sharma, Harihara Sharma, Seetharam Anjaneyulu and T. Krishnaswami, offered '*ponnadais*' (shawls adorned around the shoulders of a dignitary being honoured) to Gandhiji, who remarked that the affinity towards English in India, and more so in South India, was a kind of slavery.

> It is not difficult to break these golden shackles and obtain freedom. If you substitute Hindustani for English, it is easily done. The language spoken by a majority of Indians can become the common language of the country. This is Hindustani. Learning Hindustani through two scripts, therefore, becomes your duty. This apart, those who are involved in the work of Hindi propagation must learn the language of the province in which they are working.

As per the advice of Gandhiji, the name of Hindi Prachar Sabha was changed to Hindustani Prachar Sabha.

Students' demonstration

On 25 January, as a condemnation of the police firing in Bombay, the students of Pachaiyappa's College, Madras, staged a spirited demonstration. As they all boycotted college and started off in procession towards Hindustani Nagar, the police refused permission. Citing that the students had not sought prior approval for the procession, the police asked them to disperse. The students refused to do so, and sat in protest. In spite of Rajaji reasoning with them, they refused to move. The Students' Congress president, N. Krishnasamy, read to them the letter that Gandhiji had sent. Even after this letter was read, the students refused to budge.

Rajaji came away from there, and, after five hours, as per the suggestion of the College president, V. V. Narayanaswamy Naidu, the students moved via Nowroji Road to the grounds near Chetpet railway station, passed a Condemnation Resolution, and then dispersed.

Confusion at the prayer meeting

As had become the custom, there was noise and confusion at the day's prayer meeting. The crowds increased by the day, and there would have been a lakh people at the meeting. As soon as Gandhiji started to say a few words, which were translated into Tamil, a man from Andhra stood up and interrupted to say, "There are Telugus at this meeting also. There should also have been a Telugu translation for your speech." Gandhiji replied, "Instead of behaving thus at a prayer meeting, you could have met me ahead of it and made your request, or else sent it in writing. But you stand up at the meeting and try to browbeat me." Gandhiji tried his best to restore peace and defuse the situation, but the man refused to sit, continuing to shout at the top of his voice. This pained Gandhiji, and he hurriedly finished his speech, left the prayer meeting and returned to his place of stay.

Although the man from Andhra later expressed regret for his actions, he kept on reiterating his demand. Dr Sushila Nayyar intervened and stopped him from bothering Gandhiji any more. The man left, but Gandhiji was pleased that at least other Andhra speakers did not join him in his protest. Normally, a prayer meeting would leave him happy and spiritually at peace, but not that day. Because of this, Gandhiji decided against any translation of his speeches, and left it to the people to interact with him as they desired.

Meeting the Governor

That night, at Raj Bhavan, Guindy, Gandhiji met the Governor for discussions. The Governor's personal secretary, I. C. Allard, picked up and dropped Gandhiji for this meeting. The Governor, Sir Arthur Hope, and his wife welcomed Gandhiji. He and Gandhiji then had a private meeting lasting 80 minutes.

26 January 1946, Swarajya and Hindi

The sixth day of Gandhiji's visit was designated 'Independence Day', i.e. the day on which the independence pledge was taken. Despite his busy schedule, including four speeches on the day, he gave a few interviews in the morning. About 1000 persons involved in propagating Hindi in different states through the aegis of the Hindi Prachar Sabha attended the Sabha's conference. At this conference, inaugurated by Kaka Kalelkar, the spread of Hindustani was considered a national imperative in order to achieve 'Ishwar Rajyam', 'Rama Rajyam', or 'Khuda Rajyam'. Gandhiji further said that there should be no bar on liberally including words from other languages and provinces in Hindi.

Gandhiji's advice that those who taught Hindi should learn the languages of other provinces, and that Hindi should not be considered a rival to other languages, was well received in Madras. The *Hindu* issue of 27 January 1946 said: "The emphasis Gandhiji has placed on both has meant that, however big or useful a language may be, its importance cannot equal that of the mother tongue, and this fact is admitted by those who propagate Hindi."

Untouchability

Gandhiji said that, at the Harijan conference, the crowds that attended, together with the awakening among them, had given him much happiness. Harijan leader V. I. Munusamy Pillai garlanded him and presented a flag made out of palm leaves in three colours. Gandhiji said: "In the free India that I see in my mind's eye, there will be no untouchability. Crores of Congressmen will live and die for this. Through truth and ahimsa, Harijans must achieve their freedom."

Gandhiji's definition of freedom on this occasion deserves to be encased in gold: "True freedom does not mean that we can act as we please; it means the doing of our duty. Staying away from liquor is freedom; working for our own progress is freedom."

At the Administrative Workers' Conference on this day, since Gandhiji had insisted that everyone should speak only in their mother tongue, there were speeches in Hindustani, Tamil, Telugu, Malayalam and Kannada. Presiding over this conference, Dewan Bahadur V. Bhashyam Iyengar said, "I consider Gandhiji to be an incarnation, and in this incarnation I believe he will exterminate untouchability." By answering several queries from the workers, Gandhiji dispelled their doubts through considered responses, laced with humour.

Declaration

Gandhiji pointedly said that on this independence day next year, 1947, freedom would be gained. "Let us believe that there will be no need to take the independence pledge again next year." After the British Parliamentary group met him, it was evident that Gandhiji's declaration carried much force, and by most accounts, it is in Madras that Gandhiji first made it.

Foundation stone

The foundation stone to be laid for the building of Adi Dravidar Youth Sangam in Krishnampettai was touched and blessed by Gandhiji on this day. At first, since the lettering on the foundation stone was in English, Gandhiji refused to give his blessings. So a new stone was prepared with Telugu lettering. But did the earlier stone go waste? Would Gandhiji's financial prudence permit it? He stopped the persons who had brought the stone, and asked Satyanarayana, "Do you want this stone?" to which Satyanarayana replied that it could be used.

When Gandhiji returned from the prayer meeting, the National Muslim Mediation Group, led by Allah Pichai, with Abdul Hakim, K. V. Nooruddin Sahib, Poidu Moulvi Sahib, K. A. Ibrahim Sahib, K. Rahman Sahib, K. Moidu Sahib. P. P. Umer Koya and Haji C. Umer, met him for discussions. The celebrated singer, M. S. Subbulakshmi (1916–2004) was introduced to him by Rajaji. On Gandhiji's request she sang a few bhajans.

Not in English

During his stay here, innumerable people kept coming for his autograph, for which the Sabha authorities had made special arrangements. They collected Rs 5 each, and sent the receipts and autograph books or his photograph to Gandhiji for his signature. Gandhiji requested the autograph seekers to specify in which language they wanted him to sign. But he refused to sign in English.

27 January 1946, Exhausted

As Gandhiji had to complete a lot of work on the day, he was exhausted the next day. After his morning routine, when he returned to Mangala Bhavan, it became necessary for Thakkar Bapa to stand guard outside his room to stop any more visitors from seeing him. Normally, this is not something Thakkar Bapa would do, but the fact that he did so speaks of the impossibility for Gandhiji to engage in any more meetings or work that day.

At the prayer meeting in the morning, Gandhiji took as the theme for his speech the lyrics of the traditional Hindustani song rendered by a girl named Saraswathi Devi. After this meeting, as Gandhiji entered Mangala Bhavan, a huge crowd was waiting there to see him. So when he reappeared outside, they were ecstatic. He told them: "You have shown me unbounded love by coming to see me. I am, therefore, standing before you without going on my usual travels. The prayer meeting has been arranged at a large and comfortable place. Hence, please come with your friends for this meeting tomorrow." He said all this in Hindustani, asked A. Subbiah standing next to him to translate, and went into the house for a brief rest.

Perils of a foreign language

Dr Muthulakshmi Reddy presided over the Administration Workers' Conference on this day. Gandhiji spoke for 15 minutes at this conference, which was to be followed by the convocation ceremony of Hindi students. Those participating had assembled inside the Silver Jubilee pandal. While Gandhiji was speaking, a worker was earnestly requesting the crowd for silence, but using wrong English, and saying: "Please see there is no silence!" This evoked much laughter, and Gandhiji immediately remarked, "See the danger in using a foreign language!" (Amritha Ramasubramaniam interview)

Gandhiji was asked: "Can we seek help from Christian missionaries in independent India?" He replied: "Certainly, if anyone wholeheartedly comes forward to offer help to India, we must accept it. There is the example of the late C. F. 'Deenabandhu' Andrews, who worked for India's cause, and laid his life down for it. India definitely needs the service of those who come forward with love and commitment to work for its welfare."

Future plan

After clarifying the doubts raised by workers at the meeting, Gandhiji spoke in general terms about the plan for organisation.

> As the work that we need to do is much, I invite everyone to come forward to take responsibility. The awakening that we see in our country is due to our success in organisation. After Independence, too, it is through such organisation that we must protect our country. The main points of our organisation must

be for all to maintain the purity of bodies and soul, and ensure basic education for your children. It is through such basic education that children will learn to fulfil their own needs, and become model citizens. Educated women must go to villages and teach children not only to read and write, but cleanliness in their lives. The returns that we will get will far exceed what we spend on this organisation—that is its special feature.

Convocation dress

After this, at the 23rd Convocation of the Hindustani Prachar Sabha, the Sabha officials made their way in pairs, as per established convention, led by Gandhiji and Rajkumari Amrit Kaur. It was a splendid sight to see everyone seated on stage dressed in the traditional violet robes. A hundred brahmacharis of the Walajabad Hindu Vedic School accorded Gandhiji the welcome as per shastras. Awarding the diplomas to the students, as requested by a dignitary on stage, Gandhiji told the awardees that they must honour the oath taken by them, and serve India, and the world, by propagating Hindustani.

He presented prizes to the rank-holding students. Rajkumari Amrit Kaur delivered the convocation address. At the night conference of the Hindi *pracharak*s, the suggestion of Hindustani being taught through the scripts of both Devanagari and Urdu was debated, and then adopted by a majority vote.

Legislature and service

In the morning, Gandhiji spoke with the workers of the Kasturba Fund, and explained to them ways in which they could improve the Fund's activities. All of them should have the mindset of villagers, he added, and said it was not desirable that those involved in parliamentary work should also involve themselves in village activities. There were two reasons for this: one was that doing both together would be difficult; and secondly, the people in villages would be wrongly led to believe that village work was related to parliamentary affairs.

The missing pen

Gandhiji's ink pen went missing, causing some concern, and despite a thorough search, it could not be found. He had last used this pen at the convocation. When, after the prayer meeting, he looked for it to sign some papers, he found it missing. He swore that if this one was not found, he would never again use a fountain pen. However, Akkoor Ananthachari has written that on the third day of its loss, the fountain pen was back on the table at which Gandhiji did his normal work.

28 January 1946, The virtue of silence

The next day, even observing his day of silence, Gandhiji managed to surprise people. To ensure silence from the public at the meeting, hitherto not experienced, he worked out another device. His speech on the day that was read out at the prayer meeting was about the virtue of silence. All the songs that would normally have been sung at the meeting were just read out.

Bus journey

Dr Sushila Nayyar, Pyarelal, M. Satyanarayana and Jagannath Das went to the Harijan School in the morning with Gandhiji, who was to lay the foundation stone, and gathered all particulars. After this, when they came to the intersection of Venkatanarayana Road and Mount Road, they noticed some buses and lorries standing. Waving his hands, Gandhiji requested a bus driver to bring his vehicle nearer, which surprised the driver, who did not move. On Gandhiji's repeated beckoning, he drove the bus up. Gandhiji boarded the bus, followed by his entourage. The driver started the bus on Gandhiji's sign, drove through Mount Road and turned at Thyagaraya Road. Gandhiji espied the Kasturba Gate and Bajaj Gate, asked the driver to stop at Bajaj Gate and got down from the bus along with the others. He thereafter walked up to the Sevagram exhibition. He was shown around the exhibition by the president of the exhibition committee, K. Venkatasamy Naidu, K. Bhashyam, N. Venugopal and Duraikkannu Mudaliar.

After this he went to the Harijan Training school and inspected a new design spindle. At Bharat Café, Krishna Iyer presented a small purse. From there they drove to Hindustani Nagar and inspected the daily boarding and lodging arrangements that had been made. The doctor in charge of the dispensary, Dr K. S. Krishnan, showed him round the facility. Fees received for treatment and donations from those in the unit were presented as a purse to Gandhiji. We have only heard of fees being paid for medical treatment, never the reverse. The doctors who worked in Gandhiji's movement, though, were different. That was his strength.

When Gandhiji returned, he noticed a visually challenged person from Pollachi standing opposite the building, waiting to see him. He went up to him and stroked his cheek affectionately. When informed by persons around that it was Gandhiji who had touched him, he raised both his arms over his head in a gesture of gratitude.

Food shortage

The advisor to the Governor Sir S. V. Ramamurthy and his family met Gandhiji, who enquired about the food situation in the state. He was certain that, whatever the situation, Tamils had the resilience to surmount the problems. At the time the interim government had taken over in India, there was acute food shortage in Madras, and representatives of the State government had gone to Delhi to ask for food allotment. This did not please Gandhiji. At the Delhi prayer meeting he had referred to this and said:

> In Madras there is adequate availability of food, like peanuts and coconut. There is also enough fish, which many of the people there eat, so why should they go begging to Delhi? I know the Tamils from the days I was in South Africa. In their marches, they were served only one and a half chappatis every night as ration, yet they walked along singing happily, and cooking whatever food was available on the way. How could such people, who adjusted to the demands of the day then, be so helpless today?

Gandhiji had told Dewan Bahadur C. S. Rathinasabapathy Mudaliar and Kovai industrialist P. S. G. Ganga Naidu during his visit to Pazhani that if they were to start a gurukulam for girls in the choultry there, he would arrange for Rs 3,000 in the first year and Rs 6,000 in the second year. Tmt. Yakub Hassan met Gandhiji, and he requested her for a copy of the book she had written on the Quran.

Mistaken identity

The news about Dr Vinayakam and his wife meeting Gandhiji, and reportedly seeking his blessings before their imminent trip to Wardha to reside there, became a subject of some mirth. As was later revealed, the persons who met Gandhiji were not Dr Vinayakam and his wife, but the disciple of Dr J. C. Kumarappa, and administration employee Vinayakam and his wife. When he was employed in Maganwadi, Vinayakam had devised a wooden screw to grind paddy, and Gandhiji had praised his ability to embellish common articles into attractive artifacts.

Vinayakam had just recently got married, and his wife's name was Gomathi. Although many prominent people failed to get appointments with Gandhiji, Gomathi was fortunate enough to do so, perhaps because she was a worker's wife. She told Harihara Sharma that she wished to meet Gandhiji. Sharma directed her to Dr Sushila Nayyar, who, thinking that Gomathi Vinayakam was someone important, took her directly to Gandhiji. There were just a few press persons with him at that time. Gandhiji had the following exchange with Gomathi Vinayakam ('GV').

Gandhiji: Where does your husband work?
GV: With Dr. Kumarappa in Wardha.
G: Then I suppose you are going there?
GV: Yes. Dr Soundaram Ramachandran has said she would write to Dr Sushila Nayyar about this.
G: In that case, reach there soon. You can work in Kasturba Hospital.
GV: All right.

Listening to this exchange, the press persons there somehow misunderstood, and wrongly reported that Dr Vinayakam and his wife had visited Gandhiji.

Mirasdar Veera Pillai of Omandur village of Lalgudi Taluk, and Dr C. R. Krishnaswami Pillai met Gandhiji and donated a cheque of Rs 5,000 as initial amount to the Kasturba National Fund for establishment of a gynaecology and general hospital, and a primary education school under the Hindustani Sangam.

29 January 1946, Workers' Conference ends

The next morning, the Organisation Workers' Conference concluded. Gandhiji spoke briefly at the valedictory function, and answered few questions. When asked, "Can land be nationalised through ahimsa?", he responded:

> Yes, the tillers of the land must become its owners. The rights and duties of farmers must be properly explained by organisation workers. They must be told that they must claim their true rights through self-belief and courage. They might need to undertake satyagraha for this purpose, if needed. Zamindars are not heartless devils to keep them under subjugation, because it would not serve as a good example for those who come after them.

Gandhiji's clarification of a gram sevak who will carry out all these tasks has become famous, and is quoted in many organisational plans and books on gram swarajya.

Women's meeting

The women and children of Madras city, desirous of seeing the Mahatma up close, arranged a separate meeting in the Silver Jubilee pandal. With a view to presenting a sizeable purse to Gandhiji, a 'women's purse committee' had been formed under the presidentship of the Maharani of Vizianagaram, Vidyavati. Entry was by ticket only, and approximately 15,000 people attended. When a purse of Rs 10,000 was handed over to the Mahatma by the Maharani, Gandhiji observed that the purse on behalf of the women should have been at least Rs 1 lakh, and he exhorted her to have the balance collected later, and make up any shortfall from her own resources. The Maharani accepted to do so, which pleased Gandhiji. Tmt. Rajam Bharathi and a couple of other women presented individual purses.

Wardha Basic Education Centre

In the evening, at the convocation of the Wardha Basic Education Centre, Gandhiji appeared enthusiastic and full of ready humour. The convocation was presided over by Narahari Parikh, and 26 persons were awarded participation certificates. Gandhiji read the Tamil certificates with some effort, helped by a teacher by his side, to whom he referred his doubts. R. Vinayakam read the welcome and the Principal of the Basic Education Centre, R. V. Rudrappasamy, spoke about the scheme. The names of those receiving certificates were read out by Ko. Venkatasamy, as each one came up and received the certificate from Gandhiji. When a young woman named Baby came up to receive hers, Gandhiji wittily remarked, "Not bad, this baby is in fact a big baby!"

Congress workers' meeting

The prayer meeting that day was disrupted by noise, forcing Gandhiji to abruptly end his speech. In the evening, when he came to address the Congress workers' meeting, the workers' cheers seemed so loud as to split the sky. Gandhiji, noticing that there was no one presiding over the meeting, invited Kamaraj who was seated below, to take on the duty. Accordingly, Kamaraj presided, and requested Gandhiji to offer his advice. At this time, as many had come forward to present gifts, Gandhiji firmly declared, "I do not want money, gold, or diamonds this time."

Gandhiji began to speak in Hindustani, and asked those who could understand him to raise their hands. Some 50 people did so. Noticing that Kamaraj had not raised his hand, Gandhiji asked in surprise, "Do you, too, not know Hindi?" Then he used this to open his speech. When he finished, he answered the workers' questions.

Question: (from a man speaking partly in English and partly in Telugu) I am a Harijan and work as a sweeper in the George Town Khadi Nilayam. The people who run that establishment treat me worse than a dog. I do not allow them to touch me (at this, someone in the crowd shouted, 'It's a lie!').

Gandhiji: If it is true, it is most disturbing. All Congressmen must believe that God resides in their heart, and act as per their conscience. Everything will be all right then. If one were to talk about differences between Hindus, Muslims, outcasts and untouchables, it will only spell ruin for the nation.

Q: People say that the objective of your prayer meetings is to surreptitiously promote Hindu religion. What are your views on this?
G: One of the laws of my life is prayer. Krishna, Rama, Allah and Christ are one to me. I believe all religions are branches of the same tree. I do not conduct prayer meetings to promote Hindu or any other religion covertly. If the people have misunderstood, I am not responsible. If they want, they can attend my prayer meetings; if not, stay away.
Q: How should Congress deal with those who indulged in black marketing during the War? What punishment should they be given?
G: If I were a Congressman, I should horsewhip them (in ahimsa mode). But as I am a 100% 'ahimsavadi', I wish to say nothing.

Interviews

Gandhiji gave interviews to many people from early morning onwards. Some devotees of Shirdi Sai Baba joined in the morning prayers, and sought Gandhiji's advice in starting a gurukulam. He told them that importance should be given to the charkha and Hindustani in the gurukulam. The daughter of late Salem Vijayaraghavachariar, Seethammal, and her son, R. T. Parthasarathy, came to see Gandhiji. He emotionally told them that it was with Vijayaraghavachariar at the helm that the ahimsa-led untouchability eradication movement had become the Congress manifesto. S. Subbaier (proprietor of S. Ganesh and Company), the owner of Mangala Vilas, where Gandhiji was staying, was introduced to him. Subbaier handed over some books on politics published by Ganesh and Company to Gandhiji, including his *Indian Home Rule*. At a time (1919) when several publishers were hesitant to publish this book, it is noteworthy that Ganesh and Company brought it out.

Under the presidentship of Janammal, the Mylapore Women's Association met Gandhiji and presented a purse. Apart from this, Sindhi merchants under Kewalram Chellaram met Gandhiji to hand over a purse of Rs 10,000. Madras Congress president, Kamaraj, Vice-president, Rukmini Lakshmipathy, and secretary, M. Bhakthavatsalam, met Gandhiji for 15 minutes to seek his advice on how best to utilise the services of the heroes of the Indian National Army who had been released.

At Hindustani Nagar, a film on Gandhiji's life, made in Tamil by A. K. Chettiar and thereafter also in several languages, was screened, and viewed by many of Gandhiji's relatives and Sevagram ashramites.

30 January 1946, Writers' and artistes' conference

All conferences arranged in connection with the Silver Jubilee celebrations (except the Workers' Conference) had concluded, and the delegates had started returning to their respective places. Gandhiji participated in a conference of writers and artistes in Kannada, Telugu, Tamil and Malayalam.

V. Ramasamy, who spoke at this conference in the morning, highlighted the 'Bharathi Era' in Tamil literature and history. At first, the writers' and artistes' conference was slated to be held in English, and the addresses by the speakers had been prepared in English. However, as Gandhiji had insisted that they should either speak in their mother tongues or in Hindustani, all of them spoke in their mother tongues. When Gandhiji remarked with a laugh, "Even I am able to understand your views," everyone thought it was just a polite comment. But when, in his address, Gandhiji gave his views on the speeches made, people realised how much he had understood.

An artiste

At the artistes' function held in the afternoon as part of the Silver Jubilee celebrations of Hindustani Prachar Sabha, writers who had come for the function in the morning were also present. When Gandhiji spoke, he said he was not a litterateur, competent to talk about either Hindi or any other literature, but, that in broad terms, he could also be considered an "artiste". He explained: "I have for all these years been practising the principles of truth and ahimsa, which govern all art. All art is life. When a beautiful work of art is created, it should adhere to truth and ahimsa. Even obtaining freedom is an art."

Unusual auction

At this conference, an unusual accomplishment of Gandhiji was his auctioning of his own portrait, given to him as a gift, which fetched

Rs 350 in this gathering. On behalf of the artistes, S. N. Sumkur, who gave the welcome address, presented a photograph album containing several pictures of Gandhiji. Katturi Venkateswara Rao presided over this conference. Kambadasan sang a song. K. Rajagopalan emphasised the need to take up art with a national purpose. At the end, P. S. Krishna Iyer of Egmore Main Road was the one who bid Rs 350 and purchased Gandhiji's portrait in the auction. Gandhiji took a look at the photograph album, declared that he was not inclined to auction it even for Rs 1,000, and decided to keep it himself.

Students' meeting

In the evening, speaking at the packed Silver Jubilee pandal, Gandhiji was overjoyed to see so many students. "I have realised, not only in South Africa, where I worked alongside many people from Madras, but also now during my stay here over the last few days, that one can do much work silently. Without my saying so, the people here have understood what my objectives are, and what I desire of them." He answered a few questions from students thereafter.

No preconditions

It was clear in this meeting how very uncompromising Gandhiji was in the collection of funds. Further, he clarified, in response to a question, whether those who gave funds for a cause could lay down conditions for its use. Some students had given him a letter about fund collection. It said that, of the Rs 10,000 available, Rs 5,000 may be given to Gandhiji, and the balance would be required for other projects. In another letter from the Youth Congress Secretary, it was said that Rs 7,000 had been collected, and Gandhiji could use Rs 2,000 for the village improvement scheme.

Gandhiji read out both the letters at the meeting, and then said: "You have collected this amount for the Hindustani Prachar Sabha Fund. Hence, as per law and propriety, this money should be handed over entirely for this purpose. You should not attach any conditions as to how and where it should be spent. I do not wish to say anything beyond this."

A. RAMASAMY

Question: The organisation plan does not attract the students. What can be done?

Gandhiji: I ask the students to read the last book that I have written about the organisation plan. How can service to Harijans and hill tribes not attract you?

Q: What is your advice to students who do not exhibit tolerance?

G: The first quality a student must imbibe is tolerance. For 20 years, in the pursuit of swarajya, I have been advocating truth and ahimsa. Yet, if someone were to say that freedom can be obtained only by the sword, I would listen to him patiently. I have considered the obtaining of victory through the atom bomb (referring to the atom bombs dropped on Hiroshima and Nagasaki in August 1945 by the United States of America to gain victory over Japan). At the end of it, I have realised that truth and ahimsa are so much stronger than the bomb. The soul can never be destroyed. If only you have the conviction that violence can never win you over, victory is surely yours, because to confront violence with dharma is in itself victory.

The Indian Youth Congress secretary, V. Ganapathy, handed over a purse of Rs 6,000 to Gandhiji, promising that a further Rs 1,000 would be given the next day. On behalf of Lady Muthiah Chettiar High School, a purse was presented.

As the day's prayer meeting was yet again interrupted by noise, Gandhiji cut short his speech, pained that his advice to people to maintain peace and silence at prayer meetings seemed to go unheeded.

The evil of alcohol

In his speech, he dwelt on the deleterious effects of alcohol.

> In Madras city, I am aware that thousands of people are addicted to liquor. The ill effects of this addiction break one's heart. During the Congress regime here, there was prohibition implemented in various places. Even though revenue from liquor sales suffered as a consequence, people were much happier. Family members were getting enough to eat. If this reform had happened from below, rather than being imposed from above, it would have resulted in better benefits. However, it is only when there is abundant Grace of God that such reform will start from below.

Dr S. K. Sundaram

Before arriving at the prayer meeting, Gandhiji visited the ailing Dr S. K. Sundaram in his house, which was near the Hindustani Prachar Sabha. Dr Sundaram, who had been the Chief of Medicine at the Government General Hospital, was a nationalist and promoter of the Hindi language, and had assisted the Prachar Sabha every now and then. At the time of Gandhiji's visit, the doctor was at death's door, and keen to meet the Mahatma. When Gandhiji heard this, though he did not know Dr Sundaram, Gandhiji readily agreed to visit him at his residence, such was his magnanimity.

S. Srinivasa Sastri

Gandhiji went to the Government General hospital to call on Rt. Hon'ble Srinivasa Sastri for the second time. He also took with him T. N. Jagadeesan of the Leprosy Relief Association, because the first question Sastri had asked Gandhiji on his earlier visit was, "Has Jagadeesan come?" Attached to the Government General Hospital, Dr Jagadeesan had been treating Sastri. He himself came to Gandhiji and took him to see Sastri. On this visit, the discussion centred around the *Ramayana*. Sastri began, "You have been a blessing to me in several ways," introduced his grandson to Gandhiji, and said, "May your blessing be on him always." He quoted a Sanskrit sloka from Valmiki's *Ramayana* in illustration.

Sastri: 'Those who have not seen Rama, or those who have not been seen by Rama, will be scorned by all people in the world,' says this sloka, and it is most pertinent with respect to Gandhiji.
Gandhi: What nonsense, Sastri!
S: Do I not know that, among people today, you are great. You are a seeker of truth. On many issues, you and I have been 'North and South' in our views, and you have told me so openly. However, if not to your extent, I, too, am a worshipper of truth. The eternal truths in the *Ramayana* have deeply inspired me.

Sastri then repeated the above quote from Valmiki, translated it into English, and explained how much it applied to Gandhiji.

Dr V. H. Venkataraman, who was standing by his side, added that, if the word 'Gandhi' were to substitute the word 'Rama' in the sloka, it would be most apt. Gandhiji burst out laughing.

After the two great men spoke in confidence for ten minutes, Gandhiji took his leave. As he came out of the room, he was escorted to the adjoining room, where P. K. Rajagopalan, another patriot, had been brought for treatment, after the sentence was pronounced in the Kulasekaranpatti violence case. Rajagopalan had been transferred to this room to make it convenient for Gandhiji to visit him.

Welcome by doctors

Taking advantage of this opportunity of Gandhiji's visit to the hospital, the House Surgeons' Association of the General Hospital arranged a small welcome for him in front of the R. M. O.'s office. A few patients and members of the general public attended this function. Dr Vasanta presented a purse to Gandhiji on behalf of the House Surgeons' Association. "Do not look to opening more and more hospitals to take in patients. More than treating illness, it is important to work for prevention, and it is towards this that you must use your medical knowledge," Gandhiji advised.

Hindi Prachar Sabha employees

When Gandhiji was informed that the employees of Dakshin Bharat Hindi Prachar Sabha and its printing division personnel wished to see him, he gave them time in the morning to meet him along with their families. They were individually introduced to him. A Tiruvallikeni merchant, Krishna Das Lala, presented a purse to Gandhiji.

Leprosy eradication workers

About 30 workers involved in the leprosy eradication programme, led by Dr T. N. Jagadeesan, met Gandhiji. He thanked them for including this work in the organisation plan. A member of this group, and one belonging to the British Empire Leprosy Eradication Society, Dr T. P. N. Sloane, requested Gandhiji to stop by at Chinglepet on his return to Madras from Madurai on 4 February, and visit the leprosy sanatorium there, which had 750 patients. Miss Willheland of the South Arcot Vadattharasalur Leprosy Mission requested him to support all kinds of leprosy prevention activities. The owner of Mangala Bhavan agreed to provide a building at the Kasturba Leprosy Relief Centre in Kandacchipuram, near Villupuram (now a district and a municipality in Tamil Nadu), for the treatment of women and children.

Inscribed in Tamil

In the afternoon, as Gandhiji was starting for the writers and artistes' conference, about 60 men, women and children of the Saurashtra community met him and presented yarn spun by them and a purse. The former Mayor of Madras, J. Sivashanmugam Pillai, and some Harijan workers of Washermenpet also met Gandhiji in the afternoon, and informed him that a building for the students hostel run by the Washermenpet Adi Dravidar Sangam was being erected, and that Gandhiji may please come and bless its foundation stone laying. After making sure that the stone would be inscribed in Tamil, Gandhiji blessed their efforts.

31 January 1946, Interviews, interviews, interviews

The next day was taken up, not so much with functions, but the many interviews that Gandhiji was forced to give. With no breathing time in between, a series of people sought interviews. As a result, he had to go late to the prayer meeting and the Workers' Conference.

The Dewan of Tiruvangur, Sir C. P. Ramaswami Iyer, his son, C. R. Pattabhi Raman and family called on Gandhiji and spent about half an hour with him. Gandhiji and Sir Ramaswami Iyer spoke about the education policy of Tiruvangur and the recently established government structure in the Principality.

T. K. P. Santhanarama Udayar and his wife, belonging to Needamangalam (now a town panchayat in Thiruvarur district of Tamil Nadu), met Gandhiji and handed over a purse. The rice that had been made available for the kitchen during the Silver Jubilee Celebrations of the Hindustani Prachar Sabha was sent by Udayar and some others from Thanjavur district. Abdul Sattar from Dindigul met Gandhiji and requested that an organisation be set up to foster

Hindu-Muslim unity. Gandhiji reviewed the work being done by Kora Ramachandra Rao, who came along with Pulusu Sambamurthi. Azhagappa Chettiar and his family, as also R. M. Gaffoor, met Gandhiji. All these persons handed over individual purses. When the others had left, Chettiar had confidential discussions with him.

Not content with the funds raised for the Hindustani Prachar Sabha, Gandhiji invited some 50 prominent merchants of the city to discuss regarding raising more money. He spoke with them about his plans to raise a lakh of rupees.

Workers' Conference

In the large grounds south of the Hindustani Prachar Sabha, 30,000 workers had gathered for the Workers' Conference. As requested by P. R. K. Sharma, who had arranged this conference, some government offices and industrial establishments and factories had declared a holiday. The workers' procession that started from Royapuram swelled in numbers as it went along, and stretched for approximately a mile. Another procession, consisting of people belonging to the hunters' tribe and farmers of Ponneri Taluk, started from Sembium.

On behalf of the workers of WIMCO (Western India Match Co., a subsidiary of British Match, set up in 1923, once the leading manufacturer of safety matches in the world), T. S. Ramanujam presented a purse. This conference was remarkable for the discipline shown by these workers, who sat patiently and quietly throughout. Gandhiji was quite pleasantly surprised, and he made it a point to mention this in his speech.

Vaishnava Jana tho

At the Vidyalaya Girls' High School in Thyagaraya Nagar, the sister of one of Gandhiji's chief disciples, Dr Bharatan Kumarappa, was the principal. She had taught her students Gandhiji's favourite hymn, 'Vaishnava Jana tho,' and desired that her students sing it for him. When Dr Kumarappa told Gandhiji this, he readily agreed, and it was sung at the prayer meeting. Gandhiji took the meaning of this hymn as the core of his speech.

Guard of honour

This morning, he was faced with much work outside his planned schedule. The helpers of the Silver Jubilee celebrations had got up a special function at Hindustani Nagar. Gandhiji inspected a guard of honour presented by the workers, Indian Army heroes, the Fire Brigade, and Scouts. The Assistant Postmaster General, other high ranking authorities and postal workers were also present to greet Gandhiji. He advised them that if they wished to serve the public more effectively, they should learn Hindi.

Praise for the committee

Thereafter, he proceeded to the building where the food had been arranged. Alathur Nathamuni Chetty, K. S. Ambi Iyer and V. M. Gadigachalam were the persons in charge here. As Gandhiji entered Hindustani Nagar, he addressed the food group with a smile, "You have fed everybody except me. I understand you have prepared idli, uppuma, etc.—why did you not send these to me?" He then praised the work of the catering group, specifically for their cleanliness in service. "I have toured all over India—you have set an example for the country."

The Madras Punjab Association presented a purse of Rs 3241-25 through the Maharani of Vizianagaram, Vidyavati.

Kalluppatti Ashram

Ko. Venkatachalapathy, his wife, Meenakshi and daughter Sivarani (then a doctor), met Gandhiji, and presented him with a razor and mirror frame made by Rajan Asari of Kalluppatti Ashram. "Kalluppatti is just a 45-minute drive from Madurai—you must come there," requested Venkatachalapathy, to which Gandhiji replied, "To a young man like you, a journey of 45 minutes may not seem long, but I am an old man. It will take 2 hours to go and return, and it will exhaust me. You are inviting me to bless the ashram, are you not? My blessings are always with you."

1 February 1946, Harijan Industrial Training School

Gandhiji was excited at the foundation stone laying ceremony of the Harijan Industrial Training School at the junction of Venkatanarayana Road and Mount Road, on a land acquired from the Madras Municipal Council. Not only did he lay the foundation stone, but he handled the masonry work too. It is only after filling the spaces between the bricks with cement, spreading turmeric paste, adding vermilion and offering flowers that he returned to the dais, setting an example of 'Do what you need to do yourself'.

Naming ceremony

In this foundation stone laying ceremony, many prominent persons were present, such as Azhagappa Chettiar, who conducted the function, Madras High Court Judges Herville and Rajamannar, Sir Alladi Krishnaswami Iyer, Sir N. Gopalaswami Iyengar and others. Dewan Bahadur V. Bhashyam Iyengar read out the welcome address. The secretary of the Harijan Seva Sangam, A. V. Thakkar, furnished details about this training school. Gandhiji praised Azhagappa Chettiar for coming forward to build the school. Gandhiji suggested that the school be named after the 'father of Harijans', Thakkar Bapa (1869–1951, social worker of Gujarat who worked for the uplift of tribals). It was informed that Azhagappa Chettiar had agreed to have the building completed. H. D. Raja further said that significant funds were required to equip this school, and many people in the gathering promised on the spot to help financially; among them was the Carnatic singer and actress, N. C. Vasantakokilam (1919–51). In the auction of the silver ladle used for masonry work, S. Ramasamy Naidu bought it for Rs 2001.

An inconvenient question

In the afternoon, Gandhiji visited the Harijan Training School in Kodambakkam, and spent much time going around the facilities, observing the students at work. C. Duraikkannu Mudaliar escorted him. Observing a large number of people gathered at the western gate of the school waiting to see him, Gandhiji went up to them and said, "I will ask you a question, and you should reply without hesitation.

Is it all right?" Receiving an affirmative answer, he said, "How many among you are addicted to liquor?"

A whole lot of people raised their hands. Gandhiji continued, "Drinking is a sin. I wonder what benefit you derive from it! All of you toil hard to earn. You should not spend this away on drinking and gambling. Look wisely for productive ways to utilise this earning."

To villages

In connection with Gandhiji's visit, 18 associations involved in Harijan service had arranged for a meeting in a pandal that had been erected. He said at this meeting,

> Swami Vivekananda, who had visited this city some years ago, had exhorted all to learn Sanskrit. I hope some among the Harijans will turn out to be Sanskrit pandits. This school should not confine itself to imparting technical instruction to students to create employment opportunities. The education here must allow Harijans to prove to caste Hindus that they are in no way inferior to them. If you speak and do good, leading good lives, nobody will regard you as inferior.

During his stay in Madras, Gandhiji did not participate in any public function, other than this one at Kodambakkam Harijan Training School.

Purify through prayer

When Gandhiji arrived for prayer, he was tired. However, the peace that prevailed at this meeting pleased him. The daughters of Justice Patanjali Sastri and Sir Alladi Krishnaswami Iyer jointly sang a Hindi hymn, 'Ram Mil Megha.'

Gandhiji said (*The Hindu*, 2 February 1946):

> Temples of art are before us. Nowhere else in the world can such be seen.
>
> Going to temples and making offerings alone does not make a person pure. Purity lies within one's heart. Your aim must be to purify your hearts through prayer. A person who prays sincerely, will attain what he desires.
>
> I have always had a special respect for South India. Whenever I have come, people here have given me their unquestioning love.

But for this love of yours, I would not have been able to carry out my work so incessantly. Four languages are spoken in South India, and one cannot say that there is unity between them. This is sad. I believe, though, that the day when, not just within South India, but the differences between North and South India, too, can be eradicated, will be seen.

Interviews

T. M. Deivasigamani Achariar, Viswakarma Conference Central Committee president, met Gandhiji and handed over publicity material. This detailed the need to promote cottage industries, making products out of wood, iron and other metals.

The president of the Indian Christian Sammelan, Dr V. K. John, and another Christian leader, Dr T. S. Ramachandra Rao met Gandhiji separately to discuss the specific problems of Christians.

The poet Namakkal Ramalingam met Gandhiji in the evening, presented four of his books, and explained the contents of each. Gandhiji expressed the desire to study these books in detail, and invited the poet to his ashram in Wardha. What else could the poet say but 'yes' to this?

Gomathi and Harihara Sharma

The Mahatma had unbounded love for those who had interacted with him. The initiator of the Hindi teaching movement in South India, Harihara Sharma and his wife Gomathi had stayed for a long time at Sabarmati Ashram. On this visit, Gandhiji made it a point to ask Harihara Sharma about his wife, and was told that she was in Krishnapuram village of Tirunelveli District. Sharma was told to send her a telegram immediately, asking her to meet Gandhiji in Madurai. "It has been a long time since I saw Gomathi. I would like to meet her." Gandhiji never failed to enquire about families who were known to him.

Muthuranga Mudaliar

Congress leader Muthuranga Mudaliar came with his family to meet Gandhiji. Although he had been given an appointment, the time had not been specified. Hence, when he arrived, he was told that he had come late, and could not, therefore, meet Gandhiji. Mudaliar returned disappointed, wondering how he could have been considered as having arrived late when no time had been specified. He decided that he would eat only after meeting Gandhiji. This somehow reached the Mahatma's ears, and he declared that he, too, would not eat till he met Mudaliar. The friends then ran to Mudaliar to say that Gandhiji was waiting for him. Thereafter the two of them met and spoke.

Ma. Po. Sivagnanam

This was the first time that Ma. Po. Sivagnanam (1906–95, freedom fighter, prolific writer and founder of the Tamil Arasu Kazhagam) got to meet Gandhiji. He was taken by Rajaji and introduced to Gandhiji. "He is from the toddy tapper's community, but, more than you, he is against its consumption," Rajaji said while introducing him. Gandhiji promptly interrupted to say, "No, no, you are wrong. I am against fermented toddy, but a friend of the sweet one." Ma. Po. Si. recounts:

> It was the time during the August movement that I had just been released from jail. Noticing my extreme weakness, Gandhiji advised, 'If he takes sweet toddy, his health will improve.' Rajaji's objection to alcohol was at high pitch at that time. He told Gandhiji, 'He is the leader of my party.' 'Yes, yes, I know, that is why you have brought him separately to meet me,' was Gandhiji's retort.

T. K. Chidambaranatha

This was narrated by Keezhmoongiladi Ra. Vinayagam. One day Rajagopalachariar introduced Rasikamani T. K. Chidambaranatha (T. K. C.) Mudaliar (1882–1954, scholar, author and founding father of the Tamil renaissance movement) to Gandhiji. The conversation between Rasikamani and Gandhiji was interesting. Rajaji had said, "He is a great intellectual, and an unparalleled scholar of the *Kamba Ramayanam* (also known as *Ramavataram*, a twelfth-century Tamil epic by the poet Kambar)."

Gandhiji said, "Is that so? I have heard a lot about *Kamba Ramayanam*. Could you tell me how I could read and experience it?"

T. K. Chidambaranatha, in his characteristic way, instantly replied, "If you wish to experience the *Kamba Ramayanam*, you should be born as a Tamil in your next birth!"

Departure for Madurai

After completing his assignments in Madras, Gandhiji left at 10.30 p.m. to visit the temples of Madurai and Pazhani. He went with Rajaji, Dr Sushila Nayyar and M. Satyanarayana by car to Guindy station and boarded a special train there. The other members of Gandhiji's party entrained at Egmore station, and met him at Guindy. Rajaji, Madras Congress president Kamaraj, and L. N. Gopalaswami accompanied Gandhiji. P. S. Ramanathan of the Tiruchengode ashram also travelled with them. Hindi proponent, G. Subramaniam of Tiruchirapalli, joined them as interpreter. Engine drivers in pristine white khadi dress, having decorated the engine with the national flag and Gandhiji's portraits, presented a striking sight.

Arrangements at Madurai

When Gandhiji visited Madurai on this occasion, much preparation was required. Dr Rajan went on 30 January to supervise the arrangements for Gandhiji's prayer meeting and visit to the temple. Anticipating large crowds, the railway authorities were ready to run special trains from different places into Madurai.

Gandhiji's entourage had the train stopped at Kattuppakkam, some 25 miles from Madras, and rested for the night in the train itself—one may say it was the good fortune of Kattuppakkam railway station. The train restarted from there at 5.30 a.m. the next morning and stopped for a while at Accharappakkam station.

2 February 1946, Accharappakkam

There was a convenient bench in the train they travelled by for Gandhiji to stand and be seen by the crowd, as also sound amplification equipment. The crowds that had gathered in the early morning at Accharappakkam were disciplined. Aware that trains normally did not stop at this station, they showed their gratitude by not causing any confusion. There was a nadaswaram group playing in a village.

Disciplined crowd

The discipline that people of small villages like Accharappakkam exhibited in the presence of the Mahatma, and the consequent ease with which they could hear his speeches, was not witnessed in towns and cities like Villupuram and Tiruchi, where the disturbance caused by crowds made it virtually impossible to see and hear him.

Villupuram, Ulundurpettai, Ariyalur

At Villupuram railway station, on the grounds where the road branches off to Puduchery, 20,000 people had gathered. In spite of valiant efforts by V. Kuppuswami Iyengar, C. R. Jagadambal, V. T. Krishnaveni and men and women volunteers under them, the efforts to bring order in the crowd went in vain. Hence Gandhiji spent just about 10 minutes to allow them a glimpse of him, and returned to his compartment.

A third form student of the Town Council High School (Krishnagiri Vaidyanathan Achariar's son) had etched a portrait of Gandhiji holding a flag on a single grain of rice, which came in for much praise. An aged lady brought with her a small stone, saying that it was to be used as the foundation stone for a school to be built for Harijans, and asked Gandhiji to bless it. Gandhiji did so.

The crowds in Ulundurpettai were disciplined and quiet. Aware of Gandhiji's dietary habits, a man brought a sack of peanuts for him. A. Subramaniam from Salem came to greet Gandhiji. At Vriddhachalam, it became difficult for the train to navigate the crowds and move forward. At Ariyalur, some 7,000 people amassed peacefully, pleasing Gandhiji greatly, as he asked his group to sing 'Ram Dhun'. On behalf of the public, P. Venkatachalam Pillai presented a purse. Dr Rajan joined Gandhiji's group at this place. As the crowds at Srirangam were overflowing, there was noise and confusion at the station.

Tiruchirapalli

The two lakh people who had gathered in Tiruchirappali to see Gandhiji were disciplined till the train arrived, but no sooner had he ascended the dais that was erected near the Ceylon labour siding than they ran forward to get a better glimpse of him, resulting in pandemonium and noise. G Subramaniam translated Gandhiji's

"Please be silent, I will speak," but this had no effect on the crowd. As a result, Gandhiji got down from the dais and re-entered his railway compartment. When peace was restored, he returned to the dais. Yet again the crowd moved forward to see him, and, apprehending more indiscipline, Gandhiji went back to his compartment. Thereafter, the train started and halted before the Tiruchi junction for a couple of minutes.

He was introduced there by Dr Rajan to J. P. C. Reynolds, Railway Chief Manager, and Sidney Smith, Chief Transport Superintendent. In Tiruchi, Gandhiji's train was halted at Srirangam, Golden Rock, and Tiruchi Junction, with the halt at Golden Rock being the most successful. A largely railway workers' crowd of some 10,000 men and women sat there in disciplined silence to hear Gandhiji speak.

Manapparai

At Manapparai grounds, Gandhiji was particularly pleased to see a number of persons, including 50 women, spinning on their charkhas. He said: "I believe we shall obtain swaraj soon. The route to swaraj, and its foundation, is charkha."

At Ambatturai, a special route had been cleared for the Mahatma's train, with the signals down. The people of Chinnalappatti broke the signal wires, thereby lifting the signal's arms, and stopping the train to greet Gandhiji!

Madurai

The crowds that gathered in Madurai, and the functions organised for Gandhiji, were phenomenal. Anticipating that he would be unable to detrain at Madurai junction owing to the crowd there, Gandhiji's train was halted at a level crossing beyond Samayanallur, 10 miles away, where he, along with Pyarelal and Rajkumari Amrit Kaur got down. Prominent Madurai citizens, A. Vaidyanatha Iyer, N. M. R. Subburaman, Chidambara Bharathi, Meenakshi temple trustee R. S. Naidu and Dr Ramasubramaniam welcomed Gandhiji. Dr Ramasubramaniam drove the car that brought Gandhiji to Madurai city. Ramasubramaiam introduced the Madurai Collector, Pritchard, who had joined en route. The crowds could be seen all along the way.

A sea of humanity

The crowd which had amassed in the Madurai Competition Grounds was historic. Even the members of Gandhiji's entourage admitted that they had never before seen such a massive crowd anywhere. It was a veritable sea of humanity—not less than five lakh people! One reason for such a record turnout was that Gandhiji was visiting Madurai after 1937, that is, after nine years. Another was that this time, he was visiting only Madurai and Pazhani. A third reason was that, on this short tour, he was addressing just this one public meeting; hence, everybody gravitated to these grounds from near and far to hear him speak.

Dr Sushila Nayyar has written that there may have also been a general feeling among the people that Gandhiji was now advanced in age, and it was uncertain when they would be able to see him again. People from as far as Ceylon had come to Madurai for this meeting.

The dais on which Gandhiji and the dignitaries were seated rose like an island in the midst of this sea of people. The dais itself had been attractively erected, by courtesy of the Madurai Knitting Company and under the direct supervision of its Managing Director, N. M. R. Venkatakrishna Iyer.

Seeing the sea of humanity surrounding him, Gandhiji decided that he could not read the usual prayers he normally did at meetings. The crowd was restless, and noise levels were high. Hence he asked his grandnephew Kanu Gandhi (1928–2016, a photographer) to sing the 'Ram Bhajan.' This seemed to restore peace to an extent. Still, those at the rear of the crowd kept pushing forward to get a better glimpse of Gandhiji. This was the first sign of crowd disturbance. While the crowd in front remained quiet, those behind raised a lot of noise.

Impatient, unruly crowd

To enable people on all sides to see him, Gandhii walked up and down the stage, and then began to speak.

> I fear that I may not be able to say anything because of the noise. Those in front of the stage are quiet. If others, too, do not follow suit, it will become difficult for me to remain on this stage. My present health will not allow me to tolerate so much noise. But

seeing the people in front of me sitting peacefully, I feel I must say something at least for their sake.

Madurai is a celebrated and holy city. You have opened your temple to Harijans. Ever since it was so opened, I had been wanting to come and worship in it.

As Gandhiji was speaking, there was incessant noise from the crowd, making it impossible for him to continue. He stopped speaking, looked in the direction of the noise and said: "I understand that your noise and lack of patience are because of the love and respect you have for me. All of you desire to see me, but I wish to say only one thing—this impatient, indisciplined respect cannot be called love. If you behave in this fashion, you would lose the right to freedom."

The Congress Committees of Madurai, Ramanathapuram and Tirunelveli districts presented 25,000 hanks of khadi. S. S. Arunachala Chettiar presented a silver charkha, and the Madurai City Merchants' Clerks Association a bamboo charkha and silver inkwell and pen. Hindustani Vidyarthi Premi Mandal, and Avaniyapuram Panchayat Board gave welcome addresses at this meeting.

On behalf of the Madurai Cloth Merchants' Sangam, its president, Muhammad Abdul Karim handed over a purse of Rs 6,600, as did many others. On the dais Gandhiji was also presented a tricolour made of gold, a gold chain and two silver chains. The gold tricolour was presented by the gold merchant A. S. S. M. Somasundara Chettiar. The reason for the lack of restraint in the crowd was not just its size and the desire of so many to approach Gandhiji and seek his blessings; people in the rear could not hear what he said.

A satyagraha of sorts

Finishing his speech, and exhorting the crowd to maintain discipline, Gandhiji prepared to descend from the dais, when from all sides, the crowds surged towards the pandal. In those times, police presence for crowd control was not common. It was generally handled by Congress volunteers. The crowd on that day, however, was beyond the volunteers' control. The wooden posts all around the dais, on which the loudspeakers calling for crowd dispersal were fixed, began to collapse under the crowd's weight. Only the fence at the corner of the dais seemed intact. Seeing the rampaging crowd, Gandhiji declared, "I will remain on stage till you give me permission to leave," and lay down on the mattress that had been provided on the dais. The lights on stage were turned off, and he clapped his hands over his ears to shut off the noise.

When Gandhiji started this satyagraha of sorts, some in the crowd dispersed, while others did a counter-satyagraha of their own, determined to see him. This satyagraha and counter-satyagraha lasted one and a half hours. Despite repeated pleas by Rajaji and other leaders, the crowds refused to disperse. Eventually, they slowly began to leave. By about 8.45 p.m., the situation had significantly improved, and the noise levels decreased. Gandhiji got up and requested the stage lights to be turned on. It was then that some of the crowd still waiting to get a glimpse of him dispersed. It took some 15 minutes for him to walk from the dais to his car.

'My satyagraha failed'

The behaviour of the crowd at Madurai, and his own reaction to it, caused Gandhiji much disappointment. He seemed to have given it much thought, for on the way back to Wardha, he wrote an article entitled, 'The Lesson Taught by Madurai' for *Harijan*. In it he admitted that it was the first occasion on which his satyagraha had failed.

> There must have been at least 5 lakh people in Madurai. In that situation, the noise and restlessness could not be controlled. A satyagrahi like me should have been able to control that crowd, but for the first time my satyagraha failed. Of course, the people's satyagraha must have failed, because they showed patience when I did not speak. In spite of noise and clamour from those in the rear of the crowd, the people seated near the dais were indeed quiet and disciplined. There was, however, no let up in the pandemonium from the rear. Hence I requested all the women on the dais to get down.
>
> Only Rajaji, Kanu Gandhi and Ramakrishna Bajaj remained on stage. They requested the crowd to make way, but as soon as I got up, there was renewed confusion. I told the crowd near me that I would not be speaking, and they should disperse. They were quiet, but refused to leave.

Hence, I decided that I would sleep there till the crowd dispersed, or gave way to me. Kanu Gandhi assured me that the crowd would let me leave, and that the car was near the stage. I agreed out of my weakness. As I started to descend the strong steps of the dais, the crowd had decreased significantly, but surged forward yet again. I requested them to allow me to leave in silence, but it did not happen. At the same time it was not a crowd filled with malice. This was the only way they knew to display their love and respect for someone they held as their lord, a lord made of earth, like them, but who would not appreciate the noise made by them. The incident proved to me that I was a mentor lacking in patience and ability. If only I had been more patient, that crowd could have been better taught by me. Perhaps I could have learnt more of the discipline required to attain swarajya. Should another such situation arise, I know now how I should handle it. Still, I do not blame anyone for what happened, nobody need be ashamed.

Sivaganga Bungalow

Arrangements for Gandhiji's stay had been made at the Sivaganga Bungalow, on the northern side of the Vaigai river (this was later a Town Council office). The room upstairs that he stayed in came to be called Gandhiji Hall. As he reached the Sivaganga Bungalow, he summoned the people who had made the crowd arrangements and said, "I wish to live to the age of 125. You are planning to kill me!"

On the next day he expressed his inability to visit the Meenakshi temple. It was only after assurances were given to him that the crowds had behaved so earlier only out of bhakti and eagerness, and that Gandhiji would be driven around the four Masi Streets, and escorted into the temple without any trouble, did he agree. Although it was chilly that night, he decided to sleep on the terrace.

3 February 1946, No sleep

A. Vaidyanatha Iyer, N. M. R. Subburaman, Dr Ramasubramaniam and T. K. Rama, who had taken on the responsibility of Gandhiji's visit, had no sleep that night. From early next morning, each of them took charge of specific streets to ensure that the crowds stayed on the pedestrian platforms, and did not overflow on to the streets.

After offering prayers in the temple, Gandhiji was driven along the four Chithirai Streets and Masi Streets, to enable everyone to see him. The car was driven by the industrialist and merchant, N. M. R. Krishnamurthi. Unlike the previous day, the crowds remained peaceful and disciplined. Congress flags fluttered all over the streets.

Divine tradition

Although Gandhiji had repeatedly stated that he was not a believer in idol worship, he was seen to be divinely transported when he visited Sri Meenakshi temple. Newspersons have reported that there was an air of bhakti about Gandhiji, not normally seen, as he went about his morning chores. When he was about to get into the car for the Madurai temple, he could see from there the four *gopurams*, the large pyramidal towers over the entrance gate of the temple, which made him close his eyes and utter some silent prayer. The car took him through East Veli Street, Ramanathapuram Street and East Masi Street on the way to the temple.

From the Sivaganga Bungalow till he reached the temple, he did not speak with anyone. Even as he entered and went around the temple, he was seen to be sunk in his own thoughts, lips moving in silent prayer. Truly, Gandhiji's visit was one of intense worship—a pilgrimage, as he himself made known.

The temple's pride

Sri Meenakshi temple, built by Pandayan Emperor Sadayavarman Kulasekaran I (1190 CE–1205 CE), is one among the ancient and most hallowed temples in what is now Tamil Nadu. For hundreds of years this temple has been venerated in Halasya Puranam and Tiruvilayadal Puranam. The world-renowned works of sculpture that adorn its four entrance gateways and four gopurams were established by different kings over different periods. The Pandya and Nayak kings were largely instrumental in constructing this temple and for its renovation over the years. Even as one enters the precincts of the temple, one is overcome by a sense of divinity, and this was clearly seen on Gandhiji's countenance.

Thakkar Bapa, V. I. Musamy Pillai and Kamaraj accompanied Gandhiji to the temple. Rajaji stayed away because of a cold. Some Harijans and women entered with Gandhiji. Dr T. S. S. Rajan, the Administrative Officer and priests stood in front of the goddess Meenakshi's sanctum, and received Gandhiji with purna kumbham and full temple honours, to the accompaniment of nadaswaram music. Not just within the temple, but the streets all along Gandhiji's route were adorned with beautiful kolams.

There was a large crowd inside the temple too. Announcements had been made that entry of public into the temple would only be through passes, but all those arrangements went for a toss once Gandhiji entered the temple. It became a huge problem to escort Gandhiji into the sanctum sanctorum. However, delighted at this huge turnout, Gandhiji handled it all quite admirably.

A cherished desire fulfilled

As it was dark in the sanctum sanctorum, oil lamps had been lit on the floor for Gandhiji to find his way. An *archanai* or devotional offering was performed to the goddess in the name of Mohandas Karamchand Gandhi. The priest who conducted this archanai recited the names of the goddess at speed. Gandhiji interrupted, and requested him to recite them more slowly. It appeared that he fully absorbed the spiritual strength emanating from the goddess.

After the archanai, a turban was tied on Gandhiji's head and his forehead smeared with kumkum. He accepted the prasadam, and, after bowing to goddess Meenakshi, he paid obeisance to Lord Sundareswarar, his ceremonial image, and Sri Natarajar. An archanai was performed to Lord Sundareswarar in the Mahatma's name, He was shown the floats on which the deities were carried in procession during festivals.

At the temple marriage hall, he was garlanded and given prasadam by the temple trustees. Gandhiji spent about one and a quarter hours in the temple. He made available a photograph of his and a Hindi signature for the visitors' book. He wrote: "I am glad that the desire that I had entertained for years is fulfilled today."

Departure

Gandhiji thus completed his Madurai pilgrimage successfully, and started on his journey in the afternoon for Pazhani. There were innumerable people in front of the Sivaganga Bungalow. In spite of repeated pleas to allow Gandhiji's car to proceed, the crowd refused to give way. He, therefore, had to leave by the rear entrance.

Ottanchatthiram

Gandhiji entrained some six miles away at the Alanganallur level crossing. All along the route, crowds lined up to bid farewell. The train stopped at Chozhavandan. At Dindigul, since the people of that town and neighbouring villages had gathered to welcome him enthusiastically, making maximum noise, Gandhiji did not make a speech. Seeing the discipline of the people in Ottanchatthiram, though, Gandhiji was astonished.

"In my travel from Madras, it has been very rare for me to witness a crowd as disciplined as in your town. This discipline is good not just for you, but for our country, that, too, at a point when freedom is imminent. I believe that in a couple of months we shall obtain our freedom."

Prominent Congressman, Vadivelu Pillai, presented Gandhiji a khadi garland and a purse on behalf of the people.

The crowd at Pazhani

The Ottanchatthiram crowd was a forerunner to the crowds that would meet him at Pazhani. Gandhiji's special train was halted at a level crossing near the grounds beyond the station, where Gandhiji was to speak. He was welcomed there by prominent persons with a family of elephants. The Pazhani public meeting was in direct contrast to the one in Madurai.

There were many reasons for this. The location of the meeting was on a hillside opposite the Pazhani railway station, and the dais was erected on elevated ground, allowing everybody to see Gandhiji without obstruction. After the fiasco at the Madurai meeting, the organisers here were more alert and careful. Further, the failure of the Madurai meeting led to Dr P. N. Ramasubramaniam and the police Superintendent of the area, Spindler, placing plain-clothes policemen at the Pazhani meeting for crowd control. An able-bodied volunteer force of young men was also organised under the leadership of Lakshmipathy Raju in Pazhani for this purpose, contributing to the successful conduct of the meeting.

'I have realised the fruits of my travel'

At this meeting Gandhiji said, "I had insisted that I would visit the Madurai Meenakshi temple only if it was opened to Harijans, Hence, when I went there on this occasion, I experienced a new spiritual awakening. When I observe your discipline, I feel that I have realised the fruits of my travel."

Dr Ramasubramaniam wrote:

> After the meeting, Gandhiji expressed the desire to go out for a bit of fresh air and rest. Rajaji suggested that he could be driven to some nearby villages. Rajaji, Gandhiji, Dr Sushila Nayyar, Pazhani advocate and nationalist Sundararaja Iyer (it was at his house that Gandhiji had stayed on a previous visit) got into the car, and I drove.
>
> When the car neared a stream, Gandhiji asked whether we could sit there for a while. We did not consider this appropriate, and told him that crowds would collect here, making rest impossible for him. Gandhiji accepted this. Immediately, Sundararaja Iyer suggested that we could drive to his own village nearby, where he or his relatives had a house.
>
> We drove to that village and escorted Gandhiji into the house, where he sat against a pillar. He was taken up by the decorative work on that pillar. 'Do you see, in every house there is some work of art or other? I feel energised, and wish to write an article for *Harijan*.
>
> There was no convenient place in that house for him to sit and write this article. We went to the terrace, which was covered in dust. Dr. Sushila Nayyar and I cleaned the terrace, sprinkled water, and spread mats and boards for him to sit on and write. A couple of hurricane lanterns were also arranged, and Gandhiji sat there and wrote the article.
>
> We came down, and in the meantime, an old lady in the house came up with some 'murukkus' (dry snacks) on a plate. She did

not know that the guest in the house was the great Mahatma. She handed the plate to me and said, 'Someone seems to have come—give him these snacks.'

I took the snacks upstairs. On seeing the plate, Gandhiji said, 'O, murukku!' How do you know its Tamil name, I asked.

Gandhiji: Have you forgotten that I was with Tamils in South Africa? But, more than all this, idli is the best among all your tiffin varieties.

Me: Yes, idli is the most tasty.

Gandhiji: But I have never tasted it.

Me: You have missed a good dish.

Gandhiji: There are many such things I have missed in my life.

Temple offering

At Pazhani hill temple, only about 200 persons, including Harijans, had been specially invited. In addition there was Gandhiji, his entourage and the press people, numbering 60. All the invitees went ahead and seated themselves in rows. Gandhiji sat in the inner sanctum flanked by Thakkar Bapa and Rajaji, for the darshan of the Lord of Pazhani. As the crowd was limited, Gandhiji could have a good darshan of the Lord, while the archanai in his name was performed. Even here Gandhiji collected money for the Harijan Fund. In the visitors' book he wrote, "I was happy to be here and be able to have darshan in this temple."

Efficient arrangements for Gandhiji's visit were made by Mangala Gounder, K. R. Sundararaja Iyer, S. A. Seshaier and Sundaram Iyer.

Up the hill in a palanquin

As Gandhiji and Rajaji were carried up the hill in *menas*, small palanquins used for carrying people up a hill, the others climbed up the steps to the top. As soon as he descended from the hill, he was to visit the Harijan settlement and meet the workers. However, on account of extreme exhaustion, Gandhiji decided to go directly to his special train at the railway station. Gandhiji's visit to Pazhani was captured on film by Kovai A. Ayyamuthu, and shown along with his feature film *Kanjan*.

Essay on Pazhani

On his return journey by train, Gandhiji wrote an essay about his speech at the public meeting in Pazhani, his subsequent visit to the temple and the rituals.

> I am sure that my worship of the Lord from the base of the hill would have been heard more clearly by Him than that of a few people atop the hill shrine. Those who knew that I was definitely visiting the Lord of Pazhani on the hilltop may not understand this, because, had I not chosen to go up the hill to worship, they might have believed that some calamity would befall the nation, Further, the discipline shown by the crowd made me want to go up the hill and seek darshan. I finished my speech at around six, and hence I could reach the hill shrine by eight. Thus successfully did my pilgrimage end. One tree does not make a forest. We cannot come to any general conclusions based on this visit, but I was convinced that for India's swaraj, this was a happy augury.

Opposition to Rajaji

Let us focus on the important problem in Madras politics that arose at that time, and how it echoed during Gandhiji's Pazhani visit. When he came to the state on this occasion, the 'Anti-Rajaji Movement' was quite dominant. This had led to heated debate and argument. The matter of Gandhiji's returning to his special train without visiting the Harijan settlement in Sundararaja Iyer's village also resulted in strong differences of opinion.

Not knowing when his special train would leave Pazhani, Kamaraj could not travel in it. Gandhiji was scheduled to meet the workers who had made the welcome arrangements for his visit, but it fell through. A complaint started gaining ground that this was a plot hatched by Rajaji and his followers to prevent Kamaraj and his workers from meeting Gandhiji.

That Kamaraj could not board the train at Pazhani and had to drive up to Dindigul to join it became the topic of a communication sent by the Madras government to the Centre, showing how much importance had been attached to this incident. Ultimately, this complaint was referred to Gandhiji in writing, while he was returning by train to Madras.

In defence of Rajaji

Speaking strongly in defence of Rajaji, Gandhiji issued a detailed clarification on this in the *Harijan* issue dated 10 February 1946.

When my train halted at a station on my return from Pazhani, a person handed over a written note to me, in which strong accusations against Rajaji and L. N. Gopalaswami had been levelled. It said that these two persons do not allow anybody to come and meet me. But, as far as I am aware, the opposite is the case.

Nobody who wanted to say anything productive to me has been prevented either to speak or write to me. That this letter itself has been received by me is an example of that. Kamaraj Nadar did travel with me in the special train. He was with me at the Pazhani shrine. It is true, however, that during this trip, Rajaji and Gopalaswami were very close to me. They had arranged for this trip. Rajaji is among my oldest friends, and everyone knows that he is particularly competent in implementing my principles and methods in word and deed. I am also aware that in 1942 there had been a difference of opinion between us. I praise his courage in having openly voiced this difference then!

He is a great social reformer, and has no qualms about acting as per his convictions. His political acumen and integrity are impeccable. Hence I am saddened that there is a clique formed against him. It is a clique formed in Madras that is unable to express contempt directly within Congress. This is clear. The general public, though, have great respect for Rajaji. Even though in Madras he may not seem to have influence, I am neither an egoist [nor an] idiot not to observe the overwhelming response received from the public everywhere during my visit.

The members of the Madras Congress may take whatever decisions they consider appropriate, but do not denigrate the invaluable service rendered by Rajaji. At this present time, if I do not declare that there is no person better than him to take on responsibility, I would be doing Congress a disservice.

The problem spirals

However, instead of resolving the problem, Gandhiji's clarification only exacerbated it. Rajaji's detractors used this incident as an example to stress how Rajaji prevented people from meeting Gandhiji during his southern tour, and passed off his own views as those of Gandhiji. Those in the Madras State Congress at that time who opposed Rajaji were aggrieved at being referred to as 'clique' by Gandhiji. Kamaraj, who believed that Gandhiji was pointing to him and his supporters in this, withdrew from the Parliamentary Committee to select the Congress candidate for the Legislative Assembly elections.

Several letters and telegrams were received by Gandhiji protesting against the use of the word 'clique'. Even his devoted followers were saddened by Gandhiji's statement that large crowds had come to his meetings with the attitude of subjects desirous of seeing their king. "Can untruths come from the Mahatma's mouth?" was the feeling of some. On this issue, S. Jagannathan, then a prominent worker of the Madras Organising Committee (and later, a Bhoodan leader), went on fast in Madurai. Thereafter, the use of the word 'clique' and Kamaraj's withdrawal from the Parliamentary Committee came in for much debate in the press and among Harijans. But till the end, Gandhiji refused to take back this word.

Chief minister's election

In 1946, Kamaraj took the stand that Gandhiji's proposal to elect Rajaji as the chief minister was not acceptable. He went on to say that there were many political reasons for this, not the least being that there was a strong dislike for Rajaji in Madras, and that one must go by the majority view of the Madras Assembly members for selecting the chief minister.

At the same time, Gandhiji was not in favour of Tanguturi Prakasam (1872–1957) being elected chief minister. Kamaraj said, "We should not yet again go against what Gandhiji says," since "We could not fulfil what he desired on the first occasion." He put up Muthuranga Mudaliar as a candidate against Prakasam. However, Mudaliar lost this election. (Based on M. Bhakthavatsalam interview.)

Now let us come to the place from where the train started.

Akkaraippatti

The special train from Madurai halted at Akkaraippatti (now a village panchayat in Namakkal district). It was there that Gandhiji and his party spent the night. In the early morning, the train started from Akkaraippatti and reached Tiruchirapalli by 6 a.m.

4 February 1946, Tiruchi–Thanjavur

Gandhiji's day of silence began at Pazhani. Because of his visit to the temple and associated rituals, he started his silence late. When he met Sastri the next day, his period of silence had not ended. He remained in silence when he arrived in Tiruchi. The crowd in Tiruchi was considerably less compared to that seen when he went to Madurai from Madras. It was as silent as Gandhiji himself was. After this, he proceeded to Thanjavur. The train that had taken the chord line on its way up now switched to the main line.

At Thanjavur, about a lakh people had gathered to see Gandhiji. When his train reached Kumbakonam, the crowds were standing in knee-deep water in the Arasalar river. At the bridge, Gandhiji stood up in the special train to give darshan. Many volunteers under Dr Mahalingam were involved in crowd control. At Mayavaram, Seergazhi, Chidambaram and Cuddalore too massive crowds came to see him.

There was confusion at the Villupuram meeting, and it became difficult for the train to move from there. Stopping at Mailam, Thindivanam and Madurantakam, it halted two miles from Chinglepet near the Tirumani Leprosy Centre.

Leprosy patients at Tirumani

Gandhiji gave his darshan to leprosy patients. A child affected by the disease presented Rs 23 collected from the workers there. T. N. Jagadeesan and Dr Raja welcomed him. Gandhiji asked the patients by signs whether he could leave, and did so on their acceptance through folded hands. This event touched Gandhiji deeply. In a letter to Jagadeesan, Gandhiji wrote that he felt purified by this meeting. "I went to Madurai and Pazhani to see God, but in Tirumani, God came to see me."

From his days in South Africa, work for leprosy relief had been close to Gandhiji's heart. On his return to India, he included this as a part of his overall agenda, and helped Madras in this service as much as he did in the rest of India.

Kasturba Fund

At the beginning, leprosy relief work in India was being carried out in a limited way by Christian missionaries. When it attained widespread attention, Gandhiji adopted this work under the Kasturba Fund. In 1944, when the Kasturba Fund was established, Jagadeesan, who was spearheading the leprosy relief work in Madras, and Dr Cochrane, who was intensively involved in this service, went to meet Gandhiji at Sevagram in connection with financial assistance. Thanks to Gandhiji's support and financial help through the Kasturba Fund, women and children afflicted by leprosy were helped with adequate treatment and care.

Praise for Jagadeesan

What Gandhiji said when Jagadeesan was discussing something with him one day illustrates his humility. Jagadeesan was qualified, and had been a college professor. Having recovered from leprosy himself, he had involved himself fully in this work. Gandhiji praised him, saying: "Jagadeesan, I had thought that you had taken up this work for your personal satisfaction, and was happy. I now realise the background, and feel doubly fortunate in knowing you."

The first leprosy relief centre was established at Mazhavanthangal in South Arcot District. Jagadeesan invited Gandhiji to come and inaugurate it, but Gandhiji declined, saying, "Please invite someone else to inaugurate it. It is not a big thing to open a hospital. I will come when it needs to be closed!" Jagadeesan informed him that this work could go on for 30 to 40 years, but Gandhiji did not accept this, as he believed that leprosy could be eradicated in a definite time span.

Chinglepet

The train left Tirumani and halted near the Chinglepet School sports ground. A platform was erected on the railway line for Gandhiji. He proceeded there, sat on a chair and allowed all to see him. A similar arrangement was made at Tambaram.

In addition to Gandhiji, his entourage and some leaders, there were other officials who accompanied him on this train. As this was a special train, travelling ticket examiners Ranjit Singh of Egmore and

Sekavarma were in charge at Madras and Madurai, respectively. Food arrangements were looked after by Seetharamayya. Led by Inspector Bernard, two sub-inspectors and 20 constables took care of security. When he detrained at Guindy, Gandhiji praised these officials for their efficient service.

The Hindu praised the work of the Transport Superintendent Menon, the Railway Electrification authority Ramasubban, and the train travelling ticket inspector Swaminathan. The total collection for the Harijan Fund from the time that Gandhiji left Madras for Madurai and his return was Rs 32,000.

Prayer meeting

When Gandhiji detrained at Guindy, he was again quite exhausted. He went directly to Satyanarayana's house in Hindustani Nagar. Thereafter, he left for the prayer meeting on the grounds between Thyagaraya Road and Venkatanarayana Road. Kanu Gandhi read out Gandhiji's speech in Hindustani: "Swarajya without peace will not be complete. Without God's Grace, peace cannot be achieved. And without prayer, God's Grace cannot be obtained. This is why I have insisted on the habit of prayer."

Other meetings

From the prayer meeting, Gandhiji returned to Satyanarayana's house, where he met several people in the next hour. Sister Subbulakshmi was one. Pulusu Sambamurthy handed over Rs 10,000 from the Pethapuram Prince towards Harijan welfare work in Andhra. G. Ramabrahmam, V. Nagaiah, Soundararajan, P. Suryanarayana Jayantilal Chokhsi and Kasiappa Chetty presented a purse of Rs 27,751 from the Madras film producers, and cloth merchants for the work of the Hindustani Prachar Sabha. To discuss matters related to Indians in Malaya, R. Venkataraman met Gandhiji along with K. Bhashyam and took his blessings.

Departure

Completing his Madras visit, Madurai and Pazhani pilgrimages, Gandhiji started out from Satyanarayana's house at night. The members of the various committees of the Hindi Prachar Silver Jubilee celebrations, some Congressmen, and women, numbering about a hundred were there to see him off. Devadas Gandhi and Sir N. Gopalaswami Iyengar went with him in his car. Arrangements had been made for Gandhiji to board his special train at Ambattur.

On the way, Gandhiji stopped at Srinivasa Sastri's house (he had returned home by then from the hospital), and met him. This meeting has been recorded in the *Harijan*.

Silent communication

Monday was Gandhiji's day of silence. Realising this, Sastri was greatly disappointed. Gandhiji was replying to Sastri by writing on pieces of paper. Sastri was very surprised to learn that there were 4 to 6 lakh people at the Madurai prayer meeting, and that more than half of them were from neighbouring villages. Gandhiji's three visits to him filled Sastri with deep happiness and gratitude. He said,

> Brother, you have accorded me uncommon honour. Particularly, on this occasion, in spite of such time constraints, that you have come to see me makes me even more proud. You are closer to me than my own brothers, sons and family. It is some spiritual bond that has tied us together. I can think of nothing else. Gokhale has been one cause of this.

His softly spoken words were not heard even by the other people around. Drawing Gandhiji close, he added, "I do not wish to waste words. You know well what I want to say." Gandhiji asked him to be calm, and stood up to take his leave, because Sastri was breathless through emotion and could not speak any more.

Inseparable friend

As Gandhiji stood up, Sastri's eyes set upon the watch that was hanging on his waist, and he exclaimed, "Oh, your inseparable friend! Someone had told me that you had lost it and would no longer be using it." T. R. Venkatarama Sastri, who was standing nearby, gently corrected him, "That was his fountain pen." Srinivasa Sastri responded, "Ah, I see. So, if somebody steals your watch, would you stop using that, too?" Gandhiji smiled and shook his head to indicate that he could not function without a watch. Thereafter, they all took their leave of Sastri.

'India's true capital'

Gandhiji's visit to Madurai and Pazhani was a great success. An overall observation on this tour is necessary at this point. John Gunther (1901–70), American author, has written, "Wherever Gandhiji is becomes India's true capital." This was especially true with respect to Madras on this occasion. This was his first trip to the state after Kasturba's demise.

After the death of Bajaj, Janaki Bajaj, following in his footsteps, was responsible for making all arrangements, from erecting the pandal at the Hindustani Prachar Sabha, to the work of general administration of the Sabha. As Gandhiji had not accepted any engagements other than those at the Hindustani Prachar Sabha, he found time to meet old friends.

The Harijan Fund grows

In the wake of the Silver Jubilee function of the Hindustani Prachar Sabha, Madras Mahajan Sabha set up a Sevagram Organisation Scheme exhibition in Thyagaraja Nagar. Many artisan groups from villages participated in this exhibition. At every prayer meeting of Gandhiji, the contributions to the Harijan Fund kept increasing. Approximately Rs 800 per day was being received. Those who did not bring money, donated precious rings, earstuds and jewellery. All the articles given for this fund were displayed in this exhibition, together with their prices for sale. These included diamond jewellery, gold and silver ornaments, and beautiful works of art in sandalwood.

Place of stay

Gandhiji first stayed at the residence of the Hindustani Prachar Sabha secretary, Satyanarayana. Finding that his house could not accommodate the number of people who came to see him, he later shifted to the Mangala Bhavan nearby, where arrangements were made on the first floor for his stay. His associates stayed on the ground floor of the building. A path was created around the Hindustani Prachar Sabha for two people to walk side by side.

Whenever Gandhiji set out on a tour, he was clear about his objectives, and would strive to ensure that they were fulfilled. This was particularly evident during this visit. While the Silver Jubilee functions of the Hindustani Prachar Sabha were on, Gandhiji made sure to emphasise the importance of learning Hindi at every meeting where he spoke. On his way to Madurai, however, his focus was on untouchability eradication.

Confusion and noise

Gandhiji's prayer meetings drew large crowds, and grew by the day. At every such meeting, there had been some confusion or another in the crowd, despite Gandhiji's best efforts to quell it, with all the resources he had at his command. Some gradual improvement was seen with each passing day, but total peace at any meeting proved elusive. On one occasion, women and children almost got crushed in the crowd surging out of a meeting, and many fainted.

The restlessness and noise of the massive crowd gathered at the Madurai meeting disturbed Gandhiji greatly. That even he, the virtual incarnation of peace, was so agitated must be ascribed to the continuing confusion and noise that greeted him in meetings at Villupuram and Tiruchi en route to Madurai.

Thyagaraya Nagar

The record crowds at one meeting of Gandhiji could only be surpassed by those at another. This incomparable world leader's affection for the Tamils could only be matched by the Tamil people's profound reverence and affection for him. There was, however, no comparison to the crowds that gathered at Thyagaraya Nagar, Madras. It seemed that all trains were headed towards Thyagaraya Nagar, and the crowds were pouring in by the several thousands every hour.

On 25 January 1946, between 2 p.m. and 4.30 p.m., an estimated 20,000 people were transported by electric trains to Thyagaraya Nagar. A railway ticket counter operated at the pandal itself. At the end of the tour, Rajaji remarked, "I have accompanied Mahatma Gandhi on several tours, but I have not seen people in such large numbers, attending with obvious delight."

Gandhiji wrote, "I have not seen the importance given in this tour to my prayer meetings at any visit earlier. Hence I have asked Kanu Gandhi to sing Ram bhajan at the prayer meetings from tomorrow."

Special train

Gandhiji said that he did not want a special train for him to go to Madurai, but the railway authorities were insistent. If he were to travel by an express train, it would be impossible for other passengers to reach their destination on time, nor would they be able to control the crowds, they said. Even though Gandhiji wished to travel only by third class compartment, they made available the first class facilities in that compartment, because of which Gandhiji and party were able to sleep on the train on his visits to Madurai and Pazhani.

Further, the grounds on which the public meeting in Pazhani had been arranged belonged to the railways, making it easy for other government departments also to make arrangements there. These efficient arrangements could have been the result, not only owing to the stature of the Mahatma, but also because of the excitement that freedom was near.

An eager public

The eagerness to see Gandhiji was intense among the public. Only a select few, however, were allowed to visit him at the Sivaganga Mansion in Madurai. Only the families of eminent nationalist and Gandhian N. M. R. Subburaman, noted industrialist and Gandhian T. V. Sundaram Iyengar, along with Soundaram Ramachandran had the opportunity to call on Gandhiji. Many pleaded with the reception committee members to be allowed to meet him. One person was reported to have offered Rs 1,000, if he could meet Gandhiji, such was the eagerness evident among the people. (Interview of P. N. Ramasubramaniam)

A spiritual realisation

The theists of Madurai were delighted that Gandhiji had made this pilgrimage to visit the Madurai Meenakshi and Pazhani temples. Many spoke about this, and the connection to India's freedom. Some recounted that a rooster had crowed from the temple wall in Pazhani as Gandhiji entered the temple, and interpreted it as an auspicious sign. A devotee had drawn and distributed a picture of this. Gandhiji was not an idol worshipper, but he was no atheist to avoid going to temples. His attitude of meditation, as witnessed as he went around the Meenakshi temple, did indicate that he had experienced the divine there. He said (*The Hindu*, 4 February 1946), "While in the temple, I realised a new spiritual significance."

Had Gandhiji realised that, unless Harijans were allowed to worship in the temple, it was of no use? Or, had some new spiritual experience been awakened in him? Perhaps what he had known intellectually all along, even before visiting the Meenakshi temple, had been transformed into a spiritual realisation when he visited the temple. In his essay on the Pazhani temple, he spoke of "An augury for freedom." Gandhiji's visits to these two temples perhaps gave him a spiritual delight he had not experienced before.

What was special about the state of Madras was that it was here that Gandhiji had begun his 'service of the depressed', and it was also here that he would later announce the breaking of the chains of slavery. What more pride can Tamil Nadu now seek? Celebrate, O Tamil Nadu, and sing the glory of this great incarnation.

Revisiting an old scene

In our mind's eye we see the young Barrister-at-Law, Mohandas Gandhi of 50 years ago, in suit and bristling moustache, making himself known. Thereafter, he visited us several times over the years, and settled in our minds as the Gandhiji we all know. This Gandhiji, who had come for the Hindustani Prachar Sabha celebrations to unite the Hindus, and visit the temples, now stands at the Ambattur railway station in Madras.

Where was 1896, and where 1946? In those 50 years, how many changes had taken place in Gandhiji's life, and in Tamil history! He had raised the consciousness of Tamils in so many ways. Tamils, too, had played their part in his elevation and growth as an unparalleled leader of the people. Both must be legitimately proud. And now, after such a long and rich association, he was taking his leave from this sacred Tamil soil.

Departure at Ambattur

When he reached Ambattur railway station, some 200 people were gathered there, shouting, 'Gandhiji ki Jai'. They fell at his feet, their eyes moist with tears. When Devadas Gandhi took his leave of Gandhiji, he touched his cheeks in a manner of blessing. It was time for the train to leave. The air was rent with cries of 'Gandhiji ki Jai' as Gandhiji's feet left Ambattur and Madras. The man who left this time was Mahatma Mohandas Karamchand Gandhi, who did not again return to this hallowed land of the Tamils.

"Glory be to him, who lived a life in consonance with the word of God and Nature—a shining embodiment of the Grace of the Almighty. May his beautiful life inspire us all." (Thiru. Vi. Ka.)

Note

1. Archibald Fenner Brockway (1888–1988), British socialist, Member of Parliament, humanist and anti-war activist.

APPENDIX

A Chronology of Gandhi's Tours in Tamil Nadu, 1896–1946

1896

14 October (Wed.): Arrival in Madras

26 October: Madras Hindu Brahmagnana High School inspection; evening, public meeting in Pachaiyappa Hall

27 October: Evening, departure for Calcutta

1915 (With Kasturba)

17 April 1915 (Sat.): 6.15 p.m., from Hardwar to Madras Central Station; Mrs Besant met Gandhiji for discussions.

18 April 1915: Meeting important people

19 April 1915: Further meetings

20 April 1915: 11 a.m., visits G. Subramania Iyer's house; afternoon, discussion with Gokhale Club members

21 April 1915: Evening, welcome by South African Indians

22 April 1915: Evening, Cosmopolitan Club, meeting with members

23 April 1915: 5.30 p.m., Mahajan Sabha and State Congress Committee welcome

24 April 1915: 6 p.m., welcome to Kasturba by women; 6.15 p.m., Madras State Muslim League Tea party; 8 p.m., advocates' dinner

25 April 1915: 10 a.m., welcome by Bohras; 2.30 p.m., Abheda International Ananda Samaj girls' welcome; 3.30 p.m., Mylapore Society meeting; 6 p.m., Arya Vysya Mahasabha welcome

26 April 1915: Evening, welcome at S. Srinivasa Iyengar's house; Indian Christians' welcome

27 April 1915: Morning, Sri Ramakrishna Boys' Home; Venkataraman Ayurvedic Dispensary; Sanskrit College; evening, reception to Kasturba by Ladies' Recreation Club; 5.30 p.m., YMCA students' welcome; 6.15 p.m., meeting with degree holders at same place

28 April 1915: Morning, discussion with Pachaiyappa College professors; Model Town Council Harijan settlement; Broadway Harijan settlement; Washermenpet weaving house and dyeing shed; Rao Bahadur P. Thyagaraya Chettiar weaving factory; 6 p.m., Annie Besant welcome, Brahmagnana Sabha building

29 April 1915: 2.15 p.m., Thambu Chetty Street, Lakshmi Memorial Arya Patashala. 6 p.m., Gujaratis' welcome at Lod Govind Das' house; 8.20 p.m., to Tharangambadi by Thoothukudi Express

30 April 1915: Detrains at Mayavaram; welcome at Sembanarkoil; 9.30 a.m., welcome at Tharangambadi; 5 p.m., Tharangambadi Fort Grounds meeting

1 May 1915: Morning, Ramapuram; Thillaiyadi visits; afternoon, departure for Mayavaram; 3 p.m., arrival at Mayavaram; night, departure for Madras

2 May 1915: Madras arrival; morning, meeting with students

3 May 1915: Afternoon, lunch at Sastri's house; evening, departure for Nellore

4/5/6 May 1915: In Nellore

7 May 1915: 9 a.m, reaches Madras; 5 p.m., meeting with South African India League; 6.30 p.m., drama of Suguna Vilas Sabha; 8.30 p.m., departure for Bangalore

1916

13 February 1916 (Sun.): 2.30 p.m., arrival by Delhi Express; discussions with S. Srinivasa Iyengar and G. A. Natesan

14 February 1916: 8 p.m., Christian Propagandist Conference; speaks on swadeshi

15 February 1916: 12 noon, meets students at Victoria Hall

16 February 1916: 6 a.m., meets students at Victoria Hall; 8 a.m., speech at YMCA Hall; 6 p.m., Madras Social Work Association Annual Day; welcome by students

17 February 1916: 5.30 p.m., Christian College Societies debate inauguration; evening: departs for Poona

1917

14 September 1917: Arrival in Madras in the morning

15 September 1917: Departure from Madras in the night

1919

18 March 1919 (Tue.): 9.45 a.m., arrival in Madras by Bombay Mail; 5.30 p.m., Tiruvallikeni public meeting

19 March 1919: Evening, workers' meeting

21 March 1919: 8 a.m., Tram Workers' Association meeting

23 March 1919: Meeting with prominent persons regarding future employment prospects. The special dream he has on 22nd night/23rd morning; night, departure for Thanjavur

24 March 1919: Thanjavur arrival; public meeting

25 March 1919: Morning, departure from Thanjavur by Boat Mail to Tiruchi; 6 p.m., public meeting

26 March 1919: Morning, departure to Madurai by Boat Mail; afternoon, arrival in Madurai; public meeting; night, departure for Thoothukudi

27 March 1919: Morning, arrival in Thoothukudi; evening, procession and public meeting

28 March 1919: Morning, departure from Thoothukudi; afternoon, arrival in Madurai; changes trains for Nagerkoil; 9 p.m., arrival in Thanjavur

29 March 1919: 7 a.m., departure for Nagercoil via Salimangalam and Kambayanattham

30 March 1919: Evening, departure from Nagercoil for Madras; immediate departure for Bezawada

1920

12 August 1920 (Tue.): 9.30 a.m., arrival in Madras by Bombay Mail; evening, press interview; 5.30 p.m., public meeting

13 August 1920: Morning, meeting on Khilafat matters.

14 August 1920: Via Ambur to Vellore; morning, North Arcot District Khilafat Conference; 6 p.m., public meeting; night, return to Madras

15 August 1920: 4 a.m., return to Madras; 6 p.m., workers' meeting at George Town beach; night, departure to Kudanthai

16 August 1920: 6 a.m., arrival in Kudanthai; procession for Gandhiji and Maulana; 7.30 a.m., public meeting; 4.30 p.m., Papanasam, Needamangalam; 5.15 p.m., arrival Nagercoil; Nagore public meeting

17 August 1920: Morning, departure from Nagercoil; 10.30 a.m., Thanjavur, arrival; 12 noon, departure from Thanjavur; 1.45 p.m., arrival in Tiruchi; 3 p.m., workers' meeting; 4.30 p.m., procession to public meeting; 6 p.m., public meeting; 10 p.m., departure for Kallikkottai

18 August 1920: 3.30 a.m., arrival in Erode; meeting at Erode station; 6.30 a.m., departure for Kallikkottai; 2.30 p.m., arrival in Kallikkottai

19 August 1920: Arrival, Mangalore

20 August 1920: Arrival, Salem at 9.30 p.m.

21 August 1920: 7.30 a.m., inauguration of water tap; 8 a.m., Khilafat Conference; 10 a.m., departure for Bangalore by car; 9 p.m., departure for Madras from Bangalore

22 August 1920: Morning, arrival in Madras; meeting with Khilafat leaders; meeting Law College students; departure for Bezawada

1921 (1) (With Kasturba)

8 April 1921 (Fri.): Arrival in Madras, with Kasturba, by Calcutta Mail; proceeded to Yakub Hassan's house; morning, meeting on non-cooperation movement; evening, Marwaris' meeting; 6 p.m., public meeting at Tiruvallikeni beach front; night, meets Sathyamurthi; leaves by train for Bombay

1921 (2)

15 September 1921 (Tue.): 10 a.m., arrival in Madras; 5.30 p.m., public meeting

16 September 1921: 4.45 p.m., women's meeting; cloth merchants' meeting; 6.45 p.m., workers' meeting till 8 p.m.

17 September 1921: 6.18 a.m., departure from Madras by Boat Mail; 12 noon, reception at Villupuram station; 2 p.m., reception at Tirupathipuliyur station; 3 p.m., Parangippettai, arrival; 4 p.m., laying of foundation stone of National Girls School with Pearson; evening, departure by car for Cuddalore; 8 p.m., Cuddalore public meeting; 1 a.m., return to Parangippettai

18 September 1921: 6 a.m., departure by train from Parangippettai; 11.20 a.m., arrival in Kumbakonam (stay at choultry on Kalyanaraman Street); 3 p.m., public meeting; 5 p.m., departure from Kudanthai by Rameswaram Express; 7.30 p.m., arrival in Thanjavur; 9.30 p.m., arrival in Tiruchi

19 September 1921: 8 p.m., public meeting (the first arranged by a Town Council in the state); 11 p.m., end of public meeting

20 September 1921: Morning, Srirangam Town Council welcome; 10.15 a.m., return to Tiruchi

21 September 1921: Morning, departure by Boat Mail for Madurai; 10.45 a.m., welcome at Dindigul; 12.45 p.m., welcome by town council; 2.15 p.m., public meeting; 3.40 p.m., departure to Madurai; 6 p.m., reaches Madurai; 6.15 p.m., public meeting; 9 p.m., meeting with Women's Association, Muslim Youth Association and Gujarati merchants

22 September 1921: 7 a.m., Saurashtra people's meeting; *the first time Gandhiji appeared in dhoti and with bare body*; departure from Madurai for Karaikudi by car; 9.30 a.m., Melur, Tiruppathur, Kunrakudi, Pallangudi, Kottaiyur, Karaikudi, Amaravathi Pudur, Tiruppathur, Kunrakudi, Pallangudi; 12 noon, Kanadukathan, Pallathur, Velangudi; 1 p.m., Kottaiyur; 7 p.m., Karaikudi public meeting, Amaravathi Pudur; 8 p.m., Devakottai and return to Karaikudi

23 September 1921: Morning, departure from Karaikudi by car for Madurai; 12 noon, departure to Tirunelveli by train; 2 p.m., reaches Virudhunagar; 4.45 p.m., Gangaikondan railway station; 5.45 p.m., arrival, Tirunelveli; 7 p.m., public meeting

24 September 1921: 9 a.m., from Tirunelveli to Erode by train; 6 p.m., Dindigul

25 September 1921: 3.25 a.m., Erode, arrival (to inspect spinning at E.V.R.'s house); 2 p.m., departure for Coimbatore by train; 4.30 p.m., Tiruppur; 6.20 p.m., Singanallur (by car from here to Coimbatore); 6.40 p.m., Coimbatore; welcome by Town Council; workers' welcome at Besant House; public welcome at R. K. S. House

26 September 1921 (Gandhiji's day of silence): 4.25 p.m, departure for Salem; 12.30 a.m., stay at Salem

27 September 1921: Morning, inspection of charkhas at Kallakurichi; 8 a.m., cloth merchants at Sevvaippettai; women's meeting, Town Council welcome, meeting with weavers, inspecting students' spinning, public meeting; night, departure for Tirupathi

1925

7 March 1925 (Sat.): Morning, welcome at Basin Bridge (workers); 7.30 a.m., Central Station; procession; 9 a.m., Srinivasa Iyengar's house; 1.30 p.m., Press persons' meet; 3.30 p.m., Hindi Yuvathi Saranalayam; 4 p.m., welcome by Municipality; 6 p.m., public meeting; 7.45 p.m., departure by train for Vaikkom by Mettuppalayam Mail

8 March 1925: Morning, Salem-Erode-Pothanur

14 March 1925: 10.30 a.m., departure from Trivandrum; arrival in Kanyakumari, a look at the sea and rest; 4 p.m., temple, visit to Nagercoil; return to Trivandrum

19 March 1925: 7.30 a.m., Pothanur, arrival; welcome by workers; 10 a.m., Tiruppur, gave interview to Jayaram Naicker; 2 p.m. to 3 p.m. interview on khadi; inspection of Idumpalayam weaving centre; 5 p.m., return to Tiruppur; public meeting; night, departure for Puduppalayam; 10 p.m., Sankari Durg railway station; 11 p.m., Puduppalayam ashram

20 March 1925: Morning, essay at Gandhi Ashram; afternoon, to Rathinasabapathy Gounder's house; prayer at ashram.

21 March 1925: 4.30 a.m., prayer at ashram; 4 p.m., prayer at ashram; 7.30 p.m., public meeting; departure by Mettupalayam Mail

22 March 1925: Morning, reaches Central Station, Madras; 7.30 a.m. to 10 a.m., interviews with prominent people and Harijan leaders; 10 a.m., Narayanakadu Pudukkottai Harijans' meeting; 12 noon to 2 p.m., interviews; 3 p.m., to *The Hindu* office to unveil Kasturi Ranga Iyengar's portrait; 4.30 p.m., Cosmopolitan Club welcome; 5.30 p.m., public meeting; 8 p.m., workers' meeting

23 March 1925 (Gandhiji's day of silence): 8 p.m. to 9.15 p.m., *Ramayana* film

24 March 1925: 7.30 a.m., Sri Ramakrishna students' hostel; Mylapore Sanskrit College; Tiruvallikeni Cooperative; 8.05 a.m., Hindi Prachar Vidyalayam; 8.30 a.m., Mount Road Ayurveda Institution; 9 a.m., meeting on prohibition; meeting with Congress workers; Tamil Gurukulam talks; 3 p.m., Queen Mary's College; *Swarajya* office; 4 p.m., night school inspection at Royapuram; 5.45 p.m., Chindhatripet Congress welcome; 6 p.m., dinner at Srinivasa Iyengar's house; 7.30 p.m., welcome by Multanis, Marwaris and Gujaratis at Ekambreswarar Agraharam; 8 p.m., Peddanayakan Congress welcome; public meeting; 9.15 p.m., departure by Bombay Mail.

1927 (1) (With Kasturba)

24 August 1927 (Wed.): 7 p.m., departure from Bangalore; Sappadi Road; Hosur; Soolagiri; 10.30 a.m., arrival in Krishnagiri; 4 p.m., public meeting; return to Bangalore

30 August 1927: 12.05 p.m., arrival in Katpadi by Bangalore Express; by car to Vellore; 1 p.m., arrival at Vellore; evening, North Arcot District Association welcome; 5.30 p.m., public meeting (President, R. T. Boyer, Voorhees College Principal)

31 August 1927: Morning, women doctors' meeting; 6 p.m., Chittaranjan Park special function; 6.30 p.m., public meeting

1 September 1927: 8 a.m., by car to Gudiyattam; 5.30 p.m., public meeting at Gudiyattam; 8.45 p.m., return to Vellore

2 September 1927: 8 a.m., Arcot public meeting; 9 a.m., departure for Arni; arrival at Arni; 3.50 p.m., public meeting (ticketed); evening women's meeting; 5.45 p.m., public meeting at Arni Fort grounds

3 September 1927: 7 a.m., leave from Vellore by car; 9.45 a.m., arrival in Madras; C. F. Andrews interview; afternoon, M.S.M. Workers' Association meeting; 7 p.m., students' meeting (Mount Road)

4 September 1927: 7.30 a.m., YMCA meeting; 3 p.m., khadi merchants' meeting; 4.15 p.m., Hindu High School Alumni Association; 6 p.m., scouts inspection; 6.30 p.m., public meeting (beach)

5 September 1927: Gandhiji's day of silence

6 September 1927: 8 a.m., prohibition workers' meeting; 9 a.m., Hindi Prachar Sabha meeting; Sathyamurthi interview; Neill statue protest workers; Eekkadu Wesleyan Mission training school; 6 p.m., Tiruvallur public meeting; Poonamallee orphanage.

7 September 1927: 8 a.m., Pachaiyappa College students' meeting; tramway union workers' welcome; Neill statue discussion with satyagrahis; evening, public meeting at Royapuram

8 September 1927: 6 a.m., Perambur, Arundhatipuram welcome; 11 a.m., to Kanchipuram by car; 6 p.m., Kanchipuram public meeting

9 September 1927: 7.30 a.m., meeting with Gujaratis, Marwaris and Sindhis; 4 p.m., women's meeting at Tiruvallikeni; 5 p.m., Deshabandhu Das portrait unveiling; 6.30 p.m., Parangimalai Adambakkam meeting; night, to Cuddalore by Trivandrum Express

10 September 1927: 3.30 a.m., arrival, Cuddalore (stay at station); 6 a.m., welcome at station; 7 a.m., Municipality welcome; 6 p.m., public meeting

11 September 1927: 8 a.m., to Chidambaram; Nandanar temple foundation stone; evening, public meeting; 7 p.m., departure for Mayavaram; 9 p.m., reaches Mayavaram

12 September 1927: Gandhiji's day of silence

13 September 1927: 2.30 p.m., meeting with Municipal and Taluk Board leaders; 4.15 p.m., meeting with Isai Vellalars; 6.15 p.m., public meeting

14 September 1927: 7 a.m., departure for Kumbakonam; 8 a.m., arrival in Tiruvidaimarudur; 5.45 p.m., Kumbakonam, public meeting; night, meeting with scholars

15 September 1927: Morning, to Mannargudi; 7.30 a.m., arrival, Needamangalam; 8 a.m., Rasappan Chavadi; 8.20 a.m., reaches Mannargudi; National High School; 8. 45 a.m., Findlay College; 6.30 p.m., Mannargudi, public meeting

16 September 1927: 6 a.m., to Thanjavur; 8.15 a.m., reaches Thanjavur; 3.30–5 p.m., interview with Justice Party leaders; 5.45 p.m., Thanjavur public meeting; night, to Tiruchi

17 September 1927: 7.30 a.m., Fort Market Foundation stone function; welcome by Town Council; 4 p.m., South India Railway Workers' Sangam Foundation stone laying (Golden Rock); 6 p.m., to Lalgudi; 8 p.m., Lalgudi; 9.30 p.m., to Tiruchi

18 September 1927: 8.30 a.m., Dr Rajan Dispensary X-ray unit inauguration; afternoon, interview with Rev. Harold

20 September 1927: Morning, students' meeting; YMCA, Christians' welcome; afternoon, women's meeting; Srirangam Municipality welcome; public meeting postponed due to rain

21 September 1927: Srirangam Vivekananda Ashram welcome; 8 a.m., public meeting (Puthur Grounds); 3 p.m., to Pudukkottai; 6 p.m., arrival in Pudukkottai; 6.15 p.m., Pudukkottai public meeting

22 September 1927: 6 a.m., departure from Pudukkottai; Kuzhippirai; Ramachandrapuram; Kotthamangalam; afternoon, to Kanadukathan; 2 p.m., women's meeting

23 September 1927: 7 a.m., from Kanadukathan; Pallathur; Kottaiyur; Karaikudi; Amaravathi Pudur; Karaikudi

24 September 1927: 8 a.m., Karaikudi women's meeting; evening, Devakottai public meeting; night, Karaikudi

25 September 1927: 6.30 p.m., Karaikudi public meeting; 9 p.m., silence begins

26 September 1927: Gandhiji's day of silence

27 September 1927: 6.30 a.m., to Baganeri; Nachiarpuram; 8 a.m., Siravayal; 8.30 a.m., Tiruppathur; Swedish Mission Eye Hospital welcome; Baganeri welcome; evening, Baganeri public meeting

28 September 1927: 10 a.m., arrival, Madurai; 5.45 p.m., Municipality welcome; 6 p.m., public meeting at Tamukkam grounds

29 September 1927: Evening, welcome by Meenakshi temple shop owners; 6.30 p.m., Saurashtra community welcome

1 October 1927: 3.55 p.m., at Paramakudi; 11 p.m., reaches Madurai by Rameswaram Express (slept in train)

2 October 1927: To Virudhunagar; opening of choultry; 6 p.m., public meeting

3 October 1927: Gandhiji's day of silence

4 October 1927: 6 a.m., from Virudhunagar; 8 a.m, reaches Rajapalayam; 4 p.m., inspecting women spinning at Naickerpettai; women's meeting; Gandhi Khadi Vastralayam meeting; 6.30 p.m., public meeting

5 October 1927: To Rajapalayam in the morning; 8.15 a.m., arrival at Kazhugumalai; 9 a.m, arrival, Kovilpatti; 6 p.m., public meeting, Kovilpatti.

6 October 1927: 6 a.m., Kovilpatti to Thoothukudi by train; morning, Srivaikuntam arrival; 8 a.m., arrival, Thoothukudi; 6.30 p.m., public meeting

7 October 1927: 10 a.m., reaches Palayamkottai; 2.30 p.m., medical check-up by Dr Eswaraiah; 4 p.m., private khadi producer interview; 6 p.m., welcome by Tirunelveli Merchants' clerks; 7.15 p.m., public meeting

8 October 1927: Morning, departure from Tirunelveli; arrival, Nagercoil; public meeting; from Nagercoil to Trivandrum

8 to 15 October 1927: In Kerala

16 October 1927 (Sun.): 9 a.m., from Palakkad to Coimbatore by car; 3.30 p.m., women's meeting; 5.30 p.m., public meeting

17 October 1927: Gandhiji's day of silence

18 October 1927: 4.30 p.m., arrival, Pollachi; 5.30 p.m., public meeting at Pollachi; return to Coimbatore

19 to 21 October 1927: Rest at Coimbatore

22 October 1927: 5.30 a.m., by car to Tiruppur; Gobichettipalayam; Uthukkuli; 10.30 a.m., arrival, Tiruppur; evening, welcome at Vastralayam

23 October 1927: 3.45 a.m., inauguration of *Gita* class; to Karur; Vellakoil; Tirupur; interview; P. T. Asher and Company welcome; evening, public meeting

24 October 1927: Gandhiji's day of silence

25 October 1927: Early morning, Tiruppur to Kallikkottai; 5 a.m., Ottapalam

1927 (2) (With Kasturba)

12 November 1927: 10 p.m., arrival in Ceylon

13 November 1927: Afternoon, Chetty's association; Vivekananda Association members' welcome

30 November 1927 (Wed.): 11.30 a.m., arrival at Dhanushkodi by *Hardinge* ship; women's meeting; 6 p.m., public meeting

1 December 1927: Morning, to Ramanathapuram; evening, departure from Madras by Calcutta Mail

1927 (3)

23 December 1927 (Fri.): Arrival by Calcutta Mail; detrains at Korukkupet; 3.30 p.m., Khadi Exhibition opening

25 December 1927: Afternoon, arrival, with Congress leaders

26 December 1927 (Gandhiji's day of silence): Attends Congress meeting

27 December 1927: Congress meeting

28 December 1927: Morning, medical check-up by Dr Muthu; night, to Ahmedabad via Bombay

1929

15 May 1929 (Wed.): Arrival at Tiruttani

1933

20 December 1933 (Wed.): 8.20 a.m., arrival, Madras Central; 8.45 a.m., Ripon Buildings welcome by Corporation; 10 a.m., swadeshi, khadi exhibition; 11.30 a.m., rest; 2.15 to 2.45 p.m., meeting with untouchable movement workers; 4 p.m., Indian Women's Association meeting; 4.25 p.m., students' meeting; 4.45 p.m., Women's Association meeting; 5 p.m. to 6 p.m., rest; 6 p.m., public meeting

21 December 1933: Nariyakadu (Egmore); Periamet slums; Pallakku Maniam slum; Damodarapuram; welcome at Gopathy Narayanaswamy Chettiar Park; Vedaranyapuram; Pudupet; Perambur slum; afternoon, M. S. M. Railway workers' welcome; evening, Royapuram public meeting; 7.15 p.m., public meeting in Perambur grounds; 8.20 p.m., unveiling Besant's portrait at Wadia Park; 9 p.m., Choolaimedu public meeting

22 December 1933: Early morning, medical check-up by Dr Rangachari; Satyamurthi interview; 8.45 a.m., Harijan Seva Sangam welcome; 9.30 a.m., welcome by Gujaratis, Marwaris and Sindhis; 10 a.m., welcome by Madras Vysya Sangam; 11 a.m., Andhra Mahasabha meeting; unveiling of Nageswara Rao Panthulu's portrait; 12 noon, Kodavan Street slum; 4.15 p.m. to 5 p.m., Hindi Prachar Sabha convocation; 6 p.m., interview of leaders of backward classes; to Ennore by car

1934

22 January 1934 (Mon.): 4.30 p.m., arrival, Nagercoil; public meeting; night, reaches Kanyakumari

23 January 1934: Morning, sea bath in Kanyakumari; 6.45 p.m., from Kanyakumari; 7.30 p.m., Valliyur; Nanguneri; 9.30 p.m., Tirunelveli

24 January 1934: 6.30 a.m., interview of Aram Valarthanatha Pillai; 7 a.m., meeting with T. R. Mahadeva Iyer; naming children; inspection of scavenger quarters; distribution of money; public meeting at Courtallam Market; 9.30 a.m., arrival, Tenkasi; public meeting; reaches Courtallam; 2.15 p.m., to see the falls; 5 p.m., to Thoothukudi; 7 p.m., arrival, Thoothukudi; Prasanna Vinayakar temple; 7.30 p.m., public meeting

25 January 1934: 6 a.m., to Boltanpuram slum; 6.50 a.m., from Thoothukudi; Ettaiyapuram; 9.15 a.m., arrival, Kovilpatti; Kazhugumalai; Sankarankoil; 11.30 a.m., Rajapalayam; 12 noon, rest; 2.30 p.m., from Rajapalayam;

4.30 p.m., arrival, Sivakasi; 6 p.m., Soolakkarai; 8 p.m., Virudhunagar
public meeting; 9 p.m., Kallikudi; 9.45 p.m., Tirumangalam;
Tirupparankundram; 11.15 p.m., Madurai.

26 January 1934: 7 a.m., welcome by Merchants' Association; slum visit;
8.30 a.m., Town Council welcome; 9 a.m., students' meeting; 2 p.m.,
workers' interview; 3 p.m., women's meeting; 4 p.m., Hindi Prachar Sabha
meeting; 5.45 p.m., public meeting; 8 p.m., advice to associates; auction of
jewels and other articles

27 January 1934: Up to 2.30 p.m., rest in Madurai; 2.30 p.m., to Chettinadu;
3 p.m., South Street Melur; 5 p.m., Amaravathi Pudur; 6 p.m., Karaikudi
Town Council welcome; public meeting; 7.55 p.m., arrival, Devakottai;
night stay

28 January 1934: Morning, Devakottai Ram Nagar Harijan School foundation
stone; Sitthanur slum visit; 12.30 p.m., meeting with Nattar representatives;
compromise talks; 2 p.m., from Devakottai; Tiruppathur; public meeting;
Baganeri, public meeting; Sivaganga, public meeting; 7 p.m., Manamadurai
public meeting; 7.30 p.m., entraining at Manamadurai station; Madurai;
Dindigul

29 January 1934 (Gandhiji's day of silence): 4 a.m., Pazhani Road; 5 p.m.,
Udumalpet; 6 p.m., Pollachi; 8.30 a.m., Chettipalayam; Pothanur;
Perianaickenpalayam; Karamadai; Mettupalayam; 10.30 a.m., Coonoor

1 February 1934: 4.30 p.m., Adi Dravida group interview

2 February 1934: 3 p.m., to Kothagiri; 3.50 p.m., arrival, Kothagiri

3 February 1934: Dandakaranya slum Ottupparai Sakkiliar settlement;
5 p.m., end of public meeting

4 February 1934: Afternoon, Adi Hindus' interview; 2.45 p.m., from
Coonoor; 3.10 p.m., arrival, Ootacamund; afternoon, public meeting; Sri
Ramakrishna Mutt; Om Prakash Mutt; settlement of Vannars

6 February 1934: 7 a.m., from Coonoor to Coimbatore; Mettupalayam; Annur;
8.30 a.m., Sokkampalayam; 9.05 a.m., Karuvalur; 9.15 a.m., Avinashi;
Tirumuruganpoondi; Anuppapalayam; 10.15 a.m., Tiruppur (Rajaji
joins); 2.45 p.m., from Tiruppur; Palladam; Sulur; Ramanathapuram;
4 p.m., Coimbatore women's meeting; Harijan students' hostel; Gujaratis'
meeting; Harijan leaders' interview; public meeting; welcome at
P. S. G. Industries; Madurai Devi Balavinoda Sabha drama *Nandanar*;
Pothanur Ramakrishna Vidyalayam

7 February 1934: 7.30 a.m., start from Vidyalayam; Vidyalayalam new
building foundation stone; Kinattrukidavu; Nallattipalayam; 9.50 a.m.,
arrival Pollachi by train; 10.30 a.m., from Pollachi; 10.45 a.m.,
Komangalam Pudur; 11 a.m., arrival, Udumalpet by car; 3.10 p.m., from

Udumalpet; arrival, Vanneervalasu; 5 p.m., Pazhani; 5.30 p.m., from
Pazhani; 8.30 p.m., Dindigul, public meeting at Fort grounds; prayers at
Baluswami Choultry and stay
8 February 1934: 7 a.m., from Dindigul; 8 a.m., Vathlagundu; 9 a.m.,
Periakulam; 2 p.m., from Periakulam; Puduppatti; Theni; Pazhanichettypatti;
Veerapandi; Chinnamanur; 5.15 p.m., Cumbum.
9 February 1934: 7 a.m., from Cumbum; Kombai; Thevaram; 2.30 p.m.,
from Thevaram; 3 p.m., Bodivilakku; 5.30 p.m, by train from Theni;
Andipatti; Thottappanayakanur; Usilampatti; 7.30 p.m., Cheekkanoorani;
Chozhavandan (by car); 11.34 p.m., from Chozhavandan by train
10 February 1934: 3.50 a.m., reaches Tiruchi; 6.30 a.m., starts from place
of stay; Thennur Peerthan Juharlal Park; Srirangam; Manachanallur;
Samayapuram; Chintamani; Chintamani slum; 11 a.m., Harijan workers'
meeting; Sanatanis; interview with Harijan representatives; welcome by
Devanga Sabha; Tiruchi Taluk Board welcome; 4 p.m., women's meeting;
4.30 p.m., National College; public meeting
11 February 1934: 6.30 a.m., to Varaker slum; 7.50 a.m., by train to Karur;
Mutharasanallur; Kuzhithalai; 11.30 a.m., Karur; 3.30 p.m., public meeting;
4.30 p.m., to Erode; 5 p.m., at Kodumudi; 5.15 p.m., from Kodumudi;
6 p.m., reaches Erode; public meeting; 8 p.m., to Bhavani; 8.30 p.m., at
Bhavani; 9.45 p.m., Tiruchengode; 11 p.m., Puduppalayam
12 February 1934: Gandhiji's day of silence
13 February 1934: 7.30 a.m., public meeting; interviews with persons from
neighbouring villages
14 February 1934: 7 a.m., from Puduppalayam; 7.50 a.m., Namakkal;
Sendamangalam; Kalappanayakanpatti; Belukurichi; 10 a.m., Rasipuram;
10.10 a.m., from Rasipuram; 11 a.m., Salem; 3.30 p.m., women's meeting;
4 p.m., at Vijayaraghavachariar's house; Harijan students' hostel; Gandhi
Iyer Tiffin Street; Vysya Literary Society; public meeting; 7.20 p.m., to
Thanjavur by train
15 February 1934: 6 a.m., Thanjavur; 7.30 a.m., from Thanjavur; Ayyampettai;
8.25 a.m., Papanasam; 9 a.m., Kumbakonam; 9.05 a.m., welcome by
Viswakarma Association; 9.15 a.m., welcome by Town Council at Patel
Hall; public meeting at high school; women handed over purses; Hindi
diplomas awarded; interview to Self-Respect Group; received Gujaratis'
purse; interview to Harijans; food; rest; 2.30 p.m., to Tiruvarur; 2.50 p.m.,
Nachiarkoil; 3 p.m., Tirusirai; Kodavasal; 4.05 p.m., Koratacheri;
4.50 p.m., from Koratacheri; 5 p.m., Tiruvarur; 7.30 p.m., Nagapattinam;
public meeting

16 February 1934: 7 a.m., from Nagapattinam; 8 a.m., Nagore; 8.45 a.m., Karaikal; 9.30 a.m., Tharangambadi; 10.25 a.m., Mayavaram; 11.30 a.m., Seerkazhi; public meeting; rest; visit to K. Chidambaranatha Mudaliar's house; 3.35 p.m., Chidambaram; Thillai Samarasa Sanmana Sangam; Cosmopolitan Club; Nandanar Mutt; school; 4 p.m., Taluk Board Office; Khadi depot; 6.30 p.m., public meeting, Annamalai Nagar; 7 p.m., Annamalai University; 7.58 p.m., to Cuddalore by train; 9.06 p.m., Cuddalore; Town Council welcome; Taluk Board welcome; 10 p.m., public meeting

17 February 1934: Morning, interview with Anjalai ammal; 6.30 a.m., from Cuddalore; 8 a.m., Puducheri; 10 a.m., Panruti; 11 a.m., Gandhikuppam, Tiruvennainallur; 2.30 p.m., darshan from upstairs of Kripashram; 3 p.m., to Tiruvannamalai by car; 3.45 p.m., Tirukoilur; 4.30 p.m., Tiruvannamalai; 6 p.m., from Tiruvannamalai; 9.20 p.m., Vellore

18 February 1934: 4.15 a.m., prayer; 7.30 a.m., paper workshop, Harijan school; village meeting; visits to slums; 8.40 a.m., welcome by Town Council; public meeting; 1.05 p.m., from Vellore; 1.20 p.m., Katpadi; 2.10 p.m., Gudiyattam; 2.20 p.m., from Pallikondai; 3.15 p.m., Ambur; Periakulam; 4.05 p.m., Vaniyambadi; Nattrampalli village; 5.15 p.m., Tirupatthur; 6 p.m., Christian family ashram; 6.50 p.m., public meeting; 8 p.m., Christian ashram workers' meeting; 8.30 p.m., Kovilla Prayer House; 9.15 p.m., from Jolarpettai; 9.55 p.m., from Jolarpettai to Madras

19 February 1934 (Gandhiji's day of silence): 5.30 a.m., Perambur railway station; by car to Kodambakkam; visit by Vizianagaram Maharani Vidyavati and Ambujammal

20 February 1934: 3.30 p.m., Tamilnadu Harijan Seva Sangam meeting; 5.30 p.m., end of public meeting; to A. Rangaswami Iyengar's house for condolence

21 February 1934: 9.58 a.m., Kanchipuram; 11 a.m., end of Kanchipuram public meeting; 2.15 p.m., darshan to people from upstairs; 2.35 p.m., by car to Arni; 3.30 p.m., Walajapet; 3.45 p.m., Ranipet; 4.55 p.m., Arni Fort Grounds; 7.30 p.m., departure from Arni; 8.10 p.m., Sholingapuram; 9 p.m., Arakkonam; public meeting; by Bangalore Mail to Gadag

1937

11 January 1937 (Mon.): 5.30 p.m., arrival, Central station by Bombay Express; Hindi Prachar Sabha prayer meeting; Harihara Sharma's house; food; rest; prayer meeting; entrains at Tambaram by Trivandrum Express; welcome at Chinglepet station

12 January 1937: Morning, Dindigul railway station welcome; Madurai railway station welcome; 1.45 p.m., Tenkasi

13 January 1937: Tiruvangur Principality

14 January 1937: 5.30 p.m., arrival, Nagercoil; Nagarajaswami, Krishnaswami temples visit; 6.30 p.m., public meeting; 8 p.m., to Kanyakumari; stay at Kanyakumari

15 January 1937: 7 a.m., walk on Kanyakumari beach; temple visit; Vivekananda Library visit; 8 a.m., day of begins; 5 p.m., end of silence; interview to Hindi Premi Sabha; 5.15 p.m., from Kanyakumari; 5.30 p.m., Suchindram; Suchindram English School visit; 7.30 p.m., to Trivandrum via Nagercoil

16, 17, 18, 19 January 1937: At Tiruvangur Principality

20 January 1937: 8 p.m., arrival at Kottarakara

21 January 1937: 7 a.m., Tirukkannamaithal Vishnu temple opened by Gandhiji to Harijans; public meeting; 8 p.m., arrival, Kottarakara railway station; 10.30 p.m., entrains after dinner

22 January 1937: Morning, arrival at Tambaram railway station; to Nageswara Rao Panthulu's house; Kodambakkam Industrial School inspection; interview to the *Mail*; afternoon, meeting with Indian Christians; meeting with Srinivasa Sastri and G. A. Natesan; students' meeting; prayer; to Sevagram via Guntur

1937 (2)

26 March 1937 (Fri.): 4.50 p.m., arrival, Ponneri railway station by Grand Trunk Express; 6 p.m., visit to Mambalam Hindi Prachar Sabha; 6.30 p.m., Hindi Prachar Sabha convocation; 9.30 p.m., prayer

27 March 1937: 7.45 a.m., presides over Bharatiya Sahitya Parishad meeting; interview of Gokulam settlement inhabitants; 12 noon, discussion with Rajaji; 12.30 p.m., Hindi Sahitya Sammelan inauguration; evening, meeting with Congress members

28 March 1937: 6.40 a.m., to Kodambakkam School; 7.20 a.m., arrival Kodambakkam School; 3.30 p.m., presides over Parishad meeting; 7 p.m., press interview; 9.30 p.m., Dakshin Bharat Hindi Prachar Sabha meeting; interviews till midnight

29 March 1937: Day of silence

30 March 1937: Morning, visit to exhibition; departure for Wardha by Grand Trunk Express.

1946

21 January 1946 (Mon.): 4.15 p.m., arrival, Ambattur railway station; 4.50 p.m., arrival, Hindi Prachar Sabha; meeting with British Parliamentary Delegation secretary; 7 p.m., darshan to public

22 January 1946: 4 a.m., prayer; *Gita* Parayanam; 8.30 a.m. to 11.30 a.m., body massage; 5 p.m., interviews; 5.30 p.m., visits Hindi Prachar Sabha building; 8 p.m., meeting with Sastri at Government General Hospital

23 January 1946: Morning and evening, interviews; 5.35 p.m., prayer meeting; 7.30 p.m., meeting with Parliamentary Delegation

24 January 1946: 6 a.m., meeting with some Parliamentary Delegation members; 8.20 a.m., Organisation Workers' Conference inauguration; 3 p.m., organisation conference; 7.30 p.m., meeting with Parliamentary Delegation; 9.30 p.m., interviews

25 January 1946: Interviews till afternoon; 3 p.m., Hindi Prachar Sabha Silver Jubilee; 5.40 p.m., prayer; 6.45 p.m., to Governor's Bungalow; confidential talks with the Governor till 9 p.m.

26 January 1946: Morning, Freedom Day observed; 2.45 p.m., Organisation Workers' Conference; interviews; Hindustani propagators' conference; Harijan Mahasabha meeting; evening, prayer meeting

27 January 1946: 7.30 a.m., Kasturba Trust workers' meeting; interviews till afternoon; 1.30 p.m., Organisation Workers' Conference; Dakshin Bharat Hindi Prachar Sabha Convocation; prayer; 7.30 p.m., start of silence

28 January 1946 (Day of silence): 7 a.m., visit to Hindustani Nagar; inspection of Thyagaraya Nagar Harijan Training School site; prayer meeting; 7.30 p.m., meeting with Azhagappa Chettiar

29 January 1946: 7 a.m., final day of Organisation Workers' Conference; basic education diploma awards; 4.30 p.m., women's meeting; 5.30 p.m., prayer meeting; 7.30 p.m., Congress workers' meeting; 8.30 p.m., rest for the night

30 January 1946: 7 a.m., meeting Hindi Prachar Sabha workers and families; afternoon, interviews; 10 a.m., Students' Conference; 4 p.m., national writers' and artistes' meeting; 4.30 p.m., Students' Conference; 5.30 p.m., prayer meeting; 7.30 p.m., meeting with Rt. Hon'ble Srinivasa Sastri

31 January 1946: 7 a.m., workers' silver jubilee group meeting; afternoon, interviews; discussions with merchants; Mylapore Andhra Mahila Sabha foundation stone laying; 3 p.m., C.P.'s interview; 5.30 p.m., delayed start to workers' meeting; prayer meeting

1 February 1946: 7.15 a.m., foundation stone of Harijan Training School; interview; afternoon, meeting with Kodambakkam workers involved in Harijan welfare; 5.30 p.m., prayer meeting; 10. 30 p.m., to Madurai from

Guindy railway station; 11 p.m., halt in train at Kattuppakkam railway station for night rest

2 February 1946: 5 a.m., departure from Kattuppakkam railway station; 6.30 a.m., Acharappakkam; Villupuram; Virudachalam; 11.15 a.m., Ariyalur (Dr Rajan joins); Lalgudi; Srirangam; 1.30 p.m., Tiruchi; 5 p.m., arrival at Samayanallur; 6.30 p.m., Madurai, prayer meeting; 8.45 p.m., end of meeting

3 February 1946: 7.30 a.m., arrival at Meenakshi temple; 8.45 a.m., from Meenakshi temple; 1 p.m., to Pazhani from Madurai; 5 p.m., Pazhani, public meeting; 8 p.m., to Pazhani temple; 11 p.m., from Pazhani by special train; halt for night rest in train at Akkaraippatti station

4 February 1946: Early morning, departure from Akkaraippatti; 6 a.m., Tiruchi; 7 a.m., Thanjavur; Kumbakonam; Mayavaram; Seerkazhi; 12 noon, Cuddalore; Villupuram; Tirumani; 4 p.m., Chinglepet, Tambaram; 5 p.m., arrival Guindy railway station; 5.15 p.m., Hindi Prachar Sabha welcome; 5.30 p.m., prayer meeting; 7.45 p.m., departure from Satyanarayana's house; Sastri's house meeting; departure from Ambattur railway station